D1485381

POLITICAL COMMUNICATION: POLITICS, PRESS, AND PUBLIC IN AMERICA

LEA'S COMMUNICATION SERIES
Jennings Bryant/Dolf Zillmann, General Editors

For a complete list of other titles in LEA's Communication Series, please contact Lawrence Erlbaum Associates, Publishers.

POLITICAL COMMUNICATION: POLITICS, PRESS, AND PUBLIC IN AMERICA

Richard M. Perloff
Cleveland State University

 LAWRENCE ERLBAUM ASSOCIATES, PUBLISHERS
1998   Mahwah, New Jersey   London

NORTHWEST MISSOURI STATE
UNIVERSITY LIBRARY,
MARYVILLE, MO 64468

Figure Credits

FIG. 4.1. From Smoller (1990). *The six o' clock presidency: A theory of presidental press relations in the age of television.* Copyright 1990 by Fredric T. Smoller.

FIG. 6.1. From Hart (1994). *Verbal style and the presidency: A computer-based analysis.* Reprinted by permission of Academic Press.

FIG. 11.1. From Funkhouser (1973). The issues of the sixties: An explanatory study in the dynamics of public opinion, *Public Opinion Quarterly.* Reprinted by permission of the University of Chicago Press.

FIG. 12.1. From Dearing & Rogers (1992). AIDS and the media agenda. In T. Edgar, M. A. Fitzpatrick, & V. S. Freimuth (Eds.), *AIDS: A communication perspective* (p. 183). Copyright 1992 Lawrence Erlbaum Associates. Reprinted by permission.

FIG. 12.3. From Rogers & Dearing (1988). Agenda-setting research: What has it been, where is it going? In J. Anderson (Ed.), *Communication yearbook 11* (p. 557). Reprinted by permission of Sage Publications.

FIG. 16.1. From Adams (1987). As New Hampshire goes...In G. R. Orren & N. W. Polsby (Eds.), *Media and momentum: The New Hampshire primary and nomination politics.* Reprinted by permission of Chatham House Publishers.

FIG. 16.2. From Adams (1987). As New Hampshire goes...In G. R. Orren & N. W. Polsby (Eds.), *Media and momentum: The New Hampshire primary and nomination politics.* Reprinted by permission of Chatham House Publishers.

FIG. 17.1. From *Media Monitor*, Volume X, Number 5, Sept./Oct., 1996. Reprinted by permission of the Center for Media and Public Affairs, Washington, DC.

FIG. 17.2. From Lichter & Noyes (1995). *Good intentions made bad news: Why Americans hate campaign journalism.* Reprinted by permission of Rowman & Littlefield.

FIG. 17.3. From *Out of order* by Thomas Patterson. Copyright 1993 by Thomas Patterson. Reprinted by permission of Alfred A. Knopf, Inc.

BOX 19.1. From Simon (1990). *Road show.* Reprinted by permission of Farrar, Straus & Giroux.

Copyright © 1998 by Lawrence Erlbaum Associates, Inc.

All rights reserved. No part of this book may be reproduced in any form, by photostat, microfilm, retrieval system, or any other means, without the prior written permission of the publisher.

Lawrence Erlbaum Associates, Inc., Publishers
10 Industrial Avenue
Mahwah, New Jersey 07430

Cover transparency from the Collection of David J. and Janice L. Frent. Cover design by Kathryn Houghtaling Lacey

Library of Congress Cataloging-in-Publication-Data

Perloff, Richard M.
  Political communication : politics, press, and public in America
/ Richard M. Perloff.
    p. cm.
  Includes bibliographical references and index.
  ISBN 0-8058-1794-8 (cloth : alk. paper). — ISBN 0-8058-1795-6
(pbk. : alk. paper)
    1. Communication in politics—United States. I. Title.
  JA85.2U6P47 1997
  324'.01'4—dc21   97-21794
                                                         CIP

Books published by Lawrence Erlbaum Associates are printed on acid-free paper, and their bindings are chosen for strength and durability.

Printed in the United States of America
10 9 8 7 6 5 4 3 2 1

324.01
P45p

To my family—Julie, Michael, and Catherine

OCT 2 0 1998

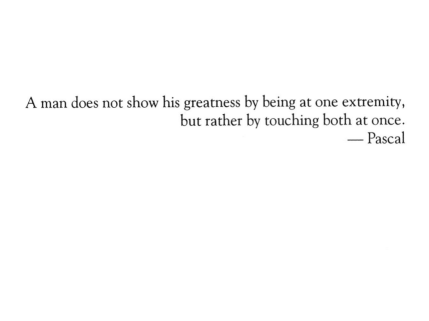

A man does not show his greatness by being at one extremity,
but rather by touching both at once.
— Pascal

Contents

Preface

Initially, one of the reasons I wanted to write a book on political communication was to showcase the knowledge we had in the field, to synthesize the facts and theories, and to trumpet the contributions that scholars had made to our knowledge of political communication effects. This remained one of my goals as I worked on the book, but in the process of writing, I found that my focus was broadening and I wanted to cover more than just the empirical body of literature. It became clear to me that an important component of the field was historical—the luminary rhetorical accomplishments of some American presidents, the constant tangle between the press and presidency, the historical roots of politics as it is practiced today and as it is studied in universities. Hence, history became a focus of my attention. I felt it was important today, when so many students are locked into the present and have little knowledge of the way that the past influences and intrudes upon the present-day practice of political communication, to provide an overview of some of the major historical issues in the study of politics and the press. Thus, the book was designed both to introduce students to contemporary political communication and to provide an historical perspective on politics and the press in America.

At the same time, as I worked on the book, it became clear to me that political communication was not something alien to me—not just the sum total of theories and methods and perspectives—but an arena in which I had some practical and personal experiences. I called on these in the book, as I covered rhetoric (thinking back to the impassioned speeches of Senator Robert F. Kennedy, for whom I did volunteer work in 1968) and in discussions of political journalism (harking back to my days as a devotee of newspapers, and particularly as a reporter for the student newspaper at the

University of Michigan during the protest era of the late 1960s and early 1970s).

Like many social scientists, I have been influenced by cognitive approaches to human behavior. I believe that a knowledge of the mind and of mental processes is critical in understanding communication effects. However, the cognitive perspective is only one of many ways to study political communication. In this book I offer a variety of perspectives on political communication, from micro-psychological to macro-political to historical.

I have also tried to describe the weaknesses and strengths of the American political communication system. If I have a bias—and I undoubtedly have many—it is to emphasize the strengths and virtues of political communication in America. I have erred on the side of accentuating the positive in order to provide a sense of hope and optimism in an age when so many people distrust politicians and the press. Politics can be an instrument of change and a force for good; after all, it is politics that gave us the United States of America, and great reforms such as Social Security and civil rights legislation. And it is the press that exposed corruption in the nineteenth century, investigated Watergate in the twentieth, and offers us the hope to link political elites and the public in the century that is nearly upon us.

I appreciate the assistance of a number of colleagues. Thanks to Everett Cataldo, Jean Dubail, Joe Frolik, Roderick Hart, Amos Kiewe, Robert Lichter, J. Anthony Maltese, Douglas McLeod, Bruce Newman, Gary Pettey, Craig Smith, J. Michael Sproule, David Weaver, and Darrell West for reading chapters of the book, and to Steve Chaffee for his thoughtful and detailed suggestions. I would also like to thank Jack McLeod for his support and encouragement over the years. Finally, I thank my father, Robert Perloff, for his reading of several chapters, and his encouraging and always reinforcing comments. Finally, I very much appreciate the assistance and support I received from Linda Bathgate, Anne Monaghan, Kathleen O'Malley, and Joe Petrowski from Lawrence Erlbaum Associates.

I

MASS MEDIA AND GOVERNMENT INSTITUTIONS

1

Introduction to Political Communication

•The Health Insurance Association of America was worried. President Bill Clinton had introduced a sweeping plan to reform health care, and the Association, a lobbying group for 270 insurance firms, was nervous that Clinton's health reform package would put insurance companies out of business.

To fight the Clinton plan, the lobbying group did what lobbying groups do in the 1990s when they want to defeat a legislative package: It hired pollsters, political consultants, and advertising professionals in an effort to influence public opinion.

The Health Insurance Association blitzed the television airwaves in the summer and fall of 1993, spending tens of millions of dollars on advertising and polling. One of its commercials, "Harry and Louise," became a campaign classic. It featured a man called Harry and a woman named Louise complaining about how government bureaucrats were forcing them to pick from a few health care plans. "Having choices we don't like is no choice at all," lamented Louise. "They choose," said Harry. "We lose," replied Louise.

Although the Harry and Louise ads grossly oversimplified and distorted Clinton's plan, they captured the national spotlight. First Lady Hillary Clinton attacked them. So, too, did influential Democrats. And, to the delight of the insurance industry, the more the Clinton administration criticized the spots, the more publicity they received. It was a public relations executive's dream.

A year later, after months of attack ads, news stories covering the campaign for and against Clinton's proposal, vitriolic commentaries on talk radio, and bureaucratic bungling by the Clinton administration, the health care reform plan was dead. And as the pundits asked what went wrong, 37 million Americans remained without health insurance, and health care costs continued to skyrocket.[1]

• Every day, from dawn to dusk, radio talk-show hosts scream and shout, and lambast and lacerate American politics and politicians. For example:

In Los Angeles, talk-show host Emiliano Limon of KFI asks, "If homeless people cannot survive on their own, why shouldn't they be put to sleep?"

In Colorado Springs, Chuck Baker of KVOR says of the attorney general, "We ought to slap Janet Reno across her face ... (and) send her back to Florida where she can live with her relatives, the gators."

In New York, the I-man, Don Imus, called Newt Gingrich "a man who would eat road kill," O. J. Simpson "a moron," Alice Rivlin a "little dwarf," Bob Novak the man with "the worst hair on the planet," and Ted Kennedy "a fat slob with a head the size of a dumpster."[2]

Imus and other talk-show hosts can be funny, irreverent, and cruel. They also attract huge audiences. Talk is now the most popular radio format after country music, commanding 15% percent of the radio market. Talk radio has sparked considerable controversy: Critics say it taints and tarnishes the nation's conversation about politics; defenders say it provides millions of Americans with a venue to express their anger and frustration with the system.

Whatever its merits, there is no doubt that people and politicians are listening. When he ran for president in 1992, Bill Clinton realized that he could reach millions of New York voters by appearing on Imus's radio program. So even as Imus mocked Clinton, calling him a "redneck bozo," Clinton appeared on his show, trading insults with Imus, and at the same time reaching the gargantuan New York radio audience. Clinton went on to win the New York primary by a huge margin.

Later when Clinton became president, Imus received a VIP tour of the White House and lunched with Clinton's communications director. But the I-man wasn't fazed by the royal treatment. The president, he claimed, "needs to be on this show a lot more than we need him."[3]

• Concerned by evidence that the public has lost confidence in the news media, dozens of news organizations have recently begun to experiment with new strategies to get the public involved in political issues.

Known as public journalism, the new movement steers clear of traditional reporting of conflict and official intrigue; instead, editors roll up their shirt sleeves and get involved in community problems, as participants rather than observers.

For example, in the fall of 1994, four Madison news media joined forces to get citizens involved in the state election campaign. The newspaper, public radio station, and two local TV stations organized town hall meetings in three Wisconsin cities to stimulate discussion of the gubernatorial race. A candidate debate, with questions from audience members, followed. The debate was simulcast live on public radio and public TV stations. Research showed that the Madison project increased knowledge of public affairs and drew people into the electoral process.[4]

The Charlotte Observer in North Carolina called on public journalism concepts in its news coverage of a much different situation—a racial conflict that had developed over the use of a city park. African-American young people had been using the park's lot as a gathering place for car cruising. This angered White residents of the neighborhood, and when city officials agreed to ban cruising from the park, the situation grew tense.

Rather than just cover the conflict, The Observer tried to find solutions to the problem. Reporters conducted lengthy interviews with the teenagers, asking them if they thought there should be more activities for young people and what would happen if the city tried to find a new spot for their cruising.

"Our reporting turned from just reporting conflict to interviewing a lot of people about what should happen, what is the solution here," explained Rick Thames, the newspaper's assistant managing editor. "The dialogue began to take place inside our newspaper that wasn't taking place in any other forum." The newspaper converge helped to defuse the crisis.[5]

From health care reform to talk radio to public journalism, the mass media are at the vortex of modern political communication. Unlike previous eras, when much of the business of politics was conducted in private back-room sessions, nowadays political campaigns are conducted in the public sector, with the mass media a major weapon in the battle for public opinion.

This book focuses on political communication and the complex interplay of influence among policymakers, the media, and the public. It traces the evolution of modern political communication, looking at changes and continuities in political media over the course of this country's history. It explores theories of political media, the impact of media in elections, and ways to improve the nation's dialogue about political issues.

As we will see, communication has always played a role in politics in the United States. It is part of the dynamic experiment in self-government that America's Founding Fathers launched over 200 years ago. The democratic ideal—the notion that people can govern themselves, elect leaders, and run a society by the rules of representative democracy—has captured the imagination of leaders and citizens in America from the beginning of the nation's history to the present day.

It is a complex system, this American system of politics and political communication, a system fraught with puzzles and paradoxes. We are a nation in which a man (Ross Perot) can rise from a middle-class background to make billions in a computer business dedicated to handling Medicare claims, then rail against the government that made him his fortune, launch a presidential campaign on a television talk show, inspire thousands of volunteers to support his candidacy, spend millions of his personal fortune on television advertising, and in 1992 capture 19% of the popular vote, an achievement that a less affluent candidate carrying the same message could never possibly have attained.

America is a nation that has more media—from newspapers to radio to television to the Internet—than any nation on earth, more coverage of the political campaign appearing in more media outlets than any other nation, a panoply of analyses, commentaries, and book-length syntheses of politics, politicians, and electoral campaigns. Yet we are a nation in which most people blithely choose to ignore the information that they can obtain from these many sources and instead opt to get most of their news from television, which even its most celebrated news anchors acknowledge is at best a headline service, never meant to be the sole source of political information for citizens in a democracy.[6]

America is a nation that celebrates democracy every Fourth of July, but increasingly finds that elections, the centerpiece of democracy, are terribly expensive affairs, costing in the hundreds of millions; they are events in which interest groups and parties trip over one another to figure out ways to use campaign finance loopholes to raise more money for electoral campaigns. The American presidential election attracts the interest of millions of Americans when conventions and presidential debates roll around, stimulates citizens to learn more about their candidates, yet nonetheless fails to rouse millions of other—more disenchanted—citizens out of their lethargy and apathy. Typically, no more than 55% of the public votes in presidential elections.

Yet for all the paradoxes and failures to live up to the ideals set forth by the Founding Fathers, the nation's political communication system has shown resilience and openness to change, from the introduction of the primary system in the early 1900s to the advent of public journalism in the early 1990s.

The manner and style in which politics is communicated in this country—a complex and controversial subject—is the focus of this book. The discussion takes us from the administration of George Washington to that of Bill Clinton, from presidential press conferences to local boosterism. The book examines the many ways in which messages are constructed and communicated from public officials through the mass media to people like you and me.

DEFINING THE TERMS

When it comes to politics, many Americans would agree with Finley Peter Dunne's fictional character, Mr. Dooley, that "politics is still th' same ol' spoort iv highway robb'ry." Study after study shows that Americans hold their elected officials in low esteem and have less confidence in government to do the right thing than they did a generation ago.[7] To many Americans, politics conjures up negative images—laundered money, shady deals, corruption in high places.

Of course, some of this exists. Talk to people in Chicago and they will regale you with stories —some steeped in myth, others based in fact—of how convicted felons have held high political office in the city of broad shoulders. As I discuss later in this book, there is reason to be concerned about ethical violations and abuses in contemporary politics. Nonetheless, there is much that is good in politics—it is politics, after all, that brought about the United States of America, and that has produced major changes including the 19th amendment that gave women the right to vote, civil rights legislation, and Social Security.

Yet for a variety of reasons, people harbor negative attitudes toward politics. There are many reasons for this, including the news media's tendency to emphasize conflict rather than efforts to build consensus, politicians' own tendency to exploit the media to showcase their opponents' vulnerabilities, and the public's predilection for simple explanations of a complex political scene. Thus when conflicts develop over legislative matters and the parties are at loggerheads, people frequently shake their heads, and say, "It's just politics." But as Samuel Popkin notes, "That's the saddest phrase in America, as if 'just politics' means that there was no stake."[8]

What is politics? Simply put, it is "the science of how who gets what and why."[9] More complexly, it is "a process whereby a group of people, whose opinions or interests are initially divergent, reach collective decisions which are generally regarded as binding on the group, and enforced as common policy."[10]

This book focuses not just on politics, but on the communication of political issues, on what an academic journal calls "press-politics" and what scholars call political communication.[11] One of the theses of this book is that you cannot understand the current political scene without appreciating the role and impact of mass media. This is hardly a controversial thesis. With the decline of political parties and the rapid diffusion of television, the mass media have come to perform many of the functions previously reserved for

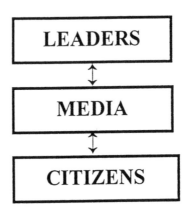

FIG. 1.1 The Major Players in Political Communication.
(Arrows denote influence of one party on another)

parties. The media have come to play an important role in the process by which leaders attempt to influence public attitudes and shape public policy. They have become the stage on which the country's political battles are fought, a forum for public discussion, and a way for citizens to talk back to the country's elites.[12]

Political communication can thus be defined as **the process by which a nation's leadership, media, and citizenry exchange and confer meaning upon messages that relate to the conduct of public policy.** There are several parts to this definition.

First, *political communication is a process*. It does not happen automatically. A leader cannot snap his or her fingers and get people to communicate. On the contrary, political communication is a complex, dynamic activity. Public officials influence journalists by supplying the raw materials of news, and journalists constrain the actions of politicians through such institutional mechanisms as deadlines and news values.

Mass media can influence citizens, but citizens also shape media agendas by indicating in opinion polls the issues that they find most important; the news media then feel an obligation (and have an economic incentive) to devote space and time to these issues. If you draw a diagram of the political communication process, you would have many bidirectional arrows showing that the arrows of influence go both ways (see Figure 1.1). Moreover, you would place the media smack dab in the middle of the process, for they play a critical role in modern political communication. While citizens and leaders do communicate directly, without the intrusion of media, this is the exception rather than the rule. Most communication between leaders and citizens occurs through the mass media, and the media play an important role in influencing the form and content of that communication.

Second, *there are three main actors who clamor for space on the public stage: leaders, the media, and the public.* This is the golden triangle of political communication. Importantly, these three agencies contain numerous subsets: there are many different types of leaders (national, state, and local; elected and appointed officials; those with power, those who aspire to power but are seen as credible by community members, etc). There are thousands of different media, running the gamut from small political newsletters and Web sites to metropolitan newspapers to corporate giants, like NBC, ABC, and CBS. And there are millions of citizens, who vary greatly in their interest in politics, their knowledge levels, and their access to the corridors of power.

Throughout this book, I use the term *elites* to refer to a nation's or a community's leaders. By elites, I mean *"political decision makers and opinion leaders in all walks of life."*[13] I distinguish elites from the public, itself a complex entity. I also refer to public opinion, defined as *"group consensus about matters of political concern which has developed in the wake of informed discussion."*[14]

A third characteristic of political communication is the exchange and interpretation of messages. Leaders, media personnel, and citizens frequently interpret messages quite differently as a function of their different positions in society and the different roles they perform in the political system. After a presidential debate, candidates will try to "spin" the outcome, arguing that they did better than expected. The media will cast a critical eye on this interpretation, and the public may lump the media and candidates together, regarding them both as part of the system of political insiders.

One of the most interesting issues in political communication is the extent to which the nation's leaders can induce the press and the public to buy their view of events—the degree to which leaders can convince the media and citizens to see events (ranging from the state of the economy to a war in a distant land) as they, the leaders, see them. Radical critics say that elites are enormously successful in getting everyone else to see things the way they do; conservative scholars aren't so sure.

Contemporary political communication is powerfully influenced by the mere fact that so much of it occurs via the mass media. We no longer see our leaders give speeches on tree stumps or from railroad cars, but we see them on television, after their speeches have been prepared by staffs of speech writers, or we read about their decisions, once these decisions have been interpreted, decoded, and encoded by reporters.

It is easy to romanticize the past and say that in the good old days of the nineteenth century, people heard their candidates speak live, in the flesh, and that things were better when voters could see the sweat on the brows of their candidates. But, as we note throughout this book, things were not necessarily better in the days of yesteryear, for candidates did not always speak clearly and honestly about the issues of the day. Nonetheless, the fact that leaders and political groups tailor their messages to the media and are exquisitely sensitive to the demands of modern media has an important impact on the content and style of political communication. Indeed, politics is communicated much differently today than in earlier eras, in large part because the modern news media function not only as conduits for communication, but also as major power centers whose structures and routines powerfully influence the content and form of politicians' communications with the public.

Finally, *the last distinguishing characteristic of political communication is that messages are concerned broadly with governance, or the conduct of public policy.* It is commonly believed that political communication is concerned only with elections, but this is not so. Politics, broadly defined, concerns the process by which society reaches consensus on policy issues. Thus political communication occurs when citizens, media, and leaders "dialogue" about issues of broad concern to elites or the public. These run the gamut from the president's decision to send troops to the Persian Gulf to a pay raise for members of Congress to a mayor's decision to run for reelection.

Since politics is fundamentally about the pursuit and use of power, political communication necessarily involves power considerations. As I discuss throughout this book, leaders, mass media, and citizens frequently jockey for control of the public agenda. Although leaders have more power than citizens and media, in that they control society's resources, they are not always able to shape the agenda —or the issues under public discussion—in the way they would like. This makes political communication dynamic and volatile.

Contextual Influences

It is important to remember that political communication occurs in a context, in a particular country or society that has developed a complex and distinctive economic, legal, and social structure. The focus of this book is political communication in America. America's political communication system, like that of other nations, is a product of its unique history—the forces, people, and cultural institutions that shaped the country's past and continue to influence its present.

In particular, political communication in America is influenced by the economic system—the fact that the means of production are owned by private interests rather than public entities. The U.S. political system is also shaped by legal forces. The First Amendment gives the news media considerable freedom to decide how they want to cover and report the news. At the same time, the First Amendment protects paid political speech, a controversial issue inasmuch as the courts have held that political action committees are entitled to spend vast sums of money on a candidate's campaign, as long as they work independently of the candidate.

The manner in which candidates, media, and citizens communicate also depends on the main features of a country's electoral system. Electoral systems differ in how they choose candidates. In some countries, like the U.S., majority rule reigns. Citizens vote for individual candidates, and the victory goes to the candidate who gets a plurality or majority of the votes cast. By contrast, several European countries choose candidates through proportional representation. In these systems, voters cast ballots for party-selected lists of candidates. Seats in the legislature are then apportioned among the political parties based on the percentage of votes each party captures in the election.[15] Political communication tends to be more candidate-centered in majority systems like the U.S. and more party-focused in nations that employ proportional representation.

Political communication in America is influenced also by historical factors—by the long tradition of press involvement in politics. Press involvement in politics in this country dates back to the 1770s when (at least some) newspapers were agitating for revolution, and has continued to the present day, when the media are there in force whenever anything that is potentially newsworthy is happening—e.g., party nominating conventions, where the number of journalists far exceeds the number of delegates, presidential debates, and the Persian Gulf War. The press has a proud—and complex—history in American politics.

Finally, we need to remember that although politics gets a bad rep these days, political communication can, or should, play a vital role in a democracy. In an ideal world, elites would use the communications media to inform and influence people, helping them improve their lot in life, and to also put aside their personal interests to work for the common good. In an ideal world, the news media would be a positive force, helping people comprehend political issues more deeply and critically. In an ideal world, the public would be enriched and invigorated by its participation in the political communication process. Of course, the realities fall short of the ideals, as we will see in this book. But the ideals remain as beacons to strive toward.

THE STUDY OF POLITICAL COMMUNICATION

The study of political communication goes back to Aristotle. Sages throughout the centuries have written about political communication, from Machiavelli in Italy to Thomas Jefferson in America. In our own time, political communication is something of a cottage industry—journalists and politicians write books, newspaper articles, and magazine features on the subject of politics and the press. Citizens also express their views about the media—often pronounced as one word by those who forget that the term encompasses newspapers, magazines, books, radio, television, and computer communication. "Everyone in a democracy is a certified media critic," Michael Schudson observes.[16] And this, he says, is as it should be.

Political communication is also a multidisciplinary field of scholarly study. It calls on research from the fields of communication, political science, psychology, sociology, and philosophy. Scholars bring a host of theories and methodologies to the study of political communication. What separates the scholar from the journalist or the ordinary citizen is the former's determination to understand the essence of political communication in a particular culture—how it works, why it often fails, what impact it has on members of society, and how it can be improved to better serve the public good.[17]

Scholarly Perspectives on Political Communication

One can approach the study of political communication from a number of vantage points. Scholars with a political science bent have examined the political and structural factors that constrain the news media and political leaders, in particular the impact of the nominating system on media coverage of electoral politics. Sociologically oriented investigators have examined the nature of media institutions, exploring the ways in which journalists navigate their roles in large bureaucratic organizations. Rhetoric scholars have explored the symbolic structure of political communications, particularly the verbal style of presidential speeches. Journalistically oriented researchers have examined how the press covers government, looking at how critically or kindly the news media treat the president, as well as other candidates for public office. Communication scholars with a psychological bent have examined the impact of political campaigns on individuals and groups.

As I discuss in chapter 10, the study of political communication has evolved and changed over the years. Election studies dominated the early research. So, too, did a concern with how the media affected individuals' beliefs and attitudes. Over the years, the field of political communication has expanded greatly. It operates at different levels of analysis, including *the individual level* (how media influence voters' cognitions about candidates), *the institutional level* (communication processes in complex media and political party organizations), and *the systemic level* (the ways in which the media influence and are influenced by the larger society or culture). A systems approach argues that to truly understand the nature of political communication, we need to look at the larger social system, and how economic, legal, political, and technological factors interrelate and constrain participants in the communication process.[18] Neo-Marxist scholars have taken systems approaches one step further, arguing that the media are closely connected with the power centers in society and invariably act to maintain the status quo rather than to shake it up. This view has both adherents and detractors.

OUTLINE OF THE BOOK

This book is designed to introduce you to what we know about political communication in America, the different perspectives on politics, the press, and the public, and to the strengths and weaknesses of particular points of view. I do not attempt to present *one* point of view on political communication. There are plenty of books that do this and do it well. Instead, I try to offer a variety of perspectives and empirical findings on political communication. I do this to help students and other readers better appreciate the way that politics is currently communicated in America, as well as the ways that intelligent people have come to grips with political communication.

I have my own biases: I think that the political communication system in America has great hope and promise, that it has produced great leaders and talented journalists, and that it has done much to educate and edify the public. I also believe that it has weaknesses that need to be addressed if we want to improve the quality of our civic discourse. In addition, I believe that we cannot understand political communication today without appreciating where we came from and how we think about the past. That is why I devote a good deal of attention to history throughout the book—to help readers see what is new and different about today, what is borrowed from yesteryear, and to call attention to the continuities that run like a stream through America's two-century-old political communication terrain.

The textbook is divided into three sections. The first focuses on the media and the institutions of government. I begin with a historical review of the press and the presidency (using the old-style term "press" synonymously with news media). I then discuss the press and presidency in today's era. The next chapters examine a critical aspect of presidential communication: rhetoric and speech-making. The last two chapters of this section focus on Congress and the media, and local government and the press.

The second portion of the book examines the theories and broad effects of political communication. Chapter 10 reviews the history of political communication scholarship. The next two chapters examine the premier theory of political communication: agenda-setting, along with its many complications and policy implications. Chapters 13 and 14 apply this line of research, as well as other perspectives discussed in the book, to the Clinton health care reform campaign. Nonelectoral media campaigns are an important part of modern political communication and are therefore deserving of special attention.

The third section of the book explores the media's role in the presidential election. These chapters look at the media's impact on the nomination process, the nature of news coverage of the campaign, political advertising, and presidential debates.

Theory plays an important part in the study of political communication, and I discuss it throughout the book. I believe that theory is most usefully appreciated when it is discussed in context, so I introduce theories in the context of particular facets of political communication. Theories of news are described in chapter 5; functional theory, as applied to local news, is discussed in chapter 9; and major theoretical approaches to the study of political media effects are introduced in chapter 10. Chapters 11 and 12 focus on agenda-setting and agenda-building, and the implications of agenda-setting for elections are noted in the last section of the book, which looks at communication in the presidential campaign.

The book covers a great deal of territory, although it does not cover everything in political communication. And, most assuredly, it does not cover the dynamic relationships among politicians, press, and public in other cultures. This book focuses on the ideas, issues, and insights that have emerged from the study of political communication in America.

Throughout the course of the book, I touch on a number of questions about the press and politics that are often raised today. You may have wondered about some of these yourself. For example:

- Is the press biased?
- How has the press covered the presidency?
- How have presidents used the media to accomplish important national goals?
- Do leaders manipulate the news and public opinion?
- Why does Congress get so much bad press?
- What does it mean to say that the media set the agenda?
- Did *The Washington Post* bring down Richard Nixon?
- Do political advertisements manipulate voters?
- Is politics just image and show?
- Why did Clinton win the 1996 election?

With these questions in mind, we now begin our exploration of political communication in America.

2

Early History of the Press and Presidency

The relationship between the presidency and the news media has long fascinated observers of the national scene. Does the president manipulate the press? Or does the press hold the upper hand? Are reporters too eager to publish what White House officials tell them? Are they too critical? Does the president manage the news? Is he victimized by a disrespectful press?

These questions strike to the heart of our inquiry into the presidency and the press. Democratic theory holds that the president and news media play different roles in a democracy: the president is charged with leading government, the press with communicating information about government to the public and providing a check on government abuses.[1] To appreciate the state of today's relations between these two institutions, we need to turn the clock backward. We cannot appreciate the continuities and changes in presidential–press relations without looking at history. This chapter looks at relations between the presidency and press from George Washington to Herbert Hoover. The next chapter continues the journey by examining the presidency and the press as they evolved in the twentieth century. What follows is an overview, based on the work of journalism historians, particularly the insightful scholarship of John Tebbel and Sarah Watts.

EARLY STRUGGLES WITH A FREE PRESS

Anyone who thinks that George Washington, the heroic general of the Revolution, the legendary father of his country, got a free ride from the

American press should think again. George Washington got gored by the newspapers of his era. "Today's presidents may think they have more press headaches than George Washington," media critic Lewis Wolfson notes, "but the news media are pussycats compared with the unrestrainedly partisan press our early presidents had to cope with."[2]

The early media did not subscribe to the norm of objectivity. They were a partisan press, vituperative in their attacks on political leaders with whom they disagreed. Two illustrious members of Washington's cabinet—Alexander Hamilton and Thomas Jefferson—established competing newspapers. Hamilton created the *Gazette of the United States*, the organ of the Federalist Party, and Jefferson helped establish the *National Gazette*, the mouthpiece of the newly formed Republican Party. The fact that two members of his Cabinet were connected with opposing newspapers must surely have frustrated Washington.

Like other architects of the Revolution, George Washington was a literate man, a voracious newspaper reader who subscribed to more than five newspapers and three magazines and insisting on getting copies of those newspapers that criticized him most stridently.

The attacks were nothing if not strident. Benjamin Franklin's grandson, Benjamin Franklin Bache (nicknamed "Lightning Rod Junior" after his grandfather's invention), gored Washington mercilessly. Bache penned:

> If ever a nation was debauched by a man, the American nation has been debauched by Washington. If ever a nation has suffered from the improper influence of a man, the American nation has suffered from the influence of Washington.[3]

Other anti-Federalist editors joined the chorus, calling Washington "treacherous," "despotic," and "a spoiled child."

The criticisms eventually got under Washington's skin. On one occasion, an observer who was on the scene chronicled that Washington "got into one of those passions when he cannot command himself, ran on much on the personal abuse which had bestowed on him, (and) defied any man on earth to produce one single act of his since he had been in the government which was not done on the purest motives."[4] Washington's reaction was not unlike those of modern presidents (such as Bill Clinton, who has railed against the media and once called a talk-radio program to complain about attacks on his presidency). Like today's presidents, Washington was outraged by press criticism.

In the end, the attacks seemed to exert little impact on the views of ordinary Americans, who loved and respected their first president immensely. Washington, though given to fits of passion after reading one of the journalistic attacks, never opted to challenge the First Amendment nor tried to silence the press. He held tenaciously to the principle of a free press and to the right of newspapers to print what they wanted. That was part of his character, Tebbel and Watts, note, adding "it was not the character of many who followed him in the highest office."[5]

When John Adams was elected to the presidency in 1796, the Federalists assumed that all would go well. It was presumed that Adams would continue Washington's programs, and that he would maintain the party's control over the ship of state. Adams had distinguished himself by his many fiery contributions to the colonial press in the years before the Revolution. It was therefore ironic that John Adams engulfed his party and the nation in one of the biggest travesties of American press history: the Sedition Act.

Trouble began brewing in 1798. Threat of war between America and France loomed, and there was concern that subversive French agents were circulating in the states. The Federalists wanted to take action against the French partisans, as well as against Irish and English exiles who were residing in America. Federalist leaders suspected the exiles wanted to overthrow the U.S. government. At the same time, the Federalists were furious with the Republican press, maintaining that it had played a critical role in the Whiskey Rebellion, a violent protest by settlers in Western Pennsylvania who refused to pay an excise tax on whiskey. Federalist partisans charged that the Republican press had whipped the settlers into frenzy by waging a wicked propaganda campaign in their newspapers.[6]

The House of Representatives proceeded to debate freedom of the press for 5 days. Jeffersonians defended the press's right to publish what it wanted. A leading defender of the press's rights, then and later, was James Madison, the brilliant architect of the Bill of Rights and the Federalist Papers. "Opinions are not the objects of legislation," Madison had written. He had reason to write this. The opinions under legislative scrutiny were those of his own party.

In the end, the Federalists carried the day. Congress passed the **Aliens Act,** which enabled the president to deport aliens whom he deemed to be subversive. It also enacted the **Sedition Act,** that held that any person who published "false, scandalous and malicious writing" against the United States government, Congress, or the president was to be punished by a fine of no more than $2,000 and a jail term not exceeding 2 years. The Sedition Act did not prohibit criticism of government, but it gave government the authority to punish those whose commentaries were deemed to be false, scandalous, and malicious. A number of editors were thrown jail because they criticized President Adams or the Army. The Federalists argued that the First Amendment did not give the newspaper the right to print false information. The Republicans viewed the Sedition Act as unconstitutional and an exercise in tyranny. Furthermore, they argued that the federal government had no right under the First Amendment to punish the press for making seditious claims.[7]

The Alien and Sedition Acts provoked a firestorm of protest from Jefferson and other political leaders. In 1800 Adams was swept from office. Thomas Jefferson became the third president of the United States, and one of his first acts was to pardon all those journalists who had been imprisoned. The Alien and Sedition Acts expired of their own accord in March, 1801. In hindsight we can see that the Sedition Act, with its attempt to punish people for speaking their minds in dissident ways, represented a dangerous precedent for a democratic society.

The new president, Thomas Jefferson, was an erudite man of arts and letters who had much to say about press and politics. An ardent defender of the free press, he wrote some 13 years before becoming president that "Were it left to me to decide whether we should have a government without newspapers or newspapers without a government, I should not hesitate a moment to prefer the latter." When he became president, Jefferson had a more complex view of press freedom. He convinced a young printer to launch a newspaper to represent his party's point of view, and he gave the printer a lucrative government printing contract.

One might think that the press would have given Jefferson an easy time of it, in view of the many luminary contributions he had made to democracy. Not so. The Federalist press tore into him, calling him a demagogue, a man lacking faith, and a man who wished to be dictator. The attacks even caused Jefferson to lament that newspapers actually misinform those who read them. At one point, Jefferson became so agitated by Federalist attacks that he suggested that Republican governors in several states target selected Federalist newspaper editors for libel. However, Jefferson was careful not to launch a whole-scale persecution, as Adams had a few years before with the Sedition Act.

During the administrations of James Madison and James Monroe, the press became embroiled in international issues—the War of 1812 in Madison's case, and the Monroe Doctrine, regarding the U.S. commitment to fledgling Central American nations, in Monroe's case. Monroe's successor, John Quincy Adams, had a stubborn, inflexible attitude toward the press.

He proved to be an unpopular president and was soundly defeated by Andrew Jackson, a man who had a much different attitude toward the press and public.

APPEALS TO THE MASS AUDIENCE

Jackson was unique among American presidents. There had been war heroes and there would be more who would follow "Old Hickory," as he came to be known, but none could equal Jackson's brash, raucous, ever-populist presence. "This tall, craggy, rough, deeply opinionated man," Tebbel and Watts note, "was about as far from the Virginia dynasty as one could get."[8] Jackson had commanded the American troops to victory against the British in New Orleans in 1814, and he had fought a duel and a gunfight. The battles had left their marks, and Jackson was often in serious physical pain. Two bullets could not be dislodged from his body, and he suffered from rheumatism and chest congestion.

Jackson was a fighter, though—a populist through and through. During his campaign for president in 1828, he capitalized on support from thousands of workers, immigrants, and traders. To the groups, he was a hero, "one of them," not a snob like John Quincy Adams. Although Jackson identified with the common person, he was canny enough to realize that there was political mileage to be gained in appealing to the masses. His supporters ran the first grass-roots campaign in American history, and they did it with the help of influential newspaper editors.

Jackson did not forget the help his newspaper friends had given him, and he showered favors upon them as president. Three of his favorites served as his "Kitchen Cabinet." During the middle of Jackson's first term, the group began *The Washington Globe*, which served as the official press organ of the Jackson administration. In exchange for editing the pro-Jackson newspaper, the newspaper received government printing contracts, and federal employees who earned at least $1,000 a year were expected to take out subscriptions. As many as 57 reporters were on the payroll of the federal government during Jackson's administration.[9] This was a flagrant example of government manipulation of the press, and it outraged Jackson's opponents. However, Jackson was merely extending a practice that had its roots in the Jefferson administration.

During Jackson's administration, "the press was at the very center of American political life," scholar Gerald Baldasty notes.[10] Newspapers were the medium by which party leaders communicated with the public. Newspapers provided a forum to discuss issues with the public, create bonds with people, and gain supporters. Even though they were unabashedly partisan and highly biased by today's standards, the party newspapers served a positive function: They put elites in touch with voters.

Historians have noted that Jackson's rise in American politics coincided with an important development in journalism: the appearance of the *penny press*, "a press for the masses."[11] These papers sold for a penny instead of the standard six cents. Adopting a different style from the party newspapers, the penny press featured human interest and crime stories in an unabashed attempt to attract a mass audience. In a sense, they fit the Jacksonian era: Just as Jackson wooed the common person, so did newspapers try to appeal to the ordinary American. The mass public now had a voice in American politics, faint though it might be.

After Jackson came a string of mediocre presidents: Van Buren, Harrison, Tyler. In 1844 Tyler ran against James Polk, whose anonymity in American politics was epitomized by the Whig party slogan, "Who is James Polk?" Polk ran a clever campaign and defeated Henry Clay because a third party candidate took away votes from Clay in New York and because Polk's Democrats encouraged fraudulent voting, a common practice in those days.

When he took office, Polk had to deal with an impending war with Mexico, a war that critics feel had its roots in an ideology of nationalism and expansionism. It was an unpopular war in many quarters. The newspapers that opposed it called it "Mr. Polk's war" in much the same way that 1960s protesters would hang the label of "Nixon's war" on President Richard Nixon.

The Mexican War was the first that the U.S. press covered in detail. By this time the entrepreneurial press was in full swing. War coverage was colorful. The nation had never seen anything like it. Reports came back from the field as quickly as the pony express and steamboats could carry them. As would be true of the Persian Gulf War a century and a half later, the press would beat the military with messages from the front lines.

The United States won the war, but the battles took their toll on James Polk. He died at the age of 53, shortly after completing his term in office.

The presidents who followed—Taylor, Fillmore, Pierce, and Buchanan—did not distinguish themselves in office. They proved to be weak presidents, unable to deal with the issue—slavery—that was splitting the country and would lead to civil war.

The 1840s and 1850s were a period of growth for the American press. The invention of the telegraph meant that news could reach the public almost immediately. It made possible the development of the nation's first wire service, the Associated Press. Newspapers like *The New York Herald* and *The New York Tribune* were read by thousands and were attracting advertising dollars. The age of the party press and of presidential subsidies to partisan newspapers was over, the final death knell sounded by the formation of the Government Printing Office in 1860. The office terminated the lucrative contracts that newspapers had signed with governments for over half a century. The stage was set for Abraham Lincoln and the newspapers of the Civil War.[12]

LINCOLN AND THE PRESS

After reading the history of the press and the Civil War, it is difficult not to be moved by the ways in which Abraham Lincoln dealt with the conflicting demands of waging war and maintaining a free press. Throughout the horrible war, Lincoln showed remarkable restraint, compassion, and respect for the principle of a free press. He did make mistakes, however, for he faced a situation that no president before or since has had to confront.

Our story begins in the 1850s when Lincoln was a rising star on the national scene. Lincoln became increasingly concerned about the great moral issue of the times—slavery—and began speaking out on the issue. One address caught the attention of leading newspaper editors of the Midwest. In his speech, Lincoln spoke passionately in favor of the abolition of slavery, holding the audience spellbound and captivating the journalists in the crowd. According to one reporter, when Lincoln was finished, "the audience sprang to their feet, and cheer after cheer told how deeply their hearts had been touched."[13] Joseph Medill, manager of *The Chicago Tribune*, was in the audience, and the speech appears to have convinced him that Lincoln was a man with a future in presidential politics.

Lincoln had a keen understanding of newspapers and was not above using editors to accomplish his political goals. He cultivated Medill and his editor, Charles Ray. Realizing that he needed their support in the 1860 presidential nomination, he made a special stopover in Chicago to show them the speech he was giving to a Republican group in New York. He asked for their comments and they were more than happy to oblige. "We toiled for hours," they reported, convinced that they had improved the speech and no doubt gratified by Lincoln's thank-yous. And yet:

> When Medill and Ray finally got the text of that famous Cooper Union Speech from New York, as it was printed in Greeley's *Tribune*, they looked eagerly for the evidences of their handiwork. There were none: Lincoln had not used even one of their suggestions. "Abe must have lost the notes out the car window," Ray said.[14]

Lincoln soon earned the support of other leading newspaper editors. In those days, editors were known to work behind the scenes for politicians—horse-trading and making delegates promises of positions in exchange for their votes in key states. Lincoln was nominated and later elected, much to the displeasure of the Southern press, which regarded him as the embodiment of evil.

In 1861 Lincoln set out for Washington, determined to preserve the union. Events were careening out of control, however. The first shots rang out at Fort Sumter in South Carolina on April 12, 1861.

The Civil War was the first American war in which government's desire to control information clashed consistently with the press's wish to print the facts as it saw them. Balancing press freedom with national security was a new issue in 1861, and Lincoln dealt with the issue complexly. He recognized that good press relations were important and made himself available to reporters. Taking tolerance to new limits, he turned the other cheek when reporters acted as though they were more important than generals. He refused to take offense when editors behaved as if they were running the war from their newsrooms. Realizing that he needed to court public opinion and that the news media represented an important way to reach the public, he cultivated reporters diligently during his time in office. Unlike many of his successors, he did not attribute hostile intentions to the press. He assumed that journalists could be a positive force, an instrument to advance his political and moral agenda.

Ultimately, Lincoln ran up against newspapers that published military secrets. The press reported the locations of General Grant's guns in Vicksburg in 1863. It revealed the details of a land and sea battle in Wilmington, North Carolina in December, 1864. The South could frequently obtain more facts from Northern newspapers than from its own espionage agents. "There is no question that lives were lost as a result, and even battles fought unnecessarily," Tebbel and Watts point out.[15]

To control the flow of information, Lincoln monitored telegraph reports and allowed his generals to restrict the movements and activities of reporters. He had a foreign correspondent thrown out of the country for describing how the Union army panicked at the Battle of Manassas. For the most part, Lincoln steered clear of imposing governmental controls because of his commitment to a free press and because, even then, presidents picked up information from reading the papers that they could not acquire elsewhere.

Lincoln was less tolerant of the Copperhead press, the newspapers that virulently opposed the war. In a move that was clearly unconstitutional, he revoked the postal privileges of one Copperhead paper, *The New York Daily News* (no relation to the present newspaper). This meant the publisher had to find other ways to distribute his newspaper. Subsequently, *The Daily News* was suspended, causing it to stop publishing for 18 months. A year and a half later, the paper was back in business, proudly publishing its criticisms of the war.

In the case of Union General Ambrose Burnside, Lincoln acted more temperately. Burnside had sent his soldiers to the offices of *The Chicago Times* at 4 a.m. in June, 1863. The troops stopped the presses, directed employees to leave the premises, and seized control of the newspaper. The Chicago Times had been particularly vitriolic in its criticism of Lincoln and had consistently ignored warnings to stop provoking antiwar sentiments. Many Chicagoans supported Burnside, disgusted by the unpatriotic stands of the paper. There was talk on the street of burning the newspaper to a crisp. It would have been easy for Lincoln to have sided with Burnside and the mobs. But he chose not to, revoking Burnside's order to suppress the paper.

Criticism of Lincoln continued throughout the war. Newspapers called him "a slang-whanging stump speaker," "a half-witted usurper," and "the Illinois ape." Articles lambasted him, charging that he was often drunk and had ordered the killing of numerous soldiers just to achieve victory. Given the terrible human costs of the war, it is easy to understand why newspapers would feel a sense of anger and frustration. Lincoln, to his credit, tolerated the invectives and allowed a variety of opposition papers to keep publishing. It was as if, Tebbel and Watts note, "pro-Nazi papers in major cities were permitted to publish and circulate in the years of the Second World War."[16]

Throughout the war, Lincoln had to struggle with an active press corps that wanted to be there to cover the battles, in much the same way as today's media want to be on the scene. Lincoln faced questions of news media coverage that no one had dealt with before. He coped remarkably well with a situation that today's presidents are grateful they do not have to face.

DEVELOPMENTS FROM 1860 TO 1900

The Civil War led to major changes in journalism. The desire to save telegraph tolls led to more concise writing. Journalists' fears that their stories would not survive government censors encouraged them to put the most important information early in the story, giving birth to the lead. The nation's appetite for the latest happenings made newspapers hot items. As a result of the Civil War, newspapers realized that circulation could be enhanced and the public could be served by providing news on a regular basis.[17]

Lincoln's successor, Andrew Johnson, became the focal point of controversy during his administration. His political blunders and outrageous public comments "aroused a storm of indignation throughout the country," observed *The New York Evening Post*.[18] In time, most newspapers and magazines joined official Washington in lambasting Johnson's Reconstruction policies. Johnson tried valiantly to save his administration, even setting up regular interviews with journalists. However, his efforts were in vain as he was denounced in major newspapers and in Congress (where he escaped impeachment by one vote).

One element of the criticism was unfair and was based, as it turned out, on an incorrect piece of information. A story that appeared in newspapers claimed Johnson was frequently drunk in public and in particular during a speech in Cleveland. It turned out that the allegation was not true and that the Cleveland drunkard was not Johnson, but the man destined to replace him in the White House: General Ulysses S. Grant.

Grant had served the country brilliantly during the Civil War, shepherding the Union to victory over the South. As president, he was unable to lead the country and presided over one of the most corrupt administrations in American history. Historians have argued that Grant's naivete when it came to political issues made him vulnerable to the shenanigans of his appointees and family members. The press dug into the scandalous affairs of the Grant Administration, giving rise to investigative reporting.

After Grant came the capable Rutherford Hayes, who was followed by James Garfield, later cut down by an assassin. Garfield's successor was Chester Arthur, a lonely and private man who made it clear he did not enjoy the public life of a president. "You have no idea how depressing and fatiguing it is to live in the same house where you work," he told one reporter, one assumes with a straight face.[19]

Arthur lasted a term. In 1884 the nation was ready for a change. New groups were mobilizing and power was shifting. Concerns about the oppressive practices of big companies were mounting. National labor unions, farmers' alliances, and reformist political movements were organizing. The age of muckraking was around the corner. Into this environment Grover Cleveland strode. I say strode because Cleveland was one of the most robust men to occupy the White House, weighing more than 300 pounds.

Cleveland had made a name for himself in Buffalo, fighting against political corruption. He became governor of New York and was nominated for president by the Democrats at their Chicago convention. Cleveland faced one political problem—and it was a whopper. While in Buffalo he had become enamored of a young woman. The two had become romantically involved, and their romance had produced a child.[20] Cleveland never married the woman, but he did provide for the youngster, making sure he was properly taken care of. The story became known to Cleveland's Republican opponents during the presidential election campaign of 1884, and they made hay of the issue. But Cleveland's honesty and integrity carried the day, and he won a very close election against Republican James Blaine.

The president's private life became public again when it was reported that the 49-year-old president was to marry a 21-year-old whom he had known for years. Cleveland had hoped to keep the matter private. For a time the press and Cleveland played cat and mouse, the press trying to find out if the president was to wed the lovely Frances Folsom, Cleveland trying to hush things up. Cleveland and Folsom made the headlines years before Kennedy and his mistresses, Gary Hart and Donna Rice, and Bill Clinton and Gennifer Flowers. There were no ground rules for covering the marriage. It was one of the first times that the press had to wrestle with balancing out the president's right to privacy with the public's right to know, and predictably they came out in favor of providing as much news as the traffic would bear. E. L. Godkin, the strong-minded editor of The Nation, had the courage to proclaim that "Nobody has a right to know everything about anybody on any occasion in life, except the police about a man convicted of a crime."[21]

As president, Cleveland displayed remarkable integrity. He worked to reduce waste in government, carefully watched the expenditures of government, and wrestled with the controversial tariff question. His policies alienated big business, which poured $3 million into the campaign of Benjamin Harrison. Harrison won, only to face Cleveland again in 1892. This time Cleveland won the election. Economic problems, labor strikes, and problems abroad plagued Cleveland's second term. It came to an end in 1896 as the nation prepared to vote for the last president to take office in the nineteenth century.

The election pit the charismatic William Jennings Bryan against William McKinley, the genteel governor of Ohio. The campaign featured parades, impassioned speeches over money (the gold standard versus silver), big business contributions to McKinley (who defended the more conservative gold coinage), and even threats by companies to workers that the election of Bryan would mean the closing of plants. McKinley won the close election, and in 1897 this quiet man from Canton, Ohio, the last veteran of the Civil War to be elected president, took the oath of office, facing the demands of a changing and increasingly diverse nation.

Newspapers were changing, too. The old press barons of the mid-nineteenth century were dying, and in their place stood Joseph Pulitzer, publisher of *The New York World*, William Randolph Hearst of *The New York Journal*, Adolph Ochs of *The New York Times*, and a host of younger editors. Newspapers were becoming more specialized as division of labor took shape in the editorial department.[22]

Sensing this, McKinley strove to get on good terms with the press, hoping to avoid the problems Cleveland had encountered when he turned a cold shoulder to the Washington press corps during his second term. McKinley's staff regularly gave reporters copies of the president's speeches in advance, and his press aide appeared twice a day to meet with journalists.

The most famous aspect of McKinley's tenure, from the perspective of the presidency and the press, is the Spanish-American War. A detailed discussion of this issue is beyond the scope of this book. Suffice it to say that some of the nation's leading dailies—*The World, The Journal, and The Sun*—had been crusading for war on their news pages for years. One celebrated story went back to 1895, three years before war broke out. In February, 1895 officials from an American steamboat disclosed that they had been fired upon by a Spanish ship. *The Sun* subsequently declared that "the next Spanish gunboat that molests an American vessel ought to be pursued and blown out of the water." In reality the shots were blank and the Spanish boat had been interested only in searching the American vessel for illegal materials.[23]

From spring of 1895 to April, 1898, when the United States and Spain went to war, there were only a handful of days in which an article about Cuba did not appear in one of the leading New York dailies.[24] It culminated in February, 1898, with the famous destruction of the U.S. war ship Maine, an explosion that *The Journal* promptly declared to be the "work of an enemy" and for which it offered a $50,000 reward.

Without question, the news coverage was jingoistic, unprofessional, and, according to press critic Godkin, "disgraceful." Its impact is harder to pin down. Myth has it that the yellow press of the era launched the Spanish-American War. This oversimplifies matters. Undoubtedly, the newspapers pushed the issue to the top of the public agenda and nudged the public toward intervention. Yet not all newspapers favored war, and it is unlikely the press would have had much impact had other political and economic factors not been operative. Prominent political leaders, including Theodore Roosevelt, were clamoring for war, the U.S. had some $50 million invested in Cuban sugar plants, and intervention fit the country's policy of manifest destiny and the emerging idea that the United States should be a major player in world affairs. Facing a nearly hegemonic pressure to go to war, McKinley, a pacifist by nature, yielded and by April, 1898, the United States was at war with Spain.

The war was colorful, but short. The quick U.S. victory elevated McKinley in the nations's eyes. He was reelected in 1900, but his second administration lasted just 6 months. It ended tragically when an assassin cut down the president in September, 1901. The nation, shocked by the assassination, mourned the death of McKinley and paid homage to this traditional man of the nineteenth century.

PRESIDENTS AND THE PRESS IN THE NEW CENTURY

The twentieth century would witness massive changes in the relationship between the presidency and the press. Both the executive branch and the mass media would grow enormously over the course of the century. In the 1880s, some 95,000 people worked for the federal government; today the number approaches 3 million. In 1900, there were 171 reporters covering Washington; now there are over 10,000. Writing in 1986, scholar Gary Orren noted that "We have witnessed the rise of both the bureaucratic and the media state, a rise more dramatic than anything contemplated by the observers half a century ago, let alone by the Founding Fathers."[25]

The growth in these institutions began with Theodore Roosevelt, who took the press and presidency by storm. A big and immensely self-confident man, Roosevelt befriended, charmed, and dominated reporters in a way that no president had before. He used the power of the office to manage and shape public opinion in important ways. "He did it with a master hand, using the newspapers like a poker player," Tebbel and Watts note.[26]

It is true that other presidents had been aware of the power of public opinion and that some, like Lincoln, had used the press to shape public sentiments. But none had the sweeping impact that Roosevelt had. He expanded the powers of the presidency and in so doing extended the influence that the president had with the press. He was the first to dream up ways to use the news media to manage opinions.[27]

Far more than his predecessors, Roosevelt recognized that news does more to shape opinion than editorials. "If he could seize the headlines and influence the way reporters wrote about him, " historian George Juergens observed, "it would not matter a great deal what the press might have to say about him on its inside pages."[28]

TR expanded the White House press room and gave reporters telephones, thereby ending the nineteenth century practice of journalists' delivering stories to telegraph aides on bicycles; he talked freely and openly with reporters, delighting those who had grown accustomed to earlier presidents' icy treatments; and he even went so far as to divide reporters into groups—those who wrote stories that reflected positively on the White House and those who did not. The former were made members of an imaginary Paradise Group and were guaranteed access to the president; the latter were banished to the Ananais Club, deprived of information about goings-on at the White House. "Small wonder, then, that the president's press reports were largely favorable," Tebbel and Watts observed.[29]

From the first day he took office, Roosevelt made it clear that he would control an exchange relationship with the press. He would give reporters access to the White House they never had before, provided they did not say where they got their stories. "If you ever hint where you got (the information)," he once said, "I'll say you are a damn liar." Scholar Carolyn Smith observed that "Roosevelt could say anything he wanted and not be held responsible for any stories reporters chose to write."[30] He was able to do this because the Washington press corps had not fully evolved into a professionalized press. Unaware that they could challenge the president and demand things from him in return, reporters tended to acquiesce to Roosevelt's directives.

But even Roosevelt found that power has its limits. Some reporters resisted Roosevelt's bullying and resented his strategy of shutting out those who disagreed with him. Newspapers criticized his programs. Reporters did investigative stories on administration activities. The president took offense at criticisms, and in particular at investigative reporting. He called newspapers like *The New York Times* liars more than once. He objected when publishers whom he had courted printed critical articles about him. The president's limitless ego and extreme self-righteousness blinded him to legitimate criticisms made by newspapers.[31]

After TR came William Howard Taft, who increased the size of the presidency but in a different way from Roosevelt. Taft was the largest man ever to occupy the Oval Office: He weighed 350 pounds. However, he was less imposing mentally and politically, and he ended up doing rather little as president.

The man who defeated Taft in 1912 was Woodrow Wilson, a government scholar by training who had been president of Princeton University. Wilson had overcome dyslexia as a child to become a man of arts and letters. Throughout his adult life he was stricken with numerous physical maladies, including severe respiratory problems and strokes. Yet he had a way of rebounding from illnesses with bursts of emotional energy.

Wilson was arrogant in his dealings with the press. He thought little of reporters' intellectual abilities and believed they should print information that served the interests of the nation as Wilson, of course, defined it. He once chastised reporters for writing about the poor health of his wife and the romantic relationships of his daughters:

> Gentlemen, I want to say something this afternoon. I am a public character for the time being, but the ladies of my household are not servants of the Government and they are not public characters. I deeply resent the treatment they are receiving at the hands of the newspapers at this time. I must ask you gentlemen to make confidential representations to the several papers which you represent about this matter.[32]

Wilson's chivalry was touching, but out of place. Journalists had a right to report on the activities of the First Family, and their stories were timid by today's standards. Wilson may have been particularly chary about press disclosures of his family's private life because he was having an affair at this time, albeit with his wife's permission. Wilson once acknowledged that "I am a vague conjectural personality, more made up on opinions and academic prepossession than of human traits and red corpuscles."[33]

Wilson was complex. At the same time as he was chastising the press, he was expanding their access to the president. He was the first president to hold regular press conferences. He met with accredited journalists at least once a week for two and a half years. Where Roosevelt had limited briefings to those who were favored by the White House, Wilson gave all accredited reporters access.

Then war intervened.

When World War I began, a British foreign secretary observed that "the lamps are going out all over Europe; we shall not see them lit again in our lifetime."[34] The war took a terrible toll on humanity. It brought great disillusionment and despair.

The United States entered the war reluctantly, but once it did, Wilson felt he needed to build morale and shape public sentiments. The United States was fighting a venal enemy, but it was one about whom most Americans knew little.[35] Wilson took extraordinary steps to enlist public support.

He announced the formation of a Committee on Public Information (CPI), headed by George Creel, a former journalist. According to Creel, the effort "was a plain publicity proposition, a vast enterprise in salesmanship, the world's greatest adventure in advertising."[36] It was America's first propaganda campaign, perhaps the most extensive effort by government to mobilize and shape public opinion—and one of the most controversial. The Committee disseminated some 100 million pamphlets and posters, sent numerous educational materials to schools, and set up a national bureau of local speakers.[37] It was not uncommon to hear speakers describing America in mythical terms. America, one lecturer said, was not the name of a country, but "a living spirit" that had "purpose and pride, and conscience." One poem said, "Life is a trifle, Honor is all, Shoulder the rifle, Answer the call."[38]

The Committee flooded newspapers with news releases, sending newspapers as many as six pounds of publicity releases a day. In May, 1917 the CPI began publishing the first government daily newspaper in the United States. It bore the ominous heading, "Published Daily under Order of the President by the Committee on Public Information."

A month later the Espionage Act was passed. It allowed the government to fine or imprison those who intentionally made false statements with the goal of interfering with military operations. The Act also denied mailing privileges to newspapers that made such statements. In the first year of the Espionage Act, 75 newspapers lost their postal privileges or kept them only by pledging not to publish information about the war. The 75 newspapers included many Socialist and German language papers.

The next year the Sedition Act was passed. This made it a criminal act to publish disloyal or abusive materials about the government or the armed forces. Socialist and labor leaders were arrested and imprisoned. Lincoln had never gone this far.

When the war finally ended, Wilson tried valiantly to sell Congress and the nation on the League of Nations. Acting boldly, he crisscrossed the country to persuade Americans that the League could be an instrument for peace and democracy. Wilson was ahead of his time in both his idealism and his method. Later in the century, Wilson's technique of taking ideas to the public would be a common strategy in the presidential arsenal.

While traveling, Wilson suffered a massive stroke. His aides did not tell the press this, saying instead he had suffered a nervous breakdown and that his condition was improving. The press and public did not learn the truth for months.

As president, Woodrow Wilson faced the unenviable task of leading the nation through a war that had originated through a complex set of circumstances. He had little time to prepare the public mind. For all its excesses, the Committee on Public Information relied more on persuasion than coercion to achieve its goals. It is hard not to sympathize with Wilson's predicament. Yet Wilson and Creel went farther than they had to, and in the process infringed on the liberties of the press and citizens.

By 1920 the nation was ready for a change. The war had sapped the energy of Americans, had taken some of its best young men, and had produced a legacy of human suffering that no one could have imagined. It is hardly surprising that the nation turned to Warren Harding, a handsome affable man with plenty of charm but little vision and less interest in the presidency. Harding had been nominated despite the fact that he had a rather checkered past: He had been a long-time gambler, had made love to his best friend's wife, and had fathered an illegitimate child. Harding figured few would find out.

Harding got on well with the press. He regularly posed for photographers and brought back press conferences, which Wilson had canceled, never having much enjoyed the interactions with reporters. Harding was more laid-back than Wilson; but he too had his rules: He insisted that reporters attending press conferences submit their questions in writing to him.

Harding ran a loose ship of state. Some of those he appointed got involved in corrupt schemes, as epitomized by the Teapot Dome Scandal. To escape the pressures, Harding scheduled a cross-country trip. He died en route of a blood clot on the brain. The new president was the quiet man from Massachusetts, Calvin Coolidge.

Known to Americans as "Silent Cal," he was arguably the least talkative, most self-contained man ever to inhabit the White House. *Baltimore Sun* reporter Frank Kent wrote that "Mr. Coolidge does not smile. He utters no greeting, does not even nod his head. There is a dour, discouraged look about him. He seems not to be pleased."[39] Coolidge was so reticent to speak that a story circulated of a woman who sat down next to the president at a dinner party and said, "You must talk to me, Mr. Coolidge. I made a bet today that I could get more than two words out of you." "You lose," Coolidge replied. And yet despite his insistence on privacy, Coolidge felt that he had an obligation to meet with reporters. He held 520 press conferences during his administration, an average of 7.8 per month. Coolidge also was the first president to use radio regularly to communicate with the public. For the shy, dour Calvin Coolidge, radio was a presidential blessing, and he used it innovatively during his term.[40]

The Republican sweep of the 1920s continued with Herbert Hoover. Hoover had terrible relations with the press. He ordered the Secret Service to prevent reporters from following him to a presidential retreat, refused to answer questions prepared in advance by reporters, called off press conferences for a time, and resurrected the practice of giving private interviews to reporters who had written stories that reflected favorably on the White House. These practices were throwbacks to an earlier era in which the president could do as he pleased with the press, but they were ill-suited to the 1920s, when both press and public felt they had a right to know what the president was doing. Hoover was later blamed for his inaction in the face of economic chaos in the United States, and he was perceived as ineffective by many members of the public. In 1932 Hoover was defeated by a man, Franklin Roosevelt, who harbored a very different philosophy of presidential communication.

CONCLUSIONS

The early history of the press and presidency is a story of change and continuity.

The newspapers of eighteenth century America bear little resemblance to today's news media. In colonial America, freedom of the press meant freedom to air anti-British sentiments. In George Washington's day, newspaper editors wrote what they wanted. They felt no obligation to give both sides of the story. As media scholar Herbert Altschull noted, "the goal of 'objectivity' was one that did not even occur to the Founders, for there did not exist in the press of their era any publisher or editor who did not see his journal as an instrument for spreading good, or truth, and not merely as a catalog of points of view."[41] Early newspapers were organs of political parties.

They churned out stories that supported the partisan positions of the Federalists, Jeffersonians, and other political factions.

Presidents in those days not only tried to influence the press; they tried to establish newspapers that supported their points of view. Jefferson convinced a printer to start up *The National Intelligencer* as his administration's political newspaper, and Jackson gave his favorite paper a lucrative government contract. It was a no-holds-barred era for both editors and presidents.

News was "invented" during the 1830s and evolved throughout the nineteenth century. For a long time there was little distinction between news and editorials. It was not until the latter part of the nineteenth century that the Washington press corps began to conceive of itself as a watchdog of government. The notion that the press was an adversary of government did not fully evolve until the twentieth century.[42]

It is important to appreciate the historical context in which presidents and the press have operated. Presidents and editors are creatures of their times, and we need to take this into account when evaluating them. It is easy to condemn the party press of the early 1830s as flagrantly biased; yet this same press put elites in touch with voters.

While there have been changes in presidential–press relations over the course of our nation's history, there also have been significant continuities. One is the friction between presidents and the news media that has occurred because the two institutions play such different roles in a democracy. Tebbel and Watts note that "in the shifting relationship between the press and presidency over nearly two centuries there has remained one primary constant—the dissatisfaction of one with the other. No president has escaped press criticism, and no president has considered himself fairly treated."[43]

There is much truth to this. Our greatest presidents have been excoriated by the press. Washington was called a patron of fraud, Jefferson a demagogue, Lincoln a half-witted usurper. The presidents who have risen to the occasion of national leadership have overlooked much of the criticism, recognizing that press scrutiny is a necessary part of democracy. And yet all presidents have found themselves frustrated with news coverage, sometimes with good reason, other times with little justification.

Tebbel and Watts say that the mutual dissatisfaction of press and presidents is the best evidence we have that the "American concept of a free press in a free society is a viable idea."[44] There is truth to this observation, but it overstates matters. It is hard to see how the press could be considered free in Adams' time if newspaper editors were thrown in jail for printing information that was critical of government, in Jackson's time if 57 journalists were on the federal payroll, in Roosevelt's era if reporters who displeased the president were deprived of access, or in Wilson's time if the government deemed it a criminal act to publish abusive information about government. The press ordinarily has been free to criticize government and to pursue its own goals, but "its freedom has never been absolute," Altschull notes, adding that it "was not intended to be by the Founding Fathers, who were pragmatists."[45]

An important continuity in presidential–press relations is the attempt of presidents to manipulate the press. Presidents have differed greatly in their attempts to influence news. The early presidents set up their own newspapers, Lincoln used charm and moral suasion, Johnson utilized personal interviews, and Roosevelt sought to influence reporters by feeding them information and offering them insider status.

It is clear from this review that the press has always been a factor in governance. And yet as the nation entered the twentieth century, there were obvious changes in the press and the presidency. Both the news media and the executive branch had grown enormously since the days of the Founding Fathers. By the end of Wilson's administration, relations between the two had become increasingly institutionalized, characterized by norms and expectations.

Our story of the colorful relationship between the news media and the president continues in the next chapter. In chapter 3 we examine how powerful presidents have influenced the media and how the media have reacted.

KEY ISSUES

Eighteenth-Century Press

Sedition Act

Penny Press

Civil War Newspapers

Privacy vs. Public's Right to Know

Press in Early 20th Century

Committee on Public Information

DISCUSSION QUESTIONS

1. In what ways are today's media similar to the media of George Washington, John Adams, and Thomas Jefferson? In what ways are they different?

2. Was Lincoln too tolerant of the Civil War press?

3. Was Woodrow Wilson justified in taking the steps he did to control the press during World War I?

3

Modern History of
the Press and Presidency

This chapter continues our historical review of the relationship between the president and the news media. The chapter examines presidential–press relations from 1933, the year that Franklin D. Roosevelt took office, to 1981, the first year of Ronald Reagan's presidency. Roosevelt expanded the powers of presidential communication, and Reagan took presidential governance into the television age. Thus, this chapter begins with Roosevelt and ends with Jimmy Carter, who preceded Reagan in the White House.

THE ROOSEVELT YEARS

Change rarely happens overnight, but with Franklin Roosevelt it did. FDR initiated numerous reforms to bolster the economy in his first 100 days. He set a new emotional tone for the nation in his now famous, then unforgettable first inaugural in which he gave the nation hope of fighting the Depression if only it could realize that "the only thing we have to fear is fear itself." In the realm of press relations, he made it clear from the first news conference that things would be different from Hoover, that he would create new ways for reporters to get information from the White House, and that he would be open to reporters' queries about his administration. He invented a new role for government and, in so doing, he greatly expanded the White House publicity apparatus. Presidential scholar Betty Winfield notes that "political scientists and historians have long acknowledged Franklin Delano Roosevelt's ability to seize, expand, test, and communicate presi-

dential powers so successfully. Roosevelt's formidable presidency has continued to be a point of political and economic reference for measuring those
presidents who followed him."[1]

Indeed it has. Roosevelt's years in office have spawned an industry of
scholarship on Roosevelt—not all of it favorable. Revisionist historians of
the press and presidency, while paying homage to FDR's powers of persuasion, have commented on the many techniques he used to manage the news,
manipulate journalists, and in some cases deceive the American public. The
fascination with Roosevelt stems from a desire to comprehend his many
accomplishments and far-reaching endeavors—but also from a deeper cu-
riosity about the psychology of the man. Roosevelt was a paradox in so many
ways. Born into a patrician family, he championed the rights of ordinary
people. A former journalist himself, he appreciated the role of the press in
a democracy; yet he developed an elaborate system to control the flow of
information. A warm, affable man with deep empathy for those, like himself,
who suffered from polio, he was manipulative, at times dishonest and cruel.

Franklin Roosevelt promised that, like his fifth cousin Theodore, he
would be a "preaching president." But where Theodore was something of a
one-man show, a virtual media star, Franklin was more discreet, more of an
operator who used his communication skills to manage the news. "You know,
I am a juggler," he once said. "I never let my right hand know what my left
hand does."[2]

FDR promised the public "a new deal" in his speech accepting the
Democratic nomination for president. He pledged to work for change. What
few knew at the time was how massive these changes would be—and how
central a role the media would play in the new administration.

It started 4 days after the inauguration with his first press conference. No
doubt most reporters who filed in to meet the president on the morning of
March 8, 1933, were curious about his intentions. Many remembered
Hoover's icy relationship with the press, his disdainful treatment of reporters, his refusal to hold press conferences. Roosevelt changed all that. He
told reporters:

> I am told that what I am about to do will become impossible, but I am going to try it.
> We are not going to have any more written questions; and, of course, while I cannot
> answer seventy-five or a hundred questions simply because I haven't got the time, I
> see no reason why I should not talk to you ladies and gentlemen off the record in just
> the way I have been doing in Albany and in the way I used to do in the Navy
> Department down here.[3]

The president then announced that four rules would govern the release of information at press conferences: *1. All stories based on announcements from the Oval Office were not to use quotations; 2. Direct quotes could be employed only when provided in writing by the press secretary; 3. Background facts would be provided to reporters, but could not be attributed to the president; and 4. Off-the-record information was to be kept confidential, to be used to help reporters understand broad trends.*

Roosevelt's announcement pleased reporters. FDR had eliminated the hated requirement of submitting questions in writing, a practice that dated back to Harding. His ban on direct quotes seemed a small price to pay for the access reporters were getting to the president and his staff. It was quite a change from Hoover. At the end of the press conference, reporters gave Roosevelt a standing ovation, the first ever given a president by the White House press. It was, one reporter said, "the most amazing performance the White House has ever seen."[4] It would be one of many such performances from the Roosevelt White House—delivered with respect and common decency, but designed to achieve other goals that were not immediately transparent to all reporters on the scene. Over the course of his administration, FDR held 998 press conferences, an average of 6.9 per month, one of the highest of all modern presidents.[5]

Throughout his years in the White House, Roosevelt had excellent rapport with the Washington press. He got to know reporters personally, joked with them, joined them in games of water polo, and shared high-level information with them, off the record of course. Journalists knew they were being used by a shrewd manipulator, Tebbel and Watts noted, "but at the same time they knew that the president's obvious affection for them was sincerely and deeply felt, and they could not help responding to it. For the first time in the history of this relationship, both sides looked forward to the press conferences."[6]

FDR also relied on his keen understanding of news. He would regularly provide guidance to reporters, saying, for instance, that "If I were going to write a story, I would write it along the lines of the decision that was taken last Saturday." The policies that FDR had embarked on were complicated. Many had their roots in economics. Realizing that they lacked the background to understand economic nuances, reporters turned to FDR to help them interpret this or that policy statement.[7] He was always happy to oblige.

Roosevelt's news management strategies worked like a charm during his first term. The newspapers were full of positive stories about New Deal programs and about this active, energetic president. For the most part, photographers respected the president's wish that no pictures be taken of his braces or crippled legs. Historian William Leuchtenburg wrote that "news photographers in the 1920s voluntarily destroyed their own plates when they showed Roosevelt in poses that revealed his handicap."[8] Photographers were similarly reticent to reveal Roosevelt's condition during his presidency. In fact, Roosevelt showed himself to be so physically active that few Americans were aware of the severity of his condition or the pain that he suffered on a daily basis.

Press coverage became more critical during FDR's second term, though it was never as bad as Roosevelt claimed. Roosevelt's plan to pack the Supreme Court got negative press as the public strongly opposed it. Columnists opposed his New Deal reforms, particularly Social Security. *Chicago Tribune* publisher Robert McCormick regularly attacked New Deal programs. He even instructed his telephone operators to answer the phone saying "Good afternoon," followed by the statement that (the number of days until the election) "remain to save your country. What are you doing to save it?"[9] Roosevelt claimed that 85% of newspapers opposed his reelection.

Roosevelt was correct that leading newspapers disapproved of his policies. Only 37% of daily newspapers endorsed him in 1936. His policies were condemned by some noted political columnists. However, scholarly studies have shown that Roosevelt exaggerated and misunderstood the nature of the criticism. While many newspaper editors appeared to have lost faith in FDR's policies, they maintained their faith in him.[10] Moreover, even when editorials criticized the president, news stories provided a more positive portrait. One study found that of 108 newspaper stories on presidential press conferences, only 6 could be classified as seriously biased against the president.[11]

Other Publicity Techniques

Roosevelt was reelected, in spite of criticisms from publishers like McCormick. His persona, if not always his ideas, resonated with the American public. Most Americans saw him as a strong and capable leader. He was able to maintain his popularity by coming up with new plans to harness the nation's work force and, from the perspective of this chapter, by cultivating the media in innovative ways. His techniques went beyond giving reporters access. They involved the creation of a government publicity apparatus.

Some of his strategies were imaginative and served the country well. Others were coercive and downright antidemocratic.

FDR appointed the first official press secretary, Stephen Early, and gave him broad powers. Early and his aides saw the media as an instrument to communicate the president's message to the people. By the end of Roosevelt's first year in office, press agents were turning out about a thousand publicity releases a month. Newspapers picked up the news releases: Over a 7-week period in 1937, *The New York Times* published 1,281 stories that seem to have had their origins in White House public relations offices.[12] These efforts did not go unnoticed. Newspapers that opposed Roosevelt called the White House efforts "propaganda," and leading reporters complained about White House attempts to control the news. From the administration's perspective, the publicity was needed to inform Americans about New Deal programs and to boost morale.

There was more. Blessed with a melodious voice, Roosevelt used radio to communicate with the public. The radio networks not only carried FDR's legendary fireside chats (see chapter 6), but also broadcast, free of charge, talks by other members of his administration. To commemorate the second anniversary of the New Deal, CBS developed a program called "Of the People, By the People, For the People." Newsreels complemented these efforts, showing FDR playing water polo and enjoying his grandchildren at Hyde Park. They portrayed Roosevelt as a vigorous, zestful man, which "helped perfect his image as the happy warrior."[13] It is hard to imagine the media developing such programs today.

Although he relied on persuasion to accomplish his goals, FDR was not above using coercion. Concerned that his opponents in the press were buying radio stations, he instructed his aides to look into ways to block these actions. He and press secretary Early planted questions at news conferences, inducing friendly reporters to ask questions the White House wanted asked. The administration banned Black reporters from attending press conferences until January, 1944.

White House information management techniques went into high gear during World War II. FDR formed an Office of War Information and an Office of Censorship, though he was careful to avoid the mistakes that Wilson had made during World War I. It has been established that before the U.S. declared war on Germany, Roosevelt worked secretly to provide military aid to the Allies, yet he did not let the press or public know what he was doing. Always the Machiavellian, Roosevelt was concerned about the threat the Nazis posed to America, but undoubtedly felt that if he showed his hand, the public would snap at it and retreat into isolationism. Perhaps the ends justified the means in World War II, especially given the horrific acts committed by the Nazis. Yet some scholars have pointed out that if FDR was so convinced of the urgency of his actions, he should have taken his case to the public as he had done so persuasively on so many other occasions.[14]

Unquestionably, Franklin Roosevelt had an important impact on presidential–press relations and on presidential communication. He showed that a dynamic personality can be a major weapon of leadership, that the mass media can play an important role in presidential governance, and that a president who understands the news media can define the news agenda.

There is no question that strong leadership was needed in the 1930s—what poet W. H. Auden called "that low dishonest decade"—and no question that Roosevelt provided it. But did he extend his control too far? Betty Winfield observes:

> Franklin D. Roosevelt's presidency brought an American victory over the Great Depression, the Germans, and the Japanese. Yet the question remains, was there also a legacy of a great victory over the control of governmental information in a democracy?[15]

THE TRANSITION TO TELEVISION: TRUMAN AND EISENHOWER

Talk about a tough act to follow—that is what faced Harry Truman when he took over the presidency following Roosevelt's death in April, 1945. The day after his inauguration, Truman confessed to reporters that "I feel as though the moon and all the stars and all the planets have fallen on me. Please, boys, give me your prayers. I need them very much."[16]

Truman, that plain-spoken native of Missouri, knew from the beginning that he would be compared to Roosevelt, but to his credit he went about his tasks in a confident manner, molding the office to fit his style rather than trying to change himself to fit FDR's mold. Truman was in many ways the opposite of Roosevelt: Where FDR was Machiavellian, and kept his cards hidden, Truman was blunt and direct; where Roosevelt cultivated the press and developed an affection for reporters, Truman kept his distance, not getting close to the Washington press corps.

His most famous encounter with the press was not with the political reporters of Washington, but with a music critic, Paul Hume of *The Washington Post*. In a review of Truman's daughter Margaret's singing recital, Hume wrote what many critics had no doubt been afraid to say. He observed that:

> Miss Truman cannot sing very well. She is flat a good deal of the time—more last night than at any time we have heard her in the past. There are few moments during her recital when one can relax and feel confident that she will make her goal, which is the end of the song.[17]

Truman exploded when he saw the review. Already angry about a statement General MacArthur had made on a different issue, he took out a piece of stationery and wrote the critic:

> Mr. Hume: I've just read your lousy review of Margaret's concert. I've come to the conclusion that you are an "eight ulcer man on four ulcer pay." It seems to me that you are a frustrated old man [Hume was 34] who wishes he could have been successful. Some day I hope to meet you. When that happens, you'll need a new nose, a lot of beefsteak for black eyes, and perhaps a supporter below![18]

This was not the last tirade Truman launched against the press. He threatened to sue *The Chicago Tribune* for libel, called *The Washington Times-Herald* "a sabotage sheet," and referred to columnists as those "whose business it is to prostitute the minds of voters."[19] These attacks reflected Truman's blunt tell-it-like-I-see-it style rather than any concerted effort to censor the press. To his credit, Truman held 334 press conferences during his tenure and answered questions on all measures of controversial issues, including the Korean War, his courageous decision to fire General Douglas MacArthur, and his seizure of the steel mills, under threat of a national strike. Truman's blunt, forceful style has since passed into myth and has served as a model for other presidents (like Bill Clinton) who sought a strong public persona.

Truman was succeeded by Dwight Eisenhower, who had served as commander of Allied Forces in Europe during World War II. Although Eisenhower was the first presidential candidate to appear in a series of televised political spots and the first to permit press conferences to be taped for TV viewing, he was uncomfortable in the role, preferring to delegate media matters to press secretary James Hagerty, widely regarded as one of the best. Hagerty protected the president well—too well, some reporters complained, remembering the press secretary's decision not to tell the press that Eisenhower had suffered a heart attack until 12 hours had elapsed.

Eisenhower's administration ended on a negative note when it was revealed that the Soviet Union had shot down a U.S. spy plane piloted by Gary Powers. Eisenhower tried the usual ploy of denial, claiming Powers had been on a weather surveillance mission. But when Soviet leaders revealed that they had captured Powers and his airplane, the president changed the story and admitted that Powers had been on an espionage mission.[20] This disclosure and the ensuing conflict between the president and the press would set the tone for the 1960s. Presidential–press relations were headed for a stormy period.

KENNEDY: CHARMING THE PRESS

John Kennedy put television on the political communication map. Before Kennedy, television was an important force in politics, but not the center-piece of modern campaigns. Kennedy expanded television's role in presi-dential communication. He used it adroitly in his 1960 campaign and devised innovative ways of exploiting its powers during his short term in office.

Kennedy was a natural for television. He was an excellent speaker, came off cool and confident on TV, and had charisma. Kennedy, Tebbel and Watts note, "was the first president who understood how to use television at a time when television was at last ready to be used."[21] The networks were increas-ing their 15-minute newscasts to a half-hour, were prepared to give presi-dents time to address the nation on television, and were willing to carry live press conferences.

The Kennedy administration came up with the idea of holding press conferences live and they were an immediate success. On the average, Kennedy held fewer press conferences than Roosevelt, Truman, and Eisen-hower, but the conferences he held were memorable. He had tremendous rapport with the White House press, a comedian's talent for using nonverbal expressions to make his point, and a keen sense of how to deflect a question so that it worked to his strategic advantage.

For the most part, the White House press liked the new president. They deferred to him and, as we know now, protected him from scandal. Reporters knew about his many dalliances with women, but they kept quiet. Television correspondent Robert Pierpoint recalls that:

> I was sitting in the White House press room one day shortly after noon. And through the corridor came a French magazine correspondent who worked for Paris Match and he said, "Bob, I've just had a very unusual experience. I have to tell somebody about it." He was somewhat agitated and said that he had been invited to have lunch with

Jackie upstairs in the private area and the President joined them, and then after lunch the President said, "Jackie, why don't you show our friend around?" She did, and brought him over to the west wing. Between the Cabinet room and the Oval Office there is a small room where the secretaries sit. As she ushered him into that room she said in French, "And there is the woman that my husband is supposed to be sleeping with." He was quite upset and didn't know what to answer; it was kind of embarrassing for him.[22]

In those days it was not considered appropriate to go public with information of such a private nature. Moreover, Kennedy was able to avoid scrutiny because so many reporters liked him. Kennedy used charm to influence the press. He knew many of the editors of large newspapers personally. He gave reporters access to the White House and socialized with them. At the same time, he leaked information strategically and played reporters off against each other. He captivated journalists early in his administration, causing some to suspend their adversarial role.[23]

Kennedy's relations with the press suffered a major blow during the Bay of Pigs crisis in April, 1961. Problems developed when *New York Times* reporter Tad Szulc got wind of the Administration's plan to land a cadre of Cuban exiles on the Cuban mainland in hopes of toppling Castro. Appealing to national security needs, Kennedy phoned the publisher of *The Times* and persuaded him to downplay the story. The Bay of Pigs invasion failed miserably, marking a major defeat for the Kennedy Administration. Later, in a fit of anger and humiliation, Kennedy rebuked the nation's newspaper publishers for printing news that helped the country's enemies. It was only later that he calmed down and said in hindsight he wished *The New York Times* had printed the story, for this might have prevented the catastrophe. However, some experts believed that Kennedy was attributing more power to the press than it actually had.[24]

For the most part, Kennedy had positive relations with reporters and he used the media to his advantage. A Hollywood film—"PT 109"— was made about JFK's war-time heroism, and countless records and books came out that celebrated the First Family. Since then, Kennedy's life has slipped into myth, which complicates efforts to evaluate his presidency and his relationship with the press. Legend has it that Kennedy was the nation's first television president and that he received universally positive press. The legend is not totally true: Truman was the first president to speak on television, Eisenhower the first to allow press conferences to be taped for television. Kennedy did not get anything like universally positive press. Newspapers criticized the Bay of Pigs fiasco, as well as JFK's delay in proposing civil rights legislation. Nonetheless, there is truth to the common mythology: Kennedy was the first president to recognize that television provided a way for presidents to appeal directly to the public and that it could be a force to mold public opinion. Like Franklin Roosevelt before him, he set a standard against which other presidents would be compared. And, like FDR, his adroit use of the news media raised new questions about government control of information.

JOHNSON: DECEIVING THE PRESS

He was a larger-than-life figure in the White House, a big brawling man who hovered over reporters, who often revealed crude and unseemly aspects of his personality as when he pulled up his shirt to show a much-surprised group of reporters how nicely an incision from a gall bladder operation had been healing, and when he moved staff meetings to the bathroom so that he could continue the discussion while he was relieving himself. He was a president who wanted it all—government funding of the war and social programs, although both cost billions; victory in Vietnam, but only a limited commitment of troops; total control over reporters and also their unfailing love and devotion. He was a Macbeth among presidents, in historian Eric Goldman's words "the tragic figure of an extraordinarily gifted President who was the wrong man from the wrong place at the wrong time under the wrong circumstances."[25]

Lyndon Johnson took office at the most tragic of circumstances—on the afternoon of November 22, 1963, after the assassination of President Kennedy in Dallas. As the shock of the assassination turned into sadness and then acceptance, the country turned to Johnson to provide leadership and to extend Kennedy's legacy. Johnson acted quickly and decisively, using skills he had acquired as majority leader of the Senate. During his first 8 months in office, he pushed major civil rights and social welfare legislation through Congress.

At first his relations with the press were positive. Reporters, like the rest of the country, wanted Johnson to succeed. And for a time he did. But Johnson found that the news management strategies he had employed in the Senate did not work in the Oval Office. In the Senate he could bully reporters into going along with him or he could offer them favors. However, success in the presidency required a more rhetorical flair, and Johnson lacked this skill.

There was another problem. Johnson, historians believe, lacked an essential confidence in himself. He frequently compared himself to others.[26] First it was FDR, who had taken the young Lyndon under his wing and become a father figure to Johnson. Johnson also compared himself, perhaps understandably, to Kennedy, but here the comparison was steeped more in anger than in love. Johnson resented Kennedy's affinity with the press and his Ivy League background. He assumed Kennedy could do as he wished with the press, but overlooked the fact that Kennedy did not escape press scrutiny or criticism. "For Johnson, the grass was perpetually greener in Kennedy's yard," journalist James Deakin wrote.[27]

Johnson should have studied American presidents more carefully. Had he done so, he might have taken as his model Harry Truman, who also followed a legendary president but who did not feel diminished by his predecessor.[28]

Not being a quitter, and determined to win the press over to his side, Johnson decided to court reporters. He flew The New York Times's James Reston and his wife over to the Texas ranch; he invited journalists over for a fish fry and extended discussions on a wide range of topics, in what became known as The Treatment. But soon hubris set in. One legendary event occurred during Easter of 1964 when Johnson shoved three reporters into his luxury car, took the wheel, and gave the group a tour of his ranch, all the while driving up to 90 miles an hour and sipping a cup of beer. A female reporter expressed concern about the speed at which they were traveling. In response, Johnson placed his large Texas hat on top of the speedometer.

When stories about this came out in the news media, and they were pretty uncritical by today's standards, Johnson was outraged. How could these reporters whom he had taken to his ranch and shown a good time come out and say these things about him? He failed to understand how his own behavior might have affected journalists; nor did he appreciate why reporters might have been motivated to write up the incidents. He took matters like this personally, which no doubt hardened his attitude toward the press.

At the same time, there were frequent occasions when Johnson said something or made claims that later turned out to be false. A Washington Star article stated that Johnson would propose a 3% pay increase for federal government workers. Johnson claimed the story was false. Shortly thereafter, he recommended the 3% pay raise. On another occasion, Johnson was asked why he ordered the Marines into the Dominican Republic. The rebels had murdered some 1,500 innocent people and had cut off their heads, the president said, adding that the rebels had been shooting at Americans. It turned out that no one had been beheaded by the rebels, and that most of the atrocities had been committed not by the insurgents, but by the military junta the U.S. was protecting. No Americans had been hurt, save two reporters. They had been shot by U.S. Marines.[29]

Johnson's biggest problems with the press—and public—came during the Vietnam War. "Johnson lied about facts in Vietnam as early as 1965," Smith notes.[30] In one case, reporters asked if new moves were planned in Vietnam. Johnson said he didn't know of any plans. Two months later, he approved an increase in the U.S. military commitment to South Vietnam and gave a green light to search-and-destroy missions. Journalists coined the term "credibility gap" to describe the discrepancy between Johnson's words and deeds. It was a nice way of saying the president was lying.

LBJ was frustrated by press coverage of Vietnam. He charged that reporters slanted stories against him. Scholarly studies indicate that, quite to the contrary, most of the news about Vietnam played up the administration's position. Daniel Hallin's systematic analysis shows that until 1968, the bulk of the news coverage was favorable to the U.S. position. Stories that referred to the North Vietnamese as the enemy were commonplace.[31] But Johnson did not see it this way. He felt the news media were against him and he tore into reporters, blasting them for asking "chicken-shit" questions. And yet Johnson was the ultimate media junkie, carrying a transistor radio wherever he went at the Texas ranch and watching all three network newscasts at once in the Oval Office. On March 31, 1968, tormented by the war, chastened by Walter Cronkite's critical documentary on Vietnam, and concerned about mounting public protests, Johnson announced he would not run for reelection. His vice president, Hubert Humphrey, ran against Richard Nixon for president that year. Nixon won in an extremely close race. After the election, Johnson returned to his native Texas.

The war took its toll on Lyndon Johnson. The sincere but misguided man who had wanted it all left the White House broken and tormented. He died a few short years later on January 22, 1973.

NIXON: ASSAULTING THE PRESS

Early Years

Nixon has become a legend in American politics, a man about whom volumes have been written and movies made. He cast a large shadow over American politics for half a century.

It is fair to say that Richard Nixon had one of the worst relationships with the press of any president. It may have been the worst, when all was said and done. Both Nixon and the press deserve blame for some of the early problems. The relational difficulties date back to the late 1940s. Nixon won election to Congress in 1946 in part by pinning a Communist label on his opponent. The charge was not altogether fair, and it led some reporters to conclude that Nixon was a politician who would resort to character assassination to get elected.[32] Then in 1952, headlines blared that Nixon had a secret political slush fund. Nixon, the Republican vice presidential candidate, took to the television airwaves to refute the charge. It later turned out that the Democratic presidential candidate, Adlai Stevenson, had a similar fund. Nixon charged that the press had given him tough treatment, but had been much easier on Stevenson.

There may be some truth to Nixon's perception. Perhaps more significantly, it was consistent with his belief, formed in the 1940s, that the press was out to get him.[33]

In 1960, Nixon ran for president and lost a close election to John Kennedy. To his credit, Nixon resisted efforts to challenge the vote, although there were persistent reports of fraud in the Democratic wards of Chicago. Nixon believed that the press favored Kennedy and that its biased treatment had hurt his campaign.

There is little doubt that most political reporters liked Kennedy better than Nixon. Nixon's biographer remarked that the press had "fawned on Kennedy" during the campaign.[34] This may be true, but there is no evidence that reporters' personal preferences influenced their stories, and it is unlikely that they influenced publishers, many of whom endorsed Nixon. But Nixon believed that reporters would not give him a fair shake. Acting on this belief, he refused to meet with reporters after a particularly confrontational news conference on September 21, 1960. Nixon aide Herbert Klein believes that this decision (rather than reporter bias) led to negative coverage and was a critical factor in Nixon's defeat.[35]

When he ran for president in 1968, Nixon made a concerted effort to pay more attention to television, advertising, and imagery. He defeated Hubert Humphrey, but remained convinced that the news media would oppose him, no matter what he did. A month after the election, he warned his cabinet that:

> the men and women of the news media approach this as an adversary relationship. The time will come when they will run lies about you, when the columnists and editorial writers will make you seem to be scoundrels or fools or both, and the

cartoonists will depict you as ogres. Some of your wives will get up in the morning and look at the papers and start to cry. Now don't let that get you down— don't let it defeat you.[36]

Presidential Strategies

Like FDR and Wilson, Nixon set up new structures to control the flow of information to the public. But while Roosevelt and Wilson had expanded government news management to achieve palpable national goals, Nixon did it to achieve personal, political goals.

Nixon's most important effort was the creation of the White House Office of Communications, which provided a more centralized and organized mechanism for White House control of information. Convinced that the press would disparage him, he felt his only recourse was to take matters into his own hands and go directly to the people. Nixon steered clear of the press wherever he could. He all but eliminated press conferences, holding fewer press conferences than Johnson or Kennedy. Instead, he focused on trying to understand and manipulate public opnion. He commissioned over 200 public opinion polls during his tenure, conducting more than 10 times as many as Kennedy and nearly twice as many as Johnson. He even commissioned a poll on Americans' opinions about media fairness toward the Nixon Administration.[37]

Nixon viewed the press as the enemy. He even called it that.[38] Based on his experiences with the media and his perceptions of those experiences, he decided that the only way he could influence the press was to apply pressure. Two months after he took office, Nixon asked White House Chief of Staff H.R. Haldeman to monitor television news reports. Haldeman told the director of the communications office that Nixon "wants, of course, the list of those who consistently slant their reports against us, such as Terry Drinkwater and Sander Vanocur and others, but it would be helpful to try to classify all of the principal people as to their general slant so that he has a feel of which ones we can count on for reliable reporting and which ones we can count on to go the other way."[39]

The president instructed members of his staff not to talk to reporters and columnists whom he deemed to be enemies of his administration. When a Nixon aide drafted a routine note to The New York Times publisher thanking him for an editorial that backed Nixon's policies, Haldeman's assistant returned the memo, noting that "the President does not correspond w/the NYT."[40]

On November 13, 1969, Vice President Spiro Agnew unleashed a major attack on the news media, hoping to rally the public against the press. Agnew accused the press of harboring a liberal, anti-Nixon bias. He laid the blame on "a small band of network commentators and self-appointed analysts," a "little group of men who...enjoy a right of instant rebuttal to every presidential (speech)." Agnew employed an old cheap trick, journalist James Deakin observed, "the small-little-known-group-operating-in-secret device."[41] In the short term, Agnew's speech worked, fueling hostility toward the press. In the long term, it backfired, for it set up a poisonous mentality in the White House that led to Watergate.

The Agnew speech spoke volumes about the administration's attitude toward the press. What particularly disturbed Nixon were the analyses that network correspondents made after his televised speeches.[42] Some analysts raised critical questions about what the president said. Nixon feared that these would carry the day with the American public. In hindsight, we can see how misguided Nixon's perceptions were. It is likely that many viewers turned off the television set when the analyses came on because they touched on politics, one of Americans' least favorite topics. The analyses undoubtedly had limited effects, the critical comments about Nixon's speech probably influencing those who disapproved of the president to begin with. Yet Nixon was convinced that the analyses would have an impact, a larger influence, he seems to have believed, than an address by a president of the United States. Years later, Nixon aides would acknowledge that Agnew's speech had been a mistake, "a great disservice to the Nixon administration."[43] But in the stormy autumn of 1969, the Nixon administration saw things differently. It decided to launch an all-out attack on the press—the press that Founding Fathers like Thomas Jefferson believed to be the bulwark of a free society.

And yet there was more. White House staff members fabricated phone calls to news organizations, trying to make it look like large numbers of ordinary citizens disapproved of the media's treatment of Nixon. A Haldeman aide sent out a memo calling on government antitrust divisions to threaten antitrust actions against menacing news organizations. The White House tried to block in court a series of news stories that traced the origins of U.S. involvement in Vietnam, in particular the deceptive actions of former presidents. Although the series, known as the Pentagon Papers, did not implicate Nixon, the administration attempted to stop its publication, seeking to legally restrain newspapers from publishing the stories. "It was the first time in American postconstitutional history that an administration had attempted to exercise prior restraint of publication, which the First Amendment had been designed to prevent," Tebbel and Watts observed.[44] The case went to the Supreme Court. The Court upheld the right of the press to publish the Pentagon Papers.

Nixon's relations with the press got worse over the course of his first term. Even as he was overseeing path-breaking accords with the Soviet Union and China and was seeing his dream of a second presidential term come to fruition, he was at war with the press, bickering with reporters, plotting against them, and setting in motion the destructive mentality that led to Watergate. In September, 1972, with *The Washington Post* turning out exposes of Watergate, Nixon showed how far he was willing to go to intimidate the press:

President: The main thing is *The Post* is going to have damnable, damnable problems out of this one. They have a television station ... and they're going to have to get it renewed.

Haldeman: They've got a radio station too.

President: Does that come up too? The point is, when does it come up?

Dean: I don't know. But the practice of non-licensees filing on top of licensees has certainly gotten more ... active ... in this area.

President: And it's going to be God damn active here.

Dean: (Laughter) (Silence)

President: Well, the game has to be played awfully rough.[45]

The Nixon administration was not the first to define the news media as an enemy and to employ coercive techniques to keep them in line. However, Nixon was unique in the extent to which he personalized press criticism and in the degree to which he was willing to endorse unethical and illegal techniques to manage the news.

Ironically, when Nixon died in 1994, the news media provided in their pages and on their airwaves an outpouring of positive sentiments that Nixon had not experienced in life. Had Nixon's efforts since leaving office to resuscitate his reputation, present himself in a favorable light, and perform the elder statesman role succeeded where antagonism and attacks had failed? Possibly in the short run, probably not in the long run. But history is only beginning to be written on the Nixon years. We can safely say that the final chapter on Nixon's relations with the news media is likely to be written and rewritten many times.

FORD AND CARTER: DOMINATED BY THE PRESS

Gerald Ford, who became president after Nixon resigned in 1974, and Jimmy Carter, who rose from obscurity to defeat Ford in 1976, had one thing in common: They never got out in front of the press and never developed a coherent strategy to dominate the media. To be sure, the news about them was not always unfavorable. But stories that appeared at critical times in their presidencies put them in a negative light, helping to undermine their support in the polls. They both had the misfortune of taking office after a decade of great acrimony between presidents and reporters. They both had to struggle with an especially assertive and adversarial press corps. Both presidents tried to ameliorate the relationship between the White House and the press, and they took strides in this direction. However, both Ford and Carter found it difficult to get on top of the media agenda.

Ford took office in August, 1974, and he created controversy almost immediately by pardoning Richard Nixon for any crimes he may have committed while president. Ford was also the butt of cruel jokes that circulated in the media, such as Lyndon Johnson's comment that Ford's years of playing college football had made him "so dumb he can't walk and chew gum at the same time." Then there were his stumbles —not political ones, but real ones. He once fell down the ramp of Air Force One; on another occasion, he bumped his head and fell when skiing. This created a feeding frenzy of speculation among reporters who asked if there was something wrong with Ford's health or if he drank too much. The comedian Chevy Chase lampooned Ford on *Saturday Night Live*.

Ford hurt himself by not developing a programmatic strategy for dealing with the media. Presidential scholar John Anthony Maltese states that "Ford's first year in office was beset by a lack of discipline within the administration itself and a laissez-faire attitude toward communications planning by the administration. Both hurt the president's image."

Ford lost to Carter in a close election, and in 1977 the one-time peanut farmer from Georgia became president of the United States.

Carter was the quintessential media candidate. Much more than Ronald Reagan or John Kennedy, who had established themselves in national politics before they ran for president, Carter used television to launch his candidacy. He had served in the Georgia legislature and as governor of Georgia from 1970 to 1974. Had it not been for his astute use of the news media during the campaign, he never would have been elected president.

As president, Carter promised an open administration and at first was highly accessible to the press. Seeking to distance himself from the authoritarian style of Richard Nixon, he adopted a decentralized approach to running the White House communications system.

Ironically, this irritated the press. The White House adopted a laid-back attitude toward photo-ops, letting all reporters in at once. This led to overcrowding and made it hard for photographers to get the pictures they needed. Researcher Frederic Smoller notes that "despite complaints about 'stage-managed' news, reporters look to the White House to coordinate coverage, which often means restricting access. Accessibility, however, was a major campaign theme, and Carter did not want to resurrect the image of an isolated president."[47] Carter also annoyed reporters by not always informing them of his moves. Wishing to preserve some of his privacy, he would go jogging at 5:30 in the morning without telling reporters. Reporters complained that Carter violated their agreements, but some critics felt that the press was behaving like a child.

Like Ford, Carter made matters more difficult for himself by insisting, at least early in his administration, on running a looser, decentralized ship of state. Unfortunately, openness has its costs. Maltese argues that in today's day and age "the president must set the agenda, maintain discipline among his spokespeople, and orchestrate media coverage of that agenda through long-term public relations planning."[48] Carter's staff eschewed this, exerting little control over what key administration officials were saying about the events of the day.

One explanation for Carter's failure was that he depended on advisers who were unschooled in the ways of Washington politics. In addition, by focusing his 1976 campaign around the media, rather than party politics, he failed to build the broad coalitions he needed to govern. His self-righteousness made it difficult for him to admit his mistakes and to change course in midstream.[49]

External events also took their toll. Carter had to deal with the oil shortage, double digit inflation, the hostage crisis in Iran, and the Soviet invasion of Afghanistan. The news brought these negative realities home to the public every day. In some cases, though, the news did more than reflect reality; it refracted it, transmitting a version of events that turned out to be damaging to Carter.

The hostage crisis illustrates this best. On November 4, 1979, militant Iranian students stormed the gates of the U.S. embassy in Tehran and seized 66 hostages. Fifty-two were held for 444 days. All were released unharmed early in 1981. The Iranian students, supporters of Ayatollah Khomeini, took the hostages to protest U.S. policy toward Iran.

Television covered the issue incessantly. Close to a third of TV newscasts focused on the story in the first 6 months. Although the hostage seizure was a bonafide issue and obviously newsworthy, there were other reasons why it generated so much television news. Researchers William Adams and Philip Heyl argue that the Iran story had all the elements television journalists look for in news: conflict, action, and good visuals. Adams and Heyl note that "Iran had it all: straightforward and fundamental conflict between two sides; a powerful elementary theme (what is or will be happening to the hostages); good footage of worried families... (and) action pictures of angry crowds in Iran and the United States, adding up to a continuing, suspenseful, telegenic narrative of nationwide appeal."[50] In general, TV oversimplified the story, neglecting to consider the historical, political, and religious dimensions. The coverage, Smoller argues, exaggerated the crisis and placed unrealistic demands on Carter.[51]

Although the hostages were eventually released, the public felt Carter had handled the crisis badly and failed to provide strong leadership. Voters rejected Carter in the 1980 election and handed the mantle of the presidency to Ronald Reagan.

CONCLUSIONS

This chapter reviewed the history of the presidency and the press from Roosevelt to Carter. Franklin Roosevelt brought the press and presidency into the modern age. He institutionalized background sessions, press secretary roles, press conferences, and White House public relations. He used his communication skills to provide leadership to the nation. FDR was unique, and the presidents who followed him employed different styles of dealing with the press. Indeed, one of the consistencies of twentieth century presidential–press relations is that the relationship depends in important ways on the personality of the president, the expectations of reporters, and the historical context. Presidents have their work cut out for them in dealing with the press. It is not an easy job. Presidents who appreciated the adversary role of the news media and were confident of their abilities to engage reporters typically had positive relations with the press. Those who resented the media's intrusion into politics and personalized press criticism generally had bad relations with reporters.

The press has reacted differently to different presidents. The White House press corps has liked certain presidents better than others, preferring those who treated them well, made their jobs easier, and conformed to their stereotypes of what a president should be like. Undoubtedly, their feelings spilled over into their work, though rarely as much as presidents believed.

The relationship between both parties has been influenced by the times. Franklin Roosevelt got away with things that presidents today would not get away with because the nation was in a depression and then a war. John Kennedy's many affairs were overlooked because it was not considered appropriate to report on such matters. Lyndon Johnson's controversial war in Vietnam received favorable coverage until 1968, as the press deferred to government elites on foreign policy matters. Much of this coverage would fall under scholar Larry Sabato's category of "*lapdog journalism*—reporting that served and reinforced the political establishment."[52]

In the late 1960s and early 1970s, news took a more critical stance toward the presidency in the wake of Johnson's Vietnam deceptions and Watergate. Sabato calls this *watchdog journalism*, in which journalists conducted independent investigations of the president's actions. From about 1974 on, Sabato argues, "political reporters have engaged in what I would call *junkyard-dog journalism*—reporting that is often harsh, aggressive, and intrusive" (italics added).[53]

The twentieth century has witnessed an expansion of both the executive branch and the news media. Franklin Roosevelt, building on Theodore Roosevelt's and Wilson's strategies, enlarged the White House public relations armamentarium. Nixon launched the White House Office of Communications, which he used to manage public opinion and intimidate the press. Nowadays presidents are expected to try to influence news coverage and to use White House publicity to manipulate public opinion. These are new developments and they have brought with them costs, as well as benefits. The White House press corps also has grown over the course of the century. It has emerged as a powerful force in Washington politics—too powerful in the view of its critics.[54]

Scholars have sought to develop principles to describe the relationship between presidents and the press. Some researchers have argued that government is most likely to restrict the press in times of stress, particularly during periods when the nation faces threats from abroad.[55] Adams imposed the Sedition Act, ostensibly to deal with a threat from France. Wilson invoked the Sedition and Espionage Acts during World War I. However, presidents must determine what constitutes a threat, and here their perceptions play an important role. Presidents have sometimes resorted to coercive news management strategies when they *perceived* that they faced serious threats. Presidents, being people, have confused their personal and political interests with those of the nation. It is for this reason that Founding Fathers like Jefferson believed that a free press was indispensable to a democratic society.

Our discussion of the history of the presidency and the press makes it clear that the basic issues that face today's chief executives are not new, but are rooted in the history of the Republic. Press criticism of presidents is not new, nor is presidential dissatisfaction with the news media. At the same time, this review makes it abundantly clear that the press–presidency relationship has gone through numerous changes over the years. With all this as backdrop, it is time to examine the dynamic relationship between the press and the presidency in our own era, dominated as it is by television and new communication technologies.

KEY ISSUES

FDR and the Press

Bay of Pigs

Press–Presidency Conflicts under Johnson and Nixon

Changes in Press Coverage with Ford and Carter

Television and the Iran Hostage Crisis

DISCUSSION QUESTIONS

1. What techniques did Franklin Delano Roosevelt employ to influence the press?

2. In today's era, FDR's polio and JFK's affairs would be big news, covered in the tabloids and conventional press. What are the pros and cons of this change in press coverage of the presidency?

3. Remembering there are two players in the press–presidency relationship, in what sense can both be blamed for some of the tensions and conflicts that developed in the 1960s and 1970s?

4

Presidents and the News in the Television Age

Today the president and the news media jointly occupy center stage. "The president of the United States ordinarily is brought to you by the news media," scholars Michael Grossman and Martha Kumar write. "Images of the White House produced by strategists who advise the president reach their audience after they are processed in the great news factories and fine craft shops of print, broadcast, and television journalism."[1]

As noted in the previous chapters, the press has always played an important part in presidential governance, but over the past half-century, its impact has grown considerably. The Founding Fathers would spin around in their graves if they observed the role that the news media play in presidential decision-making. For today, as former defense secretary Richard Cheney noted, "there is no way to do this job as president if you are not willing to think about the media as part of the process in the same way that Congress is part of the process. Consciously or unconsciously, the press often becomes an actor in the scenario."[2]

Critics argue that with the advent of political marketing techniques and sophisticated strategies to manage the news, the president is more able to manipulate the press than ever before. Other scholars disagree, noting that the news media are remarkably critical of the president; just look at how the media went after Bill Clinton on Whitewater or how much criticism George Bush received during the economic downturn of 1992, these scholars point out. In this chapter and the one that follows, I discuss these issues as I examine the complex interplay between the presidency and press in our own times. Building on the discussions in the previous chapters, I explore the ways in which presidents use the news media to advance their own agendas, the principles underlying press coverage of the presidency, and the complex interactions between these two institutions. This chapter examines presidents' techniques for influencing the news; chapter 5 looks at the nature of news coverage of the presidency.

One question may occur to you at the outset. Why, you may ask, does the president even need the press? After all, can't presidents use the authority of the office to accomplish their goals? Isn't the presidency the most powerful office in the world? The answer is that there are limits to presidential powers; "his office's constitutional and institutional prerogatives are insufficient for him to achieve many important objectives," Grossman and Kumar point out.[3] Presidents must be able to convince Congress, leaders of their party, members of the opposition, elites in the private sector, and state officials to support policy objectives. To persuade these various groups, presidents must demonstrate that they are effective leaders and that public opinion is behind them. The mass media are the major instrument for influencing public attitudes and for building an image of strong and decisive leadership.

Media differ, though, in the degree to which they allow **presidential control**. Smoller argues that media can be ordered along a continuum ranging from most controlled to least controlled.[4] As Fig. 4.1 shows, the president has the most control over presidential addresses to the nation. In these cases, the president decides what to say and when to say it. On the other end of the continuum are modalities over which the president has little control. The news fits into this category. Although presidents try to

Controlled and Uncontrolled Electronic Media

MOST CONTROLLED...			LEAST CONTROLLED
Presidential Address	Party Convention	Debate	Evening News
Political Advertisements			
Radio	Press Conference		

FIG. 4.1 Controlled and Uncontrolled Electronic Political Media (from Smoller, 1990).

influence the news—and some have done a better job than others—they ultimately cannot control what journalists decide to put on the air or write in newspapers or magazines. The White House has developed three institutional mechanisms to influence news coverage: (a) the White House Office of Communications; (b) the press secretary; and (c) press conferences. (Presidents also use oratory to achieve their political objectives, but this is a separate area of study, discussed in detail in chapters 6 and 7.)

WHITE HOUSE OFFICE OF COMMUNICATIONS

In chapters 2 and 3, I noted that presidents have used a variety of techniques to influence the media. Presidents have resorted to coercive and extralegal tactics, but these are the exceptions, not the rules. Under normal conditions, presidents employ persuasion more frequently than coercion. In an age in which presidents must go public to mold citizens' sentiments and shape policy, they find that it is more useful to court the news media than to antagonize it. To do so, they work hard to manage—or at least influence—the news that reaches the American public.

The institution that coordinates these tasks is the White House Office of Communications. According to John Anthony Maltese, the office:

> is charged with long-term public relations planning, the dissemination of "the line of-the day" to officials throughout the executive branch, and the circumvention of the White House press corps through the orchestration of direct appeals to the people (appeals that are often carefully targeted to particular constituencies in specific media markets). The goal is to set the public agenda, to make sure that all parts of the presidential team (the White House staff, cabinet officers, and other executive branch officials) are adhering to that public agenda, and to aggressively promote that agenda through a form of mass marketing. Focus groups and polling data are used to fashion presidential messages; sound-bites are written into the public pronouncements of the president and his underlings to articulate those messages; public appearances are choreographed so that the messages are reinforced by visual images; and the daily line is enforced to prevent the articulation of conflicting messages. "Surrogate speakers" take the messages to local constituencies through speaking tours while local media markets are penetrated by means of direct satellite interviews with administration officials ... The ultimate goal is to influence—to the extent possible—what news will appear in the media about the administration and its policies.[5]

Welcome to the modern White House!

White House publicity efforts evolved over the course of this century. Theodore Roosevelt, Woodrow Wilson, and Franklin Roosevelt expanded the White House publicity apparatus. As noted in chapter 3, Richard Nixon created the Office of Communications to come up with a way of circumventing the "hated" White House press corps. While current presidents do not employ the heavy-handed tactics that Nixon's team used, they have kept the office in business, adapting it to fit the needs of their administrations.

It was Ronald Reagan who recognized that the Office of Communications could be used proactively to influence news coverage and who devised ways of adapting the Office to the television age. Reagan's aides noted that Jimmy Carter had failed to use the media effectively. Furthermore, Reagan's staffers believed that Carter's failure to stay on top of the media agenda contributed to his problems in office. The Reagan team vowed not to make these mistakes. The techniques they employed profoundly influenced presidential news management. They also have raised considerable controversy. In the next section, I describe Reagan's news media strategies, using them as an exemplar of modern presidential communications.

Reagan and News Management

The first professional actor to be elected president, Reagan had a natural presence in front of the camera. During his years as governor of California, he amassed a major political resource, one that served him well in Sacramento and that would aid him in Washington: a dedicated, bright, and unusually savvy group of political advisers who were united in their belief that in presidential politics, style was as important as substance.

Strategic Principles. Reagan and his core advisers—James Baker, Richard Darman, Michael Deaver, and David Gergen—realized at the outset that they did not have the political base to sell the country on Reagan's conservative philosophy. So they used a little psychology: They tried to sell the country on Reagan the man—the charming political leader. They believed that once people saw Reagan, they would like him. And, adviser Gergen noted, "as they believe in Reagan, they would eventually come to agree with him on issues, and see him as sensible, and eventually his philosophy would have a lot more impact."[6]

Baker, Reagan's chief of staff, ran a tight ship. He and his staff picked issues carefully, making sure they focused media attention on one issue at a time. They applied the following rules of information management:

- Plan ahead
- Stay on the offensive

- Control the flow of information
- Limit reporters' access to the president
- Talk about the issues *you* want to talk about
- Speak in one voice.
- Repeat the same message many times.[7]

Reagan and his advisers did one other thing: They treated the press well. The Reagan team made it clear early on that "they were determined to work *with* the Washington establishment, including the press, and not against it."[8] Reagan's advisers socialized with leading members of the news media and made life easier for White House reporters by giving them plenty of material for their stories well in advance of deadlines. They also made a point of not setting up an adversarial relationship with reporters, of not getting angry at journalists who did negative reports.[9]

Line of the Day.   Top staff members gathered at an early morning power breakfast to decide on the "the line of the day"—the major theme that they would emphasize in that day's encounters with the press corps. "What are we going to do today to enhance the image of the President?" was the major subject of discussion, one staff member recalled. The question was "What do we want the press to cover today, and how?" he added.[10] They discussed how to market the story—whether they should try to get the president on the evening news, have top aides make announcements, or schedule a background briefing for reporters. Once key staffers had decided the line or theme of the day, they communicated that to other officials via computer or by telephone.

Reagan advisers believed—correctly—that the White House must select its issues carefully. They also maintained that it was unwise to focus on too many issues at once. In 1981, the president focused on economic reform. "In 1981 and through the first half of '82," Reagan aide Michael Deaver said, "I would not allow anything to be put on the (president's) schedule that didn't have to do with economic reform. I just said, 'That's all we're going to do'."[11]

Emphasis on Visuals.   The Reagan communication staff believed that people were moved more by television's pictures than by its words. So they worked hard to control the pictures of Reagan that people saw each night As Deaver explained:

> When the economy started to pick up toward the end of 1980, we were searching for any development that we could showcase to reflect a good trend. (Instead of making

the announcement in the press room), I had the president fly to Fort Worth (the city with the most dramatic increases in housing starts in the United States), and he made the announcement at a housing development there, surrounded by a bunch of construction workers in hard hats. You get only forty to eighty seconds on any given night on the network news, and unless you can find a visual that explains your message, you can't make it stick.[12]

Former Reagan Chief of Staff Donald Regan echoed these sentiments, noting that with Reagan "every moment of every public appearance was scheduled, every word was scripted, every place where Reagan was expected to stand was chalked with toe marks. The President was always being prepared for a performance."[13] Once when Reagan visited the demilitarized zone separating South and North Korea, his aides made certain he was dressed for the part. He appeared in a flak jacket and peered at the North Koreans across the demilitarized zone through field glasses. "I saw the toe marks for him," NBC reporter Andrea Mitchell said. "When he didn't stand on his toe mark he was signaled by one of the advance men to move over into the sunshine."[14]

Reagan's aides had good reason to try to maintain control over their boss's performances. Reagan had the habit of committing verbal gaffes. Once he said that 80% of America's air pollution had been caused by trees. On another occasion he walked into the Rose Garden with Samuel Doe, the leader of Liberia. Reagan introduced him as Chairman Moe. Taking note of these misstatements, journalist Mark Hertsgaard referred to Reagan as the "amiable dunce." In an effort to deflect the impact of those mistakes, Reagan's aides tried to show Reagan in as positive a light as they could. They arranged to have the president eat at McDonald's, ride a horse, and chop wood.[15]

Spin Control. This term came into vogue in the Reagan years. Spinning a story means *"twisting it to one's advantage, using surrogates, press releases, radio actualities, and other friendly sources to deliver the line from an angle that puts the story in the best possible light."*[16] Reagan officials felt that it was imperative to give their interpretation of events rather than letting others (such as Democrats, interest groups, or the media) relay interpretations.

During Reagan's presidency, Cabinet officers frequently found that they had to make good news out of bad. They often tried to put a good "spin" on a negative event. For example, after a 1986 summit between Reagan and Soviet Leader Gorbachev did not go as well as planned, Chief of Staff Donald Regan decided that it was important to turn around the impression that the summit had failed. Later, he described his efforts to convey a positive impression of the summit as analogous to "a shovel brigade that follows a parade down Main Street cleaning up. We … turned what was really a sour situation into something that turned out really well."[17] That, at least, was the goal.

Summary.   The Reagan White House exercised great control over Reagan's communication operations. It planned his appearances carefully, dreamed up ways to tailor speeches and announcement to television, and restricted reporters' access to the president. Did their strategies work? This is a complex issue. Reagan got his share of tough press. However, he was also able to obtain favorable coverage at critical times in his presidency. One study found that in over 90% of the pictures of Reagan shown on CBS News, the president was smiling and appeared in good spirits.[18] In part the news reflected reality: Reagan was naturally buoyant. However, research indicates that things were more complex: An important reason why so many positive images appeared is that Reagan and his aides knew how to present the president in the best possible light.

Recognizing that many people get their news from television and that television requires simple commentary and good pictures, Reagan's advisers worked hard to present Reagan in a way that was compatible with the requirements of television news. But the question remained; Had Reagan's staff substituted style for substance, thereby giving the country "a sound-bite presidency—a simplified, abbreviated, visually oriented, personalized, and thematic chief executive?"[19]

BUSH AND CLINTON'S MEDIA STRATEGIES

George Bush and Bill Clinton used some of the same strategies Reagan's advisers pioneered. They also used some of their own techniques. Both Bush and Clinton found that they were not always successful in their efforts to generate positive press. Their presidencies show that the White House Office of Communications cannot work miracles. I first identify the deficiencies in their strategies and then look at instances in which they achieved their goals.

Shortcomings in the Message

Bush ran an aggressive media campaign in 1988, but when he got to the White House he seemed unable to articulate a domestic policy agenda.

Lacking a vision or even an overall strategy, his administration got "nibbled and nicked to death by small stories because the administration (was) generating so few big stories to dominate the news."[20] Bush captured the agenda and rose enormously in the polls during the 1991 Persian Gulf War. But after the U.S. victory, the war issue faded from memory, and Americans became concerned about the economy, which was stagnating. Bush failed to put forth a convincing economic package. Absent a message, he had little to offer White House reporters and photographers in the way of good news. The White House Office of Communications could not manufacture pictures and sound bites out of thin air.

By contrast, President Clinton had a message—actually several messages. Early in his first term, he spoke in favor of traditionally liberal causes, like abortion and gay rights, as well as conservative ones, like reducing the size of government and reforming welfare. The ambiguity of his political beliefs created rhetorical problems for him. It also made it hard for him to develop a consistent "line of the day" or a coherent theme that his aides could communicate, Reagan-style, to the Washington media.

Problematic Management

George Bush deemphasized the Office of Communications early in his presidency. Perhaps to differentiate himself from the show biz-oriented Ronald Reagan, Bush downplayed the Office, and "after several years of a fairly high profile, the Office of Communications and its director shrank into relative anonymity."[21] Bush preferred to interact with reporters in private, rather than public, settings. In fact he was quite popular with some reporters. But his decision to work behind the scenes rather than "on stage" had its costs. One study reported that Bush was the focus of 336 network TV news stories during his first 100 days; Reagan had been the subject of 790 stories.[22]

The initial problem with Clinton's Office of Communications was not anonymity, but disorganization. Clinton liked to run things himself. He did not like delegating. This made for a disorganized office. There were too many meetings, too few experienced people on hand to do important tasks like speech writing, and insufficient mechanisms to get presidential decisions made quickly.[23] All this impeded the administration's efforts to send out a consistent, coherent message.

Restricting Press Access

Presidents need to be accessible to the press. Closing off the channels of communication can be a mistake, as Richard Nixon found in his 1960 presidential campaign and throughout his presidency. Presidents need reporters to communicate positive developments in their administrations, and reporters need to be in touch with the White House communications staff to do their jobs. Reagan did not meet regularly with the press, but his communications staff did. Bush, to his credit, held many news conferences and talked regularly with reporters. However, Clinton seemed to eschew the press early in his administration. He conducted held only two formal press conferences in his first 4 months of office, equaling the dismal record of Ronald Reagan.[24] And early in his administration, his new communications director, George Stephanopoulos, made a major mistake.

Stephanopoulos cut off access to a foyer in the West Wing of the White House, where Stephanopoulos and the press secretary had their offices. Reporters had used the area for more than 20 years to talk with officials and to get information quickly, as deadlines approached. Stephanopoulos explained that he wanted to travel freely from his quarters to the Oval Office. Reporters were outraged. They had wandered around the alcove undisturbed for more than 20 years. They saw no reason for the move. It is interesting to note that Reagan's media whiz, Michael Deaver, had contemplated the same change but had decided to drop it when more experienced White House hands convinced him it would needlessly antagonize the press.[25]

Bad blood developed between the White House and the press corps. Clinton and his aides bear some of the blame for treating the press corps with disdain. Reporters can be criticized for overplaying trivial issues—like a $200 haircut Clinton received while sitting in a plane on a tarmac at Los Angeles International Airport.

Positive Uses of Communications

Bush and Clinton used the media effectively at various points in their administration. Bush mounted a full-court media press in the months preceding the Persian Gulf War. His White House communications staff spoke in a unified fashion, repeated the message many times, and controlled the flow of governmental information. During the war, the Pentagon's visuals of high-technology bombing attacks on Iraq captivated the public. (This raised ethical questions about news management, as scholars have noted).[26]

Clinton's news management improved when be brought in former Reagan aide David Gergen and long-time associate Richard Morris. Gergen helped him improve his relations with the White House press, and Morris assisted the president in developing a more coherent and consistent message, long a Clinton nemesis.

Clinton used new technologies innovatively during his administration. He conducted video press conferences with local reporters in various states. Through satellite hook-ups, reporters sitting in a television station could see and hear the president on a television monitor, and the president, sitting in the White House, could view and listen to reporters. The White House also created an electronic mail address so that citizens could communicate with the president from their personal computers.

Clinton also used talk radio a great deal in his first 2 years in office. He conducted 82 radio interviews; Hillary Clinton did 80. President Clinton also invited 200 radio talk-show hosts to the White House in 1993 in an attempt to promote his health care program.[27] Ultimately, his attempt failed as talk-radio hosts condemned his health care package. In the current political environment, there is no guarantee that a president's efforts to woo the media will succeed.

Clinton and Bush were able to stay "on message" and to maintain focus on a theme at various points in their presidencies. Bush did this with the Persian Gulf War. Clinton succeeded when he went on the offensive in the 1995–1996 battle with Congressional Republicans over how to balance the federal budget. Aided by consultant Morris, Clinton adopted a more focused approach in 1996, one that seemed to net him more favorable press coverage.

Clinton's aides implemented a change in media strategy after the Republicans took control of Congress in the 1994 midterm elections. Concluding that the president was "overexposed" and that his many appearances on talk shows and town hall meetings had reduced the dignity of the office, they devoted more attention to improving relations with the Washington press corps.[28] Even today, in an era of interactive media, presidents cannot afford to ignore the conventional news media, for the press provides Americans with the bulk of their information about the presidency and also helps shape public opinion toward the chief executive.

Summary

Bush and Clinton both used the media effectively in their first presidential campaigns. However, like others before them, they found that governing is more difficult than campaigning, and that no president can control the media agenda or avoid being skewered in the press. In general, *presidents are more likely to get positive press and dominate the media agenda when they have a coherent message that resonates with the public, and when they know how to package the message for the print, broadcast, and interactive media.*

PRESS SECRETARY

The presidential press secretary is the major conduit of news and informa-tion from the president to the news media. Frequently at the president's side, the press secretary represents the president before the international media, advises the president on media matters, and announces U.S. policy to foreign and domestic elites. The press secretary is the president's most visible public relations agent; he or she releases information that the president wants released and uses words that accurately convey what the White House wants to say about a particular issue at a particular time. Today, of course, public relations is the name of the game: Reagan press secretary Larry Speakes kept a sign on his desk that read, "You don't tell us how to stage the news, we won't tell you how to cover it." To be successful, press secretaries must understand and empathize with journalists. Critics note that the main job of the press secretary is "to feed the animals" or satisfy reporters' hunger for news.[29] Feedings often take place at the **daily news briefing.** Briefings are typically held shortly before noon on weekdays.

The press secretary begins by making announcements about policy matters, presidential appointments, a presidential trip, or other issues facing the nation. The briefings give the president a mechanism to provide spin on current events and, hopefully, to set the agenda for the day's news. Given the preeminent role the president plays in American government, the news media feel obligated to report what the press secretary says. "In a sense, members of the press are 'captive' to the White House," journalist Dom Bonafede notes.[30] But the captivity cuts both ways. The press secretary is also captive to the news media's routines and their needs to get new angles on old stories. This means that the press secretary must prepare succinct statements about policy matters, must speak about issues in short sound bites, and must be ready to respond effectively to reporters who ask tough questions about administration policy. "The press secretary," note Grossman and Kumar, "acts as both manager of the message and messenger boy in what is often regarded as a theater of the absurd."[31] Far from being an omnipotent manipulator of the press, press secretaries frequently must act as reporters themselves. For one reason or another they may not know what key officials in the government are thinking about an issue, and so they must hit the streets, the phones, or computer e-mail to determine the political ramifications of the issue. The last thing they want to do, one Washington correspondent observed, is to misspeak on the network news "or, worst of all, lie to Sam Donaldson!"[32]

It is a dicey job. Presidents want their positions represented accurately. Reporters want information; some want to draw blood, hoping to generate a gaffe that will give them a good story. Foreign leaders listen closely to what the press secretary says, anxious to spot a subtle change in U.S. policy toward their countries. Verbal missteps can have serious consequences. Marlin Fitzwater, press secretary under George Bush, relates that he once responded to a question about Danish environmental policy by joking that he had Danishes for breakfast. He ended up having to formally apologize for the remark.[33] The most controversial issue that press secretaries must face is whether they should lie to protect U.S. national security. Pentagon spokesman Arthur Sylvester once said bluntly that in certain cases "government does have the right to lie." Few would disagree with him. The problem is determining when lying is justified and what constitutes a lie. Some press secretaries have had the unpleasant experience of having to lie about a military venture, only to get caught. In 1983 a CBS correspondent asked Reagan press secretary Larry Speakes if the U.S. was preparing to invade Grenada, a Caribbean island, in the wake of a coup against a U.S.-backed regime. Speakes denied an invasion was imminent, calling the idea "preposterous." Twelve hours later U.S. forces invaded Grenada.

Press secretaries must balance national security and presidential politics with the need to inform the press in a reasonably accurate fashion. Sometimes this involves tiptoeing on a narrow precipice, navigating between giving false information and speaking a truth that could be politically damaging. Long-time Washington observer Stephen Hess offered a hypothetical example of how a press secretary could walk the line by defining a reporter's question narrowly:

Q: Has the assistant secretary of state been invited to China?

A.   No. (Meaning: *He will go to China as an advisor to the vice president. It is the vice president who will be invited. Therefore, I am not lying.* Rationale: *I have to say this because protocol requires that the Chinese must first publicly extend the invitation.*)[34]

The press secretary has a complex job. There is nothing inherently wrong with a president having a press secretary, just as there is nothing wrong with companies hiring public relations agents. When press secretaries represent the president's positions accurately and keep reporters informed, they are assets to the administration. When they repeatedly distort the president's policies, in the interest of national security or to protect the president's political future, they are not advancing the cause of the presidency or the country particularly well.

PRESS CONFERENCES

The press conference is the only news-making institution that mandates an interaction between presidents and journalists. It gives presidents the chance to present their views on issues facing the nation; it also forces them to answer tough questions about policy matters. For today's presidents, who must rely on persuasion to achieve their goals, press conferences offer an opportunity to help shape the agenda and to influence public perceptions. As Carolyn Smith notes in a book on the subject:

> The main obligation of the president in this dialogue is to persuade. The main obligation of the press is to hold the president accountable for his policies and his actions. These contrary obligations produce a delicate but natural tension—a balancing act, if you will—that should be played out in each and every good press conference exchange.[35]

Presidential press conferences began with Woodrow Wilson, came of age under Franklin Roosevelt, who let reporters ask questions spontaneously and used them to publicize his programs, entered the television era with John Kennedy, who transformed them from dull Q&A sessions to media events, "degenerated into personal bickering sessions" under Richard Nixon,[36] who held as few press conferences as he could during his time in the White House, became convivial television shows under Ronald Reagan, who frequently used his acting skills to dodge questions, and continued to showcase the adversarial relationship between press and presidency under Bush and Clinton.

Press conferences have become institutionalized over the years. Presidents are expected to hold them. Reporters are expected to ask tough questions. Press conferences provide presidents with less control over outcomes than presidential speeches and more control than the evening news. Still, presidents have considerable power. They decide when a news conference will be held, what to announce to the public, which reporters will be called on, and when to call it quits. Reporters, of course, can ask tough questions of the president on any topic under the sun; they often focus their questions on a particular topic, such as Watergate (with Nixon), the Iran-Contra "arms for hostages" scandal (with Reagan), and White House ethical abuses (with Clinton). Reporters can, within the limits of modern journalism, write critical things about the president's performance or choose unflattering presidential pictures for the evening news.

Press conferences vary greatly, depending on the participants and the problems facing the nation. Smith points out that we can evaluate press conferences in terms of the quality of reporters' questions and presidents' answers. Good questions are worded cogently and accurately. They require a president to reveal something new about the administration or White House policy proposals. Good answers provide information to the public. They show that the president understands the question and the nature of the response. Good press conference exchanges "are those which reveal that the president is exercising legitimate leadership and the press is exercising its legitimate watchdog role," Smith notes.[37]

Unfortunately, all press conferences do not contain good exchanges. Sometimes reporters get their facts wrong, ask misleading questions, and raise questions that advocate policy positions. Presidents have been known to refuse to answer legitimate questions, to stonewall, and to provide vague answers that suggest they do not understand the implications of reporters' questions. Press conference exchanges reached an all-time low in 1973, as the Watergate story unfolded. CBS's Robert Pierpoint asked Nixon what it was about television news that had made him so angry. Nixon replied that Pierpoint should not assume that television aroused his anger. Then he added with a smile, "You see, one can only be angry with those he respects."

Press conferences can also be evaluated in terms of their impact on the public. Presidents hope that a press conference will increase public support of their policies and raise their standing in the polls. John Kennedy's press conferences seemed to have elevated the president's stature. Ronald Reagan's press conferences appeared to have done the same, at least until the Iran-Contra story broke in his second term.

Today, many observers feel that press conferences have deteriorated into television events. Scholars note that presidents answer only questions they want to answer, giving scripted, rehearsed responses to many questions.

Reporters, whose names are invariably flashed across the screen when they ask a question, are also concerned with their image; getting called on by the president and asking a tough question can enhance a reporter's prestige. David Gergen observes that the presidential press conference "does not serve anyone's purpose very well. They are theater for both sides; the press asks predictable questions and the president gives predictable answers."[38]

Although the press conference is a worthwhile institution, it is on the decline. Gone are the days of the Kennedy administration when the public looked forward to live encounters between the president and the White House press. Nowadays, Americans are more skeptical of both the press and the president. The networks are less interested in covering press conferences, recognizing that people will complain about interruptions in their favorite programs. Presidents don't need the press conference as much now that they can communicate directly with the public through talk radio or town hall meetings.

It will be interesting to see how the institution of the press conference adapts to the era of talk radio and interactive media, and to a time in which the public is fed up with journalists asking tough questions of elected officials. Most scholars believe that, despite its many problems, the press conference still provides a mechanism for the president to face tough questions from White House journalists, for the press to speak openly with the president, and for the public to watch the chief executive in action.

CONCLUSIONS

Presidents must dominate the agenda to govern effectively. To do this, they need to attain good press coverage and present a favorable image on television and in the nation's print media. Press conferences, press secretaries, and an assortment of communication strategies ranging from spin control to participation in town hall meetings have evolved as ways to achieve the goal of agenda control. Scholars believe that presidents are more apt to be successful in dominating the media agenda when they present a coherent message and tailor it to the needs of the print, electronic, and interactive media.

Nowadays, of course, presidents and their aides plan activities around television. Political writer Michael Kelly disdainfully notes that in our era:

the day is composed, not of hours or minutes, but of *news cycles*. In each cycle, *senior White House officials* speaking on *background* define *the line of the day. This line is echoed and amplified outside the Beltway, to real people,* who live *out there,* by the President's *surrogates,* whose appearances create *actualities* (on radio) and *talking heads* (on television).[39]

Kelly is correct that television plays an important role in the modern White House and that presidents are concerned—sometimes preoccupied— with images. Image management has become a primary concern for modern presidents, and this can have negative consequences if it supplants a concern for responsible policymaking (see discussion in chapter 7). Still, we need to remember that presidents are not omnipotent and that, faced with opposition from interest groups, the opposition party, and in some cases the press, they need to marshal resources to gain support for their programs. This means that presidents must appeal to the public and capture public support. The news media have become an important force in the battle for public opinion. As is discussed in the next chapter, the news media are autonomous institutions that have their own criteria for determining which aspects of the presidency should be highlighted, which should be downplayed, and how the president's many activities should be presented to the American public.

KEY ISSUES

White House Office of Communications

Reagan's News Management Strategies

Bush and Clinton's Media Strategies

Press Secretaries

Daily News Briefing

Press Conferences

DISCUSSION QUESTIONS

1. Ronald Reagan's media aides worked hard to influence news coverage of the president. What techniques did they employ?

2. It is often said that presidents manage the news. What are the limitations in this statement, based on the discussion in this chapter?

3. In the nineteenth century, presidents rarely worried about how they came across to the press or public. Have we gone too far in the other direction today?

4. How many presidential press conferences have you seen? What makes for a good press conference, in your opinion?

5

Covering the Presidency

This chapter examines the other half of the president–press relationship: the White House press corps. The White House is the most prestigious beat in journalism. It is also the most grueling. Reporters work in cramped quarters. They have to translate the comments of White House bureaucrats into language the ordinary person can understand. But there is glory in covering the White House. Television correspondents get to appear on TV regularly; print reporters gain fame and fortune. Once unknown to the public, today's White House reporters are media stars. They make huge salaries, far more than the ordinary Americans who read, see, and listen to what they write. They command and accept large fees on the corporate lecture circuit.

The nucleus of the White House press corps is composed of reporters from the nation's elite newspapers (*The New York Times*, *The Washington Post*, *The Wall Street Journal*), newsweeklies (*Newsweek*, *Time*, *U.S. News and World Report*), the wire services, radio news organizations (commercial radio networks and National Public Radio), and the television networks. The outer circle includes reporters from large circulation metropolitan newspapers, news services, and specialized media. Over the past 50 years, the size of the White House press corps has increased dramatically. Only 15 correspondents were on hand when Harry Truman announced that the United States was dropping a bomb on Japan. Today there are about 1,800 accredited White House reporters.[1]

As gatekeepers, White House reporters make decisions daily about what news is fit to print and which messages are appropriate to broadcast. What criteria do they use to make their judgments? As we will see, the news is not a mirror image of reality—far from it. Reporters, editors, and producers make decisions that are based on professional, organizational, economic, and even ideological factors. The White House press corps has considerable power. Writer James Fallows notes that they "have the negative power to say things about other people, in public, to which they can never really respond in kind" and "the positive power to expand other people's understanding of reality by bringing new parts of the world to their notice."[2] In this chapter we examine the White House press and its interactions with the president. We focus on these questions:

- What factors shape the news of the president that appears in the nation's news media?
- How do the media portray the president?
- Do the news media defer to presidents or do they give them tough press?

DETERMINANTS OF THE NEWS

Bias

It is commonly believed that reporters inject their political values into news stories. Like everyone else, reporters have political views. Most tend to be Democrats. A national study of journalists conducted by researchers David Weaver and Cleveland Wilhoit found that significantly more journalists described themselves as Democrats than as Republicans, or Independents. The elite reporters who cover the White House are somewhat more liberal than reporters in the country as a whole.[3]

However, this does not mean that reporters interject their political attitudes into news stories about the president. It is not true that Democratic presidents have gotten good press and Republican presidents have received negative coverage. Democrats Jimmy Carter and Lyndon Johnson got a good deal of harsh press—ABC's *Nightline* covered Carter's quagmire in Iran night after night, and CBS anchorman Walter Cronkite did a documentary in which he expressed misgivings about the war in Vietnam. On the other hand, Republican Ronald Reagan received a great deal of positive news coverage. Former *Washington Post* executive editor Benjamin Bradlee went so far as to say that "we have been kinder to President Reagan than any president that I can remember since I've been at *The Post*.[4] Clearly there is more to news of the presidency than partisan bias.

No better example of this is news coverage of Bill Clinton's presidency. You would think that if reporters were '60s-style liberal Democrats, they would have loved Bill Clinton. But Clinton received tough press in his term as president. His policy on gays in the military generated negative coverage when military and political leaders opposed it. His appointment of Zoe Baird to the post of attorney general stirred controversy when it was revealed that she had employed illegal immigrants as a nanny and chauffeur and had not paid social security taxes on their incomes, in violation of the law. It was the liberal *New York Times* that broke one of the stories.

Clinton got bad press on his health care plan, the Whitewater scandal, and his tendency to change positions on issues to suit the political climate. One study found that from 1993 to 1995, nearly two thirds of all evaluations of Clinton by reporters and sources were negative.[5] You could hardly say that the press bent over backwards to give him a break. If anything it was the other way around; reporters wanted to prove that they were *not* victims of their partisan biases and so gave Clinton tougher press than they might have given a Republican.

Modern "objective reporting" emphasizes that journalists should steer clear of putting opinions into stories. In contemporary journalism, if an event cannot be witnessed first hand, it must be confirmed by a source. Thus, journalists' pet political peeves are a much less significant determinant of the news than a host of professional and organizational factors. And yet it would be a mistake to maintain that journalists' personal views have no impact on what they write.

Journalists' biases *can* influence the news in subtle ways. Editors and producers must make decisions about the types of investigative stories or in-depth analyses they will do. Inevitably, their choices grow out of their political perspectives and attitudes. Should a news organization focus on why the U. S. economy has grown by leaps and bounds (a conservative agenda) or on corporate downsizing (a liberal agenda)? In 1996, elite media focused on the latter issue. *The New York Times* did a series examining how corporate cost-cutting had taken a toll on the American workforce, producing layoffs and the permanent elimination of jobs.[6]

People often criticize news organizations for running articles that have a political slant. What critics forget is that one of the functions of the news media is to expose wrongdoing and shine the searchlight on society's problems; to do this, journalists must have an overarching political or moral perspective. The great investigative stories of the early twentieth century—such as Upton Sinclair's expose of the Chicago meatpacking industry—were driven by a political perspective. In an ideal world, *a variety of perspectives* would drive journalism, running the gamut from conservative to radical.

It is fair to say that journalists' political views have a subtle impact on the news when the focus is on long features designed to shape the public agenda. Ordinary, run-of-the-mill news articles are not so strongly influenced by reporters' private political views, however. For the most part, news of the presidency and presidential elections (see chapter 17) are shaped less by reporters' pet political peeves than by professional journalistic factors, such as roles, news routines, organizational constraints, and politicians' news management techniques.

Routines

Journalists' routines shape the news in subtle and important ways. Routines, according to Pamela Shoemaker and Stephen Reese, are "those patterned, routinized, repeated practices and forms that media workers use to do their jobs."[7] Several routines influence reporting on the White House.

Sources. "News is not what happens, but what someone says has happened or will happen," Leon Sigal has noted.[8] Sigal points out that reporters rarely are able to witness an event first hand, but instead must depend on the observations of others. The others on whom they depend are sources, and these sources are invariably high-ranking government officials. In a now-famous study, Sigal found that nearly three fourths of all news sources quoted in *New York Times* and *Washington Post* stories were domestic and foreign government officials.[9] Official sources—key members of the political establishment—dominate the news. As Lance Bennett observes, "By any accounting, the conclusion is inescapable: Even the best journalism in the land is extremely dependent on the political messages of a small spectrum of official news sources."[10] There are good reasons why journalists turn to government sources. One observer noted that:

> The established leaders of any organization have great natural advantages. They are believed to have better sources of information. The books and papers are in their offices. They took part in the important conferences. They met the important people. They have responsibility. It is, therefore, easier for them to secure attention and speak in a convincing tone.[11]

Interestingly enough, the observer was journalist Walter Lippmann, writing in 1920. The convention of official sources has become part of political reporting, an accepted journalistic stock-in-trade.

Channels. A related determinant of news is the channel or modality that reporters use to get information. There are at least three channels: *formal (or routine), informal, and enterprise.* Routine channels include (a) official proceedings (legislative hearings, trials); (b) press releases; (c) press conferences; and (d) nonspontaneous events (speeches and ceremonies).

Informal channels include (a) background briefings; (b) leaks; (c) non-governmental proceedings, such as professional and academic conventions; and (d) reports from other news organizations, and interviews with fellow journalists.

Enterprise channels include (a) interviews conducted at the journalist's initiative; (b) spontaneous events witnessed firsthand (fires, etc.); (c) independent research; and (d) reporters' own conclusions and analyses.[12]

In his study of front page stories in *The New York Times* and *The Washington Post*, Sigal found that routine channels accounted for 58.2% of the stories, informal channels accounted for 15.7%, and enterprise 25.8%. When Sigal looked only at stories that came from Washington, he found that 72% of the channels were routine, 20% informal, and 8% enterprise.[13] Later research has confirmed these findings.[14]

Routine channels offer numerous advantages to White House reporters. As Maltese observes:

> Press releases, radio actualities, satellite feeds, fact sheets, and the like provide a torrent of easy news for the media to relay to their audience. Briefings and press conferences serve as a watering hole for packs of journalists in search of news. Well-choreographed photo opportunities provide striking visual images that reinforce the messages that White House officials want to convey, but they also give the producers of television news ready-made opportunities to get exactly what they need most: good pictures.[15]

No wonder the irreverent journalist, I.F. Stone, remarked that there is "no other city, and no other world capital, in which life is made so easy for the newspaperman."[16]

Some have argued that reliance on routine channels pushes reporters toward accepting what official sources say. There is some truth to this, but it is less true today than it was in FDR's day and in Lyndon Johnson's time, the latter a period in which reporters got much information about Vietnam through routine channels only to find that much of it was inaccurate. Nowadays it is not uncommon for information relayed through routine channels to reflect negatively on the president. In fact the major problem with reliance on routine channels is not that the information favors the

White House, but that it provides at best a superficial summary of what is going on in Washington.

In addition to obtaining information through routine modalities, reporters gain information and insights through informal channels, typically background briefings and leaks.

The White House press secretary typically conducts **briefings.** An entire terminology has evolved to describe the information that reporters are allowed to report and how they can report it. For example, information can be *on the record,* which means that the comments may be quoted and the name of the source identified; *on background,* which signifies that the source cannot be identified by name, only by status or position (as in a "senior administration official," who may in fact be the president's chief of staff); *on deep background,* which means that reporters can use the information, but cannot attribute the information to a particular source; and *off the record,* where the information is not to be quoted, but is provided to help reporters understand the larger context.[17]

Messages are also conveyed informally through **leaks,** facetiously called premature unauthorized partial disclosures.[18] Basically, a leak is information that someone in government wants disclosed. Since the official is unable to divulge it through formal channels for any number of reasons, he or she leaks it to reporters. According to Stephen Hess, there are different types of leaks, including the:

> Policy Leak (a straightforward pitch for or against a proposal using some document or insiders' information as the lure to get more attention than might be otherwise justified); Goodwill Leak (a play for future favor. The primary purpose is to accumulate credit with a reporter, which the leaker hopes can be spent at a later date); Animus Leak (used to settle grudges. Information is disclosed to embarrass another person); and the Whistle Blower Leak (going to the press may be the last resort of frustrated civil servants who feel they cannot correct a perceived wrong through regular government channels).[19]

For better or worse, leaks are a regular part of political communication in Washington. Leaks irritate presidents because they reduce the administration's control over the agenda. Yet leaks serve important functions for officials and reporters. They let officials say things they cannot easily express in public, given the strict rules of diplomatic discourse. Leaks also help reporters by giving them information they can use to write more comprehensive stories. While leaks can benefit the public, they are typically not directed at the mass audience. They are aimed at Washington insiders.[20]

The third way reporters get information is through enterprise channels. Woodward and Bernstein broke the Watergate story in this manner, interviewing sources who wanted to talk, perusing public records, and piecing together a story of collusion and corruption. Enterprise reporting is difficult because it takes time and requires that reporters be taken off regular assignments to prepare a story that may or may not pan out.

Before moving on, it should be noted that these categories—routine, informal, and enterprise channels—are rough, inexact ways to approximate the ways that reporters cover the presidency. The distinctions can sometimes get fuzzy, as when a reporter engaged in independent research (enterprise channel) gets information through a whistle blower leak. Is this enterprise reporting, use of informal channels, or both? The point to remember is that sources and routine channels play an important part in reporting on the White House.

News Values.   Journalists have long been guided by news judgments or their professional assessments of what constitutes news. They evaluate stories using such news values as conflict and controversy (conflict is more intrinsically interesting than harmony and may suggest that important issues are at stake); pervasiveness, (the more people the story affects, the more important it is); novelty (events that depart from expectations attract attention); and human interest (people tend to be interested in other people, particularly famous ones like the president and the First Family).[21]

Timeliness.   Timeliness is next to godliness in modern journalism. News must be new in America for "nothing matters more than being in the right place at the right time and filing the story before anyone else does," notes Michael Schudson. "It is the path to fame and fortune, professional advancement, and Pulitzer Prizes," he adds.[22] News organizations believe that audiences appreciate getting the latest information on a fast-breaking story and that they gravitate to news outlets that provide these facts. It is true that deadlines have probably stimulated reporters to get stories they might not otherwise have scampered after. Yet, as James Carey perceptively observes, "the latest news is not always the best and most useful news. Little is lost if the news of politics or urban life is a little old."[23]

Deadline pressure has all sorts of effects on the White House press corps. It pushes reporters to depend on official sources who can provide information quickly and efficiently. It encourages reporters to do numerous stories on what happened rather than on why something happened. It causes journalists to focus on "the fact that advances the story, not the one that explains it."[24]

Audience Appeal.   Stories are also designed to appeal to audiences and to hold audience attention. In newspapers and magazines, stories must be interesting, photographs enticing, and headlines compelling. Television news needs good pictures and engaging narrative. There is an economic, as well as a journalistic, basis to this routine. The news media, particularly television, make money by selling audience attention to advertisers. Advertisers provide between 70% to 90% of newspaper revenues, and almost all of the profits that broadcast outlets derive from news. As John McManus notes:

> News consumers trade their attention, and perhaps per-copy fees, to news providers for information. The news providers then sell that attention to advertisers for rates based on the size and commercial value (income, stage of life etc.) of the audience whose attention is delivered.[25]

To maximize profits, the print and electronic media need to attract as many consumers as possible. As McManus notes, "news programmers and newspapers are competing not in a *news market* but in a *public attention market*."[26] They need to maintain—or at least not lose—the attention of their readers, listeners, and viewers. Thus, television producers encourage reporters to "tell stories" and weave narratives rather than to rehash facts that they fear will bore viewers.[27]

Reliance on Other Journalists.   Like other workers, White House reporters are influenced by what their peers do and say. They exchange information via e-mail and look to leaders in their group for advice. Most check out *Hotline*, a prestigious digest of political news. Shoemaker and Reese observe that "lacking any firm external benchmarks against which to measure the product, journalists take consistency as their guide: consistency with other news organizations and even with themselves."[28] This can protect reporters from making egregious mistakes; it can also encourage conformity and homogeneity.[29]

Ideology

This is the most insidious—and most controversial—of all the forces that shape the news. Ideology influences how we see the world. According to Raymond Williams, ideology is *"a relatively formal and articulated system of*

*meanings, values, and beliefs, of a kind that can be abstracted as a 'world view'
or a 'class outlook.'*"[30] An ideological perspective on news media emphasizes
that the news media reflect and reinforce the dominant values of liberal
capitalist democracy. Ideologically oriented theories of the news media
make the radical argument that the news is an instrument of the ruling
classes, and that it helps to maintain the status quo and engineer mass
consent. Ideological perspectives are diverse, with some adopting a neo-
Marxist perspective and others emphasizing cultural frameworks.[31] Most
ideological theories discuss the concept of **hegemony**, defined by Shoemaker and Reese as *"the means by which the ruling order maintains its
dominance."* According to these authors, "media institutions serve a
hegemonic function by continually producing a cohesive ideology, a set of
commonsensical values and norms, that serves to reproduce and legitimate
the social structure through which the subordinate classes participate in
their own domination."[32]

The hegemony concept emphasizes that in America, government does not
have to resort to coercion to induce the public to support its policies. This would
be illegal in most circumstances, would violate American values, and would
threaten media autonomy. Instead, government uses the media to manufacture
consent through such mechanisms as concentration of ownership, government
public relations, and use of routine channels of information.

The hegemony notion has sparked a great deal of debate. Opponents
point out that the concept is difficult to falsify empirically. They also have
noted that in America there is not one ruling class, but a variety of powerful
elites, and that these groups do not always share the same goals.[33] Most
scholars find hegemony intuitively interesting, but reject its simplistic analysis of the current political scene.

One approach that bridges hegemony with more conventional approaches has been proposed by Daniel Hallin. Hallin in essence argues that
hegemony operates only under certain conditions. He contends that the
news media preserve ideological boundaries by dividing up the world into
three spheres: **the sphere of legitimate controversy, the sphere of consensus, and the sphere of deviance.**[34]

News that falls into the sphere of legitimate controversy is full of conflict
and criticisms of the president and candidates for public office. Stories that
fall into this sphere do not impinge on the basic power arrangements in
society. Hallin notes that "this is the region of electoral contests and
legislative debates, of issues recognized as such by the major established
actors of the American political process."[35]

The core region is the sphere of consensus, in which news stories touch on basic, shared American values—the region of "motherhood and apple pie." "Within this region," Hallin notes, "journalists do not feel compelled either to present opposing views or to remain disinterested observers. On the contrary, the journalist's role is to serve as an advocate or celebrant of consensual values." News of U.S. victories in the Olympics, NASA, and popular wars falls into the sphere of consensus.

The final arena is the sphere of deviance. In this area, Hallin maintains, journalism "plays the role of exposing, condemning, or excluding from the public agenda those who violate or challenge the political consensus." Stories that fall into the sphere of deviance rarely get prominent play. News about the Holocaust in World War II and AIDS victims in the early 1980s fell into this domain.[36]

Hallin's spheres are hypothetical constructs—concepts that journalists use to divide up the political and ideological universe. There are obvious complications—the boundaries between spheres are "fuzzy," as Hallin notes; there is great variability within the American media, and great fluctuation over time. Nonetheless, Hallin's notions are a useful way of describing how the news media cover controversial issues, particularly those involving the White House.

NATURE OF PRESIDENTIAL NEWS

With these theories as backdrop, let's look now at how the press has actually covered the president in the television age. I will discuss the quantity and quality of coverage.

Quantity of News

There is little question that the news media give abundant coverage to the president. Lewis Wolfson observed that "sure as the sun will rise tomorrow, the president will top America's front pages and nightly news. No single story in all of daily journalism is more heavily covered. There seems to be nothing we don't learn about a president."[37]

In a study of CBS news from 1969 to 1985, Smoller found that there was at least one presidential news story on 97% of the nightly newscasts. Approximately 20% of a typical newscast focused on the president or his administration.[38] During Bush and Clinton's administrations the networks lavished even more attention on the White House. For the first year and a half of Bush's term, approximately 38% of the newscasts focused on the president. During Clinton's first 18 months, the number rose to 57%.[39] Print and radio also focus heavily on the chief executive, but television seems to make the presidency the centerpiece of its news. Why does television lavish so much attention on the president?

The answer is that presidential news is good television. It meshes well with the routines of TV journalism. Smoller notes that there are six reasons why the networks devote so much time to the president:

1. News coverage of the president is profitable because information about the president sells.
2. By focusing on the presidency the networks are able to deliver to their affiliates a "national" news program that does not compete with local news programs.
3. White House news helps fulfill the FCC's requirement that broadcasters serve the public interest. Proximity to the president elevates network prestige.
4. White House news is cost-effective.
5. White House news is logistically easy to produce.
6. Airtime also advances the careers of correspondents assigned to the White House.[40]

Is all this coverage good or bad? There are different views here. Some scholars believe that by focusing attention on the White House, television can enhance presidential power. It can make it easier for presidents to reach and influence the public and perhaps win support for policy proposals. Others scholars take a dimmer view. They argue that by lavishing attention on the presidency, the news creates unrealistic expectations about what the president can do. Since a president cannot possibly meet these expectations, the stage is set for disappointment, increased public cynicism, and anger.

There is evidence that television may be focusing less on the president than it did in the past. Ever since the Republicans gained control of Congress in 1994, there has been a marked increase in the proportion of stories devoted to the House and Senate.[41] As long as Congress dominates the public agenda, we can expect to see Congress and the president share the television limelight.

Quality of News

Beyond quantity is the question of the quality and content of news media coverage of the president.

Stages. Scholars have proposed that there are different phases in the relationship between the president and the press. Grossman and Kumar argue that the relationship has three stages: (a) alliance, in which both sides cooperate with one another; (b) competition, in which reporters and the White House use manipulative strategies to get their way; and (c) detachment, that occurs after both sides tire of the acrimony and settle into a more formal and structured relationship.[42]

Since presidential administrations differ and the external forces that impinge on both the president and the press are not constant over time, it is difficult to formulate rules about the phases of presidential news coverage. One thing seems clear: The honeymoon between the president and the press is shorter than ever before. During Jimmy Carter's presidency, *Time* and *Newsweek* did not do critical cover stories on the president until he had been in office almost a year. With Bill Clinton, it took *Time* just 4 months to do a cover featuring the words THE INCREDIBLE SHRINKING PRESIDENT in bold and a small picture of Bill Clinton underneath. *Newsweek* did a similar cover, asking simply "What's wrong?" Media writer David Shaw noted that:

> The media battered Lyndon B. Johnson over Vietnam and savaged Richard Nixon over Watergate, but perhaps never in our nation's history—certainly not in its recent history—has a President so early in his term been subjected to a greater barrage of negative media coverage than Bill Clinton endured in his first days in office.[43]

Content and Criticisms.   At one level, the American press covers the president better than any country's news media covers its chief executive. There are thousands of stories on the president, relayed through print, electronic, and interactive media channels. Many of the stories are amazingly thorough. Some articles, particularly those in elite newspapers and specialized magazines, are chock full of insights. For its part, television gives the American public live coverage of presidential speeches and major events. It also provides visuals that convey experiences and offer powerful glimpses of the president and the White House staff.

Moreover, news media coverage of the president is diverse. Coverage differs, depending on whether you are looking at a national newspaper, a local newspaper, a wire service, a news magazine, or television. David Paletz and Kendall Guthrie found that coverage of the president in *The New York Times* centers on policy issues and policy processes. By contrast, the Associated Press wire service, that appeals to a large heterogeneous audience, relays mostly official activities transmitted through routine channels. It stays away from giving interpretations that might offend readers. CBS News presents the president as a symbolic leader, but is apt to ascribe presidential behavior to narrow political motives.[44] News coverage differs because media perform different functions and have diverse economic bases.

Yet presidential news is far from perfect. Critics have pointed out that news coverage of the White House has a number of shortcomings. It is useful to appreciate the limitations in news, as enunciated by scholars and journalists. While scholars differ in the extent to which they agree with these various criticisms, there is little doubt that our understanding of presidential news is enriched by casting a critical eye at the news business.

First, critics note that presidential news tends to be **cynical.** This is an outgrowth of journalists' conviction—call it a bias if you like—that the business of government boils down to politics, that politics is in essence a strategic game, and that politicians cannot be trusted. Journalists, critic James Fallows notes, are mostly concerned with the "how" of politics (for example, how is the president going to push for his legislative agenda?; how is he going to convince members of his own party to support his program?). Citizens, Fallows notes, are more concerned with the "what" of politics (What is the president going to do to reduce the size of government? What can the president do to make the streets safer?).[45]

Although Fallows overstates things a bit and makes voters out to be more issue-oriented than they actually are, he has a point. Journalists are cynical about politicians and are all too likely to assume that presidential decisions are based on cold, self-interested political considerations rather than on assessments of what is best for the country. Consider the following examples, provided by Fallows in a recent book on the subject:

- In February 1995, when the Democratic president and the Republican Congress were fighting over how much federal money would go to local law enforcement agencies, one network news broadcast showed a clip of Gingrich denouncing Clinton, and another of Clinton standing in front of a sea of uniformed policemen while making a tough-on-crime speech. The correspondent's sign-off line was: "But the White House likes the sound of 'cops on the beat.'" That is, the president was pushing the plan because it would sound good in his campaign ads. Whether or not that was Clinton's real motive, nothing in the broadcast gave the slightest hint of where the extra policemen would go, how much they might cost, whether there was reason to think they'd do any good. Everything in the story suggested that the crime bill mattered most only as a chapter in the *real* saga, which was the struggle between Bill and Newt.

- When health care reform was the focus of big political battles between the Republicans and Democrats, it was on the front page and the evening newscast every day. When the Clinton administration declared defeat in 1994 and there were no more battles to be fought, health-care news coverage virtually stopped too—even though the medical system still represented one seventh of the economy, even though HMOs and corporations and hospitals and pharmaceutical companies were rapidly changing policies in the face of ever-rising costs. Health care was no longer *political* news, and therefore it was no longer interesting news.[46]

News coverage of health care reform tended to focus on the narrow political aspects of the issue rather than on broader social concerns. This illustrates the second point that presidential news tends to focus on **narrow political issues.** Kathleen Hall Jamieson conducted a systematic analysis of news coverage of the health care debate in 1993 and 1994. On one occasion she had the opportunity to observe journalists as they watched First Lady Hillary Clinton present the president's health care plan. Jamieson relates that when the First Lady described the plan, reporters showed little interest. They had all heard this before and they passed notes around. But, Jamieson adds:

> As soon as she made a brief attack on the Republicans, there was a physiological reaction, this surge of adrenalin, all around me. The pens moved. The reporters arched forward. They wrote everything down rapidly. As soon as this part was over, they clearly weren't paying attention any more, They were writing on their laptops as they began constructing the story of how the First Lady had attacked the opponents.[47]

News coverage of the health care debate followed this pattern. The press focused on who would win the health care battle and which plan would pass through Congress. Comparatively fewer stories examined the content of the plans, their benefits, or liabilities. This makes sense when you consider that journalists define news as conflict and when you realize that it is easier to cover the politics of health care reform than to focus on the complex merits of the various proposals (see also chapter 14).[48]

A third characteristic of presidential news is that it focuses on **conflict and controversy,** a direct outgrowth of the need to appeal to audiences.[49] Stories about scandals—including Whitewater, Iran-Contra, and Anita Hill's accusations against Clarence Thomas during his confirmation hearings for the Supreme Court—captured a good deal of press attention. In 1996 television news was apt to portray Republicans' disagreements with Clinton over balancing the budget as a battle between titanic egos—Clinton, Gingrich, and Dole. Frequently missing from these stories, critics argued, were the ideological and philosophical origins of the differences between the political leaders. Again, Fallows observes that:

> A convenient way to think about this side of journalistic culture is to imagine a seventh grade science class in which kids are trapped and realize that they are finally going to *have* to learn the difference between metamorphic and sedimentary rocks. Then someone looks out the window and sees a fight on the playground or two dogs tangled up. The room comes alive, and by the time the teacher can get control the bell has rung.

In just the same way, a "running story" or incipient scandal can make it hard for anyone in the Washington branch of the press to concentrate on anything else. When a scandal is breaking, talk show figures wring their hands about the "agony" of Watergate or Iran-Contra; but the truth is that journalists are happier at such moments than at any other time.[50]

A fourth characteristic of presidential news (at least that which appears on television) is that it is heavily **visual.** As you know, television producers feel they need compelling visuals to hold an audience. Yet pictures tend to simplify problems. They tend to portray politics in "us versus them" and "good versus bad" terms; large gray areas are overlooked. Smoller offers an excellent example of how this works. He relates a story that was told to him by a former deputy White House press secretary under President Jimmy Carter:

> Basically, when things aren't going well at the White House, the evening news' portrayal is worse than in fact the reality is. And then when things are going well for an administration, the stories suggest that things are far better than they are. There is a tendency to extremes because television is so dependent on pictures. The Camp David peace agreement between Israel and Egypt is a good example. Those pictures of Carter and Begin and Sadat embracing are just wonderful visuals. The impression they leave is that what occurred was 100% positive. A newspaper reporter, however, might go on for two thirds of his story about what a great achievement it was. But might for the last third talk about the history of the problem and certainly how insurmountable it has been up to this point. He might also add that this achievement hasn't been as great as it may appear.[51]

Fifth, presidential news tends to be **personalized.** Personalized news, as Lance Bennett has defined it, "gives preference to the individual actors and human interest angles in events while downplaying institutional and political considerations that establish their social contexts."[52] Television is particularly apt to personalize the news because personalized stories appeal to large audiences who lack the time, motivation, or training to process more complex scenarios. Smoller notes that: "Corespondents are forced to define complicated issues and vague personalities sharply. So presidents and presidential candidates are portrayed as stereotypes—The Hatchet Man, The Klutz, The Incompetent, The Great Communicator, and The Wimp.[53] We might add "Slick Willie" to the list. Complications in presidents' personalities are neglected. Political and institutional determinants of behavior are minimized.

None of this is to say that print and electronic media do a bad job of covering the president. On the contrary, they provide the public with vast amounts of information about the president, much of it interesting and useful. But all businesses have their organizational and professional biases, and news is no different. In general, as Bennett notes, news tends to "downplay the big social, economic, or political picture in favor of the human trials and triumphs that sit at the surface of events. In place of power and process, the media concentrate on the people engaged in political combat over the issues."[54]

SCHOLARLY PERSPECTIVES

Political communication scholars have theorized about the relationship between the president and the press. In this section I focus on three major theoretical issues involving the press and president: the nature of the relationship, the role of ideology, and the part played by public opinion.

An Adversarial or Symbiotic Relationship?

The most popular model of presidential–press relations is the **adversarial view**, the one you learned in high school civics classes. According to this view, presidents are power-hungry creatures who must be "carefully watched lest they abuse their powers, exceed their mandates, commit blunders they would prefer to conceal, and elevate themselves to positions of nonaccountable authority."[55] The press's role is to serve as a watchdog on the presidency.

There are two problems with this view. First, it paints presidents as bad and reporters as good. It assumes that presidents are duplicitous figures who break their promises and connive to deceive the public. There certainly have been some presidents who fit this model, but some fit it less well than others. Furthermore, reporters are not saints: some commit ethical breaches to get stories; others are terribly cynical and resistant to change. Second, the adversarial view fails to account for the many instances in which reporters collaborate with White House sources. Typically, the relationship between reporters and government sources benefits both groups; reporters get information, and sources use journalists to reach and influence the public.

Given these shortcomings, scholars have proposed an **exchange model.** This view assumes that reporters and White House officials need and depend on each other to perform their jobs. As David Weaver and Cleveland Wilhoit note, "In accepting and providing tips and leads, in willingness to float 'trial balloons' and accept leaks and in various arrangements of quid pro quo, reporters and (politicians) are often tacit, if not intentional, partners in the news ... 'You scratch my back and I'll scratch yours.'"[56]

As we have seen, officials furnish reporters with press releases, leaks, and gritty details of inside politics. In exchange, reporters provide White House officials with publicity for their policies and with a way to reach other elites and the public. Scholars have argued that the White House and the news media are locked in a **symbiotic** relationship, in which both sides "depend on each other in their efforts to do the job for which they are responsible."[56]

The exchange model points out that far from being adversaries, reporters and White House officials, even presidents, are part of the same socioeconomic class and share some of the same social concerns. A particularly telling example occurred in 1993 when Bill and Hillary Clinton were trying to select a school for their daughter, Chelsea. The Clintons were trying to decide whether to send their daughter to a public school or to a private school, Sidwell Friends. They shared some of their concerns with political reporters who were invited to a "Renaissance Weekend" get-together in Hilton Head, South Carolina. As *New Republic* writer Jacob Weisberg tells it:

> It is not entirely surprising that the Clintons' choice (Sidwell Friends) was avidly endorsed by various TV journalists whose own kids go to or went to Sidwell: Mark Shields, Jim Lehrer, Judy Woodruff and her husband, Al Hunt (who dismissed the flap over Chelsea's schooling, saying the Clintons' decision was "simply a private matter") … (*Newsweek* political reporter Howard) Fineman and his wife, Amy Nathan, a lawyer-lobbyist, importuned Clinton to put daughter Chelsea in Sidwell Friends Academy, where their own little girl attends power-kindergarten. The Finemans got in some serious face time with Clinton at a "get acquainted" party for freshmen at which Clinton fraternized until the wee hours. No flagrant conflict of interest that. But now, whenever Fineman sees either of the Clintons, he can approach not just as a reporter asking questions, but as a fellow member of the Sidwell community.[58]

The exchange model is a useful way to view presidential–press relations, but it has its shortcomings. First if the relationship is so cooperative and loosey-goosey, then how come there is so much public animosity between the two groups? Presidents and reporters regularly criticize each other and each seems unhappy with the other. Secondly, the model pays insufficient attention to norms and role relationships between the two groups.[59] For these reasons, political communication scholars Jay Blumler and Michael Gurevitch proposed an expanded model that takes both adversarial and exchange processes into account. It emphasizes the roles both reporters and officials play in the political system, and notes that the ground rules of the relationship are open to interpretation and are governed by informal and formal modes of conflict management. Reporters and politicians are "locked into a complex set of transactions which, though mutually beneficial, also include potentials for disagreement and struggle."[60]

Both sides recognize the benefits of the relationship, but appreciate that their priorities are different. Privately, they may agree on what ails the country and respect the professional values of colleagues in the other camp. But publicly they have different roles. Both White House officials and journalists must work within the structures that their predecessors have developed. The White House has a "privileged position" in the political communication system, but it must communicate almost entirely through channels controlled by journalists.[61] Reporters can say pretty much what they want, within the constraints of objective journalism, but they are dependent on presidential sources for information.

The relationship is dynamic and transactional. The arrows of influence go from president to press and from press to president. This fact helps us understand some of the subtle nuances in the relationship. For example, although reporters recognize that the White House Office of Communications wants to put the best face on events, they resent being used by modern "spinmeisters." They also get tired of listening to White House aides spinning this event and that and at times lying straight out. Since under the rules of objective journalism, reporters cannot interject their own opinions into stories, they try to get back at presidents by employing a more subtle device. They insert those little digs at the end of their stories, comments that attribute the president's behavior to cynical political motives. Presidents and their aides get irritated when they see or hear these comments and this increases their frustration with the press. The result, Fallows notes, "is an arms race of 'attitude.'"[62]

Lap Dog or Junkyard Dog?

At various points in this chapter, I have noted that the press provides a good deal of negative coverage of presidents and their policies. Yet, as you may recall, ideologically oriented critics take the opposite point of view, arguing that the press defers to presidents, giving them coverage that borders on propaganda. Do journalists yield to presidents, letting them manipulate news routines to their advantage? Or do they provide a great deal of negative coverage of the president? Is the press a lap dog or a junkyard dog?

In support of the lap dog thesis, there is abundant evidence that the press yielded to past presidents. For example, reporters deferred to Franklin D. Roosevelt, agreeing not to quote him at press conferences and also accepting his spin on New Deal programs, even to the point of doing a special celebration of the second anniversary of the New Deal. For much of Lyndon Johnson's term in office, the media accepted his premises about Vietnam and portrayed the war as "a national endeavor," as an "American tradition," as "manly," and as right. In 1972, the majority of news organizations did *not* follow the lead of *The Washington Post* on the Watergate story; they did not pursue the story or cover it in depth. In 1991, George Bush was able to successfully manage the news during the Persian Gulf War. The news became something of a cheerleader for the United States military in January and February of 1991.[63]

And so it goes. There are many instances in which the news media supported and upheld presidential agendas, in line with what ideological models predict. But … there are also plenty of times when the press aggressively questioned the president and gave him undeniably harsh coverage. Jimmy Carter got terrible press in 1980 as stories focused on the hostage crisis and the sagging economy. In 1992 the news pounded away on the state of the economy and George Bush's inaction. Bill Clinton received primarily bad press early in his first term as president, getting pummeled on health care, Whitewater, and his position on gays in the military.[64]

How can we reconcile these two patterns of coverage? Is it ideology or an out-of-control press?

Actually, it's both.

The key factor is the extent to which *powerful elites* inside and outside government agree on a particular policy. These elites include the president, the Cabinet, Congress, the federal bureaucracy (notably, the Pentagon and the State Department), the business community, and influential interest groups. When there is consensus among these groups on a policy option, the press will follow their lead. When the president can convince these elite groups to go along with his recommendations, and official Washington speaks in one voice, the press will provide sympathetic coverage. The coverage will not be 100% sympathetic of course; however, scholars believe it will, for the most part, reflect the views of these powerful groups.[65]

It is not that the press is bullied into going along or coerced or threatened with legal action. That, happily, is not the way things work in America. The effects of ideology and hegemony are mediated by journalistic routines. Recall that journalists get information from sources, relayed primarily through formal channels. When most leaders are saying the same thing—albeit in slightly different ways—the news media have no choice but to report this. For example, the news media gave the Bush administration favorable press during the Gulf War—a conflagration that had the support of leading elites.

Things change when there is lack of consensus among key political elites. When there is disagreement between the president and Congress or among key members of the foreign policy establishment, the news will provide more critical coverage of presidential policies. Dissenting views will get a good deal of play; opponents will have considerable access to the press, at least those opponents who have clout in Washington circles. When there is conflict among leaders, the news gates open. Dissenters get quoted, polls get taken, and journalists scurry around to get quotes from the different sides.[66]

At just about all phases of the Bush and Clinton presidencies, there was disagreement among elite leaders. Notably, in 1995 when Clinton and congressional leaders could not agree on how to balance the budget to end the shutdown of government, the news was filled with stories on the budget debate. Not all were flattering to the White House.

Thus there is no simple hegemony of media, as radical critics suggest. What matters is how much consensus there is among America's leaders. To use Hallin's scheme, when presidential news falls into the sphere of consensus, journalists will provide the president with good press. The press may even provide negligible coverage of views that challenge the established policies or, if it does, it may marginalize them, subtly questioning the legitimacy of the dissident voices. But when news falls into the sphere of legitimate controversy, when there is debate and issues are regarded as fair game for discussion, the news will not celebrate the president. On the contrary, it may provide a most unflattering picture of the chief executive and his policies.

Some scholars think that official consensus is a thing of the past. Now that the Cold War is over, the president cannot easily locate common enemies. On the domestic front, Congress is increasingly setting the agenda, challenging presidential power. In an age of declining party loyalty, the president commands less allegiance from members of his own party. And political reporters, as Fallows notes, are increasingly strident; they are cynical about politics and skeptical of presidents. For this reason it is likely that (with the exception of national crises), we will see more, not less, conflict between the president and the press.

While some critics feel that such conflict is dysfunctional for society, a more philosophical perspective, one based on the Founding Fathers' respect for a balance of powers among competing political power centers, emphasizes that such conflict is healthy for the system. It allows a cacophony of voices to emerge and keeps institutions from accumulating too much power. As the press challenges the president more in the years to come, the question is whether news will be a positive force, providing an environment in which dissidents can prosper and new ideas can germinate, or a negative force, fueling public cynicism and increasing citizens' antipathy to politics.

The Role of Public Opinion

Public opinion, in some general way, influences the type of press coverage that presidents receive. When polls consistently show the public is dissatis-fied with the president, the press tends to feel emboldened to take on the chief executive and give him tougher press.[67]

On the other hand, when polls show the public strongly approves of the president or the president's policies, the press tends to give the chief executive more favorable coverage. One reason the news media were reluctant to do critical pieces on Ronald Reagan was that he seemed to have the public's support. Journalist Mark Hertsgaard argues that the press could have done more to expose Reagan's gaffes, could have raised more questions about his economic policies, and could have worked harder to uncover his role in Iran-Contra. However, they shied away from these stories. As one reporter explained at the time:

> I used to spend a lot of time writing those stories (on Reagan's gaffes), but I just gave up. You write stories once, twice, and you get a lot of mail saying, "You're picking on the guy, you guys in the press make mistakes too." And editors respond to that, so after a while the stories don't run anymore. We're intimidated.[68]

This is not to say that the press gave Reagan a free ride. He received a good deal of negative press during his presidency, just like every other president. However, Reagan may have been spared some harsher press because reporters felt the public liked Reagan and agreed with his policies. Since stories must appeal to audience members, the press was reluctant to do pieces that might turn off the audience.

Thus, public opinion influences press coverage of the president. This can be good to the extent that reporters take into account the views of their audience. It can be bad if journalists steer clear of reporting a president's mistakes for fear of alienating an audience. One thing is clear: Public opinion (and reporters' perceptions of that opinion) has an impact on political reporting that it did not have in earlier eras.

CLINTON AND THE PRESS

During the first 6 months of his administration, two of every three sources interviewed on television evaluated Clinton or his policies negatively.[69] Why did Clinton get such bad press? There are a number of reasons why Clinton got bad press early in his administration, and they help us understand the dynamics of modern press–presidential relations.

First, Clinton made policy decisions that alienated key elites. His initial decision to end the ban on gays in the military met with opposition from military and Congressional leaders. His health care reform proposals were opposed by Democratic and Republican Congressional leaders, business groups, and the insurance lobby. His policy on Bosnia drew criticism. Given the way journalism operates—getting information from key sources through routine channels—it is no wonder that Clinton got bad press. The sources journalists interviewed criticized the president's programs, and some groups actively used the media to wage campaigns against Clinton's plans. The talk-show host Rush Limbaugh was a constant thorn in Clinton's side, particularly in the early days of the Clinton administration.

A second reason Clinton got bad press was that he made political and strategic mistakes. His policy on gays in the military, while perhaps admirable from a moral point of view, was a political mistake because it alienated key constituencies. Remember that Clinton had received only 43% of the popular vote in the 1992 election and so had to tread carefully. His initial decision to lift the ban on gays in the military was not popular, and it led many in the public to believe that Clinton was just an old-fashioned liberal, not the moderate "New Democrat" he had said he was during the 1992 campaign. His health care plan was complicated and hard to understand, which did not make it easy to sell with the public or elites (see chapter 13). With his public approval ratings low at key times of his presidency, the press felt emboldened to take a tougher stand.

Thirdly, reporters were wary of giving Clinton too many breaks. They did not want to be accused of favoring the Clinton administration. Coverage of the 1992 campaign had favored Clinton over Bush—for a number of reasons not rooted in partisan bias (see chapter 17). However, reporters, particularly the more liberal members of the Washington press corps, may have been sensitive to the charge that they had let their biases influence their reporting. To obliterate the notion that they were biased, reporters may have bent over backwards to give Clinton tough press.[70]

Fourth, the press is increasingly giving presidents negative press, as discussed throughout this chapter.[71] Reporters applied a cynical, narrowly political perspective to Clinton's policies. To make matters worse, Clinton's communications office made some mistakes early on, which set up a negative dynamic.

Radical critics would argue that Clinton got bad press because some of his policies—such as health reform—threatened key elites. There is some truth to this charge, but it underplays the impact of Clinton's own management decisions.[72] Morever, Clinton faced the systemic problem of post-Cold War presidents. Deprived of a common enemy, they have difficulty unifying the country around a theme or issue. Divided government, with different government branches at war with each other, exacerbates matters.

Of course, in Clinton's case, the bad press he received early in his administration turned out to be short-lived. His press improved during the second half of his first term. One reason why Clinton got better press was because he had public opinion behind him. In the summer of 1995, with the Republicans proposing to cut back Medicare to reduce the budget deficit, Clinton successfully positioned himself as the friend of the elderly and of people in need. What's more, the Democrats embarked on an advertising campaign that accused the Republicans of making dangerous cuts in social welfare programs like Medicare. While the Republicans did propose large cuts in social programs, the Democratic ads distorted things, minimizing the extent to which Republicans sought to slow the growth of Medicare rather than slash the program to bits. The public, concerned about what it had heard about Republican cutbacks and turned off by the caustic style of Republican congressional leaders, rallied behind the president.[73]

With polls showing that the public approved of the job Clinton was doing as president, the tide shifted and the press began to cover Clinton more favorably. Moreover, the Republicans were beginning to tear into one another in the primary campaign, so reporters' conflict schema pushed them toward covering the Republicans and laying off Clinton for a while.

The president who had received rotten press early in his term turned things around late in his first term. Clinton's experience with the press points to the volatility of the current press–politics scene. A president is not going to get good press just because he (or she) is president. A president will not get good press because the chief executive accomplishes a lot in Congress in his first two years. (Congress passed a number of Clinton initiatives, including the North American Free Trade Agreement, the Brady Bill, and the Family and Medical Leave Act.) The press has its own logic for covering events—not a conspirational one nor necessarily a bad one, but one that is unique to the American media system.

CONCLUSIONS

This chapter reviewed the determinants of news coverage of the president and discussed the quantity and quality of presidential news. Although it is commonly assumed that partisan bias shapes news coverage, we have seen that this factor is not among the most important determinants of presidential news. Reporters have political biases, of course, and they make their ways into the news on some occasions, but they are less significant factors than journalistic routines, news values, and professional role relationships.

News coverage of the president provides much information about presidential appearances and events. It keeps the public informed about presidential activities and acts as a check on the abuse of presidential power. However, as critics have pointed out, news has its shortcomings: It tends to focus on narrow political issues, overemphasizes conflict, and personalizes politics, frequently neglecting to explain the complex social and economic roots of presidential policies.

The president and the press are locked in a dynamic, transactional relationship. Each affects the other. The White House has influenced the news media by creating institutional mechanisms for releasing information, including background briefings, press conferences, and photo opportunities. It continues to influence the media by providing reporters with a steady stream of information that meets the requirements of news. In times of elite consensus, presidents can flood the media with information favoring their policies, and there is a good chance that much of this information will reach the public. Increasingly, however, presidents are finding that it is not so easy to control the agenda. They must deal with Congress, powerful interest groups, and a volatile and aggressive press.

The press has influenced the presidency in a number of ways. Blumler and Gurevitch remind us that the White House gets its say "almost entirely through formats devised and controlled by journalists. Such a 'subordination' is the price they pay for their privileged access position."[74] Presidents can go around the press by giving public speeches and by doing televised town meetings. However, most people hear about these events through the news media, so journalists' judgments come back into the picture.

As noted in the last chapter, the White House Office of Communications spends considerable time trying to adapt its message to fit the electronic

As noted in the last chapter, the White House Office of Communications spends considerable time trying to adapt its message to fit the electronic media. Some scholars believe that the White House spends more time selling its message than it does formulating it. This may exaggerate matters, but it is no exaggeration to say that presidential aides spend considerable time trying to meet journalists' deadlines for news, their requests for new information, and the round-the-clock "nonstop news cycle."[75] Ideally, Fallows notes, officials would like to have time to engage in long-term planning and to think ahead about social reforms and policy innovations. But the nonstop news cycle, with its constant demand for comment and response, intervenes, like the proverbial phone call that interrupts the person who has just sat down to work. Presidential aides frequently find they are spending more time dealing with the press, with its incessant desire for new information, than in coping with the problem itself.

The media have sped up the pace of presidential decision making. Presidents cannot afford to wait long in making a decision for fear that they will be labeled indecisive by opponents (whose criticisms will most assuredly appear in the news). The press, too, has entered the fray, so presidents must consider how inaction will play on the evening news and on radio and television talk shows.

Some scholars believe the attention lavished on the president has created grandiose expectations for presidential performance. As noted earlier, the incessant television coverage of the hostage crisis may have led people to expect that the president could solve the crisis easily. Most experts believe there was little that any chief executive could have done to free the Americans any sooner.[76] Yet TV coverage, the argument goes, may have raised expectations, which led to the inevitable anger when the hostages were not released for over a year. In the same fashion, critics argue that television coverage of the 1995 budget battle between Congress and the president led the public to expect the two sides to settle sooner than was realistic.

Of course, it is also possible that television had none of these effects. And, as we see later in the book, the impact of the media on public opinion is complex and depends on a host of social and psychological factors. But there is no doubting that the media have changed the ways that the White House does business, resulting in a dynamic relationship between the president and the press that is much different from what the Founding Fathers envisioned.

KEY ISSUES

Reporter Bias

News Routines

Formal, Informal, and Enterprise Channels

Leaks

News Values

Ideological Influences on News

Shortcomings in Presidential News

Adversarial vs. Exchange Models

Public Opinion and News

DISCUSSION QUESTIONS

1. What are the main determinants of presidential news?

2. How would you defend the press against those who say it is cynical and overly concerned with narrow political issues?

3. Did Clinton get a bum rap from the press early in his presidency?

4. What bugs you most about news coverage of the president? How do you think news coverage of the White House could be improved?

6

Presidential Rhetoric

I find that the people of this country are strangely at a loss to determine the nature of their government. Some have insisted that it savors of an aristocracy; others maintain that it is a pure democracy; and a third set of theorists declare that it is nothing more nor less than a mobocracy. (Yet) the simple truth of the matter is, that their government is a pure unadulterated logocracy, or government of words—Washington Irving[1]

The basic element of politics is, quite simply, talk—Peter Hall.[2]

Politics is largely a word game. Politicians rise to power because they can talk persuasively to voters and political elites. Once in power, their daily activities are largely verbal—commands, dialogues, debates, formulation of proposals, laws, orders, decisions, and legal opinions—Doris Graber.[3]

This chapter focuses on language, in particular the language that presidents use to persuade citizens and elites. Language plays a central role in political communication. It is through words that candidates campaign for election, through words that presidents try to gain support for their policies, and through words that leaders and citizens conduct dialogues about the nation's past, present, and future. The study of political language is one of the oldest areas of academic inquiry. It dates back to ancient Greece—to Plato and Aristotle whose works on political rhetoric have survived diverse tests of time.

The term "rhetoric" conjures up many meanings; for most people, it has negative connotations. We say that a politician's speech is "mere rhetoric." We link rhetoric with propaganda and other devil terms of persuasion. "In modern times," presidential scholar Theodore Windt notes, "the word 'rhetoric' has fallen into such ill repute that it may seem disrespectful to use it in the same breath with the presidency."[4]

There are many reasons why the term "rhetoric" evokes such negative reactions in people. We have listened to candidates make vacuous statements that do not address the problems of our day. We have read critical commentaries about presidential speeches in newspapers. We have heard acquaintances, who are cynical about politicians and politics, condemn presidents and lash out at candidates for higher office. What is often forgotten is that presidents have delivered great speeches and political leaders have used oratory to inspire people. Lincoln's Gettysburg address, Franklin D. Roosevelt's first inaugural in which he intoned that "the only thing we have to fear is fear itself," and the many moving speeches of Martin Luther King are testaments to the power of political eloquence. Scholars emphasize that the term "mere rhetoric" does not do justice to the complex and profoundly human activity of political speech.

Rhetoric is a field of study that dates back centuries. "A rhetorical study," Paul Zernicke notes, "explores public discourse to determine the meaning of shared symbols. It focuses on the characteristics and significance of communication directed toward an audience."[5] *Rhetoric is concerned with the symbols that leaders use to persuade, with argumentation, with the content of political speeches, as well as the style in which the speeches are delivered.* Today, rhetoric, in the broad sense of the word, plays a major role in presidential policy making. It is at the centerpiece of presidential leadership. Roderick Hart argues that:

> The most important decision a modern president makes is not that of deciding policy but that of articulating policy in ways that will make the Congress and the people want to adopt that policy ... Even the most authoritatively worded presidential directive is impotent unless the president can convince the people that he has the power to carry out that directive and unless he can convince the press that he can convince the people.[6]

Hart goes on to argue that today, presidents no longer speak just to get elected. They speak, exhort audiences, and use the trappings of the office to achieve their political goals. In fact some scholars argue that presidents cannot attain their policy goals *unless* they can convince the public and elites to support them.

This chapter and the one that follows examine presidential rhetoric. In this chapter I review the history of presidential rhetoric, the rise of the rhetorical presidency, and the concomitant need for presidents to "go public" to gain support for their policies. I discuss how Ronald Reagan used television to lead the country, and the benefits and costs of his approach. Chapter 7 discusses different categories of presidential rhetoric, the impact of presidential speeches, and the pros and cons of the rhetorical presidency. The theme of these chapters is that presidential language matters—that it can be used for good and for ill. I concur with rhetorical scholars Craig Smith and Kathy Smith who make the simple, but telling, point that "presidents persuade ... They persuade the public, both directly and indirectly through the mass media, that they are fulfilling their obligations. And ultimately, they must persuade history. Clearly, presidential leadership entails influence through communication."[7]

HISTORICAL OVERVIEW

During the eighteenth and nineteenth centuries, presidents rarely spoke in public. The Founding Fathers distrusted popular opinion. They feared that if leaders sought to influence the populace, they would incite mob violence. To minimize the role of oratory and public opinion, the Founders set up a political system that gave power to institutions of government, such as the states, Congress, and the presidency. The Founders assumed that the president's power would flow not from his ability to stir opinions, but from the Constitution and the strategic requirements of the job.

Presidents did speak on ceremonial occasions. However, they rarely spoke about specific issues. Washington canceled plans to give a 73-page speech outlining policy recommendations. Instead he gave a general speech that emphasized virtue and the need to follow the Constitution and God. Other presidents followed Washington's lead. Even the voluble Andrew Jackson spoke through mediated channels —through formal documents and proc-lamations. Jackson's early messages and a special proclamation to Congress were submitted in written form. None of this is to say that late eighteenth and midnineteenth century politics were calm or that there were no loud voices. Quite the contrary. However, presidents rarely jumped into the rhetorical fray.[8]

In 1861, one of American's greatest orators, Abraham Lincoln, took the oath of office. In historic speeches like the Gettysburg Address, Lincoln used words to inspire Americans, to change their world views, and to mold policy. "Up to the Civil War," historian Garry Wills notes, "'the United States' was invariably a plural noun: 'The United States are a free government.' After Gettysburg, it became a singular: 'The United States is a free government.'"[9] Yet even Lincoln kept his public appearances to a minimum.

Theodore Roosevelt came up with the idea that the presidency is a "bully pulpit." By that he meant that the presidency afforded the occupant of the office the opportunity to use public address to persuade. However, it was Woodrow Wilson who took up Roosevelt's banner. Wilson believed that power lay in the ability to influence and lead mass opinion.[10] As governor of New Jersey, he had been asked why he thought he could make reforms in the state legislature, given that party leaders controlled the statehouse. "I can talk, can't I," he replied. As president, he put his ideas into practice. He spoke before Congress, breaking a habit of "presidential nonattendance" that had lasted for more than a century. He embarked on a whirlwind speaking tour to sell the country on the League of Nations. Although Wilson lost the battle for the League, he won the rhetorical war: His vision of an active, public president continues to this day.[11]

The next great rhetorical president was Franklin Delano Roosevelt. Roosevelt exploited the dominant medium of his times—radio—to unify the country and to build an agenda for his policies. Blessed with a melodious voice, Roosevelt had the ability to inspire confidence and trust. His radio talks became so popular that people even asked to hear them. Frances Perkins, FDR's labor secretary, recalled that:

> When he talked on the radio, he saw (people) gathered in the little parlor, listening with their neighbors. He was conscious of their faces and hands, their clothes and homes. His voice and his facial expression as he spoke were those of an intimate friend. I have seen men and women gathered around the radio, even those who didn't like him or were opposed to him politically, listening with a pleasant, happy feeling of association and friendship. The exchange between them and him through the medium of radio was very real. I have seen tears coming to their eyes as he told them of some tragic episode, of the sufferings of the persecuted people in Europe, of the poverty during unemployment, of the sufferings of the homeless, of the sufferings of the people whose sons had died during the war, and they were tears of sincerity and recognition and empathy.[12]

THE RHETORICAL PRESIDENCY

Roosevelt used his talks to assuage the anxieties of a worried nation. His fireside chats gave people hope. However, unlike presidents in the television era, Roosevelt did not use the media to mobilize support for his policies. As Samuel Kernell notes, "Compared with today's presidents, Roosevelt enlisted public strategies sparingly. His game remained in Washington. His interest in public opinion was motivated by a need to anticipate and, when possible, to neutralize the representatives of interested publics who might oppose his programs."[13]

Roosevelt's approach worked in his day. During the 1930s and 1940s, political elites—party leaders, interest groups, and governing coalitions—dominated Washington. A successful president had to broker deals and transact bargains with these groups. Power lay in the ability to break bread and negotiate alliances with powerful political elites. This situation has changed. Over the past 40 years, the old elite coalitions have broken down. Political parties have declined in influence (see chapter 15). New interest groups, including Mothers Against Drunk Driving, environmentalists, pro and antiabortion forces, and the Christian Coalition, have become active in politics. This means that there are no longer just one or two elite groups that presidents must deal with, but dozens. At the same time, television has made it possible for presidents to appeal directly to a mass audience "thus tearing down the communications barrier on which the Founders had relied to insulate representative institutions from direct contact with the populace."[14]

In the new political environment, presidents cannot accomplish their goals simply by negotiating with party leaders and making deals through "old boys' networks." Given the size of the budget deficit, the White House is hard pressed to offer economic incentives or pork to members of Congress in exchange for making a deal. For all of these reasons, presidents increasingly conclude that they must appeal to the public if they are to achieve their policy goals. As Marcia Whicker notes, "American government is so complex and divided, and society is so pluralistic, presidents have only limited power. Their major power stems as much from opportunities to persuade key audiences as from formal powers."[15]

This is the essence of the contemporary approach to presidential rhetoric. George Edwards argues that we have a *public presidency*, in which "the greatest source of influence for the president is public approval." Samuel Kernell maintains that presidents are increasingly *going public*, or taking their case to the people. Jeffrey Tulis has argued that there is now a *rhetorical presidency*, in which presidents must use rhetoric and mass persuasion to achieve their goals.[16]

This is not to say that presidential rhetoric always works. Some presidential speeches have failed miserably. Nor is this to say that the rhetorical presidency is a good thing. Theodore Lowi argues that the presidency has grown into a bloated institution: the White House employs too many people, the president gives too many speeches, and people expect far too much of their chief executive. To Lowi, rhetoric is a symptom of a larger problem.[17]

Our job in this chapter is to understand the role rhetoric plays in the presidency. One cannot intelligently criticize the modern White House or propose solutions without appreciating how presidents use rhetoric. Let us be clear on what we mean by the terms **rhetorical presidency** and **going** public, two key concepts in this area. The rhetorical presidency is a broad theoretical construct. It argues that:

- presidents' addresses can be as important as their policies;
- presidents' words are deeds since they bring the force and majesty of the office with them;
- even presidential directives will not achieve their goals if presidents cannot persuade the public and the press to support their aims;
- presidents have a variety of ways to influence opinions, including speeches, press conferences, and the news;
- presidential messages are the outgrowth of modern marketing techniques.

Going public is *"a strategy whereby a president promotes himself and his policies in Washington by appealing to the American public for support."*[18] The term *going public* is similar to *rhetorical presidency*. The chief difference is that the former emphasizes institutional factors because it comes from a political science perspective. Its key arguments are that:

- presidential persuasion is no longer a private game, but a very public endeavor;
- presidents are increasingly appealing to the public for support;
- going public can take different forms, including public addresses, presidential appearances, political travel, and the use of new technologies.[19]

PRESIDENT AS SPEECH-MAKER

The president is "the symbolic embodiment of the nation," Charles Euchner observes. The president represents the nation in international matters and "sets the tone" for numerous events. These include national triumphs like space exploration and tragedies such as the bombing of the federal building in Oklahoma City in 1995.[20]

Presidential speeches have become one of the most important methods for communicating policies and building mass support. As noted earlier, eighteenth and nineteenth century presidents spoke infrequently. Today that has changed. The sheer amount of presidential speechmaking tripled between 1945 and 1985. During the 1976 election campaign, Gerald Ford delivered seven times as many speeches as Dwight Eisenhower had 20 years earlier. Jimmy Carter gave an average of one speech a day during each of his years in the Oval Office.[21] Bill Clinton delivered so many speeches during his first 100 days in office that some experts thought he was becoming too accessible and was reducing the dignity of the office.[22]

"In recent years," Hart notes, "it has become possible to conceive of a corrupt president or an inept president or a truculent president, but it is not now possible to imagine a quiet president."[23]

The rise in presidential speech-making is due largely to the sharp increase in ceremonial events. Presidents are spending more time than before at *initiating ceremonies* (signing of bills, enactment of treaties, swearing in of government appointees), *honorific ceremonies* (commencement addresses, presentation of awards), *celebrative ceremonies* (patriotic celebrations, anniversary remembrances, eulogies), and *greeting/departure ceremonies* (formal welcomes of visiting heads of state, remarks after arriving in a foreign country).[24]

You undoubtedly have seen many of these events on television. Perhaps you gave them little notice. A rhetorical analysis asserts that these events serve important functions. They provide a way for a president to assert leadership. Jimmy Carter presided at the Camp David Peace Accords between Israel and Egypt in 1978, and Bill Clinton bore witness at the historic signing of a peace agreement between Israel and the Palestine Liberation Organization in 1993. Their appearances made symbolic statements about the commitment of the United States to peace in the Middle East. These kinds of statements were rare in earlier eras, before the advent of radio and television. Now presidents use them to communicate policies, to send subtle messages to diplomats abroad, and to enhance their popularity at home.

Sometimes ceremonial rhetoric can backfire. George Bush found this out when he vomited at a dinner in Japan in 1992. The picture was shown again and again over the news and made headlines across the world. It made a simple statement about George Bush that did not do justice to his policy aims. In today's day and age, unfortunate incidents and mistakes become **synecdoches**—symbols that stand for a larger and more complex whole.

How do presidents use language? To answer this question, Hart exhaustively coded presidential speeches. He compared the words and phrases presidents used with those employed by other leaders—corporate executives, social activists, political candidates, and religious prelates (see Fig. 6.1).[25] Compared with other leaders, presidents use more **optimistic language, more realism, and less complexity.** They also **refer to themselves more frequently.** Presumably, presidents find it necessary to uplift the nation's spirits (optimism), and to speak in a way all Americans can understand (high realism and low complexity). The fact that presidents refer to themselves so frequently ("I propose," "I recommend," "I am deeply

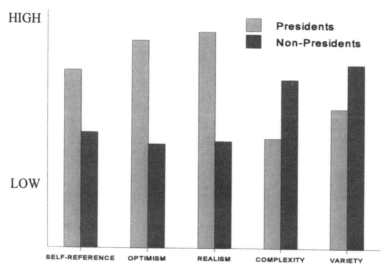

FIG 6.1 Comparisons of Presidents and Non Presidential Leaders on
Verbal Style Dimensions (from Hart, 1984).

concerned") is intriguing. It suggests that presidents believe they will be
more persuasive if they personalize political decisions and link themselves
with abstract policy matters. However, critics feel that this is part of a larger
trend toward overly personalized politics that has its roots in our dependence on television.

Although television may have led to an increase in simplicity and
self-referencing, it has not reduced the variance in presidential speech.
Different presidents speak differently.[26] Kennedy was eloquent, Johnson
informal. Nixon was self-controlled, Ford low-key. Carter was complex,
Reagan a great simplifier. Bush spoke with difficulty, Clinton was eloquent,
but not totally consistent.

And yet all these presidents faced the same rhetorical demands. Since
the Founding Fathers rejected the idea of a king or queen, America asks
that its president perform both ceremonial and political roles. This means
presidents must be authoritative, yet folksy. Presidents also have had to
adapt to the dominant medium of their times. Although all the presidents
discussed were outstanding speakers, they were not equally well suited to
television. Kennedy and Reagan spoke comfortably and naturally on the
small screen, perhaps because they were comfortable with themselves.
Johnson spoke better when he addressed live audiences than when he spoke
on national television. When speaking to a live audience, Johnson was

direct, lively, and entertaining; television brought out the worst of his presidential character. On television he was complex and overly cautious.[27] He was lugubrious and unpleasant to watch.

The Case of Carter

Jimmy Carter has fascinated rhetoricians. Carter has intrigued scholars because his leadership difficulties seem to have stemmed from rhetorical shortcomings. Carter was bright, politically astute, and deeply committed to improving America. Yet his rhetoric was singularly inappropriate to the situation.

Carter tried to "build down" the presidency. He felt that the office needed to be downsized after Watergate had shown the public what happens when power is amassed purely for its own sake. He walked down Pennsylvania Avenue after his inauguration rather than taking the ceremonial limousine ride. He referred to himself as "Jimmy Carter" not "James Earl Carter." He wore cardigan sweaters rather than the presidential suit and tie. His aims were noble, for the presidency had become far too imperious under Nixon and Johnson. Yet Carter found that even after Watergate, Americans wanted a leader who exuded the majesty of the office, who communicated grandeur as well as familiarity.

Carter created problems for himself, however. Like his nineteenth century predecessors, Carter did not like to give presidential speeches.[28] He also experimented with speech, trying on a variety of verbal styles. He never found a consistently appealing presidential persona. Over the course of his term, he became increasingly moralistic and pessimistic. His speeches used complex speech forms, making it hard for ordinary Americans to grasp his arguments. As Hart explains:

> Only a person intent on political suicide would, on national television and radio, use a sentence like the following: "To help curtail the excessive uses of credit and by dampening inflation, they [his new policies] should, along with the budget measures that I have described, speed prospects for reducing the strains which presently exist in our financial markets."[29]

For all his good ideas, Carter failed to provide compelling narratives that aroused the imagination. "Policies are grounded in historical narratives," Smith and Smith note.[30] In other words, presidents must promote their policies by showing how they are congruent with American values and rooted in national myths. Presidents must tell stories, particularly when delivering speeches over a medium—television—that emphasizes drama and simple themes. Carter failed to provide a narrative that connected with people's values and that was rooted in their experience. Instead, he concentrated on giving people "the facts."

In 1980, Carter lost his bid for reelection. A rhetorical analysis helps us appreciate why Americans did not believe Carter was an effective leader. His efforts to downgrade the office did not sit well with Americans. His speech style did not connect with ordinary people. He was pessimistic where people wanted optimism. He asked people to sacrifice for the good of the country; yet he failed to explain why they should do so or how they should follow his directives.[31] The irony is that some of Carter's arguments—his belief that the country must downsize its expectations and his insistence that the U.S. is beset by moral decay—are commonly accepted today.[32] Carter's experience leaves us with the conclusion that *successful leadership requires a match between the president's verbal style and the rhetorical demands of the situation.*

REAGAN AND THE TELEVISION PRESIDENCY

John Kennedy introduced television to the presidency, but Ronald Reagan consummated the marriage.[33]

Reagan was dubbed "The Great Communicator" because he used television masterfully during his years in office. He understood the grammar and syntax of the medium. He is to television what Franklin D. Roosevelt was to radio, Kathleen Hall Jamieson notes.[34] It could be said of Reagan as it was of Roosevelt that "his voice and his facial expression as he spoke were those of an intimate friend." Only half-facetiously, Jamieson observed that "Reagan is to television what corned beef is to rye."[35]

The rhetorical opposite of Jimmy Carter, Reagan spoke plainly, actively, and optimistically. Hart found that Reagan spoke in short sentences that were not loaded down by modifying structures. A cabdriver said, "He's the only politician I can understand." His speeches scored high in verbal activity and momentum. His choice of action words telegraphed his commitment to *doing* and *taking charge*. Most importantly, Reagan spoke positively.[36] Drawing shamelessly on American values, he delivered an upbeat, optimistic message. Consider the following comment, typical of Reagan:

> We have every right to dream heroic dreams. Those who say that we're in a time when there are no heroes, they just don't know where to look. You can see heroes every day

going in and out of factory gates. Others, a handful in number, produce enough food to feed all of us and then the world beyond. You meet heroes across a counter. And they're on both sides of that counter ... Their patriotism is deep. Their values sustain our national life.[37]

The same words would come off as schmaltzy in another speaker. In Reagan, they played well because he believed what he said and felt what he believed. And, it must be noted, Reagan had speechwriters who used words brilliantly to communicate themes.

All this helps deconstruct the notion that Reagan was a great communicator. It helps us understand what people mean they use the phrase "great communicator" to describe Reagan's verbal style. But there is more. Reagan tailored his speeches to television, using words to create memorable images. Jamieson notes that Reagan's skill in adapting his speeches to television revealed itself in four ways: (a) in his selection of props to illustrate his speeches; (b) in his ability to personify his central themes in the lives of ordinary citizens; (c) in his creativity in commandeering visual experiences we share; and (d) in his knack for narrative.[38]

Use of Televisual Props

Good speakers use props or visual devices to illustrate the arguments they are trying to make. Reagan recognized that presidents must do the same when they give television speeches. "Where other presidents used words to assert a connection with the venerated past, Reagan invites the cameras visually to meld his presidency into those of his great predecessors," Jamieson observes. "He will show as well as tell."[39]

He did this in his first inaugural. Reagan's advisers decided to hold the inaugural on the West Front of the Capitol to give the networks an opportunity to pan to the Washington Monument, the Jefferson Memorial, and the Lincoln Memorial. Before the ceremony, Reagan's television liason persuaded the networks to show the pictures of the monuments as Reagan spoke the words.[40] And so the national monuments appeared before the viewers' eyes as Reagan said, "Standing here, one faces a magnificent vista, opening up on this city's special beauty and history. At the end of this open mall are those shrines to the giants on whose shoulders we stand." It is vintage television. Rather than activating people's imaginations by eloquently quoting the Founding Fathers, Reagan instructs the modern medium to do people's cognitive work for them. His critics lament what he has done; his admirers marvel at his ability to use television to call forth powerful images.

Personifying Themes

Reagan used ordinary Americans to illustrate the major claims of his speeches.

He frequently personified his theme that America is filled with heroes by mentioning real people who displayed the traits Reagan found so impressive. He made the abstract concrete by mentioning citizens like Lenny Skutnik, who dove into the Potomac River to save a woman who had survived an airplane crash.

Personification has now become part of the grammar of presidential ceremonials. In his 1996 State of the Union speech, Bill Clinton arranged to have two firefighters who had rescued survivors of the Oklahoma City bombing on hand at the event. The camera panned to them, the audience applauded, and dignitaries seated near the firefighters rushed over to shake their hands.

Accessing Common Visual Experiences

Reagan frequently used visual evidence rather than conventional arguments to convince people to support his policies. In an effort to gather support for his decision to form a multinational force in Lebanon, he called on memories of a tragic massacre of Palestinians in Lebanon that had occurred the previous weekend. Pictures of the massacre had been repeatedly shown on American television. Rather than building a case for his policy based on logic and arguments, Reagan accessed common visual experiences.

One's first impulse is to criticize Reagan for pandering to the visual rather than making a case based on precedent and philosophy. However, it can be argued that visual evidence is just as valid as verbal argumentation.[41] Garry Wills observed that Reagan's approach "is not discursive, setting up sequences of time or thought, but associative; not a tracking shot, but montage. We make the connections."[42] In any event, Reagan called on visual images repeatedly during his presidential speeches. He frequently drew on popular novels, movies, and television dramas. Images from popular culture, Jamieson notes, were effective because "they created a strong retrievable emotional experience that large numbers share."[43]

Knack for Narrative

Instead of reciting facts or citing precedents, Reagan relied on dramatic narrative. Unlike Jimmy Carter, who often argued from factual evidence, Reagan constructed speeches by retelling stories of self-reliance, individual entrepreneurship, and the heroism of ordinary Americans. He connected his policy ideas with the myths and values of America. He provided reassurance that the country would survive and its people would prosper, despite the presence of enemies abroad and malfeasance at home. Moreover, Reagan resisted making himself the center of his narrative. Instead, he placed the American people at the core, telling them that they have what it takes to prevail.[44]

We can appreciate Reagan's knack for narrative by examining how he presented the medal of honor to a sergeant in the military on February 24, 1981. Reagan begins by recalling what happened to Vietnam veterans when they returned home after their tour of duty:

> They were greeted by no parades, no bands, no waving of the flag they had so nobly served. There's been no 'thank you' for their sacrifice. There's been no effort to honor and thus give pride to the families of more than 57,000 young men who gave their lives in that faraway war ... Back in 1970 Kenneth Y. Tomlinson wrote of what he had seen our young men do beyond and above the call of military duty in Vietnam—a marine from Texas on his way in at dawn from an all-night patrol stopping to treat huge sores on the back of an old Vietnamese man, an artillery man from New Jersey spending his free time stacking sandbags at an orphanage to protect the children from mortar attacks, an Army engineer from California distributing toys he's bought in Hong Kong to the orphans his unit had adopted.[45]

Yet, as Jamieson observes, Reagan overlooks other issues. "There is no mention," she notes, "of the possibility that the old man was the victim of U.S. napalm or that the children had been orphaned by GIs. Where those who condemn the war will select such scenes, Reagan will spend his words capturing acts the country can be proud of."[46]

Reagan's narrative played well on television. It fit the medium's preference for simple (not necessarily simplistic) stories. His use of dramatic narratives and reliance on memorable images were congruent with television's preference for the visual and the evocative.[47]

Reagan's narrative also fit television because Reagan knew how to "tell stories" before a national television audience. He was comfortable on camera and, as an actor, he knew how to communicate emotions. He was adept at using his facial expressions to communicate the three emotions that leaders must communicate: happiness/reassurance, anger/threat, and fear/evasion.[48] In other words, leaders must reassure the public, provoke anger against foreign enemies, and induce fear of unpleasant outcomes. Reagan was able to clearly and convincingly communicate these emotions.

A CRITICAL LOOK AT REAGAN'S RHETORIC

Ronald Reagan's rhetoric has stimulated controversy. Critics take note of Reagan's schmaltzy speeches, his failure to use argumentation, and his shameless use of television technology, and they argue that he pulled the wool over the eyes of the public.

They claim that he used smoke and mirrors—charm, simplistic speech, and visual images—to manipulate the American public. Reagan's admirers claim that this thesis is insulting to the American people, for it assumes they can be easily manipulated. The argument is also elitist, his supporters say, because it rejects a speech style that appeals to millions of ordinary Americans. It also assumes people were manipulated by Reagan when they may have gone along with what he said out of their own choice and volition.

This is a complex issue that gets into knotty aspects of the psychology of political communication effects. Television commentator and author Robert MacNeil acknowledges that the question of Reagan's leadership is a complex one:

> Leadership is in part being able to grasp the sort of psychic tone of your country at a particular time and respond to it and carry it in some direction. Or merely just respond to it. Reagan may have merely just responded to it. These are the kinds of things I don't talk about easily. But I think the interesting ingredient that's relevant is, How much did Reagan fool the American people and how much did he simply play into their wishes? Were they misled by the nature of his campaigning or were they led into ways they wanted to go? Was Reagan a sort of modern pied piper?

> It's my instinct about it that he very successfully delayed the apprehension of reality by this country for about a decade. He made people feel that things were better than they were, that the external dangers were greater than they were. I think the jury's out on a lot of that and my own feeling about it is that the evil that did on delaying making this country really competitive with the rest of the world and so on—may have to be balanced in history by the success that Reagan appears to have had, maybe accidentally, with the Soviet Union ... which is a very, very complicated business.[49]

If one aspect of leadership is mastering the dominant medium of the era, then Reagan was surely an excellent leader. Just as Lincoln excelled at public address and Franklin Roosevelt was a master of radio oratory, Reagan was a masterful television speaker. In our era, leadership requires an ability to reach and convince masses of citizens. Reagan clearly had what it took when it came to appealing to Americans via television.

Yet one feels unsettled when one considers that Reagan wrote none of his speeches, depended entirely on speechwriters to craft his messages, and excelled primarily at reading the messages others wrote. Notes Jamieson:

> Speaking effectively on television requires an ability both to create the illusion of eye contact with an unseen audience and to converse with a camera. Delivering from a ghosted text requires a skill at speaking someone else's words as if they were your own and investing a script with the illusion of spontaneity. Most televised speechmaking is built on these minor, but not insignificant, forms of deception.[50]

The verdict is still out on Reagan's rhetorical presidency. Unquestionably, he provided leadership. Without a doubt he inspired and reassured Americans. However, his manipulation of visual images and his reliance on other people's words leaves one troubled about the ethics of his persuasion.

The presidents who followed Reagan have also depended on speechwriters and the accoutrements of the rhetorical presidency, notably polling and marketing. We take up some of their efforts—and also examine the impact of rhetorical genres on political persuasion—in the chapter that follows.

CONCLUSIONS

Speech is the quintessential human activity, so it should not surprise us that it is the hallmark of the modern presidency.

In this chapter, I traced the evolution of presidential rhetoric. Presidents spoke rarely in the eighteenth and nineteenth centuries. Today they speak frequently, giving nearly as many speeches in nonelection years as during the quadrennial election year campaign. There are several reasons for the increase in presidential speechmaking, including the decline in political parties, the rapid growth of interest groups, the intrusion of television into politics, and the fact that presidents have less to offer political elites than they had in the old days. Presidents find that they must "go public" to maintain power and to mobilize constituent groups.

Different presidents use language differently. However, as a group presidents speak more optimistically, simply, and personally than other leaders. Presidential leadership increasingly entails skill at delivering television speeches. Ronald Reagan is the exemplar of this. He adapted his speeches to television by using televisual props, personifying central themes, evoking common visual experiences, and "telling stories." Reagan's rhetoric continues to fascinate scholars: Reagan unquestionably reassured Americans and made them feel proud of their country, yet his reliance on simple, visual arguments may have mesmerized citizens, delaying their apprehension of the social and economic problems that confronted them.

Finally, we have seen that successful rhetorical presidents have adapted their oratory to the dominant medium of the age. In our own era, television is dominant. Scholars have suggested that television has changed presidential speech-making in a number of ways. We know that the ascendance of television has been associated with an increase in personalized political speech. With televison has come more intimate rhetoric. It is possible that television reflected rather than caused this increase in personalized speech—that is, our social discourse has become more personalized and television has mirrored the increase. But if television is a mirror, it most assuredly is also a cause. Ronald Reagan once told his speechwriters that "Always remember that we are guests in people's homes." As one of his speechwriters observed, "this role of houseguest has set the tone and sensibility of modern presidential communications."[51]

KEY ISSUES

Rhetorical Presidency

Going Public

Personalized Speech

Carter's Rhetorical Problems

Reagan's Narrative

DISCUSSION QUESTIONS

1. What are the main characteristics of the rhetorical presidency?

2. If Franklin Delano Roosevelt had been born in the age of television, would he have been as persuasive as he was in the age of radio? Would he have been a rhetorical flop or a stunning success?

3. "Ronald Reagan pulled the wool over the nation's eyes." Critique or defend, using the rhetorical principles discussed in this chapter.

7

Presidential Rhetoric:
Genres and Impact

To most people, a presidential speech is a presidential speech is a presidential speech. One looks pretty much the same as another. Most of us don't pay them much mind, figuring that they're all part of that *other world, out there*—in Washington.

Rhetoric scholars take a different view of presidential speechmaking. Not only do they remind us that speechmaking is an integral part of government (we know that from the previous chapter), but they emphasize that presidential speeches differ in form as well as content, and that they can have significant effects on citizens and the nation as a whole.

There are different types of presidential oratory, although there is disagreement among rhetoric experts on the meaning of the genres and debate about which types are most important. Rhetorical forms include inaugural addresses, State of the Union addresses, veto messages, pardoning rhetoric, hortatory or moralistic addresses, farewell addresses, and crisis rhetoric. In this chapter I focus on three categories: inaugural addresses, pardoning rhetoric, and crisis rhetoric. I selected these forms for several reasons: First, they allow me to cover some of the most famous and controversial speeches of modern presidents; second, they permit me to show how a president's rhetoric can impede—and advance—the chief executive's leadership goals; and third, they allow me to touch on major issues in contemporary presidential rhetoric.

The first section of this chapter discusses different types of presidential rhetoric. The second section examines the impact of rhetoric on elites and the public, and the third portion looks at controversial issues in the rhetorical presidency.

INAUGURAL ADDRESSES

Presidential leadership begins with the inaugural address. In these speeches, presidents put forth a vision, attempt to unify the country after a fractious campaign, and try to link themselves with American myths and the nation's past.[1] Karlyn Campbell and Kathleen Jamieson argue that inaugural addresses are a special type of rhetorical discourse. In their view:

> The presidential inaugural (1) unifies the audience by reconstituting its members as the people, who can witness and ratify the ceremony; (2) rehearses communal values drawn from the past; (3) sets forth the political principles that will govern the new administration; and (4) demonstrates through enactment that the president appreciates the requirements and limitations of executive functions.[2]

Their thesis is interesting because it argues that inaugurals *do* as well as say. It asserts that inaugurals are not bland, colorless events, but dramatic encounters infused with meaning. Inaugural addresses give the audience a symbolic identity as citizens viewing an historic event. The viewing audience ceases to be a disparate group of individuals, but takes on the trappings of witnesses to an ascent to power.[3] The inaugural also calls on traditional values and time-honored principles; the president shows respect for these values and makes it clear that they will continue to guide the country in the new administration. In addition, presidents articulate the principles that will govern their administrations and demonstrate their claim to leadership by acknowledging that they appreciate the requirements and limits of executive power. In view of the heavy emphasis on ritual and myth, it should not surprise us to learn that inaugurals have a religious tinge, with presidents asking for the blessing of God.

John F. Kennedy's inaugural address fits Campbell and Jamieson's definition particularly well. As Theodore Windt observes:

> From his opening words ("We observe today not a victory of party but a celebration of freedom") to his mighty exhortation ("Ask not what your country can do for you—ask what you can do for your country"), the new president stressed the unity of the American people on this ceremonial occasion. Their ratification of his presidency was directly requested through his rhetorical questions asking them to join him in the "historic effort" upon which he and they were about to embark. Clearly he sought to reconstitute the people in a cast different from the placid people of the decade just ended and from the leadership during that decade. But even as he sought this, he did so within a celebration of "communal values of the past." The "torch has been passed

to a new generation," he declared, but that generation was "proud of its ancient heritage and unwilling to witness or permit the slow undoing of those human rights to which this nation has always been committed."[4]

Inaugurals like Kennedy's exemplify what Campbell and Jamieson call **epideictic speech,** ceremonial public address that invites contemplation, not action; praises or blames public actors or institutions; asks the audience to assess the communicator's performance; and concentrates on the present while alluding to past and future. Although there is some question as to whether all inaugurals contain epideictic features,[5] there is agreement among scholars that Campbell and Jamieson's approach provides a useful perspective on inaugural addresses. Their work helps us appreciate the ritualistic aspects of inaugurals, their dramatic qualities, the components that transcend time, as well as the flexibility they offer individual presidents, not all of whom have risen to the level of a Lincoln, a Wilson, or a Franklin Roosevelt.

PARDONING RHETORIC

The president has the authority to grant pardons for offenses against the United States. In the rhetorical presidency, the language that presidents use to frame a pardon is particularly important.

On September 8, 1974, Gerald Ford granted a "full, free, and absolute pardon" to Richard Nixon for offenses committed against the United States. Ford's announcement shocked the nation, coming as it did at 11:05 on a Sunday morning. The speech aroused considerable controversy. The president's press secretary, Gerald terHorst, resigned the day the pardon was announced. Ford later lamented that he had wished he taken a different tack in his address. Rhetoric scholars have judged Ford's speech a failure.[6]

There were several problems with Ford's address. The first was timing. The pardon was announced at a time—Sunday morning—when presidents ordinarily do not address the nation and when few reporters are covering the president. The timing suggested that Ford was trying to be secretive, that he had something to hide, perhaps (as some suspected) a deal made with Richard Nixon before Ford took office. The timing belied Ford's claim that he was trying to heal the nation's wounds.

Secondly, Ford's decision to grant Nixon a *full* pardon appeared inconsistent with his earlier announcement that he would consider granting a *conditional* pardon to young men who had evaded the draft because they had conscientiously objected to the Vietnam War. (Eight days after the Nixon pardon, Ford ordered that Vietnam War-era draft evaders and military deserters be given conditional amnesty.) Why fully pardon Nixon and not do the same for draft resisters? Ford did not adequately explain the rationale for his decision. Elsewhere, he seemed to accept Nixon's argument that forces external to Nixon had been responsible for the Watergate scandal. This did not wash with the public, which viewed Nixon as the guilty party. Finally, Ford failed to provide a strong justification for his decision. As he himself noted, he failed to make clear that judicially a pardon represents an admission of guilt.[7]

The pardon hurt Ford politically. Asked why they preferred Carter to Ford in the November, 1976, election, voters interviewed in exit polls mentioned the pardon more frequently than any other issue. "Perhaps they should have cited Ford's pardon *rhetoric*, instead," Smith and Smith observe.[8] How Ford delivered the message was nearly as important as what he said. Had he announced the pardon before a national audience during prime time, clarified the inconsistency between pardoning Nixon and granting conditional amnesty to draft evaders, and indicated more clearly that Nixon was to blame for his actions, the electoral outcome might have been different.

In the final analysis, Ford deserves credit for delivering speeches designed to heal rather than divide. His instincts were right in trying to bind the nation together after Watergate. In fairness, any presidential action regarding Richard Nixon would have stimulated controversy. Undoubtedly, Ford's long friendship with Richard Nixon influenced his decision and his choice of words. In addition, his desire not to alienate former Nixon aides, whose help he needed in his administration, played a part in his decision. Unfortunately, as Smith and Smith suggest, Ford himself became the symbol of America's ambivalence about the actions of fellow citizens (Nixon and draft evaders) who had committed offenses against the government.[9]

CRISIS RHETORIC

When the nation faces threats from foreign or domestic enemies or must deal with problems that strike to the core of the United States Constitution or must come to grips with a national tragedy, the president's oratory assumes importance. Speeches delivered under these conditions fall under the heading of crisis rhetoric. Crisis rhetoric is a broad construct, perhaps the most general and diffuse of all the rhetorical categories. There is some question as to whether crisis rhetoric constitutes a distinct genre because it is hard to distinguish crisis rhetoric from noncrisis rhetoric and difficult at times to define what we mean by "crisis."[10] Nonetheless, the area appeals to scholars because crises represent defining moments for an administration, as Robert Denton notes. "During crises," he adds, "presidents enjoy a 'near-monopoly' control over information, media access, and autonomy of decision making."[11]

Amos Kiewe defines crisis rhetoric as "the discourse initiated by decision makers in an attempt to communicate to various constituents that a certain development is critical and to suggest a certain course of action to remedy the critical situation."[12]

Rhetorical Constructions

Most of us assume that crises are objective entities, precipitated by foreign or domestic attacks. We assume that presidents react to crises. Kiewe argues that crises are rhetorical constructs. A president can decide that a particular event is a crisis, label it as such, and bring the White House persuasion factory to bear in trying to convince the country to accept this interpretation. According to this view, "crises" do not happen; they are constructed by leaders (for noble or selfish purposes).

Some events will become crises, regardless of how much a president says or how much urgency the chief executive assigns to the problem. The Japanese attack on Pearl Harbor is a case in point. Roosevelt's famous speech ("Yesterday, December 7, 1941—a date which will live in infamy ... ") helped turn shock and disbelief into resolve and commitment to avenge the brutal attack.

Other events are more ambiguous. President Truman declared a national emergency on December 16, 1950, following military setbacks in the Korean War and mounting fears about the ability of the United States to beat back Communist forces. With public support for the war dwindling, Truman decided that something needed to be done to rally public support and to convince Congress to support increased taxes to build an anti-Communist defense force in Europe. He proclaimed a state of national emergency. He told the nation that America was in danger. As Robert Ivie notes, he repeated that America was in danger a dozen times in his speech. Truman unveiled powerful symbols and employed apocalyptic rhetoric to convince the nation of the urgency of the situation. He warned that "world conquest by communist imperialism" would destroy the American way of life, including "the blessings of the freedom of worshiping." He called on Americans to meet the danger.[13]

Truman constituted the events of December, 1950 as a crisis. He conjured up a crisis mentality and used symbols to build a sense of national urgency. One's view of Truman's rhetoric is influenced by whether one believes his assessment of the Communist threat was accurate or exaggerated. Clearly, Truman was able to define the events as a crisis because the nation sympathized with his interpretation and because he used words skillfully to accomplish his goals.

Richard Nixon used crisis rhetoric differently. Carole Blair and Davis Houck take a particularly critical view. They argue that Nixon "consistently misrepresented the seriousness of events and that he did so for personal political gain ... What Nixon described to his audiences as emergencies for them were, for the most part, merely potential difficulties for his own popularity ratings."[14]

Nixon portrayed Watergate as a threat to the U.S., although it was actually his own administration that was in deep distress. He often invoked "a nameless, collective 'villian'" who urged immediate withdrawal from Vietnam; he used this caricature to justify his policies. Blair and Houck point out that another term that describes this "villain" is "dissenter." "What Nixon described frequently as the causes of crisis were the raised voices of those who disagreed with his views or actions," they add.[15] Not all critics would go as far as Blair and Houck; some would even praise Nixon for his pragmatism and his ability to articulate a vision. However, few would disagree that Nixon had a distinctive rhetoric, that he personalized crises, manufactured enemies, and that his speech-making was among the most complex of all our presidents.

Foreign Crises

Iran-Contra. Presidents do not always use crisis rhetoric effectively, as Ronald Reagan discovered in 1986 during Iran-Contra. For one of the first times in his presidency, words failed him.

In November, 1986, the nation learned that the United States had sold arms to Iran in the hopes of inducing Iran to use its influence with terrorists who held seven American hostages in Lebanon. Several weeks later, it was revealed that profits from the arms deal had been funneled to the Nicaraguan Contras, who were fighting a left-leaning government in Nicaragua that the Reagan administration opposed. The news shocked the public. The decision to sell arms to Iran violated the United States arms embargo against Iran and it seemed to contradict the president's policy of refusing to enter into negotiations with terrorists. The channeling of profits from the arms deal to the Contras violated a Congressional Amendment that prohibited the White House from giving aid to the Contras without first getting Congressional approval.

The crisis tarnished Reagan's presidency. Reagan's approval ratings dropped from 63% in October to 47% in December. He never totally regained the public's confidence. "The Iran-Contra affair cracked the teflon presidency," Zernicke concludes.[16]

Why did words fail Reagan during Iran-Contra? For several reasons:

1. Given his propensity to speak publicly, Reagan had little choice but to discuss the issues. However, Reagan was at his worst in spontaneous, unscripted encounters with the press.
2. Reagan claimed to have been outraged when he heard about the Iran-Contra affair. (It later turned out that National Security Council staff members Lieutenant Colonel Oliver North and Admiral John Poindexter had worked out the plan on the basis of their general understanding of Reagan's wishes, but without the president's specific approval.) Reagan's anger did not ring true because the plan seemed consistent with his previous rhetoric; the arms for hostages deal had been conducted by good Americans who believed in their cause, and it seemed to adhere to Reagan's humanitarian impulses.
3. Reagan could not resort to his simple, plain-speaking style since the events themselves were so complicated. Furthermore, Reagan's own attitudes seemed uncharacteristically complex. On the one hand, his humanitarian impulses led him to want to get the hostages out of Lebanon at any price. On the other hand, his aggressive foreign policy argued against this move. His support of the Contras could have led him to suggest that secret moves to overthrow the Nicaraguan government were acceptable; his role as upholder of the law required that he oppose secret aid. Simplification, Reagan's stock-in-trade, seemed rhetorically inappropriate in the case of Iran-Contra.[17]

Reagan's management style of delegating responsibilities to others backfired in the case of Iran-Contra. His style had created an environment in which zealous aides felt they could do as they pleased, as long as they committed acts that seemed to be consistent with the essence of the president's policy. North and Poindexter lied to the press and Congressional committees. The National Security Council aides circumvented U.S. policy and disobeyed the law.[18]

Although Iran-Contra shattered Reagan's "Great Communicator" image, it did not totally destroy his presidency. Reagan's personable manner and his personal popularity led Congress to shy away from undertaking a serious challenge of Reagan's presidency.[19] When the scandal died down, Reagan returned to his familiar style of employing narrative, personification, and optimistic visions of America. With the return to his old rhetoric came an increase in his popularity.[20]

Reagan's critics point out that the crisis proved that Reagan had failed to live up to the minimum responsibilities of the presidency. Rhetoric scholars emphasize that because Reagan's rhetoric failed him, the crisis turned out to be much worse for the president. Still others remind us that leadership is a transaction between leaders and followers, and that if citizens still viewed Reagan positively after Iran-Contra, then so be it—*they* must ultimately choose what traits they admire in a leader and what aspects of the chief executive's character they are willing to forgive.

The Gulf Crisis. On August 2, 1990, Iraqi tanks rolled into Kuwait. Ten days after the Iraqi invasion, the Bush administration launched a rhetorical attack on Iraqi premier Saddam Hussein. Over the course of the next 6 months, Bush's rhetoric helped define the crisis and influenced the meanings that were assigned to events.

The Bush administration decided immediately that the attack on Kuwait could not be tolerated. Bush's decision to confront Hussein struck some observers as ironic as the U.S. had given economic and military aid to Iraq for years. Perhaps, given that Hussein had violated another nation's sovereignty and had used chemical weapons against Kurdish civilians in 1988, Bush was justified in raising the rhetorical stakes. Still, it is noteworthy that the U.S. changed its posture toward Iraq so quickly and so sharply.

George Bush used symbols to evoke emotions and to influence attitudes. He relied on what Murray Edelman calls **condensational symbols.** Edelman notes that "condensational symbols evoke the emotions associated with the situation. They condense into one symbolic event, sign or act patriotic pride, anxieties, remembrances of past glories or humiliations, promises of future greatness: some one of these or all of them."[21]

Bush used two powerful condensational symbols: Munich and Adolf Hitler. Munich is the German city where British prime minister Neville Chamberlain met with Hitler in 1938 in an effort to persuade the German dictator to give up his designs on Czechoslovakia. Chamberlain left Munich claiming that we had "peace in our time." Less than 6 months later, Hitler took over Czechoslovakia, and Munich became a lasting symbol of a "failure of will in a time of moral confrontation."[22] Bush chose to paint the Kuwait situation with the brushstrokes of Munich. He argued that an attempt to appease Hussein was analogous to Chamberlain's failed attempt to appease Hitler. Bush likened Hussein to Hitler in his speeches.[23]

In Betty Glad's view, Hussein—a tyrant who by all accounts had executed opposition political leaders and had used chemical weapons against his enemies—"had many of the qualities that Bush ascribed to him."[24] Not all scholars would agree. The important point is that Bush successfully used Hitler and Munich to evoke strong emotions and memories. They helped him define the Kuwait invasion as an act that could not be left unanswered. They allowed him to define the event in terms of the valorized experiences of World War II. The two condensational symbols also helped to minimize the extent to which Vietnam came to people's minds.

Bush's rhetoric was consistent with that used by presidents in international crises. He maintained control of the facts in the situation and argued that the facts (Saddam's "naked aggression") created a new situation. He placed the crisis in the context of a battle between the forces of freedom and those of an enemy. He transformed the decision to go to war to a test of America's character.[25] Bush's rhetoric defined the crisis for the United States. Had he adopted a more passive approach or refrained from using World War II condensational symbols, the crisis would have looked very different. Conceivably, it would have been more difficult for the United States to have marshaled the political and military resources necessary to launch the air and ground attacks on Iraq in 1991.

Domestic Crises

Breaking the "No New Taxes" Pledge.   During his second year in office, George Bush was faced with an economic and political crisis brought on by years of budget deficits and serious downturns in the economy. Faced with pressure from the Democratic Congress, George Bush broke his campaign pledge not to raise taxes. This in turn infuriated Bush's supporters and, as Amos Kiewe notes, threatened to undermine the president's leadership.[26] Fortunately for Bush, just as things were beginning to unravel, the Iraqis invaded Kuwait, giving Bush an opportunity to provide leadership in the area of his greatest strength: foreign policy.

As a candidate, Bush had opted to continue Reagan's program of using tax cuts to stimulate the economy. He promised to cut capital gains taxes and he pledged in his acceptance speech at the Republican convention that he would not raise taxes. "Read my lips. No new taxes," he told the cheering crowd.

As president, Bush found that the deficit was much larger than antici-pated. Democrats argued that the economic situation had reached crisis proportions and Bush accepted their definition. It was clear that Bush's budget would not make it through Congress without an increase in taxes. On June 26, 1990, Bush agreed to reverse his pledge not to raise taxes. Fearing retribution by voters in the November elections, 100 Republican members of the House of Representatives wrote a letter to Bush saying that they were "stunned" by his decision. Bush did not help matters by announc-ing his decision in a written statement rather than a televised address to the nation.

There were alternatives available to George Bush. He could have gone before the public and clearly laid out the problem he faced, along with the policy options he had available to him. He could have gone through each of the options one by one and led the audience to the conclusion that, although it violated his campaign promise, raising taxes was the best of all the available alternatives. However, "he failed to seize the moment by pulling these points together in a coherent discourse," Smith and Smith note.[27]

National Tragedies.   When the nation is faced with a tragedy, it looks to the president for leadership and reassurance. Under these conditions, a skillful presidential orator can help people deal with their grief and adapt positively to the tragedy. Ronald Reagan rose to the occasion in January, 1986, when the space shuttle Challenger exploded. In a tender speech to America's school children, the president said:

> I want to say something to the schoolchildren of America who were watching the live coverage of the shuttle's takeoff. I know it's hard to understand, but sometimes painful things like this happen. It's all part of the process of exploration and discovery. It's all part of taking a chance and expanding man's horizons. The future doesn't belong to the fainthearted. It belongs to the brave. The Challenger crew was pulling us into the future, and we'll continue to follow them.[28]

In a similar vein, Bill Clinton consoled the nation on April 23, 1995, after the bombing of a federal building in Oklahoma City left 169 people dead. Speaking at a memorial service in Oklahoma City, Clinton said:

> You have lost too much but you have not lost everything, and you have certainly not lost America, for we will stand with you for as many tomorrows as it takes ... To my fellow Americans beyond this hall I say one thing we owe those who have sacrificed is the duty to purge ourselves of the dark forces which gave rise to this evil. There are forces that threaten our common peace, our freedom, our way of life. Let us teach our

children that the God of comfort is also the God of righteousness. Those who trouble their own house will inherit the wind. Justice will prevail.[29]

Summary

Conventional scholarship asserts that the law and the Constitution enable the nation to survive crisis and calamity. Communication scholars Campbell and Jamieson emphasize instead that the stability of the American experiment in democracy is ensured through discourse and the recurrence of rhetorical genres. They stress that it is through language that the presidency survives, reinvents itself, and adapts to changing circumstances.

Inaugurals call on traditional principles and values, link the present with the mythical past, and reconstitute the audience as honored citizens who invest the orator with the majesty of the presidency. State of the Union addresses are delivered at the same ceremonial occasion each year, thereby recognizing the authority of the president as the nation's head of state. The speeches give the president the opportunity to make policy recommendations to Congress. In the same fashion, pardoning rhetoric, veto messages, farewell addresses, and even the diffuse category of crisis rhetoric help to sustain the institution of the presidency. Campbell and Jamieson note that:

> In 1974, the long national nightmare was over, not simply because Gerald Ford pronounced those words or because Richard Nixon no longer was president, but because in Ford's speech, the citizenry heard the clearly recognizable rhetoric inviting investiture that characterizes an inaugural address.[30]

These authors emphasize that "words are deeds"—speech is action. Speech constructs and reconstructs the presidency, allowing the nation to survive an Andrew Johnson, a Warren Harding, and the second term of a Richard Nixon, as well as helping the nation adapt from a Herbert Hoover to a Franklin Roosevelt. As we have seen, the words that presidents use perform important tasks, such as reassuring the nation after national tragedies and providing the nation with the will to go on in times of crisis. Inarticulate rhetoric or inappropriate speech forms also leave their imprint, as Gerald Ford found after his address pardoning Richard Nixon, and George Bush discovered in the wake of his reversal of the "Read my lips. No new taxes" pledge.

As intriguing as the rhetorical genres approach is, it is not without its problems. Rhetorical scholars are not of one mind on whether speech forms such as inaugurals, State of the Union addresses, and crisis rhetoric constitute special genres. Some scholars argue that there are so many differences within a particular genre—different presidents have such different ways of delivering crisis speeches—that it is not useful to claim there are specific rhetorical types.[31] It might also be objected that Campbell and Jamieson focus on how rhetoric helps the system to continue, while paying insufficient attention to the ways in which rhetoric undercuts the institution of the presidency. However, there is little disagreement that words and certain rhetorical genres play a critical role in the evolution of the presidency and its adaptation to changing circumstances. Words are deeds; language matters.

CLINTON'S RHETORIC

Bill Clinton relishes rhetoric. His first inaugural showcased his rhetorical skills. He used metaphors to highlight the theme of renewal ("Now we must do the work the season demands"). He employed antithesis ("This ceremony is held in the depth of winter. But, by the words we speak and the faces we show the world, we force the spring."), and the hortatory subjunctive ("Let us put aside personal advantage").[32] However, in his inaugural Clinton failed to articulate the political values that would guide his administration. His failure to lay out a vision forecast the inconsistency of his rhetoric during his administration.

Clinton changed his position on key issues. In his 1993 State of the Union address, he began by saying "Tonight I want to talk to you about what government can do because I believe government must do more." He favored increased government spending and an activist role for government. Three years later, humbled by the Republican victories in the 1994 elections and the public's desire to downsize government, he declared that "the era of big government is over." After proposing tax increases on wealthy Americans in his 1993 budget, he told a Houston fund-raiser in October, 1995, that "you will be surprised to learn" that, like them, he thought his tax increases had been excessive. In the autumn of 1995, he told a political writer that he thought the welfare reforms he had proposed earlier in his term were too weak. This provoked a parody in the popular press:

> The Republicans call for legal reform. I totally oppose this. Well, maybe "totally" is strong and I guess I went overboard on "oppose," but may I make a tiny suggestion? I don't just want legal reform. I want *middle-class* legal reform. In particular, I want to restrict how many lawsuits can be brought against one guy who gets up every day to do the hard work of change and then can't finish his third plate of waffles before some gold-digging bimbo brings charges of sexual harassment against him even though it was obvious to any trooper in the room that she wanted it as much as he did.[33]

By publicly changing his position, Clinton came up short on one of the components of a successful rhetorical presidency: sustaining "a consistent and coherent rhetoric that coordinates the political perceptions of diverse publics."[34] As author Elizabeth Drew notes:

> Clinton's problem was that he was a big-government, or, at least, an activist-government man trying to come across as a Democrat who didn't believe in big government. Actually, he was both. He was a modern Democrat, and far from the only one, who was seeking new ways for government to help people, because of the lack of funds, because of real or perceived failures of federal programs (more were successful than was generally believed), and because big federal solutions to problems were out of style ...

> Of course, much would be made of Clinton's noted flexibility on issues. As President, he may have yielded more often than was necessary—this is an impossible thing to measure—and he may indeed have tried to please too many people, but there was no real reason to question the basic things he was for. His difficulty in articulating these things stemmed in part from the ambiguity of his own beliefs, in part from his difficulty in getting past the complexities in his own mind, and in part from the fact that there were too many cooks involved in almost every significant speech he made and every important action he took.[35]

During his first year in office, Clinton did not always present himself well. Drew notes that in presidential appearances "his mouth often hung open, which didn't look Presidential. The sight of his chunky body in his jogging shorts wasn't wonderful to behold."[36]

To his credit, Clinton took steps to deal with these problems. He hired Dick Morris, a political consultant who had previously worked for Republican candidates, to help improve his public image. Under Morris's tutelage, Clinton spoke out less frequently on issues, moved to the political center, aligned himself with condensational symbols like school uniforms and the V-chip, and endeavored to take an uncompromising position on the 1995–1996 showdown with Congress over the federal budget. Realizing the public wanted its president to take a consistent position and not equivocate, Clinton took a strong stand in favor of protecting Medicare.

Part of Clinton's success lay in his skill in using marketing and polling information. Like other presidents, Clinton relied on advice from pollsters. Polls suggested that Americans were wary of cuts in Medicare. Clinton, partly because he opposed severe cuts himself and partly because he knew that this position jelled with the public, accused the Republicans of gutting Medicare. While he was negotiating in private with Republican leaders on how to resolve the budget impasse that shut down the federal government, his staff members were developing advertisements that accused the opposition of making dangerous cuts in Medicare programs. The ads aired on network television. In fact, Clinton exaggerated the Republican position.[37] However, his position resonated with the voters. He was seen as having the guts to stand up for what he believed—not as equivocating and switching positions to suit the political climate.

In addition, his 1996 State of the Union message got high marks. He spoke well, spoke positively about the country and change, and endorsed Republican policy goals, while at the same time emphasizing that he had a more compassionate method for achieving them. During the winter of 1996, as Republican presidential candidates began attacking each other in the primaries, Bill Clinton seemed calm, reasonable, and presidential by comparison.

IMPACT

After reading about presidential rhetoric—its uses and misuses, strengths and weaknesses—you may be curious about a more pragmatic issue: Does it work? Does going public achieve a president's goals? Do presidential speeches influence public opinion and policy?

It is difficult to answer these questions because it is hard to separate a president's rhetoric from other aspects of the presidency, such as policy decisions the chief executive makes, behind-the-scenes bargaining with Congressional leaders, and news coverage of the president. Nonetheless, we can make assessments of the impact of presidential oratory, and when we do, we find that matters are more complicated than originally assumed. The complications turn out to be quite interesting.

First, **presidential speeches do not always increase public support for the president.** People are not blank slates onto which presidential rhetoric can write its message. Individuals have positions on issues and attitudes toward the president. Their attitudes influence how they will interpret presidential pronouncements. Thus, a president's supporters are more likely to cheer the president on than are the chief executive's detractors. Those who like the president and agree with White House policies are likely to *assimilate* the message—assume it is closer to their views than it really is; opponents are prone to *contrast* the communication—perceive it as farther from their beliefs than it really is.[38]

A study by Dennis Simon and Charles Ostrom bears this out. They examined the effect of presidential speeches and travel on public opinion and found "little evidence to support the proposition that such presidential activities exert a uniformly positive impact on public support."[39] This should not surprise us when we remember that some presidential speeches have failed to achieve their goals (Ford's pardon message, Bush's reversal of his "no new taxes" pledge, and Clinton's attempt to sell the public on his health care plan—see chapter 13).

Rhetoric is particularly ineffective when a president has lost public support.[40] For example, Jimmy Carter's speech-making efforts met with little success late in his administration when the public had soured on his policies. From a psychological perspective, communications are unlikely to change well-developed, strongly held attitudes. From a news media perspective, a president who lacks public support tends to get negative press as a self-fulfilling prophecy develops. This can also reduce the effects of presidential speeches.

Presidential rhetoric must compete with the gaggle of voices on the public stage. Radio talk show hosts from Rush Limbaugh to Don Imus to Howard Stern are quick to weigh in on presidential pronouncements. These shows command large audiences. Although Franklin Roosevelt had Father Coughlin to contend with, he never had to face the kind of electronic sloganeering that modern presidents have to face. Talk-show hosts are fond of ridiculing the president, and when they do, they can cause some viewers to question the words they just heard the chief executive speak.

Second, **presidential rhetoric is unlikely to influence public opinion if the president fails to make a clear and convincing case for the policy recommendations, and if the rhetoric is inconsistent with the chief executive's public image.** One reason why Clinton failed to sell the public on his health care package was it that it was too complicated. Few members of Clinton's own administration understood the plan.[41] I remember praising some of Clinton's policies to a neighbor early in the president's first term. "Yeah," the neighbor, himself a doctor, replied, "but no one can understand them."

In the previous section, I discussed several presidential speeches that failed because they did not provide a convincing logic. We also saw how Reagan's attempts to salvage his image after Iran-Contra failed because his complicated rhetoric was inconsistent with the public's view of him as a great simplifier.

Third, **presidential rhetoric will fail if it does not mobilize elite members of the president's political party.** One reason why Ronald Reagan had more success with speechmaking than Bill Clinton is that Reagan knew he could call on Republican Congressional leaders for support. Clinton, on the other hand, found that members of his own party consistently opposed his rhetoric. Congressional Democrats attacked his health plan, even though the Democratic party had long championed national health insurance.[42] Deprived of support from his own party, Clinton found that his public speeches could not carry the day.

Today, presidents cannot count on their own party for support. Presidential candidates now wage campaigns independently of political parties, and so party leaders do not feel obligated to support the president. Moreover, parties no longer speak with one voice; they are divided on many issues. The rise of candidate-centered politics has led to an increase in presidential rhetoric, but it has also put roadblocks in the way of presidential success.

For all the limits in presidential speech, there are several things it can do.

Presidential oratory can change political cognitions. Researchers have discovered that presidential speeches can influence the public agenda—specifically, they can convince people that certain issues are more important than others (see chapter 11).[43] When a president gives a speech on a particular issue—say, welfare—it makes that issue more salient to members of the public; the talk convinces them, at least for a while, that welfare is a more important policy issue than they previously believed.

Presidential speeches can influence people's feelings and attitudes. Clinton's speech after the Oklahoma City bombing reassured the public, undoubtedly helping them cope with the tragedy. War rhetoric can shape citizens' attitudes toward the crisis and can cause them to rally around the president, at least temporarily.[44]

Rhetoric can help a president hold together a fragile political coalition. Reagan's upbeat rhetoric and appeals to American individualism helped him hold the Republican party together. In the 1980s, economic conservatives did not always see eye to eye with the Religious Right, which took strong stands on moral issues such as prayer in school and abortion. Reagan's rhetoric provided a symbolic tent in which all Republicans could coexist. This helped him govern effectively.

Rhetoric helps to preserve the institution of the presidency. This restates the point made in the previous section: rhetorical genres provide the symbolic forms through which presidents can reaffirm the basic continuity of the office and can recreate the national identity. Genres also provide sufficient flexibility for presidents to articulate their own visions and to develop new directions for the country.

Presidential rhetoric can change the nature of public discourse. Presidents frequently find that they are engaged in rhetorical battles to set agendas and to influence the tone and priorities of debates. Franklin Delano Roosevelt and Theodore Roosevelt did not win all their battles with Congress and competing political leaders. However, they won the rhetorical wars, for they convinced the nation through their oratory that government had a vital role to play in improving the lot of the ordinary person. John F. Kennedy did not get nearly as much legislation passed as he would have liked. However, Kennedy's activist rhetoric ("Ask not what your country can do for you—ask what you can do for your country.") had an impact on a generation of young people, who shared Kennedy's vision, if not his politics, and set out to change America and its war in Vietnam. Contrary to his campaign promises, Ronald Reagan increased the size of the national debt. However, his antigovernment rhetoric made Newt Gingrich possible. It also sowed the seeds for elite and public efforts to trim government programs.

We are now at the crossroads of a new rhetorical age in which political leaders must decide how to frame the debate about downsizing government and how to persuade the nation to allocate scarce government resources. Presidents must decide whether to employ divisive rhetoric that emphasizes differences between competing groups or coalition-building rhetoric that tries to bridge differences between groups, but that carries with it the danger of promising all things to all people.

Finally, **rhetoric can influence public policy by mobilizing powerful interest groups and by capitalizing on favorable press coverage.** So far I have emphasized that a president can gain support for policy initiatives by appealing to the public. However, things are more complicated than this. Consider Ronald Reagan's success in getting his economic package through Congress in 1981.

Reagan succeeded in getting Congress to pass a major budget overhaul that included large budgetary reductions, increased defense spending, and tax cuts. The president circumvented Congress and took his case the public. It is commonly believed that Reagan's success with Congress was due to his ability to persuade the public to support him and to contact their legislators en masse. It is true that Reagan's success in going public was *one* reason why the bill passed. A Cabinet officer called his speech to the public "a home run with the bases loaded." Even the Democratic Speaker of the House acknowledged it was "devastating."[45] Clearly, Reagan's knack for narrative and his other communication skills helped him influence the public, which conveyed its support through opinion polls and phone calls to legislators.

There is more to it than this. Michael Schudson provides an alternative explanation of why members of Congress received so much mail supporting the president. Pointing to the growth of the conservative movement during the late 1970s and its support of Reagan, Schudson observes that: "The likeliest explanation for the burgeoning mailbags is that Reagan had successfully mobilized a new constituency, the "New Right," that had never before had one of its own in the White House."[46]

Indeed, before the president delivered a televised address, Reagan's staffers gave key conservative leaders a preview of the speech. The leaders then instructed their followers to phone, write, or telegram members of Congress. The effort worked, partly because it influenced legislators' perceptions. "Lawmakers believed their constituents supported that program and they were afraid that Mr. Reagan could galvanize that support through an adroit use of television and punish any dissidents at the polls," reporter Steven V. Roberts wrote.[47]

Perceptions also influenced White House reporters. Convinced that, as Schudson says, "a man with Reagan's evident personal charm on the television screen has practically irresistible power to shape public opinion," the press assumed that Reagan won his battles with Congress because he was a great communicator.[48] Armed with the belief that Reagan was invincible, Schudson argues that the press created the myth of the invisible Ronald Reagan. This in turn contributed to Reagan's success.[49]

ASSESSMENTS

Let us now turn to the knotty issue of the problems and virtues of presidential rhetoric. First, the bad news.

Critics argue that in the zest to promote their programs and themselves, presidents are giving too many public speeches. They are talking about important things and unimportant things. But mostly they are talking. There is a problem with this, as Hart notes:

> The natural inclination of one who speaks for a living is to become audience driven, to become less and less inclined to examine one's own thoughts analytically and more and more attentive to the often uncritical reactions of popular assemblages ... Extensive public speaking by a president begets repetition since there are only a limited number of topics confronting any given president and because so many different audiences wish to hear him speak. Repetition, in turn, begets (1) a dulling of the

intellect, (2) a growing sense that one's views are correct, and (3) the feeling that rhetorical action is equivalent to empirical action ... All of this leaves few moments for the other sorts of things we expect a president to do—namely to think. It is axiomatic that the more one speaks, the less time one has to reflect.[50]

The pressure to speak on issues can cause presidents and presidential candidates to make promises they should not make and that they cannot keep. In an earlier age, George Bush would not have felt impelled to come up with a sexy sound bite like "Read my lips. No new taxes." Had the promise not been made, the presidency might not have experienced the crisis it did in 1990. Similarly, President Clinton's decision to sign a welfare reform bill was undoubtedly influenced by his promise to reform welfare "as we know it."

A second difficulty with contemporary rhetoric stems from presidents' dependence on speechwriters to ghostwrite addresses. In the old days, presidents wrote their speeches. Today they are written for them by a horde of speechwriters. How could it be otherwise? Presidents deliver so many speeches over the course of a week that if they wrote all their addresses, they would be unable to govern. This causes problems, as Jamieson observes:

> Those who live by scripts alone may find that their own ability to think, speak, and write have gone the way of our sixth toe ... Casually and routinely delegating the responsibility for searching out the data to support claims, testing the relationship between fact and assertion, and locating the precise, expressing word may dull both a leader's disposition and ability to perform those tasks for himself. Why would we expect someone who embraces the words of others to suddenly become an active, inquiring, scrutinizing manager of information when offered a plan for aiding the Contras?[51]

Third, it is possible that the rhetorical presidency may lead to grandiose and unrealistic expectations for presidential performance. Social psychological research provides a basis for this prediction. Psychological studies tell us people view salient objects—those that stand out in a context—as particularly influential. People tend to exaggerate the causal impact of salient information.[52] Now think about the president: The chief executive stands out for people because he speaks frequently (and is nearly always covered on the news). This constant exposure to the president may cause Americans to exaggerate the chief executive's impact on policy. More generally, because the office of the presidency so frequently intrudes into their living rooms, Americans may assume that the person who occupies this office has great influence. When they discover that the president does not accomplish as much as he promised, Americans may feel betrayed.

Fourth, scholars wonder whether it is possible for presidents to speak with passion and eloquence in an electronic age. When ideas are reduced to sound bites and brevity is the soul of success, how can presidents develop arguments and thoughtful positions on issues? When presidents realize that everything they say will be dissected and analyzed in the news media, and churned and attacked on talk shows, they have little incentive to take a risk and say something ... original. When presidents must tell stories and give anecdotes to hold a television audience, how can they deliver oratory that causes people to think deeply about the nation's problems and to consider things that never were, but should be?

The final problem concerns television, the medium that presidents use to reach citizens. Television is an intimate medium. It comes into people's living rooms and is inextricably linked with their private lives. Hart argues that television has personalized the presidency.[53] As noted in chapter 6, presidents are talking more about themselves, often shamelessly discussing personal details of their lives. On television, everyone self-discloses: Guests tell tawdry tales of personal relationships on television talk shows, Marla Maples reveals her love life on *PrimeTime Live*, Lorena Bobbit talks about chopping her husband's penis on *20/20*, Nicole Simpson's relatives share their travails on program after program. Presidents, critics charge, have become just another guest on the talk show circuit. They reveal personal details about topics ranging from mothers-in-law (Carter) to preference in underwear (Clinton). The need to personally connect with voters has demeaned the presidency. Or so the criticism goes.

And now the good news. Or is there any? In fact one can argue that there are some benefits of the rhetorical presidency. The very fact that presidents talk so frequently is a good thing: It exposes Americans to presidents' words, ideas, and methods of presenting themselves. In earlier eras, people rarely heard the president. They had little basis for evaluating the president. Now the president's words are everywhere. This gives more people the chance to form their impressions of the president, to weigh the message, and to decide how to relate it to their own experiences. The emphasis on speechmaking also gives the president more opportunities to promote a policy that is judged to be in the country's best interest.

A defense of the contemporary presidency would also point to shortcomings in the criticisms previously noted.

In the nineteenth century, presidents were more apt to write their own speeches; thus the mediocre presidents of that century delivered mediocre speeches. No glory in that. What is ennobling about writing ineffective and uninspiring public oratory? In addition, there is no empirical evidence that excessive presidential speech has reduced the dignity of the office, nor that the rise in personalized speeches has demeaned the presidency. If this were the case, why was there such a hue and cry about Bill Clinton's rhetorical overexposure early in his administration. Presumably, people would be inured to personalized speeches and would just nod their heads like characters in Huxley's *Brave New World*.

It was also argued that in some sense the rhetorical age caused George Bush to make a promise regarding taxes he could not keep. In response, one can ask how it was that television or the values of an era "caused" a grown man, a president of the United States no less, to do something. Nothing forced Bush to make this promise; he chose to make it because he thought it would get him elected, and when he decided to break his word, he should be rightfully held responsible for his decision.

One can also question the argument that television militates against the delivery of eloquent, thoughtful messages. In fact we do have eloquent television speakers in our day and age—Jesse Jackson comes immediately to mind. Also, as songwriter Billy Joel sang in a different context: The good old days weren't all that good. The truth is that there were plenty of uninspiring speeches in the days when radio and stump speeches were the dominant modes of public address. And, one might ask, what is wrong with providing visual arguments and telling stories if this connects with audiences?

Still, when you look at the sum total of the critics' objections, you feel as if the country is getting shortchanged in the speech arena. Presidents hype their addresses and appearances; this sets in motion a cycle of expectations, disappointment, and cynicism. Presidents are loathe to deliver visionary addresses that outline new directions for the future.

There is one other problem in the rhetorical presidency—namely, the obsession with polling before speeches to gauge the public's attitude and with using poll results to help craft policies. Presidents today are necessarily concerned with how a speech will "play" to an audience, and they use polls regularly to guide their pronouncements. But polls are no substitute for policy, experts remind us. One of the problems with our age is that concern with the presentation of policy frequently receives more attention than the policy itself. The public perceives—sometimes correctly, sometimes not—that presidents are obsessed with presentations and never tell it like it is.

Dean Acheson, Harry Truman's secretary of state, bemoaned this tendency years ago, when he remarked about the "unfortunate preoccupation at the Kennedy White House with 'image.'" During the early 1960s, Acheson wrote Truman that:

> This is a terrible weakness. It makes one look at oneself instead of at the problem. How will I look fielding this hot line drive to short stop? This is a good way to miss the ball altogether. I am amazed looking back to how far you were from this. I don't remember a case where you stopped to think of the effect on your fortunes—or the party's for that matter—of a decision in foreign policy.[54]

Of course, we can't go back to the days of Harry Truman. Truman made his share of mistakes. But Acheson's statement highlights the difference between our era and the eras that preceded it, and it reveals a chilly shortcoming of the modern rhetorical presidency.

CONCLUSIONS

This chapter reviewed different categories of presidential rhetoric and the impact of presidential speeches. Major rhetorical forms include the inaugural address, State of the Union messages, pardoning rhetoric, and crisis rhetoric. Each rhetorical type performs different functions for the president and the country. Although there is disagreement about the utility of lumping speeches into rhetorical genres, there is agreement that official and ceremonial speeches such as those discussed in this chapter perform an important system-maintenance function. They allow the presidency to survive crises and calamities. Words are not just objects hurled into the air; they matter, and they help citizens and elites adapt to changing circumstances.

Although scholars take it for granted that we have a rhetorical presidency, in fact rhetoric is more important under certain conditions than others. Presidential speeches do not always succeed. Speeches are unlikely to succeed if they do not contain compelling arguments, are delivered at inopportune times, and if they are inconsistent with the chief executive's image. If delivered properly, presidential rhetoric can set the agenda, shape attitudes, and mobilize key elites.

Finally, there has been much criticism of the rhetorical presidency. Some of the most vociferous critics have been rhetoric scholars themselves, presumably because they appreciate oratory and lament its misuse. Critics argue that the need to "go public" has caused presidents to speak when they should be reflecting about policy and to personalize addresses when they should be crafting arguments. Defenders of the status quo note that the increase in presidential speechmaking can be a good thing if it brings issues out into the open and encourages public debate. Unfortunately, it is not clear this has happened. On the contrary, marketing techniques have proliferated, making it all too easy for presidents to emphasize selling over substance.

I close the chapter on an optimistic note. Rhetoric is a key element of leadership, and leadership can be a force for good if it makes people's lives more rewarding and more fulfilled. There is nothing in the informal rules of the modern presidency that says that presidents must speak frequently or frivolously or with excessive self-reference. Presidential rhetoric, if used properly and thoughtfully, can be an important instrument for change and effective governance. It can be used to inspire and to bring people together. Smith and Smith observe that:

> If the contemporary federal system is to work, the White House must speak. But it must speak responsibly, and to all corners of the community. It must speak clearly and persuasively of the problems facing us individually and collectively, and of the technical complexities and moral implications of the possible solutions … And, for now, it must find a way to unite … disunited communities without the help of foreign bogeymen. The task is difficult but not impossible for presidents who understand that presidential leadership requires them to build interpretive coalitions out of the needs, words, reasons, and preferences that make sense to their citizens.[55]

KEY ISSUES

Inaugural Addresses

Epideictic Speech

Pardoning Rhetoric

Crisis Rhetoric

Condensational Symbols

Impact of Rhetoric

Pros and Cons of Rhetorical Presidency

DISCUSSION QUESTIONS

1. In what ways are words deeds?

2. Would you say that President Clinton used rhetoric to advance policy goals or was he a victim of the worst aspects of the rhetorical presidency?

3. Think of an issue you deeply care about. Now, taking into account the principles discussed in this chapter, write a speech on this topic. How does it make use of rhetorical devices?

8

Congress and the Media

To appreciate how much Congressional communication has changed in the past quarter-century, consider the remark that Allard Lowenstein, an idealistic young member of the House of Representatives, made in 1970. Lowenstein, journalist Michael Green tells us, "warned that if the House was to become any more ignored than it was already, it would become as obsolete as the House of Lords and the country would simply evolve into government by Presidential decree."[1]

How things have changed!

C-SPAN now provides live coverage of House and Senate proceedings. Senators and representatives have home pages on the World Wide Web. Legislators regularly poll constituents to determine the best ways to frame controversial political issues. The news media are full of stories about Congress. Ever since the Republicans took control of Congress in 1994 and began shaping the national agenda, the print and electronic media have given Congress extensive coverage.

Yet the public remains dissatisfied with Congress, frustrated with its elected representatives, and distressed by the ways that Congress does business. This is no small matter. The fact that the citizens of the United States hold their elected representatives and the institution that houses them in low esteem is a serious problem for representative democracy.

This chapter attempts to shed light on these issues, as well as on the role that communication plays in today's Congress. The chapter is divided into four sections. The first section chronicles the changes and continuities in Congressional communication. The second part of the chapter explores how legislators use the media to reach the public. The third section describes the nature of news coverage of Congress. The final portion of the chapter offers suggestions for how to improve Congressional communication.

CONTINUITIES AND CHANGES

The story of the news media and Congress, like that of the media and the presidency, is one of continuity and change. "From the moment the House of Representatives was created," Timothy Cook notes, "its members have been preoccupied with the press."[2] The same could be said of the Senate.[3] Even in the late nineteenth century, members of Congress recognized that the media carried their words to a larger and more diverse audience than their legislative peers. Knowing this, lawmakers have worked hard to ensure that media accounts reflected favorably on their activities. In the late 1700s, it was not uncommon for reporters to be denied access to the floor if their articles were deemed inaccurate or biased. Over time this practice died a natural death. By the middle of the 1850s, with the penny press firmly established, legislators adopted a more proactive strategy: sending their speeches to reporters and constituents. By the end of the nineteenth century, Senators and House members recognized that they could influence the news by cultivating Washington reporters and providing their "spin" on events, to use the contemporary phrase.

Thus a constancy in Congress–media relations is that legislators have always recognized that the press is an important actor on the political communication stage. Another continuity is that members of Congress have long developed strategies to influence news coverage. There is where the similarities end. The relationship between Congress and the media has changed dramatically over the past 200 years.

First, **Congressional reporting** has changed. Up until about the 1840s, news about Congress consisted almost entirely of official accounts of the previous day's proceedings. Reporters were stenographers, dutifully transcribing the words that members of Congress spoke and slavishly summarizing official floor proceedings. Stenographic reporting gave way to active news gathering as the penny press developed and publishers realized that news represented a way to capture an audience and also to satisfy readers' hunger for information about the burgeoning world of politics.

In 1846 *The New York Tribune* instituted a gossip column that gave the public the "dirt" on Washington politicians. One column graphically described the behavior of Ohio congressman William Sawyer, who at 2 p.m. each day digested a sausage on the House floor. "What little grease is left on his hands he wipes on his almost bald head," the column related, adding that "his mouth sometimes serves as a finger glass, his coat sleeves and pantaloons being called into requisition as a napkin."[4]

The publication of the column about "Sausage Sawyer," as he was called, helped to change the convention of stenographic reporting. As news reporting matured during the Civil War and journalists increasingly began to see themselves as members of a profession, Congressional reporting became more active; reporters were permitted more freedom to interpret and make sense of Congressional activities. It didn't happen overnight, of course, but by the end of the nineteenth century, reporters were interviewing legislators and quoting named and unnamed Congressional sources. Over the course of the next 100 years, reporting about Congress would become increasingly feisty and aggressive.

A second change in coverage of Congress centers on **news play.** Throughout the nineteenth century, the general understanding among political experts was that Congress made the big decisions and the president implemented them. There were a number of weak one-term presidents in the late 1800s, and there was no such thing as the bully pulpit or the imperial presidency. This would await Theodore Roosevelt and his successors in the twentieth century. As Cook notes, "For most of the nineteenth century, the Congressional press corps was synonymous with the Washington press corps; Washington news was news about Congress."[5] However, the pendulum swung in the twentieth century: Today, the White House is the big story. This trend has been changing of late, but the White House is still the most prestigious beat in town.

The third change has occurred since the advent of television, and it is by far the most important. During the eighteenth and nineteenth centuries and for most of the twentieth, Congress was a closed shop, an insiders' club. During this time, the way to get bills passed and to build a personal reputation was to play "the inside game"—bargaining with colleagues, horse-trading, acquiescing to senior members of Congress, while gradually building up the record and seniority necessary to gain power and chairmanship of key committees.[6]

Private bargaining is still important in Congress, but it is not the only route to legislative success. Members of Congress spend more time today than in previous eras on **public persuasion.** They strive to gain favorable publicity for themselves and their causes. They appear on television talk shows and regularly poll their constituents to determine how best to frame controversial issues. Just as presidents have gone public, so too have members of Congress recognized that private bargaining must be combined with public persuasion. With C-SPAN televising floor activities, the networks covering controversial hearings live, and influential legislators using talk radio to promote their agendas, Congress has ceased to conduct its business exclusively behind closed doors.[7] Today, making news and seeking publicity are part of a legislator's job. Making news and maintaining a positive public image are also necessary, if not sufficient, conditions for achieving legislative success and for building political power.

THE OUTSIDE GAME

Legislators employ a variety of outside—or public persuasion—strategies to build political agendas. These strategies include direct communication with constituents, conventional news-making techniques, and use of C-SPAN, talk radio, and political marketing.

Direct and Mediated Communication

Members of Congress still meet face to face with constituents. Congressional aides spend considerable time making sure that gallery passes and tour tickets are available to visiting constituents. Members also encounter constituents when they return home, typically on weekends. The most important meetings are reserved for constituents with money and power—activists, members of interest groups, and heads of lobbying organizations. The modern campaign mandates that legislators cultivate those with financial and political resources because campaigns today cost money and require the political moxie of experienced Washington hands.

Much communication between legislators and constituents occurs through letters sent via conventional mail and through the Internet. The franking privilege allows lawmakers to mail information to constituents at government expense. Hundreds of millions of letters and newsletters are mailed out each year. Word processing programs allow legislators to personalize a stock letter. Autopens ink in the lawmaker's signature, creating the impression of real penmanship.[8]

Franking allows legislators to promote their issues and —let's face it—themselves to citizens. Critics have argued that the privilege gives incumbents an unfair advantage over those who might be interested in challenging them in a Congressional election. For this reason, the Franking Commission prohibits members of Congress from sending out mass mailings less than 60 days before an election. However, knowledgeable Congressional hands have figured out ways to get around the law. A mass mailing is defined as 500 or more letters that are fundamentally similar. Many incumbents send out a huge volume of mail in small batches or change each batch just enough so that they can claim each bundle contains a different set of letters.[9]

In addition, many members of Congress have established World Wide Web sites to communicate with constituents. House Representative Elizabeth Furse, an Oregon Democrat, used computer bulletin boards to assuage constituents' concerns about an amendment to an education bill. When constituents swamped her office with questions, Furse posted notices on bulletin boards explaining the amendment. However, most members of Congress do not use e-mail as regularly as Furse. Research indicates that the overwhelming majority of members do not respond electronically to constituents' e-mail messages.

Computer technology has the potential to greatly increase ordinary citizens' access to their representatives. It is exciting and pathbreaking. However, it has its limits. Citizens who hook up to Congressional Web sites will not necessarily gain an appreciation of the complex issues that underlie Congressional debates. Jargon-filled legislative reports that are sent over the Internet will not enhance people's understanding of the issues. Moreover, the Internet does not eliminate Congressional public relations activities. Many Web sites are filled with superpatriotic statements and Congressional self-promotion. One Minnesota senator's home page showed him against a background of an American flag and a bald eagle. Time will tell whether the World Wide Web ends up facilitating communication between legislators and the public, or whether it becomes just another way for members to publicize their accomplishments.

Conventional Newsmaking Strategies

The conventional media are still where the action is. Realizing that most people get their news and impressions of politics from the print and electronic media, legislators work hard to promote themselves in newspapers, magazines, radio, and television.

Members of Congress rely heavily on **press secretaries** to disseminate information to the news media. "The press secretary, many times, may be the most important staff member a senator can employ," a Senate handbook advised freshman senators.[10] Congressional press secretaries were once a rarity, but they are now so common and so important they have even spawned a version of the classic light bulb joke. Question: "How many press secretaries does it take to change a light bulb?" Answer: "I don't have anything on that, but I'll get back to you." Stephen Hess observes that the joke reflects both the significant role that public relations plays in the contemporary Congress and an ambivalence about the time spent on media relations.[11]

Press secretaries who work for members of the House direct most of their efforts to the local media, particularly print. "We'd rather get in (the home-town paper) than the front page of The New York Times any day," one press secretary remarked.[12] Local media—in particular, newspapers—reach representatives' constituents and are viewed positively by most members of the public. As a general rule, press releases about members of Congress are more likely to get played up in legislators' hometown media than in the national press. This makes the local news appealing to House press secretaries.

A standard technique for gaining news coverage is to schedule a press conference at which the legislator announces the regional projects that are slated for government funding, a precious commodity in this day and age. Press secretaries can also invite local dignitaries to speak at committee hearings or they can arrange media events, as when a House member shows off his or her World Wide Web site. Senators' press secretaries use similar techniques, but they usually direct their energies at larger media outlets.

Legislators' media liaisons also use high-tech communications to gain publicity. They videotape Congressional committee meetings and transmit short segments via satellite to local television news departments. Critics point out that these communications techniques work to the advantage of incumbents, who can use their offices to advertise and promote themselves. Lacking these political and psychological resources, challengers face a difficult time mounting a successful campaign.[13]

In today's media age, it is hardly surprising that legislators spend considerable time promoting themselves and their issues through the media. It is important to point out that they are not always successful. Research shows that newspapers and television stations discard a great deal of the public relations material they receive from politicians and members of Congress.[14] Thus, legislators have had to come up with additional ways to promote themselves to the public.

C-SPAN

When C-SPAN went on the air in March, 1979, no one paid much attention. There was host Brian Lamb, some makeshift tables, a blue curtain, and a C-SPAN sign, which fell down during one portion of the program. "You can't imagine how insignificant I was," Lamb related.[15]

Times have changed.

C-SPAN now is a major player on the Washington scene. It provides live coverage of Congressional committee meetings, hearings, and speeches. It gives members of Congress a way to reach citizens, and it lets ordinary people watch their representatives in action. C-SPAN (short for the Cable Satellite Public Affairs Network) began televising House proceedings in 1979. In 1986, the Senate, envious of the attention the House was receiving, decided to televise its proceedings. C-SPAN II was inaugurated. In 1996 C-SPAN initiated a third channel to carry meetings and conferences from the capital when the other two channels are occupied with other matters.

Legislators can promote themselves on C-SPAN by participating actively in floor debates. They can also address the chambers at two times of the day that are explicitly reserved for members to speak on matters of their own choosing. Members can give one-minute speeches at the beginning of the session and can address the chambers at the end of the day for hours on end.

C-SPAN is a marvelous resource: It gives members of Congress a platform to reach citizens and elites directly, and it lets ordinary people watch their representatives in action. Legislators gravitated to C-SPAN in the 1980s when they realized that it provided a less adversarial format than standard television interview programs like *Meet the Press* and *Nightline*. On C-SPAN lawmakers could speak their minds without having to worry about being interrupted by assertive journalists. In addition, while the C-SPAN audience was small, it was active in politics. According to one account, C-SPAN viewers were significantly more likely than nonviewers to donate money to candidates and to volunteer for political campaigns. And the overwhelming majority of C-SPAN viewers voted.[16]

During the 1980s, Newt Gingrich, then a new member of the House of Representatives, saw in C-SPAN a way to build support for his cause. In the early 1980s, C-SPAN attracted conservative viewers, who felt that network news programs were too liberal. Realizing this, Gingrich took advantage of the times allotted at the beginning and end of the day for speeches. Gingrich delivered fiery one-minute speeches at the beginning of the day and then gave longer speeches at the end of the day when business had been concluded. Gingrich spoke in favor of his conservative antigovernment proposals and against Democratic policies, particularly Democratic opposition of aid to the Nicaraguan Contras.

In one speech he accused several Democratic members of being "blind to communism" and challenged them to respond to his attacks. The representatives could not respond, of course, because regular business had been concluded and no one was in the chambers. Several days later, House Speaker Tip O'Neill, outraged by Gingrich's attacks, ordered the cameras to pan the empty chambers to show that no one was paying attention to Gingrich and company. O'Neill denounced Gingrich, saying, "You deliberately stood in the well before an empty House and challenged these people when you knew they would not be there. It's the lowest thing that I have ever seen in my thirty-two years in Congress."[17] But Gingrich had accomplished his mission: He had successfully used C-SPAN to publicize his charges, had brought a leading member of the opposition into the battle, and in the process had fired up his troops for the wars to come.

Thus C-SPAN has become a strategic tool in legislators' political communication arsenals. Given its small audience size, C-SPAN is not as important as the network news or the hometown paper. However, it offers lawmakers a way to communicate with constituents and, in some cases, to reach key constituent groups.

Radio Talk Shows

Talk radio is the newest—and noisiest—kid on the Congressional communication block. No one would have guessed that AM radio, which was experiencing financial problems in the late 1970s, would have come back with a vengeance in the late 1980s to influence Congressional politics. This is exactly what happened, of course. In 1988, several talk-show hosts denounced Congress's decision to vote itself a pay raise. Hosts encouraged listeners to fax and phone House and Senate leaders. The onslaught was so great that the next time the pay raise issue came before Congress, the legislature decided to do it at night and by voice vote rather than by a count of individuals.

In the 1990s, talk radio was used successfully by Republicans in their efforts to derail the Clinton agenda. It is important to remember that conservative activists gravitated to talk shows because they represented an alternative to the mainstream news media, which conservatives believed were slanted to the left.

Early in Clinton's term, Republicans were looking for a way to mobilize their diverse constituencies—the 1.7 million member Christian Coalition, antigovernment groups, gun owners, and the national organization of small business owners. They found it in talk radio. Journalists Dan Balz and Ronald Brownstein explain that:

> Technology enabled the Republicans to cement their new relationship with the talk show hosts. The key was the fax, which allowed the party to communicate with hundreds of shows—instantly. That speed revolutionized political argument. Republicans couldn't match Clinton's access to the network news, but even without such a national platform, the "blast fax" to hundreds of talk show hosts, other media outlets, and sympathetic grassroots groups allowed them to shower their response to his initiatives across the country as soon as he announced them—and sometimes before.[18]

Republican Congressional leaders—notably Speaker of the House Newt Gingrich and then-House Majority leader Dick Armey—communicated regularly with Rush Limbaugh. They frequently informed Limbaugh of the party's strategy for fighting Clinton's health care and crime bills, which conservatives believed were weighted down by government social spending. "The idea," one Republican leader explained "was to start a public education campaign that you would then roll out to a broader audience."[19]

Although it is hard to know exactly what effects talk radio had on the agenda-building process, it is clear that it helped Republicans fight Clinton's programs. Talk radio helped build opposition to President Clinton's nomination of Zoe Baird for attorney general. Republican blast faxes to sympathetic talk-radio hosts helped mobilize opposition to Clinton's health care and crime packages. Talk radio helped build opposition by inducing the mainstream media to cover conservatives' criticisms of the bills, by strengthening callers' beliefs that these programs were wrong, and by creating the appearance of widespread public opposition to the plans.[20]

The impact of conservative talk radio has been amplified by the growth of like-minded Internet Web sites. The conservative magazine, The National Review, and The Heritage Foundation, a conservative think tank, launched a Web site called Town Hall. The Christian Coalition and the National Rifle Association began computer bulletin boards. On the other side of the political spectrum, liberal groups developed Web sites to challenge the Republican Congress. A Democratic National Committee site invited users to participate in "a high-tech lynching of Speaker Gingrich," as one writer put it.[21] Users took part in a computer version of the children's game of hangman. They guessed letters of the alphabet to spell words; the goal was to come up with a combination of guesses that would show a stick figure of Gingrich hanging from a gallows, hovering above the magic word: EXTREMIST.

Critics have lamented that one of the dysfunctions of talk radio and the Internet is that they fuel the fires of extremists and encourage angry and simplistic discourse. On the other hand, long-time Congress watchers remind us that, as the representatives of a volatile people, members of the American House of Representatives and Senate have always been prone to verbal and even physical violence. In 1838, Representative William Campbell punched Representative Abram Maury near the chair of the Speaker of the House; everybody in the chambers watched. Twelve years later, in 1850, a pistol accidentally went off inside a House member's desk, causing 30 to 40 members to draw their guns.

Political Marketing

Democrats used political marketing and polling techniques brilliantly in the 1992 presidential campaign. Interest groups have used polls for years to help devise information campaign strategies. However, it was the Republican party that showed that modern polling techniques could be employed to influence midterm Congressional elections and the Congressional agenda.

Polling and marketing played a critical role in the development of the Contract With America, the 10-point platform released in the fall of 1994 that helped unify Republican candidates around a common set of ideas and which mobilized the party's major constituencies during the midterm election campaign. The Republicans swept the election, gaining the most Congressional seats in a midterm election since 1946. They took control of Congress, gaining 52 seats in the House and 8 in the Senate. There were many reasons why Republicans captured Congressional seats, notably voter dissatisfaction with the Clinton administration and with governmental performance under Democratic leadership. The GOP's Contract With America also played a part in the electoral outcome.

The Contract was a combination of conservative ideology, political coalition-building, and modern-day marketing. It called for a balanced budget amendment, major welfare reform, a capital gains tax cut, and a vote on term limits. The Contract also included a $500 per child tax credit because this was one of the Christian Coalition's top policy priorities.[22] Republican leaders promised voters that the House would vote on the Contract in the first 100 days of the new Congress. One must remember that in addition to proposing policy changes, the Contract was designed to market and promote Republican candidates running for Congress. Thus the Republicans called on experts in political marketing and polling to help them design the document.

Republican pollsters used surveys and focus groups to develop the Contract. In mid-July, polling experts showed small groups of voters a series of television commercials. Participants were given hand-held devices that let them indicate their impressions of words and slogans.

Gingrich insisted that the Contract contain 10 items because Gingrich "believed in the 'mythic power' of the number ten."[23] The exact wording of the Contract evolved in the focus groups. Republicans believed that to win the midterm elections they needed support from senior citizens. To do this they enlisted Linda DiVall, a Republican pollster who was tuned in to the power of words. *Washington Post* reporters Michael Weisskopf and David Maraniss reported:

> Several words were key to (the) strategy. "Do not say changing Medicare," DiVall stressed. Her research showed that seniors were nervous about change and likely to resist it. At a focus group in Cincinnati on March 6, when seniors were asked what words they preferred, one man offered "preserve." It had a comforting ring to it: DiVall promoted the suggestion of another respondent that they call the legislation the Medicare Preservation Act. There were other words that should be edited out of the Republican dictionary in discussions of Medicare, DiVall said. She advised the group to be "leery" of the words cut, cap and freeze— they would bring nothing but trouble and help Democrats define the process in negative terms.[24]

With the words carefully chosen and the Contract finally written, the platform was ready for *roll-out*, in the terminology of Washington politicians. After consulting with a meteorologist from Georgia, Gingrich decided that the Contract should be unveiled on September 27, 1994, because the weather forecaster told him it would not rain that afternoon. And so on a sunny Tuesday afternoon, Gingrich brought 300 Republican candidates for Congress to the Capitol's west front, where each signed the Contract With America.

Some praised the Contract because it created a mechanism for making government more accountable to voters. Others complained that it was nothing but smoke and mirrors, evolved through modern marketing. Whatever one's evaluation, there was little doubt that it exerted an impact on the national and Congressional agendas. It (coupled with the GOP victories in 1994) pushed the Clinton administration into retreating from its belief that the federal government should play a pivotal role in social change. From 1994 through 1996, the conflicts between the Clinton administration and Republicans centered less on whether the federal government should play a major role in social change than on how much federal spending should be cut back and by what date.[25]

The Contract exemplifies the current emphasis on going public and the way the outside game is played in contemporary Washington. There was one interesting irony to the entire gambit. While Republicans struggled to promote the Contract and Democrats attacked it bitterly during the campaign, a *Newsweek* poll discovered that 25% of the public thought the Contract was "a serious promise for which the new Republican Congress should be held responsible" and 24% believed it was just a campaign promise. Forty-seven percent of the public had never heard of it.[26]

Inside and Outside Games

As noted earlier in this chapter, legislators can no longer build reputations and accomplish legislative goals by exclusively playing an "inside game." Instead, members of Congress must "go public," expending energy on making news and creating images, as well as making laws. We make a mistake, however, if we assume that going public is all that is required today to achieve success in Congress. Not all business is conducted before the C-SPAN audience. Legislative know-how is still important. The more a member knows about Congressional log-rolling and parliamentary maneuvering, the better he or she will fare. Success in Congress predicts success with the media. The nation's news media lavish more attention on established leaders in Congress—such as the Speaker of the House and the Senate Majority Leader—than on nonleaders, even if those nonleaders are charming television performers.[27]

Today, successful legislators must be adept at both the inside game and the media power game. Both are important. Members of Congress need reporters to help them publicize their issues, influence the public agenda, and build a national reputation. Reporters need legislators to provide them with information, angles, and inside scoops.

PRESS COVERAGE OF CONGRESS

Quantity of Coverage

Until quite recently, news about government focused almost exclusively on the president. As Jamieson has noted, "435 members of the House and 100 members of the Senate compete for the crumbs of network time left after the president has gotten his share."[28]

One reason for this is that news about the White House fits more closely into news media routines. Presidential news is simple, personal, and easy to acquire. The story centers on the president, and White House media aides are adept at feeding reporters credible, newsworthy information in time for them to meet their deadlines. By contrast, stories about Congress are inherently more multifaceted and complex (remember Congress consists of 535 members with multiple agendas). In addition, there is no spokesperson for Congress. Reporters must scurry around getting information from different sources, which makes it difficult to provide a single, dramatic focus for a story.

Hess notes that Congress is the "quintessential talking-heads story."[29] The president can go to China, walk on the beaches of Normandy, or visit the Middle East. Since these visits represent symbolic statements, they get covered. "But the best a legislator can usually offer the cameras is a finger pointed at a recalcitrant committee witness," Hess observes.[30]

A second reason why Congress traditionally has been covered less than the White House is that Congress lumbers too slowly for the deadlines of the print and electronic media. It can take months for action to be taken on bills; thus, for long stretches of time there is no new and exciting news. In addition, the activities of Congress are complicated, for they are steeped in legal and legislative traditions. This also puts a barrier in the way of covering Congress, particularly on television.

There is some evidence this is changing. Ever since the Republicans won control of Congress in 1994 and shaped the policy agenda from 1994 through 1996, there has been an increase in the number of news stories about Congressional activities. In 1995, for the first time in recent memory, there was nearly as much network news coverage of Congress as of the president. In addition, the House got nearly twice as much network attention as the Senate, ending at least for a time the Senate's dominance of the news.[31] The House was at the vortex of activity in 1995; it was where bills emerging from the Contract With America were being proposed, introduced, and passed.

As the balance of power moves somewhat in Congress's direction, it is likely that we will see more coverage of Congress in the years to come.[32] In addition, if the House continues to influence the policy agenda, we may also see some modification of the time-honored tendency for Senators to get more coverage than House members.

Beyond the question of quantity of coverage is the controversial question of the quality and nature of Congressional news. The next sections take up this issue.

Press Coverage: 1950s–1970s

Is the news a propaganda arm of Congress or a caustic critic? Do the media give Congress free publicity or negative press?

McCarthyism. Evidence that the news media are lap dogs to Congress dates back to the early 1950s, when Wisconsin Senator Joseph McCarthy used the news media to manufacture falsehoods and to spread lies. McCarthy exploited media routines to publicly accuse American citizens of being members of the Communist party. McCarthy made his charges during the beginning of the Cold War, an era in which there was great concern about the threat the Soviet Union and China posed to America and the free world. Viewed nearly a half-century later, these fears look more like paranoia than anything grounded in reality, but at the time they were quite real.

For more than 4 years, from 1950 through 1954, McCarthy dominated the press. He would step up to the microphone and say that he held in his hand "a list of names that were made known to the Secretary of State as being members of the Communist party and who nevertheless are still working and shaping policy in the State Department." Even though the charges were bogus and manufactured, the media dutifully covered the story. Why did they do it? Why did they cover a story they knew or suspected was false? Richard Rovere asked the same questions in a book on McCarthy:

> Why did the press publish this liar's lies? McCarthy knew the answer: it was not because publishers in general wished to circulate his mendacities or even because he had achieved a glamor that made him irresistible to the readers. It was because he had achieved a high elective office, because what he said counted for something (in fact, a great deal, as time went by), in the affairs of this nation, and because there was always the possibility that there *was* a mystery witness or that he *would* force Harry Truman to testify.[33]

McCarthy charmed the press and satisfied reporters' hunger for information. More importantly, he took advantage of the principle of objectivity, which stipulated (in those days) that reporters should not put their opinions into stories, and that if a United States senator released "facts" about alleged Communists, the press had no choice but to publish the information.

These were dark days of American journalism—and American politics too, for few elected officials took McCarthy to task. This was post-World War II Cold War America, an era in which both press and government cooperated on many matters. McCarthy needed the press to make his slanderous charges, and the press let itself be coopted by McCarthy.

1940s–1970s.   During the late 1940s and early 1950s, there was relatively little criticism of Congress—or at least the criticism was mild by contemporary standards. As noted, the press gave McCarthy a platform to air his views. A few years earlier, in 1946, elite newspapers endorsed Congressional reforms of standing committees. Editorials and opinion pieces praised a Congressional pay raise. There is no way in the world a Congressional pay raise would be viewed positively in today's era, but in 1946 it was.[34]

Fast forwarding to 1965, we find that the 89th Congress, which passed Lyndon Johnson's Great Society programs and a civil rights bill, received tremendous press. Terms like "extraordinary," "outstanding record," and "matchless in our time" were used to describe the 89th Congress.[35] Some of the adulation can be explained by the fact that Congress enacted an enormous amount of legislation in a relatively short time and did so during a period of social unrest. However, viewed from the vantage point of the current era, it seems as if some of the positive press had its roots in a subtle liberal bias—in journalists' and editors' support of the Great Society.

During Watergate, Congress received a good deal of positive press for its role in investigating the crimes committed by the Nixon White House.[36] This would be one of the last times that the news media would give Congress relatively positive press. During the late 1970s, 1980s, and 1990s, the news media have subjected Congress to a great deal of criticism.

Skewering Congress

"The press on the whole has little good to report about Congress and its membership," Charles Tidmarch and John Pitney concluded after content analyzing stories that appeared in 10 newspapers during one month in 1978.[37] They found that while the majority of news about Congress is neutral, there is significantly more negative than positive information. One study conducted during the late 1970s found that the media portray Congress more negatively than either the presidency or the Supreme Court.[38]

The tone of news about Congress has become more negative since the 1970s. In 1972, three of every four judgments about Congress aired on the network news were negative. By 1992, nearly nine of ten network comments were unfavorable. In 1995, despite the fact that Congress was garnering more press than it had in years and was strongly influencing the policy agenda, it still managed to get worse press than Bill Clinton.[39] Mark Rozell concludes that "press coverage of Congress has moved from healthy skepticism to outright cynicism" and that "many reports resort to humiliating caricature."[40]

Exemplifying this coverage is an article by Tom Kenworthy, who reported on Congress for 5 years for *The Washington Post*. Kenworthy observed, "There's no shortage of buffoons, charlatans, blowhards and intellectually dishonest people on Capitol Hill. (But) perhaps a little Congress-defending is in order. Not much, mind you, but if (mass murderer) Jeffrey Dahmer deserves a defense, then Congress does too."[41]

Rubbergate.   Press coverage of Congress reached an all-time low in 1992 in the wake of the House banking scandal, what Marjorie Hershey called "the mother of all Congressional scandals."[42]

The check-bouncing story, called Rubbergate, involved the disclosure that House members frequently had overdrawn their bank accounts at the House depository. The House had long maintained a depository where representatives could keep their paychecks. The bank routinely covered members' checks when checks came in that exceeded the amount currently available in the account. Commercial banks do the same thing, but they typically penalize customers who don't have enough funds to cover a check. Records of Congressional overdrafts go back to 1830 and have been reported in annual audits since 1947. The protection afforded legislators was not illegal. However, it was unarguably a perk, and it was one that was not available to members of the public. Few knew of the practice until 1991. When the media publicized the story, it shook Congress like an earthquake. As if this were not enough, the media also got wind of the fact that members of Congress had run up large bills at the House restaurant. *The New York Times* complained that:

> Representatives have given new meaning to the expression "on the House," bouncing checks in the House bank, ignoring bills from the House restaurant, getting House officials to fix their parking tickets. All over the country voters have been smelling self-indulgence.[43]

Cartoons lampooned Congress. In one case, a woman announced that "I just saw our Congressman on TV." "Not another campaign ad," her husband moaned. "No. 'America's Most Wanted,'" the woman replied.

Public opinion toward Congress plummeted. Even people's evaluations of their own representative or senator, which are usually significantly higher than ratings of Congress as a whole, dropped to an all-time low of a 52% approval rating. Although ratings of Congress and the respondent's own representative rose after the scandal ended, they still remained in the ice-cold range. In 1994, just over 30% of the public indicated that it approved of the way Congress was doing its job. In 1996, a poll of Ohio residents found that 67% of respondents felt that political figures did not care about ordinary people, 67% did not believe they were thoughtful, and 71% believed they were corrupt.[44]

Explaining the Negativity

When research shows that news about Congress is primarily negative and that citizens hold their elected representatives in low esteem, there is unquestionably something wrong somewhere. While public disapproval of Congress has many causes, there is little doubt that exposure to negative news is an important antecedent of these attitudes. Why does news present Congress in such a negative light?

First, news does reflect reality to some extent, and the realities of Congress continue to be negative. Rubbergate happened. Five senators, dubbed the "Keating Five," *were* accused of putting pressure on federal banking regulators to help campaign contributor Charles Keating, head of a savings and loan association. A number of representatives and senators *have* gotten themselves in hot water, either by committing ethical transgressions or by getting enmeshed in sex scandals. Former House Ways and Means Chairman Dan Rostenkowski was indicted on 17 charges, notably embezzlement and misuse of government funds. Congressman Wayne Hays had a lover, Elizabeth Ray, whom he hired as a secretary even though she could not type. Robert Packwood resigned from the Senate when the Senate Ethics Committee voted to recommend he be expelled for sexual misconduct and influence peddling.

Moreover, members of Congress do not always level with the public. "Who runs (for office) by saying the problems are really difficult and that true solutions are probably nonexistent?" ask John Hibbing and Elizabeth Theiss-Morse.[45] The answer is few do, and "many run *for* Congress by running *against* Congress."[46] This further erodes the credibility of the institution.

Second, Congressional decision-making is notoriously ill-suited to the television age. As Ronald Elving notes:

> Congress would strike few public relations professionals as an attractive client. The institution tackles issues that are both technically daunting and emotionally exhaust-

ing. Its tradition-driven processes tend to the cryptic. It has few established means for helping the public understand its workings, and it operates at a handicap because it has no single institutional voice ... As it displays itself to the public in the galleries or on C-Span and the conventional news media, Congress seems tortured by intentional inactivity and delay, Byzantine procedures, and anachronistic rules. The monotony is broken by intermittent outbreaks of rancor and rhetoric leading to protracted votes on incomprehensible motions.[47]

Taking note of the process, former Speaker of the House Thomas Foley observed that "democracy in its purest forms is often not pretty." Although this is undoubtedly true, members of Congress have frequently failed to recognize that the "unpretty picture of democracy" is what citizens see on the television screens and that it can leave a lasting impression of Congress.

Third, and a corollary to the point above, is that the news media have trouble conveying complex aspects of the legislative process. It is difficult to cover tax reform and House debates about the budget deficit because they involve complicated substantive and procedural issues. In fact, coverage of domestic and foreign policy issues has dropped dramatically since 1986. From 1979 to 1985, close to 80% of television news about Congress stories focused on policy; from 1986 to 1992, the proportion had dropped to just over 50%.[48]

A fourth reason why Congress gets negative press is that the news media gravitate to scandals. Conflict, sex, and dirt are interesting to cover and fit news routines like a glove. They also have a tendency to attract huge audiences, which is especially important today, when the conventional media face increased competition from alternative outlets.

Fifth, in a related vein, political reporting has become increasingly aggressive and adversarial. Thomas Dye and Harmon Zeigler argue that journalists are guided by a "post-Watergate code of ethics" in which reporters "delve into the personal lives of public figures and other areas once considered off limits."[49] The House had a depository for over a hundred years and the House bank has long covered overdrafts. The information would never have been disclosed in an earlier era, but in 1992, journalists reported it with a near-messianic zeal.

Reporters behave much like ordinary people who hold a strong stereotype. Exceptions to the stereotype are discounted and instances that confirm the stereotype, even if they are statistically rare, are brought to bear to prove to skeptics that "you see I was right all along." Thus, cases in which members of Congress do their jobs and act responsibly are glossed over, and when a scandal breaks, it is held up to doubting Thomases to show that "you see, they are corrupt, and this is another case that proves it."

Summary.   Congressional news increasingly emphasizes scandals, conflict, and ethical abuses. To be sure, the media cover policy issues and substantive aspects of bills that Congress is considering. It is important to note that the news focuses more on policy matters than on scandals, even today.[50] However, the trend has been toward less policy news and more news about scandals and ethical transgressions. News focuses heavily on the "horse race" aspects of Congressional issues—e.g., which side is winning the debate.[51]

This discussion has focused exclusively on the news media. If you look at radio talk show discussions of Congress, you find even more negativity. Talk-show hosts and callers are extremely critical of Congress.[52] In sum, for a variety of reasons, the picture of Congress the nation gets in the print, electronic, and even interactive media is of an institution unable to act efficiently, unwilling to consider the problems of constituents, and focused incessantly on the pursuit of personal power.

PRESCRIPTIONS

Congress is more visible to the American public than ever before, but it is also more detested and more misunderstood. In the 1940s through the 1960s, most Americans did not think enough about Congress to venture much of an opinion about the institution. That has most assuredly changed. Today most Americans hold Congress in low esteem.[53] While political scientists and historians generally believe that on the whole the members of today's Congress have better qualifications and more integrity than those who served in earlier eras, the public views Congress in decidedly different terms.[54]

Is the public's dissatisfaction with Congress a cause for concern? Perhaps not, some scholars say. Hibbing and Theiss-Morse note that even though the public holds negative attitudes toward Congress, they "recognize at a more *existential* level that a system without a legislature would be dangerously flawed."[55] But Hibbing and Theiss-Morse are quick to add that the status quo is not satisfactory. Indeed, when the public views its elected representatives as lacking in integrity, when the news media focus on the seamy side of the House and Senate, and when legislators are unable to do anything to change this situation, we have a serious problem that affects the ability of our representatives to govern effectively.

Making matters more difficult is that, as Elving points out, "Congress was designed to be awkward."[56] James Madison thought that Congress ought to move slowly and deliberately. He felt that this protected the people from their worst impulses. He would have been pleased that the House passed Contract With America legislation and that the Senate blocked some of it. He thought it was wise that one legislature could check the impulses of the other. But, as Hibbing and Theiss-Morse note:

> The public does not like overly deliberate politics. They would like to see something done quickly when in fact legislatures—particularly legislatures like the U.S. Congress—are not well-equipped for rapid action. The public prefers some degree of certainty, and when there is not certainty the public wants to believe that disputes take place on the merits of the issues. The public, for the most part, does not like the partisan debates, competing interests, and compromises that many close observers of modern democratic politics believe are unavoidable. Congress is the institution in which these distasteful elements of politics are most readily visible. Thus, while Congress is sometimes viewed by the public as an enemy, we wish to call attention to the fact that it is often viewed as an enemy *because* it is so public.[57]

How can we improve things? Scholars believe that we need a three-pronged approach: Congress must work harder to explain itself to the public; the news must do a better job of covering Congress; and citizens must gain insight into their own biases and beliefs.

Turning first to **Congress**, Elving notes that there are a number of things Congress can do to improve its self-image. He suggests that Congress:

- Schedule regular debates on major issues.
- Conduct proceedings and present legislation in plain English.
- Provide simultaneous translation and commentary on C-SPAN.
- Expand the means of transmitting Congressional proceedings (e.g., through cable and the Internet).
- Multiply the opportunities for the media to hear from and question Congressional leaders at length and in depth.
- Establish a central source of institutional information.
- Subject Congress to all laws, including workplace rules.
- Pass campaign financing reform that confronts public skepticism.[58]

The news media can also improve their coverage of Congress. Lewis Wolfson suggests that the press should do more thoughtful reporting, bringing its considerable resources to bear in helping people understand Congress. He suggests that the press should:

- Follow a policy through the bureaucracy, where guidelines for administering it are set, and then down to the grass roots. Did the legislation do what Congress intended? Were there things the lawmakers failed to foresee? Is there a need for corrective action?
- Develop programs for news executives to learn more about Congress.
- Evaluate the performance of individual members.

- Encourage members to educate the public more about what really goes on in Congress.[59]

The public can also improve its understanding of Congress. A national survey conducted by Harvard University, *The Washington Post,* and the Kaiser Foundation found that two thirds of the public did not know who represented their district in the House. Half could not say whether their representative was a Democrat or a Republican.[60] This stunning lack of knowledge forces us to question exactly what public anger at Congress really means. Some of the public's anger is real—and justified. Other aspects may reflect the public's lack of understanding of Congress or a predilection for simple explanations of a complex political scene. Thus, citizens who want to gain a better appreciation of Congress might:

- Take advantage of the Internet and new resources to communicate with legislators.
- Remember that lawmakers and their aides do read mail, and they do react to comments, particularly those of organized groups.
- Introspect to see if the sources of one's anger against Congress are rooted in decisions Congress made, Congressional corruption, or one's pet peeves that have nothing to do with Congress.
- Remember you can always vote a turkey out of office.

CONCLUSIONS

"For most of the twentieth century," Cook notes, "the way to get things done and to advance a career in Washington was to play an inside game."[61] The key to this game was developing relationships and trading favors inside Congress. It is important to point out that even in the media age, private bargaining and face to face communication still occur. Negotiations on the 1995–1996 budget impasse occurred in private and behind closed doors. The 1981 Reagan budget passed in part because Republican leaders made deals on key economic packages.[62] Legislators meet face to face with key constituents and leaders of powerful lobbying organizations. But the media are now critical players on the Congressional communication scene.

The 1970s sunshine reforms opened committee and subcommittee meetings to the press and public. C-SPAN carries Congressional hearings live. More importantly, the media provide the mechanism for legislators to reach and mobilize public opinion and to build policy agendas. The Republicans used talk radio in their effort to derail the Clinton crime bill. The White House fought Republican Congressional leaders during the 1995–1996 budget impasse with poll data that showed the public blamed the Republicans for the shut-down of government. Success in Congress now requires the use of both an inside bargaining strategy and an outside media strategy. These strategies complement each other and work together in interesting, but complex, ways.

Today Congressional communication is carried out on the public stage. Opening up Congress to the public has brought many benefits. The televised Senate Hearings on Watergate helped set the stage and prepare the nation for the House vote on impeachment. Senate hearings of Anita Hill's charges that Supreme Court nominee Clarence Thomas had sexually harassed her brought an important issue out into the open. News coverage of Rubbergate had the salutary effect of revealing Congressional perks. Yet there are no free lunches (as House members discovered in 1992!), and one of the costs of the "public Congress" is that the nation has been treated to a nonstop procession of negative images and nasty portraits of its national legislature.

There are many reasons for the predominance of negative news, including legislators' own mistakes and transgressions, the Byzantine nature of Congressional decision-making, the news media's attraction to scandal, and journalistic cynicism. Part of the problem, as Hibbing and Morse-Theiss have emphasized, is that Congressional activities have become more public, which has called attention to partisan debates and messy compromises that had hitherto been conducted in private sessions. Democracy is frequently not pretty, former House Speaker Thomas Foley has remarked. He is right, and some of the public's dissatisfaction reflects a discomfort with politics as it is played and always has been played.

And yet other dimensions of the public's dissatisfaction are understandable and on target. Happily, there are a number of ways to improve the status quo, which gives us hope that dysfunctional practices and negative attitudes can be changed.

KEY ISSUES

Constancies in Congress–Media Relations

Changes in Congress–Media Relations

Congressional Newsmaking Strategies

C-SPAN

Talk Radio

Political Marketing

Press Coverage of Congress

Negative News about Congress

Public Opinion toward Congress

DISCUSSION QUESTIONS

1. In what sense could one say that Congress and the news media need each other and are engaged in a "symbiotic relationship"?

2. Why has there been so much negative news about Congress recently?

3. Decades ago, the public held Congress in higher esteem. Have things gone downhill in the days since television shined the kleig lights on Congress or are things, on balance, better today?

9

The Media and Local Politics

When most of us think about politics, we think about the president, Congress, and the big media—the networks, *The New York Times*, *Time* Magazine, and perhaps even Rush Limbaugh. We don't think about local politics—the city or the state—and how they are covered on the news. Yet the decisions local officials make inevitably affect us. In Cleveland, Ohio, where I live, fans of the professional football team, the Cleveland Browns, threatened to do bodily harm to owner Art Modell when he disclosed that he was moving the team to Baltimore. In Philadelphia, business leaders organized a group to oppose the construction of a new convention center. Workers objected too, arguing that relocating to a new part of the city would disrupt their trips to and from work. Printer Frank Busillo went so far as to vow that he would shoot any city officials who forced him to move. "I'm going to get me a couple of .44s and sit at the back of the shop with a cowboy hat and wait for 'em," Busillo said.[1]

Not all local issues evoke such violent reactions. But they frequently involve conflicts, as when homeowners organize to oppose a school levy or people protest the decision of a fast food franchise to open up a restaurant in a quaint part of town. The mass media play an important role in covering, investigating, and "cooling down" conflict situations. Local politics does not come immediately to mind when we think about political communication, but it should. People get more exercised about many local political issues than about national issues, as those examples suggest. This makes sense when you think about it. Local issues hit close to home; they impact people's jobs, neighborhoods, and their kids' schools. Recall that politics is defined as the process whereby a group of people who initially have different interests come to collective decisions that are regarded as binding on the group (see chapter 1). City and suburban issues clearly fall under the political rubric.

This chapter examines communication and local politics. The chapter focuses on newspapers because they have traditionally played a larger role than other mass media in local politics. I also concentrate more on coverage of metropolitan than state issues because the former have attracted more scholarly interest than the latter.[2]

HISTORICAL PERSPECTIVES

Phyllis Kaniss begins her book, *Making Local News*, by discussing the historical linkage between journalism and the development of cities. Kaniss observes that:

> The link between newspapers and the growth and development of cities has often been ignored in the histories of American journalism, which have focused on the role of the press in the life of the nation … And yet, in every era of American life, journalism has been tied not simply to the life of the republic but to the conditions of the individual cities which gave birth to newspapers. The first newspapers were founded in the first cities, and new newspapers spread only as urban centers spread and created new markets with their concentrations of population … Robert Park pronounced William Randolph Hearst a "great Americanizer," but it would be more accurate to call him and the other editors the "great urbanizers," for their newspapers were instrumental in teaching the new arrivals from rural areas—whether of the United States or abroad—about how to cope in the city.[3]

Late nineteenth century and early twentieth century newspapers did more than teach immigrants how to cope in the American metropolis. Magazine writers like Lincoln Steffens, Upton Sinclair, and Ida Tarbell (the early muckrakers) exposed big-time corruption in local politics, unsafe working conditions in factories, and terrible living conditions in urban areas. They also showed how big companies had irresponsibly pursued their own interests at the expense of American workers. Their stories led to major policy reforms. Journalistic exposes, along with stories designed to help immigrants adjust to America, helped to define the mission of the metropolitan newspaper. Circulation of daily newspapers increased from 3.6 million to 24.2 million between 1880 and 1909. "The city newspaper, with its massive and diverse readership, had assumed a role as an integral urban institution," Kaniss observes.[4]

The days of crusading urban journalism are long gone, of course. Gone, too, is the metaphor of the daily newspaper as the heart of urban communication, linking citizens, elites, and government.

Over the past 50 years, there has been a dramatic decline in the number of daily papers in the United States and in the number of cites that have competing newspapers. The growth of suburbs, with the concomitant increase in the number of people working outside the central city, undermined the sense of loyalty people felt to their newspapers. Radio and television have taken away numerous national advertising accounts from newspapers. The electronic media have also captured large segments of the news audience. At the same time, suburban newspapers have grown by leaps and bounds, threatening the hold city dailies traditionally had on local advertisers. To survive, metropolitan newspapers have had to adapt. They have devised section pages to appeal to different audiences (e.g., women, teenagers, business executives), used a technique called zoning to direct different news articles and advertisements to various segments of the local market, added glitzy features like color pictures, and created home pages on the World Wide Web.

The point in reviewing history has been to emphasize that the newspaper has long been an important part of the urban system. In the best of times, it energized the system, helping to introduce new ideas. In the worst of times, it slavishly supported outmoded and unfair urban practices. But for almost two centuries, newspapers have been inextricably linked with the politics of cities and small towns.

COMMUNITY SIZE AND NEWS

Theory

The dominant paradigm for understanding the role mass media play in local politics has been functional theory. Stanley Baran and Dennis Davis explain that functional theory "assumes that a society can be usefully viewed as a 'system in balance.' That is, the society consists of complex sets of interrelated activities, each of which supports the others. Every form of social activity is assumed to play some part in maintaining the system as a whole."[5]

Back in the late 1960s, Philip Tichenor, Clarice Olien, and George Donohue adapted functional theory to explain the role newspapers play in local political issues. Tichenor and his colleagues emphasize that newspapers play an important role in helping to maintain a local system. However, the scholars contend that the particular function newspapers perform differs, depending on the size of the community.[6]

In small towns and rural communities, newspapers act primarily as boosters or cheerleaders for local government. Editors see their role as helping the town grow and prosper. Tichenor et al. argued that in these small communities newspapers are apt to downplay conflict and to provide relatively little coverage of disputes among government leaders or between ordinary people and government.

Conflict coverage is rare for several reasons. First, small towns tend to be relatively homogeneous: people share similar political and religious values and often come from similar ethnic backgrounds. There simply is not as much conflict in small towns as there is in big cities, which have much more diverse populations. Furthermore, small-town publishers simply cannot afford to alienate the leading businesses in town. The newspapers are dependent on these companies for advertising, and publishers need their good will. "A newspaper in a one-industry town is unlikely to report that industry in a critical way," Tichenor and his colleagues point out.[7]

Tichenor and his associates also argue that in small towns, conflicts are frequently worked out interpersonally, before the media get wind of the dispute. There *is* conflict in small towns; people do disagree with one another. However, because most people know one another, they feel comfortable talking with each other about policy disagreements, at least minor ones. The owner of a local stationery store may call up the mayor and explain why he or she opposes a proposed change in the zoning ordinance that would allow a fast-food restaurant to open up next door. Group norms and interpersonal conflict-resolution strategies are brought to bear to contain the conflicts, so that when the newspaper reports the story, it describes an orderly and consensual set of decisions and activities.[8]

Another reason why one should not expect small-town weeklies to print much conflict information is that small communities are not structurally equipped to deal with open expressions of conflict. Conflict is seen as imperiling community solidarity.[9] The town lacks the social structures necessary to accommodate conflict; there are few organized opposition groups or institutions that mediate between the mayor's office and the larger community. Thus, during the 1950s, African-American residents of small Southern towns had no organized mechanism to express their outrage at racial segregation. The local newspaper was no help because the editor and publisher saw their roles as supporting community leaders and reinforcing the status quo.

Tichenor and his colleagues emphasize that big city newspapers serve a different function for the community. Conflict is endemic to urban areas, characterized as they are by large, heterogeneous populations, specialization of roles, numerous interest groups, and frustrations caused by disparities in wealth and status. City leaders find it more difficult than small-town mayors to resolve conflicts through interpersonal channels. As a result, they must rely on formal media channels to work out conflicts. David Demers notes that:

> Decision-making (in cities) is expected to take into account diverse perspectives and views, and such communities are structurally organized to deal with conflict, having mechanisms such as boards of inquiry (e.g., racial discrimination commissions, civilian police review boards), formal labor– management negotiators, formalized grievance procedures, and administrative law judges. Although stories and editorials that contain conflict or criticism are often viewed as threatening to the social order, such stories often play a significant role in contributing to system stability because they introduce alternative ideas or innovations that enable organizations and institutions to adapt to changing conditions.[10]

Thus, it is argued that big-city newspapers perform a different function in the community than do small-town papers. In larger, more pluralistic communities, newspapers operate more on a conflict than consensus model.[11] They call attention to social problems and provide feedback to political groups. According to functional theory, metropolitan newspapers help to maintain the system by bringing conflicts out into the open, giving dissident groups a chance to express their points of view, and providing a forum for elites to work out their differences. Tichenor, Donohue, and Olien's model is interesting because it suggests that newspapers can perform very different functions for communities, depending on how big and diverse the community is. One newspaper may stifle conflict, another may embrace it, and this is quite consistent with the model. As functional theorists, Tichenor and his colleagues believe that, in general, newspapers do more to promote and maintain the system than to change it.

Research Evidence

Many studies have examined the relationship between community structure and newspaper content. Research indicates that, as functional theory would predict, small-town newspapers tend to act as cheerleaders and consensus-builders for local government. For example, in Ripley, Ohio (population 2,500), the major cash crop is tobacco. The town hosts the Ohio Tobacco Festival, which attracted 30,000 visitors a few years ago. The 4-day fair is a major event in the sleepy Ohio town. Banks and schools close early. If this event happened in a big city, the newspaper might prominently feature the comments of anti-tobacco activists who protested the event. But in Ripley, Ohio, the school's drug and alcohol prevention officer worked as a volunteer in the main information booth, and the town's newspaper, *The Ripley Bee*, gave out free copies of the paper.[12]

Small-town and small-city newspapers tend to gloss over potential conflicts in government policies.[13] For example, David Paletz and his students compared coverage of city council meetings in *The Durham Morning Herald* with what actually occurred at council meetings in the North Carolina town.[14] The researchers noted that a large group of citizens attended one council meeting to indicate their displeasure with a proposed public housing project. Their objections led to a procedural debate among council members. When one council member said that public housing did not come under council's jurisdiction, the protesters booed and screamed. A similar suggestion by another council member led to more verbal protests from the audience. Yet the story that appeared in the newspaper portrayed the council meeting as an orderly and tidy affair:

> The respectful tone which characterizes coverage of the council stems from the reporter's belief (which is of course widely shared) that those in authority should be written about with respect (often whether they are worthy of such treatment or not) … As a result, the Durham City Council is depicted as an authority-wielding body which is organized to deal with problems efficiently; which is responsive to the needs of the people without succumbing to pressure; and which reaches its collective decisions in an impersonal, depersonalized way. Consequently, psychological distance is maintained between the council and its members, on the one hand, and the public, on the other; and the council's authority is reinforced.[15]

By contrast, big-city dailies contain a great deal of conflict information.[16] Articles describe city council members' frustration with the mayor. Front-page stories reveal how city officials mismanage public funds. News stories regularly describe conflicts between community groups and the city. In an in-depth study of Philadelphia newspaper coverage of a proposed city convention center, Kaniss found that the metropolitan newspapers initially provided positive coverage of the center; the papers stressed that the center would bring jobs and increased revenues to the city. Then when opposition groups organized, the news turned negative. It got even more negative as reporters searched for scandal and found possible conflict of interest and improprieties related to the convention center plan.[17]

Thus, the functionally oriented approach proposed by Tichenor and his colleagues receives support from empirical studies. The findings suggest that metropolitan newspapers perform important functions for cities by playing up conflict and providing a forum for city leaders, elites, and opposition

groups to "work through" conflict. Small-town newspapers perform functions for their communities by building community solidarity, giving people
pride in their home towns, and by helping to preserve traditions and rituals.
On the other hand, small-town papers' tendency to play down conflict can
be dysfunctional if it leads dissenters to express conflict in socially unaccept-
able ways or if it slows the diffusion of new ideas.

COMPLICATING FACTORS

Boosterism in the Metropolitan Press

It is time to muddy the waters by introducing some of the complexities and
subtle aspects of newspaper coverage of city developments.

Although metropolitan newspapers are much more apt to criticize local
government than small-town papers, they are not the crusading muckrakers
that Hollywood movie makers make them out to be. In fact, case study
investigations of metropolitan newspapers reveal that these papers are much
more likely to provide favorable coverage of new civic projects than is
commonly assumed. Recent research indicates that we need to update the
picture of the metropolitan press that early functional theorists provided by
considering the ways in which newspapers are adapting their formats to deal
with the changing social and economic environment.

Kaniss argues that metropolitan newspapers and electronic media have
a decided bias in favor of regional economic growth. She notes that:

> Since the news firm's profits are dependent on audience size and advertising revenues,
> the greater the total population of the locality and the healthier the economy, the
> more potential readers or viewers and advertisers the news firm can hope to attract.
> Such growth is particularly important to the metropolitan newspaper, which faces
> great economies of scale within its regional market ... As a result of this interest in
> growth, it is argued, the local news media often take on the role of a booster, much
> like an arm of the local chamber of commerce, actively promoting the kinds of policies
> and projects that would generate economic growth of the area. According to this
> theory, publishers or media owners at times muzzle their reporters' critical coverage
> of certain sacred cow public development projects that may promote growth at the
> expense of environmental quality or the sacrifice of other socially valuable uses of
> public funds.[18]

Sociologist Edward Banfield uncovered this phenomena back in 1961.
He probed the reasons why *The Chicago Tribune* strongly supported construction of a new downtown convention center. At one point Banfield

asked a *Tribune* editor why the newspaper worked so hard to mobilize support for the center. The editor responded:

> Why did we put so much time into this? Because it's good for the city. But partly from selfish motives too. We want to build a bigger Chicago and a bigger *Tribune*. We want more circulation and more advertising. We want to keep growing, and we want the city to keep growing so that we can keep growing.[18]

The idea that "what is good for the city is good for the newspaper" continues today, perhaps even more so in view of the many economic pressures on newspapers. The *San Jose Mercury* actively supported an airport construction project, even though there were adverse environmental consequences. The editors reasoned that the airport would promote air travel, which would help the region and also lead to an increase in airline advertising.

The Los Angeles Times backed a downtown redevelopment project, despite criticism that it was a "tax rip-off" that provided considerable assistance to downtown economic interests at the expense of the region as a whole. The newspaper editorialized that "Any city—and especially a city as spread out as Los Angeles—is as healthy as the sum of its parts."[20] In Cleveland, *The Plain Dealer* invariably supports the construction of new downtown projects. In particular, it provided enthusiastic and favorable coverage of a downtown sports arena and, of course, of the Rock and Roll Hall of Fame.

Newspapers have historically been identified with the city, so it should not surprise us that editors view the growth of the city in positive terms. There are certainly positive aspects of cities and good reasons to support their growth and development. However, there are other reasons why newspapers are apt to favor downtown development projects. Kaniss argues that the bias in favor of regional economic growth has its roots in economic factors and news media routines.

First, playing up civic projects can help attract suburban readers to the newspaper. But why would articles that play up downtown developments attract suburban readers? After all, they don't live in the city. The answer, Kaniss says, is that "the city is the only source of symbolism capable of drawing together the fragmented suburban market. However ironic, the city that many suburbanites rarely venture into is often the only thing they all have in common."[21] Playing up civic projects can resuscitate suburban readers' pride in the city and rekindle old-timers' memories of the city of their youth. Downtown boosterism can thus create a symbolic bond between the newspaper and suburban readers. It can enhance their identification with the city and, by extension, with the newspaper that bears the city's name.

A second reason why downtown developments get good press has its roots in reporters' dependence on city officials for their information. City officials, whose livelihood depends upon the health of the center city, can be expected to speak positively about new projects. Journalists gravitate to these official sources, as noted in chapter 5, because they are believable, provide information reliably on deadline, and are conveniently located near newspaper offices.

Third, journalists tend to accept official estimates of project costs and benefits. Kaniss notes that city planners rely on *multipliers* to estimate how many jobs will be produced by the project and how much tax revenue the project will generate. Officials also use formulas to estimate project costs. Kaniss explains:

> The choice of a multiplier of 3.5—suggesting that for every one direct job created by the project, three and one-half indirect jobs will also be generated—may indicate a surplus of benefits over costs of a new project, where the selection of a multiplier of 1.5 would not. By employing a high multiplier when estimating the impacts of a new project, a city official or city-paid consultant could therefore increase the estimated benefits of the project ... While these assumptions are crucial to the evaluation of a major project, reporters are not trained to question estimates of multipliers or inflation rates the way they are trained to probe into official acceptance of favors. For example, in covering urban renewal and redevelopment, reporters have been described as "baffled by the technical questions involved," and they are, therefore, forced to rely on local officials to explain new proposals.[22]

For example, in Philadelphia, both city newspapers accepted local officials' estimates of costs and benefits of a proposed convention center. A consulting firm's estimate that the project would cost $130 million was accepted unquestionably; subsequently, officials revised the estimate to approximately $400 million, a discrepancy of $270 million.[23]

OTHER MEDIA

Television

News is a money-maker for local TV stations; in fact, it is the major source of revenue for many local affiliates. Consequently, stations are exquisitely sensitive to attracting viewers. The more viewers a station can attract, the more money it can charge advertisers. The name of the game is ratings—estimates of the number of households tuned into a news program at a particular time. Station managers believe that success in the ratings war comes from drama and emotion ("If it bleeds, it leads") and from timeliness and rapid pacing. Longer newspaper-style coverage of city issues is simply out of the question in the competitive world of television news. Producers eschew it and, in truth, so do many viewers.

One local TV reporter summed up TV's emphasis on brevity and emotion rather nicely by citing this hypothetical situation:

> Suppose I had this great story, an exclusive from the Pope saying that God was a Woman, and I'm the only reporter to get the Pope on tape making this pronouncement. You know what my news director would say to me after my package aired? Good story, definitely a winner, but you spent too much time on the Pope talking. The package really needed some video of God.[24]

Television news does cover local government. And it does focus on such issues as the budget, schools, and elections. However, television is more likely to focus on the "human" side of government—such as how city cutbacks affect elderly residents—than on complex aspects of government policies. When government stories are covered, they are described briefly, in headline-service fashion, and always with appealing visuals. Conflict and disagreements among officials or between officials and citizens groups are favored because these are believed to capture audience attention. Moreover, local television is even more likely than newspapers to accept the viewpoints of local officials.[25]

When local officials favor a project, local TV news becomes a booster, showcasing project benefits with visuals and entertaining footage. But when elites strongly oppose a project, the news is apt to provide much more negative coverage. In either case, television news focuses more on drama and emotion than on the political, economic, and historical issues that underlie the debate. The day-to-day business of local government gets relatively little coverage on local television news. Instead, crime-related stories—murders, investigations of homicides, people's fear of walking the streets—receive considerable attention on TV news. In fact, Kaniss found that crime stories, fires, and accidents received equal or more airtime than local government and policy issues.[26]

Other Media Outlets

The big-city newspaper and local television news are not the only sources of information about local government. Today, citizens can find discussions about local government on **talk radio** (invariably negative and caustic, but always entertaining). Talk radio, as Ralph Nader said, is "the working people's medium. There's no ticket of admission. You only have to dial."[27] Thus, talk radio can serve important functions for people who feel alienated and closed off by elite media.

Another important local media outlet is **the suburban press.** More than one in three weekly newspapers are now published in suburban communities.[28] Suburban papers are able to cover community issues, such as school levies and neighborhood development projects, that are too narrowly focused for metropolitan dailies. In form and function, suburban newspapers are a cross between the consensus-oriented small-town papers and the conflict-ridden metropolitan dailies (which, as we have seen, resist reporting conflict under certain conditions themselves). Thus suburban papers give good press to high school sports heroes, which serves to promote community solidarity; at the same time, they cover neighborhood school controversies, which (at least in theory) allows the community to work out some of its conflicts.

Finally, there are a host of **city magazines, specialized newspapers, cable television stations, radio stations, and Web sites** that serve ethnic and religious groups, new immigrants, and people with alternative lifestyles. Many big cities have Jewish, Black, Hispanic, Asian immigrant, and gay newspapers. These alternative newspapers give people who have traditionally been victims of prejudice an outlet to express their feelings and concerns. Alternative newspapers typically make no pretense of being objective; many have their roots in the underground, advocacy press of the 1960s.[29]

Critics have noted that some alternative weekly papers shy away from reporting conflicts in their own communities. For example, Jewish weeklies avoid covering conflicts among Jewish fund-raising groups, Black newspapers stop short of criticizing controversial African-American leaders like Louis Farrakhan, and gay newspapers downplayed the health hazards of gay bathhouses in the 1980s. Like the small-town weeklies that Tichenor and his colleagues studied, these papers perform consensus-building rather than conflict-management functions.

Alternative newspapers can have a significant influence on political opinions. For example, gay newspapers often command a loyal following in the gay community. If a gay paper decides to target a political candidate during an election campaign for insensitive statements he or she made about gays, the article might influence readers' attitudes toward the politician, perhaps causing some to vote against the candidate.

CITY OFFICIALS AND THE NEWS

In previous chapters I discussed ways that national leaders try to secure positive press. Many of the same techniques are used by local leaders, except local leaders have fewer resources at their disposal.

Local officials scrutinize the media and cultivate reporters. They use the media to set agendas, influence policies, and to create positive images of themselves. Officials recognize that the media can be used to reach masses of people, specific constituencies, and other political elites.

To reach the masses, a mayor may release information through news releases and press conferences. Mayors use press conferences to announce policy initiatives and to float "trial balloons"—ideas that are deliberately leaked to assess public or elite reactions. They also hold press conferences to take credit for events and to deflect attention from problems. Cleveland Mayor Michael White exploited press conferences for these purposes in 1995 when Art Modell, owner of the professional football team, the Cleveland Browns, announced he was moving the team to Baltimore. White used press conferences to disclose his plans to sue Modell to keep the Browns in Cleveland. He also employed news conferences—and symbolic acts like meeting with National Football League officials—to deflect attention from pressing city problems in the police and health departments.[30]

Local officials also use the media to reach specific constituent groups. A mayor will want neighborhood residents to know that a proposal to convert a neighborhood street into a mall has received state funding. The mayor will rely on local media to publicize this accomplishment.

Local leaders also rely on the media to reach other elites. A police official may leak information about contract negotiations to help gain concessions from the union. The head of a city council may divulge a plan to cut a certain portion of the budget to test-market the idea with key civic and corporate leaders. Or a city official may leak information to settle a political grudge or to discredit a member of the administration. Naturally, some local officials and mayors are better at media manipulation than others.

Community groups also use the metropolitan media to advance their objectives. Although these groups lack the political clout and access to key reporters that government officials possess, they have become increasingly adept at using television news to capture public attention. Citizens groups have found that protests can attract the attention of television news reporters. However, such attention is typically short-lived—here today, gone tomorrow, while the problems that beset communities continue.[31]

CONSENSUS, CONFLICT, AND PUBLIC OPINION

One of the teeming issues in mass communication scholarship is whether the local media reflect and uphold the status quo, as hegemonic theorists suggest, or whether they are relentless critics of local government, as democratic theory (and thin-skinned local officials) argue. There is no simple answer to this question, because the news media are both city boosters and government critics.

As noted earlier, metropolitan newspapers are apt to give positive press to the construction of downtown developments. Consensus building frequently trumps conflict management. But conflict does not stay out of the metropolitan newspaper for long. In Cleveland, the local newspaper supported the construction of a downtown sports arena, no doubt accepting city officials' rosy predictions and multipliers. Several years later, when the arena had been constructed, and it turned out that the project cost the city $30 million more than expected, the local paper was filled with stories covering the scandal. Critics wondered why the newspaper had taken so long to criticize the project.

The Cleveland case is typical of newspaper coverage of regional developments. Newspapers initially provide positive coverage of these projects for the reasons noted earlier in the chapter. Coverage typically becomes negative when elite consensus breaks down. When members of corporate and civic elites become disillusioned with the project, or research reports commissioned by the city question initial estimates of costs and benefits, or influential community groups oppose the plan, the newspaper will dutifully report these developments. In such cases, the source routine favors the reporting of conflict information. Thus, as Bennett notes, journalists "tend to index the voices and viewpoints in stories to the range of official debate available to reporters on the news beats of decision-making institutions of government."[32]

While the public is usually a bystander in big-city policy debates, it can get into the act on issues that arouse strong community sentiments. Public opinion and news media interpretation of that opinion can influence coverage of local issues. One issue that arouses strong public passions is sports—the performance of local sports teams, the construction of new sports stadiums, and media coverage of popular sports heroes. Sports is one of the few sacred cows left in the realm of reporting; local news media are not expected to be objective about the city's baseball, basketball, or football teams. They are expected to be team boosters. A newspaper that did a series criticizing the management decisions of the city's World Series-winning baseball team would be a newspaper destined for extinction.

Yet there *are* cases in which press coverage of sports teams favors conflict over consensus. When owners of professional sports franchises make decisions that enrage large numbers of citizens, the media become populists, carrying the banner of the masses. A classic example of this type of coverage occurred in Cleveland a few years back when Art Modell announced that he was moving the Cleveland Browns to Baltimore. Modell claimed he was losing money on the Browns in Cleveland and said he was fed up with the city's failure to develop an adequate stadium renovation package. The owner announced the decision toward the end of a county-wide campaign to pass a "sin tax" on alcohol and tobacco products that would help pay for renovations to the football stadium.

Modell's decision enraged residents of Cleveland and the surrounding suburbs. Fans felt betrayed by Modell. Many questioned his claim that he was losing money and denounced him for conducting secret negotiations with Baltimore officials when voters were, in good faith, considering the merits of a sin tax that would renovate Cleveland Stadium. The public let its feelings be known soon after the story leaked out. Callers besieged radio talk shows; citizens groups organized campaigns to persuade the National Football League to oppose Modell's decision, anti-Modell signs appeared on major city thoroughfares.

The local media joined the barricades. Talk-show radio hosts denounced Modell, using intense language to express their feelings. *The Free Times*, the city's alternative newspaper, put on its cover a picture of a hand dropping a cigarette butt into a football stadium. The caption was "Hey Art! This butt's for you!" The daily newspaper, *The Plain Dealer*, blasted Modell in its editorials. It printed the phone and fax numbers of the National Football League to assist fans who wanted to register their opposition to Modell's decision.. One article even printed a song from a reader who lamented the move to Baltimore:

> **Artie, Don't Take My**
>
> **Cleveland Browns**
>
> (To the tune of "Ruby, Don't
>
> Take Your Love to Town")
>
> You've painted up your limousine

and sprayed your silver hair.

Artie, are you contemplating moving

out somewhere?

The writing on the wall tells me the deal

is going down.

Oh Artie ... don't take my Cleveland Browns ...

It's hard to love a Stadium

that's old and in demise.

And the wants and the greed of an owner your

age, Artie I realize.

But it won't be long, I've heard them say, until

you're leaving town.

Oh Artie . . . don't take my Cleveland Browns.[33]

Not all coverage in The Plain Dealer was this negative. Stories compared the offers from Baltimore and Cleveland, analyzed the reasons for Modell's decision to move the team, and even profiled the positive things the Browns' owner had done for the city. But the bulk of the discourse in the print and electronic media was critical of the Browns' owner.

Modell received negative press for many reasons, including the abrupt way he announced his decision, the massive public outcry, and the opposition from elite civic and business leaders who recognized that the Browns brought money and political clout to Cleveland. At the same time, the Cleveland mayor displayed a sophisticated appreciation of media routines as he held public rallies and mounted a legal challenge to the Browns' owner's decision to move to Baltimore. (The National Football League ultimately decided to permit Modell to move the team to Baltimore, but paved the way for Cleveland to get a new professional football team by 1999.) The mayor's public relations and rhetorical strategies netted him a great deal of positive press. Thus the local media skewered one member of the community elite—the Browns' owner—and elevated another—the city's mayor.

The Browns case and others discussed in this chapter indicate that there is no simple hegemony of media. Under normal conditions, big city newspapers contain a great deal of conflict and criticism. Local television is filled with negative news, although the stories focus less on the crimes of the system than on illegal actions of individuals. Talk radio is a bastion of what Howard Kurtz calls "raunchy talk, smug talk, self-serving talk, funny talk, (and) rumor-mongering talk."[34] Suburban weeklies and alternative newspapers regularly feature criticism of local officials and local government actions.

And yet, it must be said that for all the conflict reporting, big-city news media rarely criticize downtown developments in their formative stages. In fact, case study investigations indicate that the local media, particularly newspapers, act as cheerleaders for these developments in much the same way that small-town weeklies favor the projects proposed by their government leaders. To be sure, there is more conflict reporting in big-city newspapers than in small-town weeklies, but much of this occurs after—rather than before—powerful elites come to blows on the issues. Even in large communities, local media need the economic and political support of political leaders. Survival, particularly in an era in which the mass media are facing new economic challenges, demands that the media cooperate to some extent with civic and corporate leaders.

In sum, the news media perform diverse functions for big-city government, business interests, and the public. They build consensus and allow elites to communicate with another. However, the media also report conflict, provide a forum for public debate, and, as Kenneth Byerly notes, serve "as a unifying force in a community."[35]

On the individual level, they inform and entertain, and provide news consumers with a host of gratifications.[36] Conventional functional theory assumes that whatever the media do is good because it helps preserve the system. Scholars today would not agree with this claim. Olien, Donohue, and Tichenor have gone so far as to suggest that the local media behave more like "guard dogs" of the elite establishment than as the fabled watchdog that, as classic democratic theory had it, sat "in perpetual watch over the nobility, the church, and the popular representatives, goading them to be responsive to their constituent interest."[37] The media, they emphasize, "are dependent upon power relationships," adding that "power relationships tend to maintain themselves, and media are part of this maintenance process."[38]

Yet, somehow, through processes we do not totally understand, social change occurs—African Americans become mayors of major cities, neighborhoods refuse to accept hazardous waste sites, and communities accept the concept of home schooling, where parents educate their children at home rather than sending them to public schools. The local media have a significant impact on the social change process by introducing new ideas, creating a dialogue that puts increased pressure on community institutions to change, and by legitimizing changes that occur.[39] The news media reinforce the status quo and they change it. There is a tension between theories that emphasize system maintenance and those that focus on political change. There are no simple answers to questions about the media's impact on local government systems.

CRITICISMS AND SUGGESTIONS

There is little doubt that the news media play a vital role in urban and suburban communities. It is hard to imagine life in a city without a newspaper or in the absence of talk radio or local television news. As we have seen, the media perform important functions for communities, although the nature of their role differs, depending on the size and pluralism of the community. Yet we must resist proclaiming, with Voltaire, that this is the best of all possible worlds of local news coverage. Press critic Lewis Wolfson puts his finger on the main problems of news coverage of local government when he observes:

> The media as a whole are not interested in ideas and process—in how government gets from point A to point B in dealing with public problems or how it should get there. They focus on spot-news events and personalities ... Few news organizations will regularly probe the structure of local government and what influences policymaking. They don't consistently ask: What forces in the community affect the setting of policy? Are the policies developed practical and realistic? Is local government equipped to carry out decisions effectively? Does it solve problems or create new ones? Can a particular problem be solved by government, or are we all prisoners of politicians' promises and our own impractical expectations? Should the system be changed? Such careful exploring of officials' approach to decision making may not be many journalists' idea of "hot" news, but it may tell the real story of local government's successes and failures.[40]

Wolfson's criticism follows a long tradition of scholarly pleas for more policy-oriented and issue-based reporting. It is always easier to criticize current practices than to implement new ones, and in fairness it must be said that attempts at more policy-oriented reporting run the risk of turning off news consumers, who are frequently not interested in getting beyond the headlines or who have never developed much of an interest in local news. But today, when the federal government is transferring power to states and local municipalities, there is a pressing need for more in-depth local reporting.

Another approach to local reporting is **public journalism.** Public journalism advocates argue that news organizations have lost touch with the communities they serve. They contend that local news outlets spend too much time covering inside political games and too little on issues that genuinely concern community residents. They urge local media outlets to work harder at linking up with community residents; news organizations, they note, should find out what is on citizens' minds and then work with citizens and community leaders to solve pressing community issues. According to Jay Rosen, public journalism refers to *"an approach to journalism that tries to engage citizens in public life, improve public discussion, and reconnect journalists to the communities they serve."*[41] As the name suggests, public journalism focuses on the concerns of the public rather than on agendas put forth by elites.

Over 170 newspapers have conducted public journalism projects. For example, in the wake of concern that the 1988 presidential election campaign had been too negative and had intensified political cynicism, *The Charlotte* (North Carolina) *Observer* and *The Wichita* (Kansas) *Eagle* turned to voters to ask them what they wanted to see in the way of campaign coverage and what they thought the critical issues in the 1992 campaign were. The newpapers then provided in-depth coverage of the issues readers thought were most important and described candidates' positions on these issues.

A Dayton newspaper helped the community cope with a series of homicides committed by young people by setting up more than 400 family roundtables where family members discussed the problem over a lunch provided by the newspaper. The newspaper also published an eight-part series on youth violence, and included a resource guide for concerned parents.[42]

While such projects are laudable, we don't know what effect they had on communities and whether they actually achieved their objectives. Critics worry that public journalism will become a substitute for hard-hitting investigative reporting or for the type of news analysis that scholars like Wolfson have suggested. Others point out that the public is not informed on some issues and by asking the public its opinions, the news media run the risk of providing readers with a relatively unenlightened perspective on political issues. Still, in an era in which newspapers face declining reader-ship, most observers feel that any technique that can put the public back in touch with its newspapers has more benefits than costs.

CONCLUSIONS

I began this chapter by noting that most of us don't think about local issues when we ruminate about politics. Hopefully, the chapter has convinced you that there are interesting and important local political issues and that the news media play an important role in local government.

Functional theoretical approaches have dominated research on the me-dia and local politics. Research shows that small-town weeklies act as boosters or cheerleaders for local government. Metropolitan dailies are more apt to contain conflict and criticism of government. However, when it comes to covering regional developments, big-city editors act as partisans, and provide flattering portraits of these projects, at least in the initial stages.

Today's big-city media scene is diverse and complex. Local television stations cover government, although they typically focus on drama and emotion and are apt to take the viewpoints of city leaders. Talk radio, city magazines, suburban newspapers, alternative papers, and, increasingly, World Wide Web sites are part of the local media scene. City officials recognize that they must use the media to accomplish their policy objectives and personal goals.

One of the controversial issues in political communication research is whether the news media promote or undermine existing institutions. Re-search on local news makes it clear that the local media help to maintain existing power arrangements. Yet when the seeds for change have been sown by innovative leaders, the media can help speed the process of social change, and they can legitimize new ideas.

In the final analysis, what was true in the 1890s, during the era of growth of urban newspapers, remains true a century later: The mass media are vital community institutions, playing a host of roles in the community, helping to support and at times change existing power arrangements, and, perhaps most significantly, providing residents with a symbolic link to the larger community.

KEY ISSUES

Functional Theory

Conflict versus Consensus Coverage

Small Town versus Metropolitan Newspapers

Boosterism in the Big-City Press

City Officials' Use of Media

Public Journalism

Improving Coverage of Local Politics

DISCUSSION QUESTIONS

1.   Why do small-town newspapers act more as boosters than critics of local government? Do you think that this trend has changed in recent years?

2.   What are the benefits of metropolitan newspapers' emphasis on conflict information?

3.   Think of a controversial issue you saw covered in a local newspaper or on local TV. To what extent did the coverage favor the powers-that-be, and to what extent did it critique the government position? How do the principles discussed in this chapter help you understand this issue?

II

POLITICAL COMMUNICATION THEORIES AND EFFECTS

10

Political Communication Effects

What impact do political communications have on people? Do they change attitudes? What effect does news have on public opinion? Can it move public opinion, or are people's opinions impervious to change?

This chapter and the ones that follow examine these questions as I introduce one of the central issues in political communication research—the impact of political media on individuals. The chapter begins with a discussion of the historical origins of the field, moves to a description of the classic research, along with criticisms of the research, and concludes by introducing the major theoretical perspectives on political communication effects.

The chapters in this portion of the book differ from those in the first section in that they derive from social science theory and methods. Our interest in this section of the book and in the third section, which focuses on elections, is the impact of political communications on people. So get ready as we discuss theory, evidence, and the many ins and outs of classic and contemporary studies of political communication. First, though, a foray into history—specifically, the aftershocks of George Creel's World War I propaganda campaign.

THE STUDY OF PROPAGANDA

President Woodrow Wilson faced a problem in 1917: how to persuade Americans that a far-off war in Europe was worth fighting, and that Allied soldiers faced a venal and brutal enemy. Wilson turned to journalist George Creel, who left no stone unturned in his attempt to convince the mass public that World War I was a just and noble cause. His Committee on Public

Information (CPI) embarked on what J. Michael Sproule called "an all-pervasive system of communication that touched citizens at every possible point in their lives."[1] Sproule notes that:

> The influence of the CPI was felt in the daily routines of Americans. In the workplace, and on the streetcar and train, the worker would likely glance at CPI war posters and would often find in his or her pay envelope a pro-war flyer ... During the weekly trip to the movie house, the citizen and his family might occasionally watch one of the CPI's several war films, which enjoyed blanket bookings, and probably would listen to one of the CPI's 75,000 official Four Minute Men speakers who delivered short talks to audiences based on weekly themes set in Washington.[2]

There was more, as I noted in chapter 2. Newspaper articles depended heavily on information provided by CPI officials. In 1917, Congress passed an Espionage Act that allowed the government to fine or imprison individuals who intentionally made false statements with the goal of interfering with military operations. During the first year of the Act, 75 newspapers, including many Socialist and German language papers, lost their mailing privileges or retained them only by pledging not to publish any more information about the war.

The public supported the war, but after the armistice was signed in 1918, doubts began to surface. Critic Michael Reynolds observed that "the old values—love, honor, duty, truth— were bankrupted by a war that systematically killed off a generation of European men and permanently scarred Americans."[3] Novelist Ernest Hemingway described the psychic and physical wounds of the war in *The Sun Also Rises*.

At the same time, scholars expressed considerable concern about the impact of Creel's war-time campaign to mold public sentiments. The distortions and half-truths Creel employed in the service of the Wilson administration came under attack. Scholars believe that after the war was over, the public became increasingly disillusioned by the heavy human costs of the war, and that this disillusionment helped to make people more open to reporters' revelations that they had voluntarily written stories so as to make the American side seem more heroic than it actually had been. Looking back on post-World War I America, Sproule observes that "A new image of modern propaganda began to emerge as Americans understood how the mass media might be captured by spokesmen whose unchallenged facts could better be characterized as distortions."[4]

Leading intellectuals like John Dewey, Walter Lippmann, and Harold Lasswell expressed concern about the ability of media and government to manipulate news and information. In 1927 Lasswell wrote a book that examined how propagandistic techniques had been used during the first world war. Two years later Ralph Casey completed a dissertation at the University of Wisconsin on the effects of campaign communication. He modeled his study after Lasswell's book. While Lasswell called his book *Propaganda technique in the world war*, Casey titled his dissertation, *Propaganda technique in the 1928 election campaign*.

It is important to emphasize that these writers (e.g.., Lasswell) were making assumptions about the impact of propaganda campaigns. In those days, no one was conducting empirical studies of public opinion, so we really don't know how effective Creel's campaign or other propaganda campaigns of the era were. In addition, most Americans were probably unaware of the intellectuals' criticisms of the CPI and the war. It is likely that many Americans were proud of what the government had done to mobilize mass opinion and were relieved that the Germans had been vanquished.[5] Yet troubling questions about the war lingered, as scholars discussed the human and emotional costs of the war, the irrelevance of nineteenth-century concepts like glory and honor, and the ability of leaders to use deceptive media techniques to manipulate the masses. A new scholarly movement devoted to the exploration of propaganda was gaining adherents.[6]

At the same time, there was a growing interest among university researchers in the scientific study of attitudes, public opinion, and persuasion. Psychologists Louis Thurstone and Rensis Likert developed ways to empirically measure attitudes.[7] In 1937, Columbia University began publishing a new journal, *Public Opinion Quarterly*, which explored how scientific methods could shed light on the formation of political opinions. In the same year, the Institute for Propaganda Analysis was formed. Its scholars began to systematically examine the new and heinous forms of propaganda that were now making their way across the world, particularly in Hitler's Germany. There was also concern about the Ku Klux Klan, fascist groups in America, and Father Charles Coughlin, who used his weekly radio program to attack Wall Street, President Roosevelt, Communism, and Jews.

But in America, one person's poison can be another's meat. As humanists and social scientists lamented that propaganda could manipulate the masses, experts in the new field of public relations rejoiced in the revelation that new media techniques could be used to promote products and ideals. Edward Bernays, viewed as the founder of the modern field of public relations, cashed in on the insights of his uncle, Sigmund Freud, using the techniques of Freudian psychology to persuade the mass public to buy products and support American corporations.

Bernays worked for a time as a consultant to the American Tobacco Company. His job was to make inroads in the new expanding market of the 1920s and 1930s: women. After discussing the matter with a leading psychiatrist, Bernays decided that cigarettes represented "torches of freedom" to women, who were just breaking out of the shackles of nineteenth-century oppression. Bernays suggested to a wealthy woman he knew that she ask a group of her debutante friends to walk from 34th Street to 57th Street in New York City with cigarettes in hand. He also suggested that she contact the news media to tell them of her plans. She did, and the parade of women marching uptown, holding "torches of freedom," was an overnight success for women and the American Tobacco Company.

Bernays wrote several books on the subject of the management of public opinion, which he called "the engineering of consent." But while the title of the book suggested he was allied with the critical humanists, Bernays' theme was more middle-of-the-road. He argued that public relations specialists could occupy the middle ground between the mass public and business. Public relations, he contended, could make business more responsive to the public interest. And, to Bernays' credit, as early as 1923 he urged "ethical self-monitoring" by communication specialists as a way to guard against the potential misuses and abuses of modern social influence techniques.[8]

So, the world was changing and communication seemed to be both a blessing and a curse. America's experience with World War I propaganda left the country with an ambivalence about political communication that remains to this day. We are impressed by mass communications—awed by their power, but anxious about their effects. We marvel at their ability to promote causes and sell products, but we worry about their impact on vulnerable members of the audience.

PROPAGANDA AND COMMUNICATION RESEARCH

The early scholars of propaganda emphasized its negative aspects and, as I have noted, worried about its negative effects.[9] (See endnote 6 for a definition of propaganda). The scholarly study of propaganda was in vogue in the 1920s and 1930s; yet by the early 1940s, it had fallen out of favor. Social scientists preferred to look more dispassionately at phenomena, and tended to favor framing issues in terms of the effects of "communication" on attitudes or the role "public opinion" plays in a democracy.[10] In addition, with Europe engulfed by war and the Nazis threatening free people everywhere, it was difficult to keep hammering away at the deficiencies of the United States power structure and the impact of government propaganda campaigns.

During World War II, psychologists and sociologists conducted studies of the impact of war-time communications, such as the U.S. Army's *Why We Fight* films. The *Why We Fight* movies were developed by movie director Frank Capra of *It's A Wonderful Life* fame. Capra produced seven documentary films that were shown to hundreds of thousands of American soldiers. They were designed to explain why the Allied cause was just, to increase soldiers' resentment of the enemy, and to strengthen their motivation to fight the good fight. The films, and other war-time persuasive communications, were designed to achieve the same goals as Creel's CPI messages had sought to attain. However, the overall thrust of the World War II campaign was softer and more subtle, and it relied more on the empirical techniques of social science.

While some social scientists were working for the government during the second world war, others were out there in the heartlands, testing a different set of hypotheses and working on a different set of issues.

THE CLASSIC STUDIES

The People's Choice

No one had done it before.

No one had gone out and conducted a full-blown scientific investigation of how voters make up their minds in an election and of the impact of mass communications. This is what made Paul Lazarsfeld and his colleagues' study of voting in the 1940 election so interesting. In May, 1940, Lazarsfeld, Bernard Berelson, and Hazel Gaudet journeyed from bustling Columbia University in uptown New York City to Erie County, Ohio, located between Cleveland and Toledo. There, for 6 months, the researchers set up shop, interviewing residents of the towns and small city located on the Lake Erie shore.

Why Erie County? Lazarsfeld and his colleagues explained that they chose this site "because it was small enough to permit close supervision of the interviewers" and "because for forty years—in every presidential election in the twentieth century—it had deviated very little from the national voting trends."[11]

The study focused on the 1940 election that pitted President Franklin Delano Roosevelt, the popular incumbent and a Democrat, against Wendell Willkie, the charismatic Republican from Indiana. Roosevelt was running for an unprecedented third term, and, although there were misgivings about some of his policies, in the end the public's concerns were not serious or widespread enough to prevent FDR from defeating Willkie. He received 449 electoral votes to Willkie's 82.

The researchers probed the impact of campaign communications by conducting a survey of respondents' political predispositions and their self-reported uses of mass media (three Sandusky newspapers, a Cleveland daily, and Toledo and Cleveland radio stations). Respondents were selected through stratified sampling techniques and were interviewed at different points in the campaign. A number of intriguing results emerged from the study:

1. Social background factors—party loyalty, socioeconomic status, and religion—proved to be highly correlated with voting behavior.

2. The political media had three major influences: They activated latent political predispositions, helping to clarify and crystallize attitudes toward the candidates; they reinforced the vote intentions of strong partisans; and they converted a handful of voters.

3. Voters who were most exposed to mass media had the most fixed political attitudes. "Thus, in sheer quantity campaign propaganda reached the persons least amenable to conversion."[12]

4. Certain individuals served as **opinion leaders** for others. These persons had the greatest exposure to mass media, were most interested in the campaign and seemed to influence followers' political views.

5. The researchers also concluded that "ideas often flow *from* radio and print *to* the opinion leaders and *from* them to the less active sections of the population." They called this the **two-step flow.**

The findings, as Shearon Lowery and Melvin DeFleur note, showed that media "were not all-powerful, swaying helpless audiences uniformly and directly." On the contrary, the media had "limited effects (that were) linked to the demographic characteristics of the audiences in highly selective ways."[13]

The study also called attention to the role that interpersonal communication played in campaign decision-making. Few theorists had paid much attention to communication between people before Lazarsfeld and his colleagues conducted their study. Probably most scholars of the 1930s and 1940s would have made light of interpersonal communication, saying that whatever impact it had paled in comparison to the media. But Lazarsfeld et al. found that voters who made up their minds late in the campaign were particularly likely to mention personal influence as a factor in their vote choice. They also found that on an average day, more people reported that they participated in discussions about the campaign than said they listened to a major speech or read about election issues in the newspaper. These findings, coupled with the two-step flow idea, suggested that the prevailing notion of mass society—of atomized individuals linked with the media but alienated from one another—was definitely in need of revision.

The study results were published in 1944 in a book aptly titled *The People's Choice: How the voter makes up his mind in a presidential campaign.*[14] Today, *The People's Choice* is still regarded as a classic. It represented the first major, scientific investigation of communication in a political campaign. It introduced the panel design, a longitudinal research strategy that allows for the study of political processes over time. It compared mass media and interpersonal communication for the first time.

Opinion Leadership and News Diffusion

With the publication of *The People's Choice*, the pendulum shifted from a concern with mass media effects to an interest in small group dynamics and interpersonal communication. A number of studies were conducted in small towns and cities to probe the nature of opinion leadership and interpersonal networks.

The most comprehensive study was conducted in Decatur, Illinois. Designed to follow up on the Erie County study, it employed scientific techniques to locate opinion leaders and to explore the relationships between leaders and followers, on the one hand, and between leaders and the media, on the other. The researchers only interviewed women, and examined the role communication played in four decision-making arenas: marketing, fashion, movie-going, and public affairs. Opinion leaders in one area were found to be particularly likely to be exposed to the media relevant to that area (e.g, an opinion leader in the area of fashion was apt to read fashion magazines, a public affairs leader was likely to scrutinize news magazines.) Second, the researchers found that the two-step flow did not hold up particularly well: In three of the four domains, leaders reported that other people played a more important role in their decision-making than did the media.[15]

During the same period—the 1950s and 1960s—scholars probed the diffusion of news, or the processes by which news spreads through society. In 1963, a series of studies explored the diffusion of news of President Kennedy's assassination. Greenberg found that almost 9 in 10 respondents in his study knew of the assassination within an hour after the first announcement.[16] Other diffusion studies probed the rate at which news travels, whether the rate of diffusion is faster for certain events than others, and when word-of-mouth communication is most important.[17]

Limited Effects Model

In 1960, Joseph Klapper, a student of Paul Lazarsfeld, wrote a book entitled *The Effects of Mass Communication* that codified what was known about the sociological and psychological influences of mass media. Few could have predicted the impact that this book would have on the field of communication research.

After reviewing the available research, Klapper concluded that mass media had minimal influences on society and individuals. He noted that persuasive mass communications were unlikely to convert masses of people to one side of an issue or another. Instead, he concluded that:

1. Mass communication *ordinarily* does not serve as a necessary and sufficient cause of audience effects, but rather functions among and through a nexus of mediating factors and influences.
2. These mediating factors are such that they typically render mass communication a contributory agent, but not the sole cause, in a process of reinforcing the existing conditions.[18]

Klapper contrasted his view with the notion that the media had powerful or "hypodermic" effects. He acknowledged that the media could influence attitudes and behavior, but emphasized that they worked together with psychological and interpersonal factors—such as political predispositions, group norms, and opinion leaders. Basically, people had their minds made up before they attended to mass media; their views presumably had been formed by their upbringing, membership in groups, and interactions with important others. In most situations, Klapper argued, the media reinforced or strengthened people's preexisting sentiments.

Klapper maintained that people typically resisted persuasive messages by employing several defensive mechanisms. These consisted of: (a) **selective exposure,** the tendency to expose oneself to mass media materials one agrees with; (b) **selective perception,** the tendency to perceive information so that it fits one's preexisting point of view; and (c) **selective retention,** the predisposition to remember belief-congruent information better than belief- incongruent information. Since people were relatively closed to new information and were apt to interpret information in line with their biases, it was reasonable to suppose that mass media would be more likely to reinforce existing attitudes than to change them. The media could influence people—for example by creating opinions among individuals who did not have strong views on an issue. However, for the most part, the effects of mass media were quite limited. Klapper's book influenced a generation of social scientists. Social psychology textbooks dismissed the media, arguing instead that "stable factors" like personality, primary groups, and strongly-held values influenced political attitudes. In the 1960s and early 1970s, the University of Michigan election surveys included only a handful of items assessing media uses, and these were typically treated as examples of political participation rather than as instances of media effects.[19]

REVISING THE CLASSICS

Although Klapper had diligently reviewed the empirical literature, his conclusions seemed to fly in the face of everyday experience. If the media were so unimportant, then why were advertisers spending millions of dollars on television spots? If political communication effects were so limited, why did Kennedy and Nixon seem so concerned about the presidential debates in 1960? Americans were spending more and more time watching television; surely, their exposure to violent programs, stereotypes, and news was having some effect on their images of reality.

These observations, coupled with the development of new theories of mass communication, led scholars to revise their thinking about political communication and to reassess their interpretations of the early studies. Let's look now at the current views of the early research.

The People's Choice Revisited

When communication researchers reviewed the Erie County study in the 1970s and 1980s, they discovered that, contrary to Lazarsfeld and his colleagues' conclusions, there was ample evidence of media effects. Lee Becker, Maxwell McCombs, and Jack McLeod looked carefully at Lazarsfeld's data, focusing on a chart that broke down the sample on the basis of both partisanship and exposure to media that favored Republican and Democratic candidates. Becker and his colleagues discovered an interesting pattern of findings: 15% of Republicans who got most of their information from Republican media voted for the Democratic candidate, Franklin D. Roosevelt. However, 47% of Republicans with exposure to predominantly

Democratic media voted for FDR. A similar pattern emerged for Democrats: Democrats who had predominantly Republican media exposure were more likely to vote Republican than those who received primarily Democratic exposure.[20]

Another problem with the Erie County study stemmed from the fact that the investigators focused almost exclusively on the relationship between media exposure and voting. As Steven Chaffee and John Hochheimer observed, had Lazarsfeld and his colleagues looked at variables other than voting, they might have found more evidence of media impact. For example, Wendell Willkie emerged from nowhere to become the Republican nominee. President Roosevelt managed to convince people that the economy was getting better. The media—newspapers, magazines, radio, and newsreels—undoubtedly played a part in this.

Finally, the researchers selected a homogeneous community. This reduced the chances that they would discover instability or conflict. It made it unlikely they would observe interpersonal, ethnic, or interest group conflicts or, for that matter, intrapersonal dissonance—psychological conflict and discomfort. Had Lazarsfeld et al. picked a more heterogeneous area, like a big city, they might have discovered more fluidity, which would have provided more opportunities for the media to have exercised an impact.

Opinion Leadership

The concepts of opinion leadership and the two-step flow have also undergone considerable revision. Both have turned out to be more complex than originally assumed.

The idea that the media relay information to leaders who in turn transmit it to the mass public has not held up. As the news diffusion research indicated, people frequently receive information directly from the media. (In the high-speed world of CNN, people get information about world events almost as soon as they happen.) Researchers have pointed out that on some issues there is a one-step flow (media to public), on other issues two-step flows, and on still other issues there are multistep flows, including horizontal flows of information among leaders and followers, and upward flows, from opinion leaders to media, from followers to leaders, and from followers to media.[21]

Scholars have also distinguished between *information* and *influence*. Information may flow from the media to the mass public in one step, but influence is more complicated. It can occur in many steps. Moreover, followers can influence leaders, as when citizens faxed and phoned members of Congress during the House banking scandal of 1992. Making matters even more complicated are instances in which media sources serve as opinion leaders. Talk-show hosts like Rush Limbaugh can be viewed as influentials, who mold opinions.

Limited Effects

This brings us to Joseph Klapper, who has become the bete noire of mass communication research.[22] His conclusion that media had few effects seemed to violate common sense. His work irritated mass communication scholars, who were beginning to seriously explore the impact of mass media on individuals and society.[23] It also aggravated ideologically oriented researchers, who argue that media ideology exerts a significant impact on people's world-views.

In fact, Klapper acknowledged that the media could change attitudes under certain conditions. In addition, his conclusion that the media interact with other socialization agents has held up over time. The main problem with Klapper's work was that he harbored a narrow view of media effects.

Klapper had been educated in an era in which scholars had been preoccupied with persuasion. This made sense, given what happened during World War II—when Hitler was able to use propaganda and coercion to induce a nation to go along with his destructive political philosophy. The emphasis on persuasion also followed from the North Koreans' use of coercive social influence techniques during the Korean War and the U.S. government's preoccupation with Communist brainwashing during and after the war. During the 1950s, psychologist Carl Hovland conducted a series of experiments on the effects of persuasion that had their roots in some of these historical concerns.[24] However, persuasion is only one of many effects of political communication. In fact, news is not intended to persuade in the narrow sense of the term. It is intended to inform and interpret, and to provide a check on government. In performing these functions, news—and other media too—can have a host of effects. Yet by focusing exclusively on persuasion, and by doing so during an era marked by strong political and national sentiments, researchers were almost destined to discover that the media had minimal effects.

Contemporary scholars have pointed out that, far from having minimal effects, the media can have a host of strong influences. Let's look now at some of the revisions of Klapper's viewpoint:

First, Klapper's conclusions do not apply as well to the era of electronic media. Klapper shipped off his manuscript to the publisher in April, 1960. Had he waited 6 months, he would have observed the presidential debates between John Kennedy and Richard Nixon. Scholars believe the debates exerted a subtle impact on voters' cognitions about the candidates. The studies that Klapper reviewed, including Lazarsfeld's, had taken place in the era of print and radio. Television has had quite an impact on politics, changing the nature of presidential campaigns and profoundly influencing the nominating process.

Second, scholars now believe that the media can have a host of effects beyond changing attitudes. They can shape views about which issues are important, influence beliefs about the candidates, change assessments of the climate of public opinion, and even play a role in young people's political socialization. The "cognitive revolution" in the social sciences has left little doubt of the media's impact on political beliefs.[25]

Third, Klapper neglected to examine media effects on society and the social system. Klapper's psychological orientation led him to focus on the individual, to the exclusion of macro issues. In fact, the media have had a variety of effects on subgroups, society, and culture, including marginalization of deviant political groups, maintenance of national cohesiveness in times of tragedy, and diffusion of innovations throughout the culture.[26]

Fourth, contemporary research has provided a more complex view of the processes of selective exposure, perception, and retention. In the television era, it is harder to selectively tune into campaign information one agrees with and avoid belief-discrepant information. Television brings an endless variety of political information to people in political ads, debates, and news programs. Furthermore, psychologists have found that there is no psychological tendency to prefer supportive messages and to avoid information that clashes with one's beliefs. In addition, people may even remember information that is inconsistent with their point of view when they have well-developed knowledge structures on the issue.[27] Given that people are less selective than Klapper believed, they may be more open to news and other political communications.

Fifth, reinforcement is not a trivial effect, as Klapper seemed to imply. News and presidential rhetoric can convince people that the system is working, when in fact there are serious problems with aspects of American society. To the extent that this happens, it can inhibit change and legitimize the status quo, which is no small influence.[28]

THE POLITICS OF COMMUNICATION RESEARCH

Some of the most interesting—and controversial—criticisms of the early research in communication have come from ideologically oriented scholars, who have typically favored a radical, left-of-center political philosophy.

These scholars have observed that the early research was not objective or neutral, as the field's pioneers suggested, but was in fact supportive of (and in some cases funded by) the major arms of American capitalism. The Erie County study was funded by the Rockefeller Foundation and *Life* Magazine. The Decatur study of opinion leaders received funding from Macfadden Publications and the Roper polling firm. Klapper's volume was made possible by a grant from CBS.

Had the investigators' dependence on corporate funding sources biased or contaminated their results? One critic, Todd Gitlin, thought so, arguing that:

> The Rockefeller program insisting on underwriting only studies that were consonant with the empiricist program, and at least one instance Lazarsfeld described, the hand that paid the piper did actually and directly, and apparently despite Lazarsfeld's hesitation, call the proverbial tune.[29]

Gitlin suggested that the Decatur researchers focused only on female respondents because women were the target audience of a major magazine owned by Macfadden Publications.

In his research on this topic, Gabriel Weimann observed that the funding sources may have restricted the scope of the projects. He notes that the eminent social researcher, Theodore Adorno, felt hemmed in by the funding sources. Adorno lamented that the early radio research left little room for "critical social research." Adorno complained that:

> (the project's) charter, which came from the Rockefeller Foundation, expressly stipulated that the investigations must be performed within the limits of the commercial radio system prevailing in the United States. It was thereby implied that the system itself, its cultural and sociological consequences and its social and economic presuppositions were not to be analyzed.[30]

The funding sources may have exerted a subtle impact on the questions the researchers were asking. The fact that major media groups like the Rockefeller Foundation and Macfadden Publications were underwriting the projects may have encouraged the investigators to view politics and opinion leadership as marketing phenomena. It also may have encouraged them to focus on attitude change to the exclusion of other types of media effects, such as increased faith in the American political system.

Christopher Simpson has gone even further in his criticisms. He observes that early communication research was inextricably linked with the interests of the United States government. He argues that as social scientists became more involved in the psychological warfare projects of the U.S. government during World War II and the Cold War, their rhetoric began to change.

> The values and many of the political preconceptions of the psychological warfare projects (were) absorbed into new, "scientificized" presentations of communication theory that tended to conceal the prejudices of the early 1950s programs under a new coat of "objective" rhetoric. Basic terms in the field began to change. Terms such as *propaganda* and *psychological warfare* fell out of favor; they became instead *international communications, development,* and *public diplomacy.*[31]

Simpson traces social science involvement with the government to World War II, when leading sociologists and social psychologists helped to evaluate the Army's *Why We Fight* films. When the war was over, the Voice of America and the Central Intelligence Agency used social science techniques to assist them in psychological warfare campaigns of the early 1950s. The U.S. government was particularly interested in uncovering the "magic keys" of Communist-style brainwashing, a term popularized by the Central Intelligence Agency and made famous by the Hollywood film, *The Manchurian Candidate.*[32] Between 1951 and 1953, a group of sociologists supervised by Stuart Dodd of the University of Washington dropped millions of leaflets on rural communities and small towns in the far West. The researchers studied the diffusion and dispersal of leaflets that stated, among other things, that *Communist bombers might attack your neighborhood.*[33]

Criticizing the Critics

The humanist critics have usefully called attention to the ideological roots of the field of political communication. However, their arguments deserve scrutiny. Let's look at the charges, beginning with the claims about the funding of the early studies and moving to the arguments about the role that social science played in U.S. psychological warfare.

There is no doubt that the early studies by Lazarsfeld and his colleagues received funding from major media companies. The critics are probably correct that the funding influenced the research questions asked. However, they assume that things would have been better had the researchers pursued another option. What option should Lazarsfeld and his colleagues have pursued? How else could the researchers have obtained data about the media and opinion leaders if they had not accepted money from business groups? Wasn't it better that they conducted these studies than remained purists and done no research at all? There is little question that the early research reflected a prosystem bias, and it is useful to appreciate the possible impact that funding had on the outcomes. But one can recognize this and still appreciate the many contributions the early research made to the field of political communication.

Moving to Simpson's contentions, it is important to note at the outset that Simpson is quite correct that social scientists played a role in World War II and Cold War propaganda campaigns. The more controversial question is whether their involvement was good or bad. Few would argue that researchers should have stayed neutral during World War II. In fact, I would suggest that in view of the threat Nazi Germany posed to the United States and western civilization, a refusal to work for U.S. psychological warfare campaigns would have been immoral.

There is more debate about the appropriateness of social scientists' involvement in Cold War propaganda campaigns. Should the handful of social scientists who were asked to lend their services refused to have signed on with the CIA? The answer depends on the nature of the project, your judgments of the U.S. and Soviet positions in the Cold War, and your view of whether it is right for university researchers to get involved in Defense Department research.

Should researchers at American University have accepted a CIA contract to document the effects of drugs and electric shocks on the interrogation of prisoners? Perhaps not.[34] Should University of Washington sociologists have conducted the diffusion of leaflets study? Simpson says they should not have. He notes that many of the towns that received the message—*Communist bombers might attack your neighborhood*—were not in fact accessible to American passenger planes or Soviet bombers. His point is a good one. Still, it is important to remember that the University of Washington study was conducted in a different political era, characterized by great fears of Soviet expansionism, some of which were real, some of which were exaggerated. Moreover, the diffusion paradigm was employed to achieve a variety of prosocial goals, including speeding up the acceptance of agricultural and public health innovations.[35]

There is still debate today about the role that communication research should play in government campaigns, particularly those conducted during war-time. This issue came up most recently during the 1991 Gulf War, when the Bush Administration used public relations specialists to help mold public opinion in a direction favorable to the war.[36]

Of course, most political communication studies are not funded by the government to help develop propagandistic campaigns. Most test hypotheses derived from theory or explore topical research issues. Some scholars would argue that their research has done more to change the system than to perpetuate its problematic aspects. Nonetheless, we need to remember that the questions researchers ask are influenced by the political system in which they are operating, their own values, and the nature of the times in which they live. This does not mean that researchers should stop asking questions or quit doing studies. On the contrary, the more insight scholars have into their own orientations and perspectives, the more objective and comprehensive their analyses of communication phenomena will be.

CONTEMPORARY PERSPECTIVES

Like other fields, political communication has built upon the discoveries of the past. Today's scholars acknowledge the limitations of the early research, but they also recognize that these studies provided a foundation for the field. It would be fair to say that the following conclusions from the pioneering research of the 1940s, 1950s, and 1960s have held up over the years:

1. Although the media influence individuals and society, there are limits to their impact. Klapper and Lazarsfeld and his colleages were correct in noting that strongly held political attitudes are resistant to change. When we have strong attitudes about a subject, we are loathe to change these attitudes, regardless of what the media say.
2. Opinion leaders do influence other people. Although their impact has turned out to be more complicated and situation-bound than originally assumed, the concept of opinion leadership has survived. As Katz wrote:
    Opinion leaders are interesting, in my view, because they imply that media influence is being intercepted and reexamined in conversation. Find an opinion leader and you find a conversation. Find a conversation and you find more considered opinions and better informed actions, and thus a brake on media power.[37]
3. Media effects are complicated. They vary as a function of the person, the situation, the interaction between the person and situation, and the particular social systems variable the researcher is investigating.
4. Social science research methods help us gain insights into media effects. The questionnaire, the panel survey, experimental research, and a host of other techniques provide us with useful facts about political communication.

The criticisms of the classic studies have advanced knowledge by indicating that:

1. Conclusions about political media effects that are reached in one political era, characterized by a particular set of political arrangements and mass media, will need to be revised as the political system and dominant media change.
2. There is a more dynamic relationship between people and mass media than early theorists assumed.
3. One cannot adequately appreciate political media effects without considering the larger social system in which mass media operate.

Over the past 50 years, the study of political communication effects has expanded greatly. There are a variety of theories, research methods, and ideological perspectives on political media. Four types of theoretical perspectives have guided studies of political communication effects. The approaches are: (a) individual-centered; (b) technological; (c) systems-level; and (d) critical.

Individual-Centered Approaches

Individual-centered or psychologically-oriented approaches examine the ways that audience members use political communication and how they cognitively process political information.

A major theoretical approach is **the uses and gratifications model,** which examines both the ways audience members use mass media (for example, the time spent watching television news on an average day) and the gratifications or rewards individuals receive from the media. The starting point for uses and gratifications research is the individual member of the audience, not the media. The model asks how people bend and mold political media to suit their own needs rather than how media influence or manipulate consumers.[38]

People report that they gain a variety of gratifications from using political media, including surveillance (learning about what political leaders are like), vote guidance (to help make up one's mind about how to vote), and reinforcement (watching a presidential debate to increase one's confidence that the candidate one has selected is the best one).[39] People also derive a variety of social gratifications from tuning into talk-radio programs and from cruising campaign sites on the World Wide Web.

Another individual-level approach that has generated research is **information processing theory.** Guided by theories of human cognition and memory, information processing perspectives examine how individuals think about, process, and interpret political messages.[40]

Increasingly, individual-level approaches combine a focus on the psychology of the individual with a concern about media effects. These perspectives are transactional in that they argue that we cannot understand the impact of mass media without appreciating how the individual interprets, con-structs, and processes media messages. One approach that has gained popularity in recent years is **constructionism.** Constructionism tries to deal with the tension between an active audience—which increasingly distrusts the media—and evidence that media subtly influence audience members. According to scholars Russell Neuman, Marion Just, and Ann Crigler, constructionism:

- emphasizes the prospect of an active, interpreting, meaning-constructing audience;
- emphasizes the importance of the varying character of the communications content. Different kinds of issues are interpreted by the media and by the public in different ways; and
- focuses on what motivates people to pay attention to some public issues rather than assuming that civic duty simply requires attention to all matters political.[41]

Agenda-setting, the preeminent perspective on political communication effects, also examines the transaction between the individual and the media message.[42] Agenda-setting is discussed in detail in chapter 11.

Technological Approaches

These perspectives emphasize the technologies of communication. They contend that the technological features of a particular medium determine its impact on individuals and society. Technological approaches to political communication have typically focused on television. Scholars have argued that the superficial, fast-paced nature of television news inhibits learning, that dependence on television leads to feelings of cynicism, and that TV leads to simplistic, image-based voting. As Jack McLeod notes, "television has become a convenient scapegoat for critics at all points on the political spectrum."[43]

Daniel Dayan and Elihu Katz have proposed a particularly interesting technology-based approach. Dayan and Katz focus on *media events*, "historic occasions—mostly occasions of state—that are televised as they take place and transfix a nation or the world."[44] These include live television coverage of such diverse events as the funeral of John F. Kennedy, the Oklahoma City bombing, the Persian Gulf War, space exploration, and inaugurations.

Dayan and Katz argue that like other era's technologies —papyrus, the printing press, newspapers and radio—television influences both people and the social structure. They note that:

Television's power lies not only in the way it structures the flow of daily life, but in its consequent ability to interrupt this flow. Media events are an example of this interruptive dimension. They cancel all other programs, bring television's clock to a stop, and while they are on the air, cannot themselves be interrupted. Their performance belongs to "sacred time," bringing all social activity to a standstill. For a while, the event occupies society's "center." No matter what happens, the event has to go on.[45]

If you think for a moment about a media event that consumed your attention and that of the nation, you get a feeling for Dayan and Katz's logic.

Technological approaches are interesting. However, they frequently fail to make clear predictions about the impact that media will have on people or society, and they tend to lump a variety of factors under the technology rubric.

Systems-Level Approaches

Both individual-level and technological-driven perspectives tend to neglect the larger macroscopic system. They focus on problems caused by "trees" while forgetting that the health of trees depends to a considerable degree on the health of the forest.

Systems approaches call attention to the interrelationships among the mass media and economic, political, and cultural institutions. As J.D. Halloran observes:

What is made available by the media, and consequently what helps to shape attitudes and values, will be influenced by a whole series of economic, legal, political, professional, and technological considerations. (So,) to understand the part played by the media in our society, we must study the whole communication process (in) these appropriate contexts.[46]

Thus, to understand the role the media play in presidential elections, we need to understand the dynamics of the American system of nominating and electing candidates for the presidency. To appreciate the impact of the media on knowledge of community issues, we need to understand the interrelationships among the media and government, as discussed in chapter 9. To evaluate whether the news media are doing an adequate job of reporting on politics, we need to examine the system in which the news media operate and the factors that constrain journalists and inhibit citizens' learning from the news.

Critical Approaches

Critical theory perspectives adopt the radical neo-Marxist view that the mass media are an important arm of the ruling class. Critical theory approaches, such as hegemony (see chapter 5), argue that "the mass media play a strategic role in reinforcing dominant social norms and values that legitimize the social system."[47] Scholars in this tradition build on Marx and Engels' insight that "the class which has the means of *material* production at its disposal has control at the same time over the means of *mental* production" (italics added).[48]

While pluralistic models of mass media argue that the media are one of many institutions that vie for control in society, neo-Marxist analyses emphasize that the media are, as a general rule, closely connected with the dominant power structure of society through a host of economic, legal, and ideological mechanisms. Taking this argument to the level of effects on people, critical scholars contend that the media are a mechanism by which society's elites enforce norms and help to engineer consent with elite policies. Today's critical theorists acknowledge that the process by which the media engineer—or, as some would say, communicate—consent is complicated, involving a host of psychological, interpersonal, and macrosocial processes.

Critical perspectives take a systems approach to the mass media. However, they depart from systems approaches in their insistence that the media invariably reinforce and legitimate the dominant social structure. It should be noted that the term "critical" was invoked to be just that—critical of mainstream empirical, pluralistic approaches. The term evolved as Marxist scholars castigated political communication research in the Lazarsfeld tradition for not recognizing that values inform and influence social scientists' work.

It should be pointed out that it is possible, at least in theory, to have a critical theory that takes a conservative, rather than a radical, perspective on mass media.[49] For example, one could agree with everything that neo-Marxist scholars say about mass media, but contend that media effects are positive not negative. In addition, the claim that mass media legitimize the social system applies to all societies, not just America. The focus of critical scholars' inquiries has typically been on America, however.

Critical approaches have helped to call scholars' attention to the impact that values and ideology play in the political communication process. Unfortunately, they tend to simplify political communication effects and to make statements that cannot be empirically tested. Scholars in this tradition also tend to neglect the positive aspects of political communication in America and the ways in which the system has been able to change and reform itself from the inside.

CONCLUSIONS

This chapter reviewed the history of political communication research. Following World War I, there was great concern among intellectuals about the power of propaganda. However, humanistic studies of propaganda soon gave rise to more scientific examinations as social science theories and methods began to take hold in universities. The Erie County study, research on opinion leaders, and, finally, Klapper's book emerged from the social scientific investigations of communication phenomena that took place in the 1940s and 1950s.

As we have seen, the early studies blazed a path. They provided insights into communication effects and they suggested that we could understand media influences by applying social scientific theories and methods. But, as we have also noted, the early research had a number of limitations. Scholars have been quick to identify the various theoretical, methodological, and ideological assumptions of the early studies.

A defining feature of Lazarsfeld and his colleagues' research was the assumption that you could study political and social issues in a dispassionate, scientific way, and that researchers could separate out their own value judgments from the issues they were studying. In those days there was a great faith that social scientists could discover truth and apply it to solve social and communication problems.[50]

We have since learned that truth is much more difficult to discover than the early researchers believed, scholars' values influence the questions they ask, and the social system in which researchers work influences the ways that they approach the study of political communication and the answers they obtain. And yet contemporary scholars have not thrown up their hands in the face of these difficulties. They have adopted new theories, new techniques, and a new appreciation for methodological pluralism, or the need to study a particular phenomenon with multiple methodologies.

KEY ISSUES

Early Explorations of Propaganda

The People's Choice

Opinion Leader

Two-Step Flow

Limited Effects Model

Selective Exposure, Perception, and Retention

Criticisms of Early Empirical Research

Politics of Communication Research

Uses and Gratifications Model

Information-Processing Approach

Technological Perspective

Systems Approach

Critical Approach

DISCUSSION QUESTIONS

1. What were the major findings of *The People's Choice* study? How does the study hold up half a century later?

2. What role do you believe that opinion leaders and interpersonal communication play in election campaigns?

3. "Political communication research serves the interest of the country's elites, reinforcing the status quo." Critically discuss this statement.

11

Agenda-Setting

•Just before the U.S. Senate began holding hearings on the Watergate scandal in 1973, *The Washington Post* reported:

> Last fall, in suburban Ohio and Michigan precincts visited by *Washington Post* reporters, voters didn't know or particularly care about the bugging of the Democratic headquarters at the Watergate ...

Today, in these same precincts, the voters both know and care about the Watergate—and especially about the manner in which the man they elected to a second term is addressing himself to the scandal that has hit his party and his administration.[1]

• In November, 1986, *The New York Times* ran a front-page story on the anatomy of the drug issue. The reporter observed that:

> More than any time in memory, America this year has erupted with concern about illegal drugs.
>
> The issue suddenly spread across newspapers' front pages and nightly news broadcasts. Public concern jumped in opinion polls. And Congress, in a matter of weeks, wrote and passed antidrug legislation backed by $1.7 billion in financing.
>
> Yet statistics showed no sudden rise in drug use. While the effects of illegal drugs were severe in 1986, experts say, the problem had been bad for decades.

For many, then, a major question about drugs is "Why now?"[2]

Both of these stories illustrate how an issue that had been on the back burner, lodged in the back of the nation's consciousness, jumped to the forefront. In both cases, the mass media exerted important effects on voters' and policymakers' cognitions about the issue. In the popular lexicon, the mass media set the agenda for Watergate and for drugs. Agenda-setting, the most durable and well-known of all political media effects, is the subject of this chapter and the one that follows.

KEY TERMS

What is the most important problem facing America today? If someone gave you a list of problems—including the budget deficit, crime, and environmental pollution—which would you say was most important? Why do policymakers devote their attention to certain issues and not to others? Why do issues like homelessness and famine get so much attention in the media for a while and then disappear from view?

These questions strike to the heart of agenda-setting and a related concept, agenda-building. According to Everett Rogers and James Dearing, **agenda-setting** is *"a process through which the mass media communicate the relative importance of various issues and events to the public."* **Agenda-building** is *"a process through which the policy agendas of political elites are influenced by a variety of factors, including media agendas and public agendas."* **Agendas** are *"issues or events that are viewed at a point in time as ranked in a hierarchy of importance."*[3]

Agenda-setting research focuses on how mass media influence the **public agenda**, or the content and rankings of issues in public opinion. Agenda-building is concerned with how the media, public opinion, and political elites influence the **policy agenda**, or the political priorities of America's leaders. Agenda-building research also examines the antecedents of the **media agenda**, or the content and rankings of issues in the mass media. This chapter examines agenda-setting. Chapter 12 focuses on agenda-building and the role of media in policymaking. Implications of agenda-setting for elections are discussed in chapters 18 and 20.

UNDERSTANDING AGENDA-SETTING

Scholars have long commented on the ability of mass media to shape public sentiments. Consider the following observations:

- The press is no substitute for institutions. It is like the beam of a searchlight that moves restlessly about, bringing one episode and then another out of darkness into vision.—Walter Lippmann[4]
- The power of the press in America is a primordial one. It sets the agenda of public discussion; and this sweeping political power is unrestrained by any law. It determines

what people will talk and think about—an authority that in other nations is reserved for tyrants, priests, parties and mandarins.—Theodore White[5]

- The mass media force attention to certain issues. They build up public images of political figures. They are constantly presenting objects suggesting what individuals in the mass should think about, know about, have feelings about.—Kurt Lang and Gladys Engel Lang[6]

- The press is significantly more than a purveyor of information and opinion. It may not be successful much of the time in telling people *what to think*, but it is stunningly successful in telling its readers *what to think about* ... The world will look different to different people, depending ... on the map that is drawn for them by writers, editors, and publishers of the papers they read (italics added).— Bernard Cohen.[7]

Agenda-setting theory cautions that the news media are not likely to change people's strongly held political beliefs or attitudes. In this sense, the theory ascribes "limited effects" to the media, following Klapper's lead. But it departs from Klapper in the important sense that it emphasizes that the media can powerfully influence people's priorities—or what they perceive to be the salient problems of the country or community[8]

The term "salient" plays an important role in agenda-setting. In a sense, agenda-setting is a theory about saliences. It contends that the media select certain aspects of political reality and make these salient for individuals, causing them to stand out and dominate citizens' world views. Notice that not any effect of political media counts as agenda-setting. For agenda-setting to occur, people must come to believe the issue is more important after exposure to mass media than before.

The obverse is also true. If the media ignore a topic, it will not appear on the public agenda. As Maxwell McCombs noted, "this basic, primitive notion of agenda-setting is a truism. If the media tell us nothing about a topic or event, then in most cases it simply will not exist on our personal agenda or in our life space."[9]

McCombs makes an important point. The failure of the media to cover an event can itself have important effects. By not prominently covering the Holocaust during World War II—for a number of disturbing reasons—the media may have contributed to the perception that the extermination of the Jews was not a problem worth worrying about or doing anything about. By failing to provide in-depth coverage of the problems of inner cities until the protests of the 1950s and 1960s, the media may have promoted the widely held belief that racial injustice was a small problem, compared to all the other issues that were getting press coverage. And by waiting until the 1990s to discuss the problems caused by the expansion of big government, the media may have contributed to the perception that government largesse was not a significant issue in American society.

Agenda-setting would be a relatively uninteresting concept if it turned out that the media accurately and faithfully reflected everyday life. Then if there was a one-to-one correspondence between what people believed to be important and what the media covered in their daily reports, no one would be much impressed. What makes agenda-setting interesting is that the media do not reflect reality, but select certain aspects for coverage. They cover some stories and ignore others, give greater play to some issues than to others, and decide how to interpret and frame the issues that they cover.

The agenda-setting hypothesis postulates that the decisions that reporters and editors make have effects on the body politic. As David Weaver notes, agenda-setting assumes that *"concentration by the media over time on relatively few issues leads to the public perceiving these issues as more salient or more important than other issues."*[11]

Scholars have devised a number of ways to empirically test the agenda-setting hypothesis. They have looked to see if there is a correlation between the media agenda (issues the media cover frequently and prominently) and the public agenda (issues that the public regards as important). Researchers have compared readers of different newspapers to see if readers are sensitive to the issue that their newspaper is emphasizing. Do readers of a newspaper that focuses on Issue A believe Issue A is important? Do readers of a newspaper that gives prominent play to Issue B think B is a significant problem? Finally, scholars have conducted experiments to determine whether exposure to news stories influences viewers' rankings of national problems. Researchers have also assessed agenda-setting effects in a variety of ways, asking individuals to indicate which issues are most important to them personally, polling them on the issues they feel are most important to society as a whole, and obtaining measures of how often respondents talk about issues with their friends.[12]

EMPIRICAL RESEARCH

Correlational Evidence

There is abundant evidence that the amount of coverage given to issues in the media is significantly correlated with citizens' rankings of important issues. In a pioneering study of the 1968 election, Maxwell McCombs and Donald Shaw found that the correlation between issues emphasized by the media and those regarded as important by the public was .97.[13] (A perfect correlation is 1.0.)

G. Ray Funkhouser examined agenda-setting over the course of the decade of the 1960s. He counted the number of articles that appeared in news magazines on topics such as the Vietnam War, race relations, campus unrest, inflation, and crime. He also obtained opinion poll data on what Americans regarded as the most important problem facing the country. Funkhouser found that there was a highly significant correlation between media coverage and public opinion. As Table 11.1 shows, the more attention the press gave to issues such as Vietnam and race relations, the more people thought that these problems were important.[14]

Did this mean that media coverage was the cause of public perceptions of issue importance? That, after all, is what the agenda-setting hypothesis asserts. It turns out that the answer to this question is more complicated. There are at least three interpretations of a significant correlation between two variables: (a) Variable A can cause Variable B; (b) Variable B can cause Variable A; or (c) both A and B can be caused by a third variable, C.

In the case of agenda-setting, this means that (a) media coverage could cause citizens to change their beliefs about the nation's most important problems; (b) mass media could, at least at some level, reflect the public's beliefs about what ails the country; or (c) both media coverage and public opinion could be driven by a third variable, such as real-world conditions. For example, in Funkhouser's study, it is possible that increased U.S. involvement in Vietnam caused the media to lavish more attention on the war and led the public to regard Vietnam as a more important policy dilemma.

Unraveling the media agenda, public opinion, and real-world conditions has been one of the knottiest problems in agenda-setting research. I discuss

TABLE 11.1

Amount of Coverage Given By National Newsmagazines To Various Issues During the 1960's, and Rank Scores Of The Issues As "Most Important Problem Facing America" During That Period

Issue	Number of Articles	Coverage Rank	Importance Rank
Vietnam war	861	1	1
Race relations (and urban riots)	687	2	2
Campus unrest	267	3	4
Inflation	234	4	5
Television and mass media	218	5	12
Crime	203	6	3
Drugs	173	7	9
Environment and pollution	109	8	6
Smoking	99	9	12
Poverty	74	10	7
Sex (declining morality)	62	11	8
Women's rights	47	12	12
Science and society	37	13	12
Population	36	14	12

From Funkhouser (1973).

studies of this issue later in the chapter. However, let us see if there is, at the very least, evidence that the media cause changes in the public agenda. Two types of studies have probed this issue: *experiments*, and *longitudinal surveys*, conducted at more than one point in time.

The Question of Causality

Experimental Evidence.   Experiments can provide strong evidence that one variable causes changes in another. An experimenter can assume that the treatment has caused changes in posttreatment responses if subjects have been randomly assigned to conditions, and appropriate experimental controls have been administered. Although it may seem strange to discuss experimental design in a book on political communication, the fact is that experiments can provide unambiguous evidence that the media exert a causal impact on people's political attitudes and beliefs.

In the 1980s, Shanto Iyengar and Donald Kinder conducted a series of experiments that convincingly demonstrated that television news programs can lead viewers to adjust their perceptions of the importance of national problems.[15] The experiments were conducted at Yale University and took place over the course of a week. On the first day, research participants indicated what they believed were "the three most important problems facing the nation." For the next 4 days, participants viewed what they had been led to believe was a videotape recording of the previous evening's network newscast. In fact, the newscasts had been edited to provide substantial coverage of one national problem.

In one experiment, research participants were randomly assigned to watch one of three newscasts. A first group viewed newscasts that emphasized inadequacies in United States defense preparedness. A second group watched newscasts that focused heavily on pollution. A third group watched newscasts that emphasized skyrocketing inflation. On the final day of the experiment, participants again indicated what they thought were the three most important problems facing the country.

As Table 11.2 shows, the newscasts exerted a substantial impact on participants' beliefs. With one exception (inflation), participants who had been randomly assigned to a particular treatment came away believing that the target problem was more important than they had when they began the experimental procedures.

In the case of inflation, the news had to compete with reality: When the research was conducted, inflation was running at more than 10% a year.

TABLE 11.2

Impact of TV News on Rankings of Problem Importance

Percentage Naming Problem as One of Country's Most Serious

Problem	Before the Experiment	After the Experiment	Change: Pre to Post
Defense	33	53	20
Pollution	0	14	14
Inflation	100	100	0

From Lyengar and Kinder (1987).

Thus the newscasts had no opportunity to convince participants that inflation was a problem: they were already convinced.[16]

The results of Iyengar and Kinder's many experiments made it abundantly clear that sustained exposure to television news can cause individuals to adjust their beliefs about the importance of national problems.

Longitudinal Studies. Using a complex statistical procedure called time-series analysis, Iyengar and his associates probed the antecedents of the public's judgments of national problems. Time-series procedures allowed the investigators to determine the impact of the news on public opinion, above and beyond the effects that public opinion had on news coverage, and controlling for the impact of real-world conditions.

The research showed that television news exerts a causal impact on the public's evaluations of national problems. For example, in the case of public opinion toward energy, the investigators found that "for every seven stories broadcast, public responses citing energy as one of the country's most important problems increased by about 1%."[17] However, TV news was not the only influence on public opinion. Presidential addresses on energy actually had a somewhat stronger impact. When the president spoke on energy, he succeeded in pushing up levels of public concern by over 4%.

Public opinion toward unemployment was influenced more by actual conditions. As the unemployment rate rose, more Americans regarded joblessness as among the nation's most important problems, regardless of how the news covered it.

In sum, there is strong evidence that the media exert a causal impact on Americans' political priorities. The media's impact is consistent, though modest. Thus, as Lippmann suggested back in 1922, by shining the searchlight on certain problems but not others, and by spotlighting certain issues for longer amounts of time than others, the news media help to shape the public agenda. The process occurs subtly and without an intent to persuade the public that its opinions are wrong and in need of revision. Agenda-setting is an outgrowth of the fact that in democratic societies mass media help determine "which issues, among a whole series of possibilities, are presented to the public for attention."[18]

COMPLICATING FACTORS

Although the media influence the public agenda, they are not omnipotent. Mass media do not always shape public priorities, and they have a stronger influence under certain conditions than under others. "Most scholars of agenda-setting seem to take a contingent view of the process," note Rogers and Dearing. "Agenda-setting does not operate *everywhere*, on *everyone*, and *always*," they observe.[19] In their review of the agenda-setting research, Rogers and Dearing note that the media are *not* likely to set the agenda under three conditions:

1. *Low media credibility.* (A particular individual may regard the media in general, or the particular medium to which the individual is exposed, as low in *credibility*).
2. (*A person obtains*) *conflicting evidence from personal experience or other communication channels about the salience of the issue or news event.*
3. *The individual holds different news values than those reflected by the mass medium or media.* (The individual's reaction to a newspaper headline might be to think, "How could they regard *that* as important news?"[20]).

The other side of the coin is that the news media are apt to be particularly influential under particular conditions. Researchers have studied the impact of a host of factors on agenda-setting.

News Play.   Stories that lead off network news broadcasts have a stronger effect on public concern than ordinary stories. Lead stories are more powerful than other stories because viewers confer credibility on network news and implicitly accept TV journalists' news judgments. Lead stories are also more influential for the simple reason that they appear early in the broadcast—before viewers lose interest in the news.[21]

Audience.   Media agenda-setting effects hinge more on what audiences bring to news than on the objective characteristics of news itself. Yet there is a complex interplay between the media and audience predispositions.

Media agendas have a strong impact on those low in political involvement, the segment of the population that has little interest in politics.[22] Lacking the motivation and perhaps the skills to process political information deeply, these citizens take their cues from the media and accept journalists' views of what is most important.

At the same time, individuals who exhibit what Weaver calls *the need for orientation* are also influenced by media agendas. Those high in need for orientation perceive that politics is relevant to them personally, but say they are uncertain about how to behave in a particular political communication situation (e.g., they are uncertain who to vote for in an election). These individuals turn to the media to help them cope with the political environment, and, under some conditions, they end up accepting journalists' judgments of which issues are most important.[23]

Obtrusiveness.   Obtrusiveness refers to the extent to which individuals are personally affected by an issue, or "the degree to which the issue forces itself into lives of individuals."[24] Theorists originally hypothesized that the media would have a stronger agenda-setting effect on unobtrusive issues. As Harold Zucker noted, "The less direct experience the people have with a given issue area, the more they will rely on the news media for information and interpretation in that area."[25]

Research indicates that the media do influence political judgments on unobtrusive issues. Weaver and his colleagues found that during the primary season of an election year, the media "were instrumental in bringing before their audiences those issues and problems with which voters had minimal direct experience. The mass media seemed to introduce new areas of concern to the public agenda of issues."[26] Indeed, one of the reasons that Americans became concerned about such issues as homelessness, the budget deficit, and the nuclear arms race is that the media brought these matters to public attention.

However, like other agenda-setting processes, obtrusiveness has turned out to be more complex than originally assumed. Not all unobtrusive issues make it to the top of the public agenda. If an issue is too abstract, it may be too difficult to visualize and too hard to mentally process. Furthermore, issues involving Third World countries may not be regarded by the public as important unless they are seen as affecting the United States.[27]

There are no absolutes in the area of issue obtrusiveness. What is obtrusive for one person may be unobtrusive for another. Unemployment is obtrusive for people who have lost their jobs and for those who know others who have recently been given pink slips. For other citizens, unemployment is an unobtrusive issue. These individuals may conclude that unemployment is an important national problem because of what they have read in the newspapers or have seen on television. They may not believe that unemployment affects them personally, but may come to regard the problem as one affecting society as a whole.[28]

At the same time, it is true that the media *do* influence those who are affected personally by problems. News about unemployment does influence the political judgments of individuals who have lost their jobs; elderly individuals are significantly affected by news about Social Security; African Americans tend to be more concerned about civil rights than Whites after watching news stories about racial issues.[29]

Thus, the media set the agenda on both unobtrusive issues and issues that impinge directly on the self. Trying to synthesize this complex area, Iyengar and Kinder argue that the news has a greater effect on those personally affected by a problem early in the problem's life history. If the issue remains on the front pages and in the evening news, the media agenda will begin to exert just as strong an impact on viewers whose lives are less directly affected by the problem. Eventually, they suggest, viewers who do not experience the problem directly may come to be influenced more by the flurry of stories on the issue than the problems' victims, whose concerns have reached ceiling levels.[30]

Nature of the Issue.   Agenda-setting is frequently a function of the issue and the event. As Rogers and Dearing note, rapid-onset events, like the 1995 Oklahoma City bombing, differ drastically from slow-onset natural disaster issues such as the 1984 drought in Ethiopia. In the case of rapid-onset issues, the event leaps to the top of the media agenda soon after it happens.

In the case of slow-onset issues like a famine or a drought in a Third World nation, the problem may linger and get worse and worse until the media discover it; the media then focus intensely on the issue for a period of time, build an agenda, perhaps helping to ameliorate the problem, and then drop the issue when it no longer interests public or elite audiences.

Issues differ in the time they take to make it to the top of the public agenda.[31] Unobtrusive issues that are the focal point of complex political debates may take a long time to reach the top of the public's list of most important problems. These issues may not capture public attention if they appear at the "wrong" time, such as during a period when other controversies are dominating the media agenda or in an era when most people are not psychologically prepared to consider the larger ramifications of the issue.

CONSEQUENCES OF AGENDA-SETTING

The preceding discussion assumed that changes in the public agenda matter. But do they? What difference does it make if people change their political priorities after attending to mass media? Do changes in citizens' judgments of important problems have any impact on their evaluations of related political issues? According to the concept of **priming**, agenda-setting matters because it influences the criteria people use to evaluate their political leaders.

Based on psychological research, Iyengar and Kinder argued that the media *prime* citizens, or cause them to alter their standards for evaluating the president based on what they see and hear in the mass media. The investigators proposed that "By calling attention to some matters while ignoring others, television news influences the standards by which governments, presidents, policies, and candidates for public office are judged".[32]

There are many criteria one can use to evaluate the president, including the chief executive's integrity, competence, performance in foreign affairs, success in getting bills passed, and so on. The priming hypothesis suggests that people, preferring to rely on simple rules of thumb when making decisions, will call to mind the issues that they have seen played up in the press and that they will use these as standards for evaluating the president.

To test the priming notion, Iyengar and Kinder conducted a series of experiments. In one study, they showed a group of research participants newscasts that emphasized inadequacies in American defense preparedness. Another group did not view any news stories about defense. The priming hypothesis predicts that individuals who see a newscast dotted with defense stories will give more weight to the president's performance on defense when evaluating the president's overall performance. Consistent with the hypothesis, viewers with heavy exposure to defense stories gave twice as much weight to defense in evaluating the performance of the president than did controls. Thus, these viewers employed a criteria for evaluating the president that they might not have invoked had it not been for their exposure to television news.

Investigators have also studied priming in real-world contexts. Jon Krosnick and Donald Kinder observed that in 1986 the media lavished great attention on the Reagan Administration's covert diversion of funds to the Nicaraguan Contras. Priming suggests that Reagan's Central American policy will exert a stronger impact on the public's evaluations of Reagan's performance after than before the scandal. The results supported the prediction.[33]

In a similar fashion, after the conclusion of the 1991 Persian Gulf War, George Bush's management of the Gulf conflict loomed larger in the public's evaluation of his performance as president than did his handling of other foreign relations matters and his management of the economy.[34]

The findings are interesting, although perhaps not totally surprising. Moreover, we don't know that it was media coverage that caused these effects, as distinct from the events themselves. But taken as a whole, the priming research suggests that by focusing attention on some issues rather than others, the media not only set the agenda, but alter the standards people use to evaluate the president.

Priming also helps us understand why elected officials and candidates want to dominate the media agenda. Media coverage influences public priorities, which in turn affect the criteria people use to evaluate their leaders and those who are running for public office. Consider the plight of Cleveland Mayor Michael White. He labored hard to keep the Cleveland Browns football team in Cleveland, but was criticized for neglecting the city's serious social problems. If the news focused heavily on the deteriorating conditions in the local schools, it might prime citizens to place more emphasis on White's performance on the schools issue when evaluating his performance. But if White could get the press to concentrate on the Cleveland Browns issue—and the impact that a professional sports team has on a city—it is possible that his negotiations to keep the Browns in Cleveland would loom larger in the public's evaluation of his performance as mayor than his handling of problems in the city's infrastructure.

CONCLUSIONS

Agenda-setting is an intriguing communication concept. It has generated a voluminous amount of scholarly research—for good reason. It is a theoretical approach that captures the essence of what media in a democratic society do—allocate attention to certain issues and not others.

The early political communication research missed the mark by assuming that the media were intent on persuading people. Agenda-setting assumes that the media's major impact is in cultivating images of reality, in influencing (though not by design) the kinds of ideas people hold about the political universe. Its specific focus is the media's impact on salience judgments.

The media are not omnipotent: They do not always influence the public agenda. Moreover, the direction of causation can go from media to public, and from public to media (as when public concern with an issue forces the media to pay attention). Both the public agenda and the media agenda can also be influenced by real-world conditions, such as a sagging economy or a war. There is a complex interplay among the media agenda, public opinion, and real-world cues.

Even when the media set the agenda, they do not exert their influence in a simple unidirectional fashion. As noted in chapter 10, people bring their own biases and perspectives to mass media. The news does not inject viewers with perspectives; it suggests that certain issues are more important than others, and people (some more than others) come to accept these interpretations and adjust their political priorities accordingly.

Agenda-setting has provoked a good deal of scholarly debate. While researchers acknowledge that agenda-setting is an important concept, they have noted that there are conceptual and empirical limitations in the research literature. First, scholars have observed that we lack a convincing theoretical rationale for why media should influence public opinion, as opposed to vice versa. Second, they have noted that key terms like "agenda," "issue," "event," and even "public" have been defined imprecisely. Theoretically, this makes it possible for any effect to constitute agenda-setting. Third, critics have observed that the media and public agendas have often been measured without adequate precision and specificity.[35]

It should be clear that the common phrase "the media set the agenda" oversimplifies matters greatly. In mass communication research, terms have a very precise meaning, and, as we have seen, media agenda-setting is a complex phenomenon. But we would not want the complexity to overshadow the fact that agenda-setting is also a powerful phenomenon. As Lippmann noted years ago, the political world is "out of sight, out of mind," and rarely experienced directly; thus, we must rely on mass media to bring us images and interpretations of that world. Agenda-setting research makes the simple, but important, point that those images and interpretations can leave a mark on citizens who attend to them.

KEY ISSUES

Agenda-Setting

Agenda-Building

Public, Policy, and Media Agendas

Question of Causation

Experimental Research

Conditional Influences

Need for Orientation

Obtrusiveness

Priming

DISCUSSION QUESTIONS

1. The term "agenda-setting" is bandied about in the popular press. Now that you have read this chapter, how has your view of agenda-setting changed?

2. What evidence is there that the media exert a causal impact on the public agenda?

3. How might news have primed voters in a recent presidential election?

12

Agenda-Building

Chapter 11 introduced the concept of agenda-setting and discussed the media's impact on the public agenda. This chapter broadens the focus to the political system and examines the complex interplay among the press, government, and public. Maxwell McCombs cut to the heart of the issue in one of his many articles on agenda-setting. McCombs noted that:

> The news is not cut from whole cloth. The ingredients for the day's news are largely supplied by individuals and events quite independent of the press. And the subsequent impact of news reports rests for the most part in the hands of the political system, which must take the initiative if public concern, collective or individual, is to have major consequences. Agenda-setting, the creation of awareness and the arousal of public concern, is but one aspect of the larger process of agenda-building, a collective process in which media, government, and the public reciprocally influence each other.[1]

Early research on agenda-setting implied that the media were the major if not sole cause of changes in the public agenda. These studies took the media as the starting point and focused only on the impact of media coverage on public opinion. This approach may have been functional in the 1970s, given the paucity of research on political media effects. However, it implied that the media acted independently of other forces in the social system, when in fact the media frequently take their cues from the president, political elites, and public opinion. Subsequent studies have redressed this imbalance, and they are discussed in this chapter.

The first portion of the chapter examines the determinants of the media agenda. It focuses on the fascinating question: Who sets the media agenda? The second part of the chapter examines agenda-building on the Watergate issue. The third section takes a broader look at the agenda-building process and the role that policymakers and the public play in the construction of policy agendas. The fourth and final section focuses on the concept of *framing*, that sheds light on the "how" of agenda-setting and agenda-building. In this chapter, I cast a large net around political communication, examining the construction of agendas in areas ranging from AIDS to Watergate to investigative news reports. I discuss news about AIDS and Watergate in detail. These issues are worthy of extended discussion because they showcase the important impact that mass media exert on the agenda-building process.

THE MEDIA AGENDA

What factors shape the media agenda? What leads news organizations to focus attention on certain issues rather than others? As noted in chapter 5, news is determined by a host of personal, professional, institutional, and ideological factors. These factors determine whether news organizations will devote resources to stories and how prominently they will cover issues. To appreciate the influence of social and political forces on the media agenda, it is useful to focus on one issue in detail—coverage of AIDS in the 1980s and 1990s. By no stretch of the imagination is AIDS a typical, run-of-the-mill issue for journalists. Sometimes, though, we learn more about how people and institutions operate by looking at the unusual case than at the typical one.[2]

It is commonplace today to see stories on AIDS and to hear discussions of condoms and safe sex. It was not always like this. In the early 1980s, the news media shied away from covering AIDS issues. As James Dearing and Everett Rogers note:

> A rapidly-spreading disease that has an extremely high mortality rate might be expected to have attracted swift attention by the national mass media, the public, and by U.S. policymakers. However, the issue of AIDS did not diffuse nearly as rapidly as the disease itself ... If a scientific issue is not in the mass media, then it is not news, and if it is not news, then it does not become a public issue. AIDS did not make it onto the U.S. mass media news agenda for four years.[3]

What accounted for the reluctance of the media to cover the AIDS issue? What determined the nature of the coverage that ultimately emerged? Let's look at a few of the factors, drawing on scholarly research on the determinants of news.

Personal Attitudes

I noted in chapter 5 that journalists' personal attitudes are not major determinants of their coverage of political events. However, they can have an impact under certain conditions. James Kinsella argues that in the early 1980s, *New York Times* editors harbored prejudiced attitudes toward gays; one editor tossed around words like "faggot" and "queer" in editorial meetings. Kinsella suggests that these attitudes may have contributed to the decision to keep the AIDS epidemic off the front page of *The Times*.[4]

However, personal attitudes can cut both ways. When he learned his brother was dying of AIDS, *Newsweek* reporter Vincent Coppola pushed the magazine to do a cover story on the issue. *San Francisco Chronicle* reporter Randy Shilts brought a special passion to the story: He was gay and felt that the city's gay community was not sufficiently concerned about the threat AIDS posed to gay men's health and survival.

There is a debate about the role that personal attitudes played in coverage of AIDS. Some scholars argue that journalists' homophobic attitudes led them to downplay the AIDS story; others contend that editors took a politically correct stance and shied away from criticizing gay activists who put civil liberties ahead of the community's public health. There is no resolution to this debate since we can't know what impact journalists' attitudes had on their coverage of AIDS in the 1980s. Political communication studies suggest that whatever impact personal beliefs had on news judgments, they paled in comparison to the effects of routines and other institutional factors.

Sources

Sources, particularly those in government, are the lifeblood of news. As noted in chapter 5, the White House dominates national news, which means that presidents can set the media agenda.[5] During the 1980s, the Reagan administration did not regard AIDS as a major priority. President Reagan did not give a speech about AIDS until 1987, near the end of his second term and after over 35,000 AIDS cases had been documented by the Centers for Disease Control. The Reagan administration's apathy made it more difficult for AIDS to top the media or public agenda.

Other Reagan administration officials, such as Surgeon General C. Everett Koop, did speak out on AIDS. Scientific experts at the Centers for Disease Control also released information about the ways in which the disease was transmitted. As public health officials began talking about the epidemic proportions of the disease, the story gained legitimacy. The source routine kicked in and journalists could collect information and package it in conventional ways.

News Values

The media are quick to cover fast-onset issues, like earthquakes and bombings. They are less inclined to play up slow-onset issues, like AIDS. Such issues don't have a dramatic beginning, middle, and end; they can't be as easily reduced to sound bites. People don't die overnight of AIDS; their deaths are slow, lingering, and painful. Moreover, AIDS is an extremely complicated disease; the causes are still not understood. To do a good job of reporting on AIDS, one needs a background in medicine and public health. Few reporters have this expertise. Thus, it was more difficult to cover AIDS and to find angles that would appeal to the mass audience.

In mid-1985, two events occurred that propelled the news media to give more coverage to the AIDS issue. In July of that year it became common knowledge that actor Rock Hudson was dying of AIDS. In addition, a public controversy erupted over whether 13-year-old Ryan White, who had been diagnosed with the AIDS virus, should be permitted to attend school. These events captured the media's interest. Now AIDS was no longer a "mysterious new gay plague," but a disease that affected a world-famous actor and school children in middle America.[6]

Both events were deemed newsworthy because they jibed with journalistic news values, in particular prominence and human interest. Rock Hudson's death was "news" because it involved a prominent person. The Ryan White story was "news" because it had human drama and because it symbolically touched on an issue of great importance to most Americans—the education of their children. As Fig. 12.1 shows, these two events had a dramatic impact on news coverage of AIDS.

These incidents also transformed AIDS from a series of inexplicable, but disturbing, events to a national issue—a problem that the nation had to consider and confront.

Public Opinion

Journalists take public opinion into account when they prepare news stories and decide which issues to emphasize. They are apt to reject stories that will not appeal to the mass public and to favor those that will have general

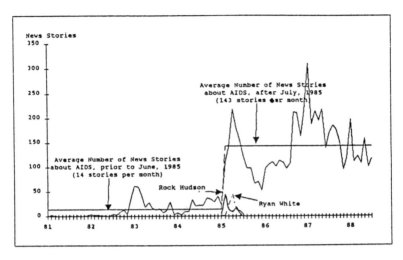

FIG. 12.1 Patterns in AIDS coverage from Dearing and Rogers (1992).

appeal. This helps explain why journalists gave prominent coverage to Rock Hudson and Ryan White and also focused on the impact of AIDS on the heterosexual population. Public concerns about AIDS, particularly the possibility that it might infect large numbers of heterosexuals, pushed the news media into covering the issue.

Another aspect of the linkage between public opinion and mass media centers on public opinion polls. In the case of AIDS, there was a complex relationship between the news agenda and the polling agenda, or the types of questions that pollsters ask. Rogers and his colleagues concluded that "media organizations sponsored polls that asked questions about AIDS and then created news stories (often several-part series) based on the poll results."[7]

Elite Media Influences

Like other professionals, journalists are influenced by the opinions of leaders in the field. In the field of journalism, *The New York Times* is a leader, and its decisions about what to cover and what not to cover influence other media outlets. *The Times's* decision not to focus on AIDS in the early 1980s suggested to other media organizations that the story was not important. Eventually, *The New York Times* did cover AIDS in depth, which undoubtedly encouraged other newspapers to do the same. Researchers call the process by which one or more media outlets influence the agenda of other media organizations **intermedia agenda-setting.**

Ideology

Although hard to quantify, ideology undoubtedly influenced news coverage of AIDS. In the early and mid-1980s, major institutions of U.S. government—the White House, the federal bureaucracy, and Congress—resisted making AIDS a major political priority. The Reagan administration focused its energies on improving the economy and on containing the Soviet Union. On the public health front, the administration showed a stronger interest in the issue of drug abuse than in AIDS. With few if any powerful elite groups pushing the AIDS issue, and many avoiding it because of the social stigma, it was hard to get the media interested in covering the story in the early 1980s.

Summary

The media were derelict at first for not doing more to cover the AIDS story. Of course, in those days most everyone in America was derelict—the government, public health officials, the public, and even some gay activists who were more concerned with preserving their freedom to engage in promiscuous sex at bathhouses than with the threat that bathhouses posed to the health and survival of the gay community.[8] Ultimately, the media decided to focus attention on AIDS, helping to put the issue on the public agenda. However, it is hard to escape the conclusion that the media might have devoted more resources to the issue had AIDS struck mainstream America rather than stigmatized groups, such as gay men and intravenous drug users.

The main point of this discussion has not been to chastise the press, but, rather, to understand the larger social and political environment in which it operates. It should be clear that the lack of coverage in the early 1980s, the dependence on scientific sources for information, the massive coverage of Magic Johnson's announcement that he had been diagnosed with the AIDS virus in 1991, the many educational stories about how the disease is transmitted, and the on-again, off-again nature of the coverage have their roots in a confluence of journalistic, political, and social system factors. The media agendas on AIDS and other issues are not cut from whole cloth. The media do not simply "set" the agenda. They help build agendas that, in most cases, have been mapped out by other political and social agencies.

WATERGATE AND AGENDA-BUILDING

Over the course of the summer and fall of 1972, *The Washington Post* doggedly followed the story of the break-in at the Democratic National Committee Headquarters at the Watergate Hotel. *The Post's* Bob Woodward and Carl Bernstein, through hard-hitting and painstaking reporting, were able to connect the Watergate burglary to the Nixon White House, were able to show that Nixon campaign funds had been involved in the break-in, and were able to document that political sabotage had played an integral role in the Nixon reelection campaign. What followed is now history: the trial of the Watergate burglars, astonishing revelations of a White House cover-up, televised hearings of Senate committee hearings, disclosure that Nixon employed a secret tape recording system in the Oval Office, the House Judiciary Committee's vote on three articles of impeachment, and Nixon's resignation on August 9, 1974.

According to popular mythology, *The Washington Post* brought the president down. Schudson observes that:

> At its broadest, the myth of journalism in Watergate asserts that two young *Washington Post* reporters brought down the president of the United States. This is a myth of David and Goliath, of powerless individuals overturning an institution of overwhelming might. It is high noon in Washington, with two white-hatted young reporters at one end of the street and the black-hatted president at the other, protected by his minions. And the good guys win. The press, truth its only weapon, saves the day.[9]

Without taking anything away from Woodward and Bernstein, who demonstrated great courage and tenacity, the fact is that *The Post* did not bring the president down. It started the ball rolling, to be sure, its reports a necessary condition for the emergence of Watergate as an issue on the national stage, but not a sufficient one. To adequately explain how events transpired in the Watergate scandal, we need to consider not just *The Post's* reports, but the larger political context in which the media work. The discussion that follows draws on Gladys Lang and Kurt Lang's book on this subject.

1972

Despite the tenacious reporting of Woodward and Bernstein (and coverage of Watergate on network news), the issue did not resonate with the American public in 1972. Few voters regarded Watergate as a decisive factor in their vote decision in the 1972 election. Honesty in government failed to develop into a major campaign issue, even among young supporters of Nixon's opponent, George McGovern.[10]

There are several reasons why Watergate did not become a major campaign issue. First, as an unobtrusive problem, Watergate required a great deal of news attention to break through people's indifference to public affairs. Not all media covered the issue in great detail, and, furthermore, the story was complicated and difficult to piece together. Watergate also had to compete with other election issues, and it was by no means the only story getting space or time in the media.

Second, the story seemed unbelievable, even to the most cynical of political observers. The idea that White House aides might approve of a break-in at Democratic party headquarters or that key presidential assistants might be involved in political espionage seemed crazy to Americans. It was inconsistent with what many voters believed—or wanted to believe—about the president; and so, according to the time-honored principle of selective perception, they discounted the information.

Third, the media described the issue in language that made the burglary seem foolish or frivolous.[11] Reporters initially accepted the White House's characterization of the break- in as a "third-rate burglary attempt." Borrowing from the then-popular television series, *Mission Impossible*, a newspaper referred to the burglary as *Mission Incredible*. The news media routinely referred to the break-in as the "Watergate caper." By using this language, the media trivialized the story, encouraging Americans to dismiss the possibility that Watergate had larger implications for the political system.

January–May 1973

Some 6 months after Nixon won a landslide victory, Watergate emerged as a major political issue. Polls indicated that Americans viewed Watergate as one of the most important problems facing the country. By early April, over 40% of the respondents interviewed in one national survey said that they believed that Richard Nixon had known about "the Watergate situation in advance."[12]

What happened? How did Watergate make the public agenda? Lang and Lang offer four explanations.

First, despite Nixon's victory in the November elections, stories about Watergate kept cropping up in the national press. The story never totally disappeared from view. The fact that Watergate was still reported in the press made it easier for the issue to penetrate the public consciousness when sensational events began occurring in 1973.

Second, a political bombshell occurred on March 23, 1973, the day before the seven Watergate defendants were scheduled to be sentenced. On this day, Judge John Sirica read a letter that he had received from one of the defendants, James McCord. The letter spoke of political pressure placed on the defendants to remain silent about others involved in the Watergate incident. It alleged that perjury had been committed during the trial. "From this point on," Lang and Lang note, "the disclosures began to fit together. They had too much plausibility to be dismissed and calls for a detailed explanation from the Administration came from both politicians and journalists."[13] From then on, the story took on a life of its own and became a major item on the media agenda.

Third, the news media began to describe Watergate with a different set of metaphors. As more and more officials became implicated in the affair, the news media stopped referring to Watergate as a "caper" and began referring to it as a full-blown political scandal. The *events* of Watergate were transformed into a major political *issue*. Watergate was described in the context of "the public's right to know" versus "executive privilege" and as an issue involving "confidence in the integrity of the government." What had once been a *caper* was now a *crisis* that rocked the very foundations of the system.[14]

A fourth reason why Watergate made the public agenda was that it became a focus of attention for America's political elites. Congress initiated an investigation of illegal campaign activities. A special prosecutor was appointed to investigate offenses arising from the burglary of the Democratic National Headquarters. The Senate Select Committee on Presidential Campaign Activities, chaired by North Carolina Senator Sam Ervin, began calling witnesses. Nixon's closest aides resigned.

These developments on the elite level virtually guaranteed that Watergate would be the major item on the nightly news and in the nation's newspapers. At the same time, the saturation coverage generated more news as policymakers responded to developments reported in the news media and tried to use the media to advance their own particular political agendas.

May 1973 and Beyond

On May 17, 1973, the networks began their gavel-to-gavel coverage of the Senate hearings on the Watergate scandal. From this point on, television took over what up to that point had been primarily a print media story. The hearings did not lead to major shifts in attitudes toward Nixon's complicity in Watergate. Instead, their impact was more subtle. After the hearings, more people regarded Watergate as a serious problem, and more Americans viewed it as a moral—and not just a political—issue.

Over the course of the year, Nixon, his political opponents, and Congressional leaders became embroiled in a fierce battle for public opinion. The battleground was the media, and public opinion polls, which tracked public attitudes toward the president and monitored support for impeachment.

Watergate was not the first time that a democratic government had faced a constitutional crisis over impeachment. But it was the first time that television had occupied center stage in an impeachment situation. TV put ordinary Americans in touch with events happening at the highest levels of government. Lang and Lang argue that television's ubiquitous presence—and the extraordinarily public nature of the process—encouraged political leaders to be responsive to societal norms and to consider the larger moral and constitutional issues involved in the crisis.

In sum, the media helped to build consensus around the Watergate issue. They did so not by directly persuading the public to change its attitudes toward impeachment. Rather, they influenced the process on a number of levels, highlighting some events rather than others, framing issues through the use of language and metaphors, linking the news to familiar political symbols, connecting the public to political elites through opinion polls, and calling on time-honored political values that forced political actors to consider the larger implications of their actions.[15]

There is still debate about whether Nixon would have been ousted from office had the events not been covered as they were in the media. Some scholars note that the system came preciously close to failing—had *The Washington Post* not stumbled on the story, had key Nixon aides not come forward with information that incriminated the president, and had a less courageous group of legislators voted on the articles of impeachment, it is entirely possible that Richard Nixon would not have been forced from power. But these events did occur. And while the press did not single-handedly bring Nixon down, it played a critical role in the process. It was, after all, the news media that dug up the dirt, kept the story on the front burner, and helped to legitimate the process by which the president of the United States was tried for high crimes and misdemeanors. In the tragedy of Watergate, the media played a complex—but decidedly positive—role.

MEDIA, PUBLIC OPINION, AND POLICYMAKING

This section focuses on a particularly important aspect of the agenda-building process: the shaping of policy agendas. **Policy agenda-building** has been defined as the process by which some problems "come to command the active and serious attention of government as prospective matters of public policy."[16] Shaping the policy agenda is a complex and controversial business. In America, there are numerous problems that compete for policymakers' attention and countless powerful and not-so-powerful groups that want to shape policies in this way or that. Which problem gets the attention of America's leaders? Which problems fall by the wayside? David Protess and his colleagues observe that:

> It is no easy matter for social problems to get on policymakers' agendas and produce corrective actions. The number of problems that policymakers might address is virtually infinite. The number that actually come to their attention is circumscribed, but each of those must still vie for policymakers' interest. Policymakers must decide which problems will receive priority attention … [17]

Deciding that something is a problem is itself an important political act. For years, policymakers viewed the plight of African Americans as a fact of life—an unfortunate, but inevitable, consequence of the Darwinian principle of survival of the fittest. This changed in the 1950s, as protests convinced leaders that prejudice and segregation were *social problems* that demanded policy attention. In the same fashion, environmental pollution, homelessness, and, most recently, the growth of the federal government have come to be seen as problems requiring attention and amelioration.

What determines whether an issue is seen as a problem and whether it commands policymakers' interest? Political scientists have identified a number of factors, including the existence of a "ripe" or favorable political climate, the expression of concern by groups inside and outside government at approximately the same time, public concern, as evidenced by opinion polls, and the articulation of specific policies to deal with the problem.[18] Furthermore, issues do not stay on the policy agenda forever. Policymakers and concerned citizens realize that they have only a fixed amount of time to make policy changes before another issue (that commands the passion of another group of leaders or activists) pushes their issue off the national agenda.

What role do mass media play in the policy-building process? To answer this question, we must consider the impact of three key players in political communication: the media, the public, and policymakers (i.e., government leaders). As Fig. 12.2 shows, each of these groups can initiate the development of policy agenda-building. The discussion that follows examines agenda-building as it has been initiated by these three groups.

Media-Initiated Agenda-Building

When you think about muckraking and crusading journalists, you probably have in mind what Protess and his colleagues refer to as **the mobilization model of investigative reporting**. This is the notion that investigative journalism arouses and mobilizes the public, which in turn pushes leaders to make reforms. The mobilization model dates back to early twentieth century muckraking, when (as legend has it) newspaper exposes of government corruption and urban squalor activated the conscience of the public, which then beat down the doors of city hall to demand immediate action (see Fig. 12-2a).

Policy agenda-building rarely follows the mobilization model. Typically, the media do not propel the public into demanding policy action. In most cases, the public plays a more passive role. This is reflected in the second model of media-instigated agenda-building, shown in Fig. 12.2b. According to this model, there is a bidirectional relationship between media and policymakers; both influence each other (and work together) to develop a policy agenda. We can appreciate this by looking at a case study example provided by Protess et al.

Media–Policymaker Alliances.   The headline, "Kidney Patients vs. the Bottom Line," introduced the dramatic *Philadelphia Inquirer* series. Describing the patients as "some of the most needy in America," the stories showed

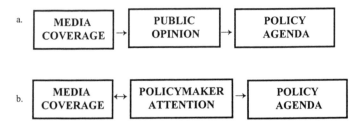

FIG. 12.2a & 12.2b Models of Agenda-Building.

how federally funded dialysis treatments centers had placed profits over the care of victims of kidney failure. They focused on how clinics had reused dialysis equipment in an effort to cut costs. The series also documented that the federal government had failed to adequately police its own kidney treatment centers.[19]

In follow-up research on the effects of the series, Protess and his associates found that the articles had only a modest impact on public beliefs. Importantly, they failed to increase concern about the profits-over-people angle of dialysis treatment centers.

By contrast, the series had a significant impact on policymakers and on the policy-making process. Two weeks after the story broke, the Pennsylvania Board of Medicine launched an investigation of a clinic that had been targeted in the articles. Four months later, a bill was introduced in Congress that recommended the imposition of strong penalties for clinics found to be providing substandard care.

The investigative articles exerted an impact on the policy-making process, but the effects seemed minimally influenced by public opinion. If anything, the investigative reports affected policymakers' perceptions directly. How had this happened? Early in the investigative process, the reporters formed a partnership with Congressional investigators who had been looking into abuses in federally funded dialysis centers. The officials needed reporters to publicize the abuses, reporters needed officials to give them access to private documents. Each side helped the other, and by the time that the stories came out, the machinery for policy-making reforms was in place and ready to move to the next stage.[20]

Thus, investigative reports rarely influence policy-making by activating and mobilizing public opinion. The role of the public in media-instigated agenda-building is typically more passive and quiescent. (While some scholars would lament the fact that public opinion plays a passive role in policy-making, others would point out that this is the way the Founding Fathers wanted things; they gave us, after all, a representative democracy, not a pure democratic form of government.)

Policymaker-Initiated Agenda-Building

Policymakers, including the president, members of Congress, and officials in the federal bureaucracy, frequently initiate the agenda-building process. They have ideas or agendas that they want to push, and they use the media to accomplish their goals. As discussed in previous chapters, government leaders employ a variety of strategies to promote agendas, including the use of press conferences, leaks, and public speeches.

The most common model of policymaker-initiated agenda-building is shown in Fig. 12.2c. A policymaker tries to move an issue to the top of the policy agenda by using the media to move public opinion, which, it is hoped, will influence the policy agenda.[21]

Presidents frequently try to influence public attitudes through rhetoric. As noted in chapter 7, the impact of rhetoric on public opinion is complex. Presidential speeches rarely influence the policy agenda simply by pushing public opinion up a few notches. As discussed earlier, journalists' perceptions of public opinion, opinion polls, and interest groups' adroit manipulation of public opinion are important mediators of the impact of presidential rhetoric on the policy agenda-building process.

Public-Initiated Agenda-Building

The public rarely initiates the agenda-building process. However, there have been cases in which public outrage has spurred media and policy elites to take action. This model of agenda-building is shown in Fig. 12.2d as an example in which public opinion influences the media agenda, which in turn affects the policy agenda.

A classic case of public-initiated agenda-building occurred in January, 1993 when a populist uprising forced President-Elect Bill Clinton to withdraw his support for Zoe Baird for the position of U.S. Attorney General.[22]

Initially, the prospects for Baird's nomination as Attorney General looked good. The majority of media reports were favorable. Then *The New York Times* revealed that Baird had hired two illegal aliens as a babysitter

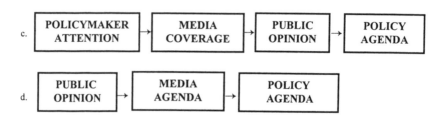

FIG. 12.2c & 12.2d Models of Agenda-Building.

and part-time driver and that she had failed to pay Social Security taxes on them. Baird's decision to knowingly hire illegal aliens was in violation of a 1986 law.

At first, both government officials and elite journalists played down the issue. They pointed out that Baird believed she was acting legally because she was sponsoring the female worker's application for U.S. citizenship. News stories quoted immigration officials as saying that the hiring of illegal aliens was relatively common and hard to police. Some elite journalists confessed they had faced similar problems hiring nannies to take care of their own kids and, consequently, could sympathize with Baird's problems.

The public was not so forgiving. Ordinary people were outraged that, as one talk-show host put it, "a woman making half a million dollars a year in a state going through a crippling and pervasive recession … could not find an out-of-work Connecticut couple to do the job."[23] Talk-show hosts were besieged by calls from angry people, many of them women who felt that it was wrong for a U.S. Attorney General-designate to have broken the law.

Pressure built as the mainstream media began covering the story of public opposition to Baird's nomination. Editorial page columnists stepped up their criticism. The popular protests nudged leading members of Congress to question and eventually oppose Baird's confirmation as Attorney General. With the White House moving away from Baird and support in Congress diminishing, Baird withdrew her name from consideration.

The Baird case demonstrates that, under some conditions, the public can influence public policy. As Benjamin Page and Jason Tannenbaum noted, the public applied reasonable ethical standards to a presidential decision, thus providing a useful corrective to the parochial and elite criteria used by White House officials. It was, they say, "a victory for democracy."[24]

Generalizations

After reviewing the voluminous agenda-setting and agenda-building litera-ture, Rogers and Dearing concluded that several general principles had emerged from the research:

1. The public agenda, once set by, or reflected by, the media agenda, influences the policy agenda of elite decision makers, and, in some cases, policy implementation;
2. The media agenda seems to have direct, sometimes strong, influence upon the policy agenda of elite decision makers, and, in some cases, policy implementation;
3. For some issues the policy agenda seems to have a direct, sometimes strong, influence upon the media agenda.[25]

Wow! Talk about complicated conclusions! But the process by which agendas are built in America is nothing if not complex—and is profoundly influenced by social, psychological, and institutional factors simultaneously operating at different places in the political system.

The mass media play an important role in agenda-building, but, as we have seen, you cannot easily separate the media from other actors in the system. News and policy agendas are frequently intertwined as both journalists and policymakers use one another to achieve their personal and professional goals. Public opinion influences the media agenda and is determined by it.

Scholars have tried to develop more precise predictions about the role the media play in policy-making. Some models emphasize that the media play a different role at different stages of the policy-making process. Others stress that there is a dynamic transactional relationship among the media, public opinion, and policy agendas, with real-world factors, such as unemployment, also influencing the process (see Fig. 12.3).[26]

In the final analysis, in a democratic society, problems must inevitably compete for media, public, and policymakers' attention. Attention, after all, is a scarce resource, and those who can capture the attention of media gatekeepers, elite decision-makers, and the general public will be most likely to see government address the problems they view as most pressing. But, in America, attention is fleeting. As Anthony Downs observed, an issue-attention cycle seems to influence public (and policymakers') attitudes toward key national problems. Downs noted that "each of these problems suddenly leaps into prominence, remains there for a short time, and then—though still largely unresolved—gradually fades from the center of public attention."[27] Policymakers have only a small amount of time in which to enact policy legislation before the next issue clamors for their attention.

FRAMING

Agenda-setting and agenda-building research tell us which issues command the attention of the public, the press, and policy elites. The scholarly studies in this area have advanced knowledge about media and politics. However, they have focused rather blandly on the content of issues emphasized by the media. What they have not considered is *how* the public, press, and policymaking elites *interpret* and *organize* the issues of the day. In recent years, researchers have adopted a transactional perspective to examine how the public and elites make sense of political information. This line of research falls under the heading of **framing.**

Frame comes from the word "framework." It refers to the context we use to comprehend complex information. Neuman, Just, and Crigler define frames as *"conceptual tools which media and individuals rely on to convey, interpret, and evaluate information."*[28] Zhongdang Pan and Gerald Kosicki view a news media frame as *" a cognitive device used in information encoding, interpreting and retrieving."*[29]

Like agenda-setting, framing can operate at different levels of analysis. We can examine the ways policymakers, journalists, and citizens frame political issues. Researchers have examined how frames operate in a variety of political communication domains.

Presidents try to encourage other elites and the public to frame, or interpret, an issue in a particular way. In 1990, George Bush framed the Iraqi invasion as a threat to the stability of the post-cold war world. Others invoked an economic frame, arguing that Bush's decision to send troops to the Gulf had more to with a determination not to let Iraq control the price or supply of oil than anything else.[30]

The media frame issues in a variety of ways. The news media may accept, reject, or question the frames that policymakers employ to interpret events. They must decide, for example, whether to describe urban riots as understandable political protests or as intolerable threats to law and order. On the local level, the news media can frame a new civic center as an exciting addition to the downtown area or as an example of government putting

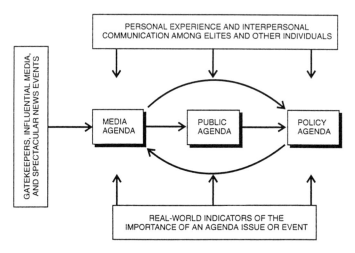

FIG. 12.3. Main Components of Agenda-Building From Rogers and Dearing (1988).

corporate needs ahead of those of the inner city.

The public also employs frames to make sense of political issues. Neuman and his colleagues argue that Americans rely on four issue frames: *human impact* (effect of events on people); *powerlessness* (helplessness of ordinary people); *economics* (e.g., the profit motive and corporate greed); and *morality* (moral values, religion, and God). People use these frames to comprehend and interpret complex events. Frames help people process the wealth of political information they encounter in everyday life.[31]

Media Effects on Frames

Just as we examined the impact of the media on the public agenda, we can also explore media effects on the frames people use to interpret political issues.

Iyengar conducted one of the first studies of framing effects.[32] He observed that television news frames issues in either an *episodic* or *thematic* fashion. Episodic news focuses on concrete events and personalities, such as a recent crime wave or the plight of a teenage mother on welfare. It typically relies on graphic pictures and hard-hitting reports. Thematic news puts events in a larger social and economic context; it tries to explain rather than graphically describe.

Noting that the networks tend to employ episodic frames for economic and organizational reasons, Iyengar examined whether these frames influence viewers' interpretation of social problems. In a series of field experiments, he showed research participants either episodic or thematic news. For example, an episodic story on poverty described a particularly bitter winter in the Midwest and showed how two families could not pay their heating bills. A thematic story on poverty juxtaposed a description of national increases in poverty with a discussion of reductions in government social programs. After watching the stories, subjects indicated what they believed were the most important causes of the problem (e.g., poverty).

Iyengar found that episodic and thematic stories encouraged the use of episodic and thematic frames respectively. Participants who saw episodic stories were more likely to explain poverty in individualistic terms, holding the poor responsible for their fate. Participants who viewed thematic stories tended to attribute poverty to societal conditions.

Iyengar argues that television's tendency to frame poverty episodically makes it more difficult for people to recognize that poverty has complex social and economic precursors. This in turn may have led people to respond more sympathetically to the argument that it is time to cut federally funded antipoverty programs. Thus, in Iyengar's view, television contributed indirectly to widely publicized shifts in public support for government social welfare spending Of course, conservatives would applaud these shifts in public sentiment, arguing that the poor are in some sense responsible for their fate. Liberals would naturally disagree.

Iyengar emphasizes that by endlessly focusing on brief snatches of problems and neglecting the larger picture, television news makes it more difficult for people to appreciate that issues are interconnected, problems have systemic roots, and leaders are responsible for proposing remedies. As a result, he says, television news shields our leaders from accepting responsibility for problems and discourages elites from making tough choices.

These claims are interesting, but unsubstantiated. Consider that the public was all too willing to hold President Bush accountable for his decision to reverse his "No New Taxes" pledge in 1990 and regarded Jimmy Carter as responsible for the nation's economic woes in 1980. Presumably, voters had considerable exposure to television news during these periods.

Thus, the impact of news frames on public opinion is complex. Research indicates that a host of factors must be considered, including people's preexisting political sentiments, their political sophistication, and the nature of the issue under consideration.[33] Contrary to the claims made by critical theorists, people are not passive victims of media frames. Conservatives reject stories that emphasize societal responsibility for poverty; liberals embrace them. Moreover, people don't share all of the media's frames. Ordinary people tend to frame issues in terms of their human impact; journalists focus more on conflict and on "good guys versus bad guys." As uses and gratifications and information-processing theories suggest, citizens actively interpret and sort out information they receive in the media.

This does not mean that media frames have no impact. On the contrary, people depend on the media to make sense of a confusing, ambiguous political world. When issues are complicated and unobtrusive, people may be particularly influenced by news frames. Vincent Price argues that "by activating some ideas rather than others the news can encourage particular trains of thought about political phenomena."[34] Once activated, these frames can then be accessed, and brought to bear in later political decision-making situations.

CONCLUSIONS

The press has always exerted an important impact on politics, from the Revolutionary War to the penny press of the 1830s, through the Civil War to the crusading journalism of the early twentieth century, and throughout the twentieth century. The power of the press lies in its ability to shape agendas and to frame events in ways that influence public opinion and policy.

In this chapter I noted that the agenda-building process is intricate and complex. The news agenda is not created out of thin air. News routines, opinion polls, influential media voices, and even ideology shape the media agenda. Once formed, the media agenda can influence public opinion, working in concert with other societal institutions. There is a complex, transactional relationship among the media, public, and policy agendas, with the directions of influence depending on the issue and the situation. Sustained coverage by mass media is typically a necessary, but not sufficient, condition for an issue to make it to the top of the policy agenda. In America, issues do not stay long on the policy or public agenda; today's problem is tomorrow's retrievable memory. Furthermore, just because an issue commands the attention of the media, the public, or policymakers does not mean that it will be solved. Environmental pollution, drug abuse, and poverty have all dominated the national agenda, but they remain intractable problems.

It should be clear from this chapter that the media do not simply "set" the agenda, by pushing a magic button on an all-powerful control panel. In many cases, the media reflect agendas cultivated by policymakers; in other cases they work with policymakers, directly and indirectly, to build agendas. And, of course, at any given time there is not one media agenda, but many agendas, with agendas varying as a function of the issue, the medium, and the dynamics of the political situation.

There is a continuing debate about whether media agenda-setting maintains the status quo or foments change. Media critics remind us that the media were slow to devote serious attention to social issues like AIDS. They note that the media are all too likely to index their coverage to the views of prominent elites who are themselves predisposed to move slowly and conservatively on policy matters.

On the other hand, the press played an important role in building the public and policy agenda on Watergate. Investigative stories have influenced policy agendas on numerous occasions—particularly when journalists formed alliances with activists in the policymaking arena. In addition, news coverage of the budget deficit in the 1980s seems to have convinced Americans that the deficit is a pressing problem deserving of policy attention.

In the final analysis, the media are one player among many in the battle to set and influence the nation's agenda. The struggle is to control the direction the nation takes and to shape the country's priorities. It is a high-stakes battle involving considerations of power politics, ideology, and strategic political marketing. While many lament that such "political games" must be fought, the fact is that they are endemic to modern democracy, inevitable in an era of mass media communication. Democratic societies must decide which problems to tackle, which to shelve, and how to develop and implement public policy. American society has developed its own set of procedures for determining which issues will command policy and media attention; they are a complex set of procedures, to be sure. The ways that America goes about deciding which problems should be tackled are not necessarily the best; they inevitably favor those at the top of the nation's pecking order, those with the most resources to expend to influence the agenda-building process. But America is nothing if not a society in change and a society in flux: power changes hands, innovative people figure out ways to influence the system, new political groups form and devise creative strategies to push proposals to the top of the nation's agenda.

KEY ISSUES

The Media Agenda on AIDS

Inter-Media Agenda-Setting

Agenda-Building in Watergate

Policy Agenda-Building

Mobilization Model of Investigative Reporting

Media–Policymaker Alliances

Policymaker-Initiated Agenda-Building

Public-Initiated Agenda-Building

Framing

DISCUSSION QUESTIONS

1. What were the main determinants of news coverage of AIDS?

2. Would Nixon have fallen from the political forest if the media had not been there to cover him?

3. In what types of situations does the public have the greatest impact on the agenda-building process?

13

The Health Care Reform Campaign

With health care costs skyrocketing and an astounding 15% of the population unable to purchase health insurance, the White House decided that action had to be taken to reform the health care delivery system. After extensive planning and much hoopla, President Bill Clinton delivered an impassioned address to Congress and the nation on September 22, 1993, calling for a sweeping overhaul of the nation's health care system.

Expectations were high as Clinton delivered his address.

A year later, health reform was dead. Neither Clinton's bill—nor any of the others—were voted on by Congress.

The campaigns waged for and against Clinton's health care plan tell us a great deal about contemporary political communication. The campaigns powerfully illustrate the principles of agenda-building discussed in the previous chapter. They also call on the many issues discussed in the first section of the book, notably presidential rhetoric and news determinants. Thus, this chapter and the one that follows focus on the campaign to reform the nation's health care, providing a multiperspectival look at the controversial health reform effort.

BEGINNINGS

Health care is one of those issues that has moved on and off the nation's agenda for years. It surfaced again in 1991. That year Harris Wofford made health care reform a centerpiece of his campaign to serve as U.S. Senator from Pennsylvania. Wofford's stunning upset victory caught the attention of Democratic party politicians, who sensed this could be a good issue for the 1992 presidential campaign.

During the 1992 primary campaign, Democratic presidential candidates introduced health care reform proposals. Newspapers described the candidates' positions on health care. Television news specials spotlighted "the health care crisis." Thus, political elites—candidates for the presidency—succeeded in getting the news media to cover the health issue. Classic media agenda-setting then ensued. From January 1992 to January 1993, the proportion of the public naming health care as the most important problem facing the nation increased from 6% to 18%. By the time Clinton delivered his speech in September, 1993, health care was seen as the second most important issue facing the country, trailing only the economy.[1]

For most people, health care reform was an obtrusive issue, one that touched their lives directly. The obtrusive aspects of the issue quickly became salient as interest groups repeatedly argued that Clinton's plan would destroy the relationship between patients and their doctor. Thus, the media not only set the agenda, they also played a critical role in framing the issue.

PRESIDENTIAL COMMUNICATION

Health care rose to the top of the policy agenda in 1993 when Bill Clinton made it clear that this issue would be a major focus of his presidency. Concerned that health care costs were rising out of control, that 37 million Americans lacked health care coverage, and that middle-class Americans were nervous that their insurance would be revoked if they changed jobs, Clinton decided to push for major reform of the nation's health care delivery system.

In a controversial move, he appointed First Lady Hillary Rodham Clinton to direct the health care reform effort. Under the First Lady's direction, the health reform task force worked around the clock, trying to fulfill the president's promise of submitting health reform legislation to Congress within the first 100 days of his presidency. However, the group alienated potential supporters by choosing not to involve Republican legislators in the policymaking process and by closing off meetings to the public and the press. Nevertheless, the task force worked methodically and in the end produced a 1,300 page document. After extensive policy analysis, polling, and high-level discussions, the Clinton plan was ready for *roll-out*—or formal introduction to the public and policy elites.

The Clinton administration set up a war room to coordinate roll-out efforts. (Hillary Clinton preferred the term "delivery room" as it seemed more relevant to the health care issue.) A 2-day event, dubbed the health care university, was held on Capitol Hill to teach members of Congress about the plan. Radio talk-show hosts were invited to broadcast from the White House's North Lawn the day after the speech. Clinton aides worked around the clock, scheduling events, coordinating rallies, and preparing counterattacks to the inevitable criticisms from Newt Gingrich and other Congressional conservatives.[2]

At 9 p.m. on September 22, 1993, Clinton strode into the House of Representatives chamber, prepared to address Congress and the nation. The speech had been written and rewritten many times. Everything had been prepared—down to the last detail. Everything except one thing, as it turned out. Journalist Elizabeth Drew relates what happened:

> Clinton entered the chamber to strong applause, said his modest thanks from the podium, glanced at the Teleprompter, and, while the ovation continued, turned to (Vice President) Gore behind him and said, "They've got the wrong speech." "You're kidding," Gore replied. "No," Clinton said. "See for yourself, it's the wrong speech." Gore, momentarily leaving his chair, summoned Stephanopoulos. Stephanopoulos and (deputy communications director) Dreyer flew out of the chamber and tried scrolling down to the health care speech— "but all we could see was the (February 17) economic speech," Dreyer said. (The economic speech had been inadvertently placed before the health care speech on the Teleprompter.) ... Clinton was now well into his speech, reading from the printed copy before him and also winging it ... So Clinton, with tens of millions watching, was reading and winging, and seeing out of the corner of his eye his speech text whizzing down the Teleprompter, until the changes were made and the text on the screen caught up with him.

Clinton stayed collected and delivered one of the best and most impassioned speeches of his Presidency.[3]

The speech laid out the principles underlying the health reform effort. Clinton did not deliver the specific proposal to Congress until October. In the proposal, Clinton recommended that there be universal coverage (health insurance for all Americans) by January 1, 1998. Employers would be required to pay for 80% of the cost of their employees' insurance premiums. (This was called the employer mandate.) The government would pick up the tab for the poor and unemployed. In addition, a system of health care alliances would be created, to be run by the states. The alliances would purchase insurance on behalf of millions of consumers, using the leveraging power of their large membership to cut the best deals with networks of hospitals and physicians. The federal government would oversee the work of the alliances and would set standards for care.

Although Clinton's speech received rave reviews, his plan—and how it was packaged rhetorically—drew criticism. There were several problems.

First, the plan was too abstruse and complicated for the American people to comprehend. Two great presidential communicators—Franklin D. Roosevelt and Ronald Reagan—knew in their gut that presidents had to make matters clear and simple for their audiences. Both FDR and Reagan had boiled down their economic reforms to simple propositions and had made certain that a fundamental theme ran through their policy proposals. By contrast, the Clinton proposal had multiple themes and employed abstract terms, such as *managed competition, mandates, and single-payer plan.* These terms "sounded heavy, bureaucratic (and) authoritarian," journalists Haynes Johnson and David Broder noted. "They were neither simple nor reassuring."[4]

Second, Clinton did not effectively employ crisis rhetoric (see chapter 7). Clinton proclaimed that the country faced a health care crisis. Yet as Rachel Holloway notes,"a 'crisis'demands public and Congressional attention … immediately." Unfortunately, the president's response to the crisis "was neither immediate nor a clear source of unity."[5] His task force lumbered for months before issuing its report. And the report it produced was so incomprehensible that it "squelched any urgency or momentum created by the 'crisis.'"[6]

Thirdly, Clinton did not frame the issue as strategically as he might have. He framed the issue in terms of universal coverage—the need to provide coverage to all Americans. He emphasized universal care because he hoped that it would help rein in costs. One reason why middle-class taxpayers pay so much for health care is that they are essentially subsidizing the health care of Americans who have no insurance. Universal coverage was proposed to shift the burden from the middle class to the system as a whole. But, as Holloway notes, Clinton began to focus on "'universal coverage' as an end in itself, ultimately creating a 'right' of health care, without articulation of the connections to the middle class, who already had health care but were discouraged by escalating costs."[7] Thus, middle- class Americans began to wonder whether the president's plan would benefit them or whether it would be another entitlement to the poor.

Fourth, there were management problems. The president should not have picked his wife to coordinate the health reform effort. No one doubted that Mrs. Clinton was a woman of immense intelligence. However, the fact that she was married to the president made it difficult for staff members and consultants to give the kind of honest feedback that is needed to improve and refashion policy proposals. As one Clinton administration official said, "The person who's in charge shouldn't sleep with the President, because if you sleep with the President, nobody is going to tell you the truth."[8]

By giving the leadership assignment to his wife and not the Department of Health and Human Services, Clinton thwarted the conventional, tried-and-true policymakng process. Had he given health care reform to the human services department, experienced government hands and key officials in the federal bureaucracy could have used their political clout to win support on Capitol Hill.

Finally, Clinton tackled too much—too fast. The task of extensively changing an industry that accounted for one seventh of the nation's economy was gargantuan, not possible to accomplish in one presidential term. The president might have had more success had he proceeded more slowly, getting some reform legislation through Congress, building consensus on new measures, and then moving to another area of health care reform. But Clinton was determined to move quickly, having made a campaign promise to submit a health care bill to Congress within the first 100 days of his presidency.

Oh, those campaign promises! Candidates have been taken to the mat by voters for not keeping promises that they never should have made in the first place. Yet candidates feel compelled to come up with simple arguments and memorable sound bites, only to regret that they succumbed at a much later date.[9] The 100-day promise harks back to FDR, who had succeeded in getting Congress to pass major New Deal reforms in his first 100 days of office. But Roosevelt had accomplished these reforms in a different era: Consensus-building in Washington was easier then, and Roosevelt could appeal to a nation groping for leadership in the midst of a worldwide Depression. Yet today's presidents, transfixed by FDR's success, saddle themselves with timetables that are impossible to adequately meet.

Clinton also was determined to make health care reform an issue in the 1994 Congressional election campaign.[10] Thus, health care reform—a complex and multifaceted issue—became just another campaign issue, driven by campaign ads and opinion polls. The campaign war mind-set may have impeded efforts to seek compromise and conciliation.

THE YEAR-LONG BATTLE FOR PUBLIC OPINION

Groups that opposed Clinton's plan realized from the outset that to defeat the Clinton proposal, they would have to win the battle of public opinion.

For some interest coalitions, the war began when Clinton delivered his address to the nation on September 22, 1993. For example:

The evening that Clinton gave his televised address, Michele Davis, a health care expert and former aide to President George Bush, worked alone in a downtown Washington office, typing a message on her word processor.

Davis was crafting a critical response to Clinton's plan. The plan, she claimed, would "force insurance companies and HMOs to ration care."[11] Soon Davis and other leaders of conservative lobbying organizations would band together, transforming a downtown office conference room to a war room for the anti-Clinton alliance. Privately calling themselves the "No Name Coalition" to keep their work hidden from the public, the groups consisted of as many as 30 organizations, including the Health Insurance Association of America and the National Federation of Independent Business. Their goal was to derail Clinton's health care reform effort, what they termed "Clintoncare."

Only those who argue that interest group lobbying is antithetical to democracy would suggest that the health care coalitions had no right to oppose Clinton's plan. Interest groups have long played a part in democratic decision-making, and one can make a good philosophical case that they have every right to try to influence presidential policy.

Moreover, business executives who opposed the Clinton plan pointed out that they had been fighting for years to control their companies' health care expenses. Now, journalists Johnson and Broder noted, "just when they were beginning to bring their health care bills down closer to the overall inflation rate, along came the Clintons with their elaborate scheme that would standardize benefits, (and) bring new governmental and quasigovernmental regulation."[12]

There were other reasons why business leaders decided to oppose the Clinton plan. Insurance and pharmaceutical CEOs who served on the board of directors of other companies lobbied against the reform package, pointing out that when government gets involved in health care, everything goes downhill. As one opponent put it, Clinton's proposal promised "the efficiency of the post office and the compassion of the IRS."[13]

In addition to their ideological opposition to government involvement in health care, insurance executives feared they would lose money if the federal bureaucracy standardized benefits.

Ideology and self-interest also explained the actions of Republican Congressional leaders. Republicans like Newt Gingrich opposed Clinton's plan because it promised to build up government—an entity which, in the view of Gingrich and his followers, was stifling individual initiative and destroying the American Dream. Republican leaders also feared that if Clinton's plan passed, it would make middle-class Americans dependent once again on government spending. This in turn would resuscitate the Democratic party's image as "the generous protector of middle-class interests," thereby striking a dagger to the heart of the Republicans' goal of winning back the critical middle-class vote.[14]

The stage was set for a lobbying battle, the likes of which had never been seen before. An estimated $200 million was spent lobbying for and against the Clinton reform package.

Leading the fight to oppose the Clinton plan were the Health Insurance Association of America, the National Federation of Independent Business, the National Restaurant Association, and the Christian Coalition. Supporting the Clinton plan were the Democratic National Committee, the California Wellness Foundation and the Kaiser Family Foundation. It was the most intense and expensive lobbying campaign in the nation's history. As Johnson and Broder note:

> In this fight, the interests demonstrated their ability to move far beyond traditional techniques of "buying" political access. They showed—at least on the opponents' side—that for the first time, they had learned to use all the tools of modern politics and political communications for their special-interest objectives. Like the officials they were trying to influence, these groups showed they could manipulate public opinion and mobilize Main Street supporters to deliver at the ballot box.[15]

Lobbyists theorized that if they could show lawmakers that the public opposed the plan, legislators would perceive that it was in their self-interest to vote down the Clinton bill. A major battle for public opinion ensued, with public opinion being operationalized not as the number of citizens who were knocking on doors demanding or opposing change, but more passively, as numbers on opinion polls—the percentage for or against, the proportion opposing or supporting the Clinton proposals.

In many ways, the battle was to control the frame. The agenda having been set, the question was which frame did the public buy into: the liberal notion that the Clinton plan was needed because government had an obligation to provide health care to all Americans; the Clintons' notion that government had to take steps to control the unending escalation of health care costs; or the Republicans' conviction that the Clinton plan was equivalent to government-run health care.

Opponents of the Clinton plan labored hard—and successfully—to convince the public that "Clintoncare" meant the intrusion of Big Government into people's private lives. The plan would force most Americans to leave their family doctors, critics charged. It would conscript Americans into health maintenance organizations (HMOs), and would take away their freedom to choose their own doctors. It would lock people into a gigantic, repressive federal bureaucracy from which there was no escape, critics vehemently argued.

These themes were played up in a multi-million dollar advertising campaign paid for by the Health Insurance Association of America (HIAA). The campaign was a classic example of issue advertising—of corporate and non-profit groups "going public."[16]

After conducting opinion polls, which showed that Americans were deeply distrustful of government, the HIAA came up with the brilliant idea of framing the Clinton plan as *government health care* not as *national health insurance*. Using the "Harry and Louise" spots described in chapter 1, the organization relied on phrases test-marketed in focus groups, such as "They choose, you lose," and "There's got to be a better way."[17]

Ads typically attempted to arouse fear by using vivid words and images. In one ad, the zigzag line of an EKG monitor appeared on the television screen. The announcer intoned that:

> Bill Clinton Wants to Socialize Health Care.
>
> Small Business Will Pay the Bill.
>
> The Largest Government Bureaucracy in History.
>
> The Bureaucracy Will Decide.
>
> The Bureaucracy Will Never See You.
>
> The Bureaucracy Will Never Examine You.
>
> Never Talk to You.
>
> Never Even See You.
>
> Limit Your Choice of Doctors.
>
> The Bureaucracy Will Dictate.
>
> The Bureaucracy Will Decide.
>
> You Will Lose Choice and Control.
>
> It's Your Health Care They're Socializing.[18]

At the end of the ad, the EKG line became flat, leaving the viewer with the impression that death would result if the Clinton plan were passed.

The interest groups also employed focus groups, sophisticated opinion polling, and "fax alerts." The National Federation of Independent Business (NFIB) sent small business owners tens of thousands of faxes that castigated the Clinton plan. Every two months, pollsters interviewed each of the 600,000 members of the NFIB. Results of the polls were delivered to members of Congress and their staff members.

The lobbying organizations also relied on the friendly persuasion of Rush Limbaugh and other conservative talk-show hosts. Limbaugh waged a fierce battle against the Clintons. One Limbaugh parody began with eerie music. A narrator, sounding a bit like the host of the old "Twilight Zone" television show, then spoke these words:

> She's a doctor with a prescription for disaster. She's Hillary Clinton and she's Doctor Hilldare.
>
> Male Voice: I don't know, Doctor. I tend to get a little heartburn after eating spicy food. What do you recommend I do?
>
> Sinister Female Voice: Heart transplant.

Evaluation

What types of appeals did the ads use? How did they try to make their case? Research by Kathleen Jamieson and Joseph Cappella and by Lynda Kaid and her colleagues focused on these questions. Jamieson and Kaid's research teams systematically analyzed the content of television ads. They reached the following conclusions:

- Advertising was more likely to be unfair than fair. Fifty-nine percent of the broadcast ads were judged to be unfair, misleading, or false.[19]
- The spots were more likely to attack a policy option than to advocate a particular proposal.
- The ads relied heavily on fear. They were more likely to arouse anxiety than to provide reassurance.
- Ads that opposed the Clinton plan were more likely to use emotional appeals than those that supported it.
- Ads opposing the Clinton plan overstated the negative effects of the Clinton reform package. They exaggerated the degree to which the plan would lead to waiting lines, big government control, and reduced choice of doctors.
- Ads supporting the Clinton plan overstated the health care problem by exaggerating the proportion of people denied coverage by their current health care plans. They also incorrectly maintained that Republican proposals would do nothing to help patients.[20]

This is not to say that the ads were all outright lies. Like many simplifications, they contained a kernel of truth. For example, it is true that by encouraging the use of health maintenance organizations and in making it more costly for people to choose their own doctors, the Clinton plan reduced Americans' choices. However, there was nothing that prohibited people who did not like the options provided in the Clinton plan to spend some of their own money to get extra health care. The claim that "Bill Clinton wants to socialize our health care" hardly fit the facts. Yet it had great appeal to a public that had grown tired of government bureaucracy.[21]

CONCLUSIONS

President Clinton launched the campaign to reform health care with a speech in September, 1993. Clinton offered path-breaking, but controversial, suggestions for how to reform the system. His overall approach had several shortcomings, from a rhetorical perspective.

Opponents mounted a serious and sophisticated campaign to derail the president's health reform effort. Spending millions on advertising and public relations, they sought to convince the public that Clinton's plan was a mistake. Using all the techniques of contemporary politics and public communications, the interest groups waged an emotional campaign to influence public opinion and policy elites.

KEY ISSUES

Rhetoric of Health Reform

Anti-Clinton Campaign

Issue Advertising

DISCUSSION QUESTIONS

1. Would health care reform have passed in 1994 if President Clinton had managed and sold the issue differently to the public and elites? Or was it doomed to fail because it seemed to smack of "Big Government Policies?"

2. What are the pros and cons of issue advertising, as employed in the health care campaign?

14

Health Care Reform:
News and Public Opinion

This chapter examines the role that news and public opinion played in the health reform campaign. It also provides a general evaluation of the campaign and the nation's debate about health reform.

NEWS COVERAGE

News Determinants

News played an important role in the agenda-building process. It provided the public with most of its information about the health care debate. The news was also the arena in which elite groups sought to influence one another, as well as the American public.

Did the news reflect the reality of the health care debate? What factors shaped news coverage?

As suggested earlier, news does not simply reflect events in the political arena. News is a product of a host of journalistic, organizational, and economic factors. In the case of health care, journalists made judgments about what to cover. They provided more than four times as much coverage of the Clinton plan than other proposals and focused more on the players' strategies than on issues.[1]

It is difficult to find evidence that personal bias influenced stories. Although the overwhelming majority of Washington reporters are Democrats, much of the coverage was critical of Clinton, especially when the Whitewater scandal surfaced in 1994. Thus, we must look to other factors to understand the determinants of health care news.

Routines exerted a major impact on news judgments. Reporters relied heavily on official sources and formal channels for information. The Clinton administration, leading members of Congress, and health care experts provided a great deal of information to reporters through formal mechanisms such as briefings and press conferences.

Information also reached reporters through informal channels, primarily leaks. It was in large part through leaks that the public learned that the Clinton administration had closed off meetings of the health task force to the public.

Throughout this book, I have discussed the impact of ideology on news. In the case of health care, the press was exposed to multiple ideologies, ranging from the liberal perspective of Congressman John Dingell of Michigan to Clinton's moderate liberalism to Gingrich's conservatism. It is difficult to find support for the hegemonic model in the health care issue. The system was at war with itself: Twenty-seven health care reform bills were proposed, Democratic Congressional committee chairmen feuded with the president, leading Republicans decided from the beginning that it would be best to torpedo any Clinton plan, and the corporate elite found itself in disagreement with the political elite running the country, even though the presidents of some of the big corporations were Democrats.

The media were caught in the middle, covering an issue that fit into what Hallin calls "the sphere of legitimate controversy."

Nature of News Coverage

How well did the news media cover the health care debate? It served society well in three ways:

- By profiling the problems in American health care, it helped set the agenda. In part because of news coverage, Americans were convinced that the health care system needed change.
- News coverage gave the public rudimentary facts about the Clinton plan and some of the issues involved in health care reform.
- News served as a check on the abuse of political power. By revealing negative aspects of the debate—such as the Clinton secrecy policy and the interest groups' campaign—the news provided a check on the abuse of power by elites.

The news had several shortcomings, rooted in the nature of contemporary journalism. In their study, Jamieson and Cappella identified a variety of limitations in news of the health care reform debate. These scholars stated that:

- Reporters tended not to cover the very real areas of agreement between Democrats and Republicans. Consensus, although necessary for the survival and passage of a health care bill, seemed uninteresting to reporters.
- Reporters were interested in conflict, sometimes to the exclusion of covering other health plans.
- Viable policy options were prematurely judged "dead" by reporters, and hence did not receive coverage.
- Two thirds of the health care reform stories in both broadcast and print news focused on strategy or legislative process. Only about a quarter of print and fewer than a fifth of broadcast stories focused on the issues of the health care debate.
- Questions of truth, fairness, and accuracy were seldom treated in journalistic coverage of the competing ad campaigns in the health care debate. More often, treatment of ads concentrated on strategy.[2]

Conflict and strategy received a great deal of coverage because these are easy to cover and fit journalistic routines. It is more difficult to carefully explain the different plans and to cover the policy debate. Journalists' tasks were made more difficult by the complexity of proposals and the technical jargon used in the different legislative plans. It was comparatively easier to cover the horse race—which plan was ahead in Congress, and which had the most public support.

There is debate among scholars as to whether the news gave too much play to conflict and strategy. Critics argue that by focusing on conflict and controversy, the news played down areas of agreement and cases in which there was bipartisan support for proposals.

Journalists counter that the media's job is not to provide consensus when there is none. They point out that leading politicians did not want to forge consensus; Newt Gingrich made it clear from the beginning that he wanted to derail the Clinton plan. Journalists note that if a national debate is brutal and divisive, the media are obligated to relay that reality to Americans.

On another point there is more agreement. Scholars and journalists acknowledge that reporters could have done a better job of clarifying the issues in the health care debate. With stories filled with technical terminology, like *portability, single-payer plan, and employer mandates*, it was difficult for ordinary Americans to make sense of health care reform and to understand the differences among the plans.

PUBLIC OPINION, MEDIA, AND POLICY

Polls

What role did public opinion play in the health care reform debate? Theory and research suggested it played an important role. The public was up for grabs, and proponents and opponents of the Clinton plan waged a battle to gain public support.

Research shows that people followed the health care debate closely, but felt that they had little knowledge of the various proposals.[3] While most Americans undoubtedly learned new information about the health care delivery system from mass media, they remained confused and ill-informed about some of the issues in the debate. For example, in early February, 1994, some 4 months after Clinton had introduced his plan, three fourths of the public did not know that Clinton had called for employer mandates (whereby employers covered 80% of the cost of employees' insurance premiums).

Shortly after the health care plan was released in the fall of 1993, nearly 6 of 10 Americans supported it. By April, 1994, there were more people who thought they would be "worse off" than "better off" if the plan were adopted. Support among the elderly dropped drastically over the course of the year.[4]

What happened? The Clinton health reform campaign failed for several reasons.

Campaign Effects

A necessary condition for persuasion is comprehension of the message, and most Americans didn't fully comprehend the Clinton plan. Most people found the complexity bewildering and irritating.

The president's rhetoric convinced people that there was a problem, but it left them with the feeling that the cure might be worse than the disease. Clinton failed to reassure the public that his plan would solve the problems he had so eloquently described.

The opposition waged a spectacularly successful campaign. It understood that people were confused about the plan—they wanted to support Clinton's proposal, but either did not understand it, were troubled by portions of it, or did not appreciate how some of Clinton's ideas (e.g., universal coverage) would solve the problems he outlined (need to control costs).

Into this morass stepped the HIAA. Their Harry and Louise spots framed the problem in a way that people could understand. Interest groups called the Clinton plan government health care. This frame resonated with Americans' distrust of the federal government. Repeated exposure to this frame in the media may have activated it, increasing the likelihood that people would use it to describe the president's health reform effort.

At the same time, opposition ads—and their coverage in the news media—played on people's fears and anxieties. The campaign seems to have succeeded in scaring people about what would happen if the Clinton bill were passed. Thus, although most Americans supported key provisions of the president's plan, they came to feel negatively toward it as they worried about the possibility that the bad things they heard and read about might actually transpire.[5]

It is important to emphasize that the ads probably had less impact on people than news coverage of the ads. "Louise," the woman in the spots, received more headline space in major newspapers on the subject of health reform than did the Senate majority leader.[6]

The ads made good stories; they fit journalistic routines. They also received coverage because the White House, particularly Hillary Clinton, denounced them. Mrs. Clinton accused the insurance industry of lying about the health care proposal. It was one of the first times that a First Lady has attacked a private industry group, and Hillary Clinton's denunciations made news. Thus, the press and the Clintons helped to "make" "Harry and Louise." Once the ads received news play—and were discussed on the talk shows—they were most assuredly a phenomenon. People assumed they were credible because they had generated so much talk.

In the end, the Clinton administration was unable to counter the arguments—factual and emotional—that were leveled against the health reform plan. Clinton's rhetorical problems were magnified by blows to his credibility that resulted from two separate developments. First, news stories disclosed incredible charges made by four Arkansas state troopers that as governor, Clinton had used the troopers to solicit women, guard him while he was having sex with the women, and cover up his romantic liaisons from his wife.

Secondly, the president was hit by a flood of stories about the Whitewater scandal. In 1978 Bill and Hillary Clinton had invested in a resort development in Arkansas called Whitewater. The scandal concerned the possibility that there had been a conflict of interest between the Clintons' involvement in Whitewater and their roles as governor and attorney in a major Little Rock firm. There were allegations that the Clintons had improperly used their political influence to help their partners survive the Whitewater deal when it went belly-up. New developments in Whitewater—milked by the Republicans and covered regularly by the media—hurt the president's credibility on health care.

How did public opinion influence policy on health care? As is typical in modern times, polls were the mechanism by which public opinion influenced public policy. Polls showed a drop in support for the president's health care plan. These results were subsequently conveyed to Congressional leaders through the news media and by partisan opponents of the plan (who, as noted earlier, were aggressively conducting opinion polls of their own). The polls reduced the president's clout with members of Congress and made it more difficult for him to use public opinion as a bargaining chip.

CONCLUSIONS AND APPRAISALS

In the end, the most expensive and intense public information campaign in history produced no government policy on health care. Congress never came close to voting on any of the various health care bills. Health care activists were dispirited; the public was confused and no doubt more cynical about the public policy process.

Had the long-drawn-out debate done any good? Health care had made it to the top of the public and policy agenda: Millions of Americans were aware that a system they thought worked perfectly had problems, and policymakers now had proposals in place that could be brought back to the floor of Congress at an appropriate time. And yet, it is a telling commentary about contemporary America that as soon as it was clear Congress would not act on health care, the issue disappeared from the media and from public view, to take its place with other unsolved problems in the storehouse of American agendas.

Had the system worked or had it failed? Some political leaders thought the system had worked. The country had rejected a national health care plan that even its proponents admitted was too ambitious and complicated. As Johnson and Broder note, "the Founders of The System created its many checks and balances to make it difficult for political power to be abused and for unwise acts to be hastily passed into law."[7]

At the same time, the policymaking process had led to changes in health care without official action.[8] The health care industry has begun to reorganize itself, shifting to managed care programs and rewarding cost-cutting practices.[9]

The great health care debate showed that the American public would not tolerate extensive government involvement in health care. However, it was silent about whether private corporations should be allowed to increase their share of the trillion-dollar health care market. Health policy analysts believe that within a few years, a handful of companies will control the bulk of the American health care market.[10]

Thus, the problems that plague the nation's health care system —lack of insurance for millions of Americans, soaring health care costs, shortcomings in managed care—are not going away. The issue of how government should come to grips with these problems is not disappearing either. The nation must still decide what role it believes is appropriate for government to play in the reform of the health care system.

From a political communication perspective, the major question is whether the system produced a healthy and informed public debate. As noted earlier, there were positive aspects to the debate: an important issue made it to the top of the public agenda, the public learned about problems in the health care system, emotional issues were aired and discussed, and policymakers were able to debate the health care issue in public, under the watchful eye of the media.[11]

And yet, the debate had its weaknesses. The news stories emphasized conflict rather than consensus and focused on strategy rather than explaining the differences among the plans and what they meant for ordinary Americans. Advertisements, relying heavily on fear appeals, were frequently misleading. Interest groups that are not accountable to the public waged a multimillion dollar campaign to sway public opinion. Blame can also be lodged at the White House for failing to provide leadership at a crucial time in the nation's history, a period when the public, media, and policy agendas converged on health care reform.

In the end, there was not a national debate about health care, but a series of national campaigns designed to sway public attitudes. This was quintessentially American in that it emphasized persuasion rather than coercion, but it left one mulling over the slogan that one of the advertisements had used in a different context: *There's got to be a better way.*[12]

KEY ISSUES

News of Health Care Campaign

Opinion Poll Findings

Campaign Effects

DISCUSSION QUESTIONS

1. How did opposition groups change public and elite attitudes toward the Clinton health care plan?

2. When all is said and done, did the system work or break down in the case of health care reform?

III

COMMUNICATION AND THE PRESIDENTIAL ELECTION

15

Presidential Campaigns: History and Overview

Electoral campaigns play a critical role in democratic societies. As Paolo Mancini and David Swanson observe, election campaigns, "select decision makers, shape policy, distribute power, and provide venues for debate and socially approved expressions of conflict … Symbolically, campaigns legitimate democratic government and political leaders, uniting voters and candidates in displays of civic piety and rituals of national renewal."[1]

Election campaigns provide people with the opportunity to give feedback to their political leaders, "to talk back to political elites," as Marion Just and her colleagues note.[2] Yet campaigns vary greatly in the extent to which they fulfill their democratic mission. Some campaigns have reaffirmed democratic principles and provided a forum for national debate. They have brought citizens into the process and forged confidence in the democratic system. Others have trivialized democratic principles, offered only a superficial debate of pressing issues, and reduced citizens' faith in democracy.

As we see in this chapter, campaigns have a long history in America; they date back to the late eighteenth century, to the time of Jefferson and Adams. The roots of today's campaign can be found in the stump speeches of yesteryear, in the passionate oratory of the nineteenth century (as well as in the negative campaigning of the 1800s). Yet today's campaigns are profoundly different from those of the past in their emphasis on candidates rather than parties, their dependence on a class of campaign professionals, and in the role the media play in conveying and interpreting candidates' messages to a highly sophisticated mass public.

In this chapter I trace the history of campaigns in America, glimpsing continuities and changes. Building on history, the second section of the chapter describes the contemporary campaign, introducing the major players and props in today's media-dominated election.

HISTORY

Early Years

Today, we are accustomed to candidates campaigning aggressively for the presidency. It was not always so. In the late 1700s and early 1800s, Gil Troy observes, "Presidential candidates were supposed to 'stand' for election, not 'run.' They did not make speeches. They did not shake hands. They did nothing to betray the slightest ambition for office. Candidates were supposed to stay on their farms in dignified silence, awaiting the people's call, as George Washington had done."[3]

The emphasis on passive campaigning was an outgrowth of the Founding Fathers' fear of monarchical government and their distrust of the popular will. Based on their experiences with Great Britain before and during the Revolution, the Founders had come to believe that it was important to keep government power in check. They feared that if candidates campaigned aggressively for the presidency, they would manipulate the masses and abuse the public trust.

The Founders' dream of a cooperative and nonpartisan system of government was not to be. Governing, even in Washington's administration, proved more difficult than imagined. Conflicts developed over a host of issues, including the national debt (even then!), and soon partisan factions developed.

By the mid-1790s, newspapers had become allied with political factions and printed vituperative attacks on leaders of the opposing group. Although candidates tried to stay above the battle, in keeping with the mores of the time, their supporters wallowed in the electoral muck. In 1796, John Adams's supporters called Jefferson "an atheist, anarchist, demagogue" and a "coward." One leading Adams supporter claimed that "if Jefferson is elected, we may see our wives and daughters the victims of legal prostitution." Four years later, Jefferson's supporters returned with a vengeance, calling Adams "a hideous, hermaphroditical character which has neither the force and firmness of a man, nor the gentleness and sensibility of a woman."[4]

By the late 1820s, political parties played a major role in presidential politics, and in 1828, Andrew Jackson's supporters waged a grass roots campaign in the general's behalf. Twelve years later, the nation experienced its first full-blown popular election campaign. The election pitted President Martin Van Buren, Andrew Jackson's able but less charismatic successor, against William Henry Harrison, a war hero and nominee of the Whig party.

Although the election did not feature political heavyweights, it engaged the voters. During this time, political parties were new and exciting—much like the religious revivals that were enchanting the nation. Millions of people attended rallies, caucuses, and conventions. "To win in politics gentlemen no longer had to persuade one another, they had to sway the crowd," Troy observes.[5]

And so in 1840 for the first time, a candidate, William Henry Harrison, took to the campaign trail to deliver an explicitly partisan speech. Songs, banners, parades, and slogans were employed to promote Harrison's candidacy. Harrison tried to appeal to rural pioneers by linking himself with two potent symbols of the era—hard cider and log cabins.

The log cabin symbol could have gotten Harrison in trouble. It suggested that Harrison was a simple farmer and backwoodsman. Although Harrison owned a log cabin in Ohio, he had not been born in one. Instead, he had been born in a two-story home in Virginia, the well-to-do son of a governor. Harrison's use of the log cabin was an early example of image advertising—the forerunner of the contemporary 30-second television spot that overlooks issues and emphasizes the candidate's background and personality.[6]

Nineteenth Century Developments

By the 1850s, presidential politics had become part of pop culture. Children got in the habit of memorizing political speeches, and their parents enjoyed attending partisan events. However, Americans remained ambivalent about candidates who campaigned too aggressively. When Whig candidate General Winfield Scott embarked on a 5-week speaking tour in 1852, he was roundly condemned for engaging in rank electioneering and pandering for votes. According to Troy, this was an example of Americans' conflicting attitudes toward politics: they wanted their presidents to be of the people and among the people, but they felt uncomfortable with too much salesmanship and too much promotion.

The nation's ambivalence continued in 1860 as Stephen Douglas crusaded for votes, while his opponent, Abraham Lincoln, took the more traditional approach and gave few stump speeches.

Arguing that only the Democrats could "save the country from Aboli-tionism and Disunion," Douglas traveled across New England, making his case. His opponents were not impressed. They distributed a pamphlet that said Douglas "talks a great deal and very loud—always about himself. Has an idea that he is a candidate for the Presidency."[7]

Lincoln's timidity reflected both his belief that it was inappropriate for candidates to mount aggressive campaigns and also a shrewd political calculation. He felt that if he made few public speeches, he would "give no offense" to voters, thereby increasing the odds that they would cast their votes for him.[8]

Lincoln was not averse to cultivating his image. He recognized he had an image problem; an Albany newspaper called him "the ugliest man in the Union." At first Lincoln tried to deflect the issue with humor. In one of his debates with Stephen Douglas in 1858, he responded to Douglas's charge that he was two-faced by saying "I leave it to my audience. If I had another face, do you think I'd wear this one?"[9]

A group of Republicans urged Lincoln to "cultivate whiskers and wear standing collars." Lincoln acquiesced—but not until after the election. Between the election and inauguration, Lincoln grew whiskers and a beard.[10]

By the 1880s, there was growing acceptance of the need for candidates to give public speeches on issues of the day. At the same time, voters were increasingly cynical about political officials, viewing them less as "public servants nobly serving democracy" than as "pigs feeding at the public trough."[11] Public opinion, newspaper stories, and party bosses' nefarious activities fueled these perceptions. Vote fraud was commonplace; historians believe that Samuel Tilden was deprived of victory in the 1876 presidential election by corrupt political bosses.

Negative campaigning was also popular, even then. In 1884, Republicans made political hay out of the fact that Democrat Grover Cleveland had fathered a child out of wedlock. "Ma! Ma! Where's my Pa?" Republicans chanted. But it was the Democrats who had the last laugh. After Cleveland won, his supporters cried out, "Ma! Ma! Where's my Pa? Gone to the White House—Ha! Ha! Ha!"[12]

There was an irony in all this. More Americans participated in elections than ever before—there were record voter turnouts of nearly 80% in the 1880s. Yet the campaigns were not significantly more positive than those of earlier (or later) eras, and they were not more likely to offer a spirited discussion of the issues.

At the turn of the century the major modes of campaign communication were the stump speech—a term derived from candidates' habit of speaking while standing on tree stumps—and newspaper coverage of the campaign.[13] Political advisers were gaining in prominence. Among the most famous was Mark Hanna, who helped manage William McKinley's successful presidential campaign in 1896. It would not be long—about 24 years, to be exact—before critics began bemoaning the influence of publicity agents on presidential candidates. The same complaint would be heard again and again in the twentieth century.

The Electronic Campaign

Radio and newsreels became major political media in the 1920s. They seemed made to order for a reserved candidate like Calvin Coolidge, who did not relish speaking before groups.

Franklin Roosevelt used radio masterfully in 1932. Yet FDR, consummate politician that he was, did not ignore personal appeals. He was the first candidate to deliver a convention speech accepting his party's nomination for president. He also campaigned in 36 states and traveled over 13,000 miles in his quest for the presidency.

In 1948 Harry Truman continued FDR's "whistlestop" tradition, traversing 32,000 miles by train and giving an average of 10 speeches a day. As Troy notes, the success of Roosevelt (and of Truman) left little doubt that the days of passive campaigning were over; from the 1940s on, candidates would campaign aggressively and would make increasing use of the electronic media.

Television became a factor in the campaign in 1952. Public relations and candidate merchandising had been slowly making their way into campaigns for years, and now advertisements—previously employed to sell products—were purchased to promote candidates for the highest office in the land.

In 1952, Eisenhower's advisers hired a New York advertising agency to do political commercials. The ads, primitive by today's standards, featured questions from citizens, followed by answers from Eisenhower. The only hitch was that the advertising executives had asked Eisenhower to record answers to a series of hypothetical questions first, and then had gone out and recruited sympathetic tourists at Radio City Music Hall to ask the questions. The ads were made to look spontaneous when they were not.

Eisenhower's opponent, Democrat Adlai Stevenson, was uncomfortable with television. Jamieson notes that he "seemed to harken to an age in which the office sought the man, not the man the office."[14] Eisenhower, aided by television but also by his image as a popular World War II hero, defeated Stevenson in a landslide.

1952 also gave us the Checkers speech, the now-classic appeal by Republican vice presidential candidate Richard Nixon. Nixon, accused of drawing on a secret trust fund to pay political expenses, took to the airwaves to defend himself. He put forth a number of arguments in his behalf. Some were compelling, such as his disclosure that Democratic candidates also had such funds; others were rhetorical sleights of hand, such as his attempt to arouse audience sympathy by mentioning that his family had received one gift, a dog named Checkers that his daughters loved. The public, unaccustomed to being wooed by politicians on television, responded favorably, and Eisenhower decided to keep Nixon on the Republican ticket. It was the first indication that television, if used effectively, could be a potent force in election campaigns.

As the 1950s wore on, it became clear that visual images were becoming an increasingly important facet of campaigns. Richard Nixon, who typically paid more attention to verbal arguments than pictures, showed an uncanny appreciation of the importance of pictures in a 1959 face-off with Soviet party chairman Nikita Khrushchev, the celebrated "kitchen debate." Journalist Christopher Matthews observes that:

> More vivid than any words spoken between the two, however, was the news photograph of the American vice president poking his finger hard into the fat Ukrainian's chest. The show of strength was actually a publicity trick. What the wirephoto didn't show was that at the moment of his finger-pointing, Nixon was actually giving Khrushchev the banal information that the speech the Soviet leader was about to make would be carried on American television. Anyone reading the next day's newspapers might have guessed that Vice President Nixon was getting the better of the tough Soviet leader on a more consequential point.[15]

By 1960, nine out of ten Americans owned television sets. Television news programs were attracting large national audiences. For the first time, the presidential candidates—Nixon and John F. Kennedy—appeared more frequently on news and public affairs programs than on paid political commercials.[16] Long before Bill Clinton, Kennedy and Nixon appeared on a television talk show, Jack Paar's "Tonight." With both candidates trying to entertain audiences, "the lines between politics and entertainment, between propriety and exploitation, blurred," Troy notes.[17]

Of course, the lines had been blurring for over a century, beginning in the 1840s when William Henry Harrison waged an image-oriented cam-

paign designed to appeal to the masses. The trend continued in the nineteenth century as candidate debates, political party rallies, and oratorial
readings of the Declaration of Independence blended politics with food and
festivities. The difference in 1960 was that the lines were being blurred by
an electronic medium that emphasized intimacy and good looks.

The Kennedy campaign capitalized on the new medium, notably in the
first presidential debate that pitted a handsome, tanned Kennedy against a
scowling, uncomfortable Richard Nixon. Kennedy won the debate for a
number of reasons (see chapter 22), and the victory, coupled with the
favorable press it attracted, provided a needed lift to Kennedy's campaign.

Kennedy beat Nixon by just over 100,000 votes. Political scientists have
ticked off a number of reasons why Kennedy won, including the cynical—but not totally implausible— explanation that he picked up votes from
corpses in corrupt Chicago wards. What was significant was that many
political observers seemed to buy a technological explanation of the vote.
They agreed with Richard Nixon, who concluded that he paid "too much
attention to what I was going to say and too little to how I would look ...
One bad camera angle on television can have far more effect on the election
outcome than a major mistake in writing a speech."[18] Nixon's explanation
was a theory—a compelling one, to be sure, but just a theory. In fact there
were a number of reasons why Kennedy won, ranging from canny political
decisions (such as putting Lyndon Johnson on the ticket) to the articulation
of a compelling vision for the country. Yet the theory that camera angles
made all the difference would persist and would influence Nixon's own
media decisions in the years to come.

With the country just recovering from Kennedy's tragic assassination in
1963, Lyndon Johnson put together a highly effective campaign in 1964 that
took advantage of his popularity, his legislative successes, and the creative
wizardry of Tony Schwartz, who developed the now-famous "Daisy" ad,
which suggested that Johnson's opponent, Barry Goldwater, might start a
nuclear war. Political marketing, though primitive by today's standards, was
an accepted part of campaigns in 1964, and both candidates hired advertising agencies to develop their television spots. The campaign touched on
issues, such as Social Security and honesty in government. However, like
other campaigns before and after, it avoided a discussion of the major issue
that would be facing the country in the years ahead. In 1964, there was
virtually no candidate discussion of the war that would tear the nation
asunder in the 1960s: Vietnam.

In 1968, a violent year in American politics that saw Martin Luther King and Robert Kennedy assassinated within a 2-month period, American voters were faced with a choice from among Richard Nixon (now determined to adapt himself to the realities of television), Vice President Hubert Humphrey, who was hopelessly associated with the Vietnam War, and independent candidate George Wallace. Forty-three percent of the public indicated it would have preferred candidates other than Humphrey or Nixon.

One of the most interesting things that came out of 1968, from a communication perspective, was Joe McGinnis's best-selling book about the Nixon campaign, *The selling of the president, 1968*. McGinnis concluded that "Nixon had been packaged and sold just like cigarettes," and that "in a presidential race, advertising is sufficiently powerful to create important public perceptions of candidates that are fundamentally different from the candidates themselves."[19]

McGinnis's book was important not because his conclusions were accurate—advertising does not have the effects McGinnis alleged; Nixon was not "packaged" in the simplistic way that McGinnis suggested. Rather, the book was noteworthy because it convinced many journalists and campaign professionals that consultants were all-powerful gurus who could, through the alchemy of polling and technology, transform weak candidates into strong ones. It also likened campaigns to merchandising, to sales and promotion. This view of campaigns—true in some ways, not so true in others—would make its way into news stories and into popular accounts of presidential elections.

In the 1970s, news came to be a key player in the nomination process as a result of party reforms enacted during the decade (see subsequent discussion). By the end of the 1970s, polling and political consultants had replaced party professionals as the main architects of campaigns. As the 1980s ended, there was great controversy about the impact of advertising consultants and campaign "handlers" on the presidential election.

As we will see, these concerns continued to be voiced in the 1990s, a decade characterized by exploding computer technologies and innovative candidate use of the new media forms, such as television talk shows, satellite hook-ups, and promotional video cassettes.

Summary

A historical review of elections in America is helpful because it shows that the problems of today's era go back at least 200 years. Negative campaigning dates back to the late eighteenth century newspaper wars between the Federalists and the Jeffersonian Republicans. Image-oriented appeals go back to William Henry Harrison in 1840. Public cynicism about politics has plagued the country for at least a century and has a number of complex roots. Americans have always demanded virtue and an "above the battle" stance from their leaders, on the one hand, and an everyman, "person of the people" stance on the other. They wanted candidates to campaign with honor and dignity, but they disdained candidates who "held too much back." Troy argues that the ambivalence stems from the fact that "the men who made our Constitution could not quite decide how much democracy Americans should enjoy or how popular an office the presidency should be."[20]

Thus, some of the same issues that occupied Americans a century or more ago consume citizens today. And yet, for all the historical continuities, there have been important changes in the ways presidential campaigns are waged. Structural, political, and technological changes in the system have transformed presidential election campaigns.

THE CONTEMPORARY CAMPAIGN

There are many players and props in the quadrennial American election drama. These include political parties, candidates, political marketing experts, the mass media, and voters.

Parties

During the nineteenth century and the first half of the twentieth, political party leaders determined who would serve as the party's nominee for president. State and national party bosses, meeting in smoke-filled rooms at nominating conventions, would decide among themselves which candidate stood the best chance of unifying the party, representing its policy positions, and winning election. A good deal of discussion, horse-trading, and political bartering went on during these closed-door sessions. In the end, party leaders could be reasonably certain that rank-and-file members would ratify their choices as they dispensed political favors to workers, chiefly jobs.

Outraged that the nomination process disenfranchised voters, early twentieth century Progressives pushed for presidential primaries. As a result of their efforts, a number of states inaugurated primaries, or direct elections of delegates to the party's nominating conventions. About a third of the states held primaries from 1912 through 1968. Yet party machines were still strong during this period, and leaders of the state organizations called the shots. Candidates entered primaries not to rack up convention delegates, but to convince party leaders they were popular or that they could overcome political disabilities. In 1960 John F. Kennedy contested primaries to show that voters would accept his candidacy, even though they knew he was a Roman Catholic.[21]

1968 changed all this. Faced with charges that party leaders had disenfranchised opponents of nominee Hubert Humphrey, and that Mayor Richard Daley had strong-armed young people in the streets of Chicago, the Democratic Party appointed a commission to make reforms in the nomination process. The commission, chaired by South Dakota Senator George McGovern, called for more open conventions and urged that primaries play a larger role in the delegate selection process. The report was adopted by the Democratic National Committee in 1971. Subsequently, state legislatures, in an effort to bring delegate selection procedures into harmony with the Democratic party's rules, enacted statutes that applied with equal force to both Democrats and Republicans.[22] As a result of the reforms and the changes in state laws, the overwhelming majority of delegates to the nominating conventions are now selected by voters in primary elections. Voters, not party leaders, essentially determine who will be the nominees of the Republican and Democratic parties.

The party reforms greatly reduced the power of political parties in America. Parties are now weaker than they were 50 years ago. There are several other reasons why parties have declined.

First, candidates can appeal directly to voters through television. In previous generations, parties interceded between voters and the candidate. Parties organized campaigns and provided voters with a great deal of their information about candidates. Today, that information comes directly from the media, typically television.

A second reason why parties have declined is that campaign finance reforms, enacted in the 1970s, have undercut the parties' ability to solicit money from conventional funding sources, such as affluent individuals and corporations. Third, the increased education of the electorate has led to more independent-mindedness and more skepticism about voting a straight party line; adding to this is voter cynicism, which makes voters more mistrustful of partisan appeals.[23]

As a result, there has been a significant increase over the years in split-ticket voting and in the percentage of voters who consider themselves Independents. This was dramatically illustrated in 1992, when 19% of the electorate cast votes for Ross Perot, who ran independently of the Democratic and Republican parties.

Parties may be down, but they are by no means out. Although voters today may be more independent than their parents and grandparents, they do not ignore party labels. Many voters still identify strongly with the Republicans or Democrats. And parties still provide the crop of candidates from which voters choose in primary campaigns.

Candidates

We are in an age of candidate-centered rather than party-dominated politics. Candidates are independent entrepreneurs who hire their own staffs, raise money independently of parties, and carefully formulate strategies for winning based on advice given by a host of campaign professionals, including pollsters and political marketing experts.

I describe the modern "marketing" campaign shortly. It must be stressed that for all the emphasis on strategy and political gamesmanship, the campaign still requires that candidates articulate issue positions and promote themselves in ways that are appealing to voters. Presidential candidates must persuade Americans to vote for them. One of the pleasant constancies of American politics is that candidates must articulate a vision of where they want to take the country and convince people that this is the best path for America to pursue. Incumbents must persuade citizens that they have met the promises they made four years earlier.

Contrary to myth, the American people are typically not bamboozled by candidate rhetoric. Ronald Reagan defeated Jimmy Carter in 1980 not because Reagan used the smoke and mirrors of television or because he relied exclusively on his skills as an actor; Reagan won because he offered the American people a vision they found appealing and because he convinced them that he would be a better leader than Jimmy Carter.

In 1992, Bill Clinton captured the public's desire for change and for a return to public purpose and societal reform. His rhetoric emphasized a covenant or partnership between the president and the American people. It fit the public's dissatisfaction with the status quo.[24]

In 1996, Clinton employed a classic incumbency style, emphasizing his accomplishments and the symbolic trappings of the presidency. For example, he announced a series of popular policies on family issues, such as the introduction of the V-chip that lets parents block violent television programs, a rule stipulating that television stations broadcast three hours a week of educational children's TV shows, and measures to discourage teenage smoking.[25]

Political Marketing

Candidates have one goal in running for election, and that is to win. From the candidate's perspective, campaigns are not about education or policy reform; they are about developing a coherent strategy that will get the candidate elected. There is nothing wrong with this goal. If people did not want to get elected to office, and did not work hard to accomplish this goal, the citizenry would not have anyone representing them in Washington. The eternal question is whether the goal of winning causes candidates to compromise their principles and to falsify their messages. I examine that question in the chapters that follow.

For purposes of the present discussion, it is important to emphasize that to win elections, candidates increasingly adopt a marketing strategy. Presidential candidates must promote their candidacies using tried-and-true marketing principles such as market segmentation, positioning, and targeting. While a marketing model would not have fit the campaign when parties dominated elections, today it provides a useful metaphor for campaign strategy.

Keep in mind that there are important differences between political and commercial marketing. Consultants do not market a candidate like advertising agencies market soap. As Bruce Newman notes, "Unlike a business, a political organization is driven not by profit but by a desire to implement a political ideology and approach to running the government."[26] In addition, political marketing operates in a more fluid and dynamic environment than does commercial marketing. A gaffe or thoughtless remark by a presidential candidate can kill the candidate's chances for election. Also, news and public opinion polls have a much greater impact in the political marketplace than in the commercial arena.

Technology plays an important role in all aspects of political marketing. Computer databases give candidates access to hundreds of thousands of voters, categorized by their demographic characteristics and their political attitudes. Databases can be very specific. Many list the name, address, and phone number of individuals who have donated to liberal, conservative, or religious, organizations; others provide demographic information on citizens who have given small amounts of money to specific causes (for example, abortion). Consultants can then contact these voters through direct mail, gearing the appeal to the voter's political predispositions and addressing the letter to the individual by name.[27]

Polls play a critical role in campaign marketing. Polls let candidates know where they stand with voters, how voters perceive their personal characteristics and issue positions, and whether their popularity is moving upward, downward, or staying the same. There are several major scientific polling techniques, including benchmark surveys, which provide general, baseline information about the public's image of candidates; trial heat surveys, which pit competing candidates against one another; tracking polls, conducted on a daily basis toward the end of a campaign to monitor changes in public sentiments; and panel surveys, in which the same group of voters is interviewed two or more times.[28]

Political consultants also employ **focus groups** to gain a more dynamic understanding of public opinion. Focus groups are *"in-depth interviews with a small number of people (usually ten to twenty) who often are selected to represent broad demographic groups."*[29] Focus groups help campaign strategists develop appeals and aid them in tailoring messages to specific subgroups.[30]

Consultants—some more than others—also rely on more controversial and nefarious techniques to probe opinions. These include oppositional research, or digging up dirty details of an opponent's personal or professional background, and push-polls, an attempt to spread lies and rumors about an opponent under the guise of legitimate research. These techniques are not the mainstay of political consulting; however, they are used and have provoked controversy.

Campaign Finance

Presidential election campaigns are enormously expensive. Television advertising, mailing of promotional material, campaign travel, polling, and paying the salaries of campaigns staffers all cost a great deal of money. In 1992, parties, candidates, and interest groups spent $550 million on the presidential campaign. In 1996, the spending exceeded $600 million.[31]

In the early 1970s, Congress, responding to mounting public and elite concerns about campaign spending, made major changes in the campaign finance laws. The new rules were designed to limit the parties' dependence on wealthy donors, discourage secret and illegal campaign contributions, and reduce the high costs of presidential campaigns. The campaign finance legislation stipulated that:

- In any election, including a primary, contributions from an individual cannot exceed $1,000 to a single candidate, $20,000 to a national political party committee, and $5,000 to other political committees, with the total not to exceed $25,000 in any one year.
- All contributions of $200 or more must be identified. All expenditures of $200 or more must be reported.
- Candidates who accept public funding cannot spend more than $10 million in their quest for the nomination and $20 million in the general election, plus a cost-of-living increment calculated from the base year of 1974.
- Major party contenders who raise $5,000 in 20 states in contributions of $250 or less, a total of $100,000, are eligible to receive matching grants during the prenomination period, which begins January 1 of the year in which the election occurs.[32]

Candidates are now responsible for paying for the lion's share of their campaign. No longer able to depend on a handful of wealthy donors (which is good), candidates must spend considerable amounts of time asking for funds from many different individuals and groups. They must solicit funds from small contributors and speak at fund-raising events attended by wealthy business executives and Hollywood celebrities (what Polsby and Wildavsky call the "Beverly Hills primary"); they also rely on direct-mail techniques that capitalize on computer databases.[33] Many candidates understandably dislike this "money-grubbing" aspect of the campaign.

Although campaign finance legislation has limited candidate expenditures in the nomination and general election periods, it has not reduced the amount of money spent on presidential campaigns. Wealthy candidates can spend unlimited amounts of money on their campaigns, provided that they do not accept public funds, in which case campaign finance regulations apply. Thus, Ross Perot spent over $68 million of his own money on the 1992 race and Steve Forbes spent $22 million of his personal fortune on advertising in the 1996 primaries.

In addition, the Supreme Court ruled in 1976 that individuals or groups could spend as much as they wanted on behalf of a presidential candidate, provided that they worked independently of the candidate's campaign. This has allowed **political action committees (PACs)** to spend vast sums of money on a candidate. It has also allowed the candidate to deny involvement with PAC-sponsored negative advertising campaigns, while at the same time reaping rewards from such campaign efforts. Another loophole is the so-called **soft money provision**, which allows PACs, interest groups, and even foreign investors to contribute unlimited amounts of money to political parties, ostensibly for activities like voter registration and get-out-the-vote drives, but actually for presidential election campaigns. There are no limits on the size of such soft-money contributions to campaigns. In a similar fashion, political parties and interest groups can spend unlimited amounts of money on so-called issue ads, ads that do not explicitly express advocacy. In 1996, special interests spent tens of millions of dollars on negative "issue spots." The Federal Election Commission was helpless to regulate these ads because they did not explicitly urge viewers to vote for or against a particular candidate.

Campaign finance is one of the most controversial aspects of the modern campaign. Critics lament the high cost of campaigns and argue that parties and PACs have made a mockery of campaign finance rules. Defenders counter that American campaigns cost less per voter than those of other western democracies. They also maintain that the First Amendment gives individuals the freedom to spend as much money as they wish on presidential campaigns.

Mass Media

It is often said that the media have changed presidential campaigns. This statement is vague and a bit misleading. The fact is that media, broadly defined, have always played an important part in campaigns. The real question is which medium dominates, how the dominant medium has changed campaigning, and whether its effects are more positive than negative.

Campaigns are now waged primarily through television. Candidates work hard to gain favorable coverage on the nightly news, spend millions of dollars on television advertising, and expend considerable energy trying to make a favorable impression in presidential debates. Other modalities, such as radio talk shows and newspapers, still count, but the major thrust of candidates' activity is toward television.

Candidates do *not* spend as much time on the campaign trail as they did 50 or more years ago. Candidates do not talk with as many voters and kiss as many babies as they did in Harry Truman's day. Television has helped change the modern campaign in several ways. Partly because of television, primaries play a more important role in the nomination process than ever before; party conventions have been transformed from hotly contested (and boss-controlled) contests for the nomination to media events designed to promote the presidential ticket; candidates schedule activities to meet the requirements of "media logic"; the campaign is organized around journalistic values, as well as party and civic values; attractive, telegenic candidates are in increasing demand; and a new class of experts—pollsters, political marketing specialists, and attorneys specializing in campaign finance law—have replaced party leaders as the key players managing presidential campaigns.[34] In fairness, it should be noted that these changes are not due entirely to television, and in an area as dynamic and complex as election campaigns it is hard to partial out the influences of nontelevision forces from those of TV. But there is little disagreement that television has changed election campaigns (see Box 15.1: On the Press Bus with Dole).

Not surprisingly, there is considerable debate about whether the current electronic campaign is worse than campaigns of yore. There is a long list of criticisms of the system: consultants have made campaigns too negative and superficial; journalists have too much power; candidates rely on personalized, rather than ideological, appeals; voters are reduced to spectators. Each criticism can be met with a counterargument: campaigns have always been negative, long before the advent of consultants and television; journalistic power is not necessarily bad, especially when compared to that wielded by party bosses; there is nothing wrong with voters' making judgments based on impressions of a candidate's personality; and voters are far more active decision-makers than critics typically assume.

What is beyond debate is that the mass media play a central role in modern campaigns. But to say this is to state the obvious. In fact, as Karol Jakubowicz notes, the media are:

> *channels for communicating* ideas and images existing or created independently of themselves, that is, channels of communication between the politicians and the public … And, of course, the media also function as *communicators*, originating messages and images and introducing them into social discourse, that is, as initiators of political communication and as communicators of their own messages (e.g., coverage and analysis of the campaign, staging of debates, interviews with candidates conducted at the media's own initiative).[35]

Furthermore, there is a tension between these two roles. The news media are used by politicians to reach national audiences, and yet journalists resent "being used," and so frequently come up with ways to assert their control, such as by asking tough questions in interviews or providing negative coverage. As we will see, we have a constant, ever-present "struggle between officials and journalists for control of the agenda and for the power to frame or interpret the important events and issues of the day."[36] That struggle is a major characteristic of today's presidential campaign, and out of that struggle new ideas, formats, and ways to communicate with the voting public have emerged.

The mass media, television in particular, have also had an important impact on the way that presidential candidates communicate with voters. Beyond causing candidates to speak in shorter sound bites (see chapter 17), TV has helped to personalize politics. Television has encouraged politicians to feel that they must reveal something of their personal lives. A medium that reaches into people's bedrooms and in which talk-show guests bare their souls (and sometimes more) is bound to leave its imprint on political leaders, who rely on television to reach and influence the voting public.

Presidents refer to themselves more frequently today than in other eras. Candidates also speak in more intimate language than did their predecessors.[37] Voters, rightly or wrongly, have come to view the campaign as a courtship, a process through which they will get to know the candidates. As noted earlier, a century ago candidates hardly spoke in public; to do so was considered gauche. Now they are not only expected to speak and campaign aggressively (for as much as an entire year), but they are also expected to "let their hair down" and let the public get to know them as people.

We see this **personalization of politics** most clearly at the nominating conventions when candidates trip over each other to disclose psychologically correct tidbits from their personal lives. For example in 1992, Al Gore shamelessly discussed his son's brush with death. Four years later, Mr. Gore was back again, this time poignantly relating his sister's death from lung cancer, right up to her last breath. Not to be outdone, President Clinton told the audience how his brother had fought to overcome his addiction to drugs. Bob Dole tearfully discussed his feelings for his parents, and Indiana governor Evan Bayh disclosed that his mother had died of breast cancer, a tidbit that had preciously little to do with Bayh's keynote address.

Voters

Elections are still decided by American voters. They must weigh the appeals of candidates, consider the trustworthiness of the contenders, and decide which candidate would make the better president.

Thousands of studies have probed the determinants of voting behavior. American voters are a complex lot. They take into account the candidates' issue positions and character. Their votes are determined by many factors, including party identification, perceptions of the extent to which the candidate shares the voter's values, and gut feelings. Moreover, as the limited effects model reminds us, voters do not begin the campaign with a totally open mind. They have positions on the issues, attitudes toward candidates, and beliefs about the political process. However, contrary to the limited effects view and congruent with the more dynamic view of campaigns that characterizes contemporary scholarship, voters do reconsider their positions over the course of a campaign. In some cases, they reassess their positions, only to return (with somewhat different arguments) to the positions they took at the beginning of the campaign; in other instances, they revise their assessments in light of information they picked up over the months-long campaign.

Voters, in short, do participate in presidential campaigns. They seek out information, tune into debates, talk shows, and newscasts, and actively process the information they pick up from these programs.

In truth, voters participate more actively in some campaigns than in others. The 1992 campaign evoked a good deal of interest, in part because Clinton's and Perot's rhetoric captured the imagination of the voters. In 1996, voters paid much less attention to the race, partly because the issues discussed by the candidates were well known to the voters and also because Clinton led Dole by such a large margin throughout the campaign. Scholars differ in their evaluations of campaigns (like 1996) that fail to engage the electorate. Some criticize these campaigns, arguing that widespread voter apathy has its roots in misleading or uninformative candidate rhetoric. Others maintain that lack of voter interest indicates that, on balance, most people are satisfied with the state of the nation.

Campaigns and Communication

There are many metaphors for the electoral campaign. Campaigns have been likened to wars, sporting events, courtships between candidates and voters, and salesmanship. It is appropriate that a book on political communication invoke a communication metaphor, noting that campaigns can be viewed as dynamic interactions between and among candidates, journalists, and voters. Marion Just and her colleagues adopt this approach, operating from a constructionist framework. They view the presidential election campaign as:

> a dynamic struggle among the actors to influence the priorities of others engaged in the process. Each player gets more information about the others as the campaign progresses, and the actions of each are modified in light of new information from other

participants. Throughout the campaign process, candidates adopt strategies that resonate with citizen priorities and do not bring down the wrath of the media; journalists try to report campaign news that will excite the audience, maintain access to the candidates, and impress their peers in the news business. And citizens, for their part, actively construct meaning about the candidates and the campaign by interpreting information in light of what they already know and value. People, in short, are neither pawns of the politicians nor dupes of the news media but can be active participants in constructing the campaign ... (The) campaign is *built* by the dynamic interactions of citizens, candidates, and news media.[38]

Campaigns are attempts to gain power, they do involve marketing considerations, and they do call on the many strategic forces discussed in this chapter. However, it is useful to remember that campaigns are also national conversations—discussions among leaders, the media, and the public. How well did the conversation go? Much depends on the attitudes of the communicators and the rules the system sets up for conducting the conversation.

CONCLUSIONS

Election campaigns are an essential aspect of democratic self-government. They give citizens the opportunity to vote their leaders up or down, and they help shape public policy. As Judith Trent and Robert Friedenberg note, elections "allow us freedom to actively participate in selecting our leaders. They are the core of democracy."[39]

They are indeed.

And yet presidential campaigns have rarely been pretty and have historically evoked criticism. Americans have always been torn between "republican virtues"—such as candidate modesty and an "above the battle" stance— and "democratic values," such as frequent candidate communication with voters, and aggressive public campaigns.[40]

Today's campaigns continue to have their negative and problematic aspects. Contemporary campaigns also differ profoundly from those that occurred in the past. Presidential elections are candidate-rather than party-centered. Quests for the presidency are now guided by principles of modern marketing; they are waged almost exclusively through the electronic media, and are enormously expensive affairs. The media convey the messages of politicians (in advertisements), initiate messages (in news programs), and convey and initiate simultaneously (in talk shows). The media are autonomous centers of power and complex, multifaceted sources of information for voters.

The third factor in the campaign equation, besides candidates and media, is the voting public. Voters shape the campaign process, actively processing political messages and relaying reactions to candidates and journalists. Voters rarely communicate directly with candidates or editors; communication is typically mediated, electronic, and, in the case of polls, rendered through numerical symbols. But this does not mean the process is any less vital than it was in 1896 when people traveled to Canton, Ohio, to hear William McKinley speak to crowds gathered outside his front porch. McKinley's speeches were "mediated" by the advice given him by ace political consultant Mark Hanna.

If there is one thing that differentiates today's campaigns from those of yesteryear, it is that so much of the campaign is conducted out in the open, under the watchful eye of the public and mass media. A half-century or more ago, presidential nominees were selected by party bosses behind closed doors. Today, they are essentially chosen by the electorate in presidential primaries. Years ago, a candidate or his advisers could have sexual dalliances and be confident the press would never report the details to the public. Today, tabloids stalk candidates and their advisers, trying to discover dirt about their sex lives. When dirt is uncovered or allegations are made, the stories become lead items in the evening news. While the public nature of today's campaign is good in that it opens up the process to more people, it also has created a whole new set of problems; foremost among them is the contempt for politics and politicians that has come with increased exposure to our presidential candidates.

Campaigns are active, dynamic, and lengthy. They can be viewed as struggles among candidate organizations, the press, and the public to control the agenda and to influence the nation's priorities. Adopting a communication metaphor, we can view these three groups as involved in a dynamic conversation about the nation's future. It is a desperately important conversation, but like all conversations, its quality and impact depends on the commitment of the communicators to the process. It is to that process that we now turn.

Box 15.1

On the Press Bus with Dole

USA Today reporter Martha T. Moore traveled with Bob Dole during the 1996 presidential campaign. She provides a bird's eye view of what it's like to cover a campaign:[41]

There's a lot of suspension of disbelief involved in traveling with a presidential candidate. Because otherwise, when you find yourself on that boardwalk, squashed between a sweaty photographer and an enormous Secret Service agent, with your arm stuck up in the air in a futile attempt to get your tape recorder somewhere near Dole, and meanwhile you're blocking the view of someone who has stood for hours in full sun to see the candidate she sincerely hopes will be the next president, you might wonder just what on Earth you are doing ...

When you are covering a presidential candidate, as this reporter learned during a first-time stint traveling with Dole, you seldom get to ask him questions, and he even more seldom answers them. But you do get a front-row seat to watch him. If the press is the window through which voters see the candidate, this is the window through which the press sees the campaign.

It's the campaign that arranges for transportation, hotel rooms, food—every three hours, just like a cruise ship— and a place for reporters to plug in their laptop computers and modems after each event.

A printed schedule—albeit usually last-minute—told us exactly when to show up, where to stand, where the phone lines were. We flew on the candidate's plane; we rode a bus in his motorcade. At his book-signing and fund-raising appearances, we swept in as a pack to a roped-off area positioned to give TV cameras the best possible picture. If the entire press corps couldn't squeeze into an event—for instance, at a Fourth of July picnic Dole attended in Bob and Susie Schemmel's back yard in Glen Ellyn, Ill.—a "pool" of one camera crew and one reporter went, then told everyone else what happened. When Dole left—whoosh, so did we ...

The traveling campaign is a kind of bubble, a vacuum. Cellular phones and computer modems are the only route out ...

Within the bubble, information is shared. If someone hears Dole say something, they tell the rest of the press corps, so that each day a common denominator of information is cobbled together and agreed upon. Maybe this is where conventional wisdom is born ...

On the one occasion when Dole wanted to talk to the press, he did it at a refueling stop in Madison, Wis. The plane landed, we joined a gaggle of local TV crews and reporters on the tarmac, Dole read a statement on welfare reform, and he answered a few shouted questions. Then he moved away from the microphones

joined a gaggle of local TV crews and reporters on the tarmac,
Dole read a statement on welfare reform, and he answered a few
shouted questions. Then he moved away from the microphones
and toward the local press, becoming completely inaudible. We
closed in, tape recorders held high. But all we ended up with was
the whine of the plane engines.

KEY ISSUES

History of Presidential Campaigns

Decline of Parties

Political Marketing

Polls

Campaign Finance Rules

Political Action Committees

Role of Mass Media

Personalization of Politics

DISCUSSION QUESTIONS

1.   If negative campaigning and image-oriented campaigns go back over a hundred
      years, what's new about today's presidential campaign?

2.   What are the similarities and differences between marketing a candidate and
      marketing a product? Is political marketing a pejorative label?

3.   Were things better when candidates pressed the flesh and talked directly to
      voters?

16

The Media and
the Nominating Process

Every so often—every couple of hours, actually—there is a reminder of … television's primacy. On a frigid, snowy New Hampshire morning, (presidential candidate Lamar) Alexander arrived at the historic town hall in Bedford (New Hampshire), and reporters quickly moved into the toasty-warm main hall. But the candidate's staff promptly hustled the media contingent outside, where the WMUR camera had been set up, and Alexander sidled up to the snowdusted podium in a stiff wind.

"We need the visual of a New Hampshire winter," explained (Alexander's) campaign aide.

Recognizing the absurdity of the situation, Alexander told the shivering reporters:

"I promise to be brief. That way we won't freeze to death."[1]

As this example illustrates, the news media play a major role in the primary election campaign. This chapter examines the impact of the media in primary elections and, more generally, in the presidential nomination process.

The American nominating campaign has three phases: **the preprimary period**, the period between the time that candidates announce their decisions to run for president and the beginning of the primaries in early February of the election year; **the presidential primaries**, which run from February to June; and the **nominating conventions,** which take place in late summer. The general election campaign traditionally kicks off after the conventions end in August. This chapter examines the news media's role in the nomination process, focusing on the impact that news exerts on candidates and voters in the critical preprimary and primary phases.

PREPRIMARY STAGE

Candidates

Many years ago, politicians could announce their candidacies at the start of the primary season. Robert F. Kennedy announced that he was a candidate for president on March 16, 1968. Although Kennedy entered the race after the New Hampshire primary, he was able to contest primaries in Indiana, Nebraska, Oregon, and California. Had Kennedy not been assassinated, the momentum from his primary victories would undoubtedly have pushed him closer to getting the Democratic nomination in Chicago.

Nowadays, candidates cannot afford to wait until March to announce their candidacies. They typically make their announcements as much as a year before the primaries begin. By August of 1995, 10 Republicans had declared their intentions to run for president in 1996. Candidates launch their candidacies earlier for several reasons.

First, under the Federal Election Campaign Act, candidates can receive matching funds on January 1 of the election year provided that they have raised at least $100,000. Thus, as Polsby and Wildavsky note, "the more money a candidate raises in the year before the election, the larger the boost given to the campaign by the sudden influx of matching funds in the short period in the election year before the first primaries and caucuses."[2]

Second, candidates need to develop large and efficient organizations to win early primaries and caucuses. As I discuss shortly, early victories are critical in modern campaigns, and candidates cannot attain success without building effective organizations.

Third, presidential aspirants need to gain coverage in the media to attract funds and to build support. It takes time to attract the interest of the nation's press corps.

The financial, organizational, and media requirements work to the advantage of established candidates from the major parties. Lesser known political figures and candidates from alternative parties lack the name recognition necessary to mount effective campaigns.

Exceptions include Steve Forbes, Ross Perot, and other wealthy candidates who have mounted campaigns on their own. In 1992, Perot launched his campaign on the Larry King television show by indicating he would run for president if volunteers in 50 states put him on the ballot.[3] Due to his personal fortune and charisma, he was able to mount an impressive challenge to Bush and Clinton in 1992.

The preprimary period has become a critical phase of the current campaign. Candidates court interest groups, influential members of the party, and the media during this period. They participate in candidate debates and straw polls conducted by state parties. They hope to score successes in these events. They further hope that their successful performances will cause leading journalists to view them as front-runners, and that their numbers will rise in public opinion polls. Good poll numbers drive press coverage and also convince wealthy donors that the candidate has a shot at the nomination. Money is critical: In 1996, the conventional wisdom was that a candidate could not win the Republican nomination without raising $20 million by the end of 1995.

News Media

Long before the nominating conventions, a front-runner—or dream candidate—emerges. The news media play a critical role in determining who this top contender is and in promoting this individual to the American people.

In some cases, candidates who achieve front-running status fall from grace. This happened during the election campaigns of 1980 and 1988.

In 1979, many political professionals and voters thought Edward Kennedy had a good chance of defeating Jimmy Carter for the Democratic presidential nomination. However, Kennedy stumbled in an interview with CBS reporter Roger Mudd. Kennedy had trouble articulating why he wanted to be president and had difficulty explaining the Chappaquiddick incident.[4]

Kennedy's popularity dropped after the interview. But it was not the interview per se that hurt Kennedy. Most Americans didn't see the interview, preferring to watch the movie *Jaws* on ABC. Instead what hurt Kennedy were the scathing criticisms he received from columnists who had watched Kennedy on CBS. In addition, political leaders who watched the program expressed disappointment. With the news media covering the aftereffects of the Kennedy interview, elites' comments filtered down to the public. Soon, the dominant opinion among the press and political elite was that Kennedy had stumbled, and that he was no longer the invincible front-runner.

Contrary to popular opinion, the news media had not *ruined* Kennedy's chances to get the nomination. Instead, Kennedy wounded himself by failing to articulate a compelling explanation for why he wanted to be president, and for proving unable to account for his actions during Chappaquiddick. The news media conveyed this reality to the public and elites. Yet they undoubtedly magnified the effect by dwelling on the Kennedy story and playing up its implications.

Subsequently, an international incident adversely affected Kennedy's nomination bid. On November 4, 1979, Iranian militants seized the U.S. embassy in Tehran and took American diplomats and aides hostage. Americans rallied around President Jimmy Carter. Carter rode the patriotic wave to early primary victories, thus ending Kennedy's hope to unseat an incumbent president.

In 1987, a candidate who was likened to the Kennedys, Gary Hart (also a front-runner during the preprimary period), dropped out of the presidential race following revelations in *The Miami Herald* that he had spent a weekend with an attractive young model, and follow-up stories in other media outlets. Again, it was not the news media that forced Hart out of the race. Hart chose to drop out after a careful assessment of his chances of winning the nomination and perusal of opinion polls that showed the public believed the incident had raised questions about his character, particularly his integrity when he refused to say whether he had ever committed adultery. But clearly it had been the news media that started the ball rolling by staking out Hart's Washington townhouse (some critics thought this was wrong) and by covering the scandal as much if not more than they had some 100 years earlier in the case of Grover Cleveland and Frances Folsom.

During other elections, candidates have used favorable news media coverage in the preprimaries to launch successful bids for the nomination and the White House. A *New York Times* story that appeared in October, 1975 stating that Jimmy Carter led the pack in an Iowa straw poll was itself a major political event.[5] Other reporters, influenced by *The Times* coverage (through the process of intermedia agenda-setting), started paying more attention to Jimmy Carter's presidential drive. This led to expanded coverage of Carter's campaign, which no doubt helped him win the Iowa caucuses in January.[6]

In 1992 Bill Clinton impressed an obscure convention of the Association of State Democratic Chairmen in Chicago. Clinton's performance netted him good press in *The Washington Post* and *The New York Times*. Two weeks later he won a straw poll at the Florida Democratic party convention. Several weeks later his picture graced the covers of major magazines. With New York Governor Mario Cuomo declaring he would not run for the presidency, Clinton was per force the front-runner!

Had the news media anointed Clinton? To some extent, they had. But Clinton would not have achieved this status had he not developed a first-rate campaign organization and had he not articulated a convincing message.

In still other cases, candidates have been declared "front-runners" or "dream candidates," only to decide after considerable testing of the political waters that they would rather not run for president. This happened most recently with Colin Powell, the former chairman of the Joint Chiefs of Staff who was seen as having the potential to win the Republican nomination and to defeat Bill Clinton in 1996.

Powell became the darling of the news media during the fall of 1995.[7] News stories speculated on the possibility that he would run. They covered his national tour to promote his autobiography, My American Journey. They featured excerpts from his book. They discussed how he had risen from a working class background in Harlem to become one of the most prominent African-American political leaders of his generation. News stories regularly reported the results of opinion polls that showed most Americans wanted Powell to run for president.

Coverage of Powell dominated campaign coverage during the fall of 1995. It was a classic example of "pack journalism"—of the press corps descending like a pack of dogs on a story. Did the media create the maybe candidacy of Colin Powell? No. Powell created the issue by indicating that he was contemplating running for president. He fed the frenzy by writing a book, which one writer called a "a campaign document from start to finish."[8] Prominent Republicans urged Powell to run, sharing their views of Powell's personal and political strengths with the press. The possibility that Powell might run then led other Republicans to wonder out loud (and in the news) whether a Powell candidacy would be good for issues about which they felt strongly (such as abortion).

Unquestionably, the news magnified the Powell "candidacy" and kept it alive on the national agenda. Had Powell decided to run, the good press he received would have sustained him for a time—but history suggests that once he became a serious candidate, his good press would have been replaced by questioning press and then by bad press.

Did the media overplay the Powell story? Possibly, although this depends on what we mean by "overplay" and the criteria we use to assess overplaying an issue.

If one views the campaign as a courtship, with candidates courting voters, then the news coverage of Powell can be seen as fulfilling a positive function—providing voters with information about a potential president. On the other hand, by implying that one candidate is far better than all the rest and by mythically building up this candidate even though the candidate has let it be known that he or she may not run, the press may have set the public up for disappointment when the candidate finally decided to end speculation and announce he was not a candidate for president. On a broader level, the enormous coverage of Powell's "candidacy" is an example of the personalization of campaign politics in that reporters were focusing not on a candidate's ideas or where the party wanted to take the country, but instead on the personality and background of a public figure. Critics thought the news resembled pop psychology more than serious journalism.

Marketing

The preprimary period has become a critical phase of the campaign. Early political events, which are meaningless in and of themselves, take on great importance because they get covered by the media and attract the attention of influential members of the party. "Straw polls" held by state party organizations attract candidates like honey attracts bees. These polls are in no way representative of the larger population of voters in the political party. They are pseudoevents that attract the party faithful, candidates, pollsters, and the media.

One such event occurred in August, 1995, in Ames, Iowa. The event was the Iowa straw poll—actually a fund-raising event that attracted 10,000 Iowa Republicans who were willing to shell out $25. (Actually, many voters got free tickets from candidates.[9])

Texas Senator Phil Gramm tied Senator Bob Dole of Kansas for first place with 24% of the vote. Both Gramm and Dole's supporters tried to put the best face on the results, in what is frequently referred to as media spin. Gramm's campaign argued that the straw poll was a key test for the Iowa caucuses in February, an indication that Dole was not invincible. Dole's managers, though they were privately unnerved by the results, publicly said "we've said consistently that straw polls are meaningless."[10]

In the final analysis, the vote made little difference in the long fight for the Republican nomination. Dole won the Iowa caucuses in February, 1996. Gramm dropped out of the race shortly after his loss.

Another weapon in candidates' preprimary armamentarium is focus group technology. Consultants use focus groups to test-market candidates' speeches announcing their candidacy for president.

On March 30, 1995 Dole's advisers tested drafts of a Dole announcement using a focus group technique, called the dial group.[11] A group of voters sat in front of a television screen, each one holding an electronic dial. As they watched excerpts from a Dole announcement speech, they turned their dials from 0 (completely disapprove) to 100 (completely approve). The dial group information was used to help select issues for emphasis in Dole's official announcement, made in April, 1995.

A unique aspect of the 1996 preprimary period was that it featured the Republican challenger (Dole) locked in a battle over the budget with an incumbent president, Bill Clinton. In November 1995, government offices shut down for a time while President Clinton and his Republican opponents tried to resolve disagreements over how to balance the federal budget.

Months before the government shut-down, Clinton approved an expensive advertising campaign directed at the Republicans. In the summer of 1995, with the Republicans proposing to cut $270 billion from Medicare (to help balance the budget), Clinton gave the green light to a series of ads that attacked the Republicans and portrayed Clinton as the protector of Medicare and the elderly. "We will defeat them in the air war!" Clinton's political consultant Dick Morris proclaimed.[12]

The Clinton ads were misleading, but they seemed to pull up the president's poll numbers in key primary states such as Pennsylvania and Ohio. So while Clinton and Dole were negotiating to balance the budget in Washington, each side was privately plotting and planning strategies for the 1996 election campaign.

Yet campaigns depend in important ways upon the men and women who run for office, and in 1996 there was an unusual relationship between Bill Clinton and Bob Dole. Professional competitors, they respected one another off the field, and even joked about it. Once during a break in the budget negotiations, Clinton called Dole to discuss ways to resolve the crisis. Dole was out, but returned the call. A personal conversation between the two men ensued, as reporter Bob Woodward relates:

> "When are we going to finish?" Dole finally asked. He was very anxious and losing his patience. He liked to be straightforward and frank. "I've got to get to Iowa. My election is in February, yours is in November."
>
> "Yeah, I know," Clinton said, sounding sympathetic.[13]

Voters

Voters typically show little interest in the preprimary process. However, voters can influence the campaign agenda. In 1992, polls and interviews showed that the public was dissatisfied with the status quo, angry at political leaders, and worried that their dreams of economic prosperity were permanently slipping away from them. The public's sour mood continued through the primary period as news of the House check-bouncing scandal spread. Trent notes that the agenda was set in the preprimary period and never changed.[14]

In 1996, the public was less engaged in the election. Its support for Colin Powell telegraphed a dissatisfaction with Clinton and his Republican opponents. Stories that appeared in the preprimary period focused on the public's cynicism about politics and its distrust of politicians.

In this election, though, citizens' impact on the campaign agenda grew out of the midterm elections of 1994, when voters gave Republicans control of Congress and seemed to voice agreement with the notion, commonly associated with Republicans, that government should be downsized, not increased.[15] But voters' message in 1994 was muddied by evidence that they did not want to totally do away with government social welfare programs, particularly Medicare. So candidates had to deal with an ambiguous message from voters: people wanted less government, undoubtedly more efficient government, but did not want government to take a totally laissez faire attitude toward its neediest citizens and certainly did not want it to eliminate Medicare and Social Security.

It is difficult to clearly discern the public agenda in the preprimary period, mostly because most people are not concerned with the election at this time. Voters also speak with a clearer voice in certain elections than in others.[16]

PRIMARIES

The primaries are the focal point of today's nominating conventions. All roads to the nominating convention must pass through the presidential primaries and caucuses. That is because the lion's share of convention delegates are selected through primaries.

As noted in chapter 15, the proportion of delegates chosen through primaries has increased dramatically over the past half-century, particularly since the Democratic reforms of 1972. More than 80% of the delegates are now chosen through primaries and caucuses.[17]

In 1996 all but one of the states held primaries or caucuses.[18] Moreover, little time elapsed between the end of one primary and the beginning of another. Between February 6, the date of the first caucus, and April 2, there was at least one primary or caucus each week. In addition, the primaries were squeezed together, so that 31 of the 50 states held primaries or caucuses between February 6 and March 26. Approximately two thirds of the convention delegates were selected in the first 2 months of the primary season, a process known as **frontloading** to suggest that the nominations are loaded up by contests that occur in the early or "front" portion of the campaign.

Contemporary campaigns have become increasingly frontloaded as states have scheduled primaries earlier to exert a greater influence on the nominating process. The fact that there is little space between primaries and that the bulk of the delegates are chosen within the first 2 months of the primary phase has concerned scholarly observers of presidential politics. Critics have lamented that frontloading increases the impact of mass media by elevating the importance of media interpretations of primary victories, magnifies the effect of candidate misstatements because candidates have only a few days to correct misimpressions, gives early primaries a disproportionate influence on the process, and puts voters in the position of having to make critical choices before they have had a chance to assimilate campaign information.

New Hampshire and Iowa

New Hampshire has been the site of America's first presidential primary since 1920. Over the years, its citizens have grown accustomed to seeing hordes of journalists and dozens of candidates trekking through snowy small towns in the dead of winter. Most residents of the Granite State seem to enjoy the attention that they receive from presidential candidates and reporters, as well as the major boost that the visitors give to the state economy.

Iowa has held caucuses to select delegates to national nominating conventions since the mid-1800s. Unlike primaries, caucuses are open meetings to choose convention delegates. The Iowa caucuses captured national attention for the first time in 1972. George McGovern campaigned heavily in the Hawkeye State that year, hoping to dispel doubts about the viability of his candidacy. The national media covered the caucuses, and they (particularly *The New York Times*) emphasized McGovern's surprisingly strong showing. The Iowa caucuses were on their way to becoming a media event as "the delegate selection procedures of both parties (were) modified to generate 'results' or 'outcomes' that would allow the media to determine 'winners' and 'losers.'"[19]

At present, Iowa and New Hampshire are super-presidential selection contests. They dwarf the other states and hover like giants over a map of the United States when one examines states in proportion to news coverage of contests for the party nominations (see Fig. 16.1 and Fig. 16.2). Iowa is typically the first or second party caucus and New Hampshire is the nation's first primary. One of the most durable findings in election research is that these two presidential events receive the lion's share of press attention and that their coverage is far out of proportion to the number of electoral votes the two states command. Consider these statistics:

- In 1996, 51 percent of all network news coverage of the primaries centered on Iowa and New Hampshire. This meant that the remaining 49% of the coverage was divided among the other 48 states that held primaries or caucuses.[20]
- In 1988, Iowa and New Hampshire, which account for just 3% of the American population, received 34% of the network news coverage of the primaries. Newscasts discussed Iowa more often than all the other states west of the Mississippi River combined.[21]
- In the 1984 Democratic primaries, the 8 million-plus voters in Illinois, Ohio, Pennsylvania, North Carolina, and California combined did not receive as much press attention as the 101,000 individuals who cast votes in the Democratic primary in New Hampshire.[22]
- On February 26, 1980, Minnesota (population 3,800,000) held its party caucuses. The caucuses had attracted only three stories on CBS and in the UPI wire service. New Hampshire, with a population of 700,000, held its primary the same day. By this date, it had managed to attract 94 stories.[23]

The massive coverage afforded Iowa and New Hampshire would not be so bad if these states represented the national electorate. But New Hamp-

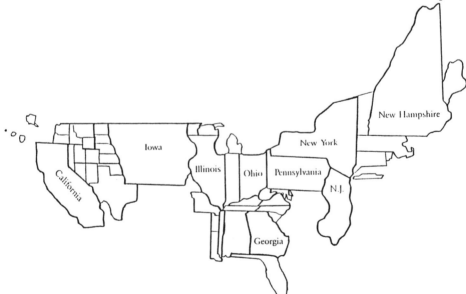

FIG. 16.1 States in Proportion to News Coverage of Contests for the 1984 Presidential Nomination. From Adams (1987).

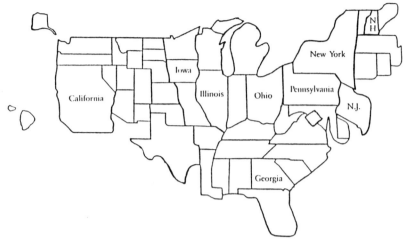

FIG. 16.2 States in Proportion to Electoral Votes. From Adams (1987).

shire is more conservative than the nation as a whole and both states have a higher proportion of whites than does the U.S. as a whole. For these reasons, scholars have been critical of the news media for focusing so heavily on these two early contests. Why does the press devote so much attention to Iowa and New Hampshire? There are several reasons.

First, news mirrors reality to some extent. Candidates spend considerable time and money campaigning in these early contests, and they regard their performance in these states as crucial. But do candidates campaign fiercely in Iowa and New Hampshire because these are critical events or are the events critical because the media treat them as such? It is probably a little bit of both, and in any event one cannot easily separate the press from electoral politics today.

Iowa and New Hampshire have traditionally been the first events of the campaign season, and the news media love firsts. "First" events are dramatic, thereby fitting one of the requirements of news. Iowa and New Hampshire also provide some of the first hard evidence of candidate performance, aside from opinion polls. They provide seemingly objective information that reporters can write up and that television anchors can discuss without fear of appearing biased. In addition, journalists view elections as a competitive, strategic game—a horse race—and fast-paced coverage of Iowa and New Hampshire fits this schema (see chapter 17). Finally, there is a long history of covering these events; they have become ritualized aspects of the quadrennial presidential election. Thus, for a variety of reasons, a caucus in mid-America and a primary on the Eastern seaboard, neither of which pretends to represent the views of registered Republicans or Democrats in the state, exerts a strong effect on the nominating process.

Effects.   Just what impact *does* winning Iowa and New Hampshire have on the nominating campaign? For one thing, victories in one or both of these contests typically produce a flurry of positive press. When Jimmy Carter won both Iowa and New Hampshire, he got himself on the cover of *Time* and *Newsweek*. More generally, as William Mayer notes, "the victorious candidate is portrayed as popular, exciting, confident, in control: in short, a leader."[24]

The political press likes to locate winners and enjoys bestowing the reward of publicity upon them. In some cases, candidates have narrowly defeated their challengers in New Hampshire and have still received the lion's share of positive press. In 1976, Carter defeated Morris Udall by less than 5,000 votes and garnered just over 28% of the total Democratic vote in New Hampshire. Yet he was declared the "clear-cut winner," and received 2,600 lines of news coverage in *Time* and *Newsweek*, compared to Udall's 96 lines.[25]

In 1996, Pat Buchanan won the New Hampshire primary with 27% of the vote, compared to Bob Dole's 26%. Buchanan received considerable positive press and was seen as a major threat to Dole's juggernaut—and suddenly a contender for the Republican nomination.

Complicating matters, candidates can also garner positive press by exceeding expectations set by journalists, pollsters, and party professionals.

In 1984, Gary Hart ran second to Walter Mondale in the Iowa caucuses. Hart received 16% of the vote, compared to Mondale's 49%. But because Hart's second-place showing was so unexpected, journalists latched onto it, eager to make a horse race out of the election. During the week following the Iowa caucuses and preceding the New Hampshire primary, Hart was the focus of more stories than Mondale. In part because of the news coverage, Hart's popularity in New Hampshire increased dramatically. Hart subsequently defeated Mondale in the Granite State 37% to 28%.[26]

In 1992 Bill Clinton proclaimed himself "the comeback kid" because he had come in second in New Hampshire. He actually garnered 25% per cent of the vote compared to winner Paul Tsongas's 35%. Clinton claimed he had exceeded *expectations*, which, he tried to imply after the campaign, were very low because of widely publicized accusations of marital infidelity and draft dodging. Although Clinton had only received one fourth of the Democratic vote in New Hampshire, he tried, with some success, to argue that his performance was really a victory because he had done better than expected (see Exhibit 16.1: Gennifer Flowers and Beyond).

In 1996, Lamar Alexander received positive press after coming in third in New Hampshire, not far behind Buchanan and Dole. Because he had exceeded "expectations," he earned the right to be treated (for a time) as a serious contender in the race. Not coincidentally, Alexander's poll numbers increased from a 13% favorable rating in January to a 34% favorable ranking

---

Exhibit 16.1
Gennifer Flowers and Beyond

Besides being a test of candidates' ability to use the media to influence voters, the primaries are also a Herculean test of our political leaders' skill in withstanding the slings and arrows of campaign attacks. Perhaps the best example of this occurred in January of 1992 when Bill Clinton was hit by charges of marital infidelity while campaigning in New Hampshire.

Clinton was the front-runner at the time. He had a message (the need for change and economic renewal), and he communicated it well. His message seemed to be registering with voters, who were also expressing concern about the economy and the course of the country in the post-Cold War era.

Then in late January, The Star, a supermarket tabloid, published a story that rocked the campaign. MY 12-YEAR AFFAIR WITH BILL CLINTON, the headline screamed, PLUS THE SECRET LOVE TAPES THAT PROVE IT! Lounge singer Gennifer Flowers was claiming that she and Clinton had enjoyed a 12-year romantic relationship and that he had once begged her to have sex with him in the men's bathroom of the Arkansas governor's mansion. Reportedly, Flowers had been paid in the six figures for talking to The Star. The conventional media were reluctant to run the story at first since it came from a newspaper tabloid and lacked hard facts. But after considerable soul-searching, the networks and the major newspapers decided to run with the story.

Critics charged that the news media had violated standards of decency and good taste. It was another example, they said, of the "tabloidization of journalism,"–of how ratings and economic pressures had pushed journalists into covering innuendo and sensational gossip. Journalists responded that it was not their job to censor the news; the public, they noted, has a right to know what is being alleged about candidates for the presidency. Citizens should be able to decide for themselves how to deal with the negative information. Both sides had a point, but the main thing was that for the first time in recent memory a newspaper tabloid had set the political agenda for the major news media.

With the story gathering momentum, the Clinton campaign planned its strategy. "This is full-scale nuclear war," press secretary Dee Dee Myers said, speaking about the battle between the press and the Clinton command group. The candidate needed to defuse the charges and maintain his position in the polls. Clinton advisers rarely publicly discussed whether the charges were true (many suspected they were). As professionals, their job was to promote the candidate and help him get *his* message across.

Clinton fought back by using the conventional media sensitively and adroitly. Clinton consultant Mandy Grunwald appeared on *Nightline* and turned the tables on Ted Koppel, telling him that the press was at fault for engaging in "trash-for-cash journalism." In essence, Grunwald reframed the issue, making press invasion of privacy – not Clinton's womanizing – the focal point.

Clinton and his wife Hillary appeared on *60 Minutes*, noting that they loved one another, cared enormously about their daughter, and had stuck with one another through thick and thin. The message was that they did not have a perfect marriage, husband Bill may have strayed, but they still were deeply committed to one another. Moreover, the Clintons suggested, their marital problems were their private concerns – not matters for the entire country to speculate about and discuss. The American people, Bill Clinton maintained, were more interested in how to deal with the problems that faced the country in the future than in events that had happened in the past.

Knowing full well that people would be watching their nonverbal, as well as verbal, interaction, the Clintons held hands from time to time in the interview. At one point in the interview, Hillary Clinton rubbed her husband's back.

Clinton's counteroffensive seemed to work. According to press reports, voters were more interested in the candidate's policy ideas than his private life. Polls showed that people overwhelmingly disapproved of the media's handling of the story and their invasion of Clinton's privacy. Political journalists themselves raised questions about the ethics of running a "sexpose" that was based on only the flimsiest of evidence. Soon, political journalism and the propriety of investigating a candidate's private life became *the* issue.

Clinton had escaped what would be the first of many brushes with political death. His success was due in part to his own ability to frame –or dance around– the issue, the public's fatigue after the Gary Hart issue with press investigations of candidates' private foibles, popular and elite dissatisfaction with negative campaign tactics in 1988, and a cyclical change in public mood that favored an emphasis upon public purpose (Clinton's mantra) over a stress on private enterprise. In another election, in another era, the same charges and Clinton's inability to directly answer his accusers' questions would have dealt his candidacy a quick and painful death. But in 1992, there was more tolerance for candidates' private indiscretions, and less willingness to accept without question the perspective of the press.

The Flowers story raised troubling questions. How far should reporters go in probing the private lives of public officials? Was anything off limits? Was society best served by having journalists report every tidbit of candidates' private lives? And if limits should be placed on what reporters covered, who should establish the limits? (see Payne & Mercuri, 1993).

Four years later, a different approach to the privacy issue surfaced. In early 1996, a novel, *Primary Colors*, was published that told the story of how an ambitious, womanizing Southern politician named Jack Stanton schemed his way to the White House, even compromising a teenage girl during the campaign. There was never any doubt that the main characters in the book were the Clintons and that other major characters were James Carville, George Stephanopoulos and their campaign aides.

For months, the author of the book was not known; the book's cover listed the author only as *Anonymous*. Then in the summer it was revealed that *Newsweek's* Joe Klein had written the book. Klein's admission rocked the media for he had persistently denied that he had written *Primary Colors*. Critic Hadley Arkes pointed out that the book contained "an amalgam of facts and fictions," adding that "the book was evidently written to present as fictions rather embarrassing facts. The first question then is: Which are the facts and which are the fictions?"

Arkes criticized Klein, suggesting that if in 1992 Klein had known certain facts about Clinton that did not place the candidate in a positive light, he should have reported them at the time, and not waited until 1996 to do so – and certainly not in the medium of fiction.

Whatever one's view about *Primary Colors*, the episode makes clear that the lines between fact and fiction – as well as between private and public, and between appropriate and inappropriate journalistic (and candidate) behavior– are not always easy to draw neatly. Candidates, reporters, and the public have had to struggle with these questions for more than 200 years, and they will continue debating them. Each generation must draw the lines and set limits that it deems most appropriate.

---

in late February after the New Hampshire vote.[27]

Candidates now play **the expectations game,** arguing that a second place or third place finish in a multicandidate race exceeded expectations and therefore allows them to declare victory. Reporters act as oddsmakers, suggesting that a candidate "must win" a primary to stay in the race or has to get at least 25% of the vote to remain a viable candidate. Based on polls, conversations with party leaders, and the outcomes of primaries, journalists informally rank candidates as front-runners, plausibles, and hopeless cases.[28] The pressure on front-runners is enormous, as columnist Russell Baker humorously points out:

Rotten luck ... Mondale, we've made you the front-runner ... Without a front-runner, we'd have nobody to suffer surprising setbacks in the early stage of the campaign, and without surprising setbacks we would be stuck with a very dull story ... It's tough, but somebody's got to make the sacrifice and be the front-runner ... Say you get only 47 percent of that boondocks vote (in New Hampshire and Iowa).

What we'll do is say, well 47 percent may not be disgraceful, but Mondale had been expected to do better, so it looks like he's all washed up … We of the press and TV do the expecting. You do the disappointing. That way we work together to give the country an entertaining story.[29]

As it turned out, Baker's warning accurately predicted the events to come—at least in the short run. After exceeding expectations in Iowa and New Hampshire in 1984, Hart did capture enormous media attention. Reporters began to suggest that Mondale could be beaten. But, in the end Mondale's superior organization and savvy use of the paid media carried the day and he won the nomination handily.

Momentum.   George Bush dubbed momentum the "Big Mo" and the name stuck. Candidates hope to win (or at least significantly exceed expectations) in Iowa or New Hampshire, benefit from the ensuing positive press, and then build a bandwagon of support that can lift them into the nomination. But does it actually work this way?

Momentum has proven to be a complex force in modern elections. In some cases, winning (or exceeding expectations) in Iowa and New Hampshire has boosted candidacies. As Robert Lichter and Richard Noyes note:

> The media attention surrounding Carter and Hart clearly boosted each man's name recognition, helping their candidacies and hurting their rivals. But that is not to say that the media deliberately, or even knowingly, intended to assist those men. Rather, both benefited from the fact that their candidacies became important news stories. That is, journalism's norms and values directed reporters to write and talk about them disproportionately during the crucial early phase of the campaign.[30]

In Carter's case, media momentum had a particularly strong impact. Carter was an unknown Georgia governor until the Iowa caucuses. After his victories in Iowa and New Hampshire and the burst of media attention, his campaign took off. His support in the polls jumped from 4% before New Hampshire to 16% after his victory.[31] He became the front-runner for the Democratic nomination and ran up a string of primary victories.

In an earlier era, a political unknown like Jimmy Carter would never have gotten nominated—certainly not on the first ballot. The media attention convinced voters and party regulars that Carter was a contender. But Carter would not have made it through the primaries if he had not developed a persuasive message. Carter intelligently and strategically centered his campaign around honesty in government, a theme especially well-suited to the post-Watergate 1976 election.

In other years, candidates have had difficulty riding the wave of victory or near-victory in New Hampshire and Iowa to success in the crucial Southern primaries that take place in March, on what has come to be known as Super Tuesday. For example, in 1996, even though he lost New Hampshire and his campaign experienced "negative momentum," Bob Dole bested his opponents on Super Tuesday and the regional primaries that followed. His organizational strength, popularity with party leaders, and name recognition among rank-and-file Republicans served him well in the primaries that followed New Hampshire.

Dole's opponent, Pat Buchanan, won New Hampshire, but never got the positive press that Carter and Hart received. In fact he received a good deal of negative press after New Hampshire as influential party leaders indicated they could not support Buchanan and lashed out at him for taking extreme positions on social issues (see Exhibit 16.2: Pulpit Candidates).

The electoral context helps determine the impact of media momentum. In 1988, Democratic Congressman Richard Gephardt won the Iowa caucuses, but received less media attention than anticipated, in part because the results on the Republican side garnered so much press. The surprise success of Rev. Pat Robertson in Iowa consumed so much attention that it eliminated Gephardt's hopes of gaining a momentous bounce from his Iowa victory.[32]

In sum, the prevailing wisdom about Iowa and New Hampshire is that: *(a) candidates cannot ignore these two states and hope to win the nomination; (b) these two contests exert effects not because of their representativeness or size but*

Exhibit 16.2
Pulpit Candidates

Question: What do Jesse Jackson, Pat Robertson, and Pat Buchanan have in common other than that they ran for president?
Answer: They are "pulpit candidates." They are politicians who, according to Stephen Wayne, *"use the campaign as a pulpit for presenting their ideas and as a vehicle for mobilizing their constituencies to promote the interests of those who were not well represented in the party and its hierarchy."*
Neither Jackson, who ran for president in 1984 and 1988, Robertson, who ran in 1988, nor Buchanan, who ran in 1992 and 1996, had a particularly good chance of winning the nomination. But they threw their hats in the ring and in so doing had a positive impact on the system.
Pulpit candidates have long been a fixture in American politics, and many have been adept at using the dominant medium of their times. Not surprisingly, Jackson, Robertson, and Buchanan used television adroitly. Jackson and Robertson are reverends who draw on their experience as religious orators to make impressive television speeches. All three have

hosted television programs: Jackson has hosted CNN's *Both sides*, Buchanan CNN's *Crossfire*, and Robertson the Christian Broadcasting Network's *700 Club*.

Each has had his share of controversy. Jesse Jackson was accused of making anti-semitic remarks, and Buchanan was widely criticized for his extremist rhetoric (peppered, as it was, by segregationist and anti-gay comments). The consistency between Robertson's religious attitudes and behavior was called into question when reporters learned that Robertson's wife was pregnant before they were married.

The news media have trouble covering pulpit candidates because they do not fit into the usual categories of presidential contenders. If reporters dismiss the candidate as not-serious, they run the risk of being wrong or of being accused of not giving an alternative candidate a chance.

In Jesse Jackson's case, the press was simultaneously accused of being too easy and too hard on the same candidate. Some critics claimed that the press was afraid to criticize Jackson because he was Black; others felt that reporters were using "condescending language delivered in patronizing tones," which suggested that they were unwilling to treat Jackson as a serious contender (see Lichter et al., 1988).

While Jackson's coverage had peaks and valleys, research on his press coverage in 1988 finds that much of the news cast Jackson in a favorable light, particularly during the Super Tuesday campaign period and the following month of primarily Midwestern races. Moreover, as Anthony Broh notes, television legitimated Jackson's candidacy. TV news treated Jackson as an important force in Democratic party politics and made it clear that "he was to receive fair treatment like any other presidential candidate because he was using established electoral procedures in an attempt to gain public office" (see Broh, 1987).

Buchanan got his share of negative press, particularly when Republican leaders complained about his extremist positions on social issues. For a time, Buchanan was the butt of jokes on late-night talk shows. David Letterman said Buchanan "is going to take a couple of days off after the New Hampshire primary and then invade Poland."

Each of these pulpit candidates employed rich and colorful rhetoric. Buchanan unleashed populist-type attacks on big business and called on a ban on immigration to protect American jobs. He sought to reach White Republicans who felt increasingly anxious about the pace of social and economic change. At the same time, critics noted that he employed a divisive rhetoric that relied on code words to attack Jews, Blacks, and gays. Robertson used religious metaphors and made "moral leadership" the focus of his presidential bid. However, his rhetoric was undermined by revelations that televangelist Jimmy Swaggart, who supported Robertson, had regularly visited prostitutes and by Robertson's less-than-moral accusations that the Bush campaign was behind the effort to release this information to the press in an effort to destroy his candidacy.

Jackson, undoubtedly the most eloquent of the three, had, as Sidney Blumenthal notes, once "countered Reagan's image of the poor – a 'welfare queen' in her Cadillac– with an equally vivid and truer line: 'They take the early bus.'" Yet although his conciliatory and unifying rhetoric stirred and greatly moved African-Americans, it failed to connect with the overwhelming majority of white Democrats, who viewed him more as the leader of a protest movement than as a potential president.

All three of these pulpit candidates accomplished political goals. Robertson energized the religiously-minded Christian Republicans, helping to make them a force in the party. Jackson helped to bring African-Americans into the party and opened the door to Colin Powell in 1995 – because of Jackson, White Americans had a schema or concept for a Black president, and this made it possible for them to consider Powell, an action that would have been unthinkable 10 or 20 years earlier. Jackson also helped to call attention to the problems that minority groups in America still face. Buchanan helped keep the concerns of White working class voters on the party agenda.

Are pulpit campaigns good for the system? As a rule, they are because they bring new voices into the system, provide disenfranchised voters with a chance to influence events, and force established candidates to confront issues they would rather not debate.

because they occur early in the primary season; (c) candidates cannot succeed in Iowa and New Hampshire without having a good organization and financial backing; (d) these two contests, coupled with media coverage and candidate spin, have a winnowing effect on the nomination—candidates who do badly in these states and get bad press as a result of their performance will not long survive the race for the presidency; and (e) winning or nearly winning these early contests is a necessary, but not sufficient, condition to gain the party nomination.

News, Primaries, and Voters

After New Hampshire, the race for the nomination intensifies. The candidates who remain in the contest face a grueling series of state and regional primaries. Candidates hustle to get good press, trying to dream up events that will get covered in the news and lining up endorsements from major party officials. They do talk-radio programs. They also sponsor television advertisements, including negative spots.

Ross Perot demonstrated that a candidate could mount a successful campaign by circumventing the news media. Perot launched his campaign on *Larry King Live* and garnered considerable support from appearances on *60 Minutes* and Phil Donahue's talk show. But Perot would not have gained in the polls in the spring of 1992 had the conventional news media decided not to run stories about him. Perot's popularity and his ability to attract volunteers suggested to reporters that he was a viable candidate, and they began to cover him. Later, when Perot became a front-runner, he was subjected to tougher press, and his poll ratings dropped.[33]

There is little question that the news media play a critical role in the nomination process by deciding which candidates should get covered and which candidates should be ignored because they are not serious contenders or because their candidacies are destined to fail.[34] Journalists, of course, have a set of criteria they use to decide which of the 30-odd candidates for the Republican and Democratic nominations should get covered (the number depends on the year). They scrutinize candidates' organization and finances, their movement in opinion polls, and their performance in primaries. They also estimate the extent to which a candidate's rhetoric is likely to appeal to voters and to fit their mood in a given election year. Thus as John Zaller notes, "the critical obstacle for every candidate is to engage the attention of the press."[35]

Some critics believe that this is the main problem with the current campaign. They argue that news media have too much power, and that the voting public is influenced in subtle, but powerful, ways by campaign news. According to critics like Thomas Patterson, people are minimally interested in the campaign in the early stages. "People are just beginning to pay attention to the campaign when the press highlights an early winner," he notes.[36]

Voters judge a candidate in part by their electability and, the argument goes, they employ the following rule of thumb: "If you really matter, you will be at the focus of mass attention, and if you are at the focus of mass attention, then you must really matter."[37] Patterson argues that lacking the motivation to carefully process the campaign, people mentally elevate candidates who get press attention and downgrade those who don't.

There is some truth to this. Studies show that when there is considerable doubt who the nominee is going to be, voters (particularly those who lack information about the candidate) are apt to prefer candidates they think are going to win.[38] Thus, during the primaries some voters do jump on the bandwagon of candidates who, in the view of political elites and the news media, have a good shot at winning the nomination. These voters also are apt to pay insufficient attention to what the candidate stands for and where he or she stands on the issues.

But more than viability considerations enter into voters' cognitive processing of candidates. Some voters may prefer a candidate because they think he or she is going to win, but others are apt to employ the opposite line of reasoning: to assume that a candidate is going to win because they think highly of the politician's personal traits (this is called the projection effect). Moreover, other aspects of media coverage seep into voters' consciousness during the primary period. People pick up information about where the candidates stand on big issues (like abortion and Medicare). They match the candidates' positions with their own if the issues are important to them. Voters also form impressions of the candidates' personality and their competence from news, talk shows, and advertising, and these influence their vote decisions.[39]

Moreover, it is not immediately clear that those voters who closely follow media reports and mentally elevate candidates whom the media regard as front-runners are making a big mistake. Wouldn't it be foolish for highly committed Republicans *not* to consider the chances that a candidate could beat an incumbent Democratic president? Didn't party leaders use the same criterion when they ran the show?

But if the news media are not the entire problem, they are not on the forefront of the solution to the issue of the primary's role in the nomination process. The fact that primaries are frontloaded means that voters who happen to live in states that hold their primaries after New Hampshire and Super Tuesday are effectively disenfranchised from the process. By the time their state gets around to holding its primary, the race has been reduced to only a couple of candidates. In some years the nomination may be effectively decided. The system—candidates, party, media, polls, and the early primaries themselves—has helped to winnow the list of contenders. Thus, voters who happen to live in states that hold primaries late are not able to meaningfully participate in the presidential selection process, whereas those who live in states that hold early primaries or caucuses exert a disproportionately large impact on the process. Moreover, there is a great deal of volatility in the process. In Patterson's view, campaign events, candidate gaffes, and journalists' need to hype a story "introduce an element of random partisanship into the campaign, which coincidentally works to the advantage of one side or another."[40]

There is little doubt that the current system, with its mad emphasis upon early contests and its unpredictable nature (exemplified by cases in which early, sometimes trivial, campaign events exert strong influences on later primary outcomes), is far from perfect; it is unquestionably an improvement upon the boss-dominated nominating system of the nineteenth century, but like all improvements upon the past, it has created unexpected problems and dilemmas.

NOMINATING CONVENTIONS

Long ago, the party convention was the centerpiece of the campaign; now it is an appendage, a 4-day-long event that ratifies the choice made by voters in the primaries, conducts party business, and promotes the ticket before a national television audience.

There are, to be sure, important things that go on at party conventions, not the least of which is the adoption of the party platform. However, from a communication perspective, conventions are primarily "four-day-long commercials for the presidential ticket and for the party as a whole."[41] Party leaders plan the convention with television in mind, preplanning events like chanting of slogans that look spontaneous when they happen, and orchestrating speeches delivered from the podium. In rhetorical terms, they seek a coherent narrative—or story line—that they can take into the fall campaign.[42]

Candidates want an orderly convention and a unified party—what Larry Smith and Dan Nimmo call "a cordial concurrence."[43] It does not always work this way. At the 1968 Democratic convention, party leaders angrily debated the rules and appeared helpless as police brutalized radical activists in the streets of Chicago. In 1988, Jesse Jackson let it be known that he felt the Democratic leadership was not giving him the role he deserved at the convention, a role he felt was due him because of his victories in the Democratic primaries. At the 1992 Republican convention, the two Pats—Buchanan and Robertson, the latter a television evangelist—unleashed brutal attacks on the Clintons, charging that the Democrats would destroy the American family and undermine the country's moral structure.

As always, there are different perspectives on the state of the current nominating convention. Some observers criticize conventions, saying they are nothing other than paid political advertisements. Others point out that this is not entirely a bad thing in that it provides the public with an opportunity to see and hear the candidates speak on the issues, without the interpretation of journalists. There is also debate about whether party leaders should disallow candidates who are bitter about losing the primary fight from delivering speeches on the grounds that they take away from the theme of party unity, or whether the leadership should permit such speeches based on the logic that one of the functions of a nominating convention is to debate issues and formulate positions on controversial policy issues.

Since elections are more about winning than debating issues, the political strategists usually carry the day at party conventions. In 1996, the Republicans carefully choreographed the political proceedings, making certain that speakers avoided discussion of abortion (a topic that provoked much controversy at the Republicans' 1992 convention). They encouraged speakers to pander to the technology, as when Elizabeth Dole gave an Oprah-style, talk-show-host speech on behalf of her husband.

Party leaders also limited speeches from the podium to 5 minutes. Given Americans' diminishing appetite for political rhetoric, and evidence that 60% of voters no longer watch conventions live on TV, Republican party leaders had a cause for concern about long-winded speeches. But even *The Weekly Standard*, a conservative Republican opinion magazine, lamented on the eve of the San Diego convention that the airtime would be filled not with compelling political rhetoric, but instead with colorful pictures, satellite hook-ups, and "all the dumbed-down schlock that cutting-edge technology allows."[44]

As *The Weekly Standard* predicted, the Republican convention (and the Democratic convention that followed) took full advantage of electronic and computer technologies. World Wide Web sites trumpeted the nominees' accomplishments. A large video wall projected the speakers' faces to the delegates and the viewers. In fact at the Democratic convention, President Clinton even spoke to the convention from a giant TV screen as he traveled by train across the Midwest; "from time to time," a columnist observed, "he beams down at the convention ... a loving apolitical presence who has paused along his route of march to extend a warm, electronic hug to those who await him."[45]

Conventions are preplanned to attract a large television audience. Events and speeches are orchestrated so they will capture the attention of the viewing audience, as well as the 15,000 reporters in attendance (there were nearly *eight* times as many journalists as delegates at the 1996 Republican convention and nearly *four* times as many reporters as delegates at the Democratic bash.)

Convention speakers frequently try to combine schmaltz with substance. They reveal personal tidbits from their past, even family tragedies. In an age of personalized politics, speakers feel that they must let their hair down a little and reveal a human and emotional side to a television audience that is used to seeing actors and actresses emote and that has come to expect personal revelations from celebrities of the nonpolitical and political kind.

Thus in 1996, Republican keynote orator Susan Molinari arranged for her Congressman husband to bring their baby along. The Democrats tugged at the audience's heartstrings by having actor Christopher Reeve, paralyzed by a horseback-riding accident, talk about sacrifice and community. Both Democrats and Republicans seemed to place entertainment values—attracting and schmoozing an audience—over civic values—educating and uplifting the electorate.

But one must be careful about writing off modern conventions as "show-biz iconography and salesmanship," as one critic put it.[46] Politics has always combined ideology, education, entertainment, and salesmanship. In the old days, convention speakers used to drone on into the night, pitching platitudes that gave political rhetoric a bad name. In 1928, Herbert Hoover told the Republican convention that "We in America today are nearer to the final triumph over poverty than ever before in the history of the land." A few short years later, the Depression made a mockery of Hoover's claim.

In the final analysis, conventions—in the old days and today—represent a formal mechanism for parties to nominate candidates and to reach consensus on their platforms. Symbolically, conventions provide parties with the opportunity to revitalize themselves and to gear up for the fall campaign. To some extent, these functions conflict with the need to attract a large audience of largely apolitical citizens and the equally important goal of capturing positive press from a news media that resents the slightest attempt to manipulate or influence the campaign agenda.

CONCLUSIONS

The American election campaign is undoubtedly the longest in the world. Candidates, by both design and necessity, begin campaigning for president as much as 2 years before the election. Ambitious and media-savvy incumbents like Bill Clinton launch advertising campaigns long before the fall election campaign. Senators and governors who plan to run for president consider the election-year implications of policy proposals that come before them. Campaigning becomes interwoven with governing.

There are three phases to the nomination campaign: preprimaries, primaries, and conventions. In the preprimaries, candidates test-market their ideas, struggle to raise money, and convince the media they are serious contenders. They then pull out all stops to win early primaries, using a variety of strategies ranging from old-fashioned campaigning (in small states like Iowa) to courting elite reporters and running television ads, which has become an accepted, if controversial, aspect of primary campaigns. Primaries have become increasingly frontloaded, which means that early primary victories—and exceeding of elusive expectations—become increasingly important. Even in an era of exploding technologies, the news media still play a critical role in helping to winnow the list of potential contenders.

This does not mean that the news media "select" the candidates. As we have seen, reporters depend upon the evaluations of party leaders and opinion polls when making their assessments of the presidential contenders. Moreover, people do not base their voting decisions simply on the knowledge that a candidate is leading the pack. Instead, they consider the candidates' personal traits, competence, and relationship with key groups in the party. Media attention is clearly a necessary, but not sufficient, condition for winning the nomination.

The real question, as Polsby and Wildavsky note, is not whether primaries or media are indispensable for presidential nominations (most assuredly they are), but which candidates "are advantaged or disadvantaged by primaries," and "are citizens' preferences more or less likely to be reflected in the results?"[47]

There is little doubt that the current system advantages media-savvy candidates who know how to communicate effectively through diverse communications media. But, as former talk-show host Pat Buchanan found in 1996, being able to talk effectively in sound bites will not overcome stiff opposition of party leaders and the absence of a unifying message. The fact that Bob Dole, an old-style campaigner who was not particularly comfortable using new media techniques, won the nomination shows that parties still matter and that candidates, like Dole, who have strong links to the party leadership, stand a fair chance of being nominated. Thus, the nomination process still gives us candidates who represent the leadership and broad rank and file of the parties.

This is not to say that the current presidential selection process is perfect. Few would deny that a process that favors pseudoevents like straw polls and early victories in unrepresentative states, and that effectively disenfranchises voters from late primary states, is the best that American democracy can offer. The nineteenth century system advantaged party bosses and excluded ordinary citizens. Today's system privileges wealthy candidates and the news media, but it gives ordinary people a greater stake in the process than did the old system. The fact that it, too, is not without problems suggests that the American nomination process is still in need of tinkering and improvement, a fact that would amuse, but not surprise, the more foresighted of the Founding Fathers.

KEY ISSUES

Preprimary Stage

Primary Campaign

Early Primary States

Frontloading

Expectations Game

Momentum

Voters and Primaries

Party Conventions

Pulpit Candidates

DISCUSSION QUESTIONS

1. What's wrong with the view that "the media created Gary Hart and Colin Powell?"

2. What impact do the media have on the nomination process? Do they have too much influence in the early phases? Why or why not?

3. Has the press gone too far in covering candidates' private lives? What limits, if any, should be placed on news coverage of candidates' private lives?

17

The Press
and the Presidential Campaign

This chapter continues the discussion of press coverage of presidential election campaigns by focusing on the biases, structure, and complexities of campaign news. The first part of the chapter discusses popular criticisms of the news. The second and third sections describe the structure of presidential news coverage, and the final section looks at controversies and complications in current scholarship on the press and the presidential campaign.

NEWS BIAS

Is the press biased?

If you ask ordinary Americans, they will tell you that the press is biased and that journalists frequently slant the news to help candidates they support. One national survey found that the majority of the public believes that journalists sometimes or often let their own political beliefs influence their reporting decisions.[1] As one New Jersey television viewer put it in a letter to ABC News, "If I could see the front page editor of *The New York Times*, I would look the person straight in the eye and say, 'Listen, pal, keep your opinions to yourself. Just give me the facts, man, just the facts.'"[2]

The allegation of press bias is probably the most frequently heard criticism of the news media in this country. Yet such allegations are hardly new. George Washington railed against the anti-Federalist newspapers of the 1790s, and Jefferson criticized newspaper editors of the early 1800s. John Adams was so infuriated by the press that he persuaded Congress to enact a Sedition Act to prohibit the publication of false and malicious statements.

Of course in the late eighteenth and early nineteenth centuries, the press really was biased; newspapers were allied with political parties and regularly printed harsh attacks on presidents and leaders of the opposing party. Their raison d'etre was to further the cause of a political party.

In our own era, the missions of the media have changed. They now perform different political, economic, and social functions for society. Yet charges of bias persist, particularly in elections, for it is here that the media seem to be most influential and carry some of the most colorful and emotional stories about political life.

Are the news media biased? It depends on what we mean by bias. Webster's Dictionary defines the word as *"an inclination of temperament or outlook (such that) the mind does not respond impartially to anything related to this object or point of view."* Using this definition, there is little doubt that the media are biased. No one can be totally impartial or objective, least of all reporters who cover politics up close. But this is not what people usually mean by bias. When audience members charge that the news media are biased, they mean that reporters slant the news to promote candidates whose positions they agree with, and denigrate candidates with whom they disagree.

It is hard to test the hypothesis that personal bias determines the news since we have to make inferences about journalists' attitudes and intentions from the results of **content analyses**, or systematic studies of the nature of media portrayals.

Even if we find that one side or another gets more favorable press, this does not mean that journalists deliberately slanted the news to further "their" candidate's cause. There are a host of reasons why candidates get good or bad press, as we will see. For example, a candidate can get favorable press because sources quoted by journalists speak positively about the candidate, because the candidate leads in the polls, or, if the candidate is an incumbent president, because the economy is running smoothly.

Candidates also get good press if they wage an effective campaign. In 1996 President Clinton ran an excellent campaign, as even his critics had to grudgingly admit. He coopted positions linked with Republicans (such as overhauling welfare) and adopted a rhetorical style that appealed to both liberals and moderates. As an incumbent, he was able to use the White House to publicize popular policy proposals such as the voluntary use of school uniforms and curfews for juveniles. In August, his staff dreamed up the clever idea of having the president travel to the Democratic convention by train, Harry Truman style. The train ride, coupled with the policy statements Clinton made as he traveled, fit media routines like a glove. So, too, did Clinton's announcement that he was designating nearly two million acres in Utah as a national monument, for the president spoke along the breathtakingly beautiful rim of the Grand Canyon, an area that provided a picture-perfect series of visuals for the evening news.

By contrast, Bob Dole, not being as natural a campaigner as Clinton, found it difficult to stage events or give speeches that generated as much positive coverage. Furthermore, when Dole made mistakes like turning down a request to address an NAACP convention on the grounds that the NAACP president was "trying to set me up," or mistakenly calling the Los Angeles Dodgers the Brooklyn Dodgers, he invited negative press. It is easy to see how people might conclude that journalists slanted the news to further Clinton's candidacy in 1996. But what really happened is that the winning candidate used the press more effectively than did the loser (see Fig. 17.1).

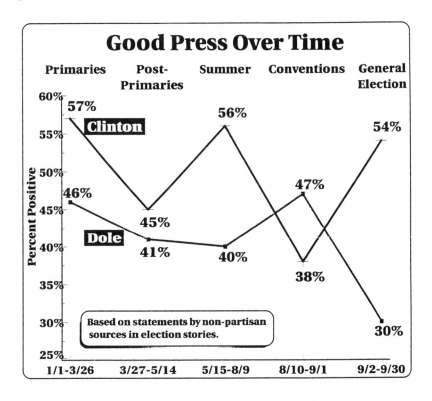

FIG. 17.1 TV News Coverage of Clinton Versus Dole, 1996.
From *Media Monitor* (1996, September/October).

It is often believed that news coverage of elections reflects a left-liberal bias. Critics argue that reporters are liberal and that they therefore slant the news to help liberal Democratic candidates. There are problems with this view as well.

It is true that Washington reporters are more likely than not to be liberal Democrats. It is also true that some Republican presidents have gotten bad press when running for reelection. For example, Michael Robinson found that network television reporters made more negative comments about the Republican ticket (Reagan–Bush) than the Democratic ticket (Mondale–Ferraro) in 1984.[3] By negative comments, Robinson did not mean opinionated statements about the candidate's political views, but reporters' interpretations of what a candidate did or said. Using this criterion, Robinson found that the Republican incumbent received significantly more negative press than did his Democratic challenger.

However, upon closer analysis, it turns out that Reagan's negative press was probably due to factors other than partisan bias.[4] Realizing that if Reagan were reelected to a second term, he would never have to face the voters again, journalists felt a special obligation to warn the electorate of problematic aspects of Reagan's presidential style. Arguably, they would have done the same for a Democratic incumbent. In addition, reporters felt exasperated at Reagan for having successfully thrown one-liners at them and for his inaccessibility during his first term in office. Negative coverage allowed journalists to "get back at" Reagan for what they saw as manipulation and exploitation. While this may be petty or peevish, it is not partisan.

Contrary to the liberal bias thesis, Democratic candidates have not always gotten an easy ride. Jimmy Carter and Michael Dukakis received a good deal of bad press in the 1980 and 1988 elections. Bill Clinton was the subject of much negative press in the 1992 primary campaign and throughout his presidency.[5]

One other argument against the view that the news media slant the news to favor Democratic candidates is the overwhelming evidence that the news devotes the same amount of time or space to Democratic and Republican candidates for the presidency. For example, in 1984, the Republicans received approximately 25,000 seconds of airtime on the network news; the Democrats garnered about 26,000 seconds. Michael Robinson, who reported these findings, concluded that this "works out to approximately six seconds more per program for the Democrats." He adds that "when one adds time spent covering Reagan as president, there is no advantage for the Democrats, but, in fact, a Democratic time deficit."[6]

This is not to say that reporters' personal feelings and partisan sentiments never influence the way they report the news. Reporters are human, and their feelings toward a candidate can influence the way they write or narrate a story. Journalists' political preferences can influence news decisions in subtle ways, as when newspapers do features on corporate downsizing (an issue that resonates with liberals) rather than on business expansion (which is popular with conservatives).[7] But for the most part, partisan political biases have less impact on what gets reported than do professional and journalistic considerations.

Elections are one area of political communication in which reporters bend over backward to give the candidates of both parties a pretty fair and equal shake. Professional norms require that they do so. There *is* bias in covering the election, but it is a different type than most people usually assume. News typically suggests that elections matter, that the two parties sharply differ on the issues, that alternative parties have little to offer voters, and that voters have an obligation to vote. Indeed, one way for journalists to appeal to the largest common denominator of news consumers or to distract people from coverage that for any number of reasons favors one or the other candidate is to proclaim that elections offer voters choices and that people have a duty to vote. Most of us would probably agree with these assumptions, but there *are* different perspectives on whether the parties differ dramatically on the issues and on how much impact elections have on public policy. Thus, the American press tends to reflect a general prodemocratic system bias in coverage of elections (see also Box 17.1).

There is another type of bias that the news displays, and this is a bias rooted in professional norms. This is a pervasive bias, one that has far greater effects than personal or partisan preferences. The next section focuses on this structural bias in American election news.

HORSE RACE NEWS

The national press is entirely concerned with "horse race" and popularity ... If thermonuclear war broke out today, the lead paragraph in tomorrow's *Washington Post* would be, "In a major defeat for President Carter ... "—Former Congressional press secretary.[8]

To a considerable extent, the news media cover elections as a game, a sporting event, a horse race. They focus on the candidates' strategy, on who is ahead in the polls, on the battle plan of the campaign, and on the political factors that underlie candidates' articulation of policy proposals. As critic

Paul Weaver notes, reporters view politics as "essentially a game played by individual politicians for personal advancement, gain or power."[9]

Thomas Patterson invokes the psychological concept of *schema* to explain how reporters approach elections. A schema is a mental structure that individuals use to process new information, retrieve old information, and make sense of situations. Patterson argues that "the dominant schema for the reporter is structured around the notion that politics is a strategic game." He adds that "when journalists encounter new information during an election, they tend to interpret it within a schematic framework according to which candidates compete for advantage."[10]

Patterson points out that the horse race is not the only way to view elections; one can also conceive of elections as methods to choose leaders, as ways to articulate policy problems, or as mechanisms to educate voters on important national issues. However, as Patterson and Robert McClure note:

> Network reporting treats a presidential election exactly like a horse race. The camera follows the entries around the country trying to capture the drama, excitement, and adventure of a grueling run for the November finish line. The opinion polls are cited frequently, indicating the candidates' positions on the track. The strengths and weaknesses of all the participants are constantly probed, providing an explanation for their position and creating drama about how the race might change as they head down the homestretch.[11]

You have undoubtedly seen these stories. A story that begins "The latest CNN tracking poll shows that the presidential race is heating up," or that discusses a candidate's strategy for winning back the Southern vote, or says that a candidate is gaining momentum, or interprets a candidate's speech on affirmative action as an attempt to woo African-American voters is employing a game schema or is an example of horse race reporting.

Although newspapers conducted straw polls as early as the 1820s and reporters have long viewed presidential elections as sporting events, there has been an upsurge of horse race news over the past 30 years, and today it is a major component of news coverage of presidential campaigns.[12] *Horse race coverage has increased in recent years for several reasons, including: (a) the proliferation of opinion polls, (b) the growth of the objectivity norm, which favors news based on "'facts" rather than opinions, (c) increased journalistic cynicism about politics following Watergate, which encourages reporters to view the election as nothing more than a strategic game, (d) candidates' tendency to openly discuss their political media strategies, and (e) the perception that voters would never follow serious coverage of issues "without the sugar coating that 'horse race' news provides."*[13]

There tends to be more horse race coverage during the presidential primaries than during any other phase of the campaign. As much as 50% of news stories focus on the horse race during the primaries.[14] There is typically less horse race news during the general election phase of the campaign as candidates, voters, and the news media concentrate more on policy issues. Nevertheless, polls and game-oriented stories get a good deal of play from September through Election Day, with horse race news predominating more in certain elections than in others.

These findings emerge from content analyses of election coverage. In a content analytic study, the scholar carefully explicates the meaning of horse race coverage, counts the number of such stories, establishes coding reliability by making sure two coders classify the story in the same manner, and computes results. Researchers typically compare the proportion of horse race coverage to news of policy issues.[15] (see Fig. 17.2).

Unquestionably, much horse race coverage consists of opinion poll reports. In the presidential elections of 1980 through 1992, the nation's major newspapers featured at least one presidential poll story per week on

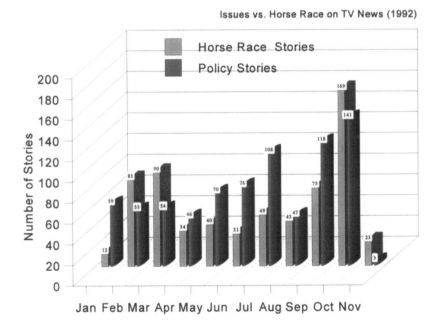

Issues vs. Horse Race on TV News (1992)

FIG. 17.2 Issues Versus Horse Race Coverage on TV News, Based on content analysis of ABC, CBS, and NBC evening newscasts, January 1, 1992 through November 2, 1992.
Note: A story may have extensively discussed both the horse race and policy issues.
(From Lichter and Noyes, 1995)

the front page from July through Election Day.[16] This, of course, did not include polls that appeared on inside pages of the newspaper, nor polls conducted by magazines or television networks.

What's more, the number of page one preelection poll stories has increased since 1980. In their study of poll stories in national newspapers, researchers Paul Lavrakas and Sandra Bauman found that in 1980, newspapers published 102 front-page poll stories; in 1992, there were 452 such stories, an increase of more than 300%.[17]

Polls focus on different aspects of the election, including voters' opinions about the issues, candidates, and the campaign. However, the lion's share of polls focus on the horse race—who is ahead and why.

Polls have become such a regular part of news coverage of the campaign that journalist Bill Kovach remarked that he had trouble recalling "how we worked before we had this tool."[18] It is now commonplace to see elite newspapers like *The New York Times* and *The Washington Post* running polls as the lead stories on page one.

Like horse race news itself, polls have proliferated because they allow journalists to present information in a seemingly unbiased fashion. They also lend an aura of scientific precision to the news page, which enhances the credibility of the newspaper. Furthermore, polls and poll-based stories allow journalists to provide an additional check on the claims of candidates and political leaders. As Thomas Mann and Gary Orren note, "armed with their own polls, reporters need not blindly accept the claims of politicians who try to peddle their own polling information."[19]

The proliferation of poll-based stories has provoked debate. Critics charge that they invite voters to view the campaign as a spectacle and that they squeeze out more substantive stories on policy issues. Defenders claim that people learn valuable information from polls and that they provide a more reliable method of tapping voter sentiments during the campaign than did old-style "seat of the pants, shoe-leather journalism."[20]

Horse Race News in Campaign '96

The 1996 election added a new wrinkle to press coverage of the horse race—namely, if an election is not close and there is no horse race to speak of, the news media will provide considerably less coverage of who's ahead, who's behind, and opinion polls than in nip-and-tuck elections, in which the outcome is in doubt. In 1996, Clinton handily defeated Dole and led Dole by double-digit margins for most of the campaign. Try as they might, the press corps had difficulty doing stories about the drama of the electoral contest. During the fall election campaign, only 18% of all television network campaign stories focused on the horse race, compared to other years in which a third or even half of all stories discussed the strategic game.[21] Whether this is an aberration or the harbinger of things to come remains to be seen. However, research suggests that when elections are close or there is some doubt as to who is going to win, the news media *will* focus on the horse race, sometimes to the exclusion of more substantive issues, such as policy problems and debates about the pros and cons of proposed solutions to pressing national problems.

OTHER STRUCTURAL BIASES

The press is not a conveyor belt that simply relays information to the public. It may not be as partisan as critics think, but it is not neutral either. To simplify complex matters and attract audiences, journalists devise **story lines or narratives**—frames that provide an overarching interpretation of campaign events. Of course, there are differences among news media outlets in the frameworks they adopt, but it is remarkable how similar the main narratives are in a given election year.[22]

Patterson has identified several major story lines. There is *the likely loser scenario* ("when a candidate trails by a wide margin in the polls, the news of his candidacy becomes less favorable"); *the losing ground scenario* ("when a candidate's support in the polls drops sharply, the news of his candidacy becomes less favorable"); and *the bandwagon story line* ("when a candidate's support in the polls increases sharply, the news of his candidacy becomes more favorable").[23] (See Fig. 17.3 for an example.)

In each of these story lines, the press makes candidate viability—success in the primaries or in the general election polls—the chief determinant of news. There is nothing sinister in reporters' adopting this approach to news gathering; it fits professional norms like objectivity and helps reporters to make sense of the campaign. But such an approach can lead to oversimplification and a tendency to force the facts to fit the theory.

In 1988, 1992, and 1996, when candidates Dukakis, Bush, and Dole fell behind in the polls, everything they did was seen as a blunder. In 1988, Patterson notes, "the same candidate (Dukakis) who had been described by *Newsweek* as 'relentless in his attack' and 'a credible candidate' was suddenly recast by the same magazine as 'reluctant to attack' and 'trying to present himself as a credible candidate.'"[24] Four years later, in an article on the first

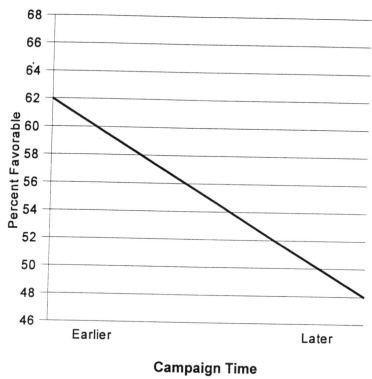

FIG. 17.3 News Portrayal of the "Losing Ground" Candidate (From Patterson, 1993) When a candidate's support in the opinion polls drops sharply, news of his candidacy becomes less favorable. *Note:* The favorability of candidates' coverage in the month before they began to lose ground (the "Earlier" category) was compared with coverage in the subsequent month (the "Later" category).

presidential debate, *Newsweek* "dismissed Bush's chances of re-election even as it dismissed his appearance: 'George Bush seemed reluctant to look the camera in the eye—even though 70 million Americans were waiting to be convinced that he should be president for another four years.'"[25]

In 1996, more than 3 months before the election, *The Washington Post* noted that Dole's "learning curve, thus far, has been painfully steep" and that some GOP officials "believe Dole only runs into trouble when he's tired; others are convinced Dole is just a poor candidate."[26] Critics suggested that the press was writing Dole off before he had even been nominated!

Dole's bad news continued throughout the fall campaign, fitting the likely loser scenario. With polls showing him trailing Clinton by as much as 20 points, news stories focused on Dole's doldrums in the Midwest ("Crucial midwest states lean toward Clinton," a *New York Times* headline blared) and on turmoil in his campaign organization.

Patterson notes that the press gravitates to *"clear-cut issues"* that frequently involve candidate gaffes, campaign controversies, and what consultant Roger Ailes calls "the orchestra pit theory" of news: "If you have two guys on a stage and one guy says, 'I have a solution to the Middle East problem,' and the other guy falls in the orchestra pit, who do you think is going to be on the evening news?"[27]

These issues fit such time-honored journalistic conceptions of news as drama, novelty, and conflict. They include relentless pack journalism coverage of Michael Dukakis's ride in a tank, Dan Quayle's criticism of the Murphy Brown television character for having a child out of wedlock, Gennifer Flowers's allegations about Bill Clinton, and Bob Dole's remark, in response to a question from *Today's* Katie Couric, that "people like you (are) always, you know, sticking up for the Democrats."

Patterson argues that these are trivial issues that are blown out of proportion by the media. Furthermore, he argues that the press overplays these campaign controversies and underplays what candidates are saying about broad issues of economic security, global problems, and government efficiency. These criticisms have sparked debate among journalists, as we will see.

What is important to remember is that news of the campaign, which to many voters seems to be chaotic, nasty, and biased, is actually governed by a set of journalistic principles and procedures. Campaigns differ, but some of the same rituals and routines occur each time.

To some degree, news reflects reality in that presidents get good press when the economy is buoyant (Clinton in 1996), and they receive bad press when the economy is floundering (Carter in 1980). But more than reality intervenes. Part of the reason why Carter got bad press was that he waged a nasty campaign and was trailing in the polls. One of the reasons that Clinton received good press in 1996 was that he led in the polls and had received such relentlessly bad press during parts of his first term that a ceiling effect had been achieved—there was a limit to how far the press could criticize Clinton without appearing biased.

In 1992, Bush got bad press in part because the economy was in a recession.[28] Government reports, released to journalists through formal channels, and interviews with economic policymakers revealed the problematic state of the economy. But the economic picture was more complicated than reporters suggested: the recession turned out to be brief by historical standards, and by the third quarter of 1992 the Gross Domestic Product was growing at the healthy rate of 4%. Thus, reality was not the entire story.

The news focused on the negative aspects of the economy because: (a) Americans were convinced the economy was stagnating, and news frequently reflects public sentiments; (b) journalists felt that they had not done enough to warn the country about some of the negative effects of Ronald Reagan's economic policies and sought to redress the imbalance in 1992; (c) reporters agreed with (or had been persuaded by) Bill Clinton that the economy was in a shambles; and (d) the "we're in a serious recession" narrative provided a simple and parsimonious explanation of complex economic events.

Journalists' emphasis on the negative aspects of the economy may not have been rooted in liberal biases.[29] And the bad economic news scenario was not an entirely unreasonable way to frame campaign news. However, the overwhelming stress on the negative components of the economy points up the important role that journalists' interpretations play in how stories are covered and how prominently they are played.

ISSUES COVERAGE

If the press just covered the horse race and candidate blunders, it would deserve the low marks it frequently gets from critics. But the news media also give extensive coverage to issues—to candidates' records, their positions on domestic and foreign policy matters, and to public policy controversies. You have probably seen or read these types of news stories.

From June through Election Day in 1988, nearly two of every three campaign news stories focused on at least one policy issue. In 1992, there was actually more discussion of the candidates' records and proposals on major issues than in 1988.[30] Chastened by criticism that in 1988 the average candidate sound bite was about 9 seconds, journalists vowed to do better in 1992. To a large extent, they succeeded.

The Washington Post provided more than 6,000 column inches of news devoted to substantive issues, such as the economy, taxes, unemployment, the budget deficit, and health care. Metropolitan dailies like *The Wichita Eagle* asked voters to identify issues that they thought were important and then worked hard to cover these issues. The television networks did regular feature segments on the issues on such programs as ABC's "American Agenda," CBS's "Eye on America," and CNN's "Democracy in America."

In 1996, the news media discussed a wide range of policy issues, including tax cuts, welfare reform, and drug abuse. Nearly half of all network campaign stories from April through September, 1996 focused on policy issues.[31] To be sure, the media differ in the extent to which they provide issue-oriented coverage. Local television news tends to provide less substantive news coverage than does network news or newspapers. Network news serves up more criticism of candidates than do the wire services.[32] Yet despite these differences, there is considerable consensus among journalists that issues constitute an important topic for news stories and that candidates issue positions should be described.

Complicating Factors

And now for the bad news: There are limits to how extensively the news media cover policy issues. First, there is typically less attention given to policy issues than to the horse race and campaign controversies. As Robert Lichter and Richard Noyes note, "part of the reason issues are shortchanged by reporters is that their definition of 'news' stresses that which is new and interesting, rather than information that is merely relevant and educational."[33]

Second, issue coverage can be brief and frequently just scratches the surface of a complex problem. During the 1992 campaign, nearly three of four issue references in a TV or newspaper story were brief—no more than a couple of sentences. Most of the references failed to provide specific details about candidates' records or issue positions.[34]

Moreover, candidates received preciously little time to present positions on the network news. The average television sound bite—or segment within a news story that shows someone speaking—dropped from 43.1 seconds in Campaign 1968 to 8.9 seconds in Campaign 1988. The overall average has fluctuated since then, rising to 9.4 seconds in 1992, dropping to 8.2 seconds in the spring of 1996.[35] (See Fig.17.4).

What this means is that candidates are shown speaking on the issues on network news programs for less than 10 seconds on a given night! There are a number of reasons why sound bites have shrunk, including economic pressures on networks to produce more fast-paced news, development of television editing technology, and candidates' desire to package campaigns for television. But, to critics of television news, the fundamental point is that presidential candidates have been squeezed out of the news.

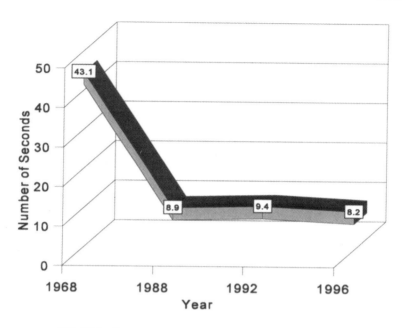

FIG. 17.4   Changes in Length of Television Sound Bite Over Time

Another shortcoming in issues coverage is that it focuses more on journalists' interpretations of candidates' ideas than on candidates' ideas themselves. Reporters, particularly on television, have become stars, and their interpretations frequently dominate the news. As Daniel Hallin observes, "Modern TV news is much more *mediated* than the TV news of the 1960s and 1970s. During the earlier period the journalist's role as a communicator was relatively passive. Frequently he or she did little more than set the scene for the candidate or another newsmaker whose speech would dominate the report."[36]

That has most assuredly changed. Lichter and Noyes reported that in the 1992 campaign, "network reporters consumed 71% of the broadcast airtime, with the remainder split among the candidates, the voters, policy experts, political strategists, etc."[37] During the 1996 primaries, reporters occupied 74% of the airtime.[38] Critics lament that voters have less opportunity to hear candidates articulate positions on the issues today than in the pretelevision era, a lamentation that has provoked its share of controversy (see Box 17.2: Sound Bite Journalism).

PRESS CRITICISM

Lamentations

The press's election coverage has come under increasing scrutiny in recent years. It has drawn fire from a host of journalists and communication scholars. Let's look now at the general tenor of the criticism, shortcomings in these critical views, and at ways of reconciling critics and defenders of the political press.

As the preceding discussion suggested, the thrust of popular criticism focuses on the press's tendency to frame the election as a game. Critics point out that the game schema is so pervasive that even stories about the issues get subsumed under the game, as when a reporter focuses less on the essence of a candidate's new policy proposal than on why the candidate has introduced the proposal, what he or she hopes to gain politically, and how the candidate has used modern technology to package the plan. Campaign coverage focuses too much on controversies, candidate gaffes, and superficial aspects of politics, critics argue.

The result, scholars note, is that news offers voters a cynical portrait of politics and politicians. Candidates are always said to be scheming. Their comments are sandwiched between journalists' observations and "wrap-up" comments. "The language of the reporter," Kathleen Kendall sardonically notes, has "replaced the candidate's language, except for the fragment or two allowed to escape from the dummy's mouth."[39] Where a century ago voters heard candidates address issues directly and in person, without any "mediation" and 30 years ago they heard candidates speak for long blocks of time on television news, today they hear journalists interpret candidates' comments more frequently than they see, hear, or read what candidates have to say about the issues.

The upshot of all this, in critics' view, is that voters receive a slanted, skewed view of campaigns. The majority of candidates' ads and speeches include considerable discussion of issues and candidate qualifications, but press coverage glosses over these in favor of discussions of the strategic game. What's more, critics note, the news frequently offers abbreviated "Cliff Notes" style discussion of issues, and is far too apt to profile negative campaign strategies. Even stories about voters emphasize the negative, such as poll stories reporting that voters believe most politicians are dishonest.

Much of this criticism is consistent with the tenets of public journalism, which emphasizes that the news media have lost touch with the communities they serve. Public journalism scholars emphasize that the news media "create disconnections" between themselves and the public by focusing on the strategic side of politics.[40] According to this view, citizens view elections primarily as a way to choose leaders and solve policy problems; by focusing on strategy and process, the news media alienate citizens and inhibit their participation in public life.

Counterarguments

There is merit in these criticisms. Indeed, lamentations about the news media have become so common and so pervasive that students frequently feel that the press constitutes the major problem with the electoral system. But there is another side to the story.

As journalists have been quick to point out, politics *is* a game and presidential candidates, being ambitious people, spend considerable time trying to figure out the best ways to win it. As discussed in the previous two chapters, candidates pay enormous attention to polls and devise media strategies based on poll results. Journalists have no choice but to cover this.

Campaigns are not just about education; they are about getting candidates elected. When candidates pull dirty tricks to get elected, journalists have an obligation to report this. Moreover, campaigns do provide a "baptism of fire" for candidates; the primaries, debates, and constant pressure to "keep one's cool" all provide a test of a candidate's mettle. If candidates commit gaffes in their pursuit of the presidency, journalists have a duty to give voters the facts, and let them make the call. Critics call coverage of campaign controversies and the horse race "unsubstantial." But people do evaluate candidates on the basis of what they say and how they carry themselves. What makes coverage of candidate misstatements any less substantial than coverage of a vague and misleading candidate proposal on the issues?

Critics argue that the press gives too little coverage to policy issues. Few would disagree that the news media could do a better job of covering policy matters. But do they give issues short shrift? Historical research indicates that, for all the superficialities of today's news, there is significantly more issue coverage in the media today than in the pretelevision era. In their analysis of newspaper election coverage from 1888 to 1988, Lee Sigelman and David Bullock found that four of the five papers they studied gave significantly more space to issues in 1988 than they had 100 years earlier. Michael Robinson and Margaret Sheehan found that print coverage of campaigns rose by more than 75% between 1940 and 1980. They also note that television provides more serious coverage of issues than did radio in the mid-1900s.[41]

Thus, Americans are getting more issue coverage than ever before, relayed through more channels than in the past—an almost infinite supply of information about candidates and issues, if we consider newspapers, magazines, television news, Web sites, and talk shows, which have offered voters large doses of substantive information.[42]

It is true that television reporters consume more airtime than candidates. It is also true that in some cases they have shut candidates out of the story and have implied that candidates' words are of little consequence. Critics often take note of these facts and suggest that things were better in the past. But this oversimplifies matters.

In 1896, when voters lined up to hear William McKinley speak on "the issues" from his front porch in Canton, they heard vague statements about the gold standard and American values, some of which were dreamed up by his campaign manager, Mark Hanna. Although sound bites were longer in 1968 than they are today, the candidates frequently were not making specific proposals; nor were they necessarily speaking more truthfully than they are today. Richard Nixon and Hubert Humphrey did not offer specific or compelling proposals to end the bloody and divisive war in Vietnam. Since sound bites were longer, voters had more opportunity to hear Nixon and Humphrey present their nostrums; but since their proposals were vague, it is not clear that the press was furthering democracy by giving the candidates more airtime to speak out on the issues.[43]

Some critics would like the press to spend less time criticizing candidates' gaffes and more time relaying their ideas to the public. But what if the candidates don't have any ideas? What about years like 1988 when candidates declined to discuss the pressing issue of the U.S. posture in a post-Cold War world, or 1996 when the major parties steered clear of discussing Social Security because they were nervous about turning off elderly voters?

The dispute between defenders of the press and critics reflects a fundamental disagreement about the role that the press should play in a democracy. Critics like Davis Merritt would like the press to do more than "tell the news;" they would like reporters to "remember that they are citizens as well as journalists."[44] They would like the news media to encourage public involvement in politics and to improve the quality of public discourse.

Political journalists traditionally are less concerned with involving the public than with acting as a watchdog on elected officials and candidates, and with pointing out their excesses. Journalists like Howell Raines respond that reporters should not become "civic stenographers" who simply convey what politicians say. In Raines' view, journalists have no business becoming "public policy missionaries" who arrogantly try to advance a particular political or social agenda. Instead, Raines argues that reporters should be "skeptical observers, critics and analysts" of electoral politics.[45]

Middle Ground?

There is clearly a role for both public journalism and time-honored horse race press coverage. There is no reason why news organizations, particularly those in smaller communities where it is easier to bring citizens and journalists together, cannot try to understand voters' concerns and help candidates meet them. Nor is there any reason why journalists should not do polls and report their results to readers and viewers.

If there is one thing that unites both press critics and defenders, it is the belief that news coverage of elections can always get better. Criticism of the news media has helped to improve news coverage. When scholars pointed out that the press had done little to question misleading political advertising claims in 1988, the news media came up with ad watches (see chapter 20). When critics pointed out that the news did not provide enough coverage of candidate speeches in 1992, newspapers began printing more excerpts from candidate speeches in 1996.

Yet some of the chronic problems that have plagued news coverage of presidential campaigns continue. The news media do not devote enough resources to exploring whether candidates' policy proposals will actually achieve their desired objectives. Journalists typically do not examine in any depth the important question of how candidates will manage the presidency and what types of decision-making styles they would bring into the Oval Office. Reporters continue to favor polls that telegraph voter discontent, rather than examining the complex origins of citizens' dissatisfaction with politics.

There is considerable room for improvement in news media coverage and, as we see in the next chapter, considerable opportunity to educate and clarify issues for voters.

CONCLUSIONS

"Journalists, politicians, academics, and the men and women in the street have a great deal of advice for the news media," Michael Schudson observes. "Everyone in a democracy is a certified media critic," he says, adding that this is as it should be.[46]

This is nowhere more true than in the area of presidential election news. The public is continually frustrated and dissatisfied with the news media. People are frequently convinced that the news reflects journalists' personal or partisan biases. In another era, such biases might have been applauded; it is good to have strong feelings and to stick up for what you believe, popular philosophers might say. But today it is assumed that the media wield great power, that the unwashed masses are helpless in their grip, and that journalists' biases can carry the day.[47]

Of course, the media do not have this power, as noted in earlier chapters. Nor does coverage typically reflect personal or partisan biases toward one candidate or another.

Journalists are human, their likes and dislikes do influence their work. Sometimes this is helpful when it leads to more passionate coverage, other times it is dysfunctional when it leads to unfair and biased reporting. In the area of presidential election news, partisan biases exert less influence than professional and journalistic considerations.

Perhaps the most important professional or structural bias is the tendency to cover the presidential election as a game or horse race. Journalists tend to evaluate candidates on the basis of their viability and electability. Polls get considerable press because they fit the canons of news. News frequently favors dramatic events, such as candidate gaffes and campaign controversies. Issues can be covered superficially, with candidates getting less broadcast airtime than journalists.

As noted earlier, these criticisms have merit. However, a historical perspective reminds us that there is more issue coverage today than a half-century ago; a cultural orientation emphasizes that, in view of America's long history of press involvement in politics, its news is likely to assign greater weight to journalists' interpretations than will other less mediacentric cultures; and a scientific analysis indicates that the news media do not operate as a monolithic entity, but cover the presidential election differently, depending on the size of the community and the nature of the medium (newspapers, talk radio, local versus network television). Lastly, a philosophical approach stresses that our view of the press will depend in no small measure on our normative assumptions: Do we feel that the news media should work primarily to encourage public involvement or mainly to critically examine the actions of political elites?

The saving grace of the political press is that it has been willing to change and make improvements. Michael Robinson points out that the twentieth century press managed to improve on its nineteenth century predecessors by treating the candidates for the presidency more fairly and dispassionately.[48] In the same fashion, today's media provide more coverage of issues, more scientific information about voters' opinions, and a more diverse menu of political recipes, when you include talk radio and the many news media Web sites. However, there are still many areas that could use improvement, and there exists in a country as big and bountiful as America numerous possibilities for improving the quality of our quadrennial conversation about politics.

Box 17.1

Campaign Humor: '96-style

David Letterman and Jay Leno on Bob Dole:

Letterman: Steve Forbes, the wacky billionaire, finished second, and he said, "Well, the problem is I just could not compete with the Bob Dole machine." And I'm thinking, what is that? Respirator or dialysis?

Leno: Bob Dole says that quitting the Senate leaves him free to roam the country. But you know, at his age, there's a fine line between roaming and just wandering off.

Letterman on Bill Clinton:

The White House is denying that anything went wrong with the confidential FBI files. They're saying the whole thing was a mistake. They say … it was a typographical error. Clinton was not ordering more files, Clinton was ordering more *fries* …

When candidates are out campaigning … they have to kiss babies. Well, it happened to Clinton over the weekend in New Hampshire … He's out there shaking hands and campaigning and somebody handed him a baby to kiss, and of course, Clinton doesn't know whether to kiss the baby or deny knowing the mother.

Box 17.2

Sound Bite Journalism

Television news has changed dramatically over the past 30 years. Critics point out that presidential election stories now revolve more around journalists than candidates. Consider the difference between these two stories, the first from the 1968 campaign, the second from 1988:[49]

1968

Bill Plante (CBS reporter, over video of Nixon striding through crowd to the podium): In Flint, Nixon made the same appeal as he did last week in the South, because the threat is the same: George Wallace. Several local unions here have endorsed Wallace. He divides the state enough so that Nixon and Humphrey are running almost even. Therefore Nixon's tactic is to convince the voters that a vote for him is the only real vote for change.

Nixon: (Speaks for 32 seconds.)

Plante (over video of Nixon shaking hands with exuberant children): Earlier Nixon brought his motorcade to a sort of scheduled unscheduled stop at the Michigan State School for the Deaf, where he told the youngsters of his Aunt Olive, a missionary though afflicted by deafness, and encouraged them. The Dean interpreted his remarks.

Nixon: When a person may not be able to hear, then he develops other qualities. Qualities of the heart. Qualities of understanding that people who may be able to hear do not develop to the same extent. It shows you that in the world in which you will be living, that your country needs you, and that what you learn here in this school will give each of you a chance to render wonderful service to this country. (44 seconds)

1988

Barry Serafin (ABC reporter): Under criticism even from some Republican party elders for not talking enough about issues, and seeking to blunt Democratic charges of callousness, Bush unveiled a new proposal called YES, Youth Engaged in Service, aimed at enlisting wealthy kids to help poor ones.

Bush: The end result, I hope, is that citizen service will become a real and living part of every young American's life.

Serafin: But by the second stop of the day ... the vice president was back to the tried and true, the one-liners that in California, for example, have helped him erase a double-digit deficit in the polls. On crime:

Bush: I support our law enforcement community.

Serafin: On education:

Bush: I will be the education president.

Serafin: And another familiar refrain:

Bush: Read my lips: No new taxes!

KEY TERMS

Campaign News Bias

Content Analysis

Horse Race News

Poll Coverage

Campaign Story Lines

Issue Coverage

Sound Bite Journalism

DISCUSSION QUESTIONS

1. What are the major structural biases in campaign news?
2. Present the pros and cons of horse race news. Would more horse race coverage in 1996 have drawn voters into the election?
3. Propose three ways to creatively use new technologies to expand issue coverage.

18

News Media Impact on Voters

"I know of no safe depository for the ultimate powers of society but the people themselves," wrote Thomas Jefferson in 1820. Jefferson went on to observe that if one thinks the people "not enlightened enough to exercise their control with a wholesome discretion, the remedy is not to take it from them, but to inform their discretion."[1]

Nearly two centuries later, Jefferson's observations still ring true. Citizens occupy a sovereign position in American democracy. Every 4 years, they exercise their "ultimate powers" by choosing to cast a vote (or to abstain from voting). They make up their minds during the presidential campaign, and today it is the media that play a critical role in "informing their discretion."

But does the system work in the idealized way that Jefferson described? Today, barely 55% of the public votes in presidential elections, many voters seem poorly informed about politics, and millions say that they are dissatisfied with the candidates and the media campaign. In this chapter, I examine these issues as I look at what voters know about politics and the impact of news on their beliefs about presidential campaigns.

THE PUBLIC'S KNOWLEDGE OF POLITICS

An informed citizenry, which understands the main issues of the day and is able to render intelligent judgments, is essential to democracy. As Bruce Buchanan notes, "One clear implication of vesting followers with the power to choose leaders is that the former must acquire sufficient information about matters under public discussion to avoid being easily duped about the facts by self-interested candidate misinformation or distortion."[2]

Is the American voting public informed? At first blush, it seems as if the answer is clearly NO. Consider the following:

- In 1987, some seven years after Congressional debate about giving aid to the Nicaraguan Contras, only one third of the American public knew that Nicaragua is in Central America.[3]
- A 1989 national survey revealed that 45% of the public did not know which party had the most members in the Senate.[4]
- In 1995, a survey found that two thirds of the American people could not name the individual who served in the House of Representatives from their Congressional district. Half did not know whether their representative was a Democrat or Republican.[5]
- Nearly half of the respondents in the 1995 survey did not know the name of the Speaker of the House of Representatives (Newt Gingrich). Three of four did not know that U.S. Senators are elected to serve 6-year terms.[6]

There are several reasons why Americans are poorly informed about political issues. Many citizens do not closely follow the news, regularly read newspapers, or tune into network newscasts. Many people are simply not interested in politics, partly because they find national issues complex and hard to comprehend and partly because they feel alienated from the system. Lacking the motivation to regularly follow public affairs, they tend not to devote much attention to print or electronic news coverage, except in the case of sensational events such as the O.J. Simpson trial about which people were phenomenally well-informed, so much so that they could tick off details about the Simpson estate, the Bronco chase, and the glove demonstration.

It is disconcerting that people are poorly informed about basic aspects of government. Clearly, increases in public education and the growth of informational media have not led to major improvements in people's knowledge of politics. However, one must be careful about inferring too much from the results of civics tests and surveys such as those described above.

Some of the survey questions tap textbook knowledge of politics, not knowledge of the current state of the country. Moreover, such tests frequently focus more on what voters don't know than on what they do. As Samuel Popkin observed a few years back:

There is much that voters *do* know about government, and many ways in which they manage to consider issues without high levels of information. They need not know what Senator Moynihan and President Bush actually said in order to be affected by news reports of their debates about Social Security; they need not know how the Japanese government works in order to be concerned about U.S.–Japanese trade issues … (People) do not need to know which party controls Congress, or the names of their senators, in order to know something about the state of the economy or proposed cuts in Social Security or the controversies over abortion. And they do not need to know where Nicaragua is, or how to describe the Politburo, in order to get information about changes in international tensions which they can relate to proposals for cutting the defense budget ... Whereas the "incompetent citizen" literature is good for telling us the many things voters do not know, it is not so good at providing clues about what they *do* know.[7]

There are other shortcomings in civics tests. They require that people remember public figures by their official titles. Relatively few Americans can accomplish this task. But large majorities can recognize the name of elected officials from a list, a task which more closely resembles the act of voting. As Robert Maranto observed, "People may not be quick to blurt out Newt Gingrich's exact title, but they likely know something about where he stands or the role he plays. After all, if no one has heard of Gingrich, how can he be widely unpopular?"[8]

Moreover, these surveys were typically conducted a year or more before the presidential election. Most people do not attend closely to politics during noncampaign periods, deciding (perhaps correctly) to leave policy matters to their elected representatives. However, people ordinarily follow politics with more diligence during presidential election campaigns, when the entire society gets into high political gear and citizens actually have a chance to influence policy outcomes.

People pick up a great deal of information during presidential campaigns. They learn where candidates stand on the issues. They assimilate information about the candidates' personal characteristics, integrity, and competence. They make judgments about the candidates, and they come to have strong feelings about what the candidates do and say.

How this all happens is the subject of the field of political psychology, which focuses on how people process political information and how they come to know what they do about politics. The consensus among scholars is that people are, for the most part, active processors of information, interpreting information based on their values and partisan preferences and constructing images of candidates and the presidential campaign.[9]

Despite their lack of textbook information and their ignorance of names and dates, people manage to pick up a great deal of information over the course of the presidential campaign. After systematically examining patterns of voter learning in the 1992 campaign, Marion Just and her colleagues concluded that:

Whereas voters in the spring were often unable to say who the candidates were and what they stood for, they had no such difficulties in the fall—even after the reentry of Perot into the race. The survey data from all four communities confirm that by the fall, respondents were better able to match the candidates with their issue positions than they had been in the spring.[10]

Moreover, it turns out that the news media play a particularly important role in imparting issue and candidate information. News helps people make judgments about the candidates' personal traits, whether they will keep their campaign promises, and whether they possess the kind of maturity voters like to see in candidates for the highest office in the land.

Campaigns differ in the extent to which they promote civic education. "If the campaign takes public concerns seriously and provides forums for political discussion," Just and her colleagues note, "it can help to reveal to individuals their power as citizens. Alternatively, if the campaign merely distracts or ignores the public and frustrates communication, the campaign may undermine the citizens' sense of their own power in the system and reinforce political cynicism."[11]

The 1992 and 1996 campaigns provided new formats for voter learning, such as town hall meeting-style presidential debates, candidate appearances on talk shows, and the provision of free television airtime for short candidate speeches. By contrast, the 1988 campaign was viewed by many scholars as deficient in that candidates skirted major national issues, the media gave heavy (and sometimes uncritical) coverage to candidates' political advertisements, and voters failed to grasp where the candidates stood on a host of domestic issues.[12]

Newspapers Versus Television

For years it was assumed that newspapers constituted the only serious source of campaign information. Television, it was believed, provided superficial and misleading facts about campaigns and American politics. Newspapers, after all, devote more space to stories, provide more depth, and allow individuals the opportunity to review difficult parts of the story, a benefit television does not provide. Consistent with these ruminations, there is considerable evidence that people who get their news from newspapers score higher on tests of comprehension than those who watch television news.[13] But is this because newspapers are a superior source of information or because people who read newspapers are more educated and cognitively skilled? It appears to be a little bit of both.[14]

It now turns out that the notion that television does a poor job of imparting political information is incorrect. There is evidence that television news can lead to as much if not more political learning than newspapers.[15] Moreover, in presidential campaigns, television helps clarify issue differences between candidates. After systematically studying the effects of television news, Steven Chaffee concluded that "the attention a person pays to campaign news on television does indeed enhance the likelihood of acquiring political issue information."[16] *Attention* appears to be a key variable, in part because it affords a better measure of television viewing than mere *exposure* to TV, and also because it underscores the point that people must be mentally engaged if they are to pick up facts and information from newscasts.

Evidence that people learn from television news runs counter to the popular wisdom that television news inhibits learning and is too "glitzy" and simplistic to teach people much about presidential campaigns. In fact, this "glitz" and simplicity may be necessary to draw in people who lack interest in (or knowledge about) politics.

None of this is to devalue the role that newspapers play in civic education. Far from it. Neuman, Just, and Crigler point out that the print media "are more factual and complete, and when the interest already exists, are a particularly efficient medium for information retrieval, but only when the citizen is motivated to do the retrieving."[17] There is little doubt that, for those who are already informed about politics, newspapers provide a wealth of information and do much to enhance knowledge of issues and candidates.

It should be emphasized, however, that in some sense the "print versus broadcast" dichotomy is a false one. Only a small minority of the public use either the print or broadcast media exclusively and steadfastly avoid information from other sources. Most people acquire campaign information from a variety of media formats, including newspapers, television news (still voters' main source of campaign information), talk shows, and (to a much lesser extent) political Web sites.[18]

Finally, even those (like me) who argue that the news media do a pretty good job of imparting campaign information are quick to acknowledge that things could be better, and that the news does not do all that it could do to clarify complex political issues. Doris Graber and Dennis Davis have pointed out television news makes learning difficult by using too many unfamiliar technical terms, failing to provide a context that would give meaning to the issues, and by distracting people with powerful visuals at the same time as the voiceover provides critical verbal information. Graber and Davis note that television newscasts—as well as print news—could benefit by taking into account how people process political information and adapting their formats to match people's routine strategies for dealing with political information.[19]

CAMPAIGN AGENDA-SETTING

Classic and contemporary studies in political communication leave little doubt that the news does not change people's basic political attitudes and ideologies. Lazarsfeld and his colleagues' Erie County study, Klapper's summary of the effects of mass communication, and a host of contemporary studies make it clear that partisan political attitudes moderate the impact of the news on electronically relevant beliefs and opinions. One recent study found that negative news about Republican President George Bush's 1992 campaign intensified Democrats' opposition to Bush. However, it had the opposite impact on Republican voters, causing them to evaluate Bush more positively, perhaps because they directed their attention to the strong points of Bush's message.[20]

We have known since the 1940s that when people are faced with messages that are inconsistent with their beliefs, they cognitively distort the information so that it is congruent with their original beliefs. Thus, it is naive to think that voters who strongly supported Bob Dole in 1996 decided to vote for Bill Clinton after exposure to news clips that showed the president in a positive light.

Having said this, there is also little doubt that the news *does* influence some types of political beliefs and attitudes. Even reinforcement of partisan attitudes—which limited effects scholars viewed as a trivial influence—can be important if it leads to greater consistency of people's thoughts and feelings about a candidate or to interpersonal discussion, which can crystallize political beliefs. Moreover, when news consistently shows a candidate in a negative light—as was true for Jimmy Carter in 1980 and George Bush in 1992—the sum total of negative images can leave an imprint on independent or undecided voters.

One of the most important effects of campaign news is agenda-setting, the influence of news on people's beliefs about what constitute the most important issues in the presidential campaign (see chapter 11). The media unquestionably influence the public agenda in presidential election years. A classic example of media agenda-setting occurred in 1992, when the press provided a drumbeat of negative coverage of the economy. The news media increased the salience of economic issues in 1992; they surfaced people's concerns that the country was on the wrong economic track.

The news media not only influenced the public agenda; they also affected the manner in which people framed economic issues. Exposure to the news convinced many voters that the economy was in bad shape and that the Bush administration should be held responsible for the country's economic woes.[21]

News coverage also appears to have *primed* some voters. Priming occurs when the media alter the standards people use to evaluate the president or candidates for the presidency. By calling attention to economic problems, such as the soaring budget deficit, crumbling real estate values, and collapsing savings and loans, the news media may have caused voters to give greater weight to the candidates' macroeconomic policies and their sensitivities to the plight of economically distressed Americans. All this played nicely into the hands of Bill Clinton, who hammered away at the economy throughout the campaign.

As we know from the research discussed in chapter 12, the media do not create agendas out of thin air. The press's emphasis on the economy was influenced by the candidates (i.e., Clinton and Perot, who focused relentlessly on economic issues), the voters, who freely discussed their economic anxieties with pollsters, and political elites, who argued that America was now paying the price for the excesses of the 1980s. The press's emphasis on the economy appears to have had the salutary effect of helping to spur a national discussion of how the country should deal with daunting issues such as the deficit and global economic competition.

During years when there is not a single overriding issue, media agenda-setting effects are more complex. Typically, when an incumbent president is up for reelection, the issues center on the president's character and performance while in office. In 1996, the campaign revolved around Clinton's record and the role government should play in the lives of Americans. In many ways, the agenda-building process began in November, 1994, when Republicans unleashed the "Contract with America," won control of Congress, and caused Bill Clinton to reassess his commitment to traditional government remedies for the nation's social and economic woes. The election, as one Congressman said, pushed the national debate away from the question of "how much bigger government should be to how much smaller it should be."[22]

News in '96 focused on a host of issues, ranging from tax cuts to economic insecurities to moral values. Critics pointed out that, for all the issue coverage, the press failed to shine the spotlight on the critical issue of how the nation should deal with the crisis in Social Security—i.e., a Social Security system that was in deep trouble and that was likely to go bust unless something was done to reverse the trend toward huge negative cash flows.[21] It was difficult for the media to make an issue of Social Security because the candidates skirted the topic, fearful as they were of alienating elderly voters, and because there was no clear elite or public consensus on how to handle the problem.

NEWS AND VOTERS CYNICISM

Political communication scholars have long argued that, in addition to shaping the public agenda, the news media strongly influence voters' attitudes toward politics and politicians. Taking note of the press's emphasis on the strategic game and its tendency to describe the campaign in negative terms, some scholars have contended that the news media intensify voters' cynicism about politics and politicians.

After studying campaign coverage from 1960 through 1992, Patterson concluded that in the 1960s, presidential candidates received primarily favorable coverage, but that today the news presents a predominately negative picture of the presidential campaign.[24] Patterson and other scholars maintain that an important reason for the increase in negative coverage is that political reporters have changed their views about campaigns. Hardened by Watergate and embittered by lies told them by officials during the Vietnam War, a generation of reporters concluded that politicians were, more often than not, liars, sneaks, and schemers who pull out all stops to win election.

At the same time as media coverage has become increasingly negative, voters have displayed more negative attitudes toward politics and politicians. Voters view the Republican and Democratic presidential nominees less favorably today than they did in the 1960s.[25] As Buchanan notes, voters "see themselves as distant participants" in the campaign, "with little at stake." They do not realize, he adds, "that the presidential campaign process belongs to them."[26] To what extent are the media to blame?

There is some evidence that the news media can increase what is popularly known as cynicism (actually a complex political variable).[27] The more people watch television news, the less interested they are in politics and the less efficacious they feel—that is, the less they feel they can influence what goes on in government.[28] However, the direction of causation remains unclear: It is possible that TV news viewing reduces political efficacy or that people who perceive that they have little influence on government gravitate to TV, either because television viewing requires little effort or because TV's frequent criticisms of public officials reinforce the cynics' outlook toward politics.

At the same time, exposure to other media can actually increase political efficacy. Regular reading of newspapers can increase interest in politics and the feeling that citizens can influence government.[29]

Interestingly, talk radio seems to have the same effect. The results of a 1995 national survey showed that regular listeners of Rush Limbaugh's radio talk show voted with greater consistency than did other Americans and reported that they had higher hopes for the Republican Congress than did other members of the electorate. Talk radio may attract those who think they can affect the system and may energize these voters, leading them to try to influence their legislators in ways that some critics may not like but that are nonetheless fully in keeping with democracy.[30]

Thus, the press does highlight the negative aspects of politics, but the jury is still out on how the coverage influences political attitudes. Negative news on television may increase voter cynicism and may strengthen beliefs that politics is nothing but a theatrical show. However, its effects do not appear to be that strong, and may be offset by exposure to other media. Moreover, even if the spin that journalists put on politics intensifies voter cynicism, it is far from the only cause of these negative attitudes. The tendency of politicians to avoid taking positions on controversial issues, the widely publicized role that consultants play in politics, voters' predilection for simple explanations of the political scene, and even the human tendency to project personal frustrations onto the larger system also contribute to the development of negative attitudes toward politics (see Box 18.1: A Reason to be Cynical?).

CONCLUSIONS

This chapter examined the impact of campaign news on voters' beliefs and attitudes. I began by looking at the public's knowledge of political issues. Although many people do poorly on civics tests and are sadly ill-informed about the nuts and bolts of American politics, they nonetheless possess a working knowledge of political issues that serves them well during presidential campaigns. People pick up a great deal of information during campaigns. What's more, voters are better informed about candidates and policy issues at the end of the campaign than at the beginning. The news media play an important role in helping people acquire political information. Yet there are many things that the news media can do to help people become more knowledgeable about politics. Scholars have offered a number of suggestions on how to make newspaper and television news more viewer-friendly.

The news media also shape the public agenda during election campaigns. They do not create agendas out of whole cloth, but, rather, reflect and amplify agendas created by candidates, elites, and voters.

One of the most controversial areas of news media impact is political cynicism. The press tends to focus on the negative aspects of campaigns. At the same time as press coverage has become more negative, the public has become more critical of presidential candidates and campaigns. We cannot say that press coverage causes voter cynicism. It is probably one of many causes of negative voter attitudes toward presidential campaigns.

Other causes include opportunistic candidate behavior, increasing concern about the role that money plays in politics, and a predilection for simple explanations of complex political problems.

The impact of media on cynicism is complex and not well understood. Some media formats, such as TV news, may, under some conditions, intensify cynicism. Other media genres, like talk shows, may increase political efficacy.

There is also evidence that people tend to be more cynical when they are poorly informed about politics. A national study conducted in 1995 found that the less Americans knew about politics, the more likely they were to say that the country was in decline. As Richard Morin notes, the less knowledgeable Americans:

> consistently say that the country's biggest problems have worsened in recent decades, including air and water quality that actually have improved. And they are less likely to know that the annual budget deficit and the number of federal workers have gone down—not up—in recent years. As a consequence, less knowledgeable Americans are much more likely to believe that actions by the federal government invariably make every problem worse, a rigid cynicism that the survey found transcends party identification or political ideology.[31]

Improving this state of affairs is important because, as Scott Keeter notes, "greater knowledge about the political process helps a person figure out what kinds of government policies are likely to be most beneficial to them, and then what political behavior on their part is most likely to further their interests."[32] Knowledge can also enhance one's appreciation of different points of view, deepen one's understanding of political issues, and increase receptivity to new approaches to national problems.

Box 18.1
A Reason to be Cynical?

On August 28, 1996, the day before President Clinton was scheduled to accept his party's nomination for president, a bombshell rocked the White House. A newspaper tabloid, *Star*, was working on a story that presidential advisor Dick Morris—the brilliant architect of Clinton's political comeback in 1995—had been involved with a call girl. In a twist that had even the most cynical of observers shaking their heads, Morris had been one of the strongest advocates of the idea that Clinton should take a tougher position on ... family issues!

Morris resigned, only to return to the public eye several days later as the press got wind that he was selling his sordid tale to a book publisher. *Newsweek* reported the details of the modern soap opera:[33]

Call it room service. On the evening of August 22, presidential adviser Dick Morris was in his $440-a-night suite at Washington's small but elegant Jefferson Hotel. Joining him was Sherry Rowlands, a call girl with whom he had allegedly been enjoying a yearlong relationship. Unbeknownst to Morris, in mid-July Rowlands, who had grown disenchanted with the rumpled New Yorker, had been trying to sell the story of her affair to the *Star* tabloid. *Star's* Richard Gooding, a former *New York Times* clerk and editor at other New York tabloids, was intrigued by the blonde's tale. It had it all: illicit sex, a description of Morris sucking her toes, accounts of the consultant blabbing White House secrets—like the discovery of life on Mars—and even letting her listen in on calls to the president ...

The wild episode seemed a fitting end to one of the wildest careers in recent American politics ... Morris had a reputation for fudging polls to make them to the candidate's liking. He wooed candidates with Pollyanna-ish talk of "permanent" leads, telling them that this ad or this speech would end his troubles ...

But Morris's ethical lapses—and absurd flights of ego—hurt him. He couldn't seem to break his ties to Republicans, sharing polling secrets with the Dole camp. And when he was found out, he blamed the indiscretion on George Stephanopoulos. He was caught demanding to be put at the head of the line at his Connecticut dentist's office, insisting that he was "running the country."

KEY ISSUES

Public's Knowledge of Politics

News Media Effects on Knowledge

Campaign Agenda-Setting

Voter Cynicism

DISCUSSION QUESTIONS

1. When it comes to the public's knowledge about politics, is the glass half empty or half full? That is, when you review survey evidence of Americans' knowledge of government, do you find yourself more critical or forgiving of the public? Why?

2. Find a news story that does a poor job of explaining political issues. Where exactly did it go wrong? Now rewrite the story, trying to make things clearer.

3. Defend the press against the charge that it focuses too much on the negative side of presidential campaigns.

4. What steps could the news media take to draw skeptical and cynical voters into the presidential campaign?

19

Political Advertising: Content

When someone mentions political advertising, what comes to mind?

Dirty tricks? Dishonesty? Glitzy Madison Avenue appeals?

Political commercials conjure up nasty images in people's minds. To many Americans, they represent what is wrong with electoral politics—the triumph of sleaze over substance, yet another example of how political professionals have hijacked the American election. Of course, candidates view advertising somewhat differently. To presidential contenders and their advisers, political ads offer a way of communicating with, and hopefully persuading, the electorate. Unlike news or debates, political advertising is under the direct control of the candidate or party.

Although political advertising encompasses promotional videocasettes and computer videos, the big bucks go for television ads, particularly in presidential campaigns. Political television advertising refers to "any programming format under the control of the party or candidate and for which time is given or purchased on a broadcast (or narrowcast) outlet."[1]

This chapter and the one that follows examine political advertising in detail. The focus is on presidential campaign commercials. This chapter examines the main features of presidential advertising—economics, strategies, and types of ads. Chapter 20 reviews the effects of political ads.

CHARACTERISTICS OF POLITICAL ADVERTISING

Ever since making their debut in presidential campaigns in 1952, televised political ads have played an important role in campaign strategy and image management. The commercials that Eisenhower developed in 1952 were primitive by today's standards: Eisenhower recorded answers to a series of hypothetical questions, his aides recruited tourists from Radio City Music Hall to pose questions, and the questions and answers were spliced together to make the ads look spontaneous.

Over the years, political advertising has become more technically and psychologically sophisticated. Numerous "advertising classics" have emerged. These include the "Daisy" commercial of 1964, which featured a little girl picking petals off a daisy as a nuclear countdown ensued; the 1984 "Morning in America" ads that featured lush images of America to showcase the accomplishments of President Reagan; Bush's 1988 "Revolving Door" attacks on Dukakis's prison furlough program; and Ross Perot's half-hour-long infomercials in 1992 and 1996 that bemoaned economic malaise.

Financial Issues

Money is the mother's milk of political advertising. In 1992 Bush, Clinton, and Perot spent $133 million on television advertising. Experts believe that even more money was spent in 1996.[2]

As noted in chapter 15, finance laws permit individuals or groups to spend as much as they want on behalf of a presidential candidate, provided that they work independently of the candidate's campaign. This has enabled political action committees (PACs) to spend vast sums of money on campaign commercials. It has also allowed candidates to deny involvement with PAC-sponsored negative advertising campaigns. A major loophole in the finance laws is the "soft money provision," which allows interest groups to contribute vast sums of money to political parties, ostensibly for general operations but actually for election campaigns.

In 1995 another ethical problem developed. President Clinton personally took charge of a Democratic National Committee (DNC) advertising campaign that was designed to attack Republican proposals to cut Medicare. The ads were sponsored by the DNC and were supposed to have nothing to do with the president's reelection campaign. However, as Bob Woodward notes:

> Clinton personally had been controlling tens of millions of dollars worth of DNC advertising. This enabled him to exceed the legal spending limits and effectively rendered the DNC an adjunct to his own reelection effort. He was circumventing the rigorous post-Watergate reforms that were designed to limit and control the raising and spending of money for presidential campaigns. His direct, hands-on involvement was risky, certainly in violation of the spirit of the law and possibly illegal.[3]

Clinton's actions raise troubling questions about campaign finance, an issue I discuss in detail in chapter 20.

Regulations

There are few legal statutes that govern political advertising. And this is as it should be, note libertarian scholars of mass media. Liberal critics of political commercials veer toward the other extreme, arguing that government should do more to protect the public from deceptive ads.

The key law that governs political ads is the equal time provision of the Federal Communications Act. The act stipulates that broadcasters must sell equal time to all legally qualified contenders for public office. But, as Patrick Devlin notes, "the key word is 'sell,' not 'give,' equal time."[4] Radio or television stations that sell time to one presidential candidate are required to provide opportunities for other legally qualified candidates to purchase broadcast time. All advertisements must contain a disclaimer that indicates which candidate or political group paid for the spot.

The equal time provision does not stipulate that a candidate must have the same number of advertisements as the opponent, only that all candidates in the same race must have equal opportunities to purchase time. Candidates who do not have the funds to purchase time are at a competitive disadvantage, but there is nothing in the law that requires broadcasters to provide them with time.

Finally, there are no formal rules governing deception in political advertising. Candidates have considerable freedom to stretch the truth and impugn their opponents' integrity. The courts have been reluctant to place limits on negative political speech, arguing that such limits are not in the best interest of democracy.[5]

Length

Political ads have shrunk over the past 40 years. Half-hour biographical commercials were used regularly in the 1950s and 1960s. Even as late as the 1970s, 4-minute spots were frequently employed. By the 1980s, and continuing into the 1990s, the overwhelming majority of presidential buys were for 60-second, 30-second and, occasionally, 15-second ads. Nowadays, the 30-second spot is the dominant time frame.[6]

Of course, there are exceptions. Over a third of Ross Perot's ads in 1992 were 30- or 60-minute spots. In 1996, Perot ran a number of half-hour spots, although they attracted far fewer viewers than they did in 1992, when one of the candidate's 30-minute infomercials captured close to 30 million television watchers. Perhaps, as Devlin notes, unconventional candidates like Perot gravitate to unconventional methods of advertising their candidacies (with more success in certain years than in others).[7]

In any case, there is little doubt that this is the age of the 30-second spot. Critics have pointed out that in earlier eras, Americans were treated to much longer speeches from their presidential contenders. Stump speeches could go on for hours. While one hesitates to defend the trend toward 30-second commercials, because they do squeeze out ideas and issues, the fact is that many of the older addresses were vague and diffuse, hardly examples of ringing political oratory.

STRATEGY: THE NOMINATION PERIOD

Years ago, political advertising did not begin in earnest until the general election campaign. However, that is no longer the way things work. Candidates run political commercials as early as the preprimary period. Indeed, in 1995 the Democratic National Committee, under President Clinton's direction, ran ads charging that the Republicans were proposing dangerous cuts in Medicare benefits. The ads were designed to shore up support for the president during budget negotiations with the Republican Congressional leadership. However, they were also viewed as the first step in his campaign for re-election, an attempt to paint the Republicans as heartless and cruel, a brushstroke which would be used again and again in the general election campaign of 1996.

Political spots are used relentlessly by candidates in the presidential primaries. Even states like Iowa and New Hampshire, which were known for their personalized campaigning, are now the sites of aggressive (and often negative) advertising blitzes. During the 1992 New Hampshire primary, the Democratic and Republican presidential candidates spent about $5.2 million on television advertising for 348,000 votes![8] Four years later, Steve Forbes surprised even seasoned professionals by spending $1.5 million on television ads in New Hampshire and Iowa within the first month of his announcement of his candidacy for the Republican nomination.

Political spots have played a key role in primary elections over the years. In the 1992 New Hampshire primary, Clinton used a variety of advertising formats—60-second issue spots, ads that invited viewers to call for a copy of Clinton's 15-page economic plan, and a 12-minute campaign video distributed to undecided voters. His advertising and thematic message helped catapult him to a second-place finish in the Granite State.

Pat Buchanan also used the paid media effectively in 1992 and 1996. For example, in 1992, he developed a simple but compelling spot criticizing George Bush ("Bush betrayed our trust. He raised our taxes. Can we afford four more years of broken promises?").

Steve Forbes's 1996 experience—spending millions on ads, but failing to win many primaries—illustrates that money does not guarantee success in the primaries. As we will see, there is much more to the alchemy of political advertising than greenbacks.

Once the primaries are over or a nominee has, for all practical purposes, been selected, candidates turn their attention to probing voters' opinion in polls and focus groups. *Nowadays, candidates develop a general strategy and try to use the conventions, news media, and advertising to hammer home their message. Advertising is not isolated from other political marketing formats, but instead is part of an overall media strategy.* Importantly, polling plays a critical role in determining the strategies candidates employ in their advertising campaigns. To appreciate the role that polling plays in political advertising campaigns, as well as the ways that consultants select thematic approaches, it is useful to look at the evolution of political advertising strategies in four recent presidential electons.

STRATEGY: RECENT ELECTIONS

1984

Republican consultant Richard Wirthlin devised a sophisticated polling strategy that made use of a "hierarchical values map" of the electorate. Arguing that values (and not issues or party loyalty) governed voters' decision-making, Wirthlin showed voters a map with 35 boxes, including education, caring about people, and world peace. Respondents were asked which candidate—Mondale or Reagan—came to mind when they thought of these values. The candidate who received the most mentions for a given value would "own" that value box.

Republican consultant Wirthlin found that Reagan owned the box below world peace, called "strengthen defense preparedness." However, Wirthlin discovered that voters were not connecting this box—Reagan's stand on national defense—with world peace. That had to be changed, Wirthlin believed. The Reagan campaign had to persuade voters to make the connection so that Reagan's efforts to build up national defense would be seen as contributing to world peace.[9]

Emerging from this analysis was the "Bear in the Woods" ad that was shown repeatedly on television during the last couple of weeks of the 1984 campaign. The ad showed a black bear walking across a mountain ridge and crossing a stream As the camera followed the bear, a deep male voice stated, "Some people say the bear is tame. Others say it is vicious and dangerous. Since no one can really be sure who's right, isn't it smart to be as strong as the bear? If there is a bear." The ad was a brilliant piece of artistry, for, as campaign specialist David Moore notes:

> The bear ... was symbolic of the Soviet Union, and indirectly the ad raised the question of how serious a threat the Russian bear was to the United States. According to Wirthlin, the ad worked. It persuaded voters to make the linkage between a strong defense and world peace, and thus by the end of the campaign, Reagan owned the World Peace box.[10]

1988

Focus groups revealed that people knew little about George Bush, beyond the fact that he had served as vice president. To remedy the problem, Bush spent the summer articulating a domestic agenda. He also did a series of positive spots to lay the foundation for his campaign. One ad showed Bush visibly enjoying himself at a picnic surrounded by children and grandchildren. As Bush's media director recalled, "People saw a George Bush they could like."[11]

The Bush campaign also depicted Democratic opponent Michael Dukakis in negative terms, based on insights gleaned from focus groups. Bush's campaign director Lee Atwater said bluntly, "We're gonna have to use research to win this campaign. You get me the stuff to beat this little bastard and put it on this three-by-five card."[12] Research indicated that people reacted negatively to Dukakis's opposition to the death penalty and to his veto of a bill requiring that school children recite the pledge of allegiance. Furthermore, focus group research showed that people were uncomfortable with Dukakis's support of a Massachusetts prison furlough program that permitted convicted murderer Willie Horton to receive 10 weekend passes from prison. On one of his leaves, Horton fled to Maryland, kidnaped a young couple, and repeatedly raped the woman. Horton was Black, the woman White.

Bush's advisers recommended that he pummel Dukakis on these issues. "Well, you guys are the experts," Bush said, signaling his acceptance of the consultants' negative advertising strategy. Over the course of the fall campaign, Bush did a series of hard-hitting ads that attacked Dukakis's record on crime and on the environment.

1992

Bill Clinton was determined not to make the mistakes that Dukakis had committed. He conducted research long before the general election to learn how voters perceived him and to identify the issues that were of paramount importance to the electorate. He also resolved to respond quickly and forcefully to attacks by Bush and Perot.

Although Clinton had clinched the Democratic nomination by the late spring of 1992, he was trailing Bush and Perot in the polls. A series of focus groups showed that Clinton was seen as a "politician going strictly for the job and power." People complained that they did not know why Clinton wanted to be president. They knew little about his background or his positions on the issues. To remedy the problem, Clinton's strategists recommended that the candidate develop an overarching message. They urged that he make "people-first economics" the centerpiece of his fall campaign. The objective, as *Newsweek*'s political reporters put it, "was to reestablish Clinton as an outsider who identified with the popular rage against Washington."[13]

At the same time, his strategists recommended that he "blitz the pop culture TV shows"—and target young voters—by appearing on MTV and Arsenio Hall, playing his saxophone. At the Democratic convention, the campaign unveiled a film biography of Clinton, "The Man from Hope," (which played off his birthplace in Hope, Arkansas). As historian Gil Troy notes, "Clinton went from being a draft-dodging, noninhaling policy wonk to the 'Man from Hope,' born in the twentieth-century version of a log cabin."[14] Ads played up these themes in the fall campaign. The strategy worked because it was congruent with Clinton's persona and his values; it was part image, part substance, and part old-fashioned political biography.

Clinton's media strategists innovatively aimed their ads at local markets in critical states. This contrasted with the usual strategy of doing national spots, purchased from the television networks. Clinton's effort not only helped him tailor his ads to local needs; it also saved the campaign money, freeing it from having to purchase ads geared to states that were already in the bag.

Fortunately for Clinton, George Bush failed to develop a coherent advertising strategy. The Bush campaign never decided on an overarching message, and it shifted directions. The campaign focused first on Bush's accomplishments, then on his conservative political stands, and later on personal attacks on Clinton. The ads telegraphed Bush's failure to develop a coherent rationale for his candidacy for a second term as president.

Ross Perot spent nearly $40 million of his own money on television advertising, a fantastic amount of money even by contemporary standards. He employed a direct "talking head" approach in his ads, nearly half of which were half-hour or one-hour spots.

1996

President Clinton launched his 1996 advertising campaign well over a year before the presidential election. Under his auspices, the Democratic National Committee ran a series of ads in the fall of 1995 that attacked Republican proposals to cut Medicare. "The Republicans are wrong to want to cut Medicare benefits," an authoritative male announcer declared. "And President Clinton is right to protect Medicare, right to defend our decision as a nation, to do what's moral, good and right by our elderly."

The ads reframed the debate over the budget from how to balance the budget and slow the growth of Medicare—the Republicans' orientation—to preserving Medicare and protecting senior citizens at the twilight of their lives. Rather than arguing that the Republicans wanted to cut Medicare to provide a tax break for the rich, Clinton emphasized that cutting Medicare benefits "was a violation of our duties and our values." In his attempt to capture the political center, Clinton emphasized values and unity rather than class warfare.[15]

Clinton began what was undoubtedly the earliest advertising campaign for reelection in American history for one critical reason: He was determined not to make the mistake he had made in the fight to reform health care, when his opponents took to the airwaves and defined the terms of the health care debate (See Box 19.3).

The early ads served as the foundation for the president's 1996 reelection campaign. Clinton would align himself with core American values and paint the Republicans as extremists. His strategy emerged from polls and focus groups that showed the public would not tolerate cuts in Medicare and was at the same time concerned with family issues such as schools, crime, and moral decay. To seize the agenda from the Republicans and to appeal to female voters, Clinton used the bully pulpit to announce "profamily policies," such as the introduction of the V-chip, measures to discourage teenage smoking, and programs to get tough on fathers who refuse to pay for child support. His campaign ads played up his commitment to family values, an issue that has become the modern equivalent of motherhood and apple pie.

Clinton's ads and marketing campaign emphasized a long-standing weapon in the president's arsenal of practical politics: A politician running for office can redefine himself by taking on popular enemies. Clinton took on the tobacco industry, the television networks, which mass produce violent programs, Republican proposals to cut Medicare, and "DoleGingrich," which (as columnists noted) the White House strategically pronounced as one word. By casting himself as the opponent of these carefully selected "bad guys," Clinton could "enhance his image as a leader looking out for the public interest without much fear of political reprisal."[16]

Clinton ran some harsh spots. One ad criticized Dole for opposing the Family Leave Act. The spot showed a young couple recalling the time they spent with their young daughter before she died. The announcer noted that the new law allows families to remain at home with a sick or newborn infant without losing their jobs. "Bob Dole led a 6-year fight against Family Leave," the announcer said. "Twelve million have used leave, but Dole's still against it."

The Dole camp objected to the ad, arguing that it was ludicrous to think that Dole "would let a child die without her parents at her side."[17] However, Dole failed to effectively rebut these and other negative spots.

The Dole campaign never developed a clear strategy for attacking Clinton or promoting Dole. Advisers went back and forth, trying to decide whether to attack Clinton for taking too many positions, for hewing too closely to the liberal line, or for ethical problems in his administration. Dole finally denounced the president's ethical record late in the campaign, calling attention to improper acquisition of FBI files by the Clinton White House and Democratic campaign finance abuses. Yet it was not clear Dole's attacks were successful, either because voters were unconcerned with the problems Dole raised or because they were willing to forgive Clinton for his ethical lapses.

To make matters worse, the Republican contender seemed to have difficulty defining himself through his ads and speeches. His tax cut plan did not resonate with voters, some of whom remembered that Dole had strongly opposed tax cuts as a senator on the grounds that they would increase the budget deficit. His spots failed to define him as a plausible alternative to Clinton, although Dole had a long and impressive record in the Senate upon which to draw. As one aide said, "It is very hard to convince people that Dole is someone other than the person they have been watching float around for the last three decades."[18]

By contrast, Clinton's ads defined the president as a candidate who cared about people and who had done things, like cutting welfare and endorsing school uniforms, that resonated with mainstream voter concerns. A clear image of the president emerged from his ads, in contrast to the fuzzy, unfocused image that came across when one watched Dole's spots. As even the conservative *Weekly Standard* remarked, Dole and running mate Jack Kemp failed to "give the American people a convincing reason to cast an affirmative for them in November."[19]

Summary

As these examples indicate, modern presidential advertising is a dynamic and complicated business. Indeed, as Montague Kern notes, "Today's consultants do not simply create an ad and launch it onto the airwaves."[20] They pretest the idea with focus groups, refine the idea through research, and consider ways of getting journalists to cover the advertising campaign. Increasingly, consultants are not making national media buys, but are purchasing spots in key markets in pivotal states.

Like it or not, presidential politics calls on the principles of marketing, packaging, and even consumer psychology. It is a fast-paced business, too, with consultants being asked to make critical decisions regarding how best to portray the candidate's strengths, how to respond to a negative ad, and how low a blow they should strike at an opponent's weak spots. As we have seen, presidential candidates employ a host of strategies in what has come to be known as "the air war."

TYPES OF POLITICAL SPOTS

Political ads do not come in one shape, size, or format. There are many different types of political spots—positive, negative, direct, indirect, issue-oriented, image-based; as many types of political spots as there are strategies for persuasion. Ads do a variety of things—they provide issue information, describe a candidate's accomplishments, create image impressions, appeal to viewers' emotions, attack the opposition, and respond to opponents' attacks (see Boxes 19.1 and 19.2).

Most political advertisements fall under one of the following categories:

- **Talking head spots,** where the candidate speaks directly to the television viewer. (All candidates have used them; in 1992, Ross Perot captured 30 million viewers with a half-hour talking head spot, "Problems.")
- **Documentary ads,** biographical spots or ads that showcase the candidate's leadership accomplishments. (These frequently contain priceless footage, such as a submarine rescuing George Bush after he was shot down in combat during World War II, and a young Bill Clinton shaking hands with President Kennedy at the White House.)
- **Testimonials,** a time-honored form of argumentation in which credible or famous people speak for or against a candidate. (The classic was Kennedy's use of Eisenhower's off-the-cuff remark at a press conference. When asked to name one thing Richard Nixon had suggested during his two terms as vice president, Eisenhower replied "If you give me a week, I might think of one.")
- **Surrogate ads,** in which the candidate does not appear in the commercial; in some cases, the ads are sponsored by independent groups. (Independent sponsorship of negative surrogate ads allows candidates to distance themselves from attack spots.)
- **Creative idea spots,** memorable ads that use powerful imagery or humor to create positive or negative images of a candidate (Positive spots like those linking Ronald Reagan with lush American images give people a chill at the end; negative ads like the 1988 "Willy Horton" spots stand out in people's minds.)
- **Prospective and retrospective policy ads.** Prospective spots assert that if elected, a candidate *will* enact a particular policy. Positive retrospective ads invite viewers to examine the incumbent's accomplishments (e.g., a Clinton ad that emphasizes the president's success in creating jobs). Negative retrospective spots encourage viewers to consider how the incumbent has broken his campaign promises (e.g., Dole's claim that Clinton reneged on his 1992 promise of a middle-class tax cut).[21]

Issues Versus Images

It is commonly believed that political ads are vacuous, meaningless drivel. Some ads do fit this description, of course. It may surprise you to learn that the overwhelming majority of presidential spots contain a good deal of issue information. They frequently describe a candidate's stand on an issue, note that the candidate shares the majority view on a policy concern, and point out shortcomings in the opponent's position. One study found that 67% of positive ads and 79% of negative ads contain substantive issue information.[22]

In early research on political advertising, scholars frequently separated issue ads from image spots. The old-fashioned view was that issue ads were good because they got voters to focus on the substance of the campaign; image spots were bad because they called attention to superficial matters, like the candidate's appearance. However, scholars now recognize that this dichotomy oversimplifies matters.

Issue ads, such as those that outline a president's foreign policy accomplishments, can enhance perceptions that the incumbent is a strong, resolute leader (an important component of the president's *image*). By the same token, image ads can provide voters with valuable information about the character or competence of the candidate. A spot that effectively portrays the challenger as a person of integrity may provide useful information to voters who worry about the incumbent's tendency to do the politically expedient thing. Such an ad focuses on the image of the candidate; yet to many voters, the character of the candidate—or lack thereof—may be a more important *issue* than the president's position on foreign or domestic policy.[23]

NEGATIVE ADVERTISING

They are the Darth Vader of modern politics, "the electronic equivalent of the plague."[24] Few dimensions of modern politics have generated as much criticism or scorn as negative political commercials.

Although candidates have traded insults and barbs for over two centuries, negative advertising is a relatively new phenomenon. Political consultants used to counsel candidates not to use negative commercials, saying they were not smart politics or that attack spots boomeranged on the candidate who sponsored them. Nowadays, negative advertising plays a prominent part in presidential election campaigns. No consultant worth his or her salt would counsel against the use of negative ads.

Why the push toward negative campaigning? There are several reasons, as Devlin notes:

1. Negative ads are memorable—more memorable than positive ads.
2. Negative ads move the numbers. Candidates see surges in polling numbers and increases in negative numbers regarding opponents.
3. Negative ads are newsworthy. Negative ads get additional free coverage in newspaper stories and television news that positive ads do not get.
4. Negative ads are more creative and ingenious than positive ads. They play, and people want to see them again.[25]

Thus far, I have used the term "negative advertising" as if it were a simple construct. In fact, as Karen Johnson-Cartee and Gary Copeland have pointed out, negative ads are complex and multidimensional; there are many types of negative ads, various thematic designs used in the transmission of negative issue appeals, and a variety of stylistic techniques for constructing negative spots.[26] Bruce Gronbeck identified three types of negative political commercials: (a) the implicative ad, involving an implication or innuendo about the opponent but no direct attack, (b) the comparative ad, incorporating an explicit comparison between the contenders; and (c) the assaultive ad ... providing a direct, personal attack on the opponent's character, motives, associates, or actions.[27]

When most people think of negative political advertising, they think of the assaultive ad. However, relatively few campaigns rely on direct attacks because they are so likely to backfire and do not touch on issues that are of interest to voters. In fact, many negative ads borrow techniques from comparative product advertising and compare the candidate directly or indirectly with the opponent. Some indirect comparison ads subtly encourage the viewer to make the comparison. For example, Johnson's 1964 "Daisy" ad never mentioned his opponent, Barry Goldwater, by name. Instead, as Johnson-Cartee and Copeland note, "Johnson tells how he views nuclear war. And by doing so, the viewers within themselves make the comparison with Goldwater."[28]

Increasingly, negative spots rely on emotional appeals, the stuff of commercial advertising.[29] The most creative ads of the campaign typically do not come out and say, "This is what is wrong with my opponent's ideas." Instead, they tell stories. For example, in Clinton's attack on Dole's policy on the Family Leave Law, the president did not outline his objections to Dole's stand, carefully explaining why it was wrong for the country. Instead, the commercial featured a couple discussing how they spent time with their young daughter before she died, and then mentioned that Dole opposed the family leave law that made such things possible. The ad tries to get voters to connect the anxiety and anger they are feeling as they watch the ad to Clinton's opponent, Bob Dole.[30]

Ads like these have detractors and defenders. Critics say these ads are manipulative and that they degrade political speech. Defenders point out that as long as negative ads state their claims accurately, they are performing a valuable function. As Bradley Smith points out:

> Although it is fashionable today to criticize negative campaigning, it can serve a valuable purpose. Bruce Felknor, a longtime "good government" advocate who once headed the Fair Campaign Practices Committee, writes that without negative advertising, "any knave or mountebank in the land may lie and steal his or her way into the White House ... Without attention-grabbing, cogent, memorable, negative campaigning, almost no challenger can hope to win unless an incumbent has just been found guilty of a heinous crime." Negative advertising need not stoop to name-calling. To suggest that a candidate for office should not point out his opponent's shortcomings, failures and broken promises is preposterous. The question is not whether an ad is negative, but whether it is truthful and relevant.[31]

CONCLUSIONS

Political advertising plays a major role in modern presidential campaigns. Advertising is governed by campaign finance laws and the equal time statue. However, political advertising is not regulated as strictly as product advertising, largely because of the freedoms afforded by the First Amendment. "Our constitution protects free political speech within broad boundaries," note Johnson-Cartee and Copeland, "even if it is in error or is judged egregious by the general population."[32]

Television ads are typically 30 seconds in length. A great deal of research and creative activity goes into ads. Dozens of ads may be created and only a few aired. Consultants who fail to move poll numbers may be fired and replaced. Successful campaigns are characterized by a combination of positive spots that build a foundation for the candidate, memorable attack ads, and visionary appeals.

Political ads are complex and multifaceted. There are different types of positive and negative ads, including documentary, testimonial, and retrospective policy spots. Both positive and negative spots tend to contain a great deal more issue information than commonly assumed. One really cannot provide a compelling case for a candidate or a persuasive denunciation of the opponent without calling on policy issue information. Typically, issue information is woven into the ad, a part of the emotional message or story that the ad is trying to tell.

Box 19.1

A Negative Clinton Ad:

"How're You Doing?" 1992

Voiceover: Remember President Bush saying "And if you elect me President, you will be better off four years from now than you are today."

Announcer: Average family income down $1,600 in two years.

Voiceover: President Bush says, "You will be better off four years from now than you are today."

Announcer: Family health care costs up $1,800 in four years.

Voiceover: President Bush says, "You will be better off in four years."

Announcer: "The second biggest tax increase in history."

Voiceover: President Bush says, "If you elect me President, you will be better off four years from now than you are today."

Announcer: Well, it's four years later. How're you doing?

Box 19.2

The Positive-Negative Ad

In 1996, the Clinton campaign developed spots that used both positive and negative appeals, as this ad illustrates:

AUDIO	VIDEO
Bob Dole attacking the president.	Dole speaking forcefully (angry expression on face).
But under President Clinton, 10 million new jobs, taxes cut for 15 million working families. Proposes tax credits for college tuition.	Clinton speaking, smiling. Man exercising. Man, woman and two children. Students talking, in caps and gowns. Numbers from tax increases.
Dole voted to raise payroll taxes, Social Security taxes, the '90 income tax increase, 900 billion in higher taxes. And look closely at his risky tax scheme. It actually raised taxes on 9 million working families. Bob Dole: 35 years in Washington. 35 years of higher taxes.	Dole talking, gesturing.

Box 19.3
Dick Morris on Political Ads

In 1994, political consultant Dick Morris went to work for his old friend from Arkansas, Bill Clinton. Morris stayed with the president for two years, helping to engineer Clinton's overwhelming victory in 1996. Under Morris's direction, Clinton and the Democrats took to the airwaves to attack Republican programs as early as the summer of 1995. An excerpt from Morris's book on the election campaign, Behind the Oval Office, appears below. His unabashed defense of political ads will trouble some and titillate others. As you read this, keep in mind that this is Morris's view of the campaign, and his perspective is heavily weighted by his own conviction that he, Dick Morris, played a key role in Clinton's electoral victory.

Why did Clinton win so easily in 1996? Why did his lead hardly vary? What was his strength with the voters that Dole could never shake?

In my opinion, the key to Clinton's victory was his early television advertising. There has never been anything even remotely like it in the history of presidential elections. In 1992, Clinton and Bush each spent about 40 million dollars on TV advertising during the primary and general elections. In 1996, the Clinton campaign and, at the president's behest, the DNC spent upwards of 85 million dollars on ads—more than twice as much! ...

(We) polled heavily to determine voters' views of the Republicans' proposed budget cuts. Drawing on this research, we identified which reductions mattered most. Broadly, cuts in Medicare, Medicaid, education, and environmental protection most upset the voters.

Based on the mall tests, we decided which ad to run and whether to combine it with elements from ads that did not do as well. We worked for hours to make the ad fit 30 seconds. Then we'd send the script to Doug Sosnik, the White House political director, who gave it to the president for his OK.

Particularly at the beginning of our ad campaign, we would then go to the Oval Office for a 10- minute meeting with the president and vice-president to win their approval ... Gore especially liked (the consultants') ability to find footage of Dole creeping around behind Gingrich at a press conference. He compared it to a scene from Jurassic Park where a particularly mobile, kangaroo-like dinosaur, the Velociraptor, would maneuver for position in a hunt. I'd worked in almost a hundred high-level political races, but never before had I worked with so many good consultants, and the thrill of it is hard to describe. I felt like a violinist suddenly surrounded by a great orchestra or a baseball player in an all-star lineup. Clinton gave us virtually unlimited budget for polling and mall testing. We spent months in war games figuring out how to handle different budget-fight scenarios or different Republican attacks on issues ...

As the ads ran their course, voters came to prefer our budget plan to the Republican version by more than two to one and trusted Clinton to balance the budget "in a way that is fair to all" over the Republicans by 12 to 15 points. We had invaded the heart of Republican territory, the very core—the advocacy of a balanced budget—and we were showing that we could do it better than they could.

KEY ISSUES

Financial Aspects of TV Ads

Legal Regulations

Length of Ads

Strategic Considerations

Types of Spots

Negative Ads

Issues vs. Images

DISCUSSION QUESTIONS

1. Which ads come to mind when you think of recent presidential campaigns? What makes these memorable?

2. Discuss the different strategies candidates use to promote themselves in political spots.

3. What are the pros and cons of negative political advertising? Now that you've read this chapter, how do you feel about negative spots?

20

Political Advertising: Effects

One of the most intriguing issues in political advertising is the impact that ads exert on the electorate. Do they sway voters, and if so, how? This chapter takes up this question, focusing also on the ethics of modern political ads.

IMPACT OF POLITICAL ADS

Before examining the effects of political commercials, it is useful to review their limits. First, ads cannot transform candidates from ordinary politicians into attractive, charismatic potential presidents. Political advertisements cannot make competent but dull campaigners into enthralling, soulful candidates.[1] No political commercial can turn capable but wooden candidates like Walter Mondale, Michael Dukakis, and Bob Dole into charismatic charmers. Smart consultants realize this, and like sculptors who recognize the strengths and limits of their clay, they take candidates as they are and try to polish and accentuate their strong points, while attempting to cover up and reframe their weaknesses.

Second, political advertisements cannot change strongly held partisan preferences. As I have noted throughout the book, people bring well-developed political attitudes to the electoral setting, and these attitudes insulate them from media effects. As Stephen Ansolabehere and Shanto Iyengar have concluded, "Advertisements induce few Republicans to vote Democratic and few Democrats to vote Republican. Exposure to an opposition candidate's advertisements, in fact, can sometimes strengthen a voter's loyalty to his or her party."[2] In addition, political spots have relatively few effects on Independent voters, many of whom are cynical about politics to begin with.[3]

362

Campaign Learning

The good news about political ads is that people learn from them. There is substantial evidence that voters become better informed about candidates' stands on the issues from watching political ads.[4] This runs counter to the conventional wisdom. But it makes sense when you remember that political ads contain considerable issue information, that people can learn from the media when they pay attention to the message, and that voters are more motivated to pay attention to political communications during the presidential election than during most other periods.

Of course, there is debate about how much people learn from political ads. Critics argue that people learn only the sketchiest of information from ads since political spots tend to be vague and diffuse and contain only information that will benefit the candidate. Defenders note that 30-second spots can contain a good deal of issue information. In their book on political advertising, Edwin Diamond and Stephen Bates offer up an example of a 24-second ad that contains a considerable amount of policy issue information:

> I believe that the question of abortion is one that ought to be reserved exclusively to a woman and her doctor. I favor giving women the unfettered right to abortion. I also favor the federal funding of abortions through Medicaid for poor women as an extension of that right to an abortion, and I oppose any statutory or constitutional limitations on that right.[5]

Naturally, few candidates would make such a clear and unambiguous statement on abortion. But Diamond and Bates's point is that there is nothing in the technology of advertising that would inhibit voter learning if a candidate did produce such a spot.

Persuasion

Ads are designed not to teach, but to persuade. How persuasive *are* presidential campaign ads? I have already noted that they rarely convert strong partisans to the other party's candidate, and that party identification helps to mediate voters' response to ads. Nonetheless, ads do solidify the support of partisans, strengthening their commitment to the party's nominees. Ads also influence weak partisans—for example, Democrats with a weak attachment to their party.

In one study, so-called weak Democrats (those who had abandoned the party in the previous election) were powerfully influenced by a Democratic advertisement, much more, as it turned out, than weak Democrats who saw a Republican ad or those who did not view an experimental commercial.[6] In addition, ads seem to have a greater effect on voters with little interest in politics. The investigators found that low-interest voters who viewed an ad from their own party's candidates shifted significantly in their voting preferences toward that candidate. As the researchers note, "These voters moved from being largely undecided or not voting back into their party's camp."[7]

Since these studies are experiments, we need to be careful about generalizing the results to the real world. In addition, they do not tell us why weak partisans and low-interest voters are more influenced by ads than strong partisans and high-interest voters. When combined with other research, these studies suggest that political advertising is likely to have its greatest effect on the subset of voters who have a weak attachment to a political party and little knowledge about politics. As Darrell West notes, "ads are developed to stir the hopes and fears of the 20% to 30% of the electorate that is undecided, not the 70% to 80% that is committed or hopeless."[8]

Agenda-Setting, Priming, and Construction of Meaning

There are a myriad of issues that clamor for public attention in a presidential election. Which issues will win out? Candidates develop marketing and advertising strategies in the hopes of inducing voters (and the news media) to focus attention on issues that *they* believe are most important.

In 1988, George Bush used advertising and news effectively to shape the agenda. After focus group research convinced him that his opponent, Massachusetts Governor Michael Dukakis, was vulnerable on the crime issue, Bush embarked on a series of ads attacking Dukakis's position on crime, particularly the state's furlough program. One prominent ad, "Revolving Door," suggested that Dukakis's furlough program had been an unmitigated disaster for Massachusetts in that it gave convicted murderers the opportunity to commit other crimes like kidnaping and rape.

Darrell West found that those who had seen this ad were more likely than those who had not to mention crime and law and order as the most important problems facing the nation.[9] Of course, this does not prove that the ad influenced people's political priorities. But consider that Marjorie Hershey found that "the proportion of respondents saying that George Bush was 'tough enough' on crime and criminals rose from 23% in July to a full 61% in late October, while the proportion saying Dukakis was not tough enough rose from 36% to 49%."[10] Also, consider that the news gave a great deal of uncritical play to the "Revolving Door" spot, as well as to other related Bush attacks on the Dukakis furlough program.

Bush's aides worked hard to shape the network news agenda and were elated when the news gave what amounted to free publicity for their attacks on Dukakis. Dukakis then miscalculated by deciding not to answer Bush's ads, preferring to take the high road and assume the public would ignore or discount the negative spots. However, as West notes, this is not what happened:

> Dukakis's decision allowed Bush to set the tone of the campaign and to define the terms of debate. It was Bush's issues—flags, patriotism, "tax and spend" liberalism, and crime—that became the agenda of the campaign. Little was heard about homelessness, rising poverty, and the unmet social needs of the Reagan years.[11]

It would be an overstatement to suggest that Bush won the election because of his ads. There were many reasons why Bush defeated Dukakis, including his association with Ronald Reagan, his experience as vice president, and the electorate's approval of the policies of the Reagan–Bush administration. However, Bush's advertising campaign played a part. It helped him define himself and control the agenda, it pushed the press to focus more on "his" issues, and it induced voters to give more attention to "his" priorities than those enunciated by Dukakis.

In 1992, it was a different story. With the economy in a recession and Perot hammering away at the budget deficit, it was a no-brainer that the economy would be a major issue in the campaign. As noted earlier, Clinton developed a strategic plan to make the economy a key issue in his campaign. The evidence is that his game plan succeeded. West found that Clinton's ads primed voters: Those who had high exposure to ads were more likely than those who had low exposure to make the economy a factor in their voting decisions. They also were more inclined to agree that Clinton had the ability to improve economic conditions.[12]

Had Clinton's advertising manipulated voters into blaming George Bush for the economy? No. But by linking himself with an issue that voters perceived to be important, convincing them that the issue should be a major consideration in their votes, and suggesting that the incumbent's policies (rather than macroeconomic factors) were to blame, Clinton mightily influenced voters' political priorities.

In 1996, the agenda was less clear-cut. The Republicans had a problem because the Democrats had co-opted many of the issues on which their party is generally perceived to be stronger. A majority of voters think that Republicans pursue wiser policies on crime and foreign affairs, and that Democrats do better in areas of unemployment and environmental protection.[13]

However, Clinton, by proving himself capable of taking moderate Republican as well as liberal Democratic positions, gave the Republicans little agenda room in which to maneuver. The president could point to his signing of a crime bill, endorsement of school uniforms, the appearance of success with missile strikes on Iraq, as well as economic accomplishments. This left Dole trying to build an agenda on his tax cut plan. However, the plan failed to excite voters, and many worried that it would increase the deficit.

To sum up, presidential advertising can influence the public agenda and can prime voters. However, it is not a panacea. As Ansolabehere and Iyengar point out, "Candidates can direct the voters' attention to an issue only if the voters are predisposed to care about that issue to begin with and only if the candidates are themselves credible messengers."[14] Moreover, advertising works in concert with other factors, such as news coverage, talk-show appearances, and presidential debates. The more that a candidate can dovetail advertising, appearances on the news, and debate commentaries, so that they all reinforce the same theme, the more successful the candidate's media messages will be.

As is now abundantly clear, political ads do not work by converting masses of voters from one side to the other. Instead, as Frank Biocca notes, "the battle of political commercials is a battle over meaning. Political spots struggle to realign the meanings of candidates, issues, and groups constructed in the mind of the voter."[15]

Negative Advertising Effects

"Negative advertising is the riskiest element of the campaign," Diamond and Bates declare.[16] They are right. Candidates can win or lose big from negative advertising campaigns. Attacks that are perceived to be too harsh, too personal, or simply unfair will boomerang on the sponsor.

Kern cited the case of a Democratic ad that attacked Republican opposition to abortion even in cases of rape or incest. The emotional Democratic spot had a young woman calling her father on the phone. "Daddy? It's Mary Ellen," a female voice says. "Daddy ... something terrible ... Daddy." A male voice interrupts. "Mr. Sawyer? This is Lieutenant Kennan at police headquarter. Your daughter has been raped ... Now she's not been harmed, but if you and Mr. and Mrs. Sawyer ... " (voice fades).[17]

Focus groups were deeply moved by the ad. "Respondents put their heads down, they avoided eye contact with the moderators, they tried not to speak to the issue," the advertising consultant reported. As a result of the group's reactions, the consultant recommended that the ad be scrapped.

Of course, other consultants have not been so prescient.

In some elections, negative ads have failed because they did not hit issues that resonated with voters. Ads that do not mention salient shortcomings in the opponent's record will have little impact. Bob Dole spent millions on negative spots in 1996, but his attacks on Clinton seemed to have little effect, perhaps because voters were well aware of the president's weaknesses but for a number of reasons preferred his record and policies to those of Senator Dole.

Negative ads *can* influence attitudes when they hit issues that are of concern to voters, and are perceived to be fair. For example, in 1992, about 50% of Clinton's ads were negative.[18] Yet they appeared to help Clinton's cause because they focused on issues that were on voters' minds, such as the recession, Bush's broken campaign pledges, and the need to make government more responsive to the needs of ordinary people.[19] Similarly, in 1996, even though Clinton ran as many if not more negative spots than Dole, he was not castigated by voters for his negative ads.[20] This seems to be because his criticisms of Dole were seen as legitimate—not below the belt—and because he seemed to offer his positions more softly than the hard-hitting, frequently-scowling Republican challenger.

Negative spots can exert a strong impact on memory. People remember negative ads better than positive ones. They also recognize negative ads more accurately and more quickly than positive spots.[21] There are many reasons for this, including the psychological tendency to attach more weight to negative than positive information, the stronger impact of negative information on already existing impressions, the better production value of negative spots, and the fact that negative spots get more news coverage than positive ads.[22]

This helps explain why candidates use negative ads, even though voters regularly complain about them. As Jill Buckley, a Democratic consultant, explained, "People say they hate negative advertising, but it works. They hate it and remember it at the same time."[23]

Combating Negative Commercials

In the old days, candidates who were targeted by negative ads were told to ignore the attacks. Voters will blame the attacker, consultants advised. Don't worry, they said; the spots will blow up in the sponsor's face.

The days of ignoring negative ads are over.

Anyone who believes that silence is the best antidote to negative ads should meet Michael Dukakis, who now freely admits that he made a mistake by not answering George Bush's attacks on his social policies in the 1988 election. By not answering Bush's ads, Dukakis gave them legitimacy. He suggested by his silence that Bush's charges just might be true. In general, Johnson-Cartee and Copeland point out, "by pursuing a strategic silence, the political leader turns over the definition of the situation to others, a very dangerous political maneuver."[24] The candidate lets others define his or her political persona, thereby abdicating the task of managing impressions and redefining one's political identity.

Silence seems to imply acquiescence to many Americans, and they dislike it. As one consultant put it, "There's one thing the American people dislike more than someone who fights dirty. And that's someone who climbs into the ring and won't fight."[25]

In a way, it is unfortunate that candidates cannot simply ignore their opponents' nasty attacks. After all, silence in the face of an adversary's criticism can be a mature way of coping with a situation. Parents counsel their children to ignore a bully's taunts and move ahead with whatever they are doing. Unfortunately, in politics, where impressions are everything and people form opinions quickly and often permanently, silence can spell doom to a campaign. Amplifying the pressure on candidates to strongly rebut negative ads is the press, which relentlessly covers the air wars and mercilessly focuses on a candidate's failure to respond to the opponent's attacks.[26]

As it turns out, candidates can counter negative ads in a variety of ways. They can: (a) confess their sins: (b) deny the charges, then turn around and attack the opposition for its use of dirty tactics; (c) reframe the issue to their own advantage; and (d) counterattack the sponsor of the negative ad.

Sophisticated campaigns also engage in a proactive strategy to combat negative commercials, called **inoculation**. This tactic, based on social psychological research, is regarded as one of the most effective ways to counter negative advertising appeals. Inoculation works in the following way: Anticipating an attack by the opponent, the candidate acknowledges the problem, even going so far as to describe the nature of the charge leveled against his or her campaign. The candidate then refutes the charge, explaining why it is hogwash. By "inoculating" the audience—introducing voters to the charge and then refuting it—the candidate (at least in theory) neutralizes the attack. He or she gets also gets credit for having shown the courage to confront the accuser.

There is considerable evidence that inoculation can neutralize an opponent's negative commercials.[27] It is used regularly in political campaigns. John F. Kennedy used it with finesse during the West Virginia primary campaign of 1960. Kennedy acknowledged that critics had questioned whether his Catholicism would interfere with his meeting the oath of office. Kennedy then rebutted the argument by noting that his faith encouraged his fulfillment of his presidential duties, adding that he was sure that no one in the state of West Virginia believed he would be a candidate for the presidency if he did not think he could meet his oath of office.

Thirty-two years later, a man who modeled himself after John Kennedy, Bill Clinton, used inoculation to protect himself against the charge that, like Michael Dukakis before him, he was greatly exaggerating the economic recovery that his state had experienced under his stewardship as governor. "To all those in this campaign season who would criticize Arkansas, come on down ... you'll see us struggling against some of the problems we haven't solved yet. But you'll also see a lot of great people doing amazing things."

In sum, candidates can reduce the impact of attacks by using a variety of proactive and reactive response strategies. Increasingly, candidates try to respond rapidly to the opposition's attack ads, even obtaining copies of the opponent's scripts before they are actually broadcast. They then prepare a refutational ad and air it within a day. While rapid response strategies work to the benefit of candidates, critics wonder whether they have a negative impact on the system. Does a system in which attacks beget more attacks tend to turn off voters, causing them to wonder whether national politics is worth the bother?

ETHICAL ISSUES

The construction of political ads is not for the faint-hearted. It is an intense, fast-paced, and often nasty business.[28] Ambition pushes candidates to go all-out to win. Inevitably, this pushes some politicians to put together advertisements that are deceptive.

The deceptions are usually subtle. Candidates cannot lie outright in ads, lest they be denounced by their opponents, the press, or the public. So under some circumstances they construct ads that are literally true, but inferentially false—that is, they invite false inferences on the part of the television viewing audience.[29]

The classic example of this is the negative advertising directed against Michael Dukakis by the Bush campaign and a pro-Bush PAC. Bush's "Revolving Door" ad attacked Dukakis's prison furlough policy. The ad used the symbol of a revolving door to symbolize Dukakis's policy of allowing prisoners to go in and out of prison, presumably forever.

In the ad, the announcer states that Dukakis's "revolving door prison policy gave weekend furloughs to first-degree murderers not eligible for parole." The words *268 escaped* are superimposed on the screen. The announcer then says, "While out, many committed other crimes like kidnaping and rape." This is the point at which the ad invites a false inference, according to Kathleen Jamieson. She notes that:

> The structure of the ad prompts listeners to hear "first-degree murderers not eligible for parole" as the antecedent referent for "many." Many of whom committed crimes? First-degree murderers not eligible for parole. Many of whom went on to commit crimes like kidnapping and rape? First-degree murderers not eligible for parole.
> But many unparoleable first-degree murderers did not escape. Of the 268 furloughed convicts who jumped furlough during Dukakis's first two terms, only four had ever been convicted first-degree murderers not eligible for parole. Of those four not "many" but one went on to kidnap and rape. That one was William Horton. By flashing "268 escaped" on the screen as the announcer speaks of "many first-degree murderers," the ad invites the false inference that 268 murderers jumped furlough to rape and kidnap. Again, the single individual who fits this description is Horton ... In Dukakis's first two terms, 268 escapes were made by the 11,497 individuals who were given a total of 67,378 furloughs.[30]

Jamieson further argues that the PAC ad that ran at the same time as "Revolving Door" encouraged viewers to think of Horton when they saw the "Revolving Door" ad. The PAC ad showed the mug shot of Horton while the announcer described Horton's crimes.[31]

None of this is illegal. But critics suggest that the Bush advertising was misleading, that it capitalized on voters' ignorance of prison furlough policies (other states had them too), and that it reinforced racial stereotyping by encouraging viewers to associate Dukakis's prison policy with a powerful symbol for racial hatred, an African-American man raping a White woman.

From the advertiser's perspective, the Horton and prison furlough material were fair game. (They had been brought up during the primaries by one of Dukakis's Democratic opponents, Al Gore.) Arguably, the fact that 268 prisoners escaped under a prison furlough program in Dukakis's state and Dukakis's unwillingness to criticize the program were serious chinks in the Democratic candidate's armor. Nonetheless, there is no getting around the fact that the "Revolving Door" spot used some televisual sleights of hand that may have led people to reach conclusions that were not based on the facts.

There have been other misleading claims in ads. In 1995, the Democrats attacked Republican plans to reduce the deficit by cutting Medicare. Their ad lambasted the Republicans for proposed cuts in Medicare, a social program that both Democrats and Republicans agreed had to be trimmed lest the country head straight into fiscal disaster. The Democratic spot implied that Clinton was the protector of Medicare, and the Republicans the enemy. But it did not mention that there was only about a 2% difference between the Republican and Clinton proposals on projected Medicare spending.[32]

Adwatches

In 1988, the television networks got into the habit of replaying the Bush campaign's attack ads. The ads were graphic and vivid and therefore good grist for the evening news. But critics objected, correctly pointing out that by rebroadcasting a candidate's negative ads, the news was blurring the distinction between advertising and news; in the process, the news was giving free publicity to one candidate and inadvertently enhancing the credibility of his spots. Furthermore in 1988, journalists were reluctant to expose inaccuracies in Bush's (and Dukakis's) advertisements, for fear of seeming biased.

Out of this controversy emerged Adwatches—an innovative method of critiquing a candidate's ads, a technique designed to reduce the impact of misleading commercials and to inform the public about claims that are erroneous or distorted. Television adwatch stories typically replay the misleading commercial, question inaccurate assumptions, and offer corrective information.

Unquestionably, adwatches are an excellent educational tool. The question is: Do they work? Unfortunately, adwatches run the risk of magnifying the impact of the misleading ad. "By repeating the advertisement itself," Ansolabehere and Iyengar note, "the adwatch may strengthen recall of the advertisement, thus making favorable information about the candidate and unfavorable information about the opponent more accessible in memory."[33] This is exactly what some researchers have found. Michael Pfau and Allan Louden discovered that the use of a full-screen television adwatch enhanced the influence of the targeted negative commercial.[34]

The good news is that, if certain precautions are followed, adwatches can call viewers' attention to misleading information. Joseph Cappella and Kathleen Jamieson found that adwatches caused viewers to regard the targeted ad as less fair and less important.[35] An adwatch is likely to be particularly effective if it (a) clearly states that viewers are watching segments from a misleading commercial; (b) makes certain that the reporter interrupts the ad to point out its erroneous claims; and (c) places corrective print information on the television screen.

Perhaps the most positive impact of adwatches has been on consultants themselves. Concerned that a graphic, but slightly misleading, advertisement would become the focus of adwatches across the country, campaign consultants have taken pains to check the accuracy of their claims. "I spent more time talking about economics and the latest statistics from the Bureau of Labor statistics and the Bureau of Census than I thought a creative person ever would in her lifetime," recalled Clinton's 1992 advertising director Mandy Grunwald.[36]

Money and Political Advertising

Does money buy elections? This question, which has been asked in America for years, is at the center of much of the controversy about elections today. With special interest groups pouring millions of dollars into election-year campaigns, political action committees, parties, and candidates spending as much as $600 million on the 1996 presidential campaign, and the parties tripping over each other to take advantage of loopholes in the campaign finance laws, there can be little doubt that money is power in American electoral politics.[37]

But how much power does money buy? This is the $64,000 (of if you prefer, the $64 million) question. In the realm of political advertising, the impact of money is complex. Steve Forbes spent millions in Iowa and New Hampshire, only to come up empty-handed. He dropped out of the race, even though he had outspent his opponents. Similarly, Ross Perot spent millions of his personal fortune in 1996, only to capture less than 10% of the vote.

But if money is not a sufficient condition for success, it surely is a necessary one. Why else would President Clinton's campaign, though it faced no opponents in the primaries, have spent more than $30 million from spring 1995 to autumn 1996 on the 1996 election campaign?[38] Steve Forbes may not have come close to capturing the Republican nomination.

But think how far he would have gone on his flat tax idea had he no money to spend.

The most persuasive evidence that money interacts with political adver- tising to influence elections comes from research on lower level elections. In a systematic study of the impact of advertising expenditures on electoral outcomes, Joseph Grush and his colleagues looked at whether the candi- dates who spent the most money on media advertising were more likely to win election than those who spent less, or had less money to spend. Focusing on low-visibility Congressional elections, Grush found that the leading spender won nearly 60% of the time. This far exceeded the proportion that one would expect on the basis of chance alone.[39]

Thus, candidates who have amassed personal fortunes are more likely to win election to low level offices. Once elected, they capitalize on their names, reputations, and the power of incumbency. Thus, incumbents are reelected with astonishing frequency.

Unquestionably, wealth provides candidates with a strategic advantage. This has caused some critics to recommend term limits for members of Congress. Other observers disagree, arguing that term limits are undemo- cratic and that there is nothing wrong with individuals spending their own personal fortunes on a political advertising campaign.

Some scholars point out that the amount of money spent on presidential advertising pales with that spent on commercial advertising. They note that the public's objection to expensive campaigns is rooted in the centuries-old ambivalence Americans have felt about aggressive efforts to win election to public office. And yet, one shudders to think how the Founding Fathers would react to data on the amount of money being spent on presidential elections and to the ways in which political parties have taken advantage of loopholes in the finance laws.

CONCLUSIONS AND PERSPECTIVES

Effects

In the previous chapter, I discussed the content and characteristics of presidential advertising. This chapter examined the social and psychological effects of ads on voters. Ads have limits. They cannot remake candi- dates—they will not alter the image candidates have negotiated with voters over the years. Political spots also cannot change strongly held partisan preferences; they do not convert voters from one side of the political aisle to the other.

Consultants recognize this and do not aim to convert partisans. Instead, they appeal to large masses of undecided voters, trying to convince these individuals that the candidate shares their perspective, and that the candidate is in touch with their sentiments on major hot-button issues of the day. Political advertising is less about persuading people in the narrow mechanistic sense of the word, and more about influencing the meaning that voters attach to events. In 1992, Bill Clinton proved himself in sync with voters' dissatisfaction with the status quo. He also helped to "access" this dissatisfaction and move it to the foreground of people's consciousness by adroitly influencing the advertising and news agendas.

This is not to say that advertising always has a strong, subtle impact. Many ads miss their mark, fail to reach the target audience, and (in the case of negative spots) totally backfire on the sponsor. Furthermore, there are some elections when even the best advertising cannot rescue a sinking candidate. When candidates face popular incumbents and voters are satisfied with the state of the nation, the odds are stacked against challengers from the get-go; it is unrealistic to expect advertising to save the day.

It is difficult to parcel out the influence of commercials from all the other forces impinging on voters during the election campaign. Clearly, political spots can affect voters' evaluations of candidates and their interpretations of political events. Ads also contribute to voters' storehouse of campaign knowledge, although even advertising consultants would agree that a campaign diet based exclusively on commercials would be an intellectually meager one.

Ethics

Misleading ads, such as the "Revolving Door" spot discussed previously, have greatly concerned critics of political advertising. And so they should. However, as lamentable as such appeals are, they pale when compared to what Johnson-Cartee and Copeland call *sewage* or *dirty politics*—"deliberate misrepresentations, half-truths, lies, or innuendos that smear a candidate's political record or personal qualifications for office."[40] Most political advertising does not fall under the rubric of "sewage politics."

Ads that contain exaggerated or misleading claims fall between the cracks. They are legitimate persuasion, but they do raise ethical issues. When ads contain such themes, it is the job of the news media to point out the distortions to the public. Adwatches have evolved as a method to accomplish this goal. Research indicates that adwatches can reduce the impact of misleading attack ads, provided that steps are taken to make certain that the corrections overwhelm the corrosive commercial.

Perhaps the greatest ethical issue involved in advertising is the age-old question of money and the corrupting influence money exerts on politics. This is not a problem with political advertising per se, but it gets tied up with political spots inasmuch as advertising is a major campaign expenditure. There are a variety of perspectives on this issue, as noted earlier.

One point of view emanates from conservative political theory. According to this view, the best solution is to leave well enough alone. Conservatives point out that the courts have consistently ruled against placing limits on what individuals or parties spend to advance their political cause. This is the essence of political freedom, conservatives emphasize; it is wrong to try to infringe on people's ability to spend money to further their own political beliefs. Furthermore, conservatives note, $600 million spent on the presidential election takes on a different meaning when one considers that the networks spend as much as $500 million to market fall television programming. Face it, conservatives note: advertising costs money.

While there is merit in this view, it has its shortcomings. The key problem is that money is not distributed equally—some groups have more of it than others, and with enormous sums of money comes the possibility of abuse. What, also, of candidates who have good ideas but no hope of advancing to square one because they can't raise money to pay for political ads?

Radicals take the opposite point of view. Government should regulate political advertising, they say. The United States should follow the example of Britain, where candidates are barred from advertising on television airwaves; only party committees are permitted to sponsor ads.[41] Furthermore, radical critics note, there is precedent for regulating certain types of ads, such as attack spots. Cigarette advertising was banned from television. Could one not argue that attack ads, while hardly cancer-producing substances, cause harm enough to the political soul to justify their regulation?

The radical proposal is fraught with problems. First, the U.S. is not Britain; in the United States, candidate-centered politics reigns. To ban candidate commercials would be to strike a dagger at the heart of free political speech. It would inhibit the type of rowdy political debate that the Founding Fathers (in their more philosophical moments) endorsed and that is protected by the First Amendment. Second, it is ridiculous to talk of regulating attack ads. Why restrict negative spots, one might ask, when they contain more issue information than positive ads? What is wrong with legitimate attacks on the opponent's issue positions? Where's the evidence that negative ads cause irreparable harm?

The third proposal, put forth by liberals, steers clear of extreme measures, but instead argues for a host of modest reforms. Suggestions include: (a) making it easier for candidates who are unfairly attacked to appeal their case to government regulatory bodies; (b) requiring that the networks review all political ads (a policy followed in the case of product advertising); (c) encouraging television stations to charge more money for negative spots; and (d) tightening federal laws governing disclosure of the sources of campaign money, even banning contributions that are not fully disclosed.[42]

These suggestions have merit, but they too are not without problems. First, when the public is complaining about "too much government," do we really want to increase the role that government plays in another aspect of political life? Second, is it wise to have the broadcast networks approving—and possibly censoring—paid political speech? Third, why should we penalize issue-oriented negative spots and reward misleading positive ones?

The final suggestion, regarding tightening federal disclosure laws, offends conservatives who abhor federal regulation. Indeed, one of the drawbacks of the plan, as proponents Larry Sabato and Glenn Simpson note, is that "the rules would drag a huge number of politically active but relatively inconsequential players into the federal regulatory framework."[43] To make certain that small players like local church groups don't get taken to court for publishing a strongly worded editorial in their newsletters, Sabato and Simpson argue that a threshold of $25,000 to $50,000 be established. If a group doesn't contribute this much money to a political campaign, it does not have to do the busywork of filing papers disclosing its financial role in the election.

An advantage of tighter disclosure laws is that they would reveal how much money lobbying organizations such as unions, trial lawyers, the Christian Coalition, and the National Organization for Women give to political campaigns. Presently, it is difficult to know how much these groups have contributed to campaigns. The proposal for stronger disclosure laws would not prevent such groups from sponsoring independent political spots (nor should it), but it would at least allow the public to know just where all the millions of campaign contributions are coming from.

When all is said and done, political advertising remains a complex, uneasy persuasion. A many-headed beast, it is primarily persuasive in nature, but also has educational dimensions; it can be deceptive or informative, is usually superficial, but is technically capable of being as detailed and thought-provoking as the market will allow. It remains, as Diamond and Bates note, "a problematic art," one that ultimately will reflect and refract the worst and the best of American culture.

KEY ISSUES

Limited Effects

Learning from Ads

Agenda-Setting

Negative Advertising Effects

Countering Negative Ads

Inoculation

Adwatches

Ethics and Political Ads

Money and Political Spots

DISCUSSION QUESTIONS

1. Is there something awry when candidates for the presidency of the United States must advertise themselves in 30-second spots? Or do advertisements represent a reasonable way for candidates to communicate with the electorate?

2. Are negative political spots deceptive? If so, how?

3. Conservatives say that in a free-enterprise society, there should be no limits placed on how much candidates can spend to get elected. Do you agree?

21

Debates: Formats and Strategies

On October 6, 1996, two celebrity contestants known to the television viewing audience as Clinton and Dole took their seats. The stage was lit and cameras rolled. The emcee announced the rules of this year's presidential debating game and then the contestants took it away.

It is tempting to view presidential debates as game shows. Like game shows, debates require contestants to compete for a prize (the presidency); they also feature nationally famous emcees and are governed by television entertainment values.[1] But debates are more than game shows: They are high stakes verbal battles for the presidency of the United States, exercises in political advocacy, and national dialogues about issues of the day. Moreover, political debates are rooted in the American experience. As Kathleen Jamieson and David Birdsell note, "The American political system grew up with debate. Colonial assemblies debated revolution, the Constitutional Convention debated the Constitution, and Congress debated the law."[2] In early America, debate was seen also as a way of educating young people, developing intellectual skills, and enlightening the populace.

Unquestionably, the most famous debates in American political history were between Abraham Lincoln and Stephen Douglas. So much has been made of the Lincoln–Douglas debates that we tend to forget several basic facts: The debates occurred not in a campaign for the presidency, but for a Senate seat from Illinois; there were seven debates in all; the debates were politically charged events (with both candidates campaigning for moderate antislavery Democratic voters); and Stephen Douglas ended up winning the election, only to lose to Lincoln in the presidential race 2 years later.

The Lincoln–Douglas debates were unique in American history. They centered on the issue of slavery, and the two debaters articulated strikingly different positions on the issue. Douglas favored popular sovereignty, the notion that the residents of a region had the right to decide if they wished to continue or abolish slavery; Lincoln argued that slavery was morally wrong and incongruent with the ideals of the Founding Fathers. Both Lincoln and Douglas used elaborate arguments and evidence; their appeals revealed a respect for the audience's intellect. They discussed issues and confronted one another. They partook in debates in the true sense of the word.[3]

Some scholars argue that since Lincoln–Douglas we have only had "counterfeit debates."[4] None of the presidential debates (from 1960 through 1996) have satisfied the core quality of a debate: verbal confrontation on a specific proposition. And yet for all their shortcomings, debates represent one of the best opportunities the electorate has to watch its presidential contenders in action, discussing issues and ideas.

Debates are spectacular combinations of entertainment and substance, showmanship and argumentation, image and issue. They are complex, intriguing, and important aspects of the presidential campaign. This chapter introduces presidential debates, examining their functions and formats, and the candidates' rhetorical strategies. Chapter 22 discusses the impact, controversies, and policy aspects of presidential debates.[5]

OVERVIEW

Debates serve important functions for candidates, the electorate, and the larger political system. These functions run at cross-purposes with one another. Notably, what may serve the interests of a presidential candidate may not necessarily advance the larger goals of civic education and public discussion. Presidential debates, it must be remembered, do not take place in a vacuum; they do not occur in rarefied academic settings. On the contrary, they occur in the loud and raucous context of a presidential campaign. They are first and foremost *political events*.

From candidates' perspective, the purpose of debates is "to win over undecided voters, to reinforce voters who have already made a decision concerning whom to vote for, and to change the minds of those who are willing to reconsider their initial judgments concerning which candidate seems more fit to serve as president."[6] Candidates, as Sidney Kraus notes, "are not interested in educating the public or in arriving at truth, but in *winning* the election."[7]

Debates serve different functions for voters. They help them see what candidates are like as people, where they stand on the issues, and whether they share voters' values.

As an institutionalized mechanism by which candidates for the presidency communicate with the electorate, debates also perform important functions for the larger political system. They are exercises in civic education, dialogues that help the nation "work through" policy conundrums, and opportunities to reassess political values.[8]

Language plays a critical role in debates. It is through language and argumentation that candidates articulate their visions and approaches to presidential leadership. Voters compare the candidates on the basis of the words they utter and the arguments they select. The system benefits when presidential debaters give us new ways of looking at old problems and when they use language to inspire and uplift us. The system suffers when candidates trot out unworkable solutions of the past, obfuscate issues, and use language that insults or diminishes us.

The mass media influence the content and style of presidential debates. As a predominately visual medium, television pushes candidates to focus on their appearance and specifically to pay attention to such factors as sweat on the brow, the color of their shirts, and the height of the podium. The news media, which gravitate to covering the debate as a horse race, influence candidates' strategic choices, particularly before and after the debate when news coverage assumes importance.

Definitional Issues

We gain insight into the problems with contemporary presidential debates by looking at how scholars have defined the term, "debate." Critic J. J. Auer argued that a debate is "*(1) a confrontation, (2) in equal and adequate time, (3) of matched contestants, (4) on a stated proposition, (5) to gain an audience decision.*"[9] Using Auer's definition, it is clear that none of the televised presidential debates could be considered authentic debates. True, they were confrontations, debaters were given equal (though perhaps not adequate) time to answer questions, and all involved matched contestants, or candidates of approximately equal stature and ability. But in no case did the candidates debate a stated proposition, such as "The federal government should reduce Medicare costs by 2%" or "There should be a lifetime limit of 5 years for welfare payments to any American family" or "The U.S. should embark immediately on a program of nuclear disarmament." In addition, none of the debates was adjudicated by a group of judges or an audience, in the classical debate tradition.

Thus, Auer argues that what we have had are "counterfeit debates." Auer is correct that we have not had authentic debates. But not all scholars would pin the "counterfeit" label on them. Myles Martel defines a political campaign debate as "*the joint appearance by two or more opposing candidates, who expound on their positions, with explicit and equitable provisions for refutation without interruption.*"[10] This definition comes closer to capturing the essence of televised presidential debates, for they really are "joint appearances" or "discussions" or "face to face encounters." These encounters give the electorate an opportunity to hear candidates speak and clash on the issues, though as George Will pointedly observes, "to label such events 'debates' is to palter with the truth in a way that would not be tolerated in labeling a loaf of bread."[11]

BACKGROUND

In 1960, for the first and only time, Congress temporarily suspended Section 315 of the Federal Communications Act—the equal time provision—to permit the networks to broadcast the presidential debates on radio and TV. Had Congress not taken this step, CBS, ABC, and NBC would by law have been forced to give equal time opportunities to the 100 other candidates (ranging from the serious to the kooky) who were running for president.

After the four Kennedy–Nixon debates of 1960, there were no debates for 16 years. This was unfortunate because the nation could have greatly benefitted from hearing its presidential contenders debate the merits of the Vietnam War. But neither Lyndon Johnson nor Richard Nixon perceived that it was in their best interest to debate.

In 1976, the candidates reasoned that debates could advance their political agendas. Congress, though, showed no inclination to suspend the equal time provision. Happily, the League of Women Voters agreed to sponsor the debates. This sidestepped the Section 315 problem. The networks could cover the debates as they would any other bona fide news event.

1976 was important in other respects. It marked the first time that an incumbent president (Gerald Ford) participated in a debate. The conventional wisdom at that time was that incumbents should not participate in debates because debating foreign policy issues would put the nation's security at risk and because debates would grant the challenger too much credibility. Neither of these outcomes occurred in 1976, thereby paving the way for future participation by incumbents. 1976 also ushered in vice presidential debates.[12]

Debates were held again in 1980. For the first time, a third candidate—Independent John Anderson—was invited to participate. In 1981, the Federal Communications Commission cleared the way for sponsorship of future debates by ruling that debates could be televised as long as a qualified sponsor arranged the event.[13]

In 1980 and 1984, presidential debates were sponsored by the League of Women Voters. However, after a series of disagreements with the political parties on the format for debates, the League bowed out. In 1987, the two major political parties formed their own debate commission, arguing that debates would proceed more smoothly if the parties were involved directly in actually planning debates; the parties also hoped to have a greater influence on the formats used in debates. The bipartisan Commission on Presidential Debates sponsored presidential and vice presidential debates in 1988 and again in 1992 and 1996.

There is no legal requirement for candidates to participate in debates. However, a refusal to debate would cause such serious political repercussions that the question is not whether to debate but when and by what rules. The perception that candidates are dragging their feet on these latter issues can also have negative political consequences. In 1992, the Bush campaign haggled with the Commission on Presidential Debates on the format for debates, refusing as late as September to accept the Commission's proposals.

Bush's delay tactics hurt him politically. In East Lansing, Michigan, a young man dressed in a chicken costume, complete with yellow feathers and webbed feet, held up a sign, GEORGE BUSH IS A CHICKEN TO DEBATE. CHICKEN GEORGE. Shortly thereafter, Chicken Georges began showing up at places where the president was scheduled to speak. In Clarksville, Tennessee, Chicken Georges brandished signs like READ MY BEAK: DON'T BE A CHICKEN. DEBATE. Needless to say, the protests were great grist for the evening news, for they suggested that Bush was engaging in fowl play. Not enjoying the negative publicity, the Bush campaign hammered out an agreement with the presidential commission.

Nowadays, with highly visible alternative candidates like Ross Perot in the race, the Commission on Presidential Debates must decide whether to limit debates to the Democratic and Republican candidates, or whether to invite alternative party contenders as well. Those who favor limiting debates to the Democratic and Republican standard bearers argue that there is no limit to the number of alternative party candidates who would have to participate, and that this invites the possibility that the public must listen to weird and kooky candidates give positions that most Americans would rather not hear. "When we put two men in the arena, " columnist William Safire noted, "one of whom is sure to be elected, we force ourselves to face reality. Which one will I make president? That is the essence of the debate process."[14]

On the other hand, those who favor letting other candidates into the debates point out that the public is woefully dissatisfied with the two major parties, alternative candidates deserve to be heard, and that third party candidates would make things interesting, perhaps even bringing some new ideas into the fray.

There is also a political slant to all this. Some of those who favor limiting the debate to two candidates do not want a third candidate (like Ross Perot) to participate because they fear that a third debater might win over those who would otherwise support their candidate (e.g., Bob Dole in 1996). Some of those who favor opening up the process to alternative candidates hope that the third debater will do just what opponents fear—this is why the Clinton campaign lobbied for including Perot in 1996.

The Commission on Presidential Debates has established a number of criteria for inclusion in debates, in particular electability and standing in the polls. Given the large number of fringe candidates who run for the presidency, the Commission wanted to make certain that only serious presidential contenders participate in debates.

In 1992, it was a no-brainer that Ross Perot would be invited, given his popularity with the public. In 1996, it was more difficult, since Perot had considerably less support. In the end, the Commission barred Perot from debates, arguing that he had no realistic chance of winning the election or of even carrying a single state. The decision sparked controversy, with critics charging that the ruling restricted the range and scope of political debate, and defenders noting that it would be unfair to include Perot and exclude other, less affluent, presidential contenders. Perot eventually appeared on CNN's *Larry King Live* after the presidential debates. Other alternative party candidates from such factions as the Libertarian, Green, and Natural Law Parties also appeared on a special installment of King's program after the first debate.[15]

FORMATS

A major issue in presidential debates is the format, or ground rules by which debates are conducted. A variety of issues have presented themselves, including the following: Should the debate focus on a particular topic? Is a panel format useful and if so, which journalists should sit on the panel? Should follow-up questions be permitted? Would it be fruitful if nonjournalists were allowed to ask questions and if so, how should citizens be selected? Since candidates want to use the debate to their strategic advantage and because different formats can work to the advantage or disadvantage of particular candidates, format issues have themselves generated considerable debate.

Anyone who doubts that format decisions can have important political ramifications should consider the experience of Richard Nixon in 1960. The Nixon campaign believed that the audience for debates would build over time, and that, therefore, the last debate would draw the largest television audience. Based on this logic, Nixon agreed that foreign policy—his specialty area—should be the focus of the fourth debate, and domestic policy—his weak link—should be the topic of the first debate. But as Nixon later acknowledged, "when the debates were held, at least 20 million more people listened to and watched the first than any of the others, including the fourth and final appearance. I turned in my best performance before the smallest audience."[16] The first debate turned out to play a pivotal role in the election campaign. It was this debate in which Nixon appeared tired and worn, and failed to take the offensive.

Negotiations about format, therefore, have assumed considerable importance in the campaign. Summarizing Ronald Reagan's negotiations in 1980, Myles Martel noted, "It would be no exaggeration to compare the 1980 presidential debate process with an advanced game of chess. Nearly every move regarding the decisions to debate, formats, strategies, and tactics, and the execution of the debates themselves, was fraught with political implications."[17]

For many years, candidates preferred the so-called **press conference format**, where reporters ask each candidate a series of questions, queries that campaigns can typically anticipate prior to the debate. As Kraus notes, "Candidates are fearful about their ability to perform in a traditional debate, and they prefer to depend on familiar format with predictable audience response rather than risk anything unknown."[18] Although the sponsoring group, like the Commission on Presidential Debates, can push for a particular format, in the end the decision about which format to adopt rests with the candidates.

From 1960 through 1988, the most common debate format was one that resembled a press conference. Reporters posed questions to the candidates, time was set aside for rebuttal, and candidates gave closing statements. Opening statements were utilized in a handful of debates, and follow-up questions were permitted in about half the presidential encounters.

In recent years, different formats have emerged, in response to widespread dissatisfaction with press panels and the feeling that ordinary people have been shut out of the campaign process. Significantly, none of the three 1996 debates used the press conference format. This is likely to continue in the years to come.

One new format, **the town hall meeting debate,** features questions from the audience, typically undecided voters chosen by polling firms. In 1992, ABC's Carole Simpson moderated a town hall debate in Richmond, Virginia. Four years later, Jim Lehrer of PBS moderated a town hall debate in San Diego.

A single moderator format dispenses with questions from the audience and reporters. Instead, the moderator asks questions of candidates and makes sure candidates abide by the rules. There are different types of single moderator debates. The 1992 vice presidential debate provided for a 5-minute discussion period during which candidates could question one another. In 1996, there was no such discussion period; instead, each candidate was given 90 seconds to respond to the interviewer's question, the opponent received 60 seconds for rebuttal, and the first candidate had another 30 seconds to reply.

Assessment.   Each of the formats for debates has strengths and weaknesses. The press conference format, which features questions from journalists, guarantees that panelists will be experienced and knowledgeable about politics. Unfortunately, journalists have often asked argumentative and accusatory questions in an effort to "trap" candidates and perhaps to show off their own intellects. Such questions can be less than useful in helping voters ferret out candidates' positions on the issues or in generating dialogue between debaters. In addition, as Susan Hellweg and her colleagues note, journalists "have frequently been guilty of asking multiple questions within the framework of a single question, making it difficult for a candidate to respond."[19] When reporters ask long, complicated questions, candidates tend not to answer the questions particularly well, either because they forget the question or, alternatively, because they take advantage of the opportunity to evade difficult parts of the question.[20]

The main virtue of the town hall meeting format is that it brings ordinary people into the political process. Rather than putting the media elite on center stage once again, it gives citizens the chance to question candidates. As one voter observed, "I think that's very important because so many of us felt like we don't have a say so."[21]

Unfortunately, ordinary people don't always ask good questions. Harking back to 1992, Robert Friedenberg asks, "What public interest was served by hearing Bush respond to the question, 'Could we cross our hearts; it sounds silly here, but could we make a commitment? You know, we're not under oath at this point, but could you make a commitment to the citizens of the United States to meet our needs and we have many, and not yours? Again, I have to repeat that, it's a real need, I think, that we all have.'"[22] In addition, the town hall meeting debate does not provide for follow-up questions, which can force interesting answers out of candidates.

Yet for all of its shortcomings, the town hall debate is a real winner with voters. Most people like it because it puts ordinary people in touch with candidates. Although the format resembles a talk show more than a debate, it does not seem to have led to a reduction in issue-based arguments. Quite the contrary. Fearing a negative reaction from voters, candidates work hard to provide cogent answers to voters' questions and treat questioners with respect.

The final format—which relies on a single moderator to ask the questions— reduces the chaos of journalists throwing question after question at candidates, and theoretically allows for follow-up questions, unlike the town meeting style debate. A problem with single moderator debates surfaced in 1992, when the discussion period turned into a free-for-all, and the moderator lost control. Provided the person in charge maintains control over the debate, single moderator formats can allow for a reasonable discussion of issues.

There is no perfect format. By using a variety of modalities, one can ensure that different constituents' needs are taken into account, and that candidates have the opportunity to excel in the format that suits their style best. This is not to say that contemporary debates always provide a high-level discussion of issues or that candidates always employ elaborate Lincoln–Douglas-style arguments. Candidates duck some questions and reinterpret others to appeal to target audiences. This is endemic in presidential debates.

RHETORICAL STRATEGIES

Debates are like advanced games of chess, observed Myles Martel, who helped Reagan prepare for the 1980 debate. Like chess games, presidential debates require the use of sophisticated and combative strategies. But the weaponry of debates, unlike chess, is words. Candidates use words and argumentative strategies to dominate the debate agenda and polish their images. Both presidential and vice presidential debaters are preoccupied with these goals. Although the stakes in vice presidential debates are considerably lower than in presidential encounters, vice presidential debates have emerged as important because they provide a means of testing the mettle of the person-who-would-be-president, and of shaping perceptions of the two-person team. Presidential and vice presidential debate strategies can be divided into three categories: predebate tactics, rhetorical strategies employed in the debate, and postdebate media strategies.

Predebate Strategies

No candidate enters a debate cold. Candidates spend days reviewing issues and preparing strategies. They rehearse speeches and try out one-liners. They participate in mock debates, with other politicians frequently standing in for the opponent.

In 1980, campaign staff members coached Ronald Reagan, telling him what to expect from President Jimmy Carter and how he might counteract Carter's strategies. The staffers urged that Reagan employ the following tactics:

1. Keep the debate focused as much as possible on Carter's record.
2. Show righteous indignation in responding to (a) Carter's attacks or innuendos that you are dangerous and (b) attacks directed at your California credentials.
3. Humor or a confident smile can also disarm Carter when he thinks he's got you where he wants you.
4. When Carter is speaking—especially when he is attacking you—look at him or take notes.
5. Wherever possible, weave your major theme into your responses: "Jimmy Carter has had his chance and has blown it ... I offer promise—hope."[23]

Reagan put these strategies into effect and turned in a deft and memorable performance in the October debate.

Another focus of predebate strategies is appearance and nonverbal behaviors. Ever since the first debate of 1960, when a tanned and athletic John F. Kennedy overwhelmed a sickly, sweaty, and half-slouched Richard

Nixon, campaign staffers have been attentive to the way candidates look and carry themselves in presidential debates.

In some elections, image consultants have given consideration to the height of the candidates, worrying that the shorter candidate looked less presidential. To adjust for the advantage that is believed to accrue to the taller candidate, consultants for the more diminutive contender leave no stones unturned. Geraldine Ferraro, the Democratic vice presidential candidate in 1984, recalls that:

> Nothing was overlooked by the two campaigns, down to the tiniest detail. My *height* compared to Bush's *was going to be a disadvantage for me*. He's over six feet. I'm five feet four inches. The Democrats didn't want him to be looking down on me or, more important, me looking up at him. Over Republican objections, we had a gently inclining ramp built out of the same material as the floor covering so that as I took my place behind the podium I would be closer to the same height as Bush without having to step up on anything.[24]

The final aspect of predebate strategizing involves manipulation of expectations. Realizing that the press will evaluate the debate in terms of who won, candidates try to lower expectations of their performance. They are particularly prone to do this when they face an opponent whose debating skills outclass their own. For example two weeks before the first Dole–Clinton debate, Dole campaign managers began deliberately poor-mouthing their man. "Surely everybody in America knows Bill Clinton is the greatest debater since Benjamin Disraeli," a Dole aide said, hoping to reduce expectations to the point that any Dole performance would count as a victory.[25] As in the presidential primaries, candidates hope to claim a victory of sorts if they exceed predebate expectations. It isn't clear this strategy works. Moreover, it *can* backfire.

Walter Mondale greatly exceeded expectations in the first presidential debate of 1984 by winning the battle of the postdebate polls. Mondale's performance raised the ante for him in the second debate. He failed to meet these expectations; at the same time, Reagan easily exceeded the lowered expectations that followed his disappointing performance in the first encounter. Already leading Mondale by a wide margin in the polls, Reagan's performance in the second debate helped put the election out of reach.

Debate Strategies

Candidates employ a host of rhetorical strategies during debates. It is helpful to review these techniques, giving examples from classic and contemporary presidential debates.

A first strategic goal of presidential debaters is to articulate a vision or express an overarching theme. Candidates use their opening and closing remarks to express this theme, and rely on their answers to specific questions to reinforce it.[26] Successful debaters realize that the televised encounter is not a debate in the classic sense, but an opportunity to create an image of themselves as experienced leaders prepared to deal with the crisis that (they suggest) faces America during the year they are running for election.

During the first debate of 1960, John F. Kennedy used his opening statement to articulate a vision (the need to get America moving again) and to create an image of himself as a bold and active leader. Using a series of verbal parallelisms (e.g., "I'm not satisfied to have 50% of our steel mill capacity unused, I'm not satisfied when many of our teachers are inadequately paid"), he articulated his displeasure with American domestic policies. Drawing on the experiences of Abraham Lincoln and Franklin D. Roosevelt and frequently using the first person pronoun "I" when suggesting what should be done to ameliorate America, Kennedy successfully set the tone and agenda for the debate.[27]

Fortunately, for Kennedy, Richard Nixon, counseled to erase his "assassin" image, acquiesced. He accepted Kennedy's theme of moving ahead, refrained from challenging JFK's criticism of eight years of Republican leadership, and chose not to present an alternative vision of America. Nixon, much to his chagrin, turned out looking weak and tepid, less the active, experienced presidential contender than the deferent and agreeable challenger. Beginning in his opening statement and continuing throughout the debate, Kennedy (calling on principles of crisis rhetoric) asserted that the nation was in the throes of a crisis and suggested that he was uniquely qualified to lead the nation in these troubled times. By failing to challenge Kennedy's framework, Nixon allowed Kennedy to define the terms of the debate.[28]

Three and a half decades later, in the 1996 presidential debates, Bill Clinton skillfully used the opening statements to summarize his accomplishments and to sketch his vision for the country. Using a classic incumbent strategy, he emphasized that his administration had delivered on its promises in the areas of jobs, deficit reduction, and welfare reform. He then tried to give voters a reason to vote for him, emphasizing that there was more work to be done and that he would help America "build that bridge to the 21st century."

By contrast, Bob Dole stressed that he empathized with Americans' problems and that his word was his bond. However, he failed to articulate a vision for the future. As a *New York Times* editorial observed, Dole "failed to provide the consistent, detailed narrative that would convince swing voters" of his positions. Dole "tries hard and means well," the conservative *Weekly Standard* observed, "but he does not weave his facts into a compelling and gripping narrative."[29]

Presidential candidates also use closing statements to articulate broad themes and create images of leadership. In his debate with Jimmy Carter in 1980, Ronald Reagan presented an optimistic vision of America, emphasizing his desire to lead a crusade "to take government off the backs of the great people of this country and turn you loose again to do those things that I know you can do so well."

Reagan invited voters to ask themselves a series of now-famous questions: "Are you better off than you were four years ago? Is it easier for you to go and buy things in stores than it was four years ago? Is America as respected throughout the world as it was?" Inviting people to answer these questions in the negative and to agree with him that America was not better off in 1980 than in 1976, Reagan offered people a reason to reject Carter and to vote for Ronald Reagan. Carter, by contrast, asked Americans to join him in a partnership, a plea that, given the problems the nation faced in 1980, seemed inappropriate. Indeed, it "could have been read as a request for assistance, suggesting implicitly that the job was too big for him."[30]

Besides expressing an overarching theme, *presidential debaters seek to identify themselves with the main aspirations of the electorate.* Successful debaters locate the qualities and characteristics that the public is looking for in a president and attempt to personify these traits.[31] A classic example was Jimmy Carter who, in 1976, recognized that in the aftermath of Watergate, the public was looking for a president who personified trustworthiness and honesty. Carter used words and arguments to emphasize that he was a man who embodied these traits, effectively contrasting himself with the incumbent, Gerald Ford.

Sixteen years later in 1992, with the electorate concerned that government had lost touch with ordinary people, Bill Clinton sought to demonstrate that he understood voters' concerns and anxieties. In an answer to a question posed by a woman named Marissa Hall, he demonstrated an ability to connect with the audience.

Ms. Hall asked the three candidates, "How has the national debt personally affected each of your lives?" The question was unclear and hard to fathom. Perot answered it directly, relating the question to himself and his background. Bush had trouble appreciating the personal import of the query, at one point confessing, "I'm not sure I get it. Help me with the question and I'll try to answer it."[32]

Clinton, who was at his best in the television talk show format, took the bull by the horns when it was his turn to respond. He turned, Oprah-style, to Ms. Hall, and asked her gently to tell him "how it affected you again? You know people who lost their jobs and lost their homes?" He continued to show empathy with the questioner, saying that "In my state, when people lose their jobs, there's a good chance I'll know them by name." He went on to expound on the economic problems that were ailing the country, and laid the blame on the policies of Presidents Reagan and Bush.

Attempts to personify a particular characteristic will not influence the audience if the characteristic is not salient to the electorate in a given election year. In the 1996 debates, Bob Dole portrayed himself as honest and reliable, trying to contrast himself on this score with President Clinton. His appeals did not take hold, largely because voters seemed to be already aware of Clinton's flaws in the character area, but were willing to ignore them, either because they were satisfied with Clinton's performance as president or realized that perfection is to be expected of saints, not presidents.

A third strategy candidates use is to go negative, criticizing the opponent's ideas or trying to cast aspersions on the opponent's leadership style, competence, or character. Criticizing the opponent's position is a classic debate strategy. Presidential debaters typically make issues the centerpiece of their attacks.

Candidates use a variety of negative techniques, including lambasting the policies of the opponent's party, or, if their adversary is the president, arguing that the president's policies have failed. Bob Dole did this repeatedly in 1996, accusing Clinton of not providing forceful leadership to curb drug use.

Presidential debaters also draw sharp contrasts between their positions and those of their adversary, as George Bush did in 1988 against Michael Dukakis. Charging that Dukakis was "a card-carrying member" of the American Civil Liberties Union ("a shorthand sobriquet for a card-carrying Communist"), Bush linked Dukakis with supposedly unpopular liberal policies and tried to suggest that his own values were much closer to those of mainstream America.[33] Bush's arguments were hardly elaborate or exemplary, but they worked; they tarnished Dukakis by implying that he was out of the cultural mainstream.

Candidates also can attack their rival directly, suggesting that the opponent is "dangerous," as Jimmy Carter did against Ronald Reagan in 1980. However, like assaultive negative advertising, these attacks can backfire or can be easily deflected by an opponent. Reagan deflected Carter's attacks by telling the audience that "I know the president's supposed to be replying to me, but sometimes, I have a hard time in connecting what he's saying with what I have said or what my positions are. I sometimes think he's like the witch doctor that gets mad when a good doctor comes along with a cure that'll work."

Debaters also use Q&A and rebuttal periods to counter their opponents' arguments and to press their own positions. Candidates frequently use statistics and evidence to bolster their arguments, as Perot did in 1992, communicating credibility with his "Step One, Step Two" introduction of his proposals. They also use pointed rhetorical questions, as Al Gore did in the 1992 vice presidential encounter, when he asked Dan Quayle, "How much longer will it take, Dan, for trickle-down economics to work?"

Like all debaters, good presidential debaters know how to use evidence and arguments to rebut their opponents' claims. If you go back and look at previous presidential debates, you find that the winning debater has effectively refuted the opposing candidates's arguments through such techniques as using evidence to point up weaknesses in the adversary's charges, identifying shortcomings in policies the opponent supports, suggesting that the opponent has misrepresented an important position, and even disarming the opposing candidate with humor.

Fourth, *candidates use a host of verbal and nonverbal persuasion tactics to maximize their credibility.* While not the most important weapons in candidates' rhetorical armor, vocal delivery, clever phrases, and nonverbal communication skills can enhance candidates' credibility. Debaters gain by speaking clearly and decisively, using one-liners strategically, and by effectively employing nonverbal communication techniques. Consider the case of the 1988 vice presidential debate.

In this debate, as Warren Decker notes, Democratic vice presidential nominee Lloyd Bentsen "handled the delivery aspects of his responses quite well. He appeared as the reasoned, self-assured, experienced person in the debate who was fully capable of being president."[34] Bentsen also showed an uncanny knowledge of how to use pauses for maximum effect. When his opponent, Senator Dan Quayle, compared himself favorably to John F. Kennedy, Bentsen replied slowly and somberly, his words gathering momentum as they were uttered:

> Senator, I served with Jack Kennedy. (Pause.) I knew Jack Kennedy. (Pause.) Jack Kennedy was a friend of mine. (Longer Pause.) Senator, you're no Jack Kennedy.[35]

Bentsen's attack broke up the audience and was played over and over again on network news programs, whose producers rejoiced in the availability of such a captivating sound bite. Candidates like Bentsen are acutely aware that the news will replay memorable sound bites, and they strive to develop one-liners before the debate.

Cognizant of the power of TV, consultants recommend that candidates maintain eye contact when expressing indignation at their opponents, that they not look downward because this suggest a lack of confidence, and that they smile at appropriate times because smiling simultaneously projects confidence and likability. The conventional wisdom is that smiling helped Reagan and Kennedy, and that Dukakis and 1984 Democratic vice president candidate Geraldine Ferraro were hurt by their "chilly demeanors."[36] (see Box 21.1: Emoting in '88) Consultants also believe that adroit use of other stage tactics, like offering a handshake to opponents, can enhance perceptions of power and credibility.

During the first 1996 debate, with voters tired of mean-spirited campaigning, both Clinton and Dole almost tripped over each other, rhetorically speaking, to convey the impression that they were nice guys, not candidates who would rip each other apart to get elected. Each complimented the other, with Clinton even saying that "You can probably tell we like each other." Each tried hard not to scowl when the opponent attacked him. They smiled a good bit during the first debate. At the end of the debate, both candidates and their wives shook hands. It was a nice moment for democracy. It was a also a moment that had been carefully scripted, for in 1996 both campaigns recognized that it was preferable to come off genteel and friendly than aggressive and feisty.

Like it or not, nonverbals are a particularly important factor in televised town hall debates, during which candidates are judged by their ability to connect with audience members. Both Bob Dole and Bill Clinton worked hard to do this during the 1996 town hall debate, with both calling the questioners by their first names. Clinton was in his element in this format, as he looked questioners in the eye, walked over to them, and at one point even asked for a show of hands to see how many members of the audience were enrolled in managed care health programs.

One of the recurring issues in political communication research is the extent to which nonverbal communication carries the day in presidential debates. I discuss this issue in the next chapter; but suffice it to say that nonverbal displays of warmth and the more general ability to connect with audiences do matter in presidential debates. However, smiles and deft maneuvers on stage will not cause most debate viewers to view a candidate positively unless these nonverbal devices are coupled with cogent arguments and persuasive rhetoric.

Summary. Candidates who offer the most compelling vision for the future, make the most persuasive linkage with the electorate's anxieties and aspirations, rebut the opponent's arguments most forcefully, and convey the most respect for audience questions ordinarily win debates. Although nonverbal communication matters, the main element of debate is argumentation—coherent statements presented in favor of one's candidacy. Interestingly, there is some evidence that candidates offer more reasons to support their claims in debates than they do in more pedestrian campaign situations. Debaters also call on issues to a considerable extent when they articulate arguments and rebuttals.[37] Indeed, rhetoricians believe that candidates "win" debates not because they look pretty, but because they argue effectively and persuasively. Candidates have a host of rhetorical goals, some revolving around the presentation of issues, others around the creation of images. However, issues and images ultimately meld into one another: Candidates use issues to convey images of leadership; and the positive images they create of themselves become issues for voters to mull over as they process the campaign.

Postdebate Strategies

After the debate is over, news media and (to some extent) public attention focuses on the quintessentially American question of who won. Candidate consultants, or handlers as they are pejoratively called, try to spin the outcome of the debate so that it favors their candidate. In interviews with reporters, they argue that their candidate did better than expected, attempt to put the best face on defeat, or sing the candidate's praises after polls show he or she won the debate. As an example, after the first presidential debate of 1996, the Clinton camp had, as one reporter put it, a "grove of little red signs, perched at the ends of sticks to mark and identify each Clinton spokesman for reporters swarming for comment."[38]

It is all a game; the consultants know they are hyping the candidate's performance, the press knows it, and voters know it too. But given the power that the news can have in shaping interpretations of debate outcomes in close elections, candidates feel they have no choice but to spin the debate as skillfully as they can.

CONCLUSIONS

Presidential debates have become part of the national political landscape, a veritable electoral institution. Debates serve a variety of functions for candidates, voters, and the larger political system. Some of these functions run at cross-purposes with one another. Candidates debate to get elected, but the strategies they employ may not always be those that encourage thoughtful discussion on the part of voters. In fact, the term "debate" is a misnomer since, contrary to the classical definition, presidential candidates do not discuss a proposition to gain an audience decision. Nonetheless, debates do provide voters with an opportunity to see and hear candidates from the major political parties discuss issues, or at least those issues that are safe to bring up and are already on the public agenda. Furthermore, debates let candidates tell their own stories, in their own words, free of the interpretations offered by reporters and the spin applied by campaign managers.

Over the years, a variety of debate formats have evolved, including the press conference, town hall meeting, and single moderator. Each has advantages and disadvantages, and at the present time, the American public seems to prefer a variety of formats for debates.

Finally, debates are nothing if not attempts at advocacy, high stakes battles in public persuasion. Candidates employ a variety of rhetorical strategies, emphasizing issues, images, verbal arguments, and nonverbal communication techniques. Candidates tailor their speeches to fit the requirements of television, compressing their oratory to fit predetermined time limits, and paying special attention to how they look and how they speak.

If Lincoln and Douglas were to step off a time machine and view our contemporary debates, no doubt they would be shocked at the spectacle and the image-making aspects of current presidential encounters. The short answers and one-liners would amaze them, men who grew up in an era of stump speeches and long-winded political oratory. They also, one assumes, would be grateful that the nation that went to war over the issue they debated was still around nearly 150 years later, still grappling with the problem of how to mix image with issue, showmanship with argumentation, and entertainment with substance.

Box 21.1

Emoting in '88

Likability and showing emotion seemed to be the keys to the second presidential debate of 1988. The key moment in that debate came when CNN anchor Bernard Shaw asked Democratic nominee Michael Dukakis this question: "Governor, if Kitty Dukakis were raped and murdered, would you favor an irrevocable death penalty for the killer?"

Dukakis answered without hesitating. "No, I don't Bernard," he replied. "And I think you know that I've opposed the death penalty during all of my life."

Public and press reaction to Dukakis's reply was swift and harsh. He had shown no emotion, critics said. Couldn't he have at least showed some emotion when asked what he'd do if his own wife had been raped and killed? He had failed the "warm and fuzzy test," television commentators observed. However, journalist Roger Simon took a different perspective in his book on the 1988 campaign.[39] In the excerpt below he raises some intriguing philosophical questions:

People across the country would express outrage over Dukakis' calm and cool answer. Yet was Dukakis' position that outrageous? (Ted Kennedy does not favor the death penalty for Sirhan Sirhan, the slayer of his brother Robert, and would not have favored it for Lee Harvey Oswald, the slayer of his brother John.) Dukakis believed that people of principle make principled decisions. And they stick to them. That is what integrity is about.

O.K., the critics said, but even if Dukakis didn't favor the death penalty, couldn't he have shown a little emotion in answering the question? After all, Dukakis' handlers had said before the debate that they were preparing him for a "Willie Horton type" question. And they had written an "emotional" answer for Dukakis. It was one in which he talked about his father, a doctor for fifty-two years, who, at age seventy-seven, had been beaten, bound and gagged by an intruder looking for drugs. And then he would talk about his elder brother, Stelian, who had been killed by a hit-and-run driver in 1973. It was an answer in which Dukakis said he knew what it was like to be a victim of crime.

But when the time came to give the answer, Dukakis did not. Instead, he told the truth. Dispassionately, he expressed his true feelings. And he was savaged for it. He was savaged for giving a sincere and unemotional answer instead of giving an insincere and emotional one.

But if he had given the prepared answer, would that really have made him any more warm? Or would it have just made him a better performer, a better actor? If he had given his prepared response, the people, press included, would have praised him. He would have been congratulated for delivering his lines as written, just as George Bush did.

By the final presidential debate, we were demanding the road show. Fool us, we were saying. Trick us. Fake a little sincerity for us.

KEY ISSUES

Defining Debates

Press Conference Format

Town Hall Meeting Debate

Single Moderator Format

Predebate Strategies

Debate Strategies

Postdebate Tactics

DISCUSSION QUESTIONS

1. Do town hall meeting debates provide an informative discussion of issues? Or are they just prime-time talk shows?

2. What are the arguments, pro and con, for including third party candidates in presidential debates?

3. What are the main rhetorical strategies candidates use in debates? Which ones work best, in your view?

22

Debates: Impact and Controversies

Debates freeze the campaign. From the time the first debate approaches to the end of the last debate, candidate communications, press coverage, and polls focus heavily on debates, even revolving around them when elections are close. Presidential debates are election-year rituals, festive occasions—the high holy days of the presidential contest.[1]

In this chapter, I continue the examination of televised presidential debates by exploring their effects and the policy controversies that have surrounded them. Let's begin by looking at their impact.

DEBATE EFFECTS

Presidential and vice presidential debates attract huge national audiences

Tens of millions of Americans tune into presidential debates. The largest audience share was captured by the presidential debates of 1960: Over 100 million people watched at least some of the Kennedy–Nixon debates. Twenty years later, nearly 81 million people watched the Reagan–Carter debate. In 1992 the critical second presidential debate attracted nearly 70 million viewers.[2] The 1996 debates also attracted a huge national audience, easily dwarfing the number of people who tuned in to the Republican and Democratic party conventions. There is little doubt that debates attract more viewers than any other single campaign event.

Yet, as these statistics suggest, the size of the audience for debates has declined over time. In 1960 and 1976, approximately 90% of the public watched at least one of the presidential debates. However, in 1984, less than 50% of Americans watched Reagan and Mondale debate, and four years later, about 40% of the public viewed the Bush–Dukakis matchups.[3]

The number of debate viewers rose in 1992, reflecting voter interest in the unconventional 1992 election and then dropped in 1996, an election that captivated far fewer Americans. In 1992, 62 million people watched the first Bush–Clinton–Perot debate, compared to 46 million who viewed the first Dole–Clinton matchup in 1996.[4]

Attention to debates tends to be sporadic. Few voters watch an entire debate from start to finish, and still fewer watch all of the presidential and vice presidential debates in a given election campaign.[5] There are many reasons why voters do not closely attend to debates. Many peoples have made up their minds before debates begin, so they have little incentive to watch. Others find debates monotonous and feel that candidates give prefabricated answers to questions. Still others are apathetic and simply don't care which candidate wins the election.

Debates do reach a broader audience than nominating conventions and news interviews. Some debates have attracted the less politicized voters who ordinarily avoid watching news. This is an achievement. However, debates are most likely to attract those who are educated, interested in politics, and follow the campaign through other sources.[6]

Voters look positively upon presidential debates, but at the same time feel debates have some shortcomings

Voters watch debates for a variety of reasons, including to learn more about the candidates' issue positions, to judge what the candidates are like as people, and to fulfill their civic duty. People seem to believe that debates are useful. They report that they derive gratifications from watching presidential debates.[7] Furthermore, voters say that they like the town hall and single interviewer debates, provided that the moderator can control the discussion.[8]

Yet people are far from satisfied with debates. They feel that candidates skirt the issues. Their eyes glaze over when candidates begin throwing statistics at each other. By the time the last debate rolls around, after enduring a year-long campaign, voters are tired; who can blame them?

Voters become better informed about candidates' issue stands and personal qualities from watching presidential debates

There is abundant evidence that people learn from debates, just as they learn from political spots. Two decades ago, Arthur Miller and Michael MacKuen concluded from a national study of 1976 debate effects that "watching the debates increased the level of manifest information that all citizens had about the candidates regardless of their education, political involvement, or general information-seeking habits."[9] This conclusion remains true today. For example, viewers of the 1996 vice presidential debate were exposed to a spirited discussion of the pros and cons of Dole's 15% tax cut plan. Theory and research strongly suggest that exposure to the debate increased voters' understanding of where the candidates stood on the tax cut issue.

Voters are more likely to learn from debates when questions are posed clearly. The more clearly stated the question, the more likely it is that the candidate will answer the question in a way that voters can understand. Voter learning is also influenced by the ways in which candidates discuss the issues. When candidates offer lucid answers to questions, voters gain. When candidates obfuscate or go off on a tangent or start talking in generalities, voters are turned off, and learning is unquestionably reduced.

Debates help to solidify voters' attitudes, bonding together thoughts and feelings about the candidates into a more cohesive whole

Voters frequently have mixed feelings about candidates, even the candidate they support. Debates help promote higher levels of cognitive consistency among party identifications, issue stands, attitudes toward the candidates, and vote intentions.[10] By watching the debates, selectively interpreting information so that it is congruent with their biases, picking up new pieces of information, possibly mentally test-marketing the notion of voting for the other candidate, and readjusting their political schema after the debate has ended, voters "bond together" and solidify different affective strands of the vote decision. Thus, voters with a weak or even strong preference for one candidate at the beginning of the debate may find themselves feeling more committed at the end of the debate.

Since most voters frequently have their minds made up before debates take place, bonding effects are more politically consequential when they occur among undecided voters. Like other political messages, debates have their greatest persuasive impact on voters with weak initial attitudes—or at least on those wavering voters who are willing to rethink their initial judgments about which candidate seems more qualified to be president.

Debates can influence voters' perceptions of presidential candidates' character and competence. But the effects are complex

Candidates hope debates will improve their image with voters, and there is evidence that a positive performance in the debate can have just this effect. A lousy performance can lead to more negative evaluations of a candidate.[11]

Challengers gain simply by sharing the stage with the incumbent and also by turning in a credible performance that convinces wavering voters that the new kid on the block has what it takes to be president. The rub is that postdebate image gains are typically short-term, not enough to overcome a large deficit in the polls.

It is commonly believed that in televised debates, visual images overwhelm words, and that candidates who look good and perform well for the cameras will win debates, regardless of what they say.[12] There is no doubting that appearances matter in debates, and that candidates like Bill Clinton who can connect with audiences hold an upper hand. However, it is facile to believe that pictures overwhelm the words debaters speak. We can appreciate the complex interplay between visual and verbal images by turning back the clock and looking at two classic presidential debates: the first presidential encounter of 1960 and the Reagan–Carter debate of 1980.

A now-famous survey taken after the first 1960 debate reported that people who saw the debate on television thought Kennedy won and those who heard it on radio thought Nixon won.[13] Presumably, Kennedy's good looks and Nixon's 5-o'clock shadow combined to put Kennedy over the top among TV viewers, whereas Nixon's debating skills carried the day among radio listeners. However, if you go back and look carefully at the original study, you find that the margin was much closer than commonly believed: 54% of those who saw the debate on television called it a draw or declined to name a winner. Of those who were willing to call the debate, 28% said Kennedy won and 18% selected Nixon.[14]

Moreover, it is commonly believed that Nixon lost on TV because he looked sweaty and sickly. As some scholars have observed, you can turn the study around by suggesting that Kennedy lost on radio because listeners were turned off by his Boston accent.[15]

Furthermore, it is likely that the *combination* of Kennedy's words and pictures is what carried the day among television viewers. As noted earlier, Kennedy articulated a compelling vision for the country. Beginning with the opening statement and continuing throughout the debate, he forcefully argued his case that the country needed new leadership in the 1960s. Quite possibly, hearing the arguments and seeing Kennedy present them as he did reinforced the idea that this *was* an exciting and vigorous potential president.

Nixon, by contrast, seemed to lack a vision or overarching theme. He failed to offer a framework that tied together his answers and opening statement. Seeing Nixon squirm and flinch, in combination with his rhetorical failures, may have raised doubts in the minds of undecided voters.

Thus, television was important in the first presidential debate, but it was not the simple "visual trumps verbal," "good looks beat bad looks" thesis that often gets played up in popular discussions of the Kennedy–Nixon encounter. Instead, it was a complex combination of words and pictures, and the ability of one candidate (Kennedy) to use the grammar of television to his advantage that accounted for his success in the first debate.

In a similar fashion, journalists argued that Reagan bested Carter in the 1980 debate because his "superior style," honed over the course of a long acting career, trumped Carter's stronger and more intelligent message. This, too, oversimplifies the effects of televised presidential debates on image assessments.

It is true that Reagan's visual appearance helped him. As one reporter noted, "Reagan's face, as seen on TV, is expressive. The president doesn't just speak with words. He speaks with a frown, a smile, or an expression of 'aw shucks.'"[16] Carter, by contrast, was less visually expressive on television. To be sure, Reagan's smile and ability to nonverbally deflect Carter's criticisms worked to his advantage. But there was more to Reagan's success than this.

Rhetorical scholars have shown that "Reagan's debating was superior in substance, as well as in style."[17] Reagan articulated an optimistic vision of America and identified himself with the main aspirations of the electorate. Carter replied only once to Reagan's attacks; Reagan replied to Carter's criticisms on 15 occasions.[18] As Kurt Ritter and David Henry note, "Reagan won the debate because he executed an effective debating strategy that combined sustained argumentation with an appealing style of presentation."[19] The head worked with the heart. The mind and body were in sync. Viewers noticed and this, coupled with the resonance of Reagan's message in the tumultuous year of 1980, put Reagan over the top in viewers' minds.

Fast forward to recent debates and you get the same message. The warmer, more handsome candidate does not always win. Certainly, Ross Perot would not qualify as a "warm and fuzzy" television-age candidate. But polls showed he won the first presidential debate of 1992.

Thus, the impact of debates on voter perceptions is complicated, with both visual and verbal information influencing voters. Unquestionably, candidates must know how to present themselves effectively on television. But more than pretty pictures are required for success in presidential debates.

Presidential debates can shape campaign dynamics

A big debate victory by a candidate, followed by good press and highly publicized gains in postdebate opinion polls, can propel a candidate forward. Experts believe that debate victories provided momentum to John F. Kennedy in 1960, Ronald Reagan in 1980, and Walter Mondale in 1984. Vice presidential debates have also influenced campaign dynamics. The Democrats gained momentum in 1976 following Walter Mondale's victory in the 1976 vice presidential debate, during which he responded forcefully to Republican vice presidential candidate Bob Dole's acerbic comment that World War II, Korea, and Vietnam had been "Democrat wars." It should be noted, however, that lopsided victories in vice presidential debates usually have fewer effects on voters than do big wins in presidential encounters.

There is no evidence that presidential debates have changed the outcome of an election, although, to be sure, many campaign specialists believe that Kennedy would not have won the 1960 election had he not defeated Nixon in the first presidential debate. Without question, debate victories provide a burst of momentum, and losses unnerve candidates and their staffs. But it is only when elections are close that debate momentum really matters. When one candidate leads the other by a large margin in the polls, as was the case in 1996, the impact of debates on campaign dynamics is minimal.

Postdebate news coverage can influence voters' perceptions of who won the debate

Traditionally, news coverage of debates has focused on the horse race and strategic game. Postdebate coverage frequently focuses on who won the debate, polls, and interviews with campaign aides. There is strong evidence that news verdicts of who won influence voter assessments.[20] Consider the case of the second debate between President Gerald Ford and Jimmy Carter in 1976.

A panelist asked Ford a question regarding the relationship between the United States and the Soviet Union. After noting that his administration had been pursuing negotiations with the Soviet Union from a position of strength, Ford blundered, "There is no Soviet domination of Eastern Europe, and there never will be under a Ford administration." Carter, in his response, took the president to task for failing to appreciate how the Soviet Union continued to dominate and suppress the nations of Eastern Europe.

The gaffe, as it came to be known, was not immediately apparent to most voters. Polls conducted the night of the debate found that 44% of respondents thought Ford had done a better job, 43% gave the debate to Carter, and the remainder was undecided. But over the course of the next day, things changed drastically, as the networks played and replayed Ford's comment and media commentators reminded voters that Ford had blundered, calling up memories of earlier Ford mishaps. Polls conducted between 5 p.m. and midnight the day after the debate showed how much difference a day can make: The verdict was now 62% Carter, 17% Ford.[21]

Although Ford's statement was factually incorrect and misleading, it was not the profound error of judgment that his opponents and journalists suggested that it was at the time. When you go back and read the transcript of this debate, you discover that what Ford had in mind was that *the people* of Poland, Rumania, and Yugoslavia did not consider themselves dominated by the Soviet Union and that each country had its own territorial integrity. Clearly, the president *knew* that the countries of Eastern Europe were under Soviet control. He appeared to have gotten carried away by his own rhetoric, gone off on a tangent, and then blundered in his assertion about the political geography of Eastern Europe.

But the news media, determined to set things right, discussed Ford's mistake endlessly, in part because it resonated with the view of journalists that Ford, for all of his political acumen, was something of a bumbler. In fairness, it must be noted that Ford compounded his problems by refusing to acknowledge that he had made a mistake. "I can be very stubborn when I think I'm right," Ford later admitted, and "I just didn't want to apologize for something that was a minor mistake."[22]

Thus, news media coverage of the Ford gaffe (coupled with Ford's own ineptness in controlling the damage) caused opinions of Ford's performance in the debate to drop dramatically, which in turn influenced judgments of Ford's competence. The upshot of it all was that Ford lost ground at an important moment in the campaign, and Carter gained an upsurge of support.

Studies of news coverage of other debates have found similar evidence that news media verdicts influence voters' evaluations of the candidates. Viewing postdebate analyses on network television influenced voters' judgments of the candidates in 1988 and 1992, with coverage typically benefitting the candidate deemed by the media to have won the debate.[23]

After exhaustively studying news of presidential debates, communication scholars James Lemert, William Elliott, James Bernstein, William Rosenberg, and Karl Nestvold concluded that "The candidate evaluated most favorably during post-debate news commentary also showed in survey respondents' perceptions as the better performer in the debate."[24] The judgment that a candidate won the debate can favorably influence perceptions of the candidate's image and even nudge voters toward supporting that candidate, provided they already agree with some of his or her issue positions.

Unlike the press of Lincoln's and Douglas's time, which was filled with partisan commentary on the debates, today's news media focus more dispassionately on the question of who won, bringing the armamentarium of polls, pundits, and public opinion professionals to coverage of debates. The news looks for the memorable moment—Ford's fumble, Bentsen's one-liner, Bush's checking his wristwatch—to symbolize the debate. Interestingly, most people do not believe that news media verdicts influence their opinions. They assume that they are immune from news media effects. The research on news verdicts suggests that all of us can be influenced by press coverage, particularly when we are not following the election carefully or are confused by complexities or ambiguities in the debaters' arguments.

BALANCE SHEET

Presidential debates have been lauded and lambasted, venerated and vilified, extolled and excoriated. Proponents praise debates, pointing out that they "serve the majority of the electorate better than any other simple campaign communication device that attempts to present both the candidates' personalities and their positions on issues."[25] Opponents object, arguing that "Debates fail to reveal the candidates' qualifications for the presidency; personality and image of the candidates eclipse the discussion of issues; and the formats of debates make for glorified press conferences, contributing little that the voter cannot hear on the campaign trail."[26]

We have now had debates in seven presidential elections. What, on balance, do we make of this rowdy institution?

First, there is little question that voters learn from presidential debates. Debates offer voters a series of opportunities to compare the candidates, side by side, rather than as they appear on packaged television commercials, in mediated spots in the news, or in reporter-dominated news stories. Viewed from the narrow perspective of providing voters with a glimpse of the men and women who would be president, where they stand on the issues, and how they present themselves, debates get high marks.

Viewed from the perspective of civic education, debates fall short. The issues that are discussed in debates are those that have made it to the top of the public agenda, those that are considered "safe" to talk about in a mass public forum. You did not hear an honest discussion of how to cut Social Security or Medicare in the 1996 debates. You did not hear a thoughtful discussion of health care reform in 1992, or of how the U.S. should posture itself in a post-Cold War world in 1988. Debates focus on issues, but typically they just scratch the surface.

A second controversy focuses on whether the words debaters speak are overshadowed by stylistic and televisual considerations, like how candidates look and their style of speech on the small screen. According to critics, debates push "television communication skills" and candidates' personal characteristics to the foreground, which is a dysfunction since these are not the skills that are most central to effectively governing the United States.[27]

It is true that debates do make candidates' personal qualities more salient, yet another example of the personalization of American politics. It is not automatically apparent that this is a bad thing. As political scientists have long argued, it is perfectly rational to focus on a candidate's personal qualities when making up one's mind how to vote. The fact that debates offer voters a mechanism for judging candidates' personal qualities and communication skills (especially in an age of television) is an advantage, not a disadvantage, of debates.

As noted earlier, candidates do not win debates on the basis of their good looks or ability to look meaningfully into a camera. Voters are not fools. Candidates who impress the electorate do so because they have developed cogent arguments, have presented themselves convincingly, and have combined verbal and nonverbal communication skills in a persuasive manner.

Critics argue that by trying to package themselves for television, relying on consultants' advice, and applying principles of social psychology to their performances, candidates are adopting a crass, manipulative philosophy toward debates. But this assumes that debaters can manipulate the audience, an assumption that is open to serious question in light of the research discussed in this book. Furthermore, as Myles Martel notes:

> To put this issue in perspective, it might be helpful to ask this question: When a person seeking a job wears his best suit for the interview, attends more meticulously than usual to grooming needs, and demonstrates more poise, better listening habits and closer attention to what he says than usual, is he being unduly manipulative? Of course not. Job interviews are imbued with image-oriented rituals rooted in the applicant's needs for survival and success. Campaign debates, too, are forms of job interviews imbued with image-oriented rituals which we need to understand before passing judgment. In fact, as far back as 2500 years ago, Aristotle wrote that the obligation of a speaker is to acquire the "faculty or power of discovering in the particular case what are the available means of persuasion." It would be foolhardy then, for any politician not to subscribe to Aristotle's dictum which includes the need to adapt to whatever medium of communication is being used.[28]

The third—and most contemporary—issue surrounding presidential debates is whether they add to, or subtract from, the legitimacy of the American presidential election. Do debates build confidence in democracy? Or do they diminish faith in the nation's democratic experiment?

Debates can serve the system well. There is evidence that debate exposure increases confidence that government is responsive to its citizens. Debates serve democracy well by the mere fact that, as Edward Hinck notes, "Candidates fight for office rhetorically, by arguing in full view of audiences that expect their leaders to symbolize their most precious democratic value: choice through rational dialogue." Furthemore, as Gladys Lang points out, "Televised debates have served as a civilizing influence on what are, or might be, bitterly fought and sometimes dirty campaigns."[29]

Persuasive as these arguments are, they do not totally convince critics, who point to acrimonious exchanges in presidential and vice presidential debates and to instances in which candidates ducked questions or found it difficult to respond to questions, because of the ambiguous and confusing ways in which they were asked. Nor do they persuade those who lament the failure of debates to focus on a single issue, such as how the nation should deal with Social Security, affirmative action, or drug abuse. For all their sparring in the 1996 debates, President Clinton and Senator Dole never *debated* these issues in any meaningful way. Instead, each relied on sound bites and catch phrases, carefully selected from previous campaign speeches.

Clearly, debates have their limits. But when scholars tally up the pros and cons of debates, most find that they end up with more checks than minutes.

Compared to what debates could be in an ideal world, debates *are* hopelessly focused on political posturing and feature shamelessly little high-level discussion. But compared to other modalities for bringing people political information, like advertising and the evening news, debates are a pretty good deal. They give voters a chance to hear the candidates speak about the issues in their own words, and they provide people with an efficient way to compare the candidates from the two major parties.

Prescriptions

No one, not even the most enthusiastic defender of presidential debates, would argue that debates are a perfect political institution. There is little question that debates can be improved to better suit the needs of the electorate.

One suggestion is to adopt a modified Lincoln–Douglas format, with candidates debating a single proposition. Freed of the shackles of panelists' or audience members' questions, candidates could tee off, giving 8-minute opening statements, followed by 6-minute restatements and rebuttals, and 4-minute segments for elaboration.[30] This is a great idea in theory, but it would never pass muster with the candidates. Candidates would be reluctant to be associated with one side of a public controversy, for fear of alienating pivotal voters from the other camp. In addition, direct confrontation with the opponent would increase the odds that a candidate would err or commit a gaffe. For these reasons, a formal debate of this type would never work in a modern presidential campaign.[31]

Thus in the real world of presidential politics, one must consider more temperate suggestions. Scholars have offered a number of suggestions to improve debates. The prescriptions include:

1. Insist that each debate focus on only two or three topics (e.g., health care, Medicare, the deficit). This would give debates more depth.
2. Continue to use multiple debate formats.
3. Give candidates more time to answer questions. Even in the age of short attention spans, voters are capable of processing answers that extend for longer than a minute and a half.
4. Consider ways of including follow-up questions in town meeting hall debates.
5. Revisit the issue of third party candidates' participation in debates so that the needs of alternative party candidates can be addressed.
6. Consider innovative formats, such as having the debate held in the House of Representatives, with the first 45 minutes a standard debate between the presidential candidates and the final 45 minutes "a version of 'question time' in the British

Parliament, with Congressional leaders shooting barbed queries at the opposition candidates."[32]

7. Develop ways to make debates relevant to those millions of Americans who find them a boring rehash of politics-as-usual.

CONCLUSIONS

Presidential debates are complex, highly political, entities. They attract huge national audiences, considerably larger than those that are captured by any other single communication activity. Yet attention is sporadic, with few viewers viewing an entire debate from start to finish.

Voters say that they find debates helpful and unquestionably want presidential candidates to debate. However, debates are no longer the novelties they were in 1960 and 1976, and citizens are eager for new formats that provide more clash between candidates and give voters more input into the process.

There is considerable learning from debates. Voters clearly acquire information about the candidates' positions on the issues and their personal characteristics. However, the fact that candidates do not debate a single proposition, that they have only 90 seconds to answer a question, and that the questions they must respond to are frequently badly worded or silly necessarily restricts the amount (and quality) of learning that takes place.

It is often said that debates favor the visual over the verbal, that pictures overpower words. However, this dichotomy greatly oversimplifies the complex interactions among visual and verbal images, and assumes that voters are easy prey for the savvy televisual manipulator.

Unquestionably, candidates who win debates are those who have mastered the television medium, which means they have shown themselves capable of compressing speech into predetermined time limits and of prowling around the stage of a large auditorium. And yet, the truth is that more than televisual sleights of hand are needed to impress an increasingly sophisticated American electorate. Debates are won by a combination of argumentation, vision, and television communication skills. The problem with many debates is not the format, but the unwillingness of candidates (being people who want to get elected and not alienate key constituencies) to freely discuss controversial issues.

Despite their shortcomings, debates symbolize one of the nation's most precious democratic values: "choice through rational dialogue."[33] As Edward Hinck observes, "When candidates no longer need to justify their actions to an audience made up of members of the community, when candidates can do as they wish in the name of democracy without accountability to the citizenry, or when candidates do what they wish and provide poor accounts to the public, then a serious problem has developed in the system."[34]

In the end, when one considers how much better presidential debates could be, one ends up feeling uneasy and dissatisfied. But when one considers how much worse the campaign would be without debates, one ends up feeling enormously relieved.[35]

KEY ISSUES

Audience for Debates

Learning Effects

Words vs. Pictures

Kennedy–Nixon Debate

News Verdicts

Reforming Debates

DISCUSSION QUESTIONS

1. Does meaningful learning take place in debates? Discuss, looking at both sides of the issue.

2. Could a candidate with great ideas, but few television communication skills, win a debate? Should he or she?

3. Are you satisfied with presidential debates? What suggestions would you make to improve debates?

23

Epilogue

On November 5, 1996, America went to the polls to elect a president. After an exhaustive year-long campaign, the voters put President Bill Clinton back in office, making him the first Democratic president since Franklin D. Roosevelt to win a second term in office.

For Clinton, it was a great personal victory. He received some of the worst press of any modern president early in his term, failed to enact a sweeping health care reform bill, and saw the opposition party, the Republicans, gain control of Congress in the midterm 1994 elections.

But Clinton, through a series of brilliant but controversial political moves, won the support of the electorate. By appealing to Democrats (in vetoes of Republican-led bills to cut government spending) and swing voters (by signing legislation that overhauled the welfare system), by presiding over a strong economy, by skillfully pointing to his record of accomplishments, and by using the communications media to advance his cause during the campaign, Clinton presented a persuasive package to voters in the autumn of 1996.

Given the state of the economy and Clinton's skills as a campaigner, it is not clear that any Republican could have defeated him in 1996. Bob Dole was at a particular disadvantage, not being a natural campaigner, drawing no strength from shaking hands and plunging into crowds of wellwishers, and lacking the president's gift of gab.[1] "To make things worse," a reporter noted, "he gives the impression of 'a man in a box,' as a staff member put it, unable to be fully himself."[2] Of course, there were other reasons why Dole went down on November 5, including the gap between some of his positions and those of the public (e.g., on tobacco and family leaves) and his failure to articulate a compelling vision for the country.

By all indications, the electorate was not totally satisfied with Clinton's performance and continued to have doubts about his character. However, people seemed to have reached a rather sophisticated understanding of the complex relationship between private traits and public performance, and the complex challenges our leaders face. In the end, as novelist Richard Ford insightfully observed:

> Americans seem to be persuaded more by a man whose active understanding of his own character appears savvy enough, even skeptical enough (apparently without giving into cynicism), to cope with a country embroiled by great insolubles. The unease and perplexity we feel in America about such "uncompromisable" matters as partial-birth abortion, gun ownership and our responsibility to our elder citizens, the unease we feel about the country itself—one in which O. J. Simpson walks, only 38 percent of those eligible bother to vote, and nobody believes what the politicians say—such unease requires a certain kind of complex man to be its leader.
> A flawed man for a flawed time? Some would certainly say so. Though I don't think it. Just a man, quite possibly, who's been in the Dark House, knows how he got there but who can still imagine light.[3]

Yet, from a political communication perspective, there was more to the 1996 election than a contest between two men, Clinton and Dole (or more, if you include the dozens of fringe candidates on the ballot, not the least of whom was Ross Perot, who raised considerable fury after he was denied a place at the presidential debates). Elections provide the nation with an opportunity to debate issues, work through conflicts, and shape policy. They are national conversations about what ail us and please us as a nation.

One of the most important issues broached in the conversation was the relationship between citizens and their government in an age of dwindling resources. At one level, the conversation was a smashing success. Our leaders discovered that citizens were upset about the state of government, through all the modern feedback mechanisms our democracy pro-vides—polls, talk radio, news, and elections themselves. Leaders of both parties then moved to take steps, in their rhetoric and policy, to reduce the size of government. For the first time in modern history, both political parties agreed with Ronald Reagan's dictum that government was part of the problem, and they took steps to build government down, not up. To their credit, the news media covered these issues thoroughly. If other elections are any guide, there is little doubt that more Americans under-stood where the candidates stood on the issues of government spending and taxes at the end of the campaign than at the beginning. The debates brought some of these issues to the fore and they offered voters an opportunity to see their leaders talk side by side about government and social issues.

Yet at other levels, the national conversation did not work out so well. There were questions about how informed voters were about the issue of cutting back government, and the consistency of their attitudes. Many Americans criticized government and said they didn't trust it, yet were loathe to cut programs from which they benefitted. Despite widely reported studies showing that people wanted to reduce the size of the federal government, there was also evidence that over 70% of the public supported increasing spending for improving education and halting the crime rate—a clear indication that the public was fickle on the government cutback issue and was susceptible to minor changes in the wording of public opinion polls.[4] Still others railed against government without fully appreciating why governments evolved in the first place.

For their part, the candidates were all too willing to put off talking about the difficult issues involved in how to use scarce government resources in a way that benefits the larger polity but does not turn a cold shoulder to the nation's most helpless citizens. Nor did they talk much about how best to confront the rising costs of government entitlement programs like Medicare and Social Security. The best candidates could say about this issue in the debates was that they would appoint a bipartisan commission to study the issue of Social Security. Economist Paul Krugman nicely summarized the problem, noting that:

> The sad truth about this year's economic debate is that the biggest issue facing the federal government—the issue that should be uppermost in our minds—is not being discussed at all. Most of what happens in our economy is beyond the reach of government policy ... There is one thing, however, the Government can and must control: its own budget. And it is heading inexorably toward fiscal disaster, as the baby boomers in the tens of millions march steadily toward the age at which they can claim Social Security and Medicare. True, the crisis is still about 15 years away. But we expect responsible adults to start preparing for their retirement decisions in advance; why shouldn't we ask the same of our Government? Unfortunately, everything that a responsible government should be doing now—raising taxes, raising the retirement age, scaling back benefits for those who can manage without them (that means for the affluent, not the poor)—is political poison.[5]

To compound things, the media did little to help us grapple with the problems that Krugman mentioned. True, they covered the candidate's speeches, such as they were. But few news organizations discussed the pros and cons of different proposals to deal with the crises in Social Security and Medicare. Few articles critically examined the merits of Democratic claims that Republicans had tried to gut Medicare in 1995 or Republican counter-arguments that the Democrats had engaged in demagoguery.

Voters showed relatively little interest in the race. Only 24% of respondents interviewed in one poll said they were following the election very closely, compared with 42% in 1992. Viewing of the debates and conventions dropped dramatically from 1992.[6] Voters' lack of interest had many causes, including the candidates' failure to say anything new, the large gap between the candidates in the polls, and disgruntlement with the modern poll-dominated campaign. Of course every election can't be a barn burner, a "real turn-on"electoral matchup like 1992. And the lack of voter interest may have reflected a satisfaction with the economy and the course the country was taking; in other words, "If it ain't broke, don't fix it"—or don't concentrate on it, for that matter.

Nonetheless, there was a silver lining in the cloudy discussions of issues that transpired in 1996. Campaigns, after all, are conversations between people and their leaders, complex discourses about the issues that face the country, dialogues that provide some indication of how far and fast the public wants to move on controversial problems. Over the course of the long campaign, citizens and candidates began to reach consensus on the kind of government they wanted in an age of dwindling resources.

As the campaign approached, in the wake of Republican victories in the 1994 elections, there was a good deal of talk about "voter anger" and dissatisfaction with Big Government. By the end of the campaign, the talk had disappeared. What happened? *Washington Post* reporter Dan Morgan observed:

> For one thing, two government shutdowns and the GOP assault on spending programs forced Americans to look beyond the talk-show abstractions portraying an evil federal establishment and define for themselves what they did and did not want from Washington. The shutdowns, which closed some national parks and caused all manner of inconveniences, provided a direct education in the sweep and reach of federal activities. It was a powerful reminder that tax dollars sent to Washington don't all disappear. They buy real things: everything from Amtrak service to school lunches....Then there is the uncertain, but lingering psychic impact of the April 1995 bombing of the Alfred P. Murrah building in Oklahoma City. In one horrifying morning, it transformed the abstraction of the "federal government" into televised pictures of frightened, bleeding people emerging from their demolished workplace. The pictures put a human face on bureaucrats, and revealed a kinder, gentler federal operation, with a day care center on the ground floor.[7]

In addition, the president and Congress delivered, giving the public some of what it wanted. The president signed a welfare reform bill and seemed to endorse the notion, which had many adherents among the public, that government needed to be reduced. Clinton appeared to have moved closer to the mainstream public sentiment that big-government solutions needed to be reevaluated, and the public appeared to have stepped back from its knee-jerk criticism of government, perhaps recognizing that government provided important services and performed vital roles. There seemed to be a greater appreciation of the complexities involved in cutting the federal government and reforming the Welfare State.[8]

In the end, the campaign, like others before it, offered people exposure to the issues and candidates, providing a spirited debate on the issues, forcing citizens to at least consider the problems that faced the country. And yet, as we have seen, the debate did not produce new ideas or proposals for solving the country's problems. Nor did it always engage the bulk of the nation's citizenry.

Such are the problems of contemporary media democracies. Or perhaps democracies in general, as the author Saul Bellow observed. "We have had some dum-dum presidents, " Bellow remarked, "but there have been no Hitlers here and no Stalins. With all its disorders, disruptions, bureaucratic idiocies, its chaotic or nihilistic state of feelings, thoughts and passions, democracy here makes more sense and perhaps is more rational than its philosophical founders might have thought possible in a country so huge and so mixed."[9]

Endnotes

Chapter 1

Note. Readers will see that I use the term "ibid" throughout the endnotes in this book. This refers to the book or article that was cited in the previous endnote.

[1]Johnson & Broder, *The system: The American way of politics at the breaking point*, chapter 10. See also Jamieson & Cappella, *Media in the middle: Fairness and accuracy in the 1994 health care reform debate.* Report of the Annenberg Public Policy Center of the University of Pennsylvania. The Health Insurance Association of America, which represents companies that sell health plans to individuals, groups, and businesses, played a pivotal role in the defeat of Clinton's reform proposal.

[2]Kurtz, *Hot air: All talk, all the time,* pp. 261–262, & 282.

[3]Ibid, p. 280. Imus didn't stop. At a March 21, 1996, Radio and Television Correspondents' Association dinner, where he was the featured speaker, Imus lampooned the president, who was sitting a few feet away from him, with cracks about Clinton's womanizing and the Whitewater scandal.

[4]Denton & Thorson, *Civic journalism: Does it work?*, Special report for the Pew Center for Civic Journalism on the "We the People" project.

[5]Glaberson, A new press role: Solving problems, *The New York Times*, October 3, 1994, p. D6.

[6]For up-to-date evidence that most voters get their news from television, see Media Studies Center, *The media & campaign 96 briefing,* April, 1996; and Ansolabehere, Behr, & Iyengar, *The media game: American politics in the television age*, pp. 43–44 for evidence that TV news has replaced the print media as the major source of political affairs information for most Americans. However, people do get information from a variety of information sources, including print, and another view of this issue can be found in Robinson & Levy, *The main source: Learning from television news.*

[7]See, for example, Tolchin, *The angry American: How voter rage is changing the nation,* pp. 108–116. Voter cynicism is a complicated issue, as I discuss in chapter 18.

[8]Quoted in Morin, Tuned out, turned off, *The Washington Post National Weekly Edition*, February 5–11, 1996, pp. 7–8.

[9]This is Sidney Hillman's view, as noted in Underhill, *FDR and Harry: Unparalleled lives,* p. 87.

[10]Miller, *The Blackwell encyclopaedia of political thought,* p. 390.

[11]The formal title of the journal is the *Harvard International Journal of Press/Politics*. See also Kalb, *The Nixon memo: Political respectability, Russia, and the press*, pp. 3–7 & 190–192.

[12]See Just, Crigler, Alger, Cook, Kern, & West, *Crosstalk,: Citizens, candidates, and the media in a presidential campaign*, p. 3.

[13]Graber, The impact of media research on public opinion studies, *Mass communication review yearbook*, 1982, p. 556.

[14]Ibid.

[15]Mancini & Swanson, Politics, media and modern democracy: Introduction. In *Politics, media, and modern democracy: An international study of innovations in electoral campaigning and their consequences*, pp. 17–18.

[16]Schudson, *The power of news*, p. 3.

[17]Important discussions of the state of political communication have emerged over the past two decades. These include, in order of publication: Chaffee (Ed.), *Political communication: Issues and strategies for research*; Kraus & Davis, *The effects of mass communication on political behavior*; Meadow, *Politics as communication*; Nimmo & Sanders (Eds.), *Handbook of political communication*; Paletz & Entman, *Media power politics*; Swanson & Nimmo (Eds.), *New directions in political communication: A resource book*; and Swanson and Mancini (Eds.), *Politics, media, and modern democracy: An international study of innovations in electoral campaigning and their consequences*. The research-oriented reader may also be interested in two journals devoted to the study of political communication, *Political Communication and Press/Politics*. Scholarly readers may also want to pursue the March, 1996, symposium on media and politics in *PS: Political Science & Politics*, and Jamieson and Cappella's article that attempts to bridge disciplinary differences btween political scientists and communication scholars, Bridging the disciplinary divide, *PS: Political Science & Politics*, 1996, pp. 13–17.

[18]See chapter 10; and McLeod & Blumler, The macrosocial level of communication science. In *Handbook of communication science*, pp. 271–322. Paranthetically, I would note that I did not discuss news media institutions in any detail in this book because this stretches into the area of news scholarship. Nor was political socialization, an intriguing area of study, discussed due to space considerations.

Chapter 2

[1]Actually, normative theories of the presidency and the press are more complicated. In colonial America, freedom of the press meant freedom to articulate anti-British views and to suppress pro-British sentiments. (See, for example, Tebbel and Watts, *The press and the presidency: From George Washington to Ronald Reagan*, p. 5). Later when Washington was faced with criticisms from the anti Federalist press, Jefferson urged the president to keep in mind that the press played an important role in a democracy. Jefferson emphasized that if the press were to remain free from government control, it must serve as a watchdog on government. It was much later that the notion of the press as an adversary of government became widely held.

[2]Wolfson, *The untapped power of the press: Explaining government to the people*, p. 13.

[3]Tebbel & Watts, *The press and the presidency*, p. 18.

[4]Ibid, p. 13.

[5]Ibid, p. 19.

[6]Ibid, pp. 23–25; Emery & Emery, *The press and America: An interpretive history of the mass media* (5th ed.), p. 101.

[7]In fairness, it should be noted that some of the editors who were thrown in jail were disreputable opportunists, willing to say or write anything about the president, whether

or not it was false (See Emery & Emery, ibid, 103). Historians have also pointed out that Adams was acting on his belief that the nation was under attack and its survival was at stake (See Tebbel & Watts, *The press and the presidency*, pp. 24–25). However, there is reason to believe that he exaggerated the threats posed by foreigners and in the process eroded basic freedoms. For a discussion of the Federalist and Jeffersonian positions on the First Amendment in this case, see Tebbel and Watts, p. 25; Wilson, *American government: Institutions and polices*, p. 502, and Bonafede, Presidents and the news media, in *The presidents and the public*, pp. 35–36. According to Wilson, Republicans acknowledged that the press could be subjected to government controls, but they did not believe that the First Amendment gave the federal government the right to punish the press for making seditious statements. If any entity had that right, Republicans argued, it was the states. Thus Wilson makes the interesting claim that debate over the Sedition Act was primarily a debate about states' rights.

[8]Tebbel & Watts, *The press and the presidency*, pp. 75–76.

[9]Bonafede, Presidents and the news media, p. 48.

[10]Baldasty, The press and politics in the age of Jackson, *Journalism Monographs*, 1984, p. 23.

[11]Emery & Emery, *The press and America*, p. 139. See also Schudson, *Discovering the news: A social history of American newspapers*, pp. 12–60.

[12]See Bonafede, Presidents and the news media, pp. 36–49; and Emery & Emery, ibid, pp. 159–173 for discussions of the development of the press during this period.

[13]Tebbel & Watts, *The press and the presidency*, p. 172.

[14]Ibid, p. 174.

[15]Ibid, p. 195.

[16]Ibid, p. 191.

[17]See Emery & Emery, *The press and America*, p. 205; Bonafede, Presidents and the news media, p. 37; Tebbel & Watts, *The press and the presidency*, p. 180.

[18]Tebbel & Watts, ibid, p. 211.

[19]Ibid, p. 251.

[20]At least, this was the claim made by the woman. Others claimed the father could have been one of a number of men who had become intimate with the woman. See Tebbel & Watts, ibid, p. 258.

[21]Ibid, p, 274

[22]Bonafede, Presidents and the news media, p. 50; Emery & Emery, *The press and America*, pp. 253–278.

[23]Tebbel & Watts, *The press and the presidency*, p. 306.

[24]Emery & Emery, *The press and America*, p. 289.

[25]Orren, Thinking about the press and government. In W. Linsky, *Impact: How the press affects federal policy-making,*, p. 4. Estimates of both the number of civilians working for government and Washington reporters are provided in Orren, pp. 2–3.

[26]Tebbel & Watts, *The press and the presidency*, p. 321.

[27]C. Smith, *Presidential press conferences: A critical approach*, p. 22.

[28]Quoted in Tebbel & Watts, *The press and the presidency*, p. 330.

[29]Ibid, p. 335.

[30]Smith, *Presidential press conferences*, p. 23.

[31]Tebbel & Watts, *The press and the presidency*, p. 339.

[32]Ibid, p. 374.

[33]Troy, *See how they ran: The changing role of the presidential candidate*, (Rev ed.), p. 128.

[34]Sir Edward Grey made the comment. Quoted in Tuchman, *The Guns of August*, p. 122.

[35]For discussion of Germany's expansionist plans and attempts to provoke war in Europe, see Fromkin, *In the time of the Americans*, pp. 66–71.

[36]Creel, *How we advertised America*, p. 4.

[37]See Jowett & O'Donnell, *Propaganda and persuasion* (2nd ed), p. 123; Vaughn, *Holding fast the inner lines: Democracy, nationalism, and the Committee on Public Information*, p. 233; and Rather, *Our times: America at the birth of the twentieth century*, p. 553.

[38]Vaughn, ibid, pp. 43–44.

[39]Quoted in Tebbel & Watts, *The press and the presidency*, p. 405.

[40]See Boller, *Presidential anecdotes*, pp. 240–241; Cornwell, *Presidential leadership of public opinion*, pp. 74–97.

[41]Altschull, *Agents of power: The media and public policy* (2nd ed.), p. 10.

[42]See Schudson, *Discovering the news*, p. 65, and Bonafede, Presidents and the news media, p. 50.

[43]Tebbel & Watts, *The press and the presidency*, p. 3.

[44]Ibid.

[45]Altschull, *Agents of power*, p. 10.

Chapter 3

[1]Winfield, *FDR and the news media*, p. 1.

[2]Warren, *The juggler: Franklin Roosevelt as wartime statesman*, p. 7.

[3]Tebbel & Watts, *The press and the presidency: From George Washington to Ronald Reagan*, pp. 440–441. FDR was not always this congenial. He once gave a hostile war correspondent an Iron Cross. He bestowed an imaginary dunce on a reporter who asked if Roosevelt planned to run for a third term. These public rebukes were rare, however (see Winfield, *FDR and the news media*, p. 68).

[4]Tebbel & Watts, *The press and the presidency*, p. 441. Some have argued that FDR did not always influence the news, but reacted to it. For an empirical examination of this thesis, see Johnson & Wanta, Exploring FDR's relationship with the press: A historical agenda-setting study, *Political Communication*, 1995, pp. 157–172.

[5]Bonafede, Presidents and the news media. In *The presidents and the public*, p. 67.

[6]Tebbel & Watts, *The press and the presidency*, p. 442.

[7]Steele, *Propaganda in an open society: The Roosevelt Administration and the media, 1933–1941*, pp. 36–37.

[8]Leuchtenburg, *Franklin D. Roosevelt and the New Deal, 1932–1940*, p. 169. See also Winfield, *FDR and the news media*, p. 16.

[9]Winfield, ibid, p. 130. Some 55 years later, radio talk–show host Rush Limbaugh would use the same canard, announcing the number of days left in Bill Clinton's term.

[10]Steele, *Propaganda in an open society*, p. 53.

[11]White, *FDR and the press*, p. 109.

[12]Winfield, *FDR and the news media*, p. 91; Steele, *Propaganda in an open society*, p. 15.

[13]Steele, ibid, p. 26.

[14]Page & Shapiro, *The rational public: Fifty years of trends in Americans' policy preferences*, p. 192. For a discussion of the gap between Roosevelt's rhetoric and reality shortly before U.S. involvement in the second world war, see Page & Shapiro, pp. 188–193.

[15]Winfield, *FDR and the news media*, p. 239.

[16]Tebbel & Watts, *The press and the presidency*, p. 454.

[17]McCullough, *Truman*, p. 828.

[18]Ibid, p. 829. Interestingly, Bill Clinton seems to have called on Truman's remark in response to a column by *New York Times* writer William Safire in which Safire called Hillary Clinton "a congenital liar" in connection with her statements about the Whitewater scandal. Clinton was quoted as saying he wanted to punch Safire in the nose for making this comment. It seems likely that Clinton's advisers were familiar with Truman's classic

remark and exploited it to polish Clinton's image. It is not clear that it had that effect. See Safire, President as pugilist, *The New York Times*, January 11, 1996, p. A15.

[19]Tebbel & Watts, *The press and the presidency*, p. 462.

[20]Bonafede, Presidents and the news media, p. 51.

[21]Tebbel & Watts, *The press and the presidency*, p. 479.

[22]Sabato, *Feeding frenzy: How attack journalism has transformed American politics*, p. 38.

[23]For discussions of JFK's relationships with the press and his management of news, see Deakin, *Straight stuff: The reporters, the White House and the truth*, pp. 163–183; Smith, *Presidential press conferences: A critical approach*, pp. 40–43; and Tebbel & Watts, *The press and the presidency*, pp. 476–489. For a discussion of his news management techniques during foreign policy crises, see Kern, Levering, & Levering, *The Kennedy crises: The press, the presidency and foreign policy*.

[24]This at least was the view of *The New York Times*'s James Reston, who was heavily involved in the Bay of Pigs decision. He later commented that "It is ridiculous to think that publishing the fact that the invasion was imminent would have avoided this disaster." See Apple, James Reston, a journalist nonpareil, dies at 86, *The New York Times*, December 8, 1995, p. B15.

[25]Goldman, *The tragedy of Lyndon Johnson*, p. 531. For discussions of Johnson's personal idiosyncracies, see Kearns, *Lyndon Johnson and the American dream*, and Miller, *Lyndon: An oral biography*.

[26]See Kearns, and Tebbel & Watts, *The press and the presidency*, pp. 491–492 for psychological profiles of Johnson. A description of LBJ's emulation of FDR appears in Leuchtenburg, *In the shadow of FDR: From Harry Truman to Ronald Reagan*, pp. 121–160.

[27]Deakin, *Straight stuff*, p. 227.

[28]At first Truman felt the ubiquitous presence of FDR and questioned whether he possessed the ability to succeed him. But as time went on, he developed his own style and gained confidence in his leadership skills. See McCullough, *Truman*, pp. 356, 529, 555.

[29]Deakin, *Straight stuff*, pp. 234–236.

[30]Smith, *Presidential press conferences*, p. 46. Some historians believe the lying about Vietnam started earlier than 1965; they argue it began in August, 1964, in the wake of the attacks on U.S. ships in the Gulf of Tonkin. For a discussion of the controversy about the Gulf of Tonkin Resolution, see Turner, *Lyndon Johnson's dual war: Vietnam and the press*, pp. 81–85.

[31]Hallin, *The "uncensored war": The media and Vietnam*.

[32]Wicker, *One of us: Richard Nixon and the American dream*, pp. 35–36, 47.

[33]Wicker, ibid, p. 107; Tebbel & Watts, *The press and the presidency*, pp. 502–503. Stevenson also received critical press for his secret fund. Whether the news media were as hard on Stevenson as they were on Nixon remains to be seen. In Nixon's view, there was no question about it. (See also Jamieson, *Packaging the presidency: A history and criticism of presidential campaign advertising*, pp. 69–75.) In recent years, critics have begun to examine Nixon's years with more empathy for Nixon. This is not to exonerate Nixon for his excesses in press relations, but to understand matters from his perspective. See Wicker, and Dubail, Hollywood history lesson, *The Plain Dealer*, January 14, 1996, p. 3–C.

[34]Ambrose, *Nixon: The triumph of a politician (1962–1972)*, p. 33; Wicker, *One of us*, p. 443.

[35]Wicker, ibid, p. 440.

[36]Tebbel & Watts, *The press and the presidency*, p. 503.

[37]Jacobs & Shapiro, The rise of presidential polling: The Nixon White House in historical perspective, *Public Opinion Quarterly*, 1995, pp. 167–168, 189–190.

[38]Maltese, *Spin control: The White House Office of Communications and the management of presidential news*, p. 42. See also Spragens, *The presidency and the mass media in the age of television*, p. 79.

[39]Maltese, ibid, p. 50.

[40]Maltese, ibid, p. 51.

[41]Deakin, *Straight stuff*, p. 284.

[42]Network reporters no longer give such detailed, incisive, and (at times) pointed commentaries on presidential speeches, in part because of Agnew's attacks and also because the networks realize that the public prefers to return to regularly scheduled programs Reporters do give mildly opinionated commentaries about presidential candidates' speeches from time to time, particularly addresses to nominating conventions.

[43]Maltese, *Spin control*, p. 57.

[44]Tebbel & Watts, *The press and the presidency*, p. 510.

[45]Spear, *Presidents and the press: The Nixon legacy*, p. 133

[46]Maltese, *Spin control*, p. 130.

[47]Smoller, *The six o'clock presidency: A theory of presidential press relations in the age of television*, p. 83.

[48]Maltese, *Spin control*, p. 150.

[49]Deakin, *Straight stuff*, p. 305.

[50]Adams & Heyl, From Cairo to Kabul with the networks 1972–1980. In *Television coverage of the Middle East*, p. 25. See also Altheide, Network news oversimplified and underexplained, *Washington Journalism Review*, pp. 28–29.

[51]Smoller, *The six o'clock presidency*, pp. 91–93. Whether television coverage had these effects is, of course, an empirical question.

[52]Sabato, Open season: How the news media cover presidential campaigns in the age of attack journalism. In *Under the watchful eye: Managing presidential campaigns in the television era*, p. 128.

[53]Ibid. Sabato notes that these are generalizations and the three periods overlap in various ways. In addition, one of the continuing issues in the study of press–presidential relations is the extent to which the press has served as a vitriolic critic, or an acquiescent stenographer, of government activities. Some of the complications are discussed in the next chapters.

[54]Sabato, *Feeding frenzy: How attack journalism has transformed American politics.*

[55]Siebert, *Freedom of the press in England, 1476–1776*, p. 10. Shaw & Bauer, Press freedom and war constraints: Case testing Siebert's Proposition II, *Journalism Quarterly*, pp. 243–254; and Winfield, *FDR and the news media*, p. 6, who distinguishes between internal and external crises.

Chapter 4

[1]Grossman & Kumar, *Portraying the president: The White House and the news media*, p. 3. It could be argued that Congress also occupies part of the stage today, given the impact Congress exerted on the public agenda in 1995 and 1996. In view of the complexity of media–government effects, it seemed useful to separate the discussions; thus this chapter and the one that follows focus on contemporary press–presidency relations, and chapter 8 examines Congress and the media.

[2]Ibid, p. 4.

[3]Ibid, p. 3.

[4]Smoller, *The six o'clock presidency: A theory of presidential press relations in the age of television*, p. 98.

[5]Maltese, *Spin control: The White House Office of Communications and the management of presidential news*, pp. 2–3. Throughout this chapter I refer to the "public agenda" and the "media agenda." These terms are used informally here; in chapters 11 and 12, I use the terms more precisely, drawing on the scientific literature on this subject.

[6]Hertsgaard, *On bended knee: The press and the Reagan presidency*, p. 107. Their strategy made good psychological sense. Persuasion theories suggest that liking can induce persuasion, and that when we feel positive affect toward a stimulus object, these feelings can generalize to other aspects of the stimulus, as suggested by classical and higher-order conditioning approaches (see Perloff, *The dynamics of persuasion*, pp. 63–69 & 155.)

[7]Hertsgaard, *On bended knee*, p. 34.

[8]Ibid, p. 43.

[9]At least, this was their goal early on. Reagan's team was certainly more likely than Carter's to try to use honey rather than vinegar to catch the media flies. Nonetheless, like other presidents, Reagan became frustrated with the press. At one point, to stop officials from leaking information, he threatened to issue a directive forbidding all but a handful of officials from talking to reporters on a not-for-attribution background basis. He also issued a series of directives that restricted the flow of government information, such as an order that two million civil servants pledge in writing not to reveal "classifiable information." (See Bonafede, Presidents and the news media. In *The presidents and the public*, pp. 68–69).

[10]Ibid, p. 35.

[11]Ibid, p. 107.

[12]Deaver, *Behind the scenes*, p. 141.

[13]Regan, *For the record*, p. 248.

[14]Hertsgaard, *On bended knee*, p. 25.

[15]See Smoller, *The six o'clock presidency*, pp. 100–104; Spear, *Presidents and the press,: The Nixon legacy*, p. 281; Hertsgaard, *On bended knee*, pp. 132–151.

[16]Maltese, *Spin control*, p. 215.

[17]Regan, *For the record*, p. 336.

[18]Paletz & Guthrie, The three faces of Ronald Reagan, *Journal of Communication*, 1987, pp. 7–23.

[19]Smoller, *The six o'clock presidency*, p. 113.

[20]Gergen, Bush's start: A presidency "on the edge of a cliff," *Washington Post*, March 5, 1989, p. C1.

[21]Maltese, *Spin control*, p. 217.

[22]Ibid

[23]Drew, *On the edge: The Clinton presidency*, pp. 185, 237, 249.

[24]Rosenstiel, *The beat goes on: President Clinton's first year with the media*, p. 8.

[25]Ibid, p. 11. See also Newman, Political marketing as a governing tool, *Werbeforschung & Praxis*, 1995, pp. 163–167.

[26]See Bennett & Paletz, *Taken by storm: The media, public opinion, and US. foreign policy in the Gulf War.*

[27]Kurtz, *Hot air: All talk, all the time*, pp. 292–293.

[28]Denton & Holloway, Clinton and the town hall meetings: Mediated conversation and the risk of being "in touch." In *The Clinton presidency: Images, issues, and communication strategies*, p. 33–34.

[29]Wolfson, *The untapped power of the press: Explaining government to the people*, p. 18.

[30]Bonafede, Presidents and the news media, p. 63.

[31]Grossman & Kumar, *Portraying the president*, p. 130.

[32]Cooper, The inside skinny on a decade with Reagan and Bush, *The Washington Post National Weekly Edition* (Oct. 30–Nov. 5, 1995), p. 39.

[33]Ibid

[34]Hess, The government/press connection: Press officers and their offices, p. 25.

[35]Smith, *Presidential press conferences: A critical approach*, p. 65.

[36]Ibid, p. 50.

[37]Ibid, p. 108. For another discussion of press conferences, see Orr, Reporters confront the president: Sustaining a counterpoised situation, *Quarterly Journal of Speech*, 1980, pp. 17–32.

[38]Quoted in Kalb & Mayer, *Reviving the presidential news conference: Report of the Harvard Commission on the presidential news conference*, p. 10.

[39]Kelly, David Gergen, Master of the game, *The New York Times Magazine*, October 31, 1993, p. 64.

Chapter 5

[1]Smoller, *The six o'clock presidency: A theory of presidential–press relations in the age of television*, p. 18.

[2]Fallows, *Breaking the news: How the media undermine American democracy*, p. 9.

[3]Weaver & Wilhoit, *The American journalist in the 1990s*, p. 7. See also Weaver & Wilhoit, *The American journalist: A portrait of U.S. news people and their work* (2nd ed.). For a different point of view, see Lichter, Rothman, & Lichter, *The media elite*; and for a critique of Lichter et al, see Gans, Are U.S. journalists dangerously liberal?, *Columbia Journalism Review* (1985, November–December), pp. 29–33.

[4]Hertsgaard, *On bended knee: The press and the Reagan presidency*, p. 3.

[5]*Media Monitor* (1995, May/June), p. 3. The Washington-based Center for Media and Public Affairs, which conducted the content analysis, notes that it codes "all explicitly positive and negative evaluations by sources and reporters, excluding ambiguous or neutral statements."

[6]An interesting discussion of press bias appears in Page, The mass media as political actors, *PS: Political Science & Politics*, 1996, p. 22.

[7]Shoemaker & Reese, *Mediating the message: Theories of influences on mass media content* (2nd ed), p. 105.

[8]Sigal, Who: Sources make the news. In *Reading the news*, p. 15.

[9]Sigal, *Reporters and officials: The organization and politics of newsmaking*, p. 122.

[10]Bennett, *News: The politics of illusion* (3rd ed), p. 108.

[11]Lippmann, *Public opinion*, p. 247.

[12]Sigal, *Reporters and officials*, p. 120.

[13]Ibid.

[14]For example, see Brown, Bybee, Wearden, & Straughan, Invisible power: Newspaper news sources and the limits of diversity, *Journalism Quarterly*, 1987, pp. 45–54. An enormous literature on sources, reporters, and news gathering has developed. In addition to sources cited here, see Gandy, *Beyond agenda-setting: Information subsidies and public policy*.

[15]Maltese, *Spin control: The White House Office of Communications and the management of presidential news*, p. 216.

[16]Stone, Many thank-yous, Mr President, *Washington Post Book World*, February 13, 1966. Quoted in Hess, *The government/press connection: Press officers and their offices*, p. 113.

[17]Bonafede, Presidents and the news media, In *The presidents and the public*, pp. 63–64.

[18]Hess, *The government/press connection*, p. 75.

[19]Ibid, pp. 77–78.

[20]See The Pentagon and the Press: Secretary of Defense William J. Perry (Interview with Marvin Kalb), *Press/Politics*, 1996, 1, p. 122.

[21]Shoemaker & Reese, *Mediating the message*, p. 111.

[22]Schudson, When: Deadlines, datelines, and history. In *Reading the news*, pp. 79–80.

[23]Carey, Why and How: The dark continent of American journalism. In *Reading the news*, p. 164.

[24]Cited in Goldman & Rajagopal, *Mapping hegemony: Television news coverage of industrial conflict*, p. 17.

[25]McManus, What kind of commodity is news? *Communication Research*, 1992, p. 788. See also Picard, *Media economics*.

[26]McManus, ibid, p. 790.

[27]Shoemaker & Reese, *Mediating the message*, p. 114.

[28]Ibid, p. 123.

[29]Page documents that many news organizations quickly rejected a Bush administration claim that the 1992 Los Angeles riots had their roots in the failed social programs of the 1960s and 1970s. See Page, Speedy deliberation: Rejecting "1960s programs" as causes of the Los Angeles riots, *Political Communication*, (1995, July–September). There were many reasons why the news media reacted in this way, as Page notes. The quick rejection may have been caused by the kind of "pack journalism" pressures alluded to in the text. The speed of the rejection suggests that liberal biases may have been at work here—as noted earlier, partisan biases are not a major determinant of news, but it would be a naive observer indeed who said they never had an impact.

[30]Williams, *Marxism and Literature*, p. 109.

[31]The literature in this area is vast. For a political economy view, see for example Curran, Gurevitch, & Woollacott, The study of the media: Theoretical approaches, in *Culture, society and the media*, pp. 11–29; and Altschull, *Agents of power: The media and public policy* (2nd ed.), who takes a comparative approach. For a cultural studies view, see Gitlin, *The whole world is watching*. A well-known work in this area is Herman and Chomsky's *Manufacturing consent; The political economy of the mass media*. Shoemaker and Reese have a useful discussion of ideological theories in their book.

[32]Shoemaker & Reese, *Mediating the message*, p. 237.

[33]See also Altheide, Media hegemony: A failure of perspective, *Public Opinion Quarterly*, 1984, pp. 476–490; and Jeffres, *Mass media: Processes and effects*, Chapter 9.

[34]Hallin, *The "uncensored war": The media and Vietnam*, pp. 116–118.

[35]Ibid.

[36]See Lipstadt, *Beyond belief: The American press and the coming of the Holocaust, 1933–1945*, and Dearing & Rogers, AIDS and the media agenda, In *AIDS: A communication perspective*, pp. 173–194.

[37]Wolfson, *The untapped power of the press: Explaining government to the people*, p. 11.

[38]Smoller, *The six o'clock presidency*, p. 45.

[39]*Media Monitor* (1994, July/August), p. 2 reports that there were 5.7 stories per night during the first year-and-a-half of Bush's administration and 8.2 a night during Clinton's first 18 months. Using Smoller's conservative estimate of 15 stories per newscast yields the percentages.

[40]Smoller, *The six o'clock presidency*, p. 17.

[41]*Media Monitor* (1995, May/June), p. 2.

[42]Grossman and Kumar, *Portraying the president*, pp. 273–298.

[43]Shaw, Not even getting a 1st chance, *Los Angeles Times*, September 15, 1993, p. A1. Empirical data back up this claim. The *Media Monitor* (1993, September/October) reported that during the first 6 month of Clinton's presidency, only 34% of the sources interviewed by television reporters evaluated Clinton positively. The corresponding figure for George Bush was 60%. See also Hughes, The "not-so-genial" conspiracy: *The New York Times* and six presidential "honeymoons," 1953–1993, *Journalism & Mass Communication Quarterly*, 1995, pp. 841–850.

[44]Paletz & Guthrie, The three faces of Ronald Reagan, *Journal of Communication*, 1987, pp. 7–23.

[45]Fallows, *Breaking the news: How the media undermine American democracy*, pp. 20–24. For an alternative view, see Raines, The Fallows Fallacy, *The New York Times*, February 25, 1996, p. A14.

[46]Fallows, ibid, pp. 27–28.

[47]Quoted in ibid, p. 224.

[48]Ibid, p. 25, though the *Media Monitor* (1994, May/June 3) reports that television coverage did devote time to policy issues, notably the debate over employer mandates and universal coverage.

[49]See Paletz & Entman, *Media power politics*, pp. 16–17.

[50]Fallows, *Breaking the news*, p. 29.

[51]Smoller, *The six o'clock presidency*, p. 29.

[52]Bennett, *News: The politics of illusion* (3rd ed.), p. 48. See Hart, Smith-Howell, & Llewellyn, The mindscape of the presidency: *Time* Magazine 1945–1985, *Journal of Communication*, 1991, pp. 6–25 for evidence suggesting that *Time* describes presidents in predominantly psychological terms, consistent with the personalized emphasis of mass media.

[53]Smoller, *The six o'clock presidency*, p. 32. Can you identify the presidents? Look at the list again. (Answer: Nixon, Ford, Carter, Reagan, Bush.)

[54]Bennett, *News: The politics of illusion*, p. 39.

[55]Blumler & Gurevitch, Politicians and the press: An essay on role relationships, In *Handbook of Political Communication*, p. 470.

[56]Weaver & Wilhoit, News media coverage of U. S. Senators in four Congresses, 1953–1974, *Journalism Monographs*, 1980. This study, while focusing on relationships between reporters and senators, can be usefully applied to president–press relationships.

[57]Grossman & Kumar, *Portraying the president, The White House and the news media*, p. 14.

[58]Weisberg, Washington's new ruling class: Clincest, *The New Republic*, April 26, 1993, p. 24.

[59]Blumler & Gurevitch, Politicians and the press, p. 474.

[60]Ibid, p. 474.

[61]Ibid, pp. 489–490.

[62]Fallows, *Breaking the news*, p. 63.

[63]See chapter 3 for a discussion of FDR's news management; Hallin, *The "uncensored war": The media and Vietnam*, for descriptions of TV coverage of Vietnam; Lang & Lang, *The battle for public opinion: The president, the press, and the polls during Watergate* for a discussion of Watergate and the press, and Bennett & Paletz, (Eds.) *Taken by storm: The media, public opinion, and U. S. foreign policy in the Gulf War* along with Kaid et al, CNN's Americanization of the Gulf War: An analysis of media, technology, and storytelling. In *The 1,000 hour war: Communication in the Gulf*, pp. 147–160, for a discussion of news and the Gulf War.

[64]For a discussion of Clinton's press, see *Media Monitor* (1995, May/June). For an alternative view on media coverage of the Clinton scandals see Sabato & Lichter, *When should the watchdogs bark?: Media coverage of the Clinton scandals.*

[65]See Alexseev & Bennett, For whom the gates open: News reporting and government source patterns in the United States, Great Britain, and Russia, *Political Communication*, 1995, pp. 395–412. See also Bennett, *News: The politics of illusion*; Bennett, The news about foreign policy, in *Taken by storm*, pp. 12–40; and Entman & Page, The news before the storm: The Iraq war debate and the limits to media independence, in *Taken by storm*, pp. 82–101.

[66]See Bennett, *News: The politics of illusion*, pp. 135–137.

[67]Paletz & Entman, *Media power politics*, p. 70.

[68]Hertsgaard, *On bended knee.* p. 148.

[69]*Media Monitor*, (1993, September/October), p. 2.

[70]For a description of 1992 campaign coverage, see Lichter & Noyes, *Good intentions make bad news; Why Americans hate campaign journalism.*
[71]See Smoller, *The six o'clock presidency*, pp. 41–60.
[72]See Drew, *On the edge; The Clinton presidency.*
[73]Morin, Taking sides in the budget battle, *The Washington Post National Weekly Edition,* November 27–December 3, 1995, p. 35.
[74]Blumler & Gurevitch, Politicians and the press, p. 490.
[75]Fallows, *Breaking the news*, pp. 182–189.
[76]Smoller, *The six o–clock presidency*, p. 93.

Chapter 6

[1]Quoted in Rodgers, *Contested truths: Keywords in American politics since Independence*, p. 7.
[2]Hall, A symbolic interactionist analysis of politics, *Sociological Inquiry*, 1972, p. 51.
[3]Graber, Political languages. In *Handbook of political communication*, p. 195.
[4]Windt, Presidential rhetoric: Definition of a discipline of study. In *Essays in presidential rhetoric*, p. xv.
[5]Zernicke, *Pitching the presidency: How presidents depict the office*, p. 5. See also Hart, *Modern rhetorical criticism*, Chapter 1 for definitions of rhetoric.
[6]Hart, *Verbal style and the presidency: A computer-based analysis*, p. 6.
[7]Smith & Smith, Introduction: Persuasion and the American presidency. In *The president and the public: Rhetoric and national leadership*, p. xi.
[8]Ceaser, Thurow, Tulis, & Bessette, The rise of the rhetorical presidency. In *Essays in presidential rhetoric*, pp. 3–8; Euchner, Presidential appearances. In *The presidents and the public*, pp. 111–113.
[9]Wills, *Lincoln at Gettysburg: The words that remade America*, p. 145.
[10]One could argue that long before Wilson, Lincoln recognized the role of public opinion and the need for the president to shape that opinion. Lincoln made the statement that "Public sentiment is everything. With public sentiment nothing can fail, without it nothing can succeed." Yet Lincoln was still a nineteenth century president in that he resisted the temptation to regularly appeal to public sentiment. See Tulis, *The rhetorical presidency*, pp. 79–83. Lincoln's successor, Andrew Johnson, tried to take his case to the public, only to find that he was roundly condemned for the attempt. See Euchner, Presidential appearances, p. 114.
[11]Kernell, *Going public: New strategies of presidential leadership* (2nd ed), p. 241. See also Ceaser et al., The rise of the rhetorical presidency, p. 9, for a discussion of Wilson's speech-making.
[12]Euchner, Presidential appearances, p. 115.
[13]Kernell, *Going public: New strategies of presidential leadership*, p. 19.
[14]Ceaser et al, The rise of the rhetorical presidency, p. 11. See Kernell, Ibid, pp. 9–52, for a discussion of the origins of "going public," and the differences between the contemporary approach and that outlined by Neustadt in his classic work, *Presidential power.*
[15]Whicker, The case AGAINST the war. In *The presidency and the Persian Gulf War*, p. 114.
[16]See Edwards, *The public presidency: The pursuit of popular support*, p. 1; Kernell, *Going public*; Tulis, *The rhetorical presidency*; and Smith & Smith, *The White House speaks: Presidential leadership as persuasion*, Chapter 1 for a critique of these approaches. See also Misciagno for a discussion of how the rhetorical presidency has to deal with increased skepticism on the part of the public, in Rethinking the mythical presidency, *Political Communication*, 1996, pp. 329–344.
[17]Lowi, *The personal president: Power invested, promise unfulfilled.*

[18]Kernell, *Going public*, p. 2.

[19]Kernell, *Going public*, chapters *1 & 2*.

[20]Euchner, Presidential appearances, p. 120.

[21]Hart, *The sound of leadership: Presidential communication in the modern age*, pp. 7–9, and Hart, *Verbal style and the presidency*, p. 2. For an alternative view, see Simon & Ostrom, The impact of televised speeches and foreign travel on presidential approval, *Public Opinion Quarterly*, 1989, pp. 58–82.

[22]Drew, George Washington was not a bubba, *The Washington Post National Weekly Edition*, December 19–25, 1994, p. 19 and Drew, *On the edge: The Clinton presidency*, p. 54.

[23]Hart, *Verbal style and the presidency*, p. 4.

[24]Hart, *The sound of leadership*, pp. 50–51. There has not been a linear increase in presidential usage of these ceremonial forms, however, and certain ceremonial types have increased more over time than others, as Hart notes in his book.

[25]Hart, *Verbal style and the presidency*, pp. 12–24.

[26]Ibid, chapter 8.

[27]Ibid, pp. 113–116.

[28]Ibid, p. 196.

[29]Ibid, p. 180.

[30]Smith & Smith, *The White House speaks*, p. 126.

[31]Such was the case when Carter gave his famous "crisis of confidence" speech. See Hart, *Verbal style and the presidency*, pp. 193–194, and Smith & Smith, *The White House speaks*, pp. 151–157 in their discussions of Carter's political jeremiads.

[32]Hart, ibid, p. 234, touches on this issue.

[33]Well, to be absolutely factual, Truman was the first president to speak on television and Eisenhower the first to allow press conferences to be taped for television. However, to pursue the romantic analogy, Truman and Eisenhower did not appreciate the way that television might seduce the American public, to quote the title of Hart's 1994 book, whereas Kennedy did. Kennedy introduced live TV news conferences and used the medium to deliver crisis addresses. Reagan used television to develop a relationship with the American public.

[34]Jamieson, *Eloquence in an electronic age: The transformation of political speechmaking*, p. 119. In this passage Jamieson also points out that the comparison of Reagan to FDR understates the knowledge and skills that Reagan brought to television speech-making. Also, for a discussion of Reagan's use of another electronic medium—radio— see Foote, Reagan on radio, *Communication Yearbook*, 1984, pp. 692–706. and for a description of opposition party access to rebut Reagan's and other presidents' speeches, see Foote, *Television access and political power: The networks, the presidency, and the "loyal opposition."*

[35]Jamieson, Ibid. See Euchner, Presidential appearances, p. 115 for the Roosevelt quote.

[36]Hart, *Verbal style and the presidency*, Chapter 8.

[37]Hart, *Verbal style and the presidency*, p. 228.

[38]Jamieson, *Eloquence in an electronic age*, p. 119. See also Denton, *The primetime presidency of Ronald Reagan: The era of the television presidency* for a discussion of Reagan's rhetoric.

[39]Jamieson, Ibid, p. 120.

[40]Henry, President Ronald Reagan's first inaugural address, 1981. In *The inaugural addresses of twentieth-century American presidents*, p. 265.

[41]Jamieson, *Eloquence in an electronic age*, pp. 126–136. Interestingly, Jamieson argues that by relying on visual evidence and personal experiences, Reagan adopted an "effeminate style" of speech. Women, she notes, tend to focus more on feelings than on facts and to "display their reactions in emotional terms" (p. 81)—much as Reagan did. Jamieson insightfully suggests that Reagan paved the way for female politicians to use this "effeminate" style in campaigning for public office. However, writing in 1988, she argues

that given their low credibility in the political realm, women run a risk by relying on the effeminate style.

[42] Wills, *Reagan's America: Innocents at home*, p. 4.

[43] Jamieson, *Eloquence in an electronic age*, p. 134.

[44] Jamieson, Ibid, p. 160. Jamieson argues that by doing this, Reagan made himself less accountable for his actions. By placing "the people" rather than himself at the center, he minimized his accountability, Jamieson argues, thus giving rise to the "Teflon president."

[45] Ibid, pp. 155–156.

[46] Ibid, p. 156.

[47] For a critical discussion of Reagan's narrative, see Smith & Smith, *The White House speaks*, pp. 212–214; Henry, President Reagan's first inaugural address, 1981, pp. 259–270; and Lewis, Telling America's story: Narrative form and the Reagan presidency, *Quarterly Journal of Speech*, 1987, 280–302. See also Fisher on narrative in *Human communication as narration: Toward a philosophy of reason, value, and action*.

[48] Lanzetta, Sullivan, Masters, & McHugo, Emotional and cognitive responses to televised images of political leaders. In *Mass media and political thought: An information-processing approach*, pp. 85–116.

[49] Quoted in Cunningham, *Talking politics: Choosing the president in the television age*, pp. 15–16.

[50] Jamieson, *Eloquence in an electronic age*, p. 132.

[51] Judge, Much more than hot air. *The Wall Street Journal*, March 11, 1996, p. A12.

Chapter 7

[1] See, for example, Smith & Smith, in *The president and the public: Rhetoric and national leadership*, p. 3.

[2] Campbell & Jamieson, *Deeds done in words: Presidential rhetoric and the genres of governance*, p. 15.

[3] Ibid, p. 16.

[4] Windt, President John F Kennedy's inaugural address, 1961. In *The inaugural addresses of twentieth- century American presidents*, pp. 189–190. (Note: In his comment, Windt does not quote Kennedy's "Ask not what your country can do for you" exhortation in its entirety, referring only to it as "his mighty exhortation ('Ask not … ')." I have filled in the rest of Kennedy's famous plea.

[5] Halford Ryan questions whether one can lump under the same category inaugurals delivered by different presidents in different historical epochs. He points out that if we assume inaugurals share the same characteristics, we may miss some of their distinctive features. Moreover, Ryan does not believe that inaugurals fit Aristotle's definition of epideictic speech for the simple reason that they do not blame or censure opponents in the fashion that Aristotle had in mind when he came up with the notion of epideictic oratory. Ryan acknowledges that conventional inaugurals can be described as epideictic, but the best ones, he notes, have been action oriented, articulating political visions. See Ryan, Introduction. In *The inaugural addresses of twentieth-century American presidents*, pp. xvi–xix, and Ryan, President Bill Clinton's inaugural address, 1993, in Ibid, p. 299. See also Hahn's review of Campbell and Jamieson's *Deeds done in words* in the *Southern Communication Journal*, 1991, p. 318.

[6] Smith & Smith, *The White House speaks*, p. 74; Campbell & Jamieson, *Deeds done in words*, Ch. 9.

[7] Smith & Smith, *The White House speaks*, pp. 67–75.

[8] Ibid, p. 75.

[9]Ibid, pp. 74–75.

[10]Kiewe, Introduction, The modern presidency and crisis rhetoric, pp. xvii–xviii, and Pratt, An analysis of three crisis speeches. Western Journal of Speech Communication, 1970, p. 194.

[11]Denton, Series Forward. In The modern presidency and crisis rhetoric, p. xi.

[12]Kiewe, Introduction, In The modern presidency and crisis rhetoric, p. xvii.

[13]Ivie, Declaring a national emergency: Truman's rhetorical crisis and the great debate of 1951. In The modern presidency and crisis rhetoric. pp. 1–5.

[14]Blair & Houck, Richard Nixon and the personalization of crisis. In The modern presidency and crisis rhetoric, p. 111.

[15]Ibid, p. 112.

[16]Zernicke, Pitching the presidency, p. 149.

[17]See also Smith & Smith, The White House speaks, pp. 215–216

[18]Smoller, The six o'clock presidency: A theory of presidential press relations in the age of television, p. 111.

[19]See Dickinson, Creating his own constraint: Ronald Reagan and the Iran-Contra crisis In The modern presidency and crisis rhetoric, p. 172.

[20]Ibid.

[21]Edelman, The symbolic uses of politics, p. 6.

[22]Goodnight, Vietnam: The metaphor and the movie. Paper presented to the Southern Speech Communication Association, Memphis, Tenn., April, 1988, p. 11.

[23]Pollock, The battle for the past: George Bush and the Gulf crisis. In The modern presidency and crisis rhetoric, pp. 210–211.

[24]Glad, Figuring out Saddam Hussein. In The presidency and the Persian Gulf War, p. 67.

[25]Windt, The presidency and speeches on international crises: Repeating the rhetorical past. In Essays in presidential rhetoric (2nd ed.), pp. 128–129. See also Pollock, The battle for the past: George Bush and the Gulf crisis.

[26]Kiewe, From a rhetorical trap to capitulation and obviation: The crisis rhetoric of George Bush's "Read my lips: No new taxes." In The modern presidency and crisis rhetoric, p. 185.

[27]Smith & Smith, The White House speaks, p. 237.

[28]Quoted in Jamieson, Eloquence in an electronic age, p. 129.

[29]Remarks by President, Governor, and Dr. Graham. The New York Times, April 24, 1995, p. B8.

[30]Campbell & Jamieson, Deeds done in words, p. 219.

[31]Ryan, Introduction. The modern presidency and crisis rhetoric, pp. xv–xix.

[32]Ryan, President Bill Clinton's inaugural address, 1993. In The inaugural addresses of twentieth-century American presidents, pp. 301–303.

[33]Quoted in Will, A weird sincerity, Newsweek, November 13, 1995, p. 94.

[34]Smith & Smith, The White House speaks, p. 192.

[35]Drew, On the edge: The Clinton presidency, pp. 127–128.

[36]Ibid, p. 136.

[37]See Samuelson, Budget charade, The Washington Post National Weekly Edition, January 1–7, 1996, p. 28.

[38]Perloff, The dynamics of persuasion, Chapter 9.

[39]Simon & Ostrom, The impact of televised speeches and foreign travel on presidential approval. Public Opinion Quarterly, 1989, p. 77.

[40]Ibid, pp. 78–79.

[41]Drew, On the edge: The Clinton presidency, p. 305.

[42]Dionne, They only look dead: Why progressives will dominate the next political era, p. 148.

[43]Behr & Iyengar, Television news, real-world cues, and changes in the public agenda. Public Opinion Quarterly, 1985, pp. 48–53.

[44]For a discussion of the "rally-round-the-flag" effect, see Mueller, *War, presidents, and public opinion*, and Mueller, *Policy and opinion in the Gulf War*. A discussion of the extensive literature on rally events is beyond the scope of this book.

[45]Kernell, *Going public: New strategies of presidential leadership* (2nd ed), pp. 130–131.

[46]Schudson, *The power of news*, p. 135.

[47]Roberts, President's coalition, *The New York Times*, October 27, 1982, p. 13.

[48]Schudson, *The power of news*, p. 137.

[49]Bodnick, "Going public" reconsidered: Reagan's 1981 tax and budget cuts, and revisionist theories of presidential power. *Congress and the Presidency*, 1990, pp. 13–28.

[50]Hart, *The sound of leadership: Presidential communication in the modern age*, pp. 195–198.

[51]Jamieson, *Eloquence in an electronic age*, pp. 220–221.

[52]Fiske & Taylor, *Social cognition*, pp. 188–190.

[53]Hart, *Seducing America: How television charms the modern voter*.

[54]McCullough, *Truman*, p. 980.

[55]Smith & Smith, *The White House speaks*, p. 247.

Chapter 8

[1]Green, M. Nobody covers the house. In *Congress and the news media*, p. 323. (Tragically, Lowenstein was shot and killed on March 14, 1980, in an insane act of political violence.)

[2]Cook, *Making laws and making news: Media strategies in the US. House of Representatives*, p. 13.

[3]One should add the caveat that in the late 1700s, House debates received more coverage than those that occurred in the Senate because House debates were more open-ended and were also regarded as more newsworthy. See Cook, *Making laws and making news*, pp. 14–15.

[4]Ibid, p. 18.

[5]Ibid.

[6]Ibid, p. 167.

[7]These developments occurred in part because of institutional reforms enacted in the 1970s, including the sunshine reforms that opened up committee and subcommittee hearings to the press and public.

[8]Elving, Brighter lights, wider windows: Presenting Congress in the 1990s. In *Congress, the press, and the public*, pp. 176–177.

[9]Sabato & Simpson, *Dirty little secrets:The persistence of corruption in American politics*, pp. 240–241.

[10]Hess, *Live from Capitol Hill!: Studies of Congress and the media*, p. 62.

[11]Ibid.

[12]Cook, *Making laws and making news*, p. 83. See also Cook, Press secretaries and media strategies in the House of Representatives: Deciding whom to pursue. *American Journal of Political Science*, 1988, pp. 1047–1069.

[13]For a discussion of how news favors incumbents over challengers, see Clarke & Evans, *Covering campaigns: Journalism in congressional elections*; See also Goldenberg & Traugott, *Campaigning for Congress*.

[14]See Polk, Eddy, & Andre, Use of congressional publicity in Wisconsin district, *Journalism Quarterly*, 1975, pp. 543–546; and Berkowitz & Adams, Information subsidy and agenda-building in local television news, *Journalism Quarterly*, 1990, pp. 723–731.

[15]Kurtz, *Hot air: All talk, all the time*, p. 166.

[16]Ibid, p. 167.

[17]Dionne, *They only look dead: Why progressives will dominate the next political era*, p. 212. See also Balz & Brownstein, *Storming the gates: Protest politics and the Republican revival*, pp. 118–121. In *Hot Air*, Kurtz points out that O'Neill could "order" cameras to pan on empty seats because the majority party in the House, not C-SPAN, controlled the cameras.

[18]Balz & Brownstein, *Storming the gates*, p. 184.

[19]Ibid, p. 185.

[20]At least that is the best guess, based on journalistic writing (see Balz & Brownstein, *Storming the gates*, pp. 179–189) and available theory (see chapter 12).

[21]Pitney, HTTP://Dems.lynch.Newt, *The Weekly Standard*, January 29, 1996, p. 13.

[22]Ibid, p. 39.

[23]Ibid, pp. 37–38.

[24]Weisskopf & Maraniss, Gingrich's war of words, *The Washington Post National Weekly Edition*, November 6–12, 1995, p. 6.

[25]Of course, you can argue that by dickering with the Republicans on cutting Medicare, Clinton was demonstrating his commitment to big government. However his rhetoric (e.g., his comment that "The era of big government is over") and his signing of welfare reform seem to argue otherwise.

[26]The *Newsweek* Poll (December 27–28, 1994), *Newsweek*, January 9, 1995, p. 28. The totals reported add up to 96%; the *Newsweek* poll does not indicate where the remaining 4% stood on the issue.

[27]Cook, *Making laws and making news*, pp. 62–68. Consistent with these findings, Entman and Page have found that the news media "calibrate news judgments rather precisely to the clout of the powerful actors whose remarks or actions are covered: the higher their power to shape newsworthy events, the more attention they receive." This tendency has obvious relevance for news about Congress. See Entman & Page, The news before the storm: The Iraq war debate and the limits to media independence. In *Taken by storm*, p. 97.

[28]Jamieson, *Eloquence in an electronic age: The transformation of political speechmaking*, p. 14. See also Kaid & Foote, How network television coverage of the president and Congress compare. *Journalism Quarterly*, 1985, pp. 59–65.

[29]Hess, *Live from Capitol Hill*, p. 104.

[30]Ibid.

[31]No Newt is good Newt, *Media Monitor*, (1995, March/April), p. 1.

[32]We need to be careful in assuming there has been a realignment from presidential news to Congressional news. There have been other periods in which Congress got big play in the news, such as during Watergate and at the beginning of Ronald Reagan's first term. Still, the ability of the 104th Congress elected in 1994 to influence the agenda, along with other historical developments, suggests that news is likely to focus more on Congress in the years to come.

[33]Quoted in Aronson, *The press and the cold war*, p. 69.

[34]Rozell, Press coverage of Congress, 1946–92. In *Congress, the press, and the public*, pp. 60–63.

[35]Ibid, p. 64.

[36]Ibid, pp. 73–81.

[37]Tidmarch & Pitney, Jr., Covering Congress. *Polity*, 1985, p. 481. See also Robinson & Appel, Network news coverage of Congress. *Political Science Quarterly*, 1979, pp. 412, 417.

[38]Miller, Goldenberg, & Erbring. Type-set politics: Impact of newspapers on public confidence. *American Political Science Review*, 1979, p. 70. Space considerations do not permit a discussion of the instances in which journalists and Congresspersons cooperate and work together, in line with the exchange model discussed in chapter 5. See Miller, Reporters and congressmen: Living in symbiosis, *Journalism Monographs*, 1978.

[39]Lichter & Amundson, Less news is worse news: Television news coverage of Congress, 1972·92. In *Congress, the press, and the public, p. 137;* No Newt is good Newt, *Media Monitor,* March/April 1995, pp. 1–3.

[40]Rozell, Press coverage of Congress, 1946–92, p. 109.

[41]Kenworthy, Keep the bums in! *The Washington Post,* April 26, 1992, p. C5.

[42]Hershey, The congressional elections. In *The election of 1992: Reports and interpretations,* p. 162.

[43]Quoted in Rozell, Press coverage of Congress, 1946–92, p. 104.

[44]Hershey, The congressional elections, p. 164; Bowman & Ladd, Public opinion toward Congress: A historical look. In *Congress, the press, and the public,* p. 47; Frolik, Ohio voters outraged by political mudslinging , *The Plain Dealer,* February 18, 1996, p. 12A. See also Hibbing & Theiss-Morse, *Congress as public enemy: Public attitudes toward American political institutions,* who remind us that there is dissatisfaction with national legislatures in European democracies as well.

[45]Hibbing & Theiss-Morse, Ibid, p. 157.

[46]Fenno, *Home style: House members in their districts,* p. 168.

[47]Elving, Brighter lights, wider windows: Presenting Congress in the 1990s. In *Congress, the press, and the public,* p. 187.

[48]Lichter & Amundson, Less news is worse news: Television news coverage of Congress, 1972–92, pp. 135–136.

[49]Dye & Zeigler, *American politics in the media age,* 2nd ed, p. 212; and Rozell, Press coverage of Congress, 1946–92, p. 110.

[50]Lichter & Amundson, Less news is worse news: Television coverage of Congress, 1972–1992, p. 136.

[51]See discussion of news of the health care debate in chapter 14.

[52]Parker, How the press views Congress. In *Congress, the press, and the public,* pp. 165–166.

[53]Bowman & Ladd, Public opinion toward Congress: A historical look, pp. 45–46.

[54]Elving, Brighter lights, wider windows: Presenting Congress in the 1990s, p. 170. Of course a real cynic would say that given the rogues and thieves who inhabited Congress in the nineteenth century, that is not saying very much.

[55]Hibbing & Theiss-Morse, *Congress as public enemy, p. 160.*

[56]Elving, Brighter lights, wider windows, p. 188.

[57]Hibbing & Theiss-Morse, *Congress as public enemy,* p. 61.

[58]Ibid, pp. 193–198.

[59]Wolfson, *The untapped power of the press: Explaining government to the people,* pp. 46–49.

[60]See Morin, Tuned out, turned off, *The Washington Post National Weekly Edition,* February 5–11, 1996, p. 6.

[61]Cook, *Making laws and making news,* p. 167.

[62]Bodnick, "Going public" reconsidered: Reagan's 1981 tax and budget cuts, and revisionist theories of presidential power. *Congress and the Presidency,* 1990, pp. 13–28.

Chapter 9

[1]Kaniss, *Making local news,* p. 202.

[2]For a discussion of news and state government, see Dunn, *Public officials and the press,* and Wolfson, *The untapped power of the press: Explaining government to the people,* chapter 8.

[3]Kaniss, *Making local news,* pp. 13, 21.

[4]Kaniss, ibid, p. 22. See Leonard, *The power of the press: The birth of American political reporting* for a critical view of muckraking and the early twentieth century political press.

[5]Baran & Davis, Mass communication theory: Foundations, ferment, and future, pp. 164–165. Of course, there are many types of functional theories and there are important differences among them. However, Baran and Davis's summary statement identifies a general characteristic that all functional approaches share.

[6]See, for example, Olien, Donohue, & Tichenor, The community editor's power and the reporting of conflict, Journalism Quarterly, 1968, pp. 243–252; Donohue, Tichenor, & Olien, Gatekeeping: Mass media systems and information control. In Current perspectives in mass communication research, pp. 41–69; and Tichenor, Donohue, & Olien, Community conflict and the press.

[7]Tichenor, Donohue, & Olien, Community conflict and the press, p. 220.

[8]See Edelstein & Schulz, The leadership role of the weekly newspaper as seen by community leaders: A sociological perspective. In People, Society and Mass Communication, pp. 221–238.

[9]Demers, Corporate newspaper structure, editorial page vigor and social change. Paper presented to the annual convention of the Midwest Association for Public Opinion Research, 1995, p. 11.

[10]Ibid, pp. 11–12.

[11]Pluralism is characterized by high role specialization, diversity of occupations, bureaucracies in government, ethnic and religious diversity, and a tendency to assess performance on meritocratic grounds rather than on primary group and family bases. See Olien, Donohue, & Tichenor, Conflict, consensus, and public opinion. In Public opinion and the communication of consent, p. 310.

[12]Long, Defending cigarettes where tobacco is king, The Plain Dealer, August 28, 1995, pp. 1–A, 4–A.

[13]An exception is when conflicts are initiated by outside agencies and in times of major social structural change. See Olien, Donohue, & Tichenor, Conflict, consensus, and public opinion, pp. 309–310.

[14]Paletz, Reichert, & McIntyre, How the media support local governmental authority, Public Opinion Quarterly, 1971, pp. 80–92

[15]Ibid, pp. 84–85. One might counterargue that maintenance of psychological distance between Council members and the public is quite appropriate and is consistent with the principles of representative democracy.

[16]See Olien et al, The community editor's power and the reporting of conflict; Tichenor et al, Community conflict and the press; Donohue, Olien, & Tichenor, Reporting conflict by pluralism, newspaper type and ownership, Journalism Quarterly, 1985, 489–499, 507; and Griffin & Dunwoody, Impacts of information subsidies and community structure on local press coverage of environmental contamination, Journalism Quarterly, 1995, pp. 271–284. Griffin and Dunwoody find partial support for the community pluralism hypothesis.

[17]Kaniss, Making local news, chapter 7.

[18]Ibid, p. 52.

[19]Banfield, Political influence, p. 231.

[20]See Kaniss, Making local news, pp. 52–55. For detailed discussion of the LA Times coverage, see Gottlieb & Wolf, Thinking big: The story of the Los Angeles Times, its publishers, and their influence on Southern California. The excerpt from the editorial appears on page 530 of their book.

[21]Kaniss, ibid, pp. 66–67.

[22]Ibid, pp. 81–82.

[23]Ibid, p. 195.

[24]Ibid, p. 108.

[25]Ibid, pp. 124–125; Berkowitz, TV news sources and news channels: A study in agenda building, Journalism Quarterly, 1987, pp. 508–513.

[26]Kaniss, *Making local news*, chapter 4.
[27]Kaniss, ibid, p. 158.
[28]Dominick, *The dynamics of mass communication* (4th ed), p. 117.
[29]See Hertog & McLeod, Anarchists wreak havoc in downtown Minneapolis: A multi-level study of media coverage of radical protest, *Journalism & Mass Communication Monographs*, 1995, for a study of how an alternative anarchist newspaper covered a radical protest.
[30]Bartimole, The big diversion, *The Cleveland Free Times*, December 6, 1995, p. 6.
[31]See Goldenberg, *Making the papers: The access of resource-poor groups to the metropolitan press*; Ryan, *Prime-time activism: Media strategies for grassroots organizing*; and Kaniss, *Making local news*, pp. 165–166, who points out that since Goldenberg made her observations in the 1970s, citizens groups have turned to local TV news to capture public attention.
[32]Bennett, The news about foreign policy. In *Taken by storm: The media, public opinion, and U.S. foreign policy in the Gulf War*, p. 31.
[33]Fans turned lament to song, *The Plain Dealer*, November 12, 1995, p. 12A.
[34]Kurtz, *Hot air: All talk, all the time*, p. 3.
[35]Byerly, *Community journalism*, p. 5. For evidence that they have this effect, see McLeod, Daily et al, Community integration, local media use, and democratic processes, *Communication Research*, 1996, pp. 179–209.
[36]There is a voluminous literature on gratifications sought and derived from mass media. See Jeffres, *Mass media processes* (2nd ed.), chapter 6, and for an interesting study of news gratifications during a newspaper strike, Elliott & Rosenberg, The 1985 Philadelphia newspaper strike: A uses and gratifications study, *Journalism Quarterly*, 1987, pp. 679–687. For a discussion of media uses and community linkages, see Stamm, *Newspaper use and community ties: Toward a dynamic theory*. For a larger perspective on news media performance in covering local, as well as national, issues, see McLeod, Kosicki, & McLeod, The expanding boundaries of political communication effects. In *Media Effects: Advances in Theory and Research*, pp. 123–162.
[37]Olien, Donohue, & Tichenor, Conflict, consensus, and public opinion, p. 305.
[38]Ibid, p. 306. Complicating matters is the fact that local news media are more than happy to cover political scandals. See, for example, Schoenbach & Becker, Origins and consequences of mediated public opinion, in *Public opinion and the communication of consent*, p. 339. Schoenbach and Becker describe news coverage of, and public opinion toward, a mayor accused of having an affair with one of his administrators.
[39]See Demers, *Corporate newspaper structure, editorial page vigor and social change*, pp. 24–25.
[40]Wolfson, *The untapped power of the press*, p. 154.
[41]Quoted in Marks, "Public journalism" aims to revitalize public life. *The Christian Science Monitor*, July 24, 1995, p. 12. See also Rosen & Merritt, *Public journalism: Theory and practice*.
[42]Shepard, Community journalism, *The responsive community*, Winter, 1994/95, pp. 30–40.

Chapter 10

[1]Sproule, Social responses to twentieth-century propaganda. In *Propaganda: A pluralistic perspective*, p. 6. See also Sproule, Propaganda studies in American social science: The rise and fall of the critical paradigm, *Quarterly Journal of Speech*, 1987, pp. 60–78.
[2]Ibid, p. 7.
[3]Reynolds, *The Sun Also Rises: A novel of the twenties*, p. 63.
[4]Spoule, Social responses to twentieth-century propaganda, p. 9.

[5]There continues to be scholarly debate about these issues. For example, Sproule argues that elite criticisms of the CPI did filter down to ordinary citizens. He notes that Army researchers evaluating the *Why We Fight* films expressed concern about this "inter-world war cynicism." Sproule, Letter to Richard M. Perloff, June 14, 1996.

[6]There was less emphasis than you might think on defining propaganda. More recently, Jowett and O'Donnell have defined propaganda as "the deliberate and systematic attempt to shape perceptions, manipulate cognitions, and direct behavior to achieve a response that furthers the desired intent of the propagandist." They have differentiated propaganda from persuasion which, in their view, is more benign and transactional. (See Jowett & O'Donnell, *Propaganda and persuasion*, 2nd ed., p. 4). Not all scholars agree. From a theoretical perspective, it is difficult to say where propaganda ends and persuasion begins. Some authors define propaganda as persuasion with negative connotations. See Perloff, *The dynamics of persuasion*, chapter 1.

[7]Interestingly, one of Thurstone's students was Samuel Stouffer who played a major role in the *American Soldier* research project during World War II. Stouffer taught at Wisconsin for a time, and one of his students was Ralph Nafziger, who would go on to play an important role in the establishment of journalism and mass communication research programs. See Sloan (Ed.), *Makers of the media mind: Journalism educators and their ideas.*

[8]See Sproule, Social responses to twentieth-century propaganda, p. 13.

[9]However, they did not appear to have a simplistic view of propaganda. If anything, their views of the impact of propaganda were sophisticated. See Chaffee and Hochheimer, The beginnings of political communication research in the United States: Origins of the "limited effects" model. In *Mass communication review yearbook*, 1985, pp. 75–104. There is little question, though, that post-World War I intellectuals viewed propaganda negatively and were especially critical of the CPI campaign.

[10]See Sproule, Propaganda studies in American social science: The rise and fall of the critical paradigm. Sproule examines the tension between the scientific and critical approaches and suggests that both approaches are useful for the study of modern social influence. Interestingly, Delia points out that communication research did not emerge as a distinct domain of scholarly study until the late 1940s and 1950s, at which time Wilbur Schramm and others in the journalism and speech fields built on and extended the early work of psychologists and sociologists, melding communication into a distinct field of study. See Delia, Communication research: A history. In *Handbook of Communication Science*, 1987, pp. 20–98. Parenthetically, it should be noted that there has been a resurgence of interest in the study of propaganda, and the field continues to arouse interest and controversy. See Jowett & O'Donnell, *Propaganda and persuasion.*

[11]Lazarsfeld, Berelson, & Gaudet, *The people's choice: How the voter makes up his mind in a presidential campaign*, p. 3.

[12]Ibid, p. 95.

[13]Lowery & DeFleur, *Milestones in mass communication research: Media effects* (3rd ed), p. 91. There is some debate as to whether Lazarsfeld et al. even expected to find large effects. For a long time, mass communication scholars believed that the early researchers subscribed to a "hypodermic needle" or "magic bullet" model of persuasion. Recent scholarship, such as Chaffee and Hochheimer's work cited above, has demolished this view, although Lazarsfeld et al.'s evident surprise at finding intepersonal effects suggests that they held to some sort of mass society perspective. For another account of the history of mass communication scholarship, see Bineham, A historical account of the hypodermic model in mass communication, *Communication Monographs*, 1988, pp. 230–246.

[14]See also the later study, conducted in Elmira, New York by Berelson, Lazarsfeld, & McPhee, *Voting.*

[15]Katz & Lazarsfeld, *Personal influence: The part played by people in the flow of mass communication.*

[16]Greenberg, Diffusion of news of the Kennedy assassination, *Public Opinion Quarterly*, 1964, pp. 225–232.

[17]DeFleur, Diffusing information, *Society*, 1988, pp. 72–81. See also Rogers, *Diffusion of innovations* (3rd ed.).

[18]Klapper, *The effects of mass communication*, p. 8.

[19]See Chaffee & Hochheimer, The beginnings of political communication research in the United States: Origins of the "limited effects" model, p. 92. Kraus and Davis also lament the influence of Klapper's "limited effects" paradigm on political communication research in *The effects of mass communication on political behavior.* Interestingly, McLeod and Blumler identify four scholars who did not accept Klapper's formulations. See McLeod & Blumler, The macrosocial level of communication science. In *Handbook of communication science*, p. 288.

[20]Becker, McCombs, & McLeod, The development of political cognitions. In *Political communication: Strategies for research*, p. 29.

[21]Weimann, *The influentials: People who influence people*, pp. 250–254.

[22]The term "bete noire" refers to someone who is disliked or avoided.

[23]An early and classic mass communication text was Wilbur Schramm's *The process and effects of mass communication.*

[24]Hovland, Janis, & Kelley, *Communication and persuasion.*

[25]Though for an alternative view, see McGuire, The myth of massive media impact: Savagings and salvagings. In *Public communication and behavior* (Vol. 1), 1986, pp. 173–257.

[26]See Wright, *Mass communication: A sociological perspective* (3rd ed).

[27]See Chaffee & Miyo, Selective exposure and the reinforcement hypothesis: An intergenerational panel study of the 1980 presidential campaign, *Communication Research*, 1983, pp. 3–36; Perloff, *The dynamics of persuasion*, chapter 9, Sears & Freedman, Selective exposure to information: A critical review, *Public Opinion Quarterly*, 1967, pp. 194–213; and Pratkanis, The cognitive representation of attitudes. In *Attitude structure and function*, 1989, pp. 84–89.

[28]Gitlin, Media sociology: The dominant paradigm, *Theory and Society*, 1978, pp. 205–253.

[29]Ibid, p. 251.

[30]Quoted in Weimann, *The influentials: People who influence people*, p. 242.

[31]Simpson, U. S. mass communication research, counterinsurgency, and scientific "reality." In *Ruthless criticism: New perspectives in U.S. communication history*, pp. 335, 340.

[32]In my book, *The dynamics of persuasion*, I traced the origins of brainwashing, noting that it was a "devil-term" that originated during the Korean War and was used to excoriate Communist-style influence techniques that, however nefarious some may have been, are better understood as complex combinations of coercion and persuasion.

[33]Simpson, U. S. mass communication research, counterinsurgency, and scientific "reality," pp. 335–340.

[34]Ibid, p. 334.

[35]Chaffee points out that Simpson inappropriately relabels "persuasion," a long-standing field of academic inquiry, "coercion," and unfairly connects "persuasion" with "domination," "subversion," and "torture." See Chaffee's review of Simpson's book in *Journal of American History* and Rogers' *A history of communication study: A biographical approach.*

[36]See Manheim, Strategic public diplomacy: Managing Kuwait's image during the Gulf conflict. In *Taken by storm: The media, public opinion, and U.S. foreign policy in the Gulf War*, pp. 131–148.

[37]Katz, Foreword. In *The influentials: People who influence people*, p. xi. In recent years, there has been increased scholarly attention directed to integrating mass and interpersonal communication concepts; contemporary researchers have tended to view interpersonal and mass communication as complementary, rather than conflicting, aspects of political communication. See Chaffee & Mutz, Comparing mediated and interpersonal communication data. In *Advancing communication science: Merging mass and interpersonal processes*, pp. 19–43, and Kinsey & Chaffee, Communication behavior and presidential approval: The decline of George Bush, *Political Communication*, 1996, pp. 281–291. For another integrative view of mass and interpersonal communication, see Lenart, *Shaping political attitudes: The impact of interpersonal communication and mass media*.

[38]Although it is not always guided by conventional psychological theories, uses and gratifications research, because it focuses on the individual, can be viewed as a "psychological communication perspective," as Rubin notes. See Rubin, Media uses and effects: A uses-and-gratifications perspective. In *Media effects: Advances in theory and research*, p. 418.

[39]See, among many articles on this subject, McLeod & Becker, Testing the validity of gratification measures through political effects analysis. In *The uses of mass communications: Current perspectives on gratifications research*, pp. 137–164. Contemporary research on the audience has expanded on the early approaches by looking at macro linkages and at how media institutions define audiences, as in Ettema & Whitney (Eds.), *Audiencemaking: How the media create the audience*.

[40]See, for example, Graber, *Processing the news: How people tame the information tide* (2nd ed), and Kraus & Perloff (Eds.), *Mass media and political thought: An information-processing approach*.

[41]Neuman, Just, & Crigler, *Common knowledge: News and the construction of political meaning*, pp. 17–18. David Swanson did pioneering work in this area, calling attention to how people mentally construct the political world. See Swanson, A constructivist approach. In *Handbook of political communication*, pp. 169–191.

[42]One can also view agenda-setting as a systems level theory if one looks at it from the perspective of "what it means to have a media system that determines which issues, among a whole series of possibilities, are presented to the public for attention." See Blumler & Gurevitch, The political effects of mass communication. In *Culture, society and the media*, p. 249.

[43]McLeod, On evaluating news media performance, *Political Communication*, 1993, p. 20.

[44]Dayan and Katz, *Media events: The live broadcasting of history*, p. 1.

[45]Ibid, p. 89. Using the interesting (but conceptually loose) definition of media events, Dayan and Katz come up with a number of hypotheses of how media events influence individuals, leisure time, institutions, and society as a whole. It is not always clear which technological features of television the authors have in mind when they discuss media events.

[46]Halloran, *Mass media and society: The challenge of research*, p. 6.

[47]Curran, Gurevitch, & Woollacott, The study of the media: Theoretical approaches, p. 14. In *Culture, society and the media*, p. 14.

[48]Marx & Engels, *The German ideology*, p. 64.

[49]Katz, Communications research since Lazarsfeld, *Public Opinion Quarterly*, 1987, p. S32.

[50]McLeod & Blumler, The macrosocial level of communication science, pp. 284–285.

Chapter 11

[1]Quoted in Weaver, McCombs, & Spellman, Watergate and the media: A case study of agenda-setting. *American Politics Quarterly*, 1975, p. 458.

[2]Kerr, Anatomy of the drug issue: How, after years, it erupted, *The New York Times*, November 17, 1986, p. A1.

[3]Rogers and Dearing, Agenda-setting research: Where has it been, where is it going? *Communication Yearbook 11*, 1988, p. 555.

[4]Lippmann, *Public Opinion*, p. 364.

[5]Quoted in Weaver et al, Watergate and the media: A case study of agenda-setting, p. 460.

[6]Lang & Lang, The mass media and voting. In *Reader in public opinion and communication* (2nd ed.), p. 468.

[7]Cohen, *The press and foreign policy*, p. 13.

[8]I will call agenda-setting a theory in this chapter for ease of discussion and because it is one of the major hypothesis-generating models in political communication research. I recognize that it would not be regarded as a theory if one invoked strict canons of the philosophy of science.

[9]McCombs, Agenda-setting research: A bibliographic essay. *Political Communication Review*, 1976, p. 3. However, as Rogers and Dearing point out, it is difficult to obtain evidence for such a claim. One would have to show that the absence of media coverage led to effects, a daunting empirical issue. The general idea, though, is interesting and worthy perhaps of experimental study.

[10]Lipstadt, *Beyond belief: The American press and the coming of the Holocaust 1933–1945*.

[11]Weaver, Media agenda-setting and public opinion: Is there a link? In *Communication yearbook 8*, 1984, p. 682.

[12]McLeod, Becker, & Byrnes, Another look at the agenda-setting function of the press, *Communication Research*, 1974, pp. 131–165.

[13]McCombs & Shaw, The agenda-setting function of mass media, *Public Opinion Quarterly*, 1972, pp. 176–185. For other correlational support for the agenda-setting hypothesis, see Protess & McCombs (Eds.), *Agenda-setting: Readings on media, public opinion, and policy-making*.

[14]Funkhouser, The issues of the sixties: An exploratory study in the dynamics of public opinion, *Public Opinion Quarterly*, 1973, pp. 62–75.

[15]Iyengar and Kinder, *News that matters*, chapter 3. (Quasiexperimental support for agenda-setting has been provided by Protess et al., in *The journalism of outrage*, discussed in chapter 12.)

[16]Ibid, p. 19.

[17]Ibid, p. 30. For other studies of the news media's causal impact on the public agenda, see Behr & Iyengar, Television news, real-world cues, and changes in the public agenda. *Public Opinion Quarterly*, 1985, pp. 38–57; Fan, *Predictions of public opinion from the mass media: Computer content analysis and mathematical modeling*; MacKuen & Coombs, *More than news: Media power in public affairs*; Tipton, Haney, & Basehart, Media agenda-setting in city and state election campaigns, *Journalism Quarterly*, 1975, pp. 15–22; and Weaver, Graber, McCombs, & Eyal, *Media agenda-setting in a presidential election: Issues, images, and interest*.

[18]Blumler & Gurevitch, The political effects of mass communication. In *Culture, society and the media*, p. 249.

[19]Rogers & Dearing, Agenda-setting research: Where has it been, where is it going?, p. 569.

[20]Ibid.

[21]Iyengar and Kinder, *News that matters*, chapter 4.

[22]See McLeod, Becker, & Brynes, Another look at the agenda-setting function of the press; and Iyengar and Kinder, ibid. For corroborative research on involvement as a moderator of the effects of priming—a concept related to agenda-setting—see Krosnick & Kinder, Altering the foundations of support for the president through priming, *American Political Science Review*, 1990, pp. 497–512; and Krosnick & Brannon, The impact of the Gulf

War on the ingredients of presidential evaluations: Multidimensional effects of political involvement, *American Political Science Review*, 1993, pp. 963–975. Suffice it to say that the moderating role of involvement is complex, varying as a function of the type of involvement one is interested in.

[23] See Weaver, Political issues and voter need for orientation. In *Agenda setting: Readings on media, public opinion, and policymaking*, pp. 131–140. Need for orientation also has complex effects on agenda-setting, as Weaver's work indicates.

[24] Yagade & Dozier, The media agenda-setting effect of concrete versus abstract issues, *Journalism Quarterly*, 1990, p. 4.

[25] Zucker, The variable nature of news media influence. In *Communication Yearbook*, 1978, p. 227.

[26] Weaver et al, *Media agenda-setting in a presidential election*, p. 104.

[27] Yagade & Dozier, The media agenda-setting effect of concrete versus abstract issues; Wanta & Hu, The agenda-setting effects of international news coverage: An examination of differing news frames, *International Journal of Public Opinion Research*, 1993, pp. 250–264.

[28] For a discussion of agenda-setting and social versus personal concerns, see Mutz, Mass media and the depoliticization of personal experience, *American Journal of Political Science*, 1992, pp. 483–508, and Weaver, Zhu, & Willnat, The bridging function of interpersonal communication in agenda-setting, *Journalism Quarterly*, 1992, pp. 856–867. Needless to say, the influence of interpersonal communication on agenda-setting is also complex, as documented by numerous studies.

[29] Iyengar & Kinder, *News that matters*, chapter 5. For evidence media can have strong effects on those personally affected by a problem or on obtrusive issues, see Erbring, Goldenberg, & Miller, Front-page news and real-world cues: A new look at agenda-setting by the media, *American Journal of Political Science*, 1980, pp. 16–49; and Demers, Craff, Choi, & Pessin, Issue obtrusiveness and the agenda-setting effects of national network news, *Communication Research*, 1989, pp. 793–812.

[30] Iyengar & Kinder, ibid.

[31] Researchers have studied the amount of time that is required for the media to influence the public agenda. See, for example, Brosius & Kepplinger, The agenda-setting function of television news: Static and dynamic views, *Communication Research*, 1990, pp. 183–211; and Salwen, *Time in agenda-setting: The accumulation of media coverage on audience issue salience*, Paper presented to the International Communication Association, 1986. Others have noted that the lag between the time that an issue appears on the media agenda to the time it appears on the public agenda depends in important ways on the issue under investigation; agenda–setting theory does not make clear predictions about what the optimal time lag should be. See Gandy, *Beyond agenda–setting: Information subsidies and public policy*, p. 7.

[32] Iyengar & Kinder, *News that matters*, p. 63.

[33] Krosnick & Kinder, Altering the foundations of support for the president through priming.

[34] Krosnick & Brannon, The impact of the Gulf War on the ingredients of presidential evaluations.

[35] For criticisms of agenda-setting research, see Swanson, Feeling the elephant: Some observations on agenda-setting research. In *Communication yearbook 11*, 1988, pp. 603–619; Lang & Lang, Watergate: An exploration of the agenda-building process. In *Mass communication review yearbook 2*, 1981, pp. 447–468; Kosicki, Problems and opportunities in agenda-setting research, *Journal of Communication*, 1993, pp. 100–127; Becker, Reflecting on metaphors, *Communication yearbook 14*, 1991, pp. 341–346; Whitney, Agenda-setting: Power and contingency, *Communication yearbook 14*, 1991, pp. 347–356; and Shaw & McCombs, *The emergence of American political issues: The agenda-setting function of the press*.

Chapter 12

[1]McCombs & Gilbert, News influence on our pictures of the world. In *Perspectives on media effects*, p. 13.

[2]See also Shoemaker (Ed), *Communication campaigns about drugs: Government, media, and the public* for a case study discussion of why the media opted to devote substantial coverage to drugs in 1986 and the impact of news stories on public opinion and policy.

[3]Dearing & Rogers, AIDS and the media agenda. In *AIDS: A communication perspective*, pp. 180–181.

[4]Kinsella, *Covering the plague: AIDS and the American media*, p. 61.

[5]A president typically can influence the media agenda by rolling out a new policy and giving public addresses, as noted in chapter 11. However, there are cases in which presidential speeches, notably the State of the Union, don't have this effect. See Gilbert, Eyal, McCombs, & Nicholas, The state of the union address and the press agenda, *Journalism Quarterly*, 1980, pp. 584–588. For a more recent study of the influence of the president on the news media agenda, see Wanta & Foote, The president-news media relationship: A time series analysis of agenda setting, *Journal of Broadcasting & Electronic Media*, 1994, pp. 437–448.

[6]Dearing & Rogers, AIDS and the media agenda, p. 182.

[7]Rogers, Dearing, & Chang, AIDS in the 1980s: The agenda-setting process for a public issue, *Journalism Monographs*, 1991, p. 43. See also Trumbo, Longitudinal modeling of public issues: An application of the agenda-setting process to the issue of global warming. *Journalism Monographs*, 152, 1995.

[8]For a discussion of this aspect of the bathhouse controversy, see Shilts, *And the band played on: Politics, people, and the AIDS epidemic*.

[9]Schudson, *Watergate in American memory: How we remember, forget, and reconstruct the past*, p. 104.

[10]Lang & Lang, *The battle for public opinion: The president, the press, and the polls during Watergate*, pp. 32–34; McLeod et al, Another look at the agenda-setting function of the press, *Communication Research*, 1974, pp. 131–165.

[11]Lang & Lang, ibid, p. 38.

[12]Ibid, pp. 44–45.

[13]Ibid, p. 51.

[14]Ibid, p. 60.

[15]Lang & Lang, *The battle for public opinion*.

[16]Elder & Cobb, Agenda-building and the politics of aging, *Policy Studies Journal*, 1984, p. 115.

[17]Protess, Cook, et al., *The journalism of outrage: Investigative reporting and agenda building in America*, pp. 238–239.

[18]See Cook & Skogan, Convergent and divergent voice models of the rise and fall of policy issues. In *Agenda-setting: Readings on media, public opinion, and policymaking*, pp. 189–206; Protess et al, *The journalism of outrage*, & Kingdon, *Agendas, alternatives, and public policies* (2nd ed.).

[19]Ibid, p. 176.

[20]It might be argued that since Congressional sources contacted *The Philadelphia Inquirer*, this is an example of policymaker-initiated agenda-building. However, it was the newspaper that transformed an idea into a coherent *issue*. A more convincing case of policymaker-initiated agenda-building occurs when an issue is clearly on the *policy agenda* and then moves to the *media agenda*.

[21]Just what the policy agenda is can be a matter of some debate. Generally speaking, the policy agenda refers to the issues that consume leading policymakers' time, attention, and resources.

[22]See Page & Tannenbaum, Populistic deliberation and talk radio, *Journal of Communication*, 1996, pp. 33–54.

[23]Ibid, p. 43.

[24]Ibid, p. 51.

[25]Excerpted from Rogers & Dearing, Agenda-setting research: Where has it been, where is it going?, *Communication Yearbook 11*, pp. 579–580.

[26]See Linksy, *Impact: How the press affects federal policy-making*; Trumbo, Longitudinal modeling of public issues: An application of the agenda-setting process to the issue of global warming; Kingdon, *Agendas, alternatives, and public policies*; and Gonzenbach's thorough analysis of agenda-building on the drug issue in *The media, the president, and public opinion: A longitudinal analysis of the drug issue, 1984–1991*.

[27]Downs, Up and down with ecology: The "issue-attention cycle," In *Agenda-setting: Readings on media, public opinion, and policymaking*, p. 27; and Hilgartner & Bosk, The rise and fall of social problems: A public arenas model, *American Journal of Sociology*, 1988, pp. 53–78.

[28]Neuman, Just, & Crigler, *Common knowledge: News and the construction of political meaning*, p. 60.

[29]Pan & Kosicki, Framing analysis: An approach to news discourse, *Political Communication*, 1993, p. 57. See also Gamson & Modigliani, Media discourse and public opinion on nuclear power: A constructionist approach, *American Journal of Sociology*, 1989, pp. 1–37.

[30]For another example of framing in news coverage of foreign policy, see Entman, Framing U. S. coverage of international news: Contrasts in narratives of the KAL and Iran Air incidents, *Journal of Communication*, 1991, pp. 6–27.

[31]Other scholars use a related concept, schema, to describe the structures people use to process information. See Lau & Sears (Eds.), *Political cognition*, and Graber, *Processing the news: How people tame the information tide* (2nd ed.) for discussions of political schema. Framing has replaced schema as the favored term in political cognition discourse because it is broader and suggests linkages with the larger political system.

[32]Iyengar, *Is anyone responsible?: How television frames political issues*.

[33]See Iyengar, ibid; Park & Kosicki, Presidential support during the Iran-Contra affair: People's reasoning process and media influence, *Communication Research*, 1995, pp. 207–236; and Pan & Kosicki, Assessing news media influences on the formation of whites' racial policy preferences, *Communication Research*, 1996, pp. 147–178.

[34]Price & Tewksbury, News values and public opinion: A theoretical account of media priming and framing. In *Progress in Communication Sciences*, 1996. See also Price, Tewksbury, & Powers, *Switching trains of thought: The impact of news frames on readers' cognitive responses*. Paper presented to the Midwest Association for Public Opinion Research, 1995.

Chapter 13

[1]Kaid, Tedesco, & Spiker, Media conflicts over Clinton policies: Political advertising and the battle for public opinion. In *The Clinton presidency: Images, issues, and communication strategies*, pp. 117–118.

[2]Drew, *On the edge: The Clinton presidency*, pp. 300–301; Johnson & Broder, *The system: The American way of politics at the breaking point*, pp. 51–52.

[3]Drew, ibid, p. 302.

[4] Johnson & Broder, *The system*, p. 154.

[5]Holloway, The Clintons and the health care crisis: Opportunity lost, promise unfulfilled. In *The Clinton presidency: Images, issues, and communication strategies*, pp. 176–177.
[6]Ibid, p. 177.
[7]Ibid, p. 178.
[8]Johnson & Broder, *The system*, p. 101.
[9]Ibid, pp. 613–614.
[10]Ibid, pp. 614–615.
[11]Ibid, p. 52.
[12]Ibid, p. 326.
[13]Ibid, p. 328.
[14]Ibid, p. 234.
[15]Ibid, p. 195.
[16]Kaid et al, Media conflicts over Clinton policies: Political advertising and the battle for public opinion.
[17]Johnson & Broder, *The system*, chapter 10.
[18]Kaid et al, Media conflicts over Clinton policies: Political advertising and the battle for public opinion, pp. 111–112.
[19]An ad was deemed unfair or misleading by Jamieson & Cappella (see citation in endnote 20) if it made a false claim, distorted evidence, exaggerated the size of an existing problem, or invited false inferences.
[20]Jamieson & Cappella, *Media in the middle: Fairness and accuracy in the 1994 health care reform debate* Report of the Annenberg Public Policy Center of the University of Pennsylvania, 1994; and Kaid et al, Media conflicts over Clinton policies: Political advertising and the battle for public opinion. My summary is based on findings from both these studies.
[21]Consider opponents' claim that the bureaucracy will dictate patients' choice of doctors. In fact the "bureaucracy" presently "dictates"—or influences—patients' choice of doctors in HMOs and managed care plans. Anyone who is a member of an HMO or a managed care plan—i.e., millions and millions of Americans—is, as a practical matter, limited in choice of doctors and hospitals. This criticism of the health care delivery system applies as much to the status quo as to Clinton's plan.

Chapter 14

[1]Jamieson & Cappella, *Media in the middle: Fairness and accuracy in the 1994 health care reform debate*. Report of the Annenberg Public Policy Center.
[2]Ibid.
[3]Blendon & Benson, *Making major changes in the health care system: Public opinion parallels between two recent debates*. Paper presented to the annual convention of the American Association for Public Opinion Research, 1996.
[4]Kaid et al, Media conflicts over Clinton policies. In *The Clinton presidency*, p. 118; Blendon & Benson, *Making major changes in the health care system*.
[5]See Perloff, *The dynamics of persuasion*, pp. 159–166 for a discussion of fear appeals.
[6]Stated by Jamieson in interview with Bill Moyers in television documentary, *The great health care debate*.
[7]Johnson & Broder, *The system*, p. 484.
[8]Molotch and his colleagues refer to this as a "leaping impact," where policy problems are ameliorated without official action. See Molotch, Protess, & Gordon, The media-policy connection: Ecologies of news. In *Political communication research: Approaches, studies, assessments*.

[9]There is, of course, continued debate about whether the move to managed care is a good thing, with critics telling horror stories about HMOs expelling doctors for ordering tests that the doctor believes to be medically necessary, but that the health plan feels would increase costs. Defenders respond that these are exceptions and that managed care represents the most cost-effective mechanism to provide quality care to Americans, particularly those who lack health insurance.

[10]Johnson & Broder, *The system*, pp. 534–535.

[11]Apologies to McCubbins, who edited *Under the watchful eye: Managing presidential campaigns in the television era*.

[12]A final complicated irony to the health care campaign is that the 104th Congress, which was Republican-controlled, passed more health care legislation than the Democratic-controlled 103rd For example, the 104th Congress approved a bill that made it easier for workers to keep health insurance if they lost or changed jobs.

Chapter 15

[1]Mancini & Swanson, Politics, media, and modern democracy: Introduction. In *Politics, media, and modern democracy: An international study of innovations in electoral campaigning and their consequences*, p. 1.

[2]Just, et al., *Crosstalk: Citizens, candidates, and the media in a presidential campaign*, p. 3.

[3]Troy, *See how they ran: The changing role of the presidential candidate*, (Rev. ed.) p. 7.

[4]Smith, Time to go negative, *The Wall Street Journal*, October 8, 1996, p. A22. See also Troy, ibid.

[5]Troy, *See how they ran*, p. 20.

[6]Jamieson, *Packaging the presidency*, pp. 8–11.

[7]Troy, *See how they ran*, p. 65.

[8]Ibid, p. 66.

[9]Jamieson, The evolution of political advertising in America. In *New perspectives on political advertising*, p. 10.

[10]Adatto, *Picture perfect: The art and artifice of public image making*, p. 73.

[11]Troy, *See how they ran*, p. 82.

[12]Johnson-Cartee & Copeland, *Negative political advertising: Coming of age*, pp. 6–7.

[13]Troy, *See how they ran*, p. 40.

[14]Jamieson, *Packaging the presidency*, p. 66.

[15]Matthews, *Kennedy & Nixon: The rivalry that shaped postwar America*, p. 125.

[16]Troy, *See how they ran*, p. 213.

[17]Ibid.

[18]Ibid, p. 215.

[19]Jamieson, *Packaging the presidency*, pp. 262–263.

[20]Troy, *See how they ran*, p. 4.

[21]Wayne, *The road to the White House 1996: The politics of presidential elections*, chapter 1.

[22]The Republican party does not use the same delegate selection process as the Democrats, and did not pass reforms quite like those recommended by McGovern (or properly the McGovern-Fraser Commission). Nonetheless, the Republicans' nominating process has more similarities to the Democrats' procedure than differences. See Bibby, NO—Brokered conventions are not desirable. In *Controversial issues in presidential selection* (2nd ed.), pp. 67–75. It should also be noted that there were many aspects to the McGovern-Fraser reforms and numerous modifications over the years. See Wayne, ibid, chapter 4.

[23]Ansolabehere, Behr, & Iyengar, *The media game*, pp. 74–77; McCubbins, Party decline and presidential campaigns in the television age, In *Under the watchful eye: Managing presidential campaigns in the television era*, pp. 9–57; and Wayne, ibid.

[24]Holloway, A time for change in American politics: The issue of the 1992 presidential election. In *The 1992 presidential campaign: A communication perspective*, pp. 129–167.

[25]See Trent & Friedenberg, *Political campaign communication: Principles and practices*, chapter 3 for a description of challenger and incumbent strategies.

[26]Newman, *The marketing of the president: Political marketing as campaign strategy*, p. 64.

[27]Newman, ibid, chapter 3; Selnow, *High-tech campaigns: Computer technology in political communication*, chapter 5.

[28]See Asher, *Polling and the public: What every citizen should know* (3rd ed), pp. 104–111. See also Richard, Polling and political campaigns. In *The practice of political communication*, pp. 25–39; and Traugott & Lavrakas, *The voter's guide to election polls*.

[29]Asher, ibid, p. 108.

[30]See Morin, Speaking of focus groups …, *The Washington Post National Weekly Edition*, June 24–30, 1996, p. 35.

[31]Polsby & Wiladvsky, *Presidential elections: Strategies and structures of American politics* (9th ed), p. 82; and Wayne, Loopholes allow presidential race to set a record, *The New York Times*, September 8, 1996, p. 1.

[32]Wayne, *The road to the White House 1996: The politics of presidential elections*, pp. 36–37.

[33]See Polsby & Wildavsky, *Presidential elections: Strategies and structures of American politics* (9th ed), chapter 3.

[34]See Swanson & Mancini, Patterns of modern electoral campaiging and their consequences; and Nimmo, Politics, media, and modern democracy: The United States, both in *Politics, media, and modern democracy*.

[35]Jakubowicz, Television and elections in post-1989 Poland: How powerful is the medium? In *Politics, media, and modern democracy*, p. 130.

[36]Mancini & Swanson, Politics, media, and modern democracy: Introduction, p. 16.

[37]Hart, *Seducing America: How television charms the modern voter*, chapter 2 See Swanson and Mancini, Patterns of modern electoral campaiging and their consequences, for a discussion of international aspects of the rise in personality politics.

[38]Just et al, *Crosstalk*, pp. 14, 43, Note that constructionism offers a framework for understanding campaign communication; it is not a theory that makes predictions about communication effects.

[39]Trent & Friedenberg, *Political campaign communication: Principles and practices* (3rd ed), p. 3.

[40]Troy, *See how they ran*.

[41]Moore, On the trail with Dole: A real media circus, *USA Today*, July 26, 1996, p. 12A.

Chapter 16

[1]Kurtz, Substance won't make the 6 o'clock news, *The Washington Post National Weekly Edition*, January 22–28, 1996, p. 12.

[2]Polsby & Wiladvsky, *Presidential elections* (9th ed), p. 69. See also Goldstein, *Guide to the 1996 presidential election*.

[3]Rosenstiel, *Strange bedfellows: How television and the presidential candidates changed American politics*, 1992, p. 164.

[4]In July, 1969 a car driven by Kennedy and carrying a young female companion plunged off a bridge in Chappaquiddick, Massachusetts. The woman was killed, and Kennedy later

pleaded guilty to leaving the scene of an accident. Although he was not held legally responsible for the woman's death, his explanations of the accident rang untrue to many people. They were left with the feeling that he was romantically involved with the woman, then tried to cover his tracks after the accident by using his influence to convince the local police to refrain from launching an investigation of his actions.

[5]Commentary by Elizabeth Drew. Quoted in Arterton, The media politics of presidential campaigns: A study of the Carter nomination drive. In Race for the presidency: The media and the nominating process, p. 39.

[6]See Winebrenner, The Iowa precinct caucuses: The making of a media event. Precinct caucuses differ from primaries in that caucuses are public meetings open to all individuals who are willing to say that they support the party whose caucus they attend. See Winebrenner, p. 49.

[7]See Smith & Lichter, Network television coverage of the 1996 presidential election campaign, Paper presented to the annual convention of the American Association for Public Opinion Research, May, 1996; Bell, The almost candidate: The media courtship of Colin Powell, Paper presented to the annual convention of the American Association for Public Opinion Research, May, 1996; and Edwards, Candidate coverage of a non-candidate: The media, citizen Powell, and public opinion, Paper presented to the annual convention of the International Communication Association, May, 1996.

[8]Fineman, Powell on the march, Newsweek, September 11, 1995, p. 28.

[9]Keen, Gramm relishes straw poll tally, USA Today, August 21, 1995, p. 4A.

[10]Woodward, The Choice, p. 244.

[11]Ibid, pp. 158–159.

[12]Ibid, p. 238.

[13]Ibid, p. 342.

[14]Trent, The early campaign. In The 1992 presidential campaign: A communication perspective, p. 53.

[15]Balz & Brownstein, Storming the gates, pp. 55–58.

[16]At this stage of the electoral process, candidates rely heavily on polls to decipher public opinion.

[17]The remainder are reserved for party officials, through a complicated set of procedures.

[18]Kansas was the only state not to hold a primary or caucus. In Kansas, the state party committees selected delegates at party conventions. This was a fluke that may have had its roots in the fact that it was a foregone conclusion that the Republican candidate would be Kansas's native son, Bob Dole. Perhaps influenced by Republicans, Democrats decided to follow suit. Officials at the Federal Election Commission told me about this unusual event and noted that all other states held primaries or caucuses in 1996.

[19]Winebrenner, The Iowa precinct caucuses: The making of a media event, p. 49.

[20]Media Monitor, May/June 1996, p. 1.

[21]Lichter, Amundson, & Noyes, The video campaign: Network coverage of the 1988 primaries, pp. 12–14.

[22]Adams, As New Hampshire goes. In Media and momentum: The New Hampshire primary and nomination politics, p. 42.

[23]Robinson & Sheehan, Over the wire and on TV: CBS and UPI in campaign '80, p. 34.

[24]Mayer, The New Hampshire primary: A historical overview. In Media and momentum, p. 14. In addition, Arterton notes that early primary victories are followed by an increase in the number of reporters who travel regularly with the candidate. See Arterton, The media politics of presidential campaigns: A study of the Carter nomination drive. In Race for the presidency: The media and the nominating process.

[25]See Patterson, Out of order, p. 41.

[26]Lichter & Noyes, *Good intentions make bad news: Why Americans hate campaign journalism*, p. 10.

[27]Keeter, *Public opinion dynamics in the Republican presidential nomination of 1996: Why Dole won; why the rest fell short*. Paper presented to the annual convention of the American Association for Public Opinion Research, May, 1996.

[28]Robinson & Sheehan, *Over the wire and on TV*, p. 76.

[29]Baker, Handicappers, *The New York Times Magazine*, February 6, 1983, p. 12.

[30]Lichter & Noyes, *Good intentions make bad news*, p. 10.

[31]Adams. As New Hampshire goes …, p. 56.

[32]See Polsby & Wildavsky, *Presidential elections* (9th ed.), chapter 4. Press effects also differ, depending on whether there is a front-runner in the campaign; see Johnson, The seven dwarfs and other tales: How the networks and select newspapers covered the 1988 Democratic primaries, *Journalism Quarterly*, 1993, pp. 311–320.

[33]Zaller, The rise and fall of candidate Perot: Unmediated versus mediated politics—Part 1. *Political Communication*, 1994, pp. 357–390.

[34]For a discussion of how press routines can adversly affect lesser-known candidates, see Meyrowitz, The problem of getting on the media agenda: A case study in competing logics of campaign coverage. In *Presidential campaign discourse: Strategic communication problems*, pp. 35–67.

[35]Zaller, The rise and fall of candidate Perot, p. 379.

[36]Patterson, *Out of order*, p. 186.

[37]Ibid, p. 187.

[38]See Bartels, *Presidential primaries and the dynamics of public choice*; Brady & Johnston, What's the primary message: Horse race or issue journalism?, in *Media and momentum*, pp. 127–186; and Cantril, *The opinion connection: Polling, politics, and the press*, chapter 2.

[39]See Pfau, Diedrich, Larson, & Van Winkle, Relational and competence perceptions of presidential candidates during primary election campaigns, *Journal of Broadcasting & Electronic Media*, 1993, pp. 275–292; and Kennamer & Chaffee, Communication of political information during early presidential primaries: Cognition, affect, and uncertainty. In *Communication Yearbook 5*, 1985. For evidence that voters make sense out of the primary campaign and do a reasonable job processing campaign information, see Popkin, *The reasoning voter: Communication and persuasion in presidential campaigns*, and Geer, *Nominating presidents: An evaluation of voters and primaries*. (For a less positive assessment of voters' processing of primary campaign communication, see Keeter & Zukin, *Uninformed choice: The failure of the new presidential nominating system*).

[40]Patterson, *Out of order*, p. 52.

[41]Polsby & Wildavsky, *Presidential elections* (9th ed.), p. 160.

[42]Timmerman & Smith, The 1992 presidential nominating conventions: Cordial concurrence revisited. In *The 1992 presidential campaign: A communication perspective*, pp. 65-87.

[43]Smith & Nimmo, *Cordial concurrence: Orchestrating national party conventions in the telepolitical age*.

[44]Tell, Don't dumb down the convention, *The Weekly Standard*, August 5, 1996, p. 10.

[45]Feagler, Act one: Night of miracles raises curtain on big show, *The Plain Dealer*, August 28, 1996, p. 2A

[46]Rich, New Deal lite, *The New York Times*, August 28, 1996, p. A15.

[47]Polsby & Wildavsky, *Presidential elections* (9th ed.), p. 138.

Chapter 17

[1]See Lichter & Noyes, *Good intentions make bad news: Why Americans hate campaign journalism* for a discussion of the results of this September 22, 1992 poll conducted by the Times Mirror Center for the People & the Press.

[2]Read on ABC's *Primetime*, March, 11, 1993.

[3]Clancey & Robinson, General election coverage: Part I. In *The mass media in campaign '84: Articles from Public Opinion Magazine*, p. 28. This analysis did not code visual messages, where Reagan excelled. In her analysis of 1984 campaign news, Graber suggested that pictures favored Reagan and that TV gave heavy coverage to leadership traits like the ability to communicate well on TV, which were Reagan's strong suits. See Graber, Kind pictures and harsh words: How television presents the candidates. In *Elections in America*, pp. 115–141. Thus, findings on good and bad press are influenced by how researchers define their terms in content analytic studies. One can focus on visual displays of candidates, comments about the candidates made by sources, and journalists' comments.

[4]Ibid, pp. 32–33.

[5]See chapter 5 of this book for a discussion of Clinton's bad press early in his first term. Evidence that Carter received bad press is reported in Robinson & Sheehan, *Over the wire and on TV*, chapter 5. Dukakis received negative press, like all presidential candidates, though not quite as much as critics have suggested. Research indicates that he received slightly less positive press than Bush (32% positive compared with Bush's 37% positive.) See Lichter & Noyes, *Good intentions make bad news*, p. 60.

[6]Robinson, The media in campaign '84, Part II: Wingless, toothless, and hopeless. In *The mass media in campaign '84*, p. 35. See also chapter 4 in *The media in the 1984 and 1988 presidential campaigns* edited by Stempel & Windhauser.

[7]See Semetko, Blumler, Gurevitch, & Weaver, *The formation of campaign agendas: A comparative analysis of party and media roles in recent American and British elections*, chapter 5 for evidence of the influence of partisanship on regional newspaper, but not national television, coverage of the U. S. presidential election.

[8]Robinson & Sheehan, *Over the wire and on TV: CBS and UPI in campaign '80*, p. 140.

[9]Weaver, Is television news biased?, *The public interest*, 1972, p. 69.

[10]Patterson, *Out of order*, p. 57. See also Jamieson, The subversive effects of a focus on strategy in news coverage of presidential campaigns. In *1-800-President*, pp. 35–61; and Kerbel, *Edited for television: CNN, ABC, and the 1992 presidential campaign*.

[11]Patterson & McClure, *The unseeing eye: The myth of television power in national elections*, pp. 41–42. For a precise definition of horse race news, see Sigelman & Bullock, Candidates, issues, horse races, and hoopla: Presidential campaign coverage, 1888–1988, *American Politics Quarterly*, 1991, p. 14. (The term "horse race" dates back years, to an era in which horse races were popular spectator sports.)

[12]Sigelman & Bullock, ibid. For a discussion of polling history, see Herbst, *Numbered voices: How opinion polling has shaped American politics*. In addition, for an analysis of horse race themes in newspaper poll stories, see Miller & Denham, Horserace, issue coverage in prestige newspapers during 1988, 1992 elections, *Newspaper Research Journal*, 1994, pp. 20–28. For a critical view, see also Joslyn, Election campaigns as occasions for civic education. In *New directions in political communication: A resource book*, pp. 86–119.

[13]Robinson & Sheehan, *Over the wire and on TV*, p. 151.

[14]Stanley & Niemi, *Vital statistics on American politics*, 1988, p. 57. See also Smith & Lichter, *Network television coverage of the 1996 presidential election campaign*, Paper presented to the annual convention of the American Association for Public Opinion Research, 1996.

[15]Stories can discuss both horse race and policy matters, and researchers take this into account in their coding as well.

[16]Lavrakas & Bauman, Page one use of presidential pre-election polls: 1980–1992. In *Presidential polls and the news media*, p. 39. See also Stovall & Solomon, The poll as a news event in the 1980 presidential campaign, *Public Opinion Quarterly*, 1984, pp. 615–623.

[17]Ibid, p. 41. See also Miller & Denham, Horserace, issue coverage in prestige newspapers during 1988, 1992 elections.

[18]Kovach, A user's view of the polls, *Public Opinion Quarterly*, 1980, p. 567; See also Stovall & Solomon, The poll as a news event in the 1980 presidential campaign; and Ratzan, The real agenda setters: Pollsters in the 1988 presidential campaign, *American Behavioral Scientist*, 1989, pp. 451–463.

[19]Mann & Orren, To poll or not to poll..and other questions. In *Media polls in American politics*, p. 4.

[20]A comprehensive discussion of the ins and outs of election polling and their pros and cons is beyond the scope of this book. For a useful discussion of the pros and cons of polling, see Dionne, The illusion of technique: The impact of polls on reporters and democracy. In *Media polls in American politics*. See also Rhee, How polls drive campaign coverage: The Gallup/CNN/USA Today tracking poll and USA Today's coverage of the 1992 presidential campaign, *Political Communication*, 1996, pp. 213–229.

[21]*Media Monitor*, (1996, September/October), Take this campaign—Please!, p. 2. These findings reflect news coverage of the 1996 campaign from the end of the primaries through September 30.

[22]See Just, et al., *Crosstalk*, chapter 5, for evidence that the news media demonstrate substantial consensus in candidate coverage; at the same time, these authors find noteworthy differences in news coverage in different media markets and media outlets.

[23]Patterson, *Out of order*, pp. 118, 120, & 122.

[24]Ibid, pp. 109–110.

[25]Ibid, p. 120.

[26]Harden, Wounded by his own sound bites, *The Washington Post National Weekly Edition*, July 22–28, 1996, p. 14.

[27]Quoted in Runkel, *Campaign for president: The managers look at '88*, p. 136. For a study of press coverage of candidate character, see King, The flawed characters in the campaign: Prestige newspaper assessments of the 1992 presidential candidates' integrity and competence, *Journalism & Mass Communication Quarterly*, 1995, pp. 84–97.

[28]See Lichter & Noyes, *Good intentions make bad news*, for a description of Bush's bad press in 1992.

[29]This remains a provocative issue. Based on a careful analysis of network television sound bites in the 1992 campaign, Lowry and Shidler conclude that the Bush–Quayle ticket received significantly more negative bites than Clinton–Gore and Perot–Stockdale. They argue that the data are consistent with the hypothesis of liberal bias. There are other interpretations of the data, too, but Lowry and Shidler make an interesting case. See Lowry & Shidler, The sound bites, the biters, and the bitten: An analysis of network TV news bias in campaign '92, *Journalism & Mass Communication Quarterly*, 1995, pp. 33–44.

[30]Lichter & Noyes, *Good intentions make bad news*, p. 88 & pp. 54–55.

[31]*Media Monitor*, (1996, September/October), Take this campaign— Please!, p. 3.

[32]See Just, et al., *Crosstalk*, chapter 5, for a discussion of local news; and Robinson & Sheehan, *Over the wire and on TV*, pp. 110–115. See also Mondak's discussion of the role newspapers play in the electoral process in *Nothing to read: Newspapers and elections in a social experiment*.

[33]Ibid, p. 80.

[34]Ibid, p. 95. In a similar fashion, research indicates that the press provides inadequate coverage of presidential candidates' abilities to manage the presidency, such as their decision-making styles and management skills. See Graber & Weaver, Presidential performance criteria: The missing element in election coverage, *Press/Politics*, Winter, 1996, pp. 7–32. In 1996, Bob Woodward's book, *The choice*, provided such information; notably, Woodward had more freedom to make judgments about Dole and Clinton's management styles in a book than he would have in *The Washington Post*. Nonetheless, it is possible that, with some forethought, the press could provide more information about candidates' management styles (though no doubt, if they did, critics would point out that journalists were venturing too many of their own interpretations!)

[35]See Hallin, Sound bite news: Television coverage of elections, 1968–1988, *Journal of Communication*, pp. 5–24; and Adatto, *Picture perfect: The art and artifice of public image making*, p. 2; Lowry & Shidler, The sound bites, the biters, and the bitten: An analysis of network TV news bias in campaign '92;. and Media Monitor, The bad news campaign: TV news coverage of the GOP primaries, March/April 1996; Harmon & Pinkleton, *Broadcast news as a source of political information: Shrinking sound bites revisited*, Paper presented to the annual convention of the Association for Education in Journalism and Mass Communication, 1994; and Media Monitor, 1996, September/October, Take this campaign—Please!, p. 2. Different findings emerge because elections differ and because researchers measure sound bites in different ways (e.g., Lowry & Shidler counted bites of candidates and noncandidates, e.g., candidate aides).

[36]Hallin, Sound bite news: Television coverage of elections, 1968–1988, p. 9.

[37]Lichter & Noyes, *Good intentions make bad news*, p. 246. Paralleling these findings is interesting evidence that in the U.S., election news stories are more likely to be initiated by the journalist than by the political party, whereas in Britain, there is a higher proportion of party-initiated news stories. See Semetko, Blumler, Gurevitch, & Weaver, *The formation of campaign agendas*, pp. 156–157. Just, et al. (see *Crosstalk*, chapter 5) find that in the 1992 U.S. election, journalist-initiated stories were more visually negative than stories originated by candidates. Of course, it is not clear that the U.S. electorate would best be served by changing things so that more stories originated with the candidate and inducing journalists to take a more positive approach.

[38]Media Monitor, 1996, March/April, The bad news campaign.

[39]Kendall, Public speaking in the presidential primaries through media eyes, *American Behavioral Scientist*, 1993, p. 250. See also Kendall, The problem of beginnings in New Hampshire: Control over the play. In *Presidential campaign discourse: Strategic communication problems*, pp. 9–12.

[40]Merritt, *Public journalism and public life: Why telling the news is not enough*, p. 69.

[41]Sigelman & Bullock, Candidates, issues, horse, races and hoopla, p. 18, and Robinson & Sheehan, *Over the wire and on TV*, pp. 162–163.

[42]In 1992, television talk shows offered significantly more substantive discussion of issues than did network evening news programs. See Lichter & Noyes, *Good intentions make bad news*, pp. 246–247. Interestingly, in 1992, newspapers provided twice as much news about the campaign as did television, as Just, et al., note in *Crosstalk*, p. 96.

[43]One can also question the assumption that longer sound bites mean higher quality political discourse. It is possible for a long-winded candidate to say less in a long sound bite than a fluent candidate says in a short bite. For an interesting discussion of this issue, see Russomanno & Everett, Candidate sound bites: Too much concern over length?, *Journal of Broadcasting & Electronic Media*, 1995, pp. 408–415.

[44]Merritt, *Public journalism & public life: Why telling the news is not enough*, p. 113.

[45]Raines, The Fallows fallacy, *The New York Times*, February 25, 1996, p. E14.

[46]Schudson, *The power of news*, p. 3.

[47]Scholars have a term for the tendency to believe that mass media exert strong effects on the body politic and specifically the belief that media have a stronger impact on others than the self. It is called the third-person effect. See Perloff, Third-person effect research 1983–1992: A review and synthesis. *International Journal of Public Opinion Research*, 1993, pp. 167–184.

[48]Robinson & Sheehan, *Over the wire and on TV*, pp. 304–305.

[49]Hallin, Sound bite news: Television coverage of elections, 1968–1988, *Journal of Communication*, 1992, pp. 7 & 9.

Chapter 18

[1]Quoted in Buchanan, *Electing a president: The Markle commission research on campaign '88*, p. 19.

[2]Ibid, p. 22.

[3]Popkin, *The reasoning voter: Communication and persuasion in presidential campaigns*, p. 35. For a cross-national study of citizens' foreign affairs knowledge, see Bennett, Flickinger, Baker, Rhine, & Bennett, Citizens' knowledge of foreign affairs, *Press/Politics*, 1996, pp. 10–29.

[4]Delli Carpini & Keeter, Stability and change in the U. S. public's knowledge of politics, *Public Opinion* Quarterly, 1991, p. 592.

[5]See Morin, Tuned out, Turned off, *The Washington Post National Weekly Edition*, February 5–11, 1996, p. 6 for a summary of the results of the study conducted by *The Post*, the Kaiser Family Foundation and Harvard University in November and December of 1995.

[6]Ibid

[7]Popkin, *The reasoning voter*, pp. 42–43, p. 213.

[8]Maranto, Of masses and morons, *The Weekly Standard*, February 26, 1996, p. 19.

[9]See Popkin, *The reasoning voter*; McGraw & Lodge, Political information processing: A review essay, *Political Communication*, 1996, pp. 131–142, and Rahn & Cramer, Activation and application of political party stereotypes: The role of television. *Political Communication*, 1996, pp. 195–212. For an examination of media processing strategies, see Fredin, Kosicki, & Becker, Cognitive strategies for media use during a presidential campaign, *Political Communication*, 1996, 23–42. Finally, see Cavanaugh, *Media effects on voters: A panel study of the 1992 presidential election*, for another study of voters' cognitions about the presidential campaign.

[10]Just, et al., *Crosstalk*, p. 187.

[11]Ibid, p. 6.

[12]See Buchanan, *Electing a president*, chapter 5, for evidence of lack of voter learning in the '88 campaign.

[13]See, for example, Robinson & Davis, Television news and the informed public: An information-processing approach, *Journal of Communication*, 1990, pp. 106–119. See also Robinson & Levy, News media use and the informed public: A 1990s update, *Journal of Communication*, 1996, pp. 129–135, who find that regular viewing of PBS's *MacNeil/Lehrer NewsHour* and CSPAN also predicted high information scores. These are among the many scholarly studies on this topic, a full discussion of which is beyond the scope of this book.

[14]See Bennett et al., Citizens' knowledge of foreign affairs; Neuman, Just, & Crigler, *Common knowledge: News and the construction of political meaning*, chapter 6. See also Owen, *Media messages in American presidential elections* for a discussion of media reliance.

[15] Neuman et al., *Common knowledge*, chapter 5; these authors also find that television is particularly successful in imparting information about abstract and distant issues, a

finding that suggests TV news may be particularly effective in teaching voters about complex issues like the budget deficit. See also Chaffee, Zhao, & Leshner, Political knowledge and the campaign media of 1992, *Communication Research*, 1994, pp. 305–324.

[16]Zhao & Chaffee, Campaign advertisements versus television news as sources of political issue information, *Public Opinion Quarterly*, 1995, p. 51. See also Chaffee, Zhao, & Leshner, ibid; and McLeod & McDonald, Beyond simple exposure: Media orientations and their impact on political processes, *Communication Research*, 1985, pp. 3–33, for an early investigation of television news attention effects.

[17]Neuman et al., *Common knowledge*, p. 92. For a similar conclusion, see Chaffee & Frank, How Americans get political information: Print versus broadcast news, *The Annals of the American Academy of Political and Social Science,*, 1996, pp. 48–58.

[18]For evidence that most voters get their news from television, see *The media & campaign 96 briefing*, Media Studies Center, April, 1996. The verdict is still out on whether televised talk shows enhance campaign learning. See Weaver & Drew, Voter learning in the 1992 presidential election: Did the "nontraditional" media and debates matter?, *Journalism Quarterly*, 1995, pp. 7–17. McLeod et al reported that in 1992, traditional media like newspapers had a greater impact on learning than nontraditional formats like talk shows. See McLeod, Guo, et al., The impact of traditional and nontraditional media forms in the 1992 presidential election, *Journalism & Mass Communication Quarterly*, 1996, pp. 401–418; and Weaver, What voters learn from media, *The Annals of the American Academy of Political and Social Science*, 1996, pp. 41–42. With regard to political Web Sites, a Freedom Forum poll reported that although more than 25% of voting-age Americans have access to the Internet or an on-line service, less than 5% of Americans report that they have visited a politically oriented Internet site. See *The media & campaign 96 briefing*. Interestingly, the Freedom Forum study reports that despite the tremendous growth in the Internet and the large number of on-line users, the overwhelming majority of voters still report that they get most of their information about the campaign from the conventional media—television, newspapers, and radio.

[19]Graber, Why voters fail information tests: Can the hurdles be overcome?, *Political Communication*, 1994, pp. 331–346. Davis, News and politics. In *New directions in political communication: A resource book*, pp. 147–184.

[20]Joslyn & Ceccoli, Attentiveness to television news and opinion change in the fall 1992 presidential campaign, *Political Behavior*, 1996, 141–170.

[21]Hetherington, The media's role in forming voters' national economic evaluations in 1992, *American Journal of Political Science*, 1996, pp. 372–395. For a discussion of the role of economic considerations in voters' 1992 decision-making calculus, see Miller, Economic, character, and social issues in the 1992 presidential election, *American Behavioral Scientist*, 1993, pp. 315–327.

[22]New York representative Bill Paxson quoted in Wines, Republicans face plight that hurt Democrats in 1994, *The New York Times*, May 5, 1996, p. 15.

[23]Carter & Shipman, Rethinking social security, *The Plain Dealer*, August 10, 1996, p. 11–B.

[24]Patterson, *Out of order*, pp. 19–21. For evidence of press negativity in the 1996 election, see Lichter & Smith, Why elections are bad news: Media and candidate discourse in the 1996 presidential primaries, *Press/Politics*, 1996, pp. 15–35.

[25]Patterson, *Out of order*, p. 23.

[26]Buchanan, *Electing a president*, p. 155.

[27]See Austin & Pinkleton, Positive and negative effects of political disaffection on the less experienced voter, *Journal of Broadcasting & Electronic Media*, 1995, 215–235.

[28]Robinson, Public affairs television and the growth of political malaise: The case of "The selling of the Pentagon," *American Political Science Review*, 1976, pp. 409–432, though see Norris, Does television erode social capital? A reply to Putnam, *PS: Political Science &*

Politics, 1996, p. 474–480. For experimental evidence, see Cappella & Jamieson, *Public cynicism and news coverage in campaigns and policy debates: Three field experiments*, Paper presented to the annual convention of the American Political Science Association, 1994; and Cappella & Jamieson, News frames, political cynicism, and media cynicism, *The Annals of the American Academy of Political and Social Science*, 1996, pp. 71–84.

[29]Norris, ibid, though see Miller, Goldenberg, & Erbring, Type-set politics: Impact of newspapers on public confidence, *American Political Science Review*, 1979, pp. 67–84, who find that readers of newspapers that contain a good deal of criticism of political institutions are more distrustful of government, though not necessarily less efficacious.

[30]See Brossard, Rush's "dittoheads" know what they don't like, *The Washington Post National Weekly Edition*, February 5–11, 1996, p. 8; and Newhagen, who finds that political self-efficacy predicts use of a television call-in show, in Self-efficacy and call-in political television show use, *Communication Research*, 1994, pp. 366–379. See also Hollander, The new news and the 1992 presidential campaign: Perceived vs. actual political knowledge, *Journalism & Mass Communication Quarterly*, 1995, pp. 786–798; and Lemert, Elliott, Rosenberg, & Bernstein, *The politics of disenchantment: Bush, Clinton, Perot, and the press*, chapter 5, who find that contrary to popular belief, during the 1992 campaign, heavy talk show viewers were highly educated, high in internal political efficacy, and more knowledgeable about candidates' policy ideas than were light viewers.

[31]Morin, Tuned out, turned off, p. 6.

[32]Quoted in ibid. See also Delli Carpini & Keeter, *What Americans know about politics and why it matters*.

[33]Cooper, The Morris meltdown, *Newsweek*, September 9, 1996, pp. 32, 36, 37.

Chapter 19

[1]Kaid & Holtz-Bacha, An introduction to parties and candidates on television. In *Political advertising in western democracies: Parties & candidates on television*, p. 2. See this book for a discussion of the role political advertising plays in election campaigns in European nations.

[2]Devlin, Political commercials in American presidential elections. In *Political advertising in western democracies: Parties & candidates on television*, p. 189; Wayne, Loopholes allow presidential race to set a record, *The New York Times*, September 8, 1996, p. 1.

[3]Woodward, *The Choice*, p. 354.

[4]Devlin, Political commercials in American presidential elections, p. 190. See also Kaid, Political advertising. In *Handbook of political communication*, p. 252; and Johnson-Cartee & Copeland, *Negative political advertising: Coming of age*, pp. 253–254.

[5]Johnson-Cartee and Copeland note that candidates who make libelous claims about their opponents can be sued under libel laws. But it is difficult for candidates to win libel suits because of restrictions set up by the classic *New York Times* versus Sullivan case. See Johnson-Cartee & Copeland, ibid, chapter 7.

[6]Devlin, Political commercials in American presidential elections, pp. 190–191. See also Kern, *30- second politics: Political advertising in the eighties*.

[7]Devlin, Contrasts in presidential campaign commercials of 1992, *American Behavioral Scientist*, 1993, p. 288.

[8]Devlin, Television advertising in the 1992 New Hampshire presidential primary election, *Political Communication*, 1994, p. 82.

[9]Moore, *The superpollsters: How they measure and manipulate public opinion in America*, p. 218.

[10]Ibid. Interestingly, for all of the emphasis devoted to the "Bear in the Woods" spot, the ad did not influence people's concerns with peace and arms control; it did have its greatest

effect on men and persons aged 30 to 44, however. See West, *Air wars: Television advertising in election campaigns, 1952–1992,* pp. 112–114.

[11]Devlin, Contrasts in presidential campaign commercials of 1988, *American Behavioral Scientist,* 1989, p. 393.

[12]Troy, *See how they ran: The changing role of the presidential candidate,* (Rev ed.), p. 258.

[13]Goldman, DeFrank, Miller, Murr, & Mathews, Quest for the presidency 1992, p. 270. The game plan was known as the "Manhattan Project," after the top-secret mission to build an atomic bomb, which was also engaged in a race against time.

[14]Troy, *See how they ran,* p. 266. See also Goldman et al, ibid, pp. 665–666 for a description of the plan for the pop culture blitz. See Morreale for a description of Clinton's campaign film in *The presidential campaign film: A critical history.*

[15]Bennet, Liberal use of "extremist" is the winning strategy, *The New York Times,* November 7, 1996, p. B7.

[16]Maraniss, The comeback kid's last return, *The Washington Post National Weekly Edition,* September 2–8, 1996, p. 9.

[17]See Bennet, Dole campaign says it has hardly begun to fight as Clinton storms the airwaves, *The New York Times,* September 11, 1996, p. A13.

[18]Seelye, Dole replaces top aides in effort to sharpen his message, *The New York Times,* September 6, 1996, p. A10.

[19]Tell, Saving the GOP from Dole-Kemp '96, *The Weekly Standard,* p. 12.

[20]Kern, *30-second politics,* p. 207.

[21]See Devlin, Political commercials in American presidential elections, pp. 193–196; and Johnson-Cartee & Copeland, *Negative political advertising: Coming of age.*

[22]Kaid & Johnston, Negative versus positive television advertising in U. S. presidential campaigns, 1960–1988, *Journal of Communication,* 1991, p. 59.

[23]For discussions of issues versus image in political spots, see Devlin, Political commercials in American presidential elections, pp. 186–205. See also Kaid & Holtz-Bacha, Political advertising across cultures: Comparing content, styles, and effects. In *Political advertising in western democracies: Parties & candidates on television* (these authors provide a definition of the two terms on p. 225); Louden, Voter rationality and media excess: Image in the 1992 presidential campaign, in *The 1992 presidential campaign: A communication perspective,* pp. 169–187; & Shyles, The televised political spot advertisement: Its structure, content, and role in the political system, in *New perspectives on political advertising,* pp. 107–138.

[24]West, *Air wars: Television advertising in election campaigns, 1952–1992,* p. 51.

[25]Devlin, Political commercials in American presidential elections, pp. 198–199.

[26]See Johnson-Cartee & Copeland, *Negative political advertising: Coming of age.*

[27]Quoted in Johnson-Cartee & Copeland, *Negative political advertising: Coming of age,* p. 17. See Gronbeck, *The rhetoric of negative political advertising: Thoughts on the senatorial race ads in 1984.* Paper presented to the annual convention of the Speech Communication Association, 1985. See also Gronbeck, Negative narratives in 1988 presidential campaign ads, *Quarterly Journal of Speech,* 1992, pp. 333–346; and Merritt, Negative political advertising: Some empirical findings, *Journal of Advertising,* 1984, pp. 27–38.

[28]Johnson-Cartee & Copeland, *Negative political advertising: Coming of age,* p. 48.

[29]See, for example, Kern & Wicks, Television news and the advertising-driven new mass media election: A more significant local role in 1992? In *The 1992 presidential campaign: A communication perspective,* pp. 189–206.

[30]Interestingly, voters believed that Dole ran a more negative campaign than Clinton in 1996; yet Clinton ran a great many negative ads. An informal study suggested only 5 of the 31 Clinton–Gore commercials broadcast from the summer of 1995 through October

21, 1996, were entirely positive. See Bennet, Clinton makes use of negative ads, *The New York Times*, October 22, 1996, p. A12.

[31]Smith, Time to go negative, *The Wall Street Journal*, October 8, 1996, p. A22.

[32]Johnson-Cartee & Copeland, *Negative political advertising: Coming of age*, p. 269.

Chapter 20

[1]See Diamond & Bates, *The spot: The rise of political advertising on television* (3rd ed), chapter 15.

[2]Ansolabehere & Iyengar, *Going negative: How political advertisements shrink and polarize the electorate*, p. 64.

[3]There continues to be a debate about whether negative advertising reduces voter turnout. Conflicting findings have been reported in this area. See Ansolabehere & Iyengar, ibid; and Brians & Wattenberg, *The turnout effects of negative advertising in a presidential campaign*, Paper presented to the annual convention of the American Political Science Association, 1995.

[4]See Brians & Wattenberg, Campaign issue knowledge and salience: Comparing reception from TV commercials, TV news, and newspapers, *American Journal of Political Science*, 1996, pp. 172–193; Just , Crigler, & Wallach, Thirty seconds or thirty minutes: What viewers learn from spot advertisements and candidate debates, *Journal of Communication*, 1990, pp. 120–133; and West, *Air wars*, chapter 5.

[5]Diamond & Bates, *The spot: The rise of political advertising on television* (3rd ed), pp. 377–378.

[6]Ansolabehere & Iyengar, *Going negative*, pp. 75–76.

[7]Ibid, p. 80.

[8]West, *Air wars*, p. 155.

[9]Ibid, p. 112.

[10]Hershey, The campaign and the media. In *The election of 1988: Reports and interpretations*, pp. 95–96.

[11]West, *Air wars*, p. 119.

[12]Ibid, pp. 138–140. For evidence gleaned from an experimental approach to priming and advertising, see Schleuder, McCombs, & Wanta, Inside the agenda-setting process: How political advertising and TV news prime viewers to think about issues and candidates. In *Television and political advertising, Volume 1: Psychological processes*, pp. 265–309.

[13]Ansolabehere & Iyengar, *Going negative*, chapter 4.

[14]Ibid, p. 88.

[15]Biocca, Viewers' mental models of political messages: Toward a theory of the semantic processing of television. In *Television and political advertising, Volume 1: Psychological processes*, p. 27. For other studies of cognitive processing of political advertising, see Christ, Thorson, & Caywood, Do attitudes toward political advertising affect information processing of televised political commercials?, *Journal of Broadcasting & Electronic Media*, 1994; Hitchon & Chang, Effects of gender schematic processing on the reception of political commercials for men and women candidates, *Communication Research*, 1995, pp. 430–458; and Roberts, Political advertising: Strategies for influence, in *Presidential campaign discourse: Strategic communication problems*, pp. 179–199.

[16]Diamond & Bates, *The spot* (3rd ed), p. 355.

[17]Kern, *30-second politics*, p. 124.

[18]Devlin, Contrasts in presidential campaign commercials of 1992, p. 287; See also Kaid, Political advertising in the 1992 campaign. In *The 1992 presidential campaign: A communication perspective*, pp. 116–117.

[19]Indeed, there is evidence that issue attack ads exert a more positive impact on attitudes toward the sponsor than do image or character attack spots. See Roddy & Garramone, Appeals and strategies of negative political advertising, *Journal of Broadcasting & Electronic Media*, 1988, p. 425; Pfau & Burgoon, The efficacy of issue and character attack message strategies in political campaign communication, *Communication Reports*, 1989, p. 53; and Shapiro & Rieger, Comparing positive and negative political advertising on radio, *Journalism Quarterly*, 1992, pp. 135–145.

[20]An informal study revealed that only 5 of the 31 Clinton-Gore ads broadcast from the summer of 1995 through October 21, 1996, were entirely positive. See Bennet, Clinton makes use of negative ads, *The New York Times*, October 22, 1996, p. A12. As Bennet notes, voters perceived that Dole was running a more negative campaign than the president.

[21]For evidence that negative ads are remembered and recognized better than positive spots, see Shapiro & Rieger, Comparing positive and negative political advertising on radio, and Newhagen & Reeves, Emotion and memory responses for negative political advertising: A study of television commercials used in the 1988 presidential election. In *Television and political advertising, Vol 1: Psychological processes*, pp. 197–220.

[22]For evidence of the negativity effect, see Kellerman, The negativity effect and its implications for initial interaction, *Communication Monographs*, 1984, pp. 37–55.

[23]Quoted in Johnson-Cartee & Copeland, *Negative political advertising: Coming of age*, p. 15.

[24]Ibid, p. 223.

[25]Quoted in ibid, p. 224.

[26]Lemert, Elliott, Bernstein, Rosenberg, & Nestvold conclude that a candidate's failure to effectively rebut attacks probably has a greater negative impact on how the candidate is covered by the news media than it does on the attitudes of the voting public. See *News verdicts, the debates, and presidential campaigns*, p. 259.

[27]See Pfau & Burgoon, Inoculation in political campaign communication, *Human Communication Research*, 1988, pp. 91–111; and Pfau & Kenski, *Attack politics: Strategy and defense*. There are many variables that determine the effectiveness of political inoculations, as these studies show.

[28]While campaigns vary in how much they rely on negative tactics, there are a variety of dirty techniques available. These include computer-based oppositional research, designed to get dirt on opponents' personal lives, and push-polls, which use opinion research in a manipulative way, as when phone interviewers provide respondents with derogatory information about the opponent, then ask individuals their views of the two candidates, and release the results to the press. See Sabato & Simpson, *Dirty little secrets: The persistence of corruption in American politics*.

[29]This phrase has originated with Kathleen Jamieson. See the discussion of negative ads in her book, *Dirty politics: Deception, distraction, and democracy*. The notion that an ad that invites false inferences is deceptive is quite consistent with the definition of advertising deception proposed by consumer behavior researchers—i.e., if the ad leaves the typical consumer with an impression different from what would be expected if the consumer had "reasonable knowledge", and if the impression is "factually untrue or potentially misleading." Using this definition, Bush's "Revolving Door" spot would be deceptive. See Engel & Blackwell, *Consumer behavior (4th ed.)*, p. 295.

[30]Jamieson, ibid, pp. 19–20.

[31]Research suggests that the PAC ad had a particularly strong effect; we know that independently sponsored ads can be more effective than candidate-sponsored spots. See Garamone, Effects of negative political advertising: The roles of sponsor and rebuttal, *Journal of Broadcasting & Electronic Media*, 1985, pp. 147–159.

[32]Woodward, *The choice*, p. 322.

[33]Ansolabehere & Iyengar, *Going negative*, p. 141.

[34]Pfau & Louden, Effectiveness of adwatch formats in deflecting political attack ads, *Communication Research*, 1994, pp. 325–341. See also McKinnon, *Mediating political mudslinging or magnifying advertising effects: An experimental study of adwatch effects on voters' evaluations of candidates and their ads*, Paper presented to the annual convention of the Association for Education in Journalism and Mass Communication, 1995; and Kaid, Tedesco, & McKinnon, Presidential ads as nightly news: A content analysis of 1988 and 1992 televised adwatches, *Journal of Broadcasting & Electronic Media*, 1996, pp. 297–308.

[35]Cappella & Jamieson, Broadcast adwatch effects: A field experiment, *Communication Research*, 1994, pp. 342–365. There remain a variety of provocative explanations of how adwatches influence attitudes toward the targeted ad, as these authors and other scholars have noted.

[36]Ibid, p. 345, though see Kern & Wicks, Television news and the advertising-driven new mass media election: A more significant local role in 1992? In *The 1992 presidential campaign: A communication perspective*, pp. 189–206.

[37]See, for example, Wayne, Loopholes allow presidential race to set a record, *The New York Times*, September 8, 1996, p. 1.

[38]The money behind Clinton's campaign, *The Washington Post National Weekly Edition*, September 2–8, 1996, p. 12.

[39]Grush, McKeough, & Ahlering, Extrapolating laboratory exposure research to actual political elections, *Journal of Personality and Social Psychology*, 1978, pp. 257–270.

[40]Ibid, p. 259.

[41]Ansolabere & Iyengar, *Going negative*, p. 151.

[42]This list of suggestions is based on reforms suggested by Ansolabehere & Iyengar, ibid, chapter 7; and Sabato & Simpson, *Dirty little secrets*, chapter 11. For a comprehensive view of campaign finance reform, see also Magleby & Nelson, *The money chase: Congressional campaign finance reform*.

[43]Sabato & Simpson, ibid, p. 332.

Chapter 21

[1]Drucker & Hunold creatively suggested the analogy between debates and game shows in The debating game, *Critical Studies in Mass Communication*, 1987, pp. 202–207. See also Schroeder, Watching between the lines: Presidential debates as television, *Press/Politics*, 1996, pp. 57–75.

[2]Jamieson & Birdsell, *Presidential debates: The challenge of creating an informed electorate*, p. 17.

[3]For a compelling discussion of Lincoln–Douglas, see Zarefsky, *Lincoln, Douglas, and slavery: In the crucible of public debate*.

[4]This phrase originated with Auer, The counterfeit debates. In *The great debates: Kennedy vs. Nixon, 1960*, p. 149. It should be noted that there have been a handful of political debates that focused on single propositions, such as a 1948 radio debate between Thomas Dewey and Harold Stassen on the question of outlawing communism in the U. S. Few debates have risen to the rhetorical heights of Lincoln-Douglas, however. See also Kraus, *Televised presidential debates and public policy*; and Meyer & Carlin, The impact of formats on voter reaction. In *The 1992 presidential debates in focus*, pp. 69–83.

[5]It should be noted that debates also occur in other phases of the presidential election campaign, such as the primaries where the number of debates have increased sharply in recent years. In addition, candidates for other political offices frequently debate. For

purposes of cohesiveness, this chapter and the one that follows focus only on presidential election debates, with a minor consideration of vice presidential debates.

[6]Hinck, *Enacting the presidency: Political argument, presidential debates, and presidential character*, p. 2.

[7]Kraus, *Televised presidential debates and public policy*, p. 30.

[8]See Hinck, *Enacting the presidency*, chapter 1.

[9]Auer, The counterfeit debates, p. 146.

[10]Martel, *Political campaign debates: Images, strategies, and tactics*, p. 3.

[11]Will, A partial home run, *Newsweek*, October 14, 1996, p. 98.

[12]See Friedenberg, Patterns and trends in national political debates: 1960–1992. In *Rhetorical studies of national political debates: 1960–1992* (2nd ed.), pp. 235–259. Actually, it could be argued that the fourth 1960 debate, which did not feature an incumbent, put the national security more at risk than any debate held, with its discussion of the merits of helping the anti–Castro freedom fighters. Both candidates knew that a covert CIA plan was afoot to help the freedom fighters, a plan that would later go by the name of the Bay of Pigs. See Matthews, *Kennedy & Nixon*, chapter 11.

[13]Martel, *Political campaign debates*, p. 174.

[14]Safire, Brush off the "pollbearers," *The New York Times*, September 16, 1996, A15.

[15]CNN could do this because a 1983 FCC ruling stipulated that broadcast stations could sponsor so-called debates and invite whomever they wished to participate without violating the equal time provision.

[16]Nixon, *Six crises*, p. 324.

[17]Quoted in Kraus, *Televised presidential debates and public policy*, p. 33.

[18]Ibid, p. 33.

[19]Hellweg, Pfau, & Brydon, *Televised presidential debates: Advocacy in contemporary America*, p. 23. See also Bitzer and Rueter's thorough analysis of the 1976 debates in *Carter vs. Ford: The counterfeit debates of 1976*; Eveland, McLeod, & Nathanson, Reporters vs. undecided voters: An analysis of the questions asked during the 1992 presidential debates, *Communication Quarterly*, 1994, pp. 390–406.

[20]Matera & Salwen, Unwieldy questions? Circuitous answers?: Journalists as panelists in presidential election debates, *Journal of Broadcasting & Electronic Media*, 1996, pp. 309–317.

[21]Meyer & Carlin, The impact of formats on voter reaction, p. 79. Some researchers have argued that voters' agenda has not been adequately reflected in debates. See Meadow & Jackson-Beeck, A comparative perspective on presidential debates: Issue evolution in 1960 and 1976. In *The presidential debates: Media, electoral, and policy perspectives*, pp. 33–58.

[22]Friedenberg, The 1992 presidential debates. In *The 1992 presidential campaign: A communication perspective*, p. 101.

[23]Martel, *Political campaign debates*, p. 21.

[24]Quoted in Kraus, *Televised presidential debates and public policy*, p. 60.

[25]Clines, "Ask not ... " " ... military-industrial complex ... " " ... but fear itself ... ", *The New York Times*, September 25, 1996, p. A8.

[26]See Friedenberg, Patterns and trends in national political debates: 1960–1992.

[27]Windt, The 1960 Kennedy-Nixon presidential debates. In *Rhetorical studies of national political debates: 1960–1992*, pp. 1–27.

[28]See Hinck, *Enacting the presidency*, chapter 2.

[29]The attack that fizzled, *The New York Times*, October 17, 1996, p. A14; Tell, Saving the GOP from Dole-Kemp '96, *The Weekly Standard*, October 21, 1996, p. 11.

[30]Hinck, *Enacting the presidency*, p. 120.

[31]Friedenberg, Patterns and trends in national political debates: 1960–1992, p. 255.

[32]Depoe & Short-Thompson, Let the people speak: The emergence of public space in the Richmond presidential debate. In *The 1992 presidential debates in focus*, p. 93.

[33]Ryan, The 1988 Bush-Dukakis presidential debates. In *Rhetorical studies of national political debates: 1960–1992*, p. 153.

[34]Decker, The 1988 Quayle-Bentsen vice presidential debate. In *Rhetorical studies of national political debates: 1960–1992*, p. 178.

[35]Quoted in ibid, p. 179.

[36]Ferraro's case was complicated: As the first woman vice presidential candidate, she felt she had to project strength, which pushed her away from showing her familiar smile; on the other hand, had she smiled more frequently, she might have signaled that she was not a serious candidate. Such are the double binds female candidates experience.

[37]See discussion in Hellweg et al., *Televised presidential debates*, pp. 46–50. There is solid evidence that debates contain a great deal of issue content. See Sears & Chaffee, Uses and effects of the 1976 debates: An overview of empirical studies. In *The great debates: Carter vs. Ford, 1976*, pp. 228–229.

[38]Bennet, In spin wars after the debate, Clinton campaign takes lead. *The New York Times*, October 8, 1996, p. 1.

[39]Simon, *Road show*, pp. 292–293.

Chapter 22

[1]It was former secretary of state James Baker who first said that "the debates … have a way of freezing campaigns." Quoted in Lemert, Elliott, Bernstein, Rosenberg, & Nestvold, *News verdicts, the debates, and presidential campaigns*, p. 240. Dayan & Katz, in *Media events: The live broadcasting of history*, invoke a religious metaphor to describe macro events like presidential events. Theirs is a technological approach to political communication, as noted in chapter 10.

[2] 1980 and 1992 audience statistics appeared in Carlin, A rationale for a focus group study. In *The 1992 presidential debates in focus*, pp. 6–7.

[3]Ibid; and Trent & Friedenberg, *Political campaign communication: Principles and practices* (3rd ed), p. 229.

[4]Voters' interest: Then and now, *USA Today*, October 11, 1996, p. 4A (With data compiled by Nielsen Media Research).

[5]Sears & Chaffee, Uses and effects of the 1976 debates: An overview of empirical studies. In *The great debates: Carter vs. Ford, 1976*, p. 231. Although these data come from 1976, there is no reason to believe that attention paid to debates has increased since then. If anything, it is probably lower than in 1976 for reasons suggested in the text.

[6]McLeod, Durall, Ziemke, & Bybee, Reactions of young and older voters: Expanding the context of effects. In *The great debates: Carter vs. Ford, 1976*, pp. 348–367; and Sears & Chaffee, Uses and effects of the 1976 debates: An overview of empirical studies, pp. 232–233.

[7]McLeod, Durall, Ziemke, & Bybee, ibid; Sears & Chaffee, ibid, p. 228; and Lemert, Elliott, Bernstein, Rosenberg, & Nestvold, *News verdicts, the debates, and presidential campaigns*, chapter 9.

[8]Meyer & Carlin, The impact of formats on voter reaction. In *The 1992 presidential debates in focus*, chapter 5; and Carlin, Implications for future debates. In *The 1992 presidential debates in focus*, chapter 14. See also Lemert, Elliott, Rosenberg, & Bernstein, *The politics of disenchantment*, chapter 10 for a description of reactions to 1992 formats.

[9]Miller & MacKuen, Informing the electorate: A national study. In *The great debates: Carter vs. Ford, 1976*, p. 290. See also Sears & Chaffee, Uses and effects of the 1976 debates;

Hellweg, Pfau, & Brydon, *Televised presidential debates*, chapter 5; and for recent evidence of learning effects, Chaffee, Zhao, & Leshner, Political knowledge and the campaign media of 1992, *Communication Research*, 1994, pp. 305–324.

[10]Sears & Chaffee, ibid, p. 244; these authors came up with the notion that "affective strands" are "bonded together" through debate viewing.

[11]For evidence of image effects see Hellweg, Pfau, & Brydon, *Televised presidential debates*, chapter 4; Lemert, Elliott, Bernstein, Rosenberg, & Nestvold, *News verdicts, the debates, and presidential campaigns*; and Pfau & Eveland, Debates versus other communication sources: The pattern of information and influence. In *The 1992 presidential debates in focus*, pp. 155–173.

[12]Hellweg, Pfau, & Brydon, ibid, p. 77. For an interesting article in this area, see Morello, Visual structuring of the 1976 and 1984 nationally televised presidential debates: Implications, *Central States Speech Journal*, 1988, pp. 233–243.

[13]The study, "Debate score: Kennedy up, Nixon down," appeared in *Broadcasting*, November 7, 1960, pp. 27–29. See also Vancil & Pendell, The myth of viewer-listener disagreement in the first Kennedy-Nixon debate, *Central States Speech Journal*, 1987, pp. 16–27.

[14]See Vancil & Pendell, ibid.

[15]Schudson, *The power of news*, p. 117. See also Kraus, Winners of the first 1960 televised presidential debate between Kennedy and Nixon, *Journal of Communication*, 1996, pp. 78–96.

[16]Reporter John Dillin quoted in Hellweg, Pfau, & Brydon, *Televised presidential debates*, p. 84. See also discussion of Reagan's rhetoric in chapter 6 of the present book.

[17]Ritter & Henry, The 1980 Reagan-Carter presidential debate. In *Rhetorical studies of national political debates, 1960–1992* (2nd ed.), p. 87.

[18]Ibid, p. 82. See, in particular, Tiemens, Hellweg, Kipper, & Phillips, An integrative verbal and visual analysis of the Carter-Reagan debate, *Communication Quarterly*, 1985, pp. 34–42.

[19]Ritter and Henry, The 1980 Reagan-Carter presidential debate, p. 87.

[20]Lemert, Elliott, Bernstein, Rosenberg, & Nestvold, *News verdicts, the debates, and presidential campaigns*, chapter 3. Kraus and Ross, in a study of polling on presidential debates, find that polls are less likely to focus on issues separating the candidates than on who won the debate and the personal characteristics of candidates. See Kraus & Ross, Polling on presidential debates, 1960–1992, *The Public Perspective*, August/September, 1996, pp. 57–59.

[21]Results of a poll taken by Ford's pollster, Robert Teeter, reported in Berquist, The 1976 Carter-Ford presidential debates, in *Rhetorical studies of national political debates, 1960–1992*, p. 36. For stronger evidence of news media impact on postdebate judgments in 1976, see Patterson, *The mass media election: How Americans choose their president*.

[22]Ford, *A time to heal*, p. 424.

[23]Lemert, Elliott, Bernstein, Rosenberg, & Nestvold, *News verdicts, the debates, and presidential campaigns*; and Lemert, Elliott, Rosenberg, & Bernstein, *The politics of disenchantment: Bush, Clinton, Perot, and the press*.

[24]Lemert et al., *News verdicts, the debates, and presidential campaigns*, p. 253.

[25]Kraus, Voters win, *Critical Studies in Mass Communication*, 1987, p. 215.

[26]Ibid. See also Meadow, A speech by any other name, *Critical Studies in Mass Communication*, 1987, pp. 207–210.

[27]Meadow, A speech by any other name, p. 209.

[28]Martel, *Political campaign debates*, p. 3.

[29]Evidence of debate effects on perceived legitimacy is from Sears & Chaffee, Uses and effects of the 1976 debates, p. 248. Quotes in this paragraph are from, respectively, Hinck, *Enacting the presidency*, p. 7; and Lang, Still seeking answers, *Critical Studies in Mass*

Communication, p. 212. From a rhetorical perspective, these functions would be termed epideictic, a concept touched on in chapter 7.

[30]See Jamieson & Birdsell, *Presidential debates*, pp. 201–203.

[31]Meyer & Carlin, The impact of formats on voter reaction, pp. 71–72. Of course, such a format might work in a Congressional or lower-level political race.

[32]Broder, Making debates more useful, *The Plain Dealer*, October 23,1996, p. 11B.

[33]Hinck, *Enacting the presidency*, p. 7.

[34]Ibid.

[35]Apologies to Robinson & Sheehan, *Over the wire and on TV*, p. 305, whose last two sentences I have quoted and gently paraphrased, applying them to the debate context.

Epilogue

[1]Apple, A muted Dole persona, *The New York Times*, September 26, 1996, p. A15.

[2]Ibid.

[3]Ford, The master of ambiguity, *The New York Times*, October 17, 1996, p. A15.

[4]Tolchin, *The angry American: How voter rage is changing the nation*, p. 134.

[5]Krugman, First, do no harm. *The New York Times*, September 4, 1996, p. A15.

[6]Kurtz, Hey! Is anyone listening? *The Washington Post National Weekly Edition*, October 21–27, 1996, p. 21.

[7]Morgan, A revolution derailed, *The Washington Post National Weekly Edition*, October 28–November 3, 1996, p. 21.

[8]This is suggested in a column by Klein, Where the anger went, *Newsweek*, November 4, 1996, p. 33.

[9]Bellow, Mr. Sugarman's pledge of allegiance, *The Chicago Tribune*, August 25, 1996, Section 1A, p.3.

References

Adams, W. C. (1987). As New Hampshire goes … In G. R. Orren & N. W. Polsby (Eds.), *Media and momentum: The New Hampshire primary and nomination politics* (pp. 42–59). Chatham, NJ: Chatham House.

Adams, W. C., & Heyl, P. (1981). From Cairo to Kabul with the networks, 1972–1980. In W. C. Adams (Ed.), *Television coverage of the Middle East* (pp. 1–39). Norwood, NJ: Ablex.

Adatto, K. (1993). *Picture perfect: The art and artifice of public image making*. New York: Basic Books.

Alexseev, M. A., & Bennett, W. L. (1995). For whom the gates open: News reporting and government source patterns in the United States, Great Britain, and Russia. *Political Communication, 12*, 395–412.

Altheide, D. L. (1981). Network news oversimplified and underexplained. *Washington Journalism Review, 3*, 28–29.

Altheide, D. L. (1984). Media hegemony: A failure of perspective. *Public Opinion Quarterly, 48*, 476–490.

Altschull, J. H. (1995). *Agents of power: The media and public policy* (2nd ed.). White Plains, NY: Longman.

Ambrose, S. E. (1989). *Nixon: The triumph of a politician (1962–1972)*. New York: Simon and Schuster.

Ansolabehere, S., Behr, R., & Iyengar, S. (1993). *The media game: American politics in the television age.* New York: Macmillan.

Ansolabehere, S., & Iyengar, S. (1995). *Going negative: How political advertisements shrink and polarize the electorate.* New York: Free Press.

Apple, R. W., Jr. (1995, December 8). James Reston, a journalist nonpareil, dies at 86. *The New York Times*, A1, B15.

Apple, R. W., Jr. (1996, September 26). A muted Dole persona. *The New York Times*, A15.

Arkes, H. (1996, August 5). Primary fictions. *The Weekly Standard*, 13–14.

Aronson, J. (1990). *The press and the cold war*. New York: Monthly Review Press.

Arterton, F. C. (1978). The media politics of presidential campaigns: A study of the Carter nomination drive. In J. D. Barber (Ed.), *Race for the presidency: The media and the nominating process* (pp. 26–54). Englewood Cliffs, NJ: Prentice-Hall.

Asher, H. (1995). *Polling and the public: What every citizen should know* (3rd ed). Washington, DC: Congressional Quarterly Press.

Auer, J. J. (1962). The counterfeit debates. In S. Kraus (Ed.), *The great debates: Kennedy vs. Nixon, 1960* (pp. 142–150). Bloomington, IN: Indiana University Press.

Austin, E. W., & Pinkleton, B. E. (1995). Positive and negative effects of political disaffection on the less experienced voter. *Journal of Broadcasting & Electronic Media, 39*, 215–235.

Baker, R. (1983, February 6). Handicappers. *The New York Times Magazine*, 12.

Baldasty, G. J. (1984). The press and politics in the age of Jackson. *Journalism Monographs, 89*, 1–28.

Balz, D., & Brownstein, R. (1996). *Storming the gates: Protest politics and the Republican revival.* Boston: Little, Brown.

Banfield, E. (1961). *Political influence.* New York: Free Press.

Baran, S. J., & Davis, D. K. (1995). *Mass communication theory: Foundations, ferment, and future.* Belmont, CA: Wadsworth.

Bartels, L. M. (1988). *Presidential primaries and the dynamics of public choice.* Princeton: Princeton University Press.

Bartimole, R. (1995, December 6). The big diversion. *The Cleveland Free Times,* 6.

Becker, L. B. (1991). Reflecting on metaphors (commentary on Reese). In J. A. Anderson (Ed.), *Communication yearbook 14* (pp. 341–346). Newbury Park, CA: Sage.

Becker, L. B., McCombs, M. E., & McLeod, J. M. (1975). The development of political cognitions. In S. H. Chaffee (Ed.), *Political communication: Strategies for research* (pp. 21–63). Newbury Park, CA: Sage.

Behr, R. L., & Iyengar, S. (1985). Television news, real-world cues, and changes in the public agenda. *Public Opinion Quarterly,* 49, 38–57.

Bell, T. (1996). *The almost candidate: The media courtship of Colin Powell.* Paper presented to the annual convention of the American Association for Public Opinion Research, Salt Lake City, May, 1996.

Bellow, S. (1996, August 25). Mr. Sugarman's pledge of allegiance. *The Chicago Tribune,* Section 1A, 3.

Bennet, J. (1996, September 11). Dole campaign says it has hardly begun to fight as Clinton storms the airwaves. *The New York Times,* A13.

Bennet, J. (1996, October 8). In spin wars after the debate, Clinton campaign takes lead. *The New York Times,* A1.

Bennet, J. (1996, October 22). Clinton makes use of negative ads. *The New York Times,* A12.

Bennet, J. (1996, November 7). Liberal use of "extremist" is the winning strategy. *The New York Times,* B1, B7.

Bennett, S. E., Flickinger, R. S., Baker, J. R., Rhine, S. L., & Bennett, L. L. M. (1996). Citizens' knowledge of foreign affairs. *Press/Politics,1* (2), 10–29.

Bennett, W. L. (1994). The news about foreign policy. In W. L. Bennett & D. L. Paletz (Eds.), *Taken by storm: The media, public opinion, and U. S. foreign policy in the Gulf War* (pp. 12–40). Chicago: University of Chicago Press.

Bennett, W. L. (1996). *News: The politics of illusion* (3rd ed.). White Plains, NY: Longman.

Bennett, W. L., & Paletz, D. L. (Eds.). (1994). *Taken by storm: The media, public opinion, and U. S. foreign policy in the Gulf War.* Chicago: University of Chicago Press.

Berelson, B., Lazarsfeld, P. F., & McPhee, W. (1954). *Voting.* Chicago: University of Chicago Press.

Berkowitz, D. (1987). TV news sources and news channels: A study in agenda building. *Journalism Quarterly,* 64, 508–513.

Berkowitz, D. & Adams, D. B. (1990). Information subsidy and agenda-building in local television news. *Journalism Quarterly,* 67, 723–731.

Berquist, G. (1994). The 1976 Carter-Ford presidential debates. In R. V. Friedenberg (Ed.), *Rhetorical studies of national political debates, 1960–1992* (2nd ed., pp. 29–44). Westport, CT: Praeger.

Bibby, J. F. (1994). NO—Brokered conventions are not desirable. In G. L. Rose (Ed.), *Controversial issues in presidential selection* (2nd ed., pp. 67–75). Albany: State University of New York Press.

Bineham, J. L. (1988). A historical account of the hypodermic model in mass communication. *Communication Monographs,* 55, 230–246.

Biocca, F. (1991). Viewers' mental models of political messages: Toward a theory of the semantic processing of television. In F. Biocca (Ed.), *Television and political advertising, Volume 1: Psychological processes* (pp. 27–89). Hillsdale, NJ: Lawrence Erlbaum Associates.

Bitzer, L., & Rueter, T. (1980). *Carter vs. Ford: The counterfeit debates of 1976.* Madison: University of Wisconsin Press.

Blair, C., & Houck, D. W. (1994). Richard Nixon and the personalization of crisis. In A. Kiewe (Ed.), *The modern presidency and crisis rhetoric* (pp. 91–118). Westport, CT: Praeger.

Blendon, R. J., & Benson, J. M. (1996). *Making major changes in the health care system: Public opinion parallels between two recent debates.* Paper presented to the annual convention of the American Association for Public Opinion Research, Salt Lake City.

Blumenthal, S. (1991). *Pledging allegiance: The last campaign of the cold war.* New York: Harper Perennial.

Blumler, J. G., & Gurevitch, M. (1981). Politicians and the press: An essay on role relationships. In D. D. Nimmo & K. R. Sanders (Eds.), *Handbook of political communication* (pp. 467–493). Newbury Park, CA: Sage.

Blumler, J. G., & Gurevitch, M. (1982). The political effects of mass communication. In M. Gurevitch, T. Bennett, J. Curran, & J. Woollacott (Eds.), *Culture, society and the media* (pp. 236–267). New York: Methuen.

Bodnick, M. A. (1990). "Going public" reconsidered: Reagan's 1981 tax and budget cuts, and revisionist theories of presidential power. *Congress and the Presidency, 17*, 13–28.

Boller, P. E., Jr. (1996). *Presidential anecdotes*. New York: Penguin.

Bonafede, D. (1990a). The presidents and the public. In *The presidents and the public* (pp. 1–11). Washington, DC: Congressional Quarterly Press.

Bonafede, D. (1990b). Presidents and the news media. In *The presidents and the public* (33–73). Washington, DC: Congressional Quarterly Press.

Bowman, K., & Ladd, E. C. (1994). Public opinion toward Congress: A historical look. In T. E. Mann & N. J. Ornstein (Eds.), *Congress, the press, and the public* (pp. 45–58). Washington, DC: American Enterprise Institute and Brookings Institution.

Brady, H. E., & Johnston, R. (1987). What's the primary message: Horse race or issue journalism? In G. R. Orren & N. W. Polsby (Eds.), *Media and momentum: The New Hampshire primary and nomination politics* (pp. 127–186). Chatham, NJ: Chatham House.

Brians, C. L., & Wattenberg, M. P. (1995, September). *The turnout effects of negative advertising in a presidential campaign*. Paper presented to the annual convention of the American Political Science Association, Chicago.

Brians, C. L., & Wattenberg, M. P. (1996). Campaign issue knowledge and salience: Comparing reception from TV commercials, TV news, and newspapers. *American Journal of Political Science, 40*, 172–193.

Broder, D. (1996, October 23). Making debates more useful. *The Plain Dealer*, 11–B.

Broh, C. A. (1987). *A horse of a different color: Television's treatment of Jesse Jackson's 1984 presidential campaign*. Washington, DC: Joint Center for Political Studies.

Brosius, H. B., & Kepplinger, H. M. (1990). The agenda-setting function of television news: Static and dynamic views. *Communication Research, 17*, 183–211.

Brossard, M. A. (1996, February 5–11). Rush's "dittoheads" know what they don't like. *The Washington Post National Weekly Edition*, 8.

Brown, J. D., Bybee, C., Wearden, S., & Straughan, D. (1987). Invisible power: Newspaper news sources and the limits of diversity. *Journalism Quarterly, 64*, 45–54.

Buchanan, B. (1991). *Electing a president: The Markle commission research on campaign '88*. Austin: University of Texas Press.

Byerly, K. (1961). *Community journalism*. Philadelphia: Chilton.

Campbell, K. K., & Jamieson, K. H. (1990). *Deeds done in words: Presidential rhetoric and the genres of governance*. Chicago: University of Chicago Press.

Cantril, A. H. (1991). *The opinion connection: Polling, politics, and the press*. Washington, DC: Congressional Quarterly Press.

Cappella, J. N., & Jamieson, K. H. (1994a, September). *Public cynicism and news coverage in campaigns and policy debates: Three field experiments*. Paper presented at the annual convention of the American Political Science Association, New York.

Cappella, J. N., & Jamieson, K. H. (1994b). Broadcast adwatch effects: A field experiment. *Communication Research, 21*, 342–365.

Cappella, J. N., & Jamieson, K. H. (1996). News frames, political cynicism, and media cynicism. *The Annals of the American Academy of Political and Social Science, 546*, 71–84.

Carey, J. W. (1986). Why and how: The dark continent of American journalism. In R. K. Manoff & M. Schudson (Eds.), *Reading the news* (pp. 146–196). New York: Pantheon.

Carlin, D. B. (1994a). A rationale for a focus group study. In D. B. Carlin & M. S. McKinney (Eds.), *The 1992 presidential debates in focus* (pp. 3–19). Westport, CT: Praeger.

Carlin, D. B. (1994b). Implications for future debates. In D. B. Carlin & M. S. McKinney (Eds.), *The 1992 presidential debates in focus* (pp. 205–215). Westport, CT: Praeger.

Carter, M. N., & Shipman, W. G. (1996, August 10). Rethinking social security. *The Plain Dealer*, 11–B.

Casey, R. (1929). *Propaganda technique in the 1928 election campaign*. Unpublished doctoral dissertation, University of Wisconsin.

Cavanaugh, J. W. (1995). *Media effects on voters: A panel study of the 1992 presidential election*. Lanham, MD: University Press of America.

Ceaser, J. W., Thurow, G. E., Tulis, J., & Bessette, J. M. (1987). The rise of the rhetorical presidency. In T. Windt & B. Ingold (Eds.), *Essays in presidential rhetoric* (2nd ed., pp. 3–22). Dubuque, Iowa: Kendall/Hunt.

Chaffee, S. H. (Ed. 1975). *Political communication: Issues and strategies for research*. Newbury Park, CA: Sage.

Chaffee, S. H. (1995). Review of *Science of Coercion: Communication Research and Psychological Warfare, 1945–1960. Journal of American History, 82,* 345–346.

Chaffee, S. H., & Frank, S. (1996). How Americans get political information: Print versus broadcast news. *The Annals of the American Academy of Political and Social Science, 546,* 48–58.

Chaffee, S. H., & Hochheimer, J. L. (1985). The beginnings of political communication research in the United States: Origins of the "limited effects" model. In M. Gurevitch & M. R. Levy (Eds.), *Mass communication review yearbook* (Vol. 5, pp. 75–104). Newbury, Park, CA: Sage.

Chaffee, S. H., & Miyo, Y. (1983). Selective exposure and the reinforcement hypothesis: An intergenerational panel study of the 1980 presidential campaign. *Communication Research, 10,* 3–36.

Chaffee, S. H., & Mutz, D. C. (1988). Comparing mediated and interpersonal communication data. In R. P. Hawkins, J. M. Wiemann, & S. Pingree (Eds.), *Advancing communication science: Merging mass and interpersonal processes.* (pp. 19–43). Newbury Park, CA: Sage.

Chaffee, S. H., Zhao, X., & Leshner, G. (1994). Political knowledge and the campaign media of 1992. *Communication Research, 21,* 305–324.

Christ, W. G., Thorson, E., & Caywood, C. (1994). Do attitudes toward political advertising affect information processing of televised political commercials? *Journal of Broadcasting & Electronic Media, 38,* 251–270.

Clancey, M., & Robinson, M. J. (1985). General election coverage: Part I. In M. J. Robinson & A. Ranney (Eds.), *The mass media in campaign '84: Articles from Public Opinion Magazine* (pp. 27–33). Washington, DC: American Enterprise Institute for Public Policy Research.

Clarke, P., & Evans, S. H. (1983). *Covering campaigns: Journalism in congressional elections.* Stanford, CA: Stanford University Press.

Clines, F. X. (1996, September 23). "Ask not ..." "... military-industrial complex ..." "... but fear itself ..." *The New York Times,* A8.

Cohen, B. C. (1963). *The press and foreign policy.* Princeton: Princeton University Press.

Cook, F. L., & Skogan, W. G. (1991). Convergent and divergent voice models of the rise and fall of policy issues. In D. L. Protess & M. McCombs (Eds.), *Agenda setting: Readings on media, public opinion, and policymaking* (pp. 189–206). Mahwah, NJ: Lawrence Erlbaum Associates.

Cook, T. E. (1988). Press secretaries and media strategies in the House of Representatives: Deciding whom to pursue. *American Journal of Political Science, 32,* 1047–1069.

Cook, T. E. (1989). *Making laws and making news: Media strategies in the U. S. House of Representatives.* Washington, DC: Brookings Institution.

Cooper, M. (1995, October 30–November 5). The inside skinny on a decade with Reagan and Bush. *The Washington Post National Weekly Edition, 39.*

Cooper, M. (1996, September 9). The Morris meltdown. *Newsweek, 32–37.*

Cornwell, E. E., Jr. (1965). *Presidential leadership of public opinion.* Bloomington: Indiana University Press.

Creel, G. (1920). *How we advertised America.* New York: Harper & Row.

Cunningham, L. (1995). *Talking politics: Choosing the president in the television age.* Westport, CT: Praeger.

Curran, J., Gurevitch, M., & Woollacott, J. (1982). The study of the media: Theoretical approaches. In M. Gurevitch, T. Bennett, J. Curran, & J. Woollacot (Eds.), *Culture, society and the media* (pp. 11–29). London: Methuen.

Davis, D. K. (1990). News and politics. In D. L. Swanson & D. Nimmo (Eds.), *New directions in political communication: A resource book* (pp. 147–184). Newbury Park, CA: Sage.

Dayan, D., & Katz, E. (1992). *Media events: The live broadcasting of history.* Cambridge, MA: Harvard University Press.

Deakin, J. (1984). *Straight stuff: The reporters, the White House and the truth.* New York: William Morrow.

Dearing, J. W., & Rogers, E. M. (1992). AIDS and the media agenda. In T. Edgar, M. A. Fitzpatrick, & V. S. Freimuth (Eds.), *AIDS: A communication perspective* (pp. 173–194). Hillsdale, NJ: Lawrence Erlbaum Associates.

Deaver, M. (with M. Herskowitz). (1987). *Behind the scenes.* New York: William Morrow.

Decker, W. D. (1994). The 1988 Quayle-Bentsen vice presidential debate. In R. V. Friedenberg (Ed.), *Rhetorical studies of national political debates, 1960–1992* (2nd ed., pp. 167–185). Westport, CT: Praeger.

Debate score: Kennedy up, Nixon down. (1960, November 7). *Broadcasting, 27–28.*

DeFleur, M. L. (1988). Diffusing information. *Society, 25,* 72–81.

Delia, J. G. (1987). Communication research: A history. In C. R. Berger & S. H. Chaffee (Eds.), *Handbook of communication science* (pp. 20–98). Newbury Park, CA: Sage.

Delli Carpini, M. X., & Keeter, S. (1991). Stability and change in the U. S. public's knowledge of politics. *Public Opinion Quarterly, 55*, 583–612.

Delli Carpini, M. X., & Keeter, S. (1996). *What Americans know about politics and why it matters.* New Haven, CT: Yale University Press.

Demers, D. P. (1995). *Corporate newspaper structure, editorial page vigor and social change.* Paper presented to the annual convention of the Midwest Association for Public Opinion Research, Chicago.

Demers, D. P., Craff, D., Choi, Y. H., & Pessin, B. M. (1989). Issue obtrusiveness and the agenda-setting effects of national network news. *Communication Research, 16*, 793–812.

Denton, F., & Thorson, E. (1995). *Civic journalism: Does it work?* Report for Pew Center for Civic Journalism, Washington, DC.

Denton, R. E., Jr. (1988). *The primetime presidency of Ronald Reagan: The era of the television presidency.* Westport, CT: Praeger.

Denton, R. E., Jr. (1994). Series forward. In A. Kiewe (Ed.), *The modern presidency and crisis rhetoric* (pp. ix–xi). Westport, CT: Praeger.

Denton, R. E., Jr., & Holloway, R. L. (1996). Clinton and the town hall meetings: Mediated conversation and the risk of being "in touch." In R. E. Denton, Jr., & R. L. Holloway (Eds.), *The Clinton presidency: Images, issues, and communication strategies* (pp. 17–41). Westport, CT: Praeger.

Depoe, S. P., & Short-Thompson, C. (1994). Let the people speak: The emergence of public space in the Richmond presidential debate. In D. B. Carlin & M. S. McKinney (Eds.), *The 1992 presidential debates in focus* (pp. 85–98). Westport, CT: Praeger.

Devlin, L. P. (1989). Contrasts in presidential campaign commercials of 1988. *American Behavioral Scientist, 32*, 389–414.

Devlin, L. P. (1993). Contrasts in presidential campaign commercials of 1992. *American Behavioral Scientist, 37*, 272–290.

Devlin, L. P. (1994). Television advertising in the 1992 New Hampshire presidential primary election. *Political Communication, 11*, 81–99.

Devlin, L. P. (1995). Political commercials in American presidential elections. In L. L. Kaid & C. Holtz-Bacha (Eds.), *Political advertising in western democracies: Parties & candidates on television* (pp. 186–205). Thousand Oaks, CA: Sage.

Diamond, E., & Bates, S. (1992). *The spot: The rise of political advertising on television* (3rd ed.). Cambridge: MIT Press.

Dickinson, G., (1994). Creating his own constraint: Ronald Reagan and the Iran-Contra crisis. In A. Kiewe (Ed.), *The modern presidency and crisis rhetoric* (pp. 155–177). Westport, CT: Praeger.

Dionne, E. J., Jr. (1992). The illusion of technique: The impact of polls on reporters and democracy. In T. E. Mann & G. R. Orren (Eds.), *Media polls in American politics* (pp. 150–167). Washington, DC: Brookings Institution.

Dionne, E. J., Jr. (1996). *They only look dead: Why progressives will dominate the next political era.* New York: Simon & Schuster.

Dominick, J. R. (1993). *The dynamics of mass communication* (4th ed.). New York: McGraw-Hill.

Donohue, G. A., Olien, C. N., & Tichenor, P. J. (1985). Reporting conflict by pluralism, newspaper type and ownership. *Journalism Quarterly, 62*, 489–499, 507.

Donohue, G. A., Tichenor, P. J., & Olien, C. N. (1972). Gatekeeping: Mass media systems and information control. In F. G. Kline & P. J. Tichenor (Eds.), *Current perspectives in mass communication research* (pp. 41–69). Newbury Park, CA: Sage.

Downs, A. (1991). Up and down with ecology: The "issue-attention cycle." In D. L. Protess & M. McCombs (Eds.), *Agenda-setting: Readings on media, public opinion, and policymaking* (pp. 27–33). Hillsdale, NJ: Lawrence Erlbaum Associates.

Drew, E. (1994). *On the edge: The Clinton presidency.* New York: Simon & Schuster.

Drew, E. (1994, December 19–25). George Washington was not a bubba. *The Washington Post National Weekly Edition,* 19.

Drucker, S. J., & Hunold, J. P. (1987). The debating game. *Critical Studies in Mass Communication, 4*, 202–207.

Dubail, J. (1996, January 14). Hollywood history lesson. *The Plain Dealer,* 3–C.

Dunn, D. (1969). *Public officials and the press.* Reading, MA: Addison-Wesley.

Dye, T. R., & Zeigler, H. (1986). *American politics in the media age* (2nd ed.). Monterey, CA: Brooks/Cole.

Edelman, M. (1967). *The symbolic uses of politics.* Urbana: University of Illinois Press.

Edelstein, A. S., & Schulz. J. B. (1964). The leadership role of the weekly newspaper as seen by community leaders: A sociological perspective. In L. A. Dexter & D. M. White (Eds.), *People, society and mass communication* (pp. 221–238). New York: Macmillan.

Edwards, G. C. III (1983). *The public presidency: The pursuit of popular support.* New York: St. Martin's Press.

Edwards, J. L. (1996, May). *Candidate coverage of a non-candidate: The media, citizen Powell, and public opinion.* Paper presented to the annual convention of the International Communication Association.

Elder, C. D., & Cobb, R. W. (1984). Agenda-building and the politics of aging. *Policy Studies Journal, 13,* 115–129.

Elliott, W. R., & Rosenberg, W. L. (1987). The 1985 Philadelphia newspaper strike: A uses and gratifications study. *Journalism Quarterly, 64,* 679–687.

Elving, R. D. (1994). Brighter lights, wider windows: Presenting Congress in the 1990s. In T. E. Mann & N. J. Ornstein (Eds.), *Congress, the press, and the public* (pp. 171–206). Washington, DC: American Enterprise Institute and Brookings Institution.

Emery, E., & Emery, M. (1984). *The press and America: An interpretive history of the mass media* (5th ed.). Englewood Cliffs, NJ: Prentice-Hall.

Engel, J. F., & Blackwell, R. D. (1982). *Consumer behavior* (4th ed.). Chicago: Dryden Press.

Entman, R. M. (1991). Framing U. S. coverage of international news: Contrasts in narratives of the KAL and Iran Air incidents. *Journal of Communication, 41*(4), 6–27.

Entman, R. M., & Page, B. I. (1994). The news before the storm: The Iraq war debate and the limits to media independence. In W. L. Bennett & D. L. Paletz (Eds.), *Taken by storm: The media, public opinion, and U. S. foreign policy in the Gulf* (pp. 82–101). Chicago: University of Chicago Press.

Erbring, L., Goldenberg, E. N., & Miller, A. H. (1980). Front-page news and real-world cues: A new look at agenda-setting by the media. *American Journal of Political Science, 24,* 16–49.

Ettema, J. S., & Whitney, D. C. (Eds.). (1994). *Audiencemaking: How the media create the audience.* Newbury Park, CA: Sage.

Euchner, C. C. (1990). Presidential appearances. In *The presidents and the public* (pp. 109–129). Washington, DC: Congressional Quarterly Inc.

Eveland, W. P., Jr., McLeod, D. M., & Nathanson, A. I. (1994). Reporters vs. undecided voters: An analysis of the questions asked during the 1992 presidential debates. *Communication Quarterly, 42,* 390–406.

Fallows, J. (1996). *Breaking the news: How the media undermine American democracy.* New York: Pantheon.

Fan, D. P. (1988). *Predictions of public opinion from the mass media: Computer content analysis and mathematical modeling.* New York: Greenwood.

Fans turned lament to song. (1995, November 12). *The Plain Dealer,* 12A.

Feagler, D. (1996, August 28). Act one: Night of miracles raises curtain on big show. *The Plain Dealer,* 2A.

Fenno, R. F., Jr. (1978). *Home style: House members in their districts.* Boston: Little, Brown.

Fineman, H. (1995, September 11). Powell on the march. *Newsweek,* 26–31.

Fisher, W. R. (1987). *Human communication as narration: Toward a philosophy of reason, value, and action.* Columbia, SC: University of South Carolina Press.

Fiske, S. T., & Taylor, S. E. (1984). *Social cognition.* Reading, MA: Addison-Wesley.

Foote, J. S. (1984). Reagan on radio. In R. N. Bostrom and B. H. Westley (Eds.), *Communication yearbook 8* (pp. 692–706). Thousand Oaks, CA: Sage.

Foote, J. S. (1990). *Television access and political power: The networks, the presidency, and the "loyal opposition."* Westport, CT: Praeger.

Ford, G. R. (1979). *A time to heal.* New York: Harper & Row.

Ford, R. (1996, October 17). The master of ambiguity. *The New York Times,* A15.

Fredin, E. S., Kosicki, G. M., & Becker, L. B. (1996). Cognitive strategies for media use during a presidential campaign. *Political Communication, 13,* 23–42.

Friedenberg, R. V. (1994a). Patterns and trends in national political debates: 1960–1992. In R. V. Friedenberg (Ed.), *Rhetorical studies of national political debates, 1960–1992.* (2nd ed. pp. 235–259). Westport, CT: Praeger.

Friedenberg, R. V. (1994b). The 1992 presidential debates. In R. E. Denton, Jr. (Ed.), *The 1992 presidential campaign: A communication perspective* (pp. 89–110). Westport, CT: Praeger.

Frolik, J. (1996, February 18). Ohio voters outraged by political mudslinging. *The Plain Dealer,* 1A, 12A, 13A.

Fromkin, D. (1995). *In the time of the Americans.* New York: Alfred Knopf.

Funkhouser, G. R. (1973). The issues of the sixties: An exploratory study in the dynamics of public opinion. *Public Opinion Quarterly, 37,* 62–75.

Gamson, W. A., & Modigliani, A. (1989). Media discourse and public opinion on nuclear power: A constructionist approach. *American Journal of Sociology, 95,* 1–37.

Gandy, O. (1982). *Beyond agenda-setting: Information subsidies and public policy.* Norwood, NJ: Ablex.

Gans, H. (1985, November–December). Are U. S. journalists dangerously liberal? *Columbia Journalism Review,* 24(4), 29–33.

Garramone, G. M. (1985). Effects of negative political advertising: The roles of sponsor and rebuttal. *Journal of Broadcasting & Electronic Media, 29,* 147–159.

Geer, J. G. (1989). *Nominating presidents: An evaluation of voters and primaries.* Westport, CT: Greenwood.

Gergen, D. (1989, March 5). Bush's start: A presidency "on the edge of a cliff." *The Washington Post,* C1.

Gilbert, C. H., McCombs, M. E., & Nicholas, D. (1980). The state of the union address and the press agenda. *Journalism Quarterly, 57,* 584–588.

Gitlin, T. (1978). Media sociology: The dominant paradigm. *Theory and Society, 6,* 205–253.

Gitlin, T. (1980). *The whole world is watching.* Berkeley: University of California Press.

Glaberson, W. (1994, October 3). A new press role: Solving problems. *The New York Times,* D6.

Glad, B. (1993). Figuring out Saddam Hussein. In M. L. Whicker, J. P. Pfiffner, & R. A. Moore (Eds.), *The presidency and the Gulf War* (pp. 65–89). Westport, CT: Praeger.

Goldenberg, E. N. (1975). *Making the papers: The access of resource-poor groups to the metropolitan press.* Lexington, MA: Lexington Books.

Goldenberg, E. N., & Traugott, M. W. (1984). *Campaigning for Congress.* Washington, DC: Congressional Quarterly Press.

Goldman, E. F. (1969). *The tragedy of Lyndon Johnson.* New York: Alfred Knopf.

Goldman, P., DeFrank, T. M., Miller, M., Murr, A., & Mathews, T. (1994). *Quest for the presidency 1992.* College Station, TX: Texas A&M University Press.

Goldman, R., & Rajagopal, A. (1991). *Mapping hegemony: Television news coverage of industrial conflict.* Norwood, NJ: Ablex.

Goldstein, M. L. (1995). *Guide to the 1996 presidential election.* Washington, DC: Congressional Quarterly.

Gonzenbach, W. J. (1996). *The media, the president, and public opinion: A longitudinal analysis of the drug issue, 1984–1991.* Mahwah, NJ: Lawrence Erlbaum Associates.

Goodnight, G. T. (1988). *Vietnam: The metaphor and the movie.* Paper presented to the annual convention of the Southern Speech Communication Association, Memphis, TN.

Gottlieb, R., & Wolf, I. (1977). *Thinking big: The story of the Los Angeles Times, its publishers, and their influence on southern California.* New York: G. P. Putnam Sons.

Graber, D. A. (1980). *Mass media and American politics.* Washington, DC: Congressional Quarterly Press.

Graber. D. A. (1981). Political languages. In D. D. Nimmo & K. R. Sanders (Eds.), *Handbook of political communication* (pp. 195–223). Newbury Park, CA: Sage.

Graber, D. A. (1982). The impact of media research on public opinion studies. In D. C. Whitney, E. Wartella, & S. Windahl (Eds.), *Mass communication review yearbook* (Vol. 3, pp. 555–564). Newbury Park, CA: Sage.

Graber, D. A. (1987). Kind words and harsh pictures: How television presents the candidates. In K. L. Schlozman (Ed.), *Elections in America* (pp. 115–141). Boston: Allen & Unwin.

Graber, D. A. (1988). *Processing the news: How people tame the information tide* (2nd ed.) New York: Longman.

Graber, D. A. (1994). Why voters fail information tests: Can the hurdles be overcome? *Political Communication, 11,* 331–346.

Graber, D. A., & Weaver, D. (1996). Presidential performance criteria: The missing element in election coverage. *Press/Politics, 1(1),* 7–32.

Green, M. (1974). Nobody covers the House. In R. O. Blanchard (Ed.), *Congress and the news media* (pp. 322–331). New York: Hastings House.

Greenberg, B. S. (1964). Diffusion of news of the Kennedy assassination. *Public Opinion Quarterly, 28,* 225–232.

Griffin, R. J., & Dunwoody, S. (1995). Impacts of information subsidies and community structure on local press coverage of environmental contamination. *Journalism & Mass Communication Quarterly, 72,* 271–284.

Gronbeck, B. E. (1985, November). *The rhetoric of negative political advertising: Thoughts on the senatorial race ads in 1984.* Paper presented to the annual convention of the Speech Communication Association, Denver.

Gronbeck, B. E. (1992). Negative narratives in 1988 presidential campaign ads. *Quarterly Journal of Speech, 78,* 333–346.

Grossman, M. B., & Kumar, M. J. (1981). *Portraying the president: The White House and the news media.* Baltimore: Johns Hopkins Press.

Grush, J. E., McKeough, K. L., & Ahlering, R. F. (1978). Extrapolating laboratory exposure research to actual political elections. *Journal of Personality and Social Psychology, 36,* 257–270.

Hahn, D. (1991). Review of *Deeds done in words: Presidential rhetoric and the genres of governance. Southern Communication Journal, 56,* 318.

Hahn, D. F. (1994). The 1992 Clinton-Bush-Perot presidential debates. In R. V. Friedenberg (Ed.), *Rhetorical studies in national political debates, 1960–1992* (2nd ed. pp. 187–210). Westport, CT: Praeger.

Hall, P. M. (1972). A symbolic interactionist analysis of politics. *Sociological Inquiry, 42,* 35–75.

Hallin, D. C. (1986). *The "uncensored war": The media and Vietnam.* New York: Oxford Press.

Hallin, D. C. (1992). Sound bite news: Television coverage of elections, 1968–1988. *Journal of Communication, 42(2),* 5–24.

Halloran, J. D. (1974). *Mass media and society: The challenge of research.* Leicester: Leicester University Press.

Harden, B. (1996, July 22–28). Wounded by his own sound bites. *The Washington Post National Weekly Edition,* 14.

Harmon, M. D., & Pinkleton, B. E. (1994, August). *Broadcast news as a source of political information: Shrinking sound bites revisited.* Paper presented to the annual convention of the Association for Education in Journalism and Mass Communication, Atlanta.

Hart, R. P. (1984). *Verbal style and the presidency: A computer-based analysis.* Orlando: Academic Press.

Hart, R. P. (1987). *The sound of leadership: Presidential communication in the modern age.* Chicago: University of Chicago Press.

Hart, R. P. (1990). *Modern rhetorical criticism.* Glenview, IL: Scott, Foresman.

Hart, R. P. (1994). *Seducing America: How television charms the modern voter.* New York: Oxford University Press.

Hart, R. P., Smith-Howell, D., & Llewellyn, J. (1991). The mindscape of the presidency: *Time* Magazine, 1945–1985. *Journal of Communication, 41(3),* 6–25.

Hellweg, S. A., Pfau, M., & Brydon, S. R. (1992). *Televised presidential debates: Advocacy in contemporary America.* New York: Praeger.

Henry, D. (1993). President Ronald Reagan's first inaugural address, 1981. In H. Ryan (Ed.), *The inaugural addresses of twentieth-century American presidents* (pp. 259–270). Westport, CT: Praeger.

Herbst, S. (1993). *Numbered voices: How opinion polling has shaped American politics.* Chicago: University of Chicago Press.

Herman, E., & Chomsky, N. (1988). *Manufacturing consent: The political economy of the mass media.* New York: Pantheon.

Hershey, M. R. (1989). The campaign and the media. In G. M. Pomper (Ed.), *The election of 1988: Reports and interpretations* (pp. 73–102). Chatham, NJ: Chatham House.

Hershey, M. R. (1993). The congressional elections. In G. Pomper (Ed.), *The election of 1992: Reports and interpretations* (pp. 157–189). Chatham, NJ: Chatham House.

Hertog, J. K., & McLeod, D. M. (1995). Anarchists wreak havoc in downtown Minneapolis: A multi-level study of media coverage of radical protest. *Journalism & Mass Communication Monographs, 151,* 1–48.

Hertsgaard, M. (1988). *On bended knee: The press and the Reagan presidency.* New York: Farrar Strauss Giroux.

Hess, S. (1991). *Live from Capitol Hill!: Studies of Congress and the media.* Washington, DC: Brookings Institution.

Hetherington, M. (1996). The media's role in forming voters' national economic evaluations in 1992. *American Journal of Political Science, 40,* 372–395.

Hibbing, J. R., & Theiss-Morse, E. (1995). *Congress as public enemy: Public attitudes toward American political institutions.* Cambridge: Cambridge University Press.

Hilgartner, S., & Bosk, C. L. (1988). The rise and fall of social problems: A public arenas model. *American Journal of Sociology, 94,* 53–78.

Hinck, E. A. (1993). *Enacting the presidency: Political argument, presidential debates, and presidential character*. Westport, CT: Praeger.

Hitchon, J. C., & Chang, C. (1995). Effects of gender schematic processing on the reception of political commercials for men and women candidates. *Communication Research, 22*, 430–458.

Hollander, B. A. (1995). The new news and the 1992 presidential campaign: Perceived vs. actual political knowledge. *Journalism & Mass Communication Quarterly, 72*, 786–798.

Holloway, R. L. (1994). A time for change in American politics: The issue of the 1992 presidential election. In R. E. Denton, Jr. (Ed.), *The 1992 presidential campaign: A communication perspective* (pp. 129–167). Westport, CT: Praeger.

Holloway, R. L. (1996). The Clintons and the health care crisis: Opportunity lost, promise unfulfilled. In R. E. Denton, Jr. & R. L. Holloway (Eds.), *The Clinton presidency: Images, issues, and communication strategies* (pp. 159–187). Westport, CT: Praeger.

Hovland, C. I., Janis, I., & Kelley, H. H. (1953). *Communication and persuasion*. New Haven: Yale University Press.

Hughes, W. J. (1995). The "not-so-genial" conspiracy: The New York Times and six presidential "honeymoons," 1953–1993. *Journalism and Mass Communication Quarterly, 72*, 841–850.

Ivie, R. L. (1994). Declaring a national emergency: Truman's rhetorical crisis and the great debate of 1951. In A. Kiewe (Ed.), *The modern presidency and crisis rhetoric.* (pp. 1–18). Westport, CT: Praeger.

Iyengar, S. (1991). *Is anyone responsible?: How television frames political issues*. Chicago: University of Chicago Press.

Iyengar, S., & Kinder, D. R. (1987). *News that matters*. Chicago: University of Chicago Press.

Jacobs, L. R., & Shapiro, R. Y. (1995). The rise of presidential polling: The Nixon White House in historical perspective. *Public Opinion Quarterly, 59*, 163–195.

Jakubowicz, K. (1996). Television and elections in post-1989 Poland: How powerful is the medium? In D. L. Swanon & P. Mancini (Eds.), *Politics, media, and modern democracy: An international study of innovations in electoral campaigning and their consequences* (pp. 129–154). Westport, CT: Praeger.

Jamieson, K. H. (1984). *Packaging the presidency: A history and criticism of presidential campaign advertising*. New York: Oxford.

Jamieson, K. H. (1986). The evolution of political advertising in America. In L. L. Kaid, D. Nimmo, & K. R. Sanders (Eds.), *New perspectives on political advertising* (pp. 1–20). Carbondale, IL: Southern Illinois Press.

Jamieson, K. H. (1988). *Eloquence in an electronic age: The transformation of political speechmaking*. New York: Oxford University Press.

Jamieson, K. H. (1992). *Dirty politics: Deception, distraction, and democracy*. New York: Oxford University Press.

Jamieson, K. H. (1993). The subversive effects of a focus on strategy in news coverage of presidential campaigns. In *1-800-president* (pp. 35–61). New York: Twentieth Century Fund Press.

Jamieson, K. H., & Birdsell, D. S. (1988). *Presidential debates: The challenge of creating an informed electorate*. New York: Oxford.

Jamieson, K. H., & Cappella, J. N. (1995). *Media in the middle: Fairness and accuracy in the 1994 health care reform debate*. Report by the Annenberg Public Policy Center of the University of Pennsylvania.

Jamieson, K. H., & Cappella, J. N. (1996). Bridging the disciplinary divide. *PS: Political Science & Politics, 29*, 13–17.

Jeffres, L. W. (1986). *Mass media: Processes and effects*. Prospect Heights, IL: Waveland Press.

Jeffres, L. W. (1994). *Mass media: Processes* (2nd ed.). Prospect Heights, IL: Waveland Press.

Johnson, H., & Broder, D. S. (1996). *The system: The American way of politics at the breaking point*. Boston: Little, Brown.

Johnson, T. J. (1993). The seven dwarfs and other tales: How the networks and select newspapers covered the 1988 Democratic primaries. *Journalism Quarterly, 70*, 311–320.

Johnson, T. J., & Wanta, W. (1995). Exploring FDR's relationship with the press: A historical agenda-setting study. *Political Communication, 12*, 157–172.

Johnson-Cartee, K. S., & Copeland, G. A. (1991). *Negative political advertising: Coming of age*. Hillsdale, NJ: Lawrence Erlbaum Associates.

Joslyn, M. R., & Ceccoli, S. (1996). Attentiveness to television news and opinion change in the fall 1992 presidential campaign. *Political Behavior, 18*, 141–170.

Joslyn, R. A. (1990). Election campaigns as occasions for civic education. In D. L. Swanson & D. Nimmo (Eds.), *New directions in political communication: A resource book* (pp. 86–119). Newbury Park, CA: Sage.

Jowett, G. S., & O'Donnell, V. (1992). *Propaganda and persuasion* (2nd ed.). Newbury Park, CA: Sage.

Judge, C. S. (1996, March 11). Much more than hot air. *The Wall Street Journal*, A12.

Just, M. R., Crigler, A. N., Alger, D. E., Cook, T. E., Kern, M., & West, D. M. (1996). *Crosstalk: Citizens, candidates, and the media in a presidential campaign*. Chicago: University of Chicago Press.

Just, M. R., Crigler, A. N., & Wallach, L. (1990). Thirty seconds or thirty minutes: What viewers learn from spot advertisements and candidate debates. *Journal of Communication, 40(3),* 120–133.

Kaid, L. L. (1981). Political advertising. In D. Nimmo & K. R. Sanders (Eds.), *Handbook of political communication* (pp. 249–271). Thousand Oaks, CA: Sage.

Kaid, L. L. (1994). Political advertising in the 1992 campaign. In R. E. Denton, Jr. (Ed.), *The 1992 presidential campaign: A communication perspective* (pp. 111–127). Westport, CT: Praeger.

Kaid, L. L., & Foote, J. (1985). How network television coverage of the president and Congress compare. *Journalism Quarterly, 62,* 59–65.

Kaid, L. L, & Holtz-Bacha, C. (1995a). An introduction to parties and candidates on television. In L. L. Kaid & C. Holtz-Bacha (Eds.), *Political advertising in western democracies: Parties & candidates on television* (pp. 1–7). Thousand Oaks, CA: Sage.

Kaid, L. L., & Holtz-Bacha, C. (1995b). Political advertising across cultures: Comparing content, styles, and effects. In L. L. Kaid & C. Holtz-Bacha (Eds.), *Political advertising in western democracies: Parties & candidates on television* (pp. 206–227). Thousand Oaks, CA: Sage.

Kaid, L. L., & Johnston, A. (1991). Negative versus positive television advertising in U. S. presidential campaigns, 1960–1988. *Journal of Communication, 41(3),* 53–64.

Kaid, L. L., Myrick, R., Chanslor, M., Roper, C., Hovind, M., & Trivoulidis, N. (1994). CNN's Americanization of the Gulf War: An analysis of media, technology, and storytelling. In T. A. McCain & L. Shyles (Eds.), *The 1,000 hour war: Communication in the Gulf* (pp. 147–160). Westport, CT: Greenwood.

Kaid, L. L., Tedesco, J. C., & McKinnon, L. M. (1996). Presidential ads as nightly news: A content analysis of 1988 and 1992 televised adwatches. *Journal of Broadcasting & Electronic Media, 40,* 297–308.

Kaid, L. L., Tedesco, J. C., & Spiker, J. A. (1996). Media conflicts over Clinton policies: Political advertising and the battle for public opinion. In R. E. Denton, Jr. & R. L. Holloway (Eds.), *The Clinton presidency: Images, issues, and communication strategies* (pp. 103–121). Westport, CT: Praeger.

Kalb, M. L. (1994). *The Nixon memo: Political respectability, Russia, and the press.* Chicago: University of Chicago Press.

Kalb, M. L., & Mayer, F. (1988). *Reviving the presidential news conference: Report of the Harvard Commission on the presidential news conference.* Cambridge, MA: Joan Shorenstein Barone Center on the Press, Politics, and Public Policy.

Kaniss, P. (1991). *Making local news.* Chicago: University of Chicago Press.

Katz, E. (1987). Communications research since Lazarsfeld. *Public Opinion Quarterly, 51,* S25–S45.

Katz, E. (1994). Foreword. In G. Weimann, *The influentials: People who influence people* (pp. ix–xi). Albany: State University of New York Press.

Katz, E., & Lazarsfeld, P. F. (1955). *Personal influence: The part played by people in the flow of mass communication.* Glencoe, IL: Free Press of Glencoe.

Kearns, D. (1976). *Lyndon Johnson and the American dream.* New York: Harper & Row.

Keen, J. (1995, August 21). Gramm relishes straw poll tally. *USA Today,* 4A.

Keeter, S. (1996, May). *Public opinion dynamics in the Republican presidential nomination of 1996: Why Dole won; why the rest fell short.* Paper presented to the annual convention of the American Association for Public Opinion Research, Salt Lake City.

Keeter, S., & Zukin, C. (1983). *Uninformed choice: The failure of the new presidential nominating system.* New York: Praeger.

Kellerman, K. (1984). The negativity effect and its implications for initial interaction. *Communication Monographs, 51,* 37–55.

Kelly, M. (1993, October 31). David Gergen, Master of the game. *The New York Times Magazine,* 62–71, 80, 94, 97, 103.

Kendall, K. E. (1993). Public speaking in the presidential primaries through media eyes. *American Behavioral Scientist, 37,* 240–251.

Kendall, K. E., (1995). The problem of beginnings in New Hampshire: Control over the play. In K. E. Kendall (Ed.), *Presidential campaign discourse: Strategic communication problems* (pp. 1–34). Albany: State University of New York Press.

Kennamer, J. D., & Chaffee, S. H. (1982). Communication of political information during early presidential primaries: Cognition, affect, and uncertainty. In M. Burgoon (Ed.), *Communication Yearbook 5* (pp. 627–650). New Brunswick, NJ: Transaction Books.

Kenworthy, T. (1992, April 26). Keep the bums in! *The Washington Post*, C5.

Kerbel, M. R. (1994). *Edited for television: CNN, ABC, and the 1992 presidential campaign*. Boulder, CO: Westview Press.

Kern, M. (1989). *30–second politics: Political advertising in the eighties*. New York: Praeger.

Kern, M., Levering, P. W., & Levering, R. B. (1983). *The Kennedy crises: The press, the presidency, and foreign policy*. Chapel Hill, NC: University of North Carolina Press.

Kern, M., & Wicks, R. H. (1994). Television news and the advertising-driven new mass media election: A more significant local role in 1992? In R. E. Denton, Jr. (Ed.), *The 1992 presidential campaign: A communication perspective* (pp. 189–206), Westport, CT: Praeger.

Kernell, S. (1993). *Going public: New strategies of presidential leadership* (2nd ed.) Washington, DC: Congressional Quarterly Press.

Kerr, P. (1986, November 17). Anatomy of the drug issue: How, after years, it erupted. *The New York Times*, A1, B6.

Kiewe, A. (1994a). Introduction. In A. Kiewe (Ed.), *The modern presidency and crisis rhetoric.* (pp. xv–xxxvii). Westport, CT: Praeger.

Kiewe, A. (1994b). From a rhetorical trap to capitulation and obviation: The crisis rhetoric of George Bush's "Read my Lips: No New Taxes." In A. Kiewe (Ed.), *The modern presidency and crisis rhetoric* (pp. 179–201). Westport, CT: Praeger.

King, E. G. (1995). The flawed characters in the campaign: Prestige newspaper assessments of the 1992 presidential candidates' integrity and competence. *Journalism & Mass Communication Quarterly, 72*, 84–97.

Kingdon, J. W. (1995). *Agendas, alternatives, and public policies* (2nd ed.). New York: HarperCollins.

Kinsella, J. (1988). *Covering the plague: AIDS and the American media*. New Brunswick, NJ: Rutgers University Press.

Kinsey, D. F., & Chaffee, S. H. (1995). Communication behavior and presidential approval: The decline of George Bush. *Political Communication, 13*, 281–291.

Klapper, J. T. (1960). *The effects of mass communication*. New York: The Free Press.

Klein, J. (1996, November 4). Where the anger went. *Newsweek*, 33.

Kosicki, G. M. (1993). Problems and opportunities in agenda-setting research. *Journal of Communication, 43*, 100–127.

Kovach, B. (1980). A user's view of the polls. *Public Opinion Quarterly, 44*, 567–571.

Kraus, S. (1987). Voters win. *Critical Studies in Mass Communication, 4*, 214–216.

Kraus, S. (1988). *Televised presidential debates and public policy*. Hillsdale, NJ: Lawrence Erlbaum Associates.

Kraus, S. (1996). Winners of the first 1960 televised presidential debate between Kennedy and Nixon. *Journal of Communication, 46*(4), 78–96.

Kraus, S., & Davis, D. K. (1976). *The effects of mass communication on political behavior.* University Park, PA: Pennsylvania State University Press.

Kraus, S., & Perloff, R. M. (Eds., 1985). *Mass media and political thought: An information- processing approach*. Newbury Park, CA: Sage.

Kraus, S., & Ross, M. (1996, August/September). Polling on presidential debates, 1960–1992. *The Public Perspective*, 57–59.

Krosnick, J. A., & Brannon, L. A. (1993). The impact of the Gulf War on the ingredients of presidential evaluations: Multidimensional effects of political involvement. *American Political Science Review, 87*, 963–975.

Krosnick, J. A., & Kinder, D. R. (1990). Altering the foundations of support for the president through priming. *American Political Science Review, 84*, 497–512.

Krugman, P. R. (1996, September 4). First, do no harm. *The New York Times*, A15.

Kurtz, H. (1996, January 22–28). Substance won't make the 6 o'clock news. *The Washington Post National Weekly Edition*, 12.

Kurtz, H. (1996, October 21–27). Hey! Is anyone listening? *The Washington Post National Weekly Edition*, 6.

Kurtz, H. (1996). *Hot air: All talk, all the time.* New York: Times Books.

Lang, G. E. (1987). Still seeking answers. *Critical Studies in Mass Communication, 4*, 211–214.

Lang, G. E., & Lang, K. (1981). Watergate: An exploration of the agenda-building process. In G. C. Wilhoit & H. de Bock (Eds.), *Mass communication review yearbook 2* (pp. 447–468). Newbury Park, CA: Sage.

Lang, G. E., & Lang, K. (1983). *The battle for public opinion: The president, the press, and the polls during Watergate.* New York: Columbia University Press.

Lang, K., & Lang, G. E. (1966). The mass media and voting. In B. Berelson & M. Janowitz (Eds.), *Reader in public opinion and communication* (2nd ed.). New York: The Free Press.

Lanzetta, J. T., Sullivan, D. G., Masters, R. D., & McHugo, G. J. (1985). Emotional and cognitive responses to televised images of political leaders. In S. Kraus & R. M. Perloff (Eds.), *Mass media and political thought: An information-processing approach* (pp. 85–116). Newbury Park, CA: Sage.

Lasswell, H. (1927). *Propaganda technique in the world war.* New York: Knopf.

Lau, R. R., & Sears, D. O. (Eds., 1986). *Political cognition.* Hillsdale, NJ: Lawrence Erlbaum Associates.

Lavrakas, P. J., & Bauman, S. L. (1995). Page one use of presidential pre-election polls: 1980–1992. In P. J. Lavrakas, M. W. Traugott, & P. V. Miller (Eds.), *Presidential polls and the news media* (pp. 35–49). Boulder, CO: Westview Press.

Lazarsfeld, P. F., Berelson, B., & Gaudet, H. (1944). *The people's choice: How the voter makes up his mind in a presidential campaign.* New York: Columbia University Press.

Lemert, J. B., Elliott, W. R., Bernstein, J. M., Rosenberg, W. L., & Nestvold, K. J. (1991). *News verdicts, the debates, and presidential campaigns.* New York: Praeger.

Lemert, J. B., Elliott, W. R., Rosenberg, W. L., & Bernstein, J. M. (1996). *The politics of disenchantment: Bush, Clinton, Perot, and the press.* Cresskill, NJ: Hampton Press.

Lenart, S. (1994). *Shaping political attitudes: The impact of interpersonal communication and mass media.* Newbury Park, CA: Sage.

Leonard, T. C. (1986). *The power of the press: The birth of American political reporting.* New York: Oxford Press.

Leuchtenburg, W. E. (1963). *Franklin D. Roosevelt and the New Deal, 1932–1940.* New York: Harper and Brothers.

Leuchtenburg, W. E. (1983). *In the shadow of FDR: From Harry Truman to Ronald Reagan.* Ithaca: Cornell University Press.

Lewis, W. F. (1987). Telling America's story: Narrative form and the Reagan presidency. *Quarterly Journal of Speech, 73*, 280–302.

Lichter, S. R., & Amundson, D. R. (1994). Less news is worse news: Television news coverage of Congress, 1972–92. In T. E. Mann & N. J. Ornstein (Eds.), *Congress, the press, and the public* (pp. 131–140). Washington, DC: American Enterprise Institute and Brookings Institution.

Lichter, S. R., Amundson, D., & Noyes, R. (1988). *The video campaign: Network coverage of the 1988 primaries.* Washington, DC: American Enterprise Institute for Public Policy.

Lichter, S. R., & Noyes, R. E. (1995). *Good intentions make bad news: Why Americans hate campaign journalism.* Lanham, MD: Rowman & Littlefield.

Lichter, S. R., Rothman, S., & Lichter, L. S. (1986). *The media elite.* Bethesda, MD: Adler & Adler.

Lichter, S. R., & Smith, T. (1996). Why elections are bad news: Media and candidate discourse in the 1996 presidential primaries. *Press/Politics,1*(4),15–35.

Linsky, M. (1986). *Impact: How the press affects federal policy-making.* New York: W. W. Norton.

Lippmann, W. (1941). *Public opinion.* New York: Macmillan.

Lipstadt, D. E. (1986). *Beyond belief: The American press and the coming of the Holocaust 1933–1945.* New York: The Free Press.

Long, K. L. (1995, August 28). Defending cigarettes where tobacco is king. *The Plain Dealer*, 1A, 4A.

Louden, A. (1994). Voter rationality and media excess: Image in the 1992 presidential campaign. In R. E. Denton, Jr. (Ed.), *The 1992 presidential campaign: A communication perspective* (pp. 169–187). Westport, CT: Praeger.

Lowery, S. A., & DeFleur, M. L. (1995). *Milestones in mass communication research: Media effects* (3rd ed.). White Plains, NY: Longman.

Lowi, T. J. (1985). *The personal president: Power invested, promise unfulfilled.* Ithaca: Cornell University Press.

Lowry, D. T., & Shidler, J. A. (1995). The sound bites, the biters, and the bitten: An analysis of network TV news bias in campaign '92. *Journalism & Mass Communication Quarterly, 72,* 33–44.

MacKuen, M. B., & Coombs, S. L. (1981). *More than news: Media power in public affairs.* Newbury Park, CA: Sage.

Magleby, D. B., & Nelson, C. J. (1990). *The money chase: Congressional campaign finance reform.* Washington, DC: Brookings Institution.

Maltese, J. A. (1994). *Spin control: The White House Office of Communications and the management of presidential news* (2nd ed.). Chapel Hill: University of North Carolina Press.

Mancini, P., & Swanson, D. L. (1996). Politics, media, and modern democracy: Introduction. In D. L. Swanson & P. Mancini (Eds.), *Politics, media, and modern democracy: An international study of innovations in electoral campaigning and their consequences* (pp. 1–26). Westport, CT: Praeger.

Manheim, J. B. (1994). Strategic public diplomacy: Managing Kuwait's image during the Gulf conflict. In W. L. Bennett & D. L. Paletz (Eds.), *Taken by storm: The media, public opinion, and U. S. foreign policy in the Gulf War* (pp. 131–148). Chicago: University of Chicago Press.

Mann, T. E., & Orren, G. R. (1992). To poll or not to poll … and other questions. In T. E. Mann & G. R. Orren (Eds.), *Media polls in American politics* (pp. 1–18). Washington, DC: Brookings Institute.

Maraniss, D. (1996, September 2–8). The comeback kid's last return. *The Washington Post National Weekly Edition,* 8–9.

Maranto, R. (1996, February 26). Of masses and morons. *The Weekly Standard,* 19–20.

Marks, A. (1995, July 24). "Public journalism" aims to revitalize public life. *The Christian Science Monitor,* 12.

Martel, M. (1983). *Political campaign debates: Images, strategies, and tactics.* New York: Longman.

Marx, K., & Engels, F. (1970). *The German ideology.* (First published in full in 1932). London: Lawrence and Wishart.

Matera, F. R., & Salwen, M. B. (1996). Unwieldy questions? Circuitous answers?: Journalists as panelists in presidential election debates. *Journal of Broadcasting & Electronic Media, 40,* 309–317.

Matthews, C. (1996). *Kennedy & Nixon: The rivalry that shaped postwar America.* New York: Simon & Schuster.

Mayer, W. G. (1987). The New Hampshire primary: A historical overview. In G. R. Orren & N. W. Polsby (Eds.), *Media and momentum: The New Hampshire primary and nomination politics* (pp. 9–41). Chatham, NJ: Chatham House.

McCombs, M. E. (1976). Agenda-setting research: A bibliographic essay. *Political Communication Review, 1,* 1–7.

McCombs, M. E. & Gilbert, S. (1986). News influence on our pictures of the world. In J. Bryant & D. Zillmann (Eds.), *Perspectives on media effects* (pp. 1–15). Hillsdale, NJ: Lawrence Erlbaum Associates.

McCombs, M. E., & Shaw, D. L. (1972). The agenda-setting function of mass media. *Public Opinion Quarterly, 36,* 176–185.

McCubbins, M. D. (1992). Party decline and presidential campaigns in the television age. In M. D. McCubbins (Ed.), *Under the watchful eye: Managing presidential campaigns in the television era* (pp. 9–57). Washington, DC: Congressional Quarterly Press.

McCullough, D. (1992). *Truman.* New York: Simon & Schuster.

McGraw, K. M., & Lodge, M. (1996). Political information processing: A review essay. *Political Communication, 13,* 131–142.

McGuire, W. J. (1986). The myth of massive media impact: Savagings and salvagings. In G. Comstock (Ed.), *Public communication and behavior* (Vol. 1, pp. 173–257). New York: Academic Press.

McKinnon, L. M. (1995, August). *Mediating political mudslinging or magnifying advertising effects: An experimental study of adwatch effects on voters' evaluations of candidates and their ads.* Paper presented to the annual convention of the Association for Education in Journalism and Mass Communication, Washington, DC.

McLeod, J. M. (1993). On evaluating news media performance. *Political Communication, 10,* 16–22.

McLeod, J. M., & Becker, L. B. (1974). Testing the validity of gratification measures through political effects analysis. In J. G. Blumler & E. Katz (Eds.), *The uses of mass communications: Current perspectives on gratifications research* (pp. 137–164). Thousand Oaks, CA: Sage.

McLeod, J. M., Becker, L. B., & Byrnes, J. E. (1974). Another look at the agenda-setting function of the press. *Communication Research, 1,* 131–165.

McLeod, J. M., & Blumler, J. G. (1987). The macrosocial level of communication science. In C. R. Berger & S. H. Chaffee (Eds.), *Handbook of communication science* (pp. 271–322). Newbury Park, CA: Sage.

McLeod, J. M., Daily, K., Guo, Z., Eveland, W. P., Jr., Bayer, J., Yang, S., & Wang, H. (1996). Community integration, local media use, and democratic processes. *Communication Research, 23,* 179–209.

McLeod, J. M., Durall, J. A., Ziemke, D. A., & Bybee, C. R. (1979). Reactions of young and older voters: Expanding the context of effects. In S. Kraus (Ed.), *The great debates: Carter vs. Ford, 1976* (pp. 348–367). Bloomington, IN: Indiana University Press.

McLeod, J. M., Guo, Z., Daily, K., Steele, C. A., Huang, H., Horowitz, E., & Chen, H. (1996). The impact of traditional and nontraditional media forms in the 1992 presidential election. *Journalism & Mass Communication Quarterly, 73,* 401–416.

McLeod, J. M., Kosicki, G. M., & McLeod, D. M. (1994). The expanding boundaries of political communication effects. In J. Bryant & D. Zillmann (Eds.), *Media effects: Advances in theory and research* (pp. 123–162). Hillsdale, NJ: Lawrence Erlbaum Associates.

McLeod, J. M., & McDonald, D. G. (1985). Beyond simple exposure: Media orientations and their impact on political processes. *Communication Research, 12,* 3–33.

McManus, J. H. (1992). What kind of commodity is news? *Communication Research, 19,* 787–805.

Meadow, R. G. (1980). *Politics as communication.* Norwood, NJ: Ablex.

Meadow, R. G. (1987). A speech by any another name. *Critical Studies in Mass Communication, 4,* 207–210.

Meadow, R. G., & Jackson–Beeck, M. (1978). A comparative perspective on presidential debates: Issue evolution in 1960 and 1976. In G. F. Bishop, R. G. Meadow, & M. Jackson-Beeck (Eds.), *The presidential debates: Media, electoral, and policy perspectives* (pp. 33–58). New York: Praeger.

Media Monitor. (1993, September/October). The honeymoon that wasn't: TV news coverage of President Clinton's first six months. Washington, D. C. : Center for Media and Public Affairs.

Media Monitor. (1994, May/June). Diagnosing health care reform: How TV news has covered President Clinton's health security act. Washington, DC: Center for Media and Public Affairs.

Media Monitor. (1994, July/August). They're no friends of Bill: TV news coverage of the Clinton administration. Washington, DC: Center for Media and Public Affairs.

Media Monitor. (1995, March/April). No Newt is good Newt: Media coverage of the new G. O. P. Congress. Washington, DC: Center for Media and Public Affairs.

Media Monitor. (1995, May/June). The invisible man: TV news coverage of President Bill Clinton, 1993–1995. Washington, DC: Center for Media and Public Affairs.

Media Monitor. (1996, March/April). The bad news campaign: TV news coverage of the GOP primaries. Washington, DC: Center for Media and Public Affairs.

Media Monitor. (1996, May/June). Whose campaign did you see?: Primary perspectives from the press, the pols, the polls, and TV's pranksters. Washington, DC: Center for Media and Public Affairs.

Media Monitor. (1996, September/October). Take this campaign—please!: TV news coverage of the 1996 presidential election. Washington, DC: Center for Media and Public Affairs.

Media Studies Center (1996, April). *The media and campaign 96 briefing.* New York: Media Studies Center.

Merrit, S. (1984). Negative political advertising: Some empirical findings. *Journal of Advertising, 13,* 27–38.

Merritt, D. (1995). *Public journalism and public life: Why telling the news is not enough.* Mahwah, NJ: Lawrence Erlbaum Associates.

Meyer, J., & Carlin, D. B. (1994). The impact of formats on voter reaction. In D. B. Carlin & M. S. McKinney (Eds.), *The 1992 presidential debates in focus* (pp. 69–83). Westport, CT: Praeger.

Meyrowitz, J. (1995). The problem of getting on the media agenda: A case study in competing logics of campaign coverage. In K. E. Kendall (Ed.), *Presidential campaign discourse: Strategic communication problems* (pp. 35–67). Albany: State University of New York Press.

Miller, A. H. (1993). Economic, character, and social issues in the 1992 presidential election. *American Behavioral Scientist, 37,* 315–327.

Miller, A. H., Goldenberg, E. N., & Erbring, L. (1979). Type-set politics: Impact of newspapers on public confidence. *American Political Science Review, 73,* 67–84.

Miller, A. H., & MacKuen, M. (1979). Informing the electorate: A national study. In S. Kraus (Ed.), *The great debates: Carter vs. Ford, 1976* (pp. 269–297). Bloomington, IN: Indiana University Press.

Miller, D. (1987; Ed.). *The Blackwell encyclopaedia of political thought.* New York: Basil Blackwell.

Miller, M. (1981). *Lyndon: An oral biography.* New York: G. P. Putnam's Sons.

Miller, M. M., & Denham, B. (1994). Horserace, issue coverage in prestige newspapers during 1988, 1992 elections. *Newspaper Research Journal, 15,* 20–28.

Miller, S. H. (1978). Reporters and Congressmen: Living in symbiosis. *Journalism Monographs, 53*, 1–25.

Misciagno, P. S. (1996). Rethinking the mythic presidency. *Political Communication, 13*, 329–344.

Molotch, H., Protess, D. L., & Gordon, M. T. (1987). The media-policy connection: Ecologies of news. In D. L. Paletz (Ed.), *Political communication research: Approaches, studies, assessments* (pp. 26–48). Norwood, NJ: Ablex.

Mondak, J. J. (1995). *Nothing to read: Newspapers and elections in a social experiment.* Ann Arbor: University of Michigan Press.

The money behind Clinton's campaign. (1996, September 2–8). *The Washington Post National Weekly Edition*, 12.

Moore, D. W. (1992). *The superpollsters: How they measure and manipulate public opinion in America.* New York: Four Walls Eight Windows.

Moore, M. T. (1996, July 26). On the trail with Dole: A real media circus. *USA Today*, 12A.

Morello, J. T. (1988). Visual structuring of the 1976 and 1984 nationally televised presidential debates: Implications. *Central States Speech Journal, 39*, 233–243.

Morgan, D. (1996, October 28–November 3). A revolution derailed. *The Washington Post National Weekly Edition*, 21–22.

Morin, R. (1995, November 27–December 3). Taking sides in the budget battle. *The Washington Post National Weekly Edition*, 35.

Morin, R. (1996, February 5–11). Tuned out, turned off. *The Washington Post National Weekly Edition*, 6–8.

Morin, R. (1996, June 24–30). Speaking of focus groups ... *The Washington Post National Weekly Edition*, 35.

Morreale, J. (1993). *The presidential campaign film: A critical history.* Westport, CT: Praeger.

Morris, D. (1997). *Behind the oval office: Winning the presidency in the nineties.* New York: Random House.

Mueller, J. (1973). *War, presidents and public opinion.* New York: Wiley.

Mueller, J. (1994). *Policy and opinion in the Gulf War.* Chicago: University of Chicago Press.

Mutz, D. C. (1992). Mass media and the depoliticization of personal experience. *American Journal of Political Science, 36*, 483–508.

Neuman, W. R., Just, M. R., & Crigler, A. N. (1992). *Common knowledge: News and the construction of political meaning.* Chicago: University of Chicago Press.

Neustadt, R. E. (1980). *Presidential power: The politics of leadership from FDR to Carter.* New York: John Wiley. (Originally published in 1960.)

Newhagen, J. E. (1994). Self-efficacy and call-in political television show use. *Communication Research, 21*, 366–379.

Newhagen, J. E., & Reeves, B. (1991). Emotion and memory responses for negative political advertising: A study of television commercials used in the 1988 presidential election. In F. Biocca (Ed.), *Television and political advertising, Volume 1: Psychological processes* (pp. 197–220). Hillsdale, NJ: Lawrence Erlbaum Associates.

Newman, B. I. (1994). *The marketing of the president: Political marketing as campaign strategy.* Thousand Oaks, CA: Sage.

Newman, B. I. (1995, May). Political marketing as a governing tool. *Werbeforschung & Praxis*, 163–167.

Newsweek Poll. (1995, January 9), *Newsweek*, 28.

Nimmo, D. (1996). Politics, media, and modern democracy: The United States. In D. L. Swanson & P. Mancini (Eds.), *Politics, media, and modern democracy: An international study of innovations in electoral campaigning and their consequences* (pp. 29–47). Westport, CT: Praeger.

Nimmo, D., & Sanders, K. R. (Eds.) (1981). *Handbook of political communication.* Newbury Park, CA: Sage.

Nixon, R. M. (1962). *Six crises.* Garden City, NY: Doubleday.

Norris, P. (1996). Does television erode social capital? A reply to Putnam. *PS: Political Science & Politics, 29*, 474–480.

Olien, C. N., Donohue, G. A., & Tichenor, P. J. (1968). The community editor's power and the reporting of conflict. *Journalism Quarterly, 45*, 243–252.

Olien, C. N., Donohue, G. A., & Tichenor, P. J. (1995). Conflict, consensus, and public opinion. In T. L. Glasser & C. T. Salmon (Eds.), *Public opinion and the communication of consent* (pp. 301–322). New York: Guilford Press.

Orr, C. J. (1980). Reporters confront the president: Sustaining a counterpoised situation. *Quarterly Journal of Speech, 66*, 17–32.

Orren, G. R. (1986). Thinking about the press and government. In M. Linsky, *Impact: How the press affects federal policymaking* (pp. 1–20). New York: W. W. Norton.

Owen, D. (1991). *Media messages in American presidential elections*. New York: Greenwood.

Page, B. I. (1995). Speedy deliberation: Rejecting "1960s programs" as causes of the Los Angeles riots. *Political Communication, 12*, 245–261.

Page, B. I. (1996). The mass media as political actors. *PS: Political Science & Politics, 29*, 20–24.

Page, B. I., & Shapiro, R. Y. (1992). *The rational public: Fifty years of trends in Americans' policy preferences*. Chicago: University of Chicago Press.

Page, B. I., & Tannenbaum, J. (1996). Populistic deliberation and talk radio. *Journal of Communication, 46*(2), 33–54.

Paletz, D. L., & Entman, R. M. (1981). *Media power politics*. New York: The Free Press.

Paletz, D. L., & Guthrie, K. K. (1987). The three faces of Ronald Reagan. *Journal of Communication, 37*(4), 7–23.

Paletz, D., Reichert, P., & McIntyre, B. (1971). How the media support local government authority. *Public Opinion Quarterly, 35*, 80–92.

Pan, Z., & Kosicki, G. M. (1993). Framing analysis: An approach to news discourse. *Political Communication, 10*, 55–75.

Pan, Z., & Kosicki, G. M. (1996). Assessing news media influences on the formation of whites' racial policy preferences. *Communication Research, 23*, 147–178.

Park, E., & Kosicki, G. M. (1995). Presidential support during the Iran-Contra affair: People's reasoning process and media influence. *Communication Research, 22*, 207–236.

Parker, K. C. (1994). How the press views Congress. In T. E. Mann & N. J. Ornstein (Eds.), *Congress, the press, and the public* (pp. 157–170). Washington, DC: American Enterprise Institute and Brookings Institution.

Patterson, T. E. (1980). *The mass media election: How Americans choose their president*. New York: Praeger.

Patterson, T. E. (1993). *Out of order*. New York: Alfred Knopf.

Patterson, T. E., & McClure, R. D. (1976). *The unseeing eye: The myth of television power in national elections*. New York: G. P. Putnam.

Payne, J. G., & Mercuri, K. (1993). Private lives, public officials: The challenge to mainstream media. *American Behavioral Scientist, 37*, 291–301.

Perloff, R. M. (1993). *The dynamics of persuasion*. Hillsdale, NJ: Lawrence Erlbaum Associates.

Perloff, R. M. (1993). Third-person effect research 1983–1992: A review and synthesis. *International Journal of Public Opinion Research, 5*, 167–184.

Pfau, M., & Burgoon, M. (1988). Inoculation in political campaign communication. *Human Communication Research, 15*, 91–111.

Pfau, M., & Burgoon, M. (1989). The efficacy of issue and character attack message strategies in political campaign communication. *Communication Reports, 2*, 52–61.

Pfau, M., Diedrich, T., Larson, K. M., & Van Winkle, K. M. (1993). Relational and competence perceptions of presidential candidates during primary election campaigns. *Journal of Broadcasting & Electronic Media, 26*, 275–292.

Pfau, M., & Eveland, W. P., Jr. (1994). Debates versus other communication sources: The pattern of information and influence. In D. B. Carlin & M. S. McKinney (Eds.), *The 1992 presidential debates in focus* (pp. 155–173). Westport, CT: Praeger.

Pfau, M., & Kenski, H. C. (1990). *Attack politics: Strategy and defense*. New York: Praeger.

Pfau, M., & Louden, A. (1994). Effectiveness of adwatch formats in deflecting political attack ads. *Communication Research, 21*, 325–341.

Picard, R. G. (1989). *Media economics*. Thousand Oaks, CA: Sage.

Pitney, J. J., Jr. (1996, January 29). HTTP://Dems. lynch. Newt. *The Weekly Standard*, 13–14.

The Pentagon and The Press: Secretary of Defense William J. Perry (Interview with Marvin Kalb). (1996, Winter). *Press/Politics, 1*, 121–126.

Polk, L. D., Eddy, J., & Andre, A. (1975). Use of congressional publicity in Wisconsin district. *Journalism Quarterly*, 543–546.

Pollock, M. A. (1994). The battle for the past: George Bush and the Gulf crisis. In A. Kiewe (Ed.), *The modern presidency and crisis rhetoric* (pp. 203–224). Westport, CT: Praeger.

Polsby, N. W., & Wildavsky, A. (1996). *Presidential elections: Strategies and structures of American politics* (9th ed.). Chatham, NJ: Chatham House.

Popkin, S. L. (1991). *The reasoning voter: Communication and persuasion in presidential campaigns.* Chicago: University of Chicago Press.

Pratkanis, A. R. (1989). The cognitive representation of attitudes. In A. R. Pratkanis, S. J. Breckler, & A. G. Greenwald (Eds.), *Attitude structure and function* (pp. 71–98). Hillsdale, NJ: Lawrence Erlbaum Associates.

Pratt, J. W. (1970). An analysis of three crisis speeches. *Western Journal of Speech Communication, 34,* 194–203.

Price, V., & Tewksbury, D. (1996). News values and public opinion: A theoretical account of media priming and framing. In G. Barnett & F. J. Boster (Eds.), *Progress in the communication sciences.* Norwood, NJ: Ablex.

Price, V., Tewksbury, D., & Powers, E. (1995). *Switching trains of thought: The impact of news frames on readers' cognitive responses.* Paper presented to the annual convention of the Midwest Association for Public Opinion Research, Chicago.

Protess, D. L., Cook, F. L., Doppelt, J. C., Ettema, J. S., Gordon, M. T., Leff, D. R., & Miller, P. (1991). *The journalism of outrage: Investigative reporting and agenda building in America.* New York: Guilford Press.

Protess, D. L., & McCombs, M. E. (Eds.; 1991). *Agenda-setting: Readings on media, public opinion, and policymaking.* Hillsdale, NJ: Lawrence Erlbaum Associates.

Rahn, W. M., & Cramer, K. J. (1996). Activation and application of political party stereotypes: The role of television. *Political Communication, 13,* 195–212.

Raines, H. (1996, February 25). The Fallows fallacy. *The New York Times,* E14.

Rather, D. (Ed.;1996). *Our times: America at the birth of the twentieth century* (Based on the landmark study by Mark Sullivan). New York: Scribner.

Ratzan, S. C. (1989). The real agenda setters: Pollsters in the 1988 presidential campaign. *American Behavioral Scientist, 32,* 451–463.

Regan, D. T. (1988). *For the record.* New York: Harcourt Brace Jovanovich.

Remarks by President, Governor and Dr. Graham (1995, April 24). *The New York Times,* B8.

Reynolds, M. S. (1988). *The sun also rises: A novel of the twenties.* Boston: Twayne.

Rhee, J. W. (1996). How polls drive campaign coverage: The Gallup/CNN/USA Today tracking poll and USA Today's coverage of the 1992 presidential campaign. *Political Communication, 13,* 213–229.

Rich, F. (1996, August 28). New deal lite. *The New York Times,* A15.

Richard, P. B. (1994). Polling and political campaigns. In G. H. Stempel (Ed.), *The practice of political communication* (pp. 25–39). Englewood Cliffs, NJ: Prentice-Hall.

Ritter, K., & Henry, D. (1994). The 1980 Reagan-Carter presidential debate. In R. V. Friedenberg (Ed.), *Rhetorical studies of national political debates, 1960–1992* (2nd ed., pp. 69–93). Westport, CT: Praeger.

Roberts, M. S. (1995). Political advertising: Strategies for influence. In K. E. Kendall (Ed.), *Presidential campaign discourse: Strategic communication problems* (pp. 179–199). Albany: State University of New York Press.

Roberts, S. V. (1982, October 27). President's coalition. *The New York Times,* 13.

Robinson, J. P., & Davis, D. K. (1990). Television news and the informed public: An information-processing approach. *Journal of Communication, 40(3),* 106–119.

Robinson, J. P., & Levy, M. R. (1986). *The main source: Learning from television news.* Thousand Oaks, CA: Sage.

Robinson, J. P., & Levy, M. R. (1996). News media use and the informed public: A 1990s update. *Journal of Communication, 46(2),* 129–135.

Robinson, M. J. (1976). Public affairs television and the growth of political malaise: The case of "The selling of the Pentagon." *American Political Science Review, 70,* 409–432.

Robinson, M. J. (1985). The media in campaign 1984, Part II: Wingless, toothless, and hopeless. In M. J. Robinson & A. Ranney (Eds.), *The mass media in campaign '84: Articles from Public Opinion Magazine* (pp. 34–39). Washington, DC: American Enterprise Institute for Public Policy Research.

Robinson, M. J., & Appel, K. R. (1979). Network news coverage of Congress. *Political Science Quarterly, 94,* 407–418.

Robinson, M. J., & Sheehan, M. A. (1983). *Over the wire and on TV: CBS and UPI in campaign '80.* New York: Russell Sage Foundation.

Roddy, B. L., & Garramone, G. M. (1988). Appeals and strategies of negative political advertising. *Journal of Broadcasting & Electronic Media, 32,* 415–427.

Rodgers, D. T. (1987). *Contested truths: Keywords in American politics since Independence*. New York: Basic Books.

Rogers, E. M. (1987). *Diffusion of innovations* (3rd ed.). New York: The Free Press.

Rogers, E. M. (1994). *A history of communication study: A biographical approach*. New York: The Free Press.

Rogers, E. M., & Dearing, J. (1988). Agenda-setting research: Where has it been, where is it going? In J. Anderson (Ed.), *Communication yearbook 11* (pp. 555–594). Thousand Oaks, CA: Sage.

Rogers, E. M., Dearing, J. W. & Chang, S. (1991). AIDS in the 1980s: The agenda-setting process for a public issue. *Journalism Monographs, 126*, 1–47.

Rosen, J., & Merritt, D., Jr. (1994). *Public journalism: Theory and practice*. Dayton, OH: Kettering Foundation.

Rosenstiel, T. (1993). *Strange bedfellows: How television and the presidential candidates changed American politics, 1992*. New York: Hyperion.

Rosenstiel, T. (1994). *The beat goes on: President Clinton's first year with the media*. New York: Twentieth Century Fund Press.

Rozell, M. J. (1994). Press coverage of Congress, 1946–92. In T. E. Mann & N. J. Ornstein (Eds.), *Congress, the press, and the public* (pp. 59–129). Washington, DC: American Enterprise Institute and Brookings Institution.

Rubin, A. M. (1994). Media uses and effects: A uses-and-gratifications perspective. In J. Bryant & D. Zillmann (Eds.), *Media effects: Advances in theory and research* (pp. 417–436). Hillsdale, NJ: Lawrence Erlbaum Associates.

Runkel, D. R. (Ed.). (1989). *Campaign for president: The managers look at '88*. Dover, MA: Auburn House.

Russomanno, J. A., & Everett, S. E. (1995). Candidate sound bites: Too much concern over length? *Journal of Broadcasting & Electronic Media, 39*, 408–415.

Ryan, C. (1991). *Prime time activism: Media strategies for grassroots organizing*. Boston: South End Press.

Ryan, H. (1993a). Introduction. In H. Ryan (Ed.), *The inaugural addresses of twentieth-century American presidents* (pp. xv–xix). Westport, CT: Praeger.

Ryan, H. (1993b). President Bill Clinton's inaugural address, 1993. In H. Ryan (Ed.), *The inaugural addresses of twentieth-century American presidents* (pp. 299–310). Westport, CT: Praeger.

Ryan, H. (1994). The 1988 Bush-Dukakis presidential debates. In R. V. Friedenberg (Ed.), *Rhetorical studies of national political debates* (2nd ed., pp. 145–166). Westport, CT: Praeger.

Sabato, L. J. (1991). *Feeding frenzy: How attack journalism has transformed American politics*. New York: The Free Press.

Sabato, L. J. (1992). Open season: How the news media cover presidential campaigns in the age of attack journalism. In M. McCubbins (Ed.), *Under the watchful eye: Managing presidential campaigns in the television era* (pp. 127–151). Washington, DC: Congressional Quarterly Press.

Sabato, L. J., & Lichter, S. R. (1994). *When should the watchdogs bark?: Media coverage of the Clinton scandals*. Washington, DC: University Press of America.

Sabato, L. J., & Simpson, G. R. (1996). *Dirty little secrets: The persistence of corruption in American politics*. New York: Times Books.

Safire, W. (1996, January 11). President as pugilist. *The New York Times*, A15.

Safire, W. (1996, September 16). Brush off the "pollbearers." *The New York Times*, A15.

Salwen, M. B. (1986, May). *Time in agenda-setting: The accumulation of media coverage on audience issue salience*. Paper presented at the annual meeting of the International Communication Association, Chicago.

Samuelson, R. J. (1996, January 1–7). Budget charade. *The Washington Post National Weekly Edition*, 28.

Schleuder, J., McCombs, M., & Wanta, W. (1991). Inside the agenda-setting process: How political advertising and TV news prime viewers to think about issues and candidates. In F. Biocca (Ed.), *Television and political advertising, Volume 1: Psychological processes* (pp. 265–309). Hillsdale, NJ: Lawrence Erlbaum Associates.

Schoenbach, K., & Becker, L. B. (1995). Origins and consequences of mediated public opinion. In T. L. Glasser & C. T. Salmon (Eds.), *Public opinion and the communication of consent* (pp. 323–347). New York: Guilford Press.

Schramm, W. (Ed.). (1954). *The process and effects of mass communication*. Urbana: University of Illinois Press.

Schroeder, A. (1996). Watching between the lines: Presidential debates as television. *Press/Politics, 1*, 57–75.

Schudson, M. (1978). *Discovering the news: A social history of American newspapers.* New York: Basic Books.

Schudson, M. (1986). When: Deadlines, datelines, and history. In R. K. Manoff & M. S. Schudson (Eds.), *Reading the news* (pp. 79–108). New York: Pantheon.

Schudson, M. (1992). *Watergate in American memory: How we remember, forget and reconstruct the past.* New York: Basic Books.

Schudson, M. (1995). *The power of news.* Cambridge, MA: Harvard University Press.

Sears, D. O., & Chaffee, S. H. (1979). Uses and effects of the 1976 debates: An overview of empirical studies. In S. Kraus (Ed.), *The great debates: Carter vs. Ford, 1976* (pp. 223–261). Bloomington, IN: Indiana University Press.

Sears, D. O., & Freedman, J. L. (1967). Selective exposure to information: A critical review. *Public Opinion Quarterly, 31,* 194–213.

Seelye, K. Q. (1996, September 6). Dole replaces top aides in effort to sharpen his message. *The New York Times,* A10.

Selnow, G. W. (1994). *High-tech campaigns: Computer technology in political communication.* Westport, CT: Praeger.

Semetko, H., Blumler, J. G., Gurevitch, M., Weaver, D. H. with Barkin, S., & Wilhoit, G. C. (1991). *The formation of campaign agendas: A comparative analysis of party and media roles in recent American and British elections.* Hillsdale, NJ: Lawrence Erlbaum Associates.

Shapiro, M. A, & Rieger, R. H. (1992). Comparing positive and negative political advertising on radio. *Journalism Quarterly, 69,* 135–145.

Shaw, D. (1993, September 15). Not even getting a 1st chance. *The Los Angeles Times,* A1.

Shaw, D. L. (1977). The press agenda in a community setting. In D. L Shaw & M. E. McCombs (Eds.), *The emergence of American political issues: The agenda-setting function of the press* (pp. 19–31). St. Paul, MN: West.

Shaw, D. L., & Bauer, S. W. (1969). Press freedom and war constraints: Case testing Siebert's Proposition II. *Journalism Quarterly, 46,* 243–254.

Shepard, A. C. (1994/95). Community journalism. *The Responsive Community, 5,* 30–40.

Shilts, R. (1987). *And the band played on: Politics, people, and the AIDS epidemic.* New York: St. Martin's Press.

Shyles, L. C. (1986). The televised political spot advertisement: Its structure, content, and role in the political system. In L. L. Kaid, D. Nimmo, & K. R. Sanders (Eds.), *New perspectives on political advertising* (pp. 107–138). Carbondale, IL: Southern Illinois University Press.

Shoemaker, P. J. (Ed.). (1989). *Communication campaigns about drugs: Government, media, and the public.* Hillsdale, NJ: Lawrence Erlbaum Associates.

Shoemaker, P. J., & Reese, S. D. (1996). *Mediating the message: Theories of influences on mass media content* (2nd ed.). White Plains, NY: Longman.

Siebert, F. (1952). *Freedom of the press in England 1476–1776.* Urbana: University of Illinois Press.

Sigal, L. V. (1973). *Reporters and officials: The organization and politics of newsmaking.* Lexington, MA: D. C. Heath.

Sigal, L. (1986). Who: Sources make the news. In R. K. Manoff & M. Schudson (Eds.), *Reading the news* (pp. 9–37). New York: Pantheon.

Sigelman, L., & Bullock, D. (1991). Candidates, issues, horse races, and hoopla: Presidential campaign coverage, 1888–1988. *American Politics Quarterly, 19,* 5–32.

Simon, D. M., & Ostrom, C. W., Jr. (1989). The impact of televised speeches and foreign travel on presidential approval. *Public Opinion Quarterly, 53,* 58–82.

Simon, R. (1990). *Road show.* New York: Farrar, Straus, Giroux.

Simpson, C. (1993). U. S. mass communication research, counterinsurgency, and scientific "reality." In W. S. Solomon & R. W. McChesney (Eds.), *Ruthless criticism: New perspectives in U. S. communication history* (pp. 313–348). Minneapolis: University of Minnesota Press.

Sloan, W. D. (Ed.). (1990). *Makers of the media mind: Journalism educators and their ideas.* Hillsdale, NJ: Lawrence Erlbaum Associates.

Smith, B. A. (1996, October 8). Time to go negative. *The Wall Street Journal,* A22.

Smith, C. (1990). *Presidential press conferences: A critical approach.* New York: Praeger.

Smith, C. A., & Smith, K. B. (1985). Introduction: Persuasion and the American presidency. In C. A. Smith & K. B. Smith (Eds.), *The president and the public: Rhetoric and national leadership* (pp xi–xxiii). Lanham, MD: University Press of America.

Smith, C. A., & Smith, K. B. (1994). *The White House speaks: Presidential leadership as persuasion.* Westport, CT: Praeger.

Smith, L. J., & Nimmo, D. (1991). *Cordial concurrence: Orchestrating national party conventions in the telepolitical age.* Westport, CT: Praeger.

Smith, T. J., & Lichter, S. R. (1996, May). *Network television coverage of the 1996 presidential election campaign.* Paper presented to the annual convention of the American Association for Public Opinion Research, Salt Lake City.

Smoller, F. T. (1990). *The six o'clock presidency: A theory of presidential press relations in the age of television.* New York: Praeger.

Spear, J. C. (1984). *Presidents and the press: The Nixon legacy.* Cambridge, MA: MIT Press.

Spragens, W. C. (1978). *The presidency and the mass media in the age of television.* Washington, DC: University Press of America.

Sproule, J. M. (1987). Propaganda studies in American social science: The rise and fall of the critical paradigm. *Quarterly Journal of Speech, 73,* 60–78.

Sproule, J. M. (1989). Social responses to twentieth-century propaganda. In T. J. Smith (Ed.), *Propaganda: A pluralistic perspective* (pp. 5–22). New York: Praeger.

Sproule, J. M. (1996, June 14). Letter to Richard M. Perloff.

Stamm, K. (1985). *Newspaper use and community ties: Toward a dynamic theory.* Norwood, NJ: Ablex.

Stanley, H. W., & Niemi, R. A. (1988). *Vital statistics on American politics.* Washington, DC: Congressional Quarterly Press.

Steele, R. W. (1985). *Propaganda in an open society: The Roosevelt administration and the media, 1933–1941.* Westport, CT: Greenwood.

Stempel, G. H. III, & Windhauser, J. W. (Eds.; 1991). *The media in the 1984 and 1988 presidential campaigns.* New York: Greenwood Press.

Stone, I. F. (1966, February 13). Many thank-yous, Mr. President. *The Washington Post Book World.*

Stovall, J. G., & Solomon, J. H. (1984). The poll as a news event in the 1980 presidential campaign. *Public Opinion Quarterly, 48,* 615–623.

Swanson, D. L. (1981). A constructivist approach. In D. D. Nimmo & K. R. Sanders (Eds.), *Handbook of political communication* (pp. 169–191). Thousand Oaks, CA: Sage.

Swanson, D. L. (1988). Feeling the elephant: Some observations on agenda-setting research (commentary on Rogers and Dearing). In J. Anderson (Ed.), *Communication yearbook 11* (pp. 603–619). Thousand Oaks, CA: Sage.

Swanson, D. L., & Mancini, P. (Eds.). (1996a). *Politics, media, and modern democracy: An international study of innovations in electoral campaigning and their consequences.* Westport, CT: Praeger.

Swanson, D. L, & Mancini, P. (1996b). Patterns of modern electoral campaigning and their consequences. In D. L. Swanson & P. Mancini (Eds.), *Politics, media, and modern democracy: An international study of innovations in electoral campaigning and their consequences* (pp. 247–276). Westport, CT: Praeger.

Swanson, D. L., & Nimmo, D. (Eds.) (1990). *New directions in political communication: A resource book.* Thousand Oaks, CA: Sage.

Tebbel, J., & Watts, S. M. (1985). *The press and the presidency: From George Washington to Ronald Reagan.* New York: Oxford.

Tell, D. (1996, August 5). Don't dumb down the convention. *The Weekly Standard,* 9–10.

Tell, D. (1996, October 21). Saving the GOP from Dole-Kemp '96. *The Weekly Standard,* 11–12.

Tichenor, P. J., Donohue, G. A., & Olien, C. N. (1980). *Community conflict and the press.* Thousand Oaks, CA: Sage.

Tidmarch, C. M., & Pitney, J. J., Jr. (1985). Covering Congress. *Polity, 17,* 463–483.

Tiemens, R. K., Hellweg, S. A., Kipper, P., & Phillips, S. L. (1985). An integrative verbal and visual analysis of the Carter-Reagan debate. *Communication Quarterly, 33,* 34–42.

Timmerman, D. M., & Smith, L. D. (1994). The 1992 presidential nominating conventions: Cordial concurrence revisited. In R. E. Denton, Jr. (Ed.), *The 1992 presidential campaign: A communication perspective* (pp. 65–87). Westport, CT: Praeger.

Tipton, L. P., Haney, R. D., & Basehart, J. R. (1975). Media agenda-setting in city and state election campaigns. *Journalism Quarterly, 52,* 15–22.

Tolchin, S. J. (1996). *The angry American: How voter rage is changing the nation.* Boulder: Westview Press.

Traugott, M. W., & Lavrakas, P. J. (1996). *The voter's guide to election polls.* Chatham, NJ: Chatham House.

Trent, J. S. (1994). The early campaign. In R. E. Denton, Jr. (Ed.), *The 1992 presidential campaign: A communication perspective* (pp. 43–64). Westport, CT: Praeger.

Trent, J. S., & Friedenberg, R. V. (1995). *Political campaign communication: Principles and practices* (3rd ed.). Westport, CT: Praeger.

Troy, G. (1996). *See how they ran: The changing role of the presidential candidate.* (Rev. ed.). Cambridge, MA: Harvard University Press.

Trumbo, C. (1995). Longitudinal modeling of public issues: An application of the agenda-setting process to the issue of global warming. *Journalism & Mass Communication Monographs, 152,* 1–57.

Tuchman, B. (1962). *The guns of August.* New York: Macmillan.

Tulis, J. K. (1987). *The rhetorical presidency.* Princeton: Princeton University Press.

Turner, K. J. (1985). *Lyndon Johnson's dual war: Vietnam and the press.* Chicago: University of Chicago Press.

Underhill, R. (1996). *FDR and Harry: Unparalleled lives.* Westport, CT: Praeger.

Vancil, D. L., & Pendell, S. D. (1987). The myth of viewer-listener disagreement in the first Kennedy-Nixon debate. *Central States Speech Journal, 38,* 16–27.

Vaughn, S. (1980). *Holding fast the inner lines: Democracy, nationalism, and the Committee on Public Information.* Chapel Hill, NC: University of North Carolina Press.

Voters' interest: Then and now. (1996, October 11). *USA Today,* 4A.

Wanta, W., & Foote, J. (1994). The president-news media relationship: A time series analysis of agenda-setting. *Journal of Broadcasting & Electronic Media, 38,* 437–448.

Wanta, W., & Hu, Y. W. (1993). The agenda-setting effects of international news coverage: An examination of differing news frames. *International Journal of Public Opinion Research, 5,* 250–264.

Warren, K. F. (1991). *The juggler: Franklin Roosevelt as wartime statesman.* Princeton: Princeton University Press.

Wayne, L. (1996, September 8). Loopholes allow presidential race to set a record. *The New York Times,* 1, 19.

Wayne, S. J. (1996). *The road to the White House 1996: The politics of presidential elections.* New York: St. Martin's Press.

Weaver, D. H. (1984). Media agenda-setting and public opinion: Is there a link? In R. N. Bostrom (Ed.), *Communication yearbook 8* (pp. 680–691). Thousand Oaks, CA: Sage.

Weaver, D. H. (1991). Political issues and voter need for orientation. In D. L. Protess & M. E. McCombs (Eds.), *Agenda setting: Readings on media, public opinion, and policymaking* (pp. 131–139). Hillsdale, NJ: Lawrence Erlbaum Associates.

Weaver, D. H. (1996). What voters learn from media. *The Annals of the American Academy of Political and Social Science, 546,* 34–47.

Weaver, D. H., & Drew, D. (1995). Voter learning in the 1992 presidential election: Did the "nontraditional" media and debates matter? *Journalism Quarterly, 72,* 7–17.

Weaver, D. H., Graber, D. A., McCombs, M. E., & Eyal, C. H. (1981). *Media agenda- setting in a presidential election: Issues, images, and interest.* New York: Praeger.

Weaver, D. H., McCombs, M. E., & Spellman, C. (1975). Watergate and the media: A case study of agenda-setting. *American Politics Quarterly, 3,* 458–472.

Weaver, D. H., & Wilhoit, G. C. (1980). News media coverage of U. S. Senators in four Congresses, 1953–1974. *Journalism Monographs, 67,* 1–34.

Weaver, D. H., & Wilhoit, G. C. (1991). *The American journalist: A portrait of U. S. news people and their work* (2nd ed.). Bloomington: Indiana University Press.

Weaver, D. H., & Wilhoit, G. C. (1992). *The American journalist in the 1990s.* Arlington, VA: Freedom Forum World Center.

Weaver, D. H., Zhu, J. H., & Willnat, L. (1992). The bridging function of interpersonal communication in agenda-setting. *Journalism Quarterly, 69,* 856–867.

Weaver, P. H. (1972). Is television news biased? *The Public Interest, 27,* 57–74.

Weimann, G. (1994). *The influentials: People who influence people.* Albany: State University of New York Press.

Weisberg, J. (1993, April 26). Washington's new ruling class: Clincest. *The New Republic,* 22–27.

Weisskopf, M., & Maraniss, D. (1995, November 6–12). Gingrich's war of words. *The Washington Post National Weekly Edition,* 6–8.

West, D. M. (1993). *Air wars: Television advertising in election campaigns, 1952–1992.* Washington, DC: Congressional Quarterly Press.

Whicker, M. L. (1993). The case AGAINST the war. In M. L. Whicker, J. P. Pfiffner, & R. A. Moore (Eds.), *The presidency and the Persian Gulf war* (pp. 111–129). Westport, CT: Praeger.

White, G. J. (1979). *FDR and the press*. Chicago: University of Chicago Press.

White, T. H. (1961). *The making of the president: 1960*. New York: Atheneum.

Whitney, D. C. (1991). Agenda-setting: Power and contingency (commentary on Reese). In J. A. Anderson (Ed.), *Communication yearbook 14* (pp. 347–356). Newbury Park, CA: Sage.

Wicker, T. (1991). *One of us: Richard Nixon and the American dream*. New York: Random House.

Will, G. F. (1995, November 13). A weird sincerity. *Newsweek, 94*.

Will, G. F. (1996, October 14). A partial home run. *Newsweek, 98*.

Williams, R. (1977). *Marxism and literature*. New York: Oxford University Press.

Wills, G. (1987). *Reagan's America: Innocents at home*. New York: Doubleday.

Wills, G. (1992). *Lincoln at Gettysburg: The words that remade America*. New York: Simon & Schuster.

Wilson, J. Q. (1986). *American government: Institutions and policies*. Lexington, MA: D. C. Heath.

Windt, T. O., Jr. (1987a). Presidential rhetoric: Definition of a discipline of study. In T. Windt & B. Ingold (Eds.), *Essays in presidential rhetoric* (2nd ed.; pp. xv–xliii). Dubuque, IA: Kendall/Hunt.

Windt, T. O., Jr. (1987b). The presidency and speeches on international crises: Repeating the rhetorical past. In T. Windt & B. Ingold (Eds.), *Essays in presidential rhetoric* (2nd ed., pp. 125–134). Dubuque, IA: Kendall/Hunt.

Windt, T. O., Jr. (1993). President John F. Kennedy's inaugural address, 1961. In H. Ryan (Ed.), *The inaugural addresses of twentieth-century American presidents* (pp. 181–193). Westport, CT: Praeger.

Windt, T. O., Jr. (1994). The 1960 Kennedy-Nixon presidential debates. In R. V. Friedenberg (Ed.), *Rhetorical studies of national political debates, 1960–1992* (2nd ed., pp. 1–27). Westport, CT: Praeger.

Winebrenner, H. (1987). *The Iowa precinct caucuses: The making of a media event*. Ames, IA: Iowa State University Press.

Wines, M. (1996, May 5). Republicans face plight that hurt Democrats in 1994. *The New York Times*, 1, 15.

Winfield, B. (1994). *FDR and the news media*. New York: Columbia University Press.

Wolfson, L. W. (1985). *The untapped power of the press: Explaining government to the people*. New York: Praeger.

Woodward, B. (1996). *The choice*. New York: Simon & Schuster.

Wright, C. R. (1986). *Mass communication: A sociological perspective* (3rd ed.). New York: Random House.

Yagade, A., & Dozier, D. M. (1990). The media agenda-setting effect of concrete versus abstract issues. *Journalism Quarterly, 67*, 3–10.

Zaller, J. (1994). The rise and fall of candidate Perot: Unmediated versus mediated politics—Part 1. *Political Communication, 11*, 357–390.

Zarefsky, D. (1990). *Lincoln, Douglas, and slavery: In the crucible of public debate*. Chicago: University of Chicago Press.

Zernicke, P. H. (1994). *Pitching the presidency: How presidents depict the office*. Westport, CT: Praeger.

Zhao, X., & Chaffee, S. H. (1995). Campaign advertisements versus television news as sources of political issue information. *Public Opinion Quarterly, 59*, 41–65.

Zucker, H. G. (1978). The variable nature of news media influence. In B. D. Ruben (Ed.), *Communication yearbook 2* (pp. 225–240). New Brunswick: Transaction Books.

Author Index*

*Indexes authors whose names appear in text. Numerous citations also appear in Endnotes, with complete bibliographic material in References.

Subject Index

7455